C000183339

STREET ATLAS

Leicestershire and Rutland

First published in 2000 by

Philip's, a division of
Octopus Publishing Group Ltd
2-4 Heron Quays, London E14 4JP

Second edition 2003
Third impression with revisions 2005

ISBN-10   0-540-08488-3 (spiral)
ISBN-13   978-0-540-08488-3 (spiral)

© Philip's 2005

Ordnance Survey®

This product includes mapping data licensed
from Ordnance Survey® with the permission of
the Controller of Her Majesty's Stationery Office.
© Crown copyright 2005. All rights reserved.
Licence number 100011710.

Printed and bound in Spain
by Cayfosa-Quebecor

Contents

Digital Data

The exceptionally high-quality mapping found in this atlas is available as digital data in TIFF format, which is easily convertible to other bitmapped (raster) image formats.

The index is also available in digital form as a standard database table. It contains all the details found in the printed index together with the National Grid reference for the map square in which each entry is named.

For further information and to discuss your requirements, please contact Philip's on 020 7644 6932 or james.mann@philips-maps.co.uk

(22a)	**Motorway** with junction number
	Primary route – dual/single carriageway
	A road – dual/single carriageway
	B road – dual/single carriageway
	Minor road – dual/single carriageway
	Other minor road – dual/single carriageway
	Road under construction
	Tunnel, covered road
	Rural track, private road or narrow road in urban area
	Gate or obstruction to traffic (restrictions may not apply at all times or to all vehicles)
	Path, bridleway, byway open to all traffic, road used as a public path
	Pedestrianised area
DY7	**Postcode boundaries**
	County and unitary authority boundaries
	Railway, tunnel, railway under construction
	Tramway, tramway under construction
	Miniature railway
Walsall	**Railway station**
	Private railway station
South Shields	**Metro station**
	Tram stop, tram stop under construction
	Bus, coach station

Acad	**Academy**	Inst	**Institute**	Recn Gd	**Recreation Ground**
Allot Gdns	**Allotments**	Ct	**Law Court**		
Cemy	**Cemetery**	L Ctr	**Leisure Centre**	Resr	**Reservoir**
C Ctr	**Civic Centre**	LC	**Level Crossing**	Ret Pk	**Retail Park**
CH	**Club House**	Liby	**Library**	Sch	**School**
Coll	**College**	Mkt	**Market**	Sh Ctr	**Shopping Centre**
Crem	**Crematorium**	Meml	**Memorial**	TH	**Town Hall/House**
Ent	**Enterprise**	Mon	**Monument**	Trad Est	**Trading Estate**
Ex H	**Exhibition Hall**	Mus	**Museum**	Univ	**University**
Ind Est	**Industrial Estate**	Obsy	**Observatory**	W Twr	**Water Tower**
IRB Sta	**Inshore Rescue Boat Station**	Pal	**Royal Palace**	Wks	**Works**
		PH	**Public House**	YH	**Youth Hostel**

◆	**Ambulance station**
◆	**Coastguard station**
◆	**Fire station**
◆	**Police station**
✚	**Accident and Emergency entrance to hospital**
H	**Hospital**
+	**Place of worship**
i	**Information Centre** (open all year)
P	**Parking**
P&R	**Park and Ride**
PO	**Post Office**
X	**Camping site**
	Caravan site
▶	**Golf course**
X	**Picnic site**
Prim Sch	**Important buildings, schools, colleges, universities and hospitals**
River Medway	**Water name**
	River, weir, stream
	Canal, lock, tunnel
	Water
	Tidal water
	Woods
	Built up area
Church	**Non-Roman antiquity**
ROMAN FORT	**Roman antiquity**
87 / 228	**Adjoining page indicators and overlap bands** The colour of the arrow and the band indicates the scale of the adjoining or overlapping page (see scales below)

■ The small numbers around the edges of the maps identify the 1 kilometre National Grid lines

■ The dark grey border on the inside edge of some pages indicates that the mapping does not continue onto the adjacent page

The scale of the maps on the pages numbered in blue is 5.52 cm to 1 km • 3½ inches to 1 mile • 1: 18103

0 — ¼ — ½ — ¾ — 1 mile
0 — 250m — 500m — 750m — 1 kilometre

The scale of the maps on pages numbered in red is 11.04 cm to 1 km • 7 inches to 1 mile • 1: 9051.4

0 — 220 yards — 440 yards — 660 yards — ½ mile
0 — 125m — 250m — 375m — ½ kilometre

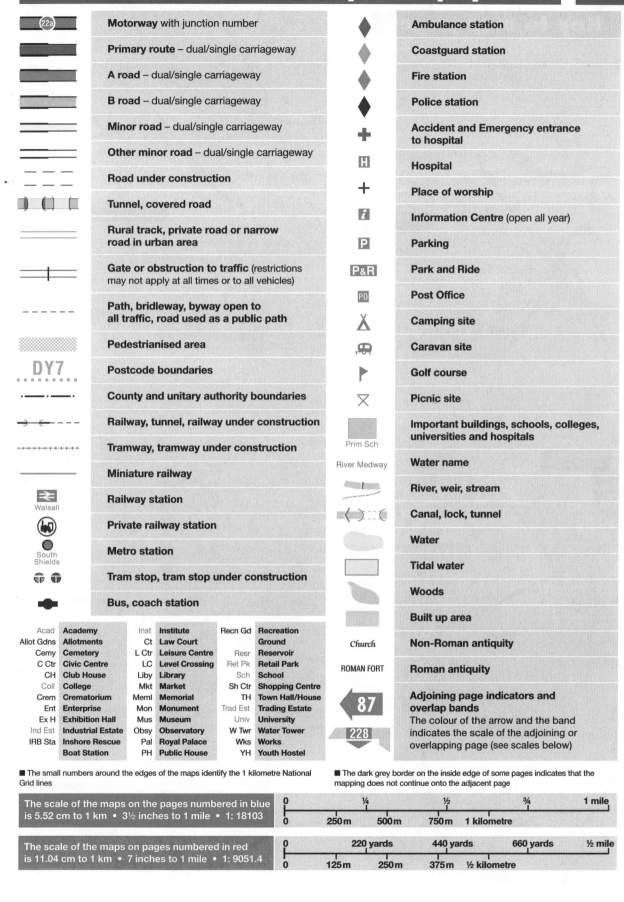

IV

Key to map pages

122	Map pages at 3½ inches to 1 mile
59	Map pages at 7 inches to 1 mile

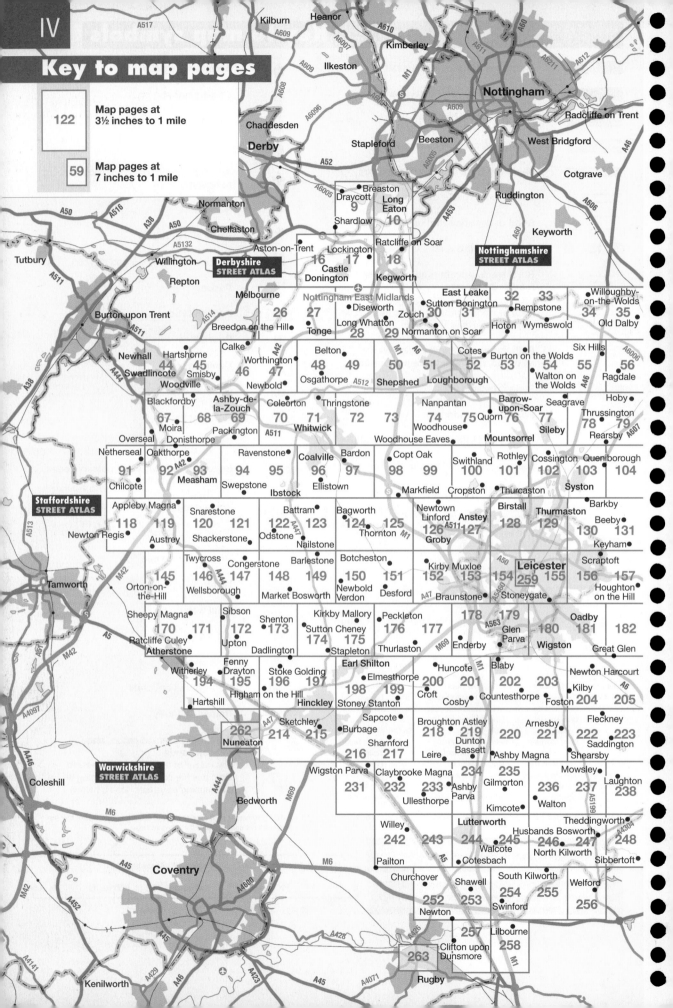

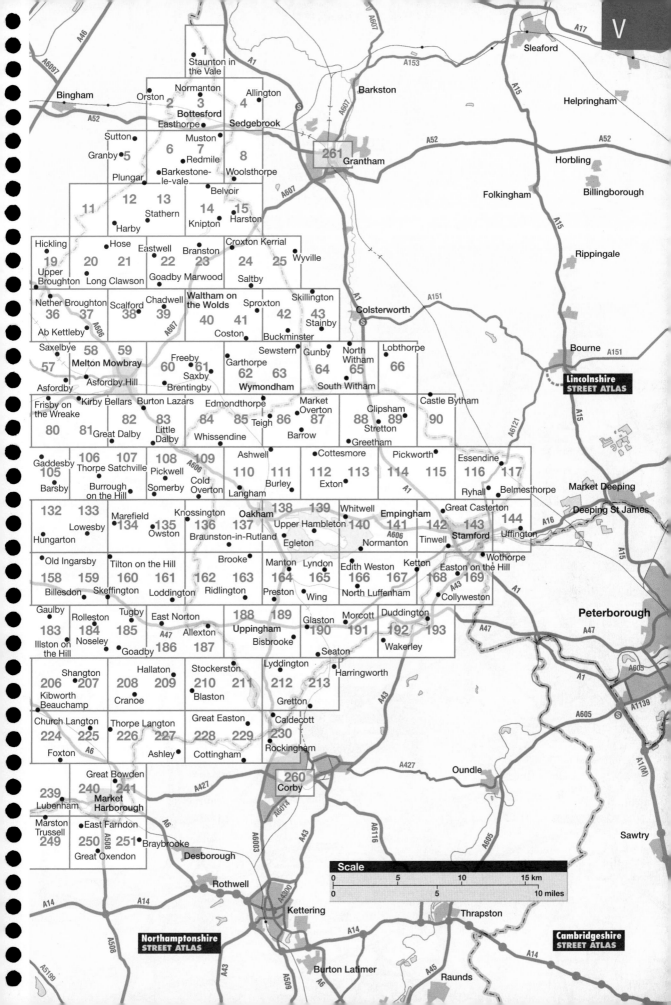

V

Staunton in the Vale 1

Normanton 3 Allington 4
Orston Bingham 2 Bottesford
Easthorpe Sedgebrook

Sutton Muston 7 8
Granby 5 6 Redmile Woolsthorpe
Plungar Barkestone-le-vale Belvoir

11 12 13 14 15
Harby Stathern Knipton Harston

Hickling Hose Eastwell Branston Croxton Kerrial
19 20 21 22 23 24 25 Wyville
Upper Broughton Long Clawson Goadby Marwood Saltby

Nether Broughton Scalford Chadwell Waltham on the Wolds Sproxton Skillington
36 37 38 39 40 41 42 43 Stainby
Ab Kettleby Coston Buckminster

Saxelbye 58 59 Sewstern Gunby North Witham Lobthorpe
57 Melton Mowbray 60 Freeby 61 Garthorpe 62 63 64 65 66
Asfordby Asfordby Hill Saxby Brentingby Wymondham South Witham

Frisby on the Wreake Kirby Bellars Burton Lazars Edmondthorpe Market Overton Castle Bytham
80 81 82 83 84 85 86 87 Clipsham 88 89 90
Great Dalby Little Dalby Whissendine Teigh Barrow Stretton Greetham

Gaddesby 106 107 108 109 Ashwell Cottesmore Pickworth Essendine
105 Thorpe Satchville Pickwell 110 111 112 113 114 115 116 117
Barsby Burrough on the Hill Somerby Cold Overton Langham Burley Exton Ryhall Belmesthorpe

132 133 Marefield Knossington Oakham 138 139 Whitwell Empingham Great Casterton 144
Lowesby 134 135 136 137 Upper Hambleton 140 141 142 143 Uffington
Hungarton Owston Braunston-in-Rutland Egleton Normanton Tinwell Stamford

Old Ingarsby Tilton on the Hill Brooke Manton Lyndon Edith Weston Ketton Easton on the Hill
158 159 160 161 162 163 164 165 166 167 168 169
Billesdon Skeffington Loddington Ridlington Preston Wing North Luffenham Collyweston

Gaulby Rolleston Tugby East Norton 188 189 Glaston Morcott Duddington
183 184 185 186 187 Uppingham 190 191 192 193
Illston on the Hill Noseley Goadby Allexton Bisbrooke Seaton Wakerley

Shangton Hallaton Stockerston Lyddington
206 207 208 209 210 211 212 213 Harringworth
Kibworth Beauchamp Cranoe Blaston Gretton

Church Langton Thorpe Langton Great Easton Caldecott
224 225 226 227 228 229 230
Foxton Ashley Cottingham Rockingham

Great Bowden
239 240 241
Lubenham Market Harborough
Marston Trussell East Farndon
249 250 251 Braybrooke
Great Oxendon

Barkston
Sleaford
Helpringham

Grantham 261

Horbling
Billingborough

Folkingham
Rippingale

Colsterworth

Bourne

Lincolnshire STREET ATLAS

Market Deeping
Deeping St James

Peterborough

Oundle

Sawtry

Corby 260

Desborough
Rothwell
Kettering

Thrapston

Burton Latimer
Raunds

Cambridgeshire STREET ATLAS

Northamptonshire STREET ATLAS

Scale
0   5   10   15 km
0   5   10 miles

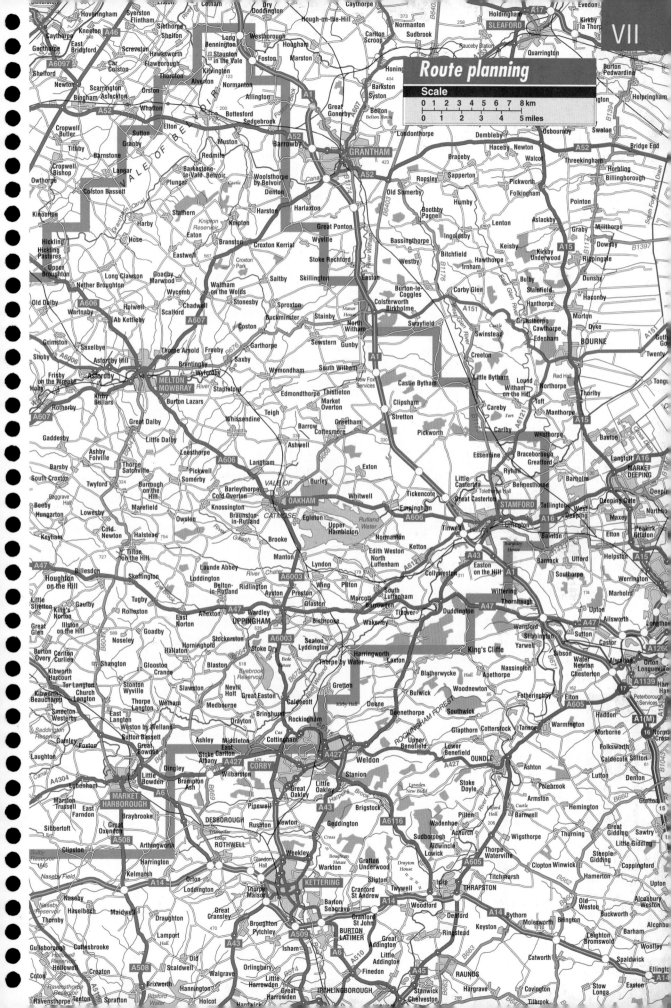

Route planning

Scale

0 1 2 3 4 5 6 7 8 km

0 1 2 3 4 5 miles

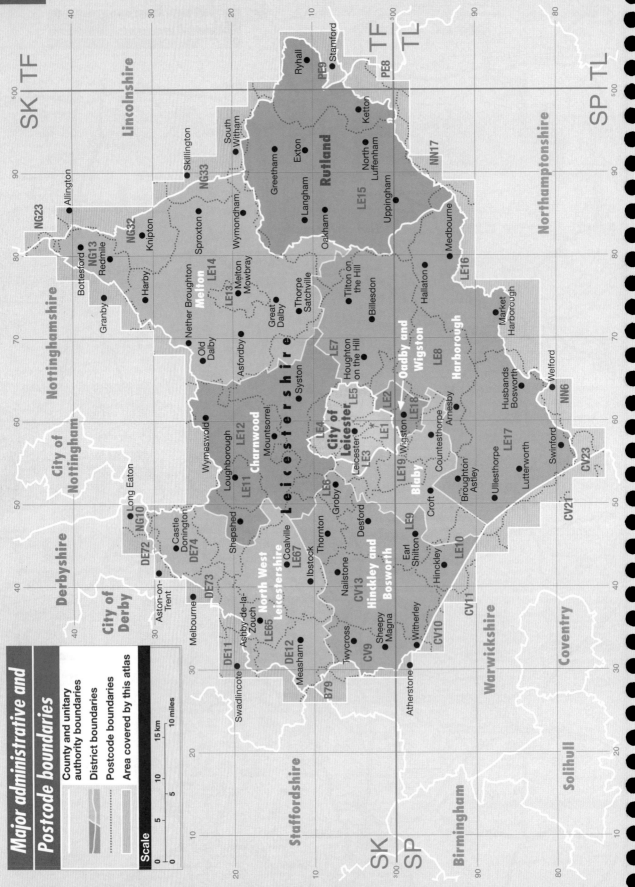

Major administrative and Postcode boundaries

County and unitary authority boundaries
District boundaries
Postcode boundaries
Area covered by this atlas

Scale

0   5   10   15 km
0   5   10 miles

Lincolnshire

Nottinghamshire

City of Nottingham

Derbyshire

City of Derby

Staffordshire

Birmingham

Solihull

Coventry

Warwickshire

Northamptonshire

Leicestershire

Rutland

Melton

Charnwood

North West Leicestershire

Hinckley and Bosworth

Blaby

City of Leicester

Oadby and Wigston

Harborough

SK TF
SK TF
TF TL
SP TL
SK SP

Allington
Bottesford
Redmile
Granby
Harby
Long Eaton
Aston-on-Trent
Melbourne
Swadlincote
Measham
Twycross
Sheepy Magna
Witherley
Atherstone
Ashby-de-la-Zouch
Castle Donington
Shepshed
Coalville
Ibstock
Nailstone
Thornton
Groby
Desford
Earl Shilton
Hinckley
Croft
Broughton Astley
Lutterworth
Ullesthorpe
Swinford
Welford
Husbands Bosworth
Market Harborough
Medbourne
Hallaton
Arnesby
Countesthorpe
Wigston
Leicester
Syston
Houghton on the Hill
Tilton on the Hill
Billesdon
Uppingham
Oakham
Langham
North Luffenham
Ketton
Stamford
Ryhall
Exton
Greetham
South Witham
Skillington
Knipton
Sproxton
Wymondham
Melton Mowbray
Great Dalby
Thorpe Satchville
Nether Broughton
Old Dalby
Asfordby
Wymeswold
Loughborough
Mountsorrel

NG23
NG13
NG32
NG33
NG10
DE72
DE74
DE73
DE11
DE12
B79
CV9
CV13
CV10
CV11
CV21
CV23
LE65
LE67
LE12
LE11
LE6
LE9
LE10
LE8
LE17
LE16
LE15
LE14
LE13
LE7
LE4
LE3
LE1
LE2
LE5
LE19
LE18
NN6
NN17
PE8
PE9

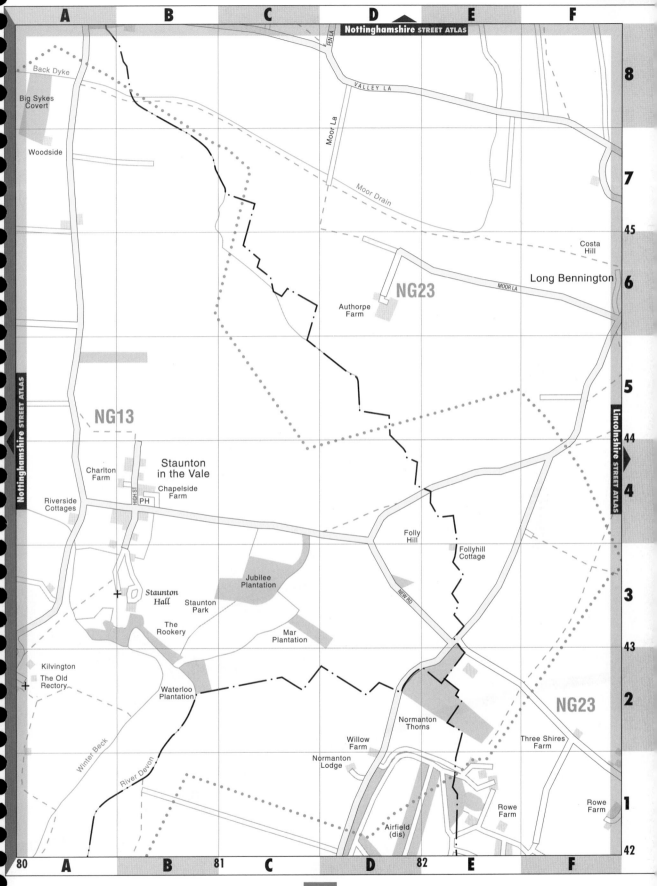

Back Dyke

Big Sykes Covert

Woodside

VALLEY LA

FEN LA

Moor La

Moor Drain

Costa Hill

NG23

MOOR LA

Long Bennington

Authorpe Farm

NG13

Staunton in the Vale

Charlton Farm

HIGH ST

PH

Chapelside Farm

Riverside Cottages

Jubilee Plantation

Staunton Hall

Staunton Park

Folly Hill

Follyhill Cottage

The Rookery

Mar Plantation

NEW RD

Kilvington

The Old Rectory

Waterloo Plantation

NG23

Normanton Thorns

Winter Beck

River Devon

Willow Farm

Three Shires Farm

Normanton Lodge

Rowe Farm

Rowe Farm

Airfield (dis)

Nottinghamshire STREET ATLAS

Lincolnshire STREET ATLAS

8

7

45

6

5

44

4

3

43

2

1

42

80 A   B 81 C   D 82 E   F

3

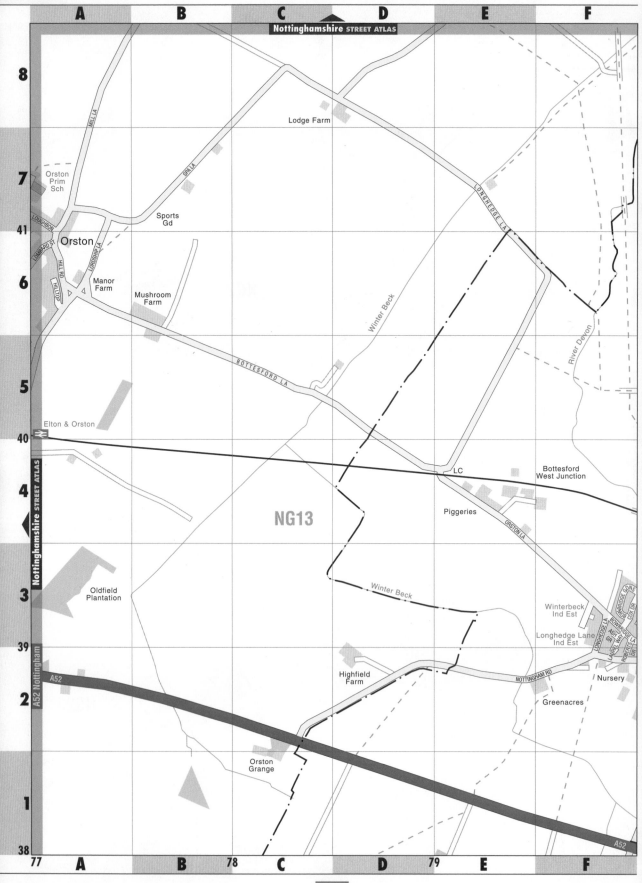

Lodge Farm

Orston Prim Sch

Sports Gd

Orston

Manor Farm

Mushroom Farm

Winter Beck

LONGHEDGE LA

River Devon

BOTTESFORD LA

Elton & Orston

LC

Bottesford West Junction

Piggeries

ORSTON LA

NG13

Oldfield Plantation

Winter Beck

Winterbeck Ind Est

Longhedge Lane Ind Est

LONGHEDGE LA

BOWBRIDGE GDNS

BOWBRIDGE RD

CMK DR

ASH WAY

LAUREL GR

ROBERTS DR

NOTTINGHAM RD

Nursery

Highfield Farm

A52

A52 Nottingham

Greenacres

Orston Grange

A52

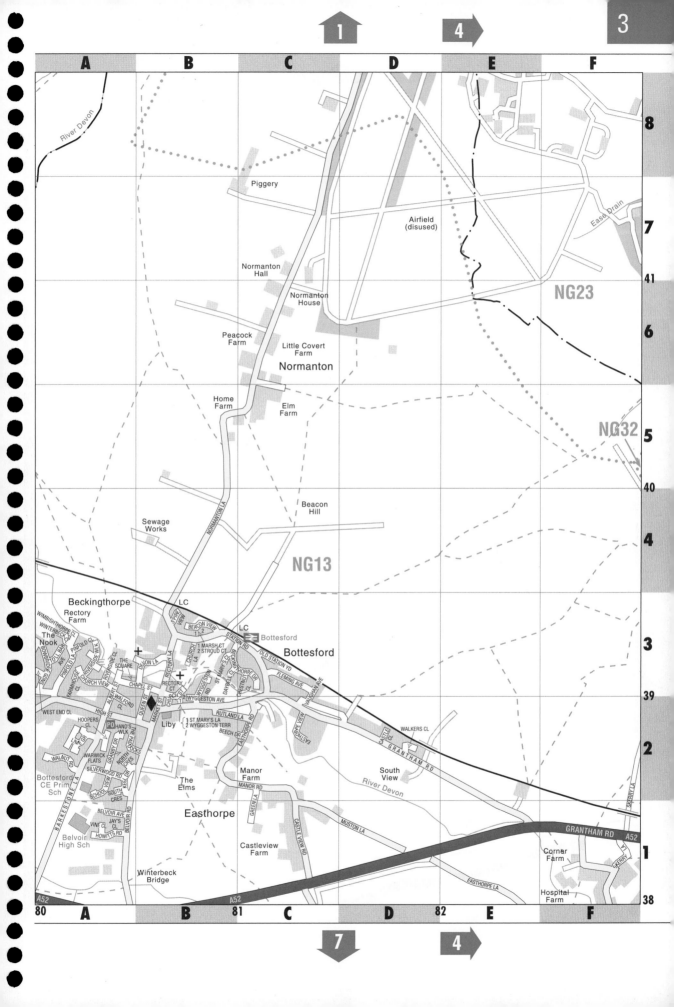

Lincolnshire STREET ATLAS

A   B   C   D   E   F

8

The Ashes

Camp (dis)

Thackson's Well Farm

SEWSTERN LA

The Spinney

Ease Drain

7

Moss' Plantation

NG23

41

LOWFIELDS LA

Lowfield Farm

The Bungalow

ROSTON LA

6

Stonepit Plantation

Allington with Sedgebrook CE Prim Sch

Hillside Plantation

PARK RD

MARSTON LA

Allington Hall

PARK AVE

BURTON'S LA

Allington

SIDE ST

GONERBY LA

5

West Wong Plantation

THE GREEN

PO

PH

THE PADDOCK

MAIN ST

BOTTOM ST

Old Rectory

Manor House

MANOR PADDOCK

DALESTORTH CT

LAMBERT RD

BACK LA

SEWSTERN LA

40

Endcliffe Farm

BOTTESFORD RD

SEDGEBROOK RD

PEACH LA

THE CRESCENT

ALLINGTON GDNS

Salt Well (Chalybeate)

Glebe Farm

WEST WAY

4

NG32

Viking Way

ALLINGTON RD

3

Debdale Barn

Keeper's Plantation

39

The Debdale

Manor Farm

SKEVERY LA

2

NG13

Barra-Don

Station Farm

1

A52

GRANTHAM RD

Cox's Walk Farm

LC

CHURCH LA

PH

Manor House

CHURCH LA

WHATONS YD

A52

38

83   A   B   84   C   D   85   E   F

Lincolnshire STREET ATLAS

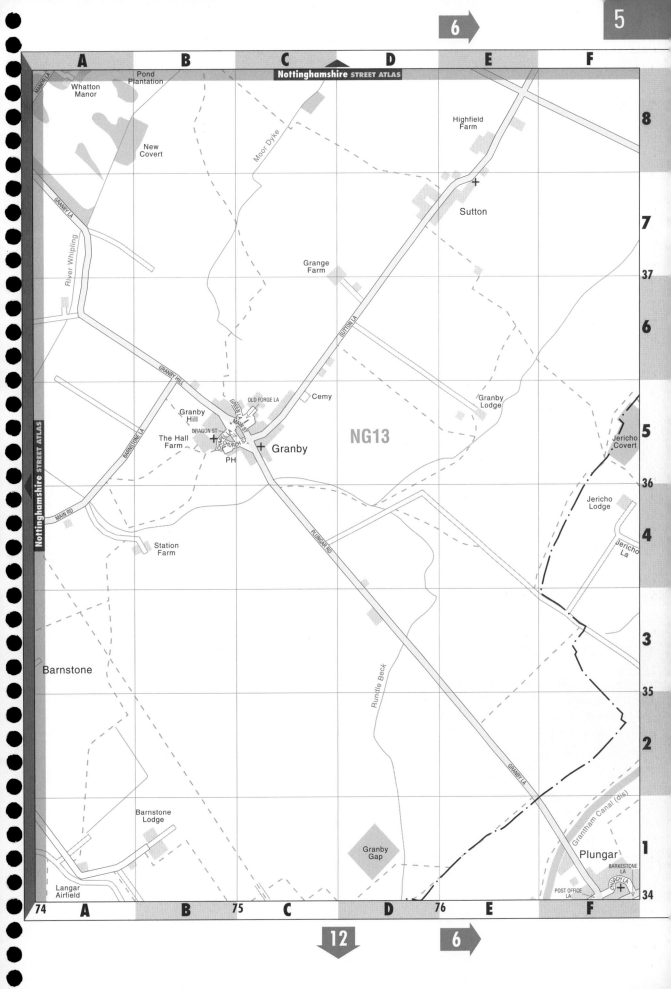

5

6

A B C D E F

8

7

37

6

5

36

4

3

35

2

1

34

Whatton Manor

Pond Plantation

New Covert

MANOR LA

GRANBY LA

River Whipling

GRANBY HILL

BARNSTONE LA

MAIN RD

The Hall Farm

Granby Hill

BRAGON ST

CHAPEL LA

MAIN ST

CHURCH ST

GREEN LA

PH

OLD FORGE LA

Cemy

Granby

Moor Dyke

Grange Farm

SUTTON LA

Highfield Farm

Sutton

Granby Lodge

NG13

Jericho Covert

Jericho Lodge

Jericho La

JERICHO LA

Station Farm

PLUNGAR RD

Rundle Beck

Barnstone

Barnstone Lodge

Granby Gap

GRANBY LA

Plungar

Grantham Canal (dis)

BARKESTONE LA

POST OFFICE LA

CHURCH LA

Langar Airfield

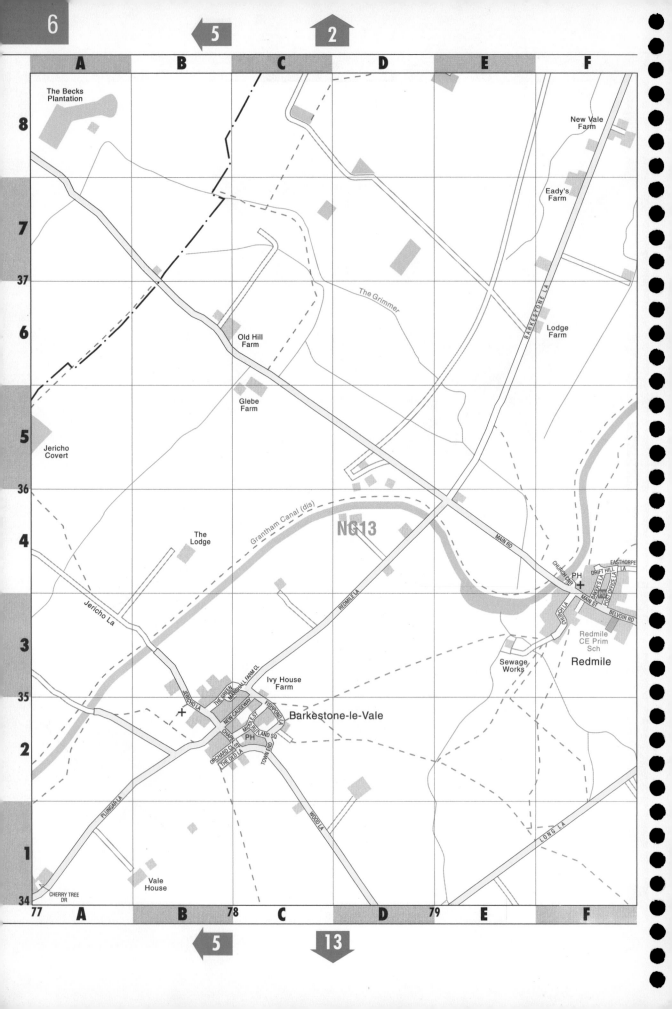

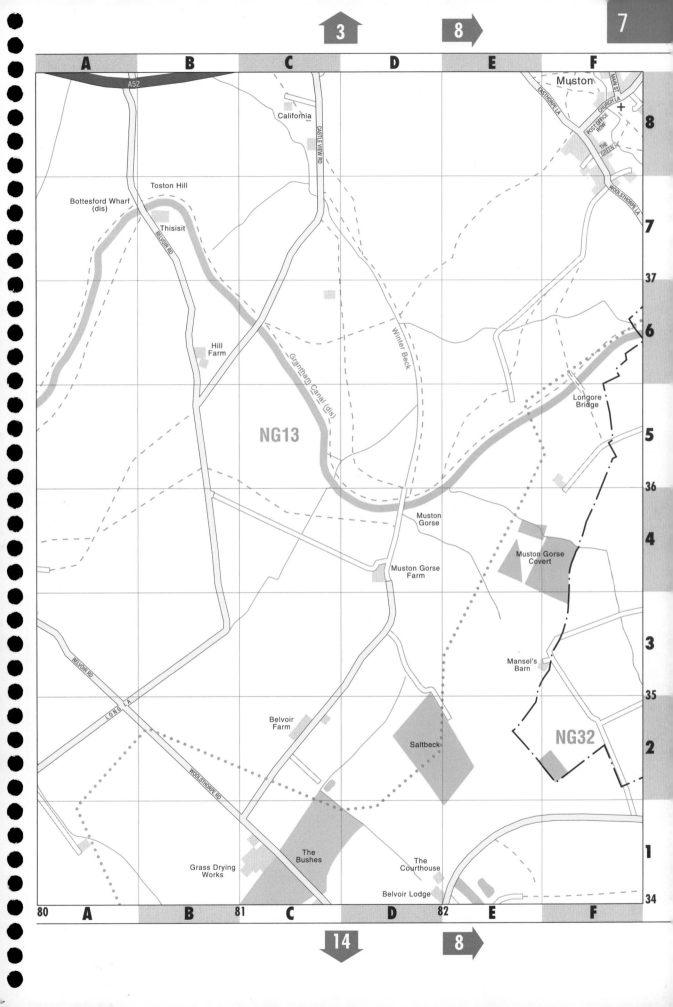

3
8
14
8

A B C D E F

Muston

A52

California

CASTLE VIEW RD

EASTHORPE LA

POST OFFICE ROW

CHURCH LA

MAIN ST

THE GREEN

WOOLSTHORPE LA

Toston Hill

Bottesford Wharf (dis)

Thisisit

BELVOIR RD

Hill Farm

Grantham Canal (dis)

Winter Beck

NG13

Longore Bridge

Muston Gorse

Muston Gorse Covert

Muston Gorse Farm

Mansel's Barn

NG32

BELVOIR RD

LONG LA

Belvoir Farm

Saltbeck

WOOLSTHORPE RD

Grass Drying Works

The Bushes

The Courthouse

Belvoir Lodge

80 A 81 B C 82 D E F

8
7
37
6
5
36
4
3
35
2
1
34

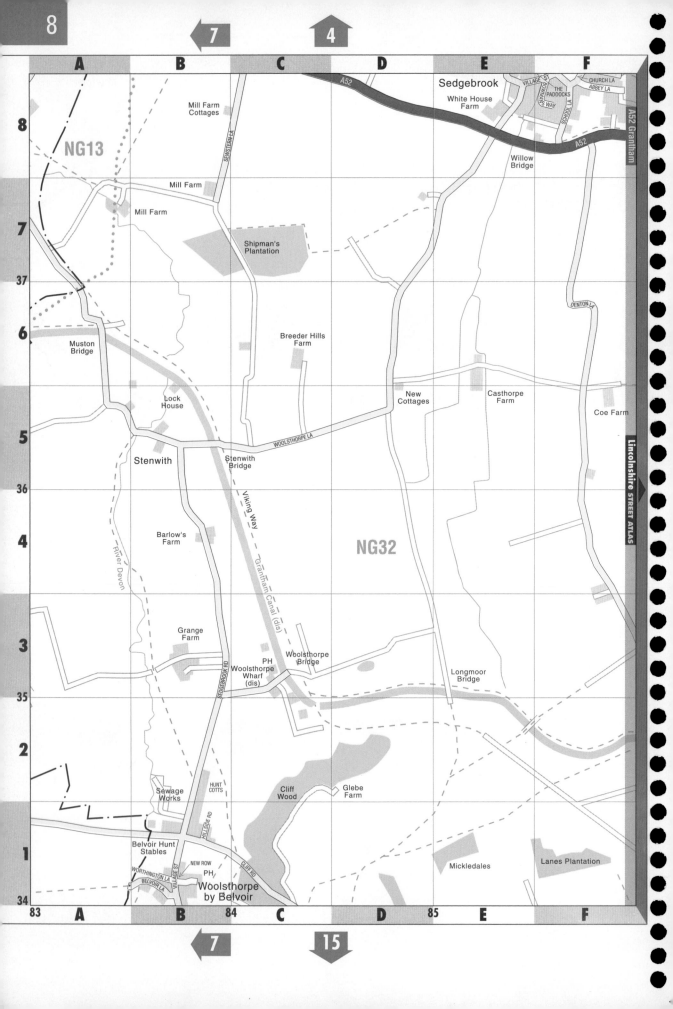

7   4

A   B   C   D   E   F

Sedgebrook

NG13

Mill Farm
Cottages

White House
Farm

A52 Grantham

8

Mill Farm

Mill Farm

Shipman's
Plantation

Willow
Bridge

7

37

DENTON LA

6

Muston
Bridge

Breeder Hills
Farm

Lock
House

New
Cottages

Casthorpe
Farm

Coe Farm

5

Stenwith

Stenwith
Bridge

WOOLSTHORPE LA

36

Viking Way

Barlow's
Farm

4

NG32

Lincolnshire STREET ATLAS

River Devon

Grantham Canal (dis)

Grange
Farm

3

Woolsthorpe
Bridge

Longmoor
Bridge

SEDGEBROOK RD

PH
Woolsthorpe
Wharf
(dis)

35

2

HUNT
COTTS

Cliff
Wood

Glebe
Farm

Sewage
Works

HILLSIDE RD

Belvoir Hunt
Stables

Mickledales

Lanes Plantation

1

NEW ROW
PH

VILLAGE ST

CLIFF RD

WORTHINGTON LA

Woolsthorpe
by Belvoir

BELVOIR LA

34

83   A   B   84   C   D   85   E   F

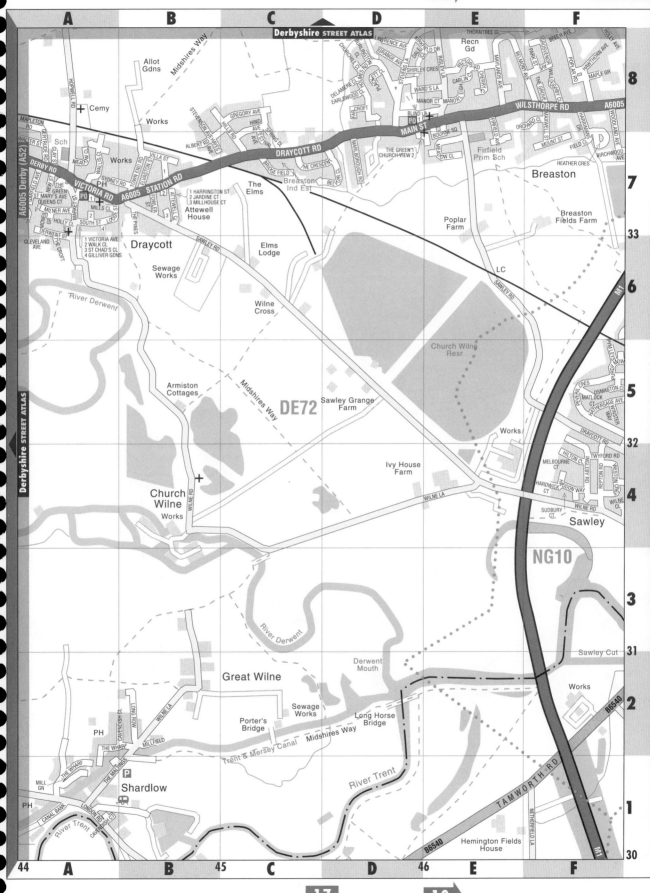

Derbyshire STREET ATLAS

Derbyshire STREET ATLAS

A **B** **C** **D** **E** **F**

8

Allot Gdns

Midshires Way

Works

Cemy

Hopwell Rd

Mapleton Rd

Walter St

Gertrude Rd

Clay La

Derby Rd

A6005 Derby (A52)

Sch

Old Hall

Walls Cl

Works

Villa St

Stevenson Ave

Albert Rd

Hills Rd

Hind Ave

Spring Cl

Festival Ave

Gregory Ave

DRAYCOTT RD

Lawrence Ave

Grange Ave

Burlington

Churchill Cl

Delamere Cl

Earlswood Cl

Far Croft

Shirley Cres

Dale Rd

Stevens La

Risley La

Carlin

Cherry

Ward's La

Manor Ct

Manor

Thorntree Cl

Recn Gd

Belmont Rd

Maylands Ave

Wilsthorpe Rd

A6005

Grosvenor

Willoughby Rd

The Grove

Poplar Rd

Beech Ave

Hawthorn Ave

Holly Rd

Maple Gr

8

The Green

New St

St Mary's Ave

Queens Ct

Milner Ave

Money La

Holly Cl

South St

The Croft

Derwent St

Market St

Ellaston St

Fowler St

Attewell Cl

PO

The Pines

Sawley Rd

VICTORIA RD

A6005 STATION RD

PH

Sydney Rd

Mills Cl

1 HARRINGTON ST
2 JARDINE CT
3 MILLHOUSE CT

The Elms

Attewell House

Bridge Field

The Crescent

Marlborough Rd

The Green
Church View 2

Bourne Sq

Main St

Blind La

PO

Firfield
Prim Sch

Field Cl

Mount St

Orchard Cl

Maxwell St

Harriman's La

Birchwood Ave

Woodland Ave

Heather Cres

Breaston

7

Cleveland Ave

1 VICTORIA AVE
2 WALK CL
3 ST CHAD'S CL
4 GILLIVER GDNS

Draycott

Sewage Works

Elms Lodge

Breaston
Ind Est

Poplar
Farm

LC

Sawley Rd

Breaston
Fields Farm

33

River Derwent

Wilne Cross

Armiston Cottages

Midshires Way

DE72

Sawley Grange
Farm

Church Wilne
Resr

Works

M1

Pevenil Cres

Matlock

Osmaston Cl

Hathersage Ave

Winster Way

DRAYCOTT RD

Hilton Cl

Ingleby Rd

Twyford Rd

Repton Cl

Weston Cres

Melbourne
Ct

Wilne Cl

Pymleye Rd Mow

5

32

Church
Wilne

Wilne Rd

Works

Ivy House
Farm

WILNE LA

Hardwick
Ct

Soddon Way

Sudbury
Ct

Wilne Rd

Sawley

4

NG10

3

River Derwent

Sawley Cut

31

Great Wilne

Long Row

Wilne La

Wilne Rd

Derwent
Mouth

Sewage
Works

Long Horse
Bridge

Works

B6540

2

PH

The Wharf

Cavendish Cl

Millfield

Porter's
Bridge

Midshires Way

Trent & Mersey Canal

River Trent

Tamworth Rd

Netherfield La

1

Mill
Gn

The Wharf

The Maltings

P

Shardlow

PH

Canal Bank

London Rd

Cavendish Ct

River Trent

B6540

Hemington Fields
House

M1

30

44 **A** 45 **B** **C** 46 **D** **E** **F**

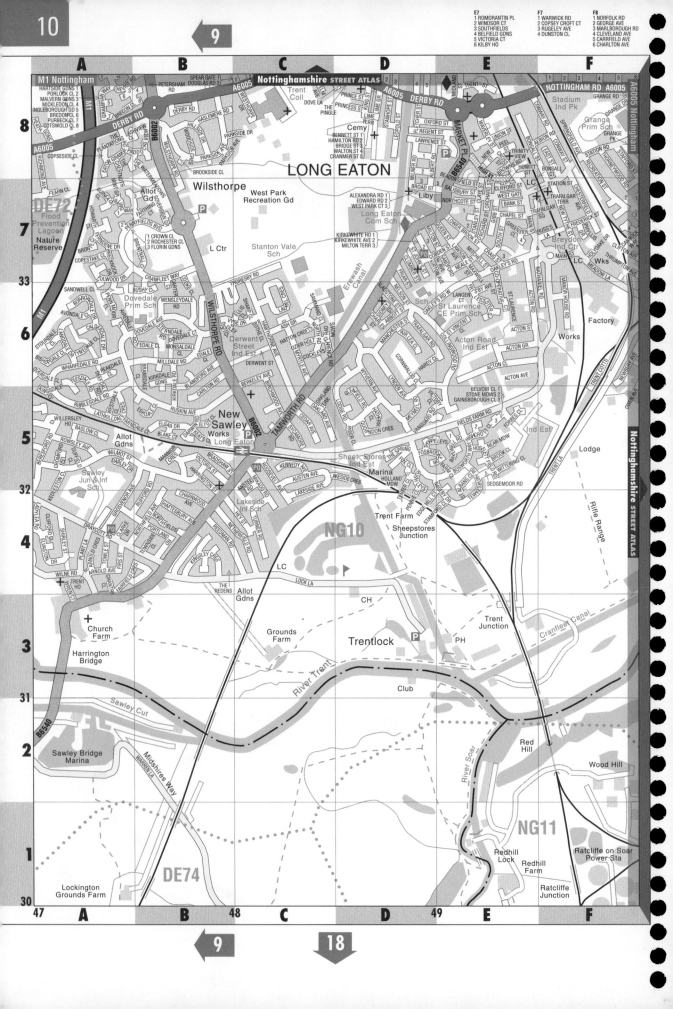

Nottinghamshire STREET ATLAS

LONG EATON

Wilsthorpe

West Park
Recreation Gd

DE72

New
Sawley

NG10

NG11

DE74

Harrington
Bridge

Trentlock

Sawley Bridge
Marina

Red
Hill

Wood Hill

Ratcliffe on Soar
Power Sta

Nottinghamshire STREET ATLAS

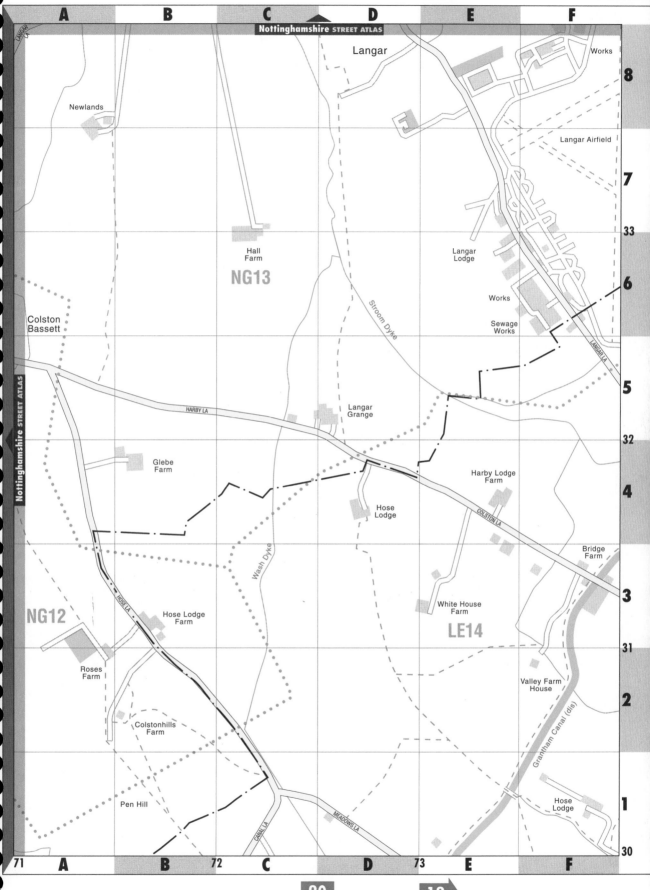

Nottinghamshire STREET ATLAS

Langar

Works

Newlands

Langar Airfield

8

7

33

Hall
Farm

NG13

Langar
Lodge

6

Works

Stroom Dyke

Colston
Bassett

Sewage
Works

LANGAR LA

5

HARBY LA

Langar
Grange

32

Glebe
Farm

Harby Lodge
Farm

4

COLSTON LA

Hose
Lodge

Wash Dyke

Bridge
Farm

3

NG12

HOSE LA

Hose Lodge
Farm

White House
Farm

LE14

31

Roses
Farm

Valley Farm
House

Grantham Canal (dis)

2

Colstonhills
Farm

Pen Hill

Hose
Lodge

1

CANAL LA

MEADOWS LA

30

Nottinghamshire STREET ATLAS

71 A   B 72 C   D 73 E   F

11
5

A B C D E F

8

7

33

6

5

32

4

3

31

2

1

30

NG13

Plungar

PH

Langar Airfield

Rundle Beck

Lodge Farm

Woodland Farm

Stathern Lodge

HARBY LA

White House

LONG LA

Lodge Farm

Stathern Bridge

P

CANAL LA

LE14

Uncle Nork's Tea Room & Farm

Glebe Farm

Grantham Canal (dis)

Washdyke Farm

PENN LA

Langar Bridge

LANGAR LA

Harby CE Prim Sch

P

Harby

BOYER'S ORCH

PINFOLD PL

STATHERN RD

HARBY LA

CITY RD

SWALLOWS DR

VALEBROOK RD

COLSTON LA

NETHER ST

BURTON CL

SCHOOL LA

STENSON'S LA

BURDEN LA

DUCKMAN'S LA

WALNUT PADDOCK

PINFOLD LA

GAS WLK

PO

Works

PH

MAIN ST

Manor Ho

THE RED CAUSEWAY

GREEN LA

Sewage Works

HOSE LA

Lodge Farm

WALTHAM LA

Willow Farm

PASTURE LA

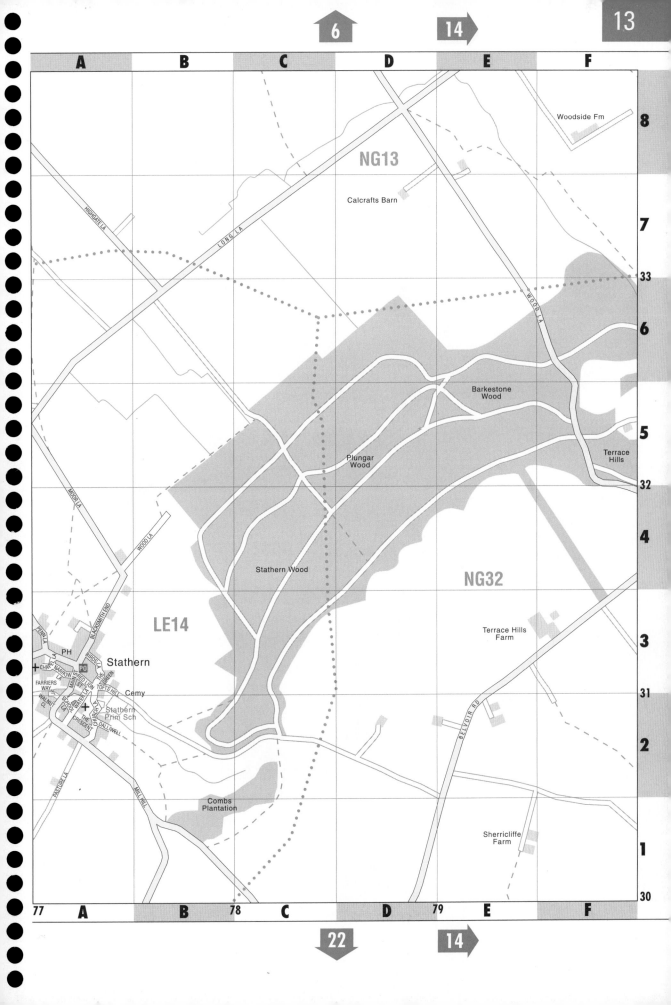

A   B   C   D   E   F

8

NG13

West Wong

The Ash
Beds

Belvoir

Belvoir Castle
(restored)

Clayfield Cottage

7

Fir
Holt

Dairy Cottage

Mausoleum

Middlesdale

33

Church Thorns

Duchess
Gardens

Briery Wood

Kennel Wood

Old Park Wood

Blackberry Hill

Kennels

6

Reeded
Cottage

High Leys

Briery Cottage

Sir John's
Belt

Carlisle
Wood

Knipton Pasture

5

Windsor Hill

Frog
Hollow

King's
Wood

32

High Leys
Farm

Granby
Wood

Knipton
Lodge

4

Hart's Barn

NG32

The Priory

Granby
Cottages

Glebe Farm

Knipton

3

Middle Barn

Bunkers Wood

Granby
Farm

PO

PH

Rectory

31

2

Reservoir
Wood

Knipton Resr

Reservoir
Cottage

Nursery
Plantation

1

Keeper's
Lodge

Cedar
Hill

30

80   A   B   81   C   D   82   E   F

WOOD LA

BELVOIR RD

The Carrier

KNIPTON LA

PASTURE LA

NURSERY LA

FINNS LA

CHURCH HILL

THE OLD HILL

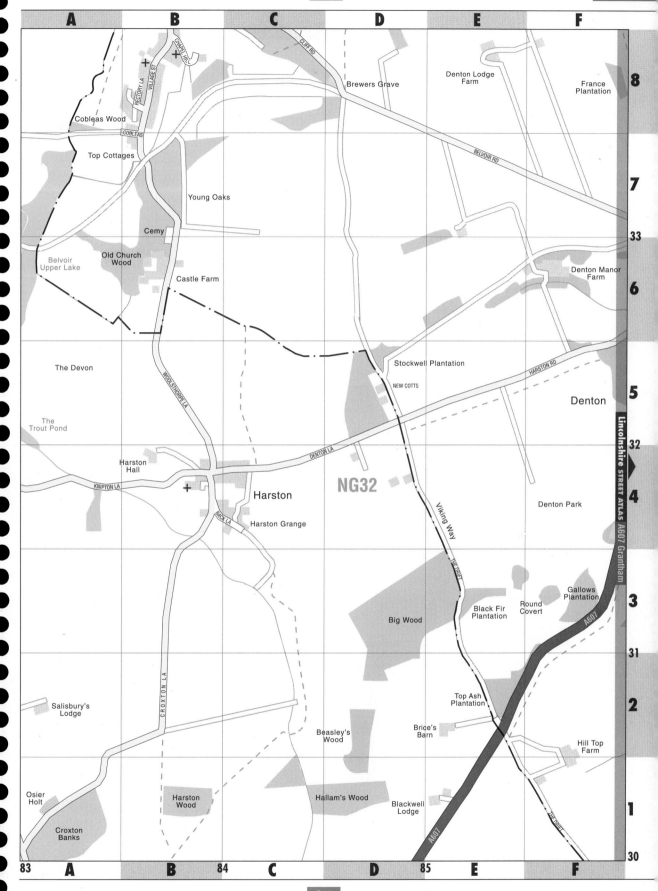

A B C D E F

8
7
33
6
5
32
4
3
31
2
1
30

Cobleas Wood
CHAPEL HILL
RECTORY LA
VILLAGE ST
Top Cottages
COBLEAS
Young Oaks
Cemy
Old Church Wood
Belvoir Upper Lake
Castle Farm
WOOLSTHORPE LA
The Devon
The Trout Pond
Harston Hall
KNIPTON LA
BACK LA
Harston
Harston Grange
NG32
Salisbury's Lodge
CROXTON LA
Osier Holt
Croxton Banks
Harston Wood
Beasley's Wood
Hallam's Wood
Blackwell Lodge
Brice's Barn
Top Ash Plantation
Big Wood
Black Fir Plantation
Round Covert
Gallows Plantation
Denton Park
Denton
DENTON LA
Viking Way
THE DRIFT
A607
THE DRIFT
Hill Top Farm
Stockwell Plantation
NEW COTTS
HARSTON RD
Denton Manor Farm
Denton Lodge Farm
France Plantation
Brewers Grave
CLIFF RD
BELVOIR RD

Lincolnshire STREET ATLAS A607 Grantham

83 A B 84 C D 85 E F

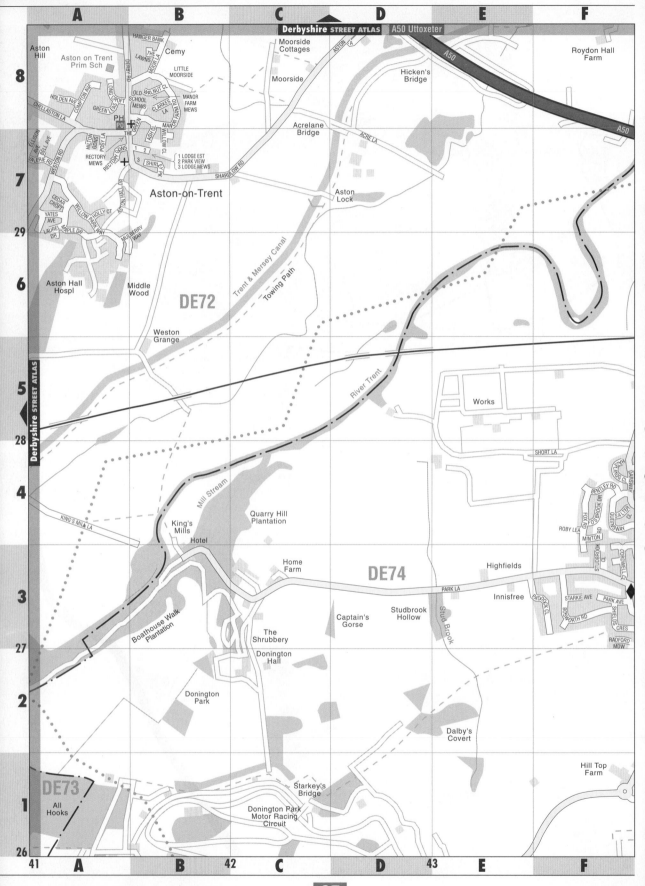

A50 Uttoxeter

Aston Hill

Aston on Trent Prim Sch

Cemy

HANGER BANK

THE LAWNS

LITTLE MOORSIDE

Moorside Cottages

Moorside

Roydon Hall Farm

Hicken's Bridge

A50

HOLDEN AVE

COMPTON AVE

LONG CROFT

GREEN LEYS

DERBY RD

MOOR LA

OLD SCHOOL MEWS

CLARKES MEWS

MANOR FARM MEWS

Acrelane Bridge

ACRE LA

CHELLASTON LA

PH PO

THE GREEN

ASH CL

WILLOW CL

ELLISON AVE

BELL AVE

WESTON RD

HILTON GDNS

POST LA

RECTORY MEWS

RECTORY GDNS

1 2

3

SHIRLEY PK

1 LODGE EST
2 PARK VIEW
3 LODGE MEWS

Aston Lock

VALERIE RD

RD THE NOOK

SHARDLOW RD

Aston-on-Trent

CEDAR CROFT

YATES AVE

LAUREL DR

MAPLE DR

WILLOW PARK WAY

HOLLY CT

MULBERRY WAY

Trent & Mersey Canal

Towing Path

Aston Hall Hospl

Middle Wood

DE72

Weston Grange

River Trent

Works

SHORT LA

Mill Stream

King's Mills

Hotel

Quarry Hill Plantation

KING'S MILL LA

Home Farm

DE74

Highfields

Park La

DARSWAY

HAZEL GRGE CL

BENTLEY RD

FOX LA

FOSBROOK DR

SALTER CL

QUEENS OWN

ROBY LEA

MINTON

STUDBROOK CL

CROWELL CL

Innisfree

PADDOCK CL

STARKIE AVE

PARK AVE

Boathouse Walk Plantation

The Shrubbery

Captain's Gorse

Studbrook Hollow

Stud Brook

BOSWORTH RD

SHIELDS CRES

RADFORD MDW

Donington Hall

Donington Park

DE73

All Hooks

Dalby's Covert

Hill Top Farm

Starkey's Bridge

Donington Park Motor Racing Circuit

41

42

43

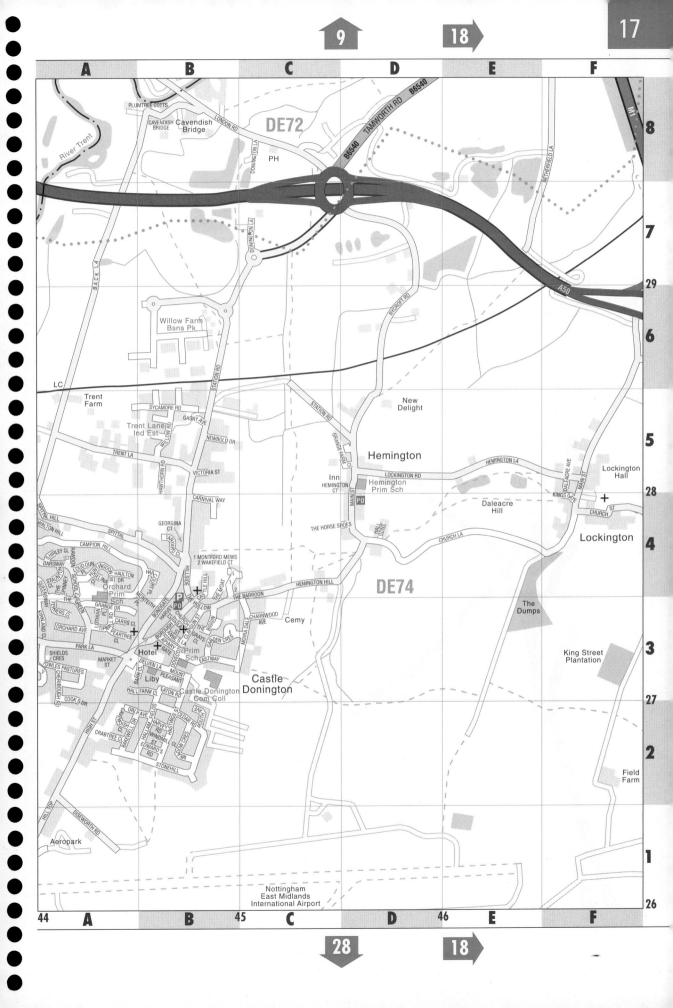

A B C D E F

8

Grounds Farm
Cottages

Power
Sta

Mason's
Barn

7

WARREN LA

RATCLIFFE LA

RATCLIFFE LA

A453

A453 Nottingham

Nottinghamshire STREET ATLAS

29

24a

M1

A50

Ratcliffe
on Soar

D PARK CL

6

Barn
Farm

Manor
Farm

Green Spot
Wood

NG11

5

Park

Long Lane
Farm

Willow
Farm

The
Bungalow

River Soar

March
Covert

Midshires Way

LONG LA

KEGWORTH RD

28

CHURCH ST

Hotel

DE74

Allot
Gdns

Kingston   Brook

Kingston
on Soar

A50

A453

KEGWORTH RD

Manor
Farm

KINGSTON LA

4

24

A6

A453

3

Factory

Sewage
Works

Kegworth

Bridge
Farm
PH

Works

STATION RD

P

Computer
Centre

CURTIS GR

JEFFARES
CL

SIDE LEY

LEATHERLANDS

MOORE AVE

NEW ST

BRIDGE FIELDS

FREDERICK AVE

KIRK AVE

VELLE

BORO

WALTON
CT

MILL LA

2

PEPPERS DR

STONEHILLS

SIBSON DR

WINDMILL WAY

Hotel

NINE ACRES

PLUMMER
LA

Kegworth
Mus

NOTTINGHAM RD

THE O

Kegworth
Prim Sch

1 WINSER CT
2 TOMS CT
3 CHURCH GATE
4 MARKET PL

Sewage
Works

27

DERBY RD

PACKINGTON HILL

COPENHALL

SUTH

MOUNT
PLEASANT

BROADHILL

BARDGATE

BRIGNOLL

HIGH ST

PO

NORMAN
CT

Old Cut

Liby

ASHBY RD

LANE

WEST BANK MEWS

OLDERSHAW AVE

BULSTODE
PL

STAF

SOHO

SQ

PLEASANT PL

THE CROFT

HEAFIELD DR

LE12

SPRINGFIELD

LANGLEY DR

ACRE

2
1

3
4

ASHBY RD

FOXHILLS

WHATTON RD

ST ANDREW'S RISE

SUTTON RD

Cemy

HILLSIDE

BURLEY RISE

BEDFORD
CL

ROBERTS CL

GEYARD

GEYARD

CRES

SHEPHERD WLK

KIRBY DR

THOMAS RD

Alton
Lodge

LONDON RD

NEW BRICKYARD LA

A6

26

A453

M1

Molehill
Farm

Broad
Hill

47 A B 48 C D 49 E F

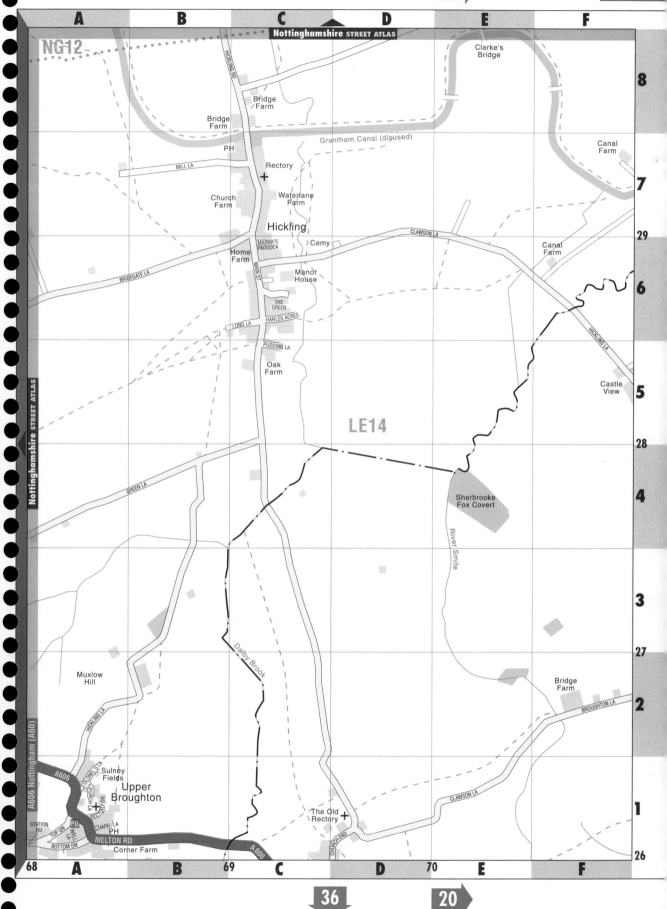

Nottinghamshire STREET ATLAS

Nottinghamshire STREET ATLAS

NG12

Clarke's Bridge

Bridge Farm

Bridge Farm

HICKLING RD

PH

MILL LA

Rectory

Church Farm

Waterlane Farm

Grantham Canal (disused)

Canal Farm

Hickling

MARSH'S PADDOCK

Cemy

CLAWSON LA

Canal Farm

Home Farm

MAIN ST

Manor House

BRIDEGATE LA

THE GREEN

HARLES ACRES

LONG LA

PUDDING LA

Oak Farm

LE14

Castle View

HICKLING LA

Sherbrooke Fox Covert

GREEN LA

River Smite

Muxlow Hill

Dalby Brook

Bridge Farm

BROUGHTON LA

HICKLING LA

A606 Nottingham (A60)

Sulney Fields

COLONEL'S TA

CHURCH LA

RECTORY DR

Upper Broughton

A606

The Old Rectory

CLAWSON LA

STATION RD

PO

TOP GN

WELL

CHAPEL LA

PH

BOTTOM GN

MELTON RD

A606

Corner Farm

CHURCH END

19
11

A B C D E F

8

Grantham Canal (disused)
Long Clawson Bridge
Hose Thorns
Marriott's Bridge
Wash Dyke
MEADOWS LA
Bridge House
CANAL LA
The Grange
STROUD'S CL
Hose
Works
Hose Lodge
CHAPEL LA
HOME CL
COAL LA
HARBY LA
PASTURES
PH
THE GREEN
MIDDLE CHURCH CL
DAIRY LA
ST
CHURCH
BOLTON LA
WLK
Hose CE Prim Sch
The Farm
PH

7

River Smite

29

6

CANAL LA
Dam Dyke

Brook Farm
Glebe Farm

HOSE LA

5

Castle View

Highfield Farm

28

LE14

Hall Farm

4

HICKLING LA

WATER LA

PAGET'S END
EAST END
PH
Long Clawson CE Prim Sch
PO
Barkers Farm
BARKERS FI ELD
THE SANDS
SCHOOL LA
PH

3

West End Farm
CHURCH LA
BACK LA
Long Clawson

HOLYTREE LA
WEST END
STOKES PADDOCK
CLAXTON RISE

27

BROUGHTON LA
Hill Farm
KINGS RD
MILL LA

Cemy
WALTHAM LA

2

CORONATION AVE
Mill Farm
Brookhill Cottage

MELTON RD
SANDPIT LA
Windmill (disused)

Slyborough Hill
Old Mill House

1

Sandpit Farm

26

71 A B 72 C D 73 E F

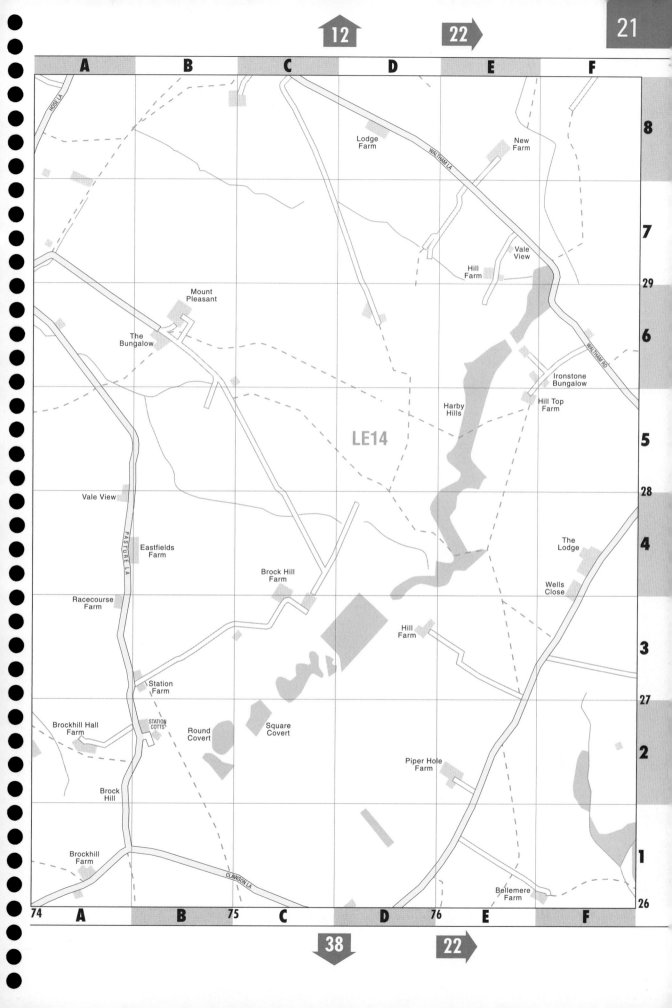

21
13

A B C D E F

8

High Leas
Farm

Eaton
Lodge

Thorn
Hills

BELVOIR RD

Lodge Farm

Sunnydene

NG32

7

Cemy

PH

EATON
CT

VICARAGE LA

LINGS CL

BLUE POTS LA

CHURCH LA

PO

29

STATHERN RD

Eaton

ELM LA

Home
Farm

MAIN ST

WATER LA

CHAPEL ST

MAIN ST

Eastwell

Castlehill
Farm

6

West End
Farm

STANLEYS LA

PO

The
Old Rectory

STALFORD RD

HALL LA

The
Hall

WALTHAM LA

5

Hall Farm

Crossroads Farm
Mus

28

Glebe Farm

WALTHAM RD

4

LE14

White
Lodge

Green
Lodge

GREEN LA

STATION RD

3

27

2

Manor
Farm

TOWNS LA

The Hall

KEMP LA

Goadby
Marwood

Goadby Hall
Farm

WYCOMB LA

PO

MAIN ST

1

26

21
39

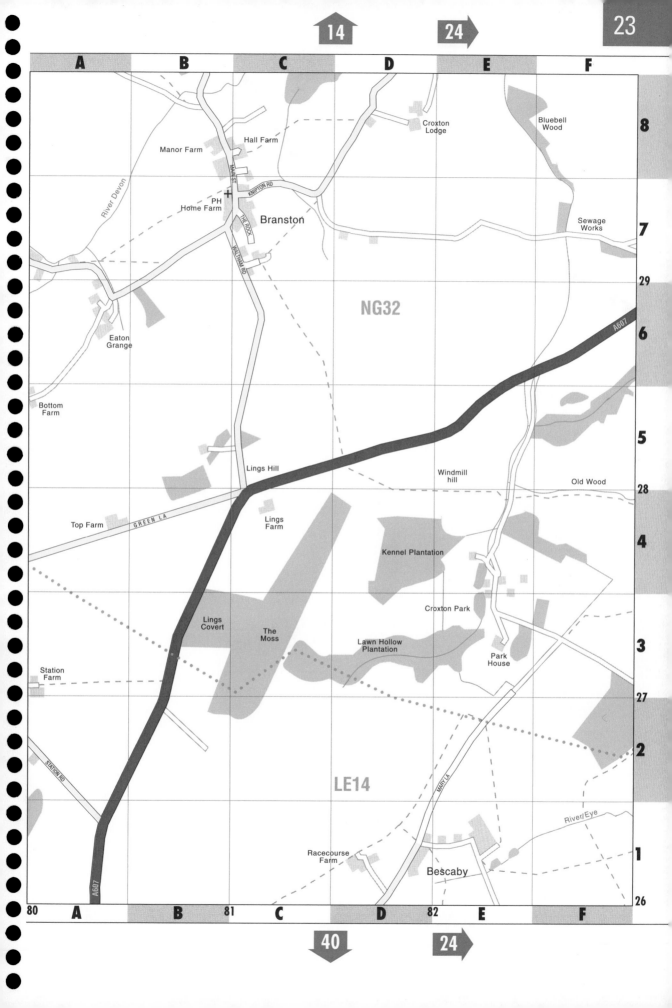

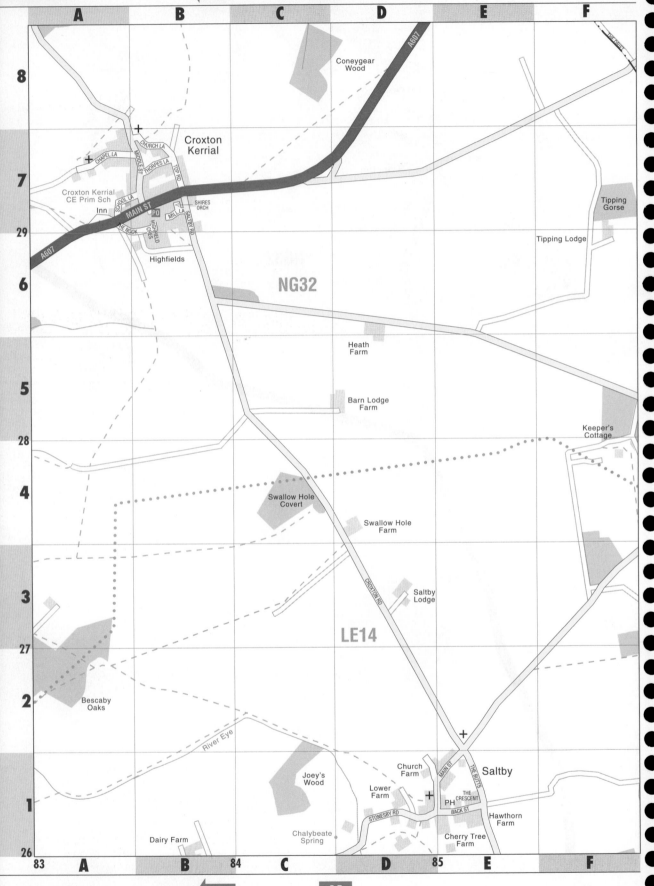

A   B   C   D   E   F

8

Coneygear Wood

A607

Croxton Kerrial

7

CHURCH LA
CHAPEL LA
MIDDLE ST
THORPES LA
TOP RD

Croxton Kerrial
CE Prim Sch

SCHOOL LA

SHIRES ORCH

29   Inn   MAIN ST   PO   THE NOOK   MILL LA   SALTBY RD   HIGHFIELD CRES

Tipping Gorse

Tipping Lodge

A607

Highfields

6   NG32

Heath Farm

5

Barn Lodge Farm

Keeper's Cottage

28

4   Swallow Hole Covert

Swallow Hole Farm

3   CROXTON RD   Saltby Lodge

LE14

27

2   Bescaby Oaks

River Eye

Church Farm

MAIN ST   THE BUTS   Saltby

Joey's Wood

Lower Farm

PH   THE CRESCENT

1   STONESBY RD   BACK ST   Hawthorn Farm

Dairy Farm   Chalybeate Spring   Cherry Tree Farm

26

83   A   B   84   C   D   85   E   F

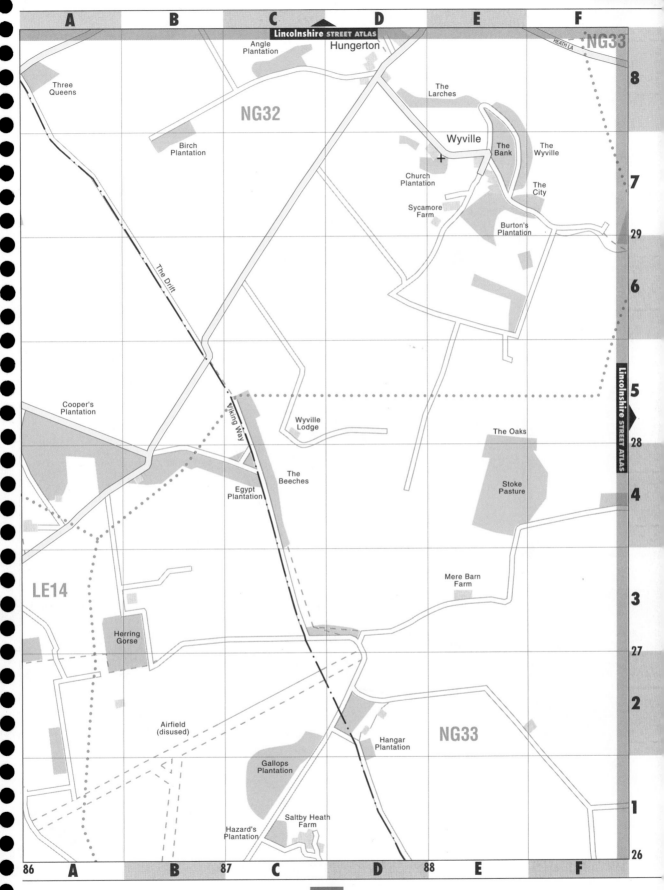

Hungerton

Angle Plantation

The Larches

Three Queens

NG32

Wyville

The Bank

The Wyville

Birch Plantation

Church Plantation

The City

Sycamore Farm

Burton's Plantation

The Drift

Cooper's Plantation

Viking Way

Wyville Lodge

The Oaks

Egypt Plantation

The Beeches

Stoke Pasture

LE14

Mere Barn Farm

Herring Gorse

Airfield (disused)

NG33

Hangar Plantation

Gallops Plantation

Saltby Heath Farm

Hazard's Plantation

HEATH LA

NG33

Lincolnshire STREET ATLAS

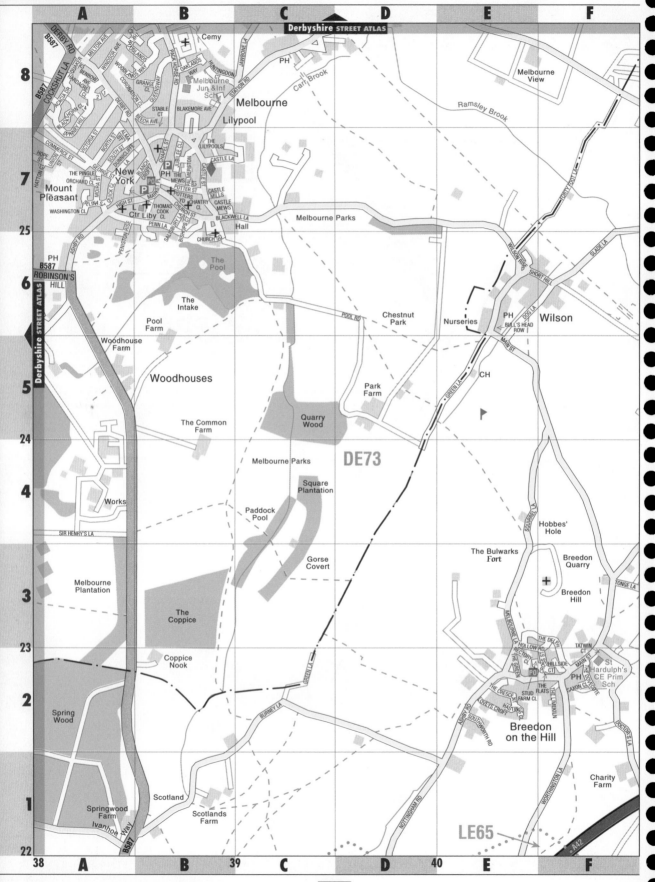

Derbyshire STREET ATLAS

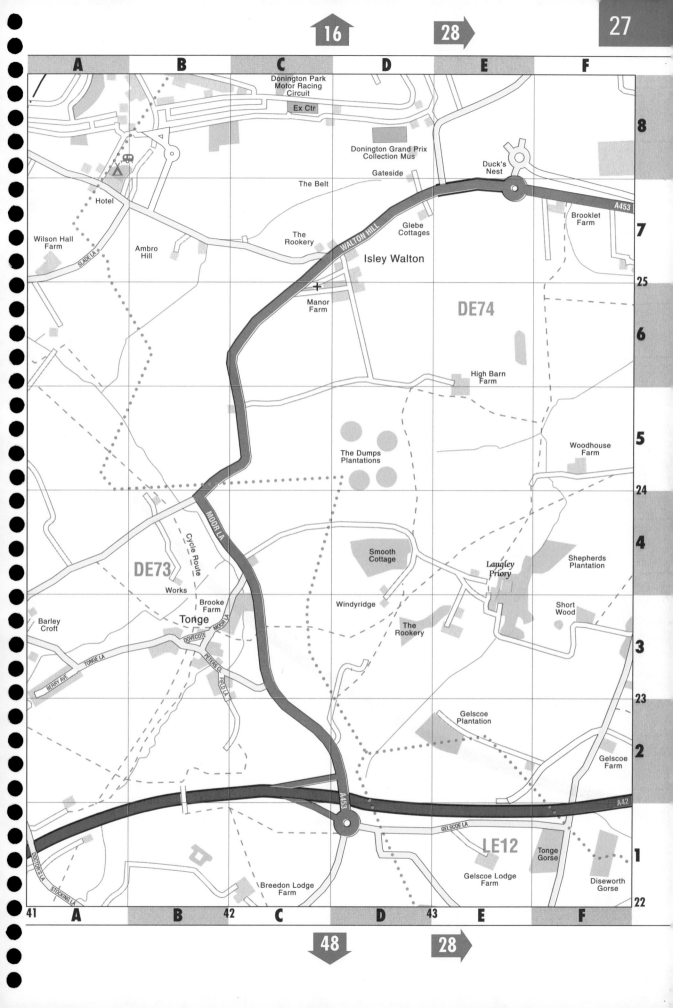

27
17

A · B · C · D · E · F

8

Nottingham
East Midlands
International Airport

ANSON RD

DAKOTA RD

VANGUARD RD

BEVERLEY RD

ARGOSY RD

Finger
Farm

DOVE RD

P

P

VISCOUNT RD

P

VISCOUNT RD

AMBASSADOR RD

ASHBY RD

Hotel

A453

A453

7

A453

Charnock
Hill

Bleak
House

GRIMES GATE

Donington Park
Services

M1

25

GREEN LA

HYAM'S LA

23a

6

Wartoft
Grange

Diseworth
CE
Prim Sch

PH

SHAKESPEARE DR

HALL GATE

CLEMENTS GATE

LONG HOLDEN

THE BONLEY

SHAKESPEAR CL

ORCHARD CL

BROOKSIDE

Diseworth

A42

THE GREEN

THE WOODCROFT

PAGE LA

LADY GATE

5

The Green

Diseworth Brook

DE74

Town
End

Wood Nook
Farm

24

WEST END

M1

4

LONG MERE LA

WESTMEADOW LA

3

New Wood

23

Little Rise
Farm

LE12

2

Scaffacre
Farm

Westmeadow Brook

Riste
Farm

DRY POT LA

Glebe
Farm

A42

David's
Hill

1

Long Mere
Farm

WV8

22

44 · A · B · 45 · C · D · 46 · E · F

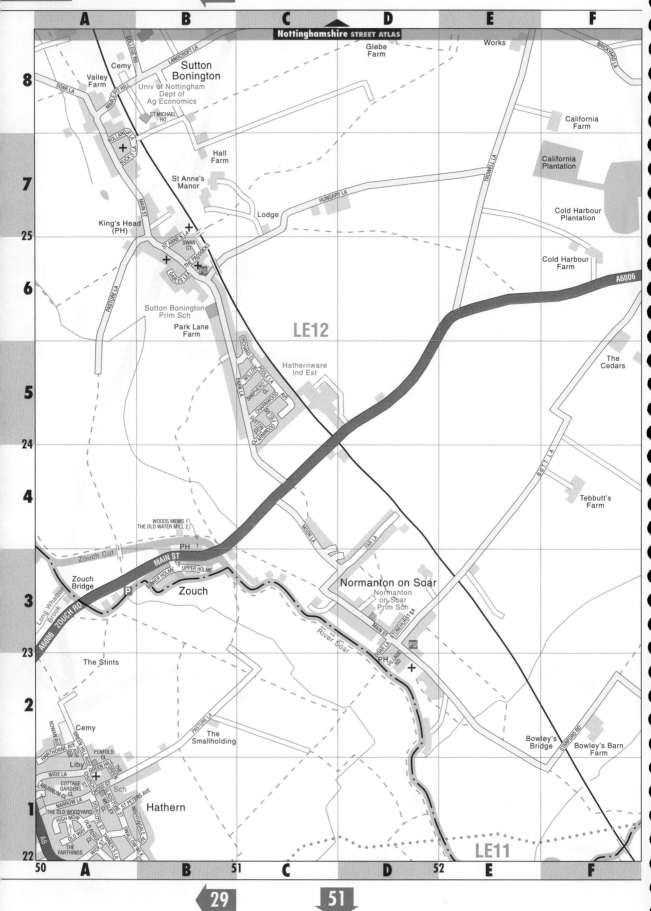

A B C D E F

Glebe Farm

Works

BRICKYARD LA

Cemy

Valley Farm

Sutton Bonington

Univ of Nottingham Dept of Ag Economics

St Michael Ho

Hall Farm

California Farm

California Plantation

St Anne's Manor

HUNGARY LA

Lodge

Cold Harbour Plantation

King's Head (PH)

ST ANNE'S LA

SWAN CT

THE PADDOCKS

PO

Cold Harbour Farm

A6006

Sutton Bonington Prim Sch

Park Lane Farm

LE12

The Cedars

Hathernware Ind Est

BUTT LA

Tebbutt's Farm

WOODS MEWS
THE OLD WATER MILL 2

PH

MAIN ST

UPPER HOLME

Zouch Cut

Zouch Bridge

LOWER HOLME

P

Zouch

Normanton on Soar

Normanton on Soar Prim Sch

FAR LA

MOOR LA

A6006 ZOUCH RD

River Soar

PO

SPH VILLAGE RD

The Stints

The Smallholding

PASTURE LA

Bowley's Bridge

STANFORD RD

Bowley's Barn Farm

Cemy

Liby

Sch

Hathern

LE11

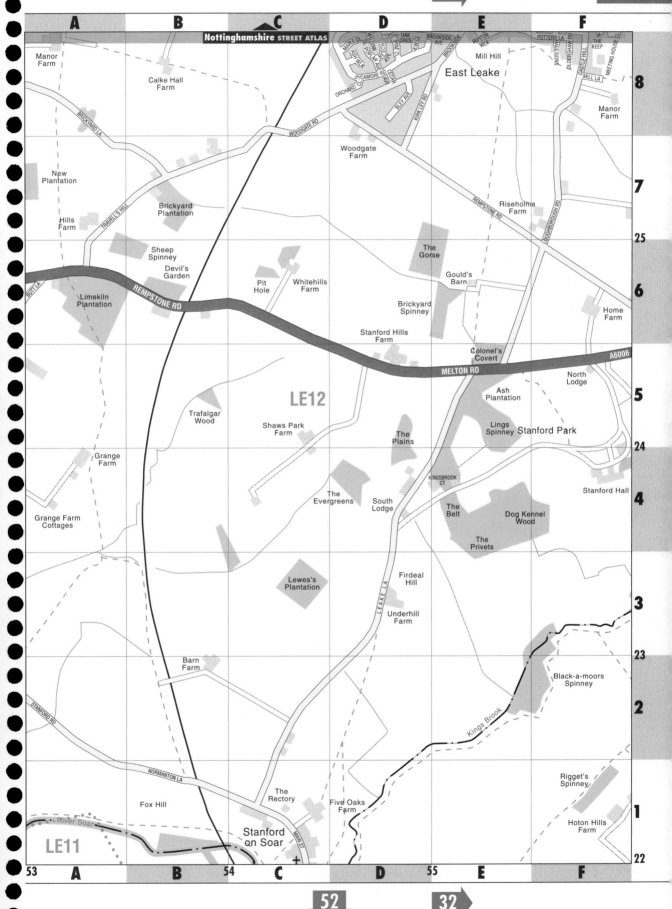

A   B   C   D   E   F

Nottinghamshire STREET ATLAS

Manor Farm

Calke Hall Farm

BRICKYARD LA

New Plantation

Hills Farm

TRAVELL'S HILL

Brickyard Plantation

Sheep Spinney

Devil's Garden

BUTT LA

Limekiln Plantation

REMPSTONE RD

Pit Hole

Whitehills Farm

Woodgate Farm

WOODGATE RD

MAPLE CL
ASH WLK
WILLOW CL
POPLAR AVE
PINE CL
BEECH AVE
CEDAR
SEW CL
OAK CRES
BROOKSIDE AVE
BROOKSIDE
ORCHARD CL
SYCAMORE RD
KIRKLEY RD
BLEY AVE

BURTON WLK
POTTERS LA
TEL HILL GDNS
OLDERSHAW RD
CASTLE HILL
MEETING HOUSE CL
MILL LA
THE KEEP

Mill Hill

East Leake

Manor Farm

REMPSTONE RD

Riseholme Farm

LOUGHBOROUGH RD

The Gorse

Gould's Barn

Brickyard Spinney

Home Farm

Stanford Hills Farm

Colonel's Covert

MELTON RD

A6006

LE12

Trafalgar Wood

Shaws Park Farm

The Plains

Ash Plantation

Lings Spinney

Stanford Park

North Lodge

Grange Farm

The Evergreens

South Lodge

KINGSBROOK CT

The Belt

Dog Kennel Wood

The Privets

Stanford Hall

Grange Farm Cottages

Lewes's Plantation

LEAKE LA

Firdeal Hill

Underhill Farm

STANFORD RD

Barn Farm

Kings Brook

Black-a-moors Spinney

NORMANTON LA

The Rectory

Five Oaks Farm

Rigget's Spinney

Fox Hill

River Soar

Stanford on Soar

MAIN ST

Hoton Hills Farm

LE11

8
7
25
6
5
24
4
3
23
2
1
22

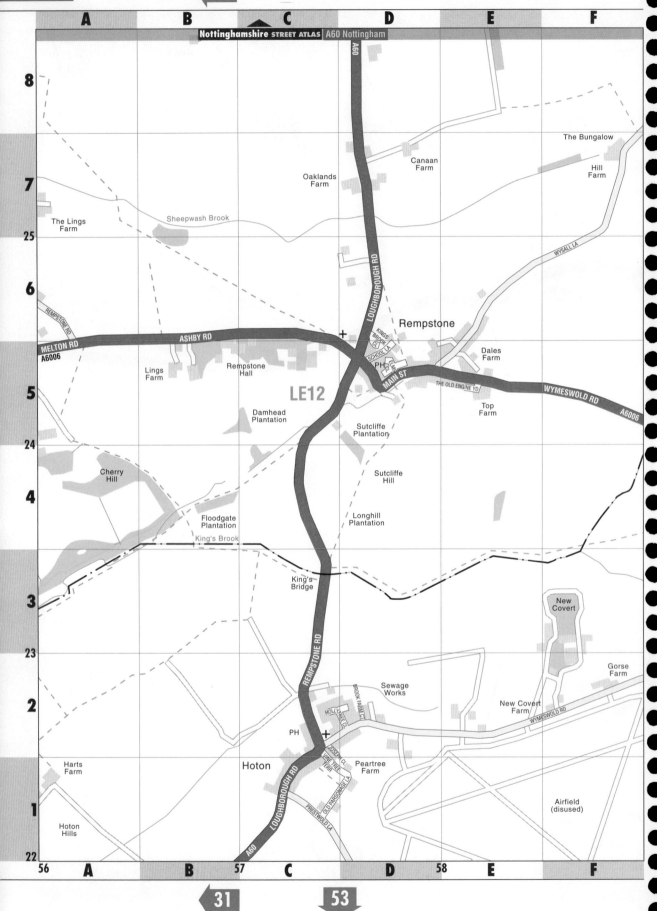

Nottinghamshire STREET ATLAS | A60 Nottingham

A **B** **C** **D** **E** **F**

A60

8

The Bungalow

Canaan
Farm

7

Oaklands
Farm

Hill
Farm

25

Sheepwash Brook

WYSALL LA

The Lings
Farm

6

LOUGHBOROUGH RD

REMPSTONE RD

Rempstone

MELTON RD

ASHBY RD

KINGS
BROOK
CL

Dales Farm

A6006

SCHOOL LA

PH

Lings
Farm

Rempstone
Hall

THE OLD ENGINE YD

MAIN ST

WYMESWOLD RD

5

LE12

Top
Farm

A6006

Damhead
Plantation

Sutcliffe
Plantation

24

Cherry
Hill

Sutcliffe
Hill

4

Floodgate
Plantation

Longhill
Plantation

New
Covert

King's Brook

3

King's
Bridge

23

Gorse
Farm

REMPSTONE RD

Sewage
Works

New Covert

2

BROOK FARM CL

New Covert
Farm

WYMESWOLD RD

HOLLYTREE CL

PH

Harts
Farm

JOSEPH CL

Hoton

VINE TREE
TERR

Peartree
Farm

Airfield
(disused)

LOUGHBOROUGH RD

OLD PARSONAGE LA

1

PRESTWOLD LA

Hoton
Hills

A60

22

56 **A** 57 **B** **C** 58 **D** **E** **F**

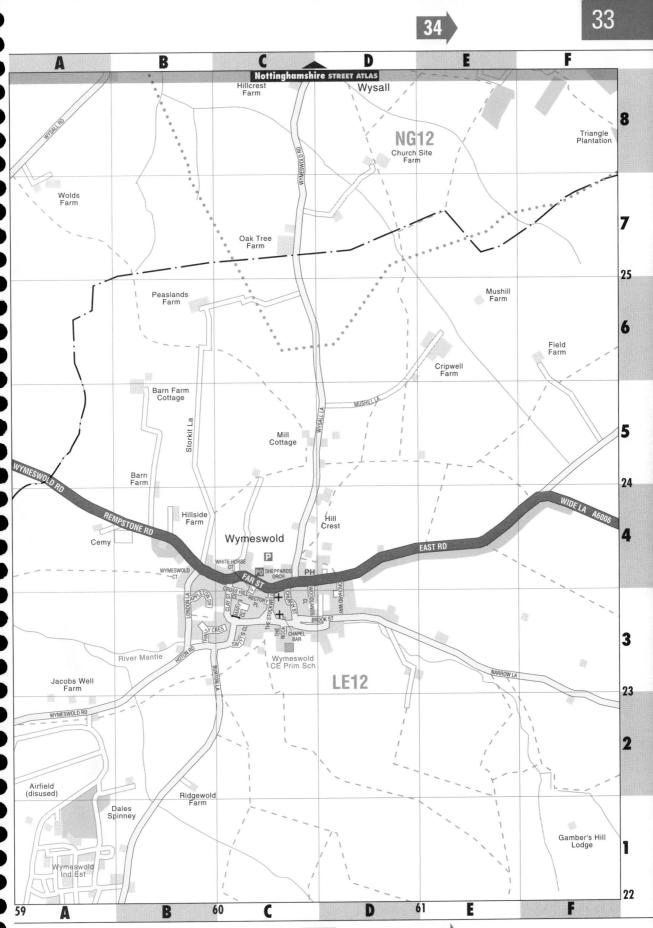

Nottinghamshire STREET ATLAS

Wysall

Hillcrest Farm

NG12

Church Site Farm

Triangle Plantation

WYSALL RD

Wolds Farm

Oak Tree Farm

Mushill Farm

Peaslands Farm

WYMESWOLD RD

Barn Farm Cottage

Cripwell Farm

Field Farm

Storkit La

Mill Cottage

WYSALL LA

MUSHILL LA

Barn Farm

WYMESWOLD RD

Hillside Farm

REMPSTONE RD

Hill Crest

WIDE LA A6006

Cemy

Wymeswold

EAST RD

WHITE HORSE CT

P

WYMESWOLD CT

PO

SHEPPARDS ORCH

FAR ST

PH

LONDON LA

APPLETON DR

CLAY ST

CROSS HILL CL

MARY'S CL

RECTORY PL

CHURCH ST

WOODLANDS CL

ORCHARD WAY

TRINITY CRES

SWIFT'S CL

THE STOCKWELL

THE NOOK

BROOK ST

CHAPEL BAR

HOTON RD

BURTON LA

River Mantle

Wymeswold CE Prim Sch

LE12

NARROW LA

Jacobs Well Farm

WYMESWOLD RD

Airfield (disused)

Ridgewold Farm

Dales Spinney

Gamber's Hill Lodge

Wymeswold Ind Est

NG12

Nottinghamshire STREET ATLAS

8

Eclpool
Field

Willoughby-on-the-Wolds

WIDMERPOOL LA

MILL LA

Bryans La

7

Willoughby
Gorse

Old Hall
Farm

MANOR CT

CHURCH LA

FIELD FARM
CL

CROSS HILL

NEW
ROW

Willoughby
Prim Sch

MAIN ST

PO

PH

WESTHORPE

BROOK FARM CT

Green La

CHAPEL LA

LONDON LA

25

BACK LA

Midshires Way

Barrack
Cottages

6

5

Turnpost
Farm

24

Kingston Brook

HADES LA

OCCUPATION LA

LE14

4

A6006

Dungehill
Farm

LE12

Eller's
Gorse

Lakeside

3

Hill
Farm

WIDE LA

Ella's Farm

Pasture
Lodge

23

Highthorn
Farm

2

Common
Farm

NARROW LA

Wymeswold
Lodge

Willoughby Fields
Farm

PADDY'S LA

A6006

A46

1

LE14

Wolds
Farm

The
Lodge

22

62

A

B

63

C

D

64

E

F

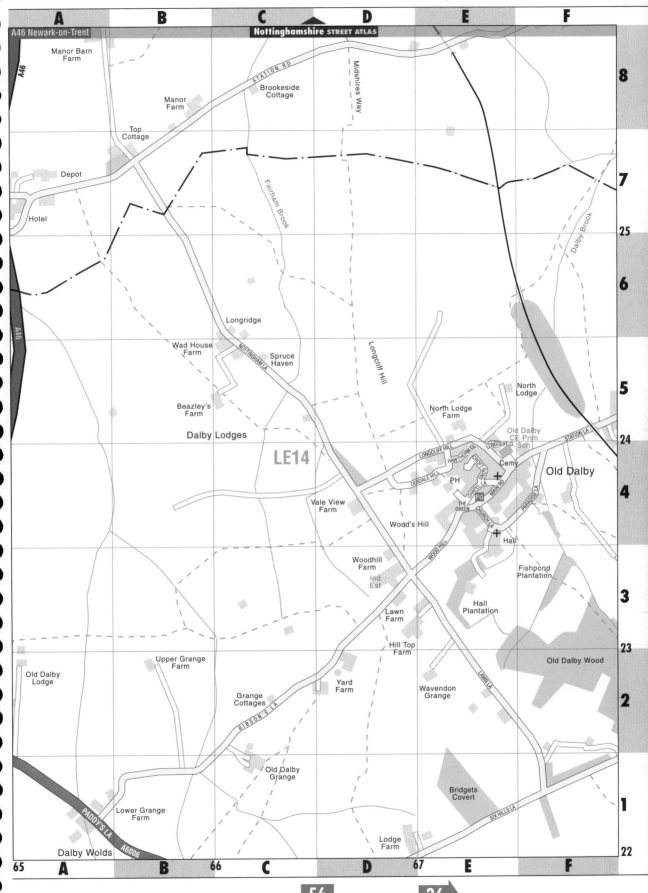

A46 Newark-on-Trent

Nottinghamshire STREET ATLAS

Manor Barn Farm

A46

Manor Farm

Top Cottage

STATION RD

Brookeside Cottage

Midshires Way

8

Depot

7

Hotel

Fairham Brook

25

A46

6

Longridge

Wad House Farm

NOTTINGHAM LA

Spruce Haven

Longcliff Hill

North Lodge

5

Beazley's Farm

North Lodge Farm

Old Dalby CE Prim Sch

STATION LA

24

Dalby Lodges

LE14

LONGCLIFF HILL

HAWTHORN CL

CROFT GDNS

LONGCLIFF CL

Cemy

Old Dalby

DERDALE HILL

CHAPEL LA

MAIN RD

PARADISE LA

Vale View Farm

PH

PO

4

Wood's Hill

THE GREEN

CHURCH LA

Hall

Woodhill Farm

WOOD HILL

Fishpond Plantation

Ind Est

3

Lawn Farm

Hall Plantation

Hill Top Farm

23

Upper Grange Farm

Old Dalby Wood

Old Dalby Lodge

Yard Farm

Wavendon Grange

LAWN LA

2

Grange Cottages

GIBSON'S LA

Old Dalby Grange

Bridgets Covert

1

PADDY'S LA

Lower Grange Farm

A6006

Lodge Farm

SIX HILLS LA

22

Dalby Wolds

35
19

A **B** **C** **D** **E** **F**

8

Nether Broughton

CHURCH END

Moat Farm

A606

HEADECK LA

PARNHAM'S CL

CHAPEL LA

MIDDLE LA

BLACKSMITHS CL

KING ST

DAIRY LA

Manor Farm

MAIN RD

7

Works

PH

The Grange

NOTTINGHAM RD

25

GREAVES AVE

THE CRESCENT

QUEENSWAY

PRINCES RD

6

Hatton Lodge

Broughton Lodges

Playing Field

EARLS CL

MARQUIS RD

DUKES RD

OLD DALBY LA

Broughton Lodge

Lodge Farm

A606

5

STATION LA

Old Dalby Trad Est

SIGNAL RD

FLAGSTAFF RD

APPLESART RD

MAIN ST

Crown Bsns Pk

STATION LA

BOMBARD RD

WESTERN RD

FIELDWORK RD

BICYCLE RD

24

Railway Research Station

BOILERHOUSE RD

Greenhill Farm

Broughton Hill

4

Crompton's Plantation

LE14

Stonepit Spinney

Marriott's Spinney

Berlea Farm

Green Hill

3

Friars Well Farm

23

Saxelbye Lodge

Barnes Hill Plantation

Marriott's Wood

Friars Well

SIX HILLS LA

Air Shafts

Grimston Tunnel

Old Dalby Wood

2

Tunnel Farm

Ten Acres Plantation

Saxelbye Wood

1

PERKINS LA

Grimston Gorse

Barn Farm

Saxelbye Pastures

22

Hillside Farm

A **B** **C** **D** **E** **F**

68 69 70

35
57

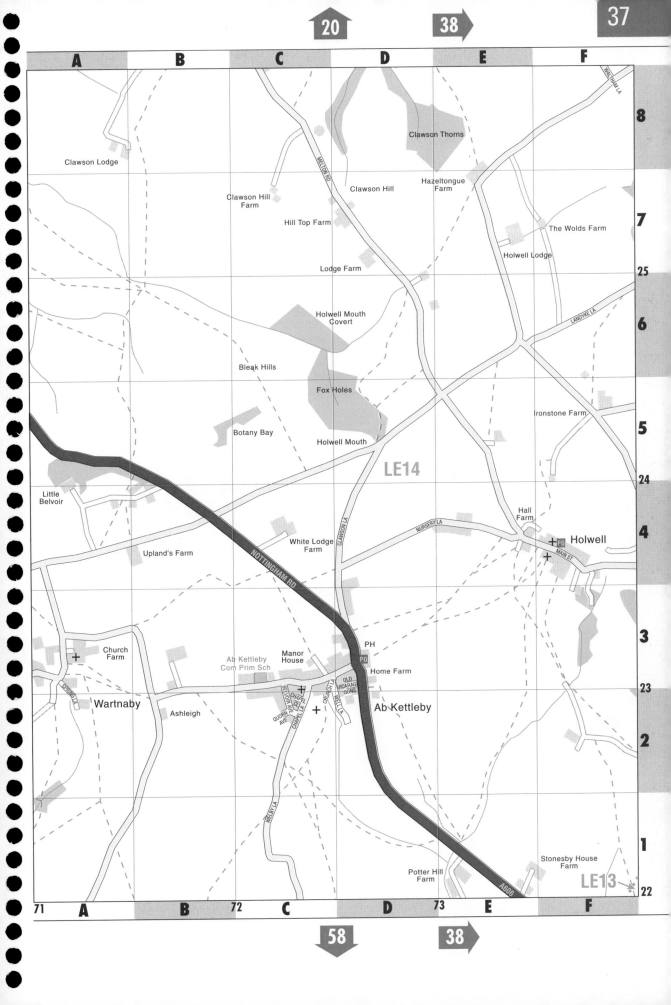

37 21

A B C D E F

8

CLAWSON LA

Cranyke
Farm

Wolds
Farm

LIONVILLE
COTTS

Deben
Farm

Red House
Farm

LANDYKE LA

7

The
Cottage

Mawbrook
Lodge

25

Landyke Lane
Farm

Old Brickyard
Cottages

6

Mawbrook
Farm

Manor
House

The
Willows

Scalford

5

Grange
Farm

The
Elms

KING'S
CL

KING ST

PH

PO

SANDY LA

Cemy

PH
SOUTH
CL

QUEEN'S
CL

NEW ST

SCHOOL LA

CHURCH ST

Scalford
CE Prim
Sch

24

HIGH ST

SOUTH ST

Netherhall
Barn

4

LE14

Mill Top
Farm

Clayfield
Farm

THORPE SIDE

Brown's
Hill

Scalford
Lodge

3

Scalford
Hall

23

Sans
Souci

Cumberland
Lodge

Scalford Brook

Old Hills
Wood

Long-gate
Lodge

2

Old
Hills

MELTON RD

MELTON SPINNEY RD

LE13

Glebe
Farm

Melton
Spinney

1

Scalford
Gorse

SCALFORD RD

22

LE13

Melton
Spinney
Farm

74 A B 75 C D 76 E F

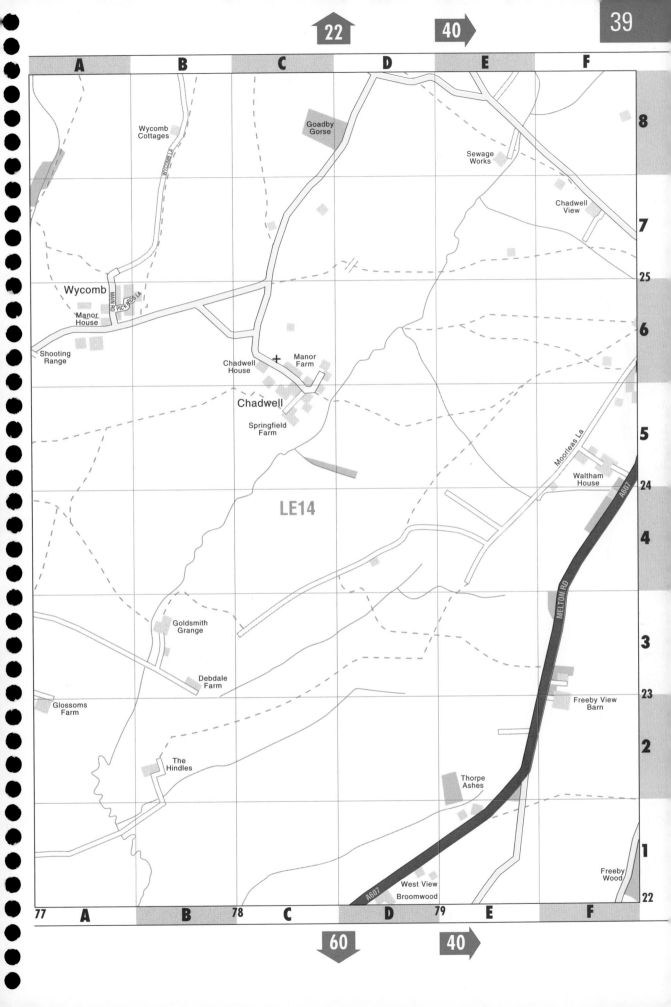

A B C D E F

8
7
25
6
5
24
4
3
23
2
1
22

Wycomb Cottages

Goadby Gorse

Sewage Works

Chadwell View

WYCOMB LA

Wycomb

MAIN RD PICKLOUS LA

Manor House

Shooting Range

Chadwell House

Manor Farm

Chadwell

Springfield Farm

LE14

Mooreas La

A607

Waltham House

MELTON RD

Goldsmith Grange

Debdale Farm

Glossoms Farm

The Hindles

Freeby View Barn

Thorpe Ashes

A607

West View Broomwood

Freeby Wood

77 A B 78 C D 79 E F

39
23

A B C D E F

8

Mast
Radio
Station

MARY LA

7

Hall
Farm

Waltham on the
Wolds

THE COURTYARD

MERE RD

25

GOADBY RD

THE
PADDOCK

BURGINS LA

WINDSOR
RD

PH

CHURCH LA

PO

Stoneleigh
Farm

BESCABY LA

MELTON RD

HIGH ST

TWELLS
RD

MILL LA

ROSE
COTTS

6

MANOR
CT

Waltham on the Wolds
CE Prim Sch

FAIR
FIELD

Allot
Gdns

The
Mount

STONESBY RD

WALTHAM RD

Church
Farm

THE
GREEN

BACK LA

PO

MAIN ST

Manor
Farm

Cemy

Mast

Wr Twr

Stonesby

CHAPEL LA

5

A607

Rectory

Gorse
Farm

KING STREET LA

24

LE14

4

3

Waltham
Stud Farm

TV Mast

Stonesby
Spinney

23

Waltham
Lodge

Covert
Farm

2

Waltham Pasture
Farm

Waltham
New Covert

GIPSY NOOK

Strifts
Plantation

1

Waltham
Thorns

Freeby Wood

22

80 A 81 B C 81 D 82 E F

39
61

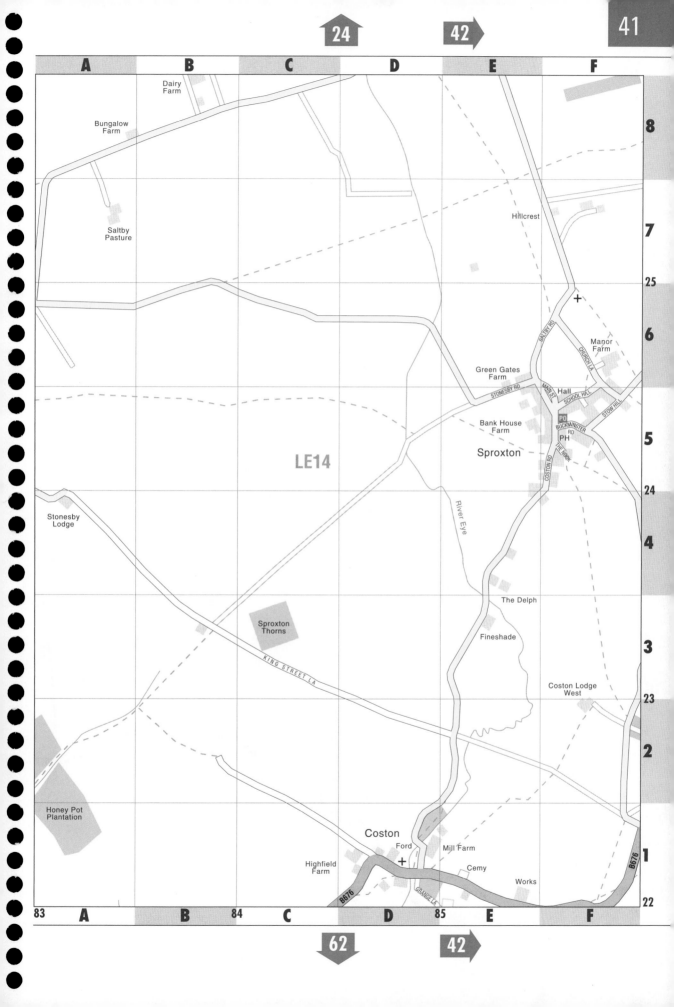

A B C D E F

8

7

25

6

NG33

LE14

5

24

4

Annises
Plantation

Sproxton Lodge

Viking Way

Cringle Brook

Gorse
Plantation

Jackson's
Plantation

Bottom
Plantation

Cams Hill

The Ashes
(Wr Twr)

New
Rookery

3

23

Park
Oaks

Buckminster Park

Parkside
Wood

The
Roundle

Buckminster
Hall

Hanby
House

Viking Way

THE DRIFT

2

Gorse Close
Plantation

Manor House
Farm

Buckminster

BACK ST

MAIN ST

PH

Manor
Farm

STAINBY RD

B676

East
Plantation

SPROXTON RD

PO

Grange Farm

COW ROW

1

Royce's
Plantation

B676

Brick Yard
Wood

COSTON RD

SCHOOL LA

Old School
House

Buckminster
Prim Sch

22

86 A B 87 C D 88 E F

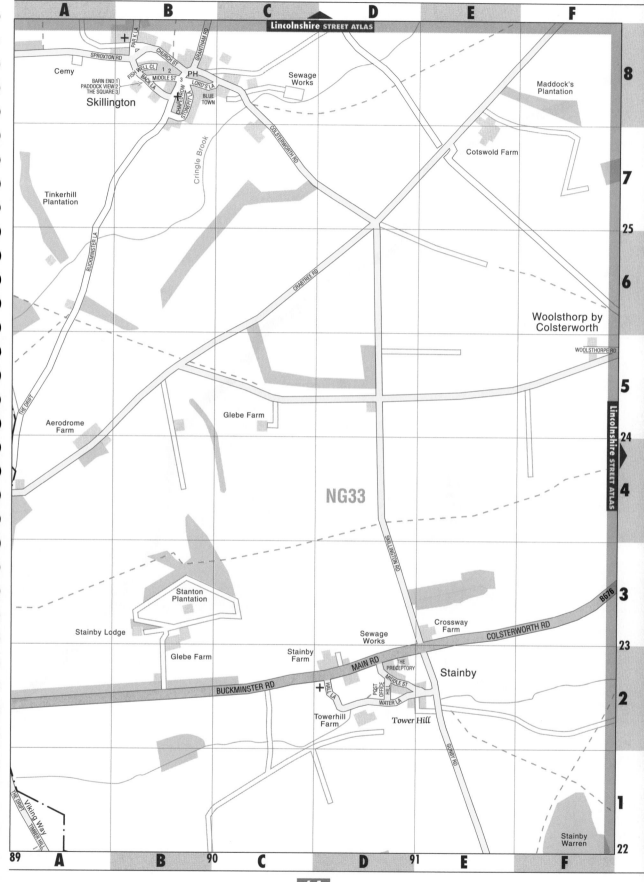

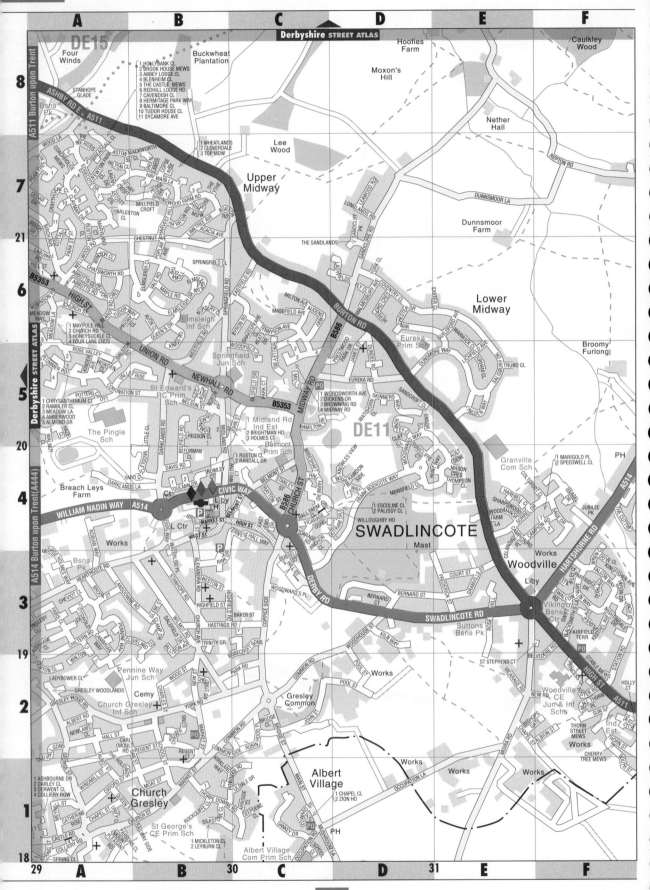

Derbyshire STREET ATLAS

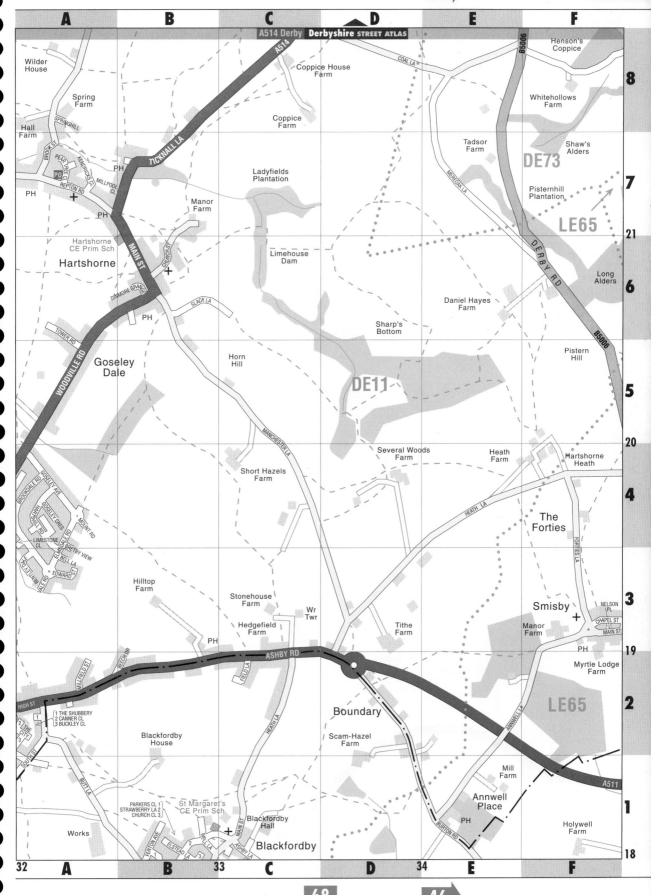

A B C D E F

A514

COAL LA

B5006

Henson's Coppice

Wilder House

Coppice House Farm

Whitehollows Farm

8

Spring Farm

SPRINGHILL

TICKNALL LA

Coppice Farm

Tadsor Farm

Shaw's Alders

DE73

BROCK ST

PEAR TREE CL

KENDRICKS CL

MILLPOOL CL

PO

Hall Farm

PH

MEROAK LA

Pisternhill Plantation

7

REPTON RD

CHURCH ST

Manor Farm

Ladyfields Plantation

LE65

21

PH

PH

MAIN ST

Hartshorne CE Prim Sch

Limehouse Dam

DERBY RD

Long Alders

6

Hartshorne

SLACK LA

DUNMORE GRANGE

PH

Sharp's Bottom

Daniel Hayes Farm

TOWER RD

WOODVILLE RD

Goseley Dale

Horn Hill

Pistern Hill

B5006

5

DE11

BROOKDALE RD

GOSELEY AVE

GOSELEY DRES

MANCHESTER LA

Several Woods Farm

Heath Farm

Hartshorne Heath

20

Short Hazels Farm

MOUNT RD

BRETBY VIEW

LIMESTONE CL

ELMSDALE RD

BELL LA

4

HEATH LA

FORTIES LA

The Forties

PG

BENTLEY RD

VALE RD

EDWARD

Hilltop Farm

Stonehouse Farm

Wr Twr

Smisby

NELSON PL

CHAPEL ST

MAIN ST

3

MILLFIELD ST

BEECH DR

Hedgefield Farm

PH

Tithe Farm

Manor Farm

PH

Myrtle Lodge Farm

PH

ASHBY RD

FIELD LA

19

HIGH ST

1 THE SHUBBERY
2 CANNER CL
3 BUCKLEY CL

HEATH LA

Boundary

ANNWELL LA

LE65

2

SOUTH ST

THE CITY

Blackfordby House

Scam-Hazel Farm

Mill Farm

BUTT LA

A511

PARKERS CL 1
STRAWBERRY LA 2
CHURCH CL 3

St Margaret's CE Prim Sch

MAIN ST

Blackfordby Hall

BURTON RD

PH

Annwell Place

1

FENTON AVE

ELSTEAD LA

WELL LA

ASHBY LA

Works

Blackfordby

Holywell Farm

18

45

Derbyshire STREET ATLAS

A   B   C   D   E   F

Calke

8

DE73

Standley's Barn

Archer's Alders

Heathend Plantation

Dimminsdale

Southwood House

Southwood

Crusoe's Plantation

7

Southwood Farm

CALLAN'S LA

PH

Heath End

Ley Farm

Home Farm

21

Heath End Farm

Ferrers Ctr for Arts & Crafts

Heath Farm

The Coppice

6

Pisternhill Plantation

HEATH LA

South Wood

Rough Heath

Staunton Harold Hall

Dogkennel Pool

DE11

Pisternhill Farm

New Plantation

5

LE65

Southwood Farm

Wicket Nook

CALLAN'S LA

20

Mosley's Plantation

Old Parks Farm

B5006

Bryan's Coppice

4

Pistern Hills Farm East

Old Parks

Park Place

3

DERBY RD

Black Ditches

Ivanhoe Way

MAIN ST

19

Lount Wood

Old Parks Farm

P

2

Sewage Works

Old Parks House

Woodcote

Tunnel Wood

Western Old Parks Farm

NOTTINGHAM RD

B587

B5006

Gilwiskaw Brook

Cliftonthorpe

CLIFTON THORPE MDWS

Eastern Old Parks

A511

1

SMISBY RD

A511

B587

18

Mast

45   69

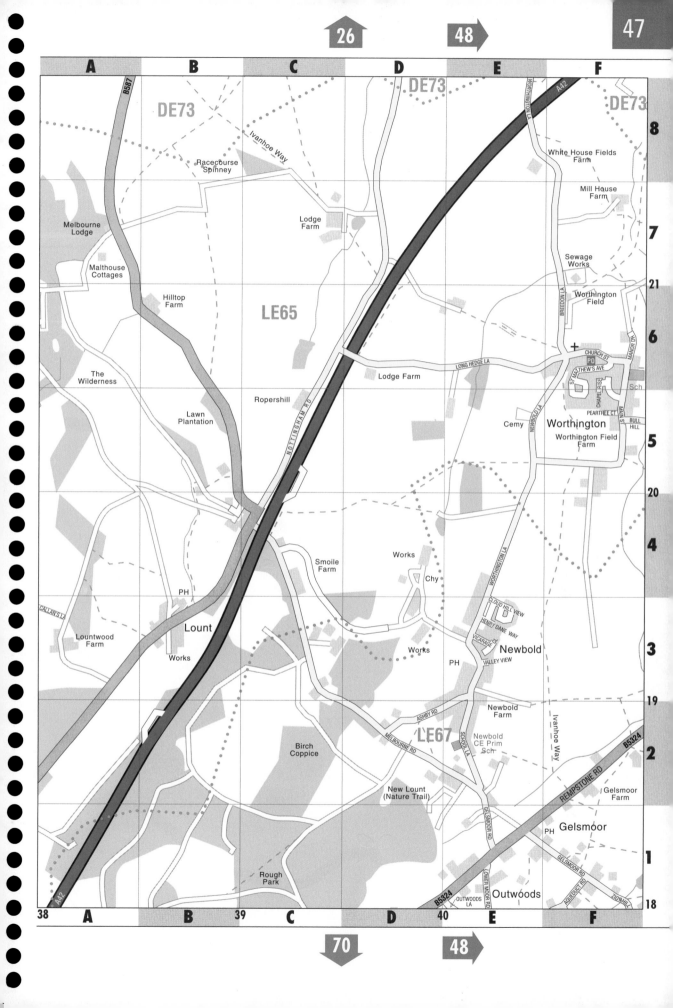

A B C D E F

8

DE73

STOCKING LA

Brandgate Farm

Asplin Wood

Top Merril Grange

Cloud Wood

Pasture Wood

Cloud Hill Quarry

7

LE65

Hillparks Farm

21

Breedon Brand Farm

Wayside Farm

6

BREEDON LA

Fields Farm

B5324

Breedon Brand

Greaveley Farm

LE12

5

Barrow Hill

PH

Cemy

DODGEFORD LA

20

Brand House Farm

Barrow Hill Farm

Forest View Farm

Osgathorpe Hall Farm

Brookside Farm

4

LOWER BRAND

ASHBY RD

West End

ORCHARD CL

DAWSON'S RD

JARMETT'S LA

Church View

CHURCH LA

Cottage Farm

Osgathorpe

PH

CHAPEL LA

St Marys CL

Cottage Farm CL

3

Brand Farm

Vinegar Hill

Stordon Grange

Osgathorpe House

MAIN ST

PH

TEMPSTONE RD

PH

19

B5324

ELDER LA

TOP RD

STORDON LA

SHARROW'S RD

Abbey Ford Farm

Grace Dieu Brook

2

Griffydam

LE67

Junction House

Sewage Works

GRACE DIEU LA

Griffydam Prim Sch

A512

THE TENTAS

MIDDLE RD

BOTTOM RD

NOTTINGHAM RD

Griffy Hill House

Cinder Hill Farm

Grace Dieu Priory

A512

1

SCHOOL LA

CLAY LA

Ivanhoe Way

A512

Mill Farm

PH

LILY BANK

ASHBY RD

LOUGHBOROUGH RD

The Manor Farm

Grace Dieu Manor Sch

Thringstone Prim Sch

18

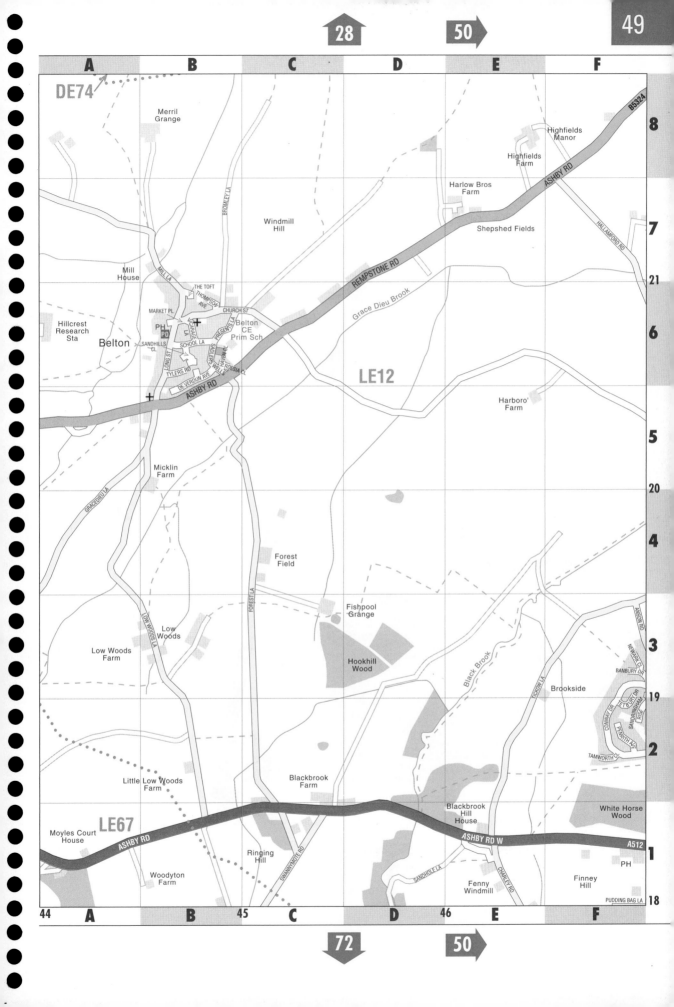

49 29

A B C D E F

8
7
21
6
5
20
4
3
19
2
1
18

SHEPSHED

LE12

LE11

B5324

M1

Piper Wood

Oakley Wood

Hathern Hill

Lounds Farm

Bedlam Barn Farm

GOLDEN SQ

SHEPSHED RD

PEAR TREE LA

HATHERN DR

Woodlands Farm

Shepshed Fields

OAKLEY 2ND

Black Brook

HALLAMFORD RD

Shepshed Mill Farm

HATHERN RD

Sewage Works

The Hermitage

Tyler-Brigg Farm

Carr Bridge

Carr Hill

FIELD AVE
NORK CL
NURSERY RD
POD DR
WORTLEY CL
TYLER CT
PIER CL
HIGHFIELD RD
RINGWOOD RD
LANSDOWNE RD
OAKLEY CL
OAKLEY RD
MANOR CL
BELTON ST
NEW WLK
PATERSON PL
HARRIMAN CL
CHAPEL ST
BRIDGE ST
BRIDGE ST
BLACK BROOK CL
DOVECOTE
MARKET PL
COUNTRYMANS WAY
BOUNDARY WAY

BUTTHOLE LA

1 WOODMANS WAY
2 SHEPHERDS CL
3 PLOUGHMANS DR
4 BLACKSMITHS AVE
5 COACHMANS CT
6 WOODLANDS DR
7 LANSDOWNE AVE

St Botolph's CE Prim Sch

Hind Leys Com Coll

Bunker Hill

Shepshed High Sch

White Lodge

Temple of Venus

Home Covert

LOUGHBOROUGH RD
CHURCH GATE
CHURCH ST
DANVERS RD
THE LANT
BEECH CL
FOREST ST
FREEHOLD ST
BERESFORD CT
KIRKHILL
GARENDON RD
CAMBRIDGE ST
FORMAN RD
PARK AVE

St Winefride's RC Prim Sch

THE PADDOCK
MOORFIELD PL
WIGHTMAN CL
LAMBERT AVE
LACEY CT
CHALLOTTEE
ST WINEFRIDE RD

Oxley Prim Sch

CHATSWORTH RD
BLACKBROOK CL
THORPE RD
GLENFIELDS
GLENMORE AVE
MCCARTHY RD
NEVILLE CL
GLENMORE RD
FACTORY ST
PARK RISE
SALMON MEWS
BRITANNIA ST
HALL CROFT
FIELD ST
BULL RING
PI CL

Liby

LITTLE HAW LA
LONGCLIFFE RD
GRANGE RD
OXLEY RD
THE MEADOWS
HOWARD CL
SPRINGFIELD RD
DOMONT CL
RING FENCE
ST JAMES CL
OXFORD ST
KING'S RD
ST MARK ST
CENTRAL AVE
ST BOTOLPH ST
SULLINGTON RD
COTTON CROFT
HARLEY CL
BROOKSIDE CL
SPRING LA

Newcroft Prim Sch

CONWAY DR
NORWICH CL
LUDLOW PL
ANSON RD
BALMORAL AVE
ST BERNARD'S
WINDSOR DR
CAERNARVON CL
BEAUMARIS CRES
ROCKINGHAM RD
ARUNDEL CL
BELVOIR WAY

Gelders Hall Ind Est

Cemy

THE PARADE

GRIFFIN CL

Ind Est

GELDERS HALL RD
OLD STATION CL
HOLT RISE
NEWLANDS AVE
NOOK CL
POLDEN
COOMBE CL
BRENDON CL
TEMPLE CL
SNOWDON
PENNINE CL
FAIRWAY RD
TRUEWAY DR
PORLOCK CL
WICKLOW CL
MALVERN AVE
LEICESTER RD
LINLEY AVE
ARBURY DALE
FURLEY
QUANTOCK CL
PENTLAND CL
PURBECK CL
QUORN AVE
CHEV
MENDIP
FAIRWAY AVE
HARRINGTON
CHE
ROMWAY
WOOD CL
PEARTREE AVE
JUMBOW WAY
WESTON
CUMBRIAN WAY
SMILBY WAY
NIXON CL
THE INLEYS
COACH RD
BEECH CL

Shepshed Nook

Cow Hill

Oxley Gutter

Shortcliff Brook

A512 ASHBY RD W   ASHBY ROAD CENTRAL   ASHBY RD E   A512

23

A512

M1

Hurst Farm

BRICK KILN LA
MOSCOW LA
TOON CL
IVESHEAD RD
CROWSON CL
MORLEY LA
INGLEBERRY RD
B591

PH

47 48 49

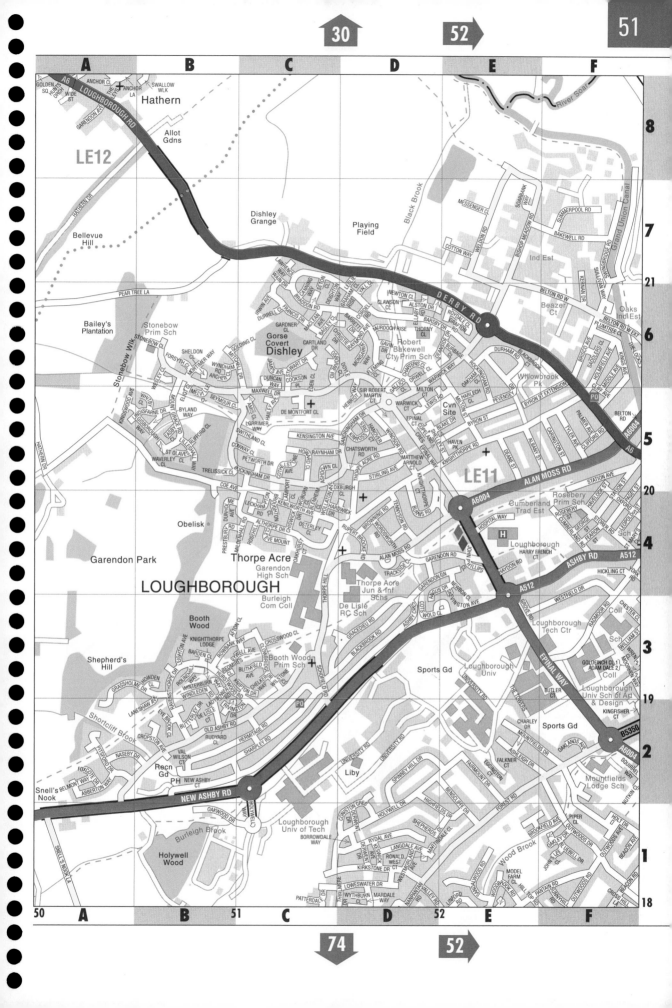

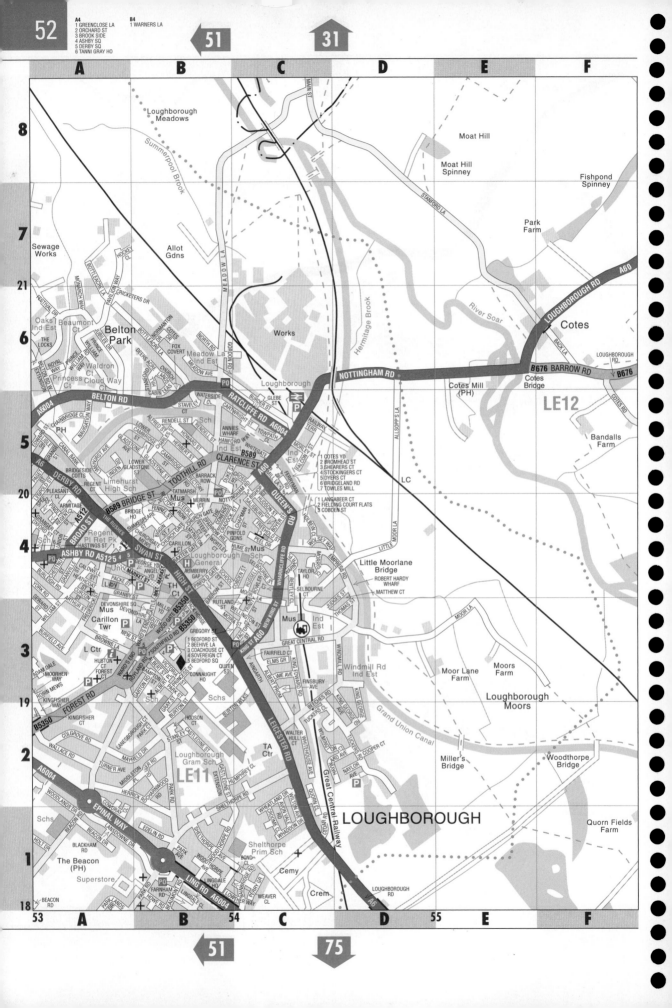

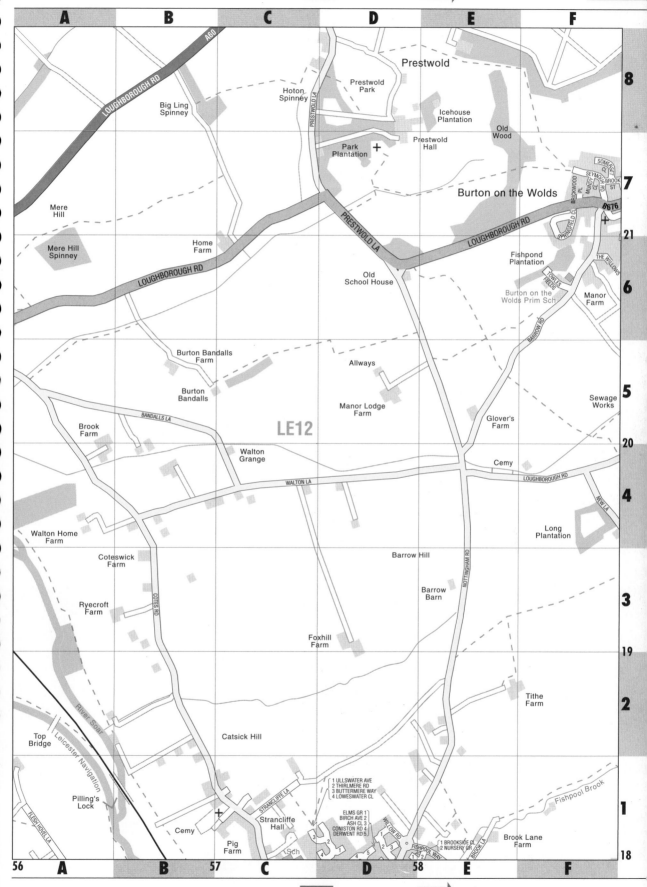

A B C D E F

8

Prestwold

Prestwold Park

Hoton Spinney

Icehouse Plantation

Old Wood

LOUGHBOROUGH RD

A60

Big Ling Spinney

PRESTWOLD LA

Park Plantation

Prestwold Hall

7

SOMERSET CL

BRICKWOOD PL

SEYMOUR CL

MUNDY CL

BROOK ST

Burton on the Wolds

B676

21

Mere Hill

Home Farm

PRESTWOLD LA

LOUGHBOROUGH RD

SPRINGFIELD CL

THE WILLOWS

Mere Hill Spinney

LOUGHBOROUGH RD

Old School House

Fishpond Plantation

TOWLES FIELDS

6

Burton on the Wolds Prim Sch

Manor Farm

Burton Bandalls Farm

Allways

BARROW RD

5

Sewage Works

LE12

Manor Lodge Farm

Glover's Farm

Burton Bandalls

BANDALLS LA

Brook Farm

Walton Grange

Cemy

20

WALTON LA

LOUGHBOROUGH RD

Walton Home Farm

NEW LA

4

Coteswick Farm

Long Plantation

COTES RD

Barrow Hill

Ryecroft Farm

Barrow Barn

NOTTINGHAM RD

3

Foxhill Farm

19

River Soar

Tithe Farm

2

Top Bridge

Leicester Navigation

Catsick Hill

Fishpool Brook

Pilling's Lock

STRANCLIFFE LA

1 ULLSWATER AVE
2 THIRLMERE RD
3 BUTTERMERE WAY
4 LOWESWATER CL

Fishpool Brook

1

FLESH HOVEL LA

Cemy

Strancliffe Hall

ELMS GR 1
BIRCH AVE 2
ASH CL 3
CONISTON RD 4
DERWENT RD 5

WILLOW RD

FISHPOOL WAY

BROOK LA

1 BROOKSIDE CL
2 NURSERY GR

Brook Lane Farm

Pig Farm

Sch

18

56 A B 57 C D 58 E F

A   B   C   D   E   F

8

The Cliff
Cliff Farm
Cliff House Farm
West View
Works

MELTON RD   B676

Valley Farm
Harrow Farm

Cemy
HUNTINGDON CL

7

Hurst Hill Farm
Horse Leys Farm
Keeper's Lodge

B676
PH
ST ANDREWS CL
ST PETER'S RD
ST LEONARDS CL
HALL DR
ST MARY'S CL

21

SEALS
SOWTERS LA

LE14

Burton Hall
Sturdee Poultry Farm
Rancliff Wood

6

Four Acre Wood

The Clump
Walton Brook

Middle Plantation
Lime Hole Plantation
Shuttlewood's Farm

Meadow View

5

Bailiff's Covert
Top Farm

Three Oaks
White Lodge Farm

20

LOUGHBOROUGH RD
THE GREEN
SIX HILLS RD

PH

SCHOOL HILL
POPLAR HILL
Middle Farm

4

Walton on the Wolds   LE12

NEW LA
The Manor House
BLACK LA

North Farm

Fishpool Brook

3

19

Seagrave Grange

2

PAUDY LA
BIG LA
PAUDY CROSS ROADS

Cream Lodge

Home Farm

1

Barrow Fields Farm
Rose Farm
Whitehouse Farm

OXEN
MELTON RD
MUCKLE GATE LA
GREEN LA

18
59   A   B   60   C   D   61   E   F

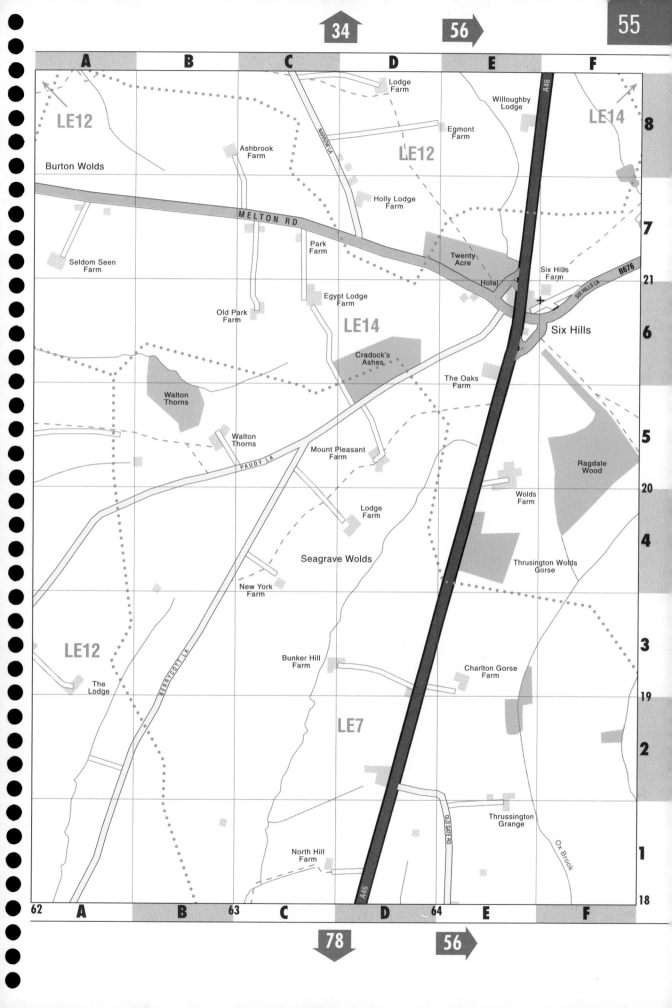

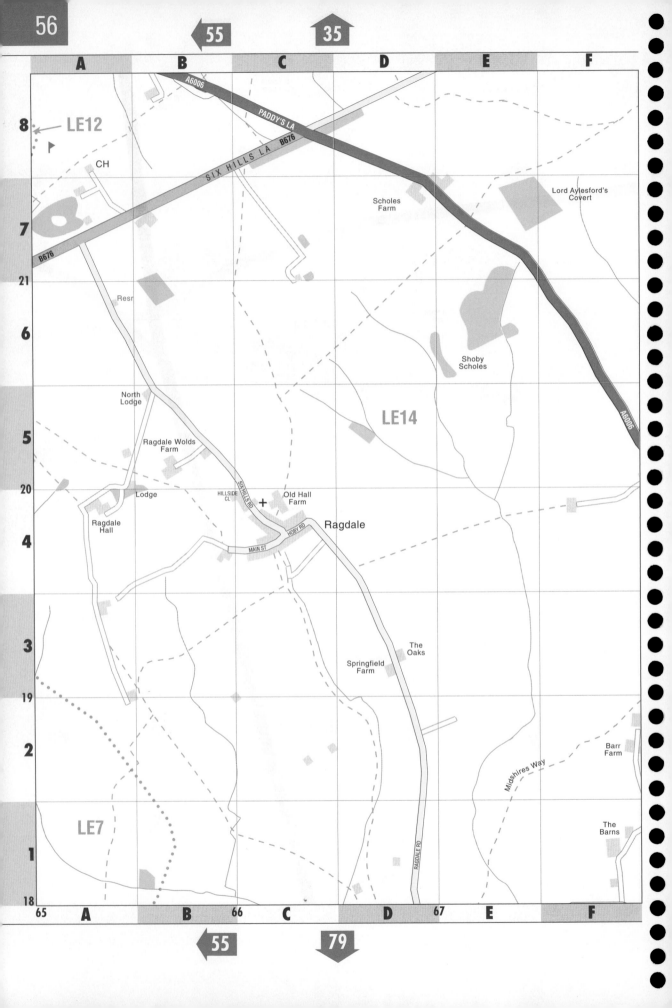

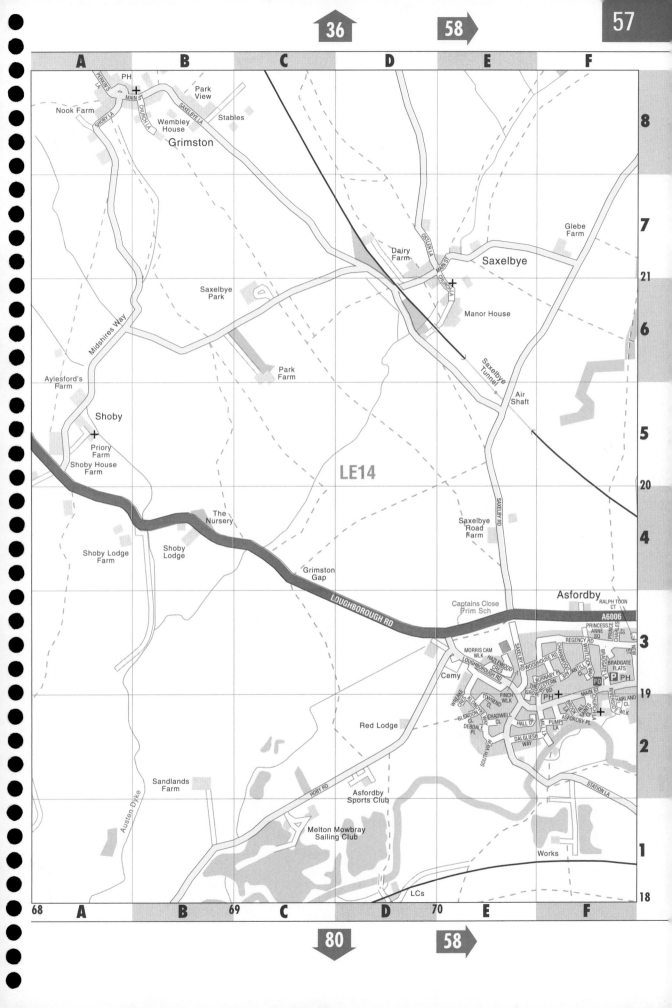

36
58
80
58

A   B   C   D   E   F

8

7

21

6

5

20

4

3

19

2

1

18

68   A   B   69   C   D   70   E   F

PH
Nook Farm
PERKINS LA
SHOBY LA
MAIN ST
CHURCH LA
SAXELBYE LA
Park View
Stables
Wembley House
Grimston

Saxelbye Park

Midshires Way

Aylesford's Farm

Shoby

Priory Farm
Shoby House Farm

Park Farm

LE14

The Nursery

Shoby Lodge Farm
Shoby Lodge

Grimston Gap

LOUGHBOROUGH RD

Dairy Farm

USTIER LA
MAIN ST
CHURCH LA
Saxelbye

Glebe Farm

Manor House

Saxelbye Tunnel

Air Shaft

SAXELBY RD

Saxelbye Road Farm

Captains Close Prim Sch

Asfordby
RALPH TOON CT

A6006

PRINCESS ANNE SQ
REGENCY RD
CHARLES ST
NEW ST
BRADGATE FLATS
WHITLOCK WAY
ANTILL CL
CHARNWOOD RD
WOODHOUSE RD
SAXELBY RD
MORRIS CAM WLK
HAZLEWOOD CRES
LOUGHBOROUGH RD
Cemy
BURNABY PL
THE WESTERN
GROVE
FINCH WLK
TOWNEND CL
WREAKE CRES
KLONDYKE WAY
GLENDON CL
DEBDALE PL
CHADWELL CL
HALL OR
MILL LA
PUMP LA
BROOK ST
ASFORDBY PL
HARLAND CL
WLK
RIVERSIDE
MAIN ST
CHURCH LA
PH
P PH
PO
PH

Red Lodge

Sandlands Farm

HOBY RD

Asfordby Sports Club

Melton Mowbray Sailing Club

Austen Dyke

DALGLIESH WAY
SOUTH VIEW

STATION LA

Works

LCs

57
37

A B C D E F

8

Cant's
Thorns

Ash
Plantation

Oak
Plantation

Potter
Hill

A606

NOTTINGHAM RD

A606

7

WELBY LA

Sysonby Lodge
Farm

Welby
Grange

Hilltop
Farm

21

+

Welby

ST BARTHOLOMEWS WAY

WELBY LA

6

JAMES LAMBERT DR

5

Asfordby
Farm

LE14

Works

LE13

20

WELBY RD

4

Remount
Depot

3

A6006

THE CRESCENT

COWMAN CL

JUBILEE AVE

Playing
Field

NORTH VIEW CL
NORTH ST
ROSEBERY AVE
BROOK CRES

MAIN RD

MAIN RD

Asfordby
Tunnel

ST JOHNS RD
WEST SIDE
EAST SIDE
SOUTH ST
WELBY RD
PO

Asfordby
Hill

+

Halfway
House

ASFORDBY RD

A6006

CH

Sysonby

BRAMLINGTON CL
COLLINGWOOD CRES

CHETWYND DR

RIVERSIDE RD

MELTON RD

19

MAIN ST
SARSON CL

Asfordby
Valley

Home
Farm

GLEBE RD
CROPTON RD
STANTON LA

Asfordby Hill
Prim Sch

The
Grange House

Butt
Close

+

SYSONBY GRANGE LA

2

The Hollies

Sysonby Grange
Farm

Sewage
Works

1

STATION LA

White Lodge

LC

MAIN ST
WASHDYKE LA

PO

+

Old Lock
Water

River Wreake

Mill

LEICESTER RD

A607

18

71 A 72 B C 73 D E F

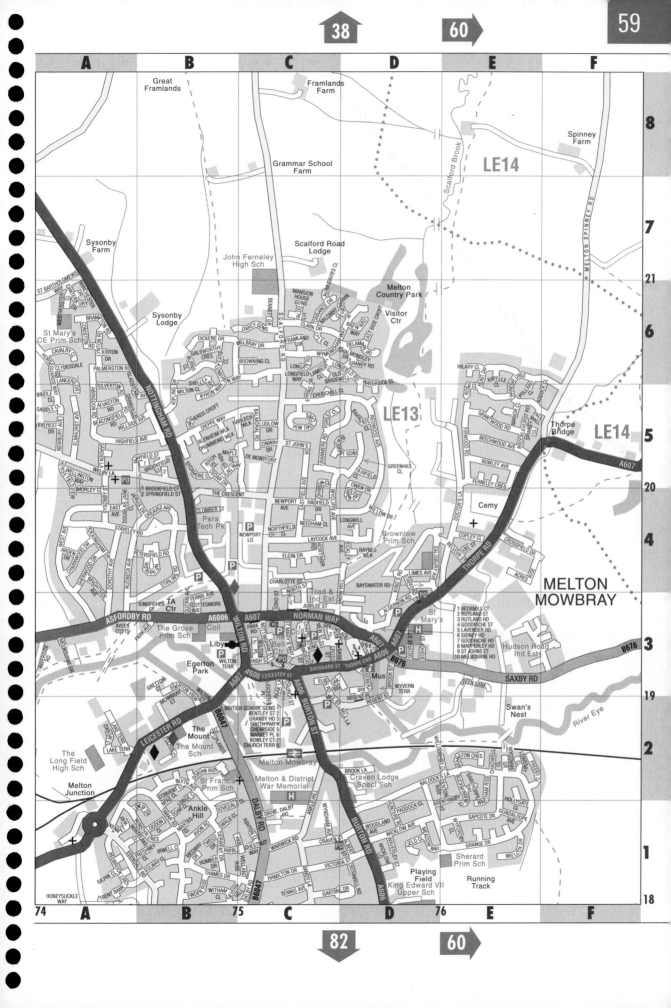

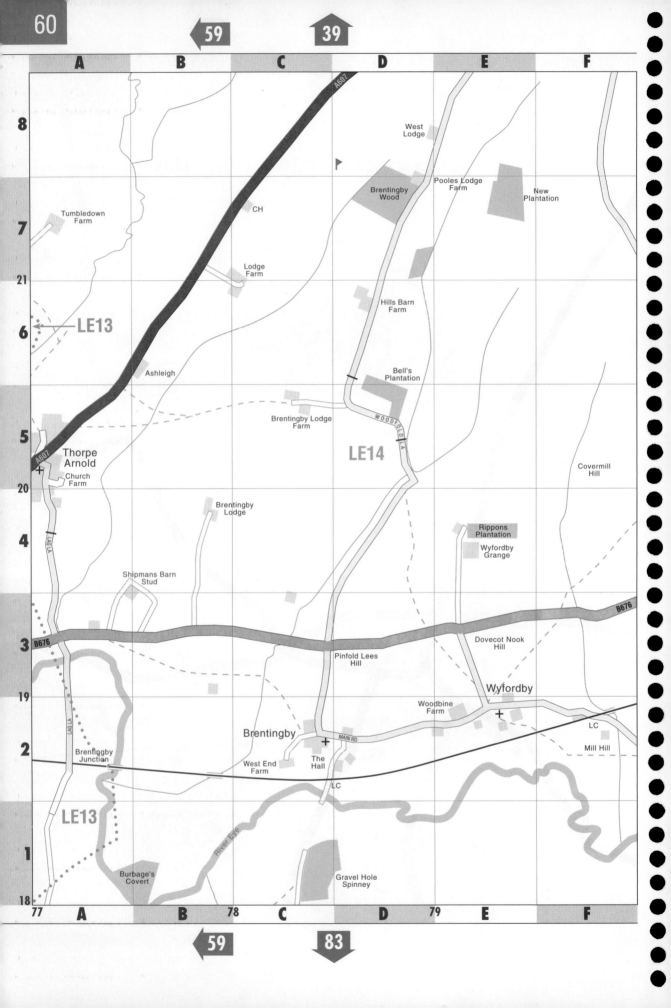

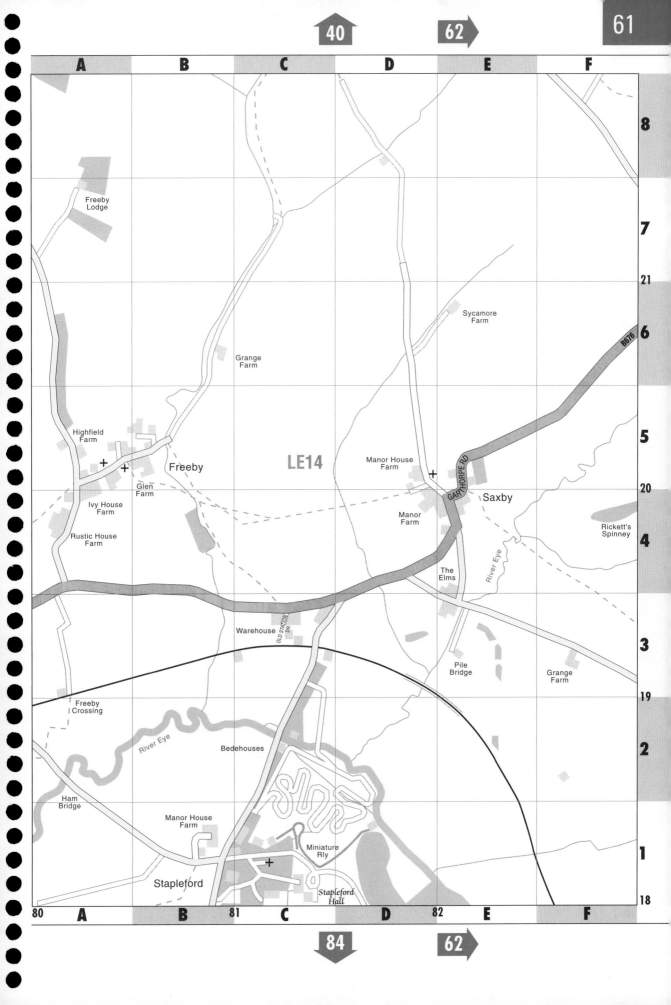

A B C D E F

8

7

21

Freeby
Lodge

Sycamore
Farm

6 B676

Grange
Farm

5

Highfield
Farm

Manor House
Farm

+ +
Freeby

GARTHORPE RD

Glen
Farm

Saxby 20

Ivy House
Farm

LE14

Manor
Farm

Rickett's
Spinney

4

Rustic House
Farm

The
Elms

River Eye

Warehouse

OLD STATION DR

Pile
Bridge

Grange
Farm

3

19

Freeby
Crossing

River Eye

Bedehouses

2

Ham
Bridge

Manor House
Farm

Miniature
Rly

1

Stapleford

Stapleford
Hall

18

A B C D E F

8

7

21

Coston Rd

Grange Farm

THE ROW

+

B676

6

Garthorpe

Garthorpe Race Course

Hall Farm

B676

Grange Farm

Coston Lodge

GRANGE LA

Hall Farm

5

LE14

Garthorpe Lodge

Old Close Plantation

Mount Pleasant Farm

20

4

3

The Old Grammar School

Wymondham Windmill (dis)

The Mill

BUTT LA

Red House

BRICKYARD LA

19

MELTON RD

St Peter's CE Prim Sch

GRETTON GDNS

PH

PO

2

WEST END

ROOKERY LA

MEADOWS RISE

SYCAMORE PL

BURSNELLS LA

SPRINGS

CHAPEL LA

CHURCH LA

+

MAIN ST

+

WYK

SUSPELA

NEWMIN

SLISH LA

Manns Farm

WYMONDHAM DRIFT

GLEBE RD

Rookery House

Wymondham

EDMUNDTHORPE RD

The Grange

1

The Grange Cottage

Sewage Works

18

83 A B 84 C D 85 E F

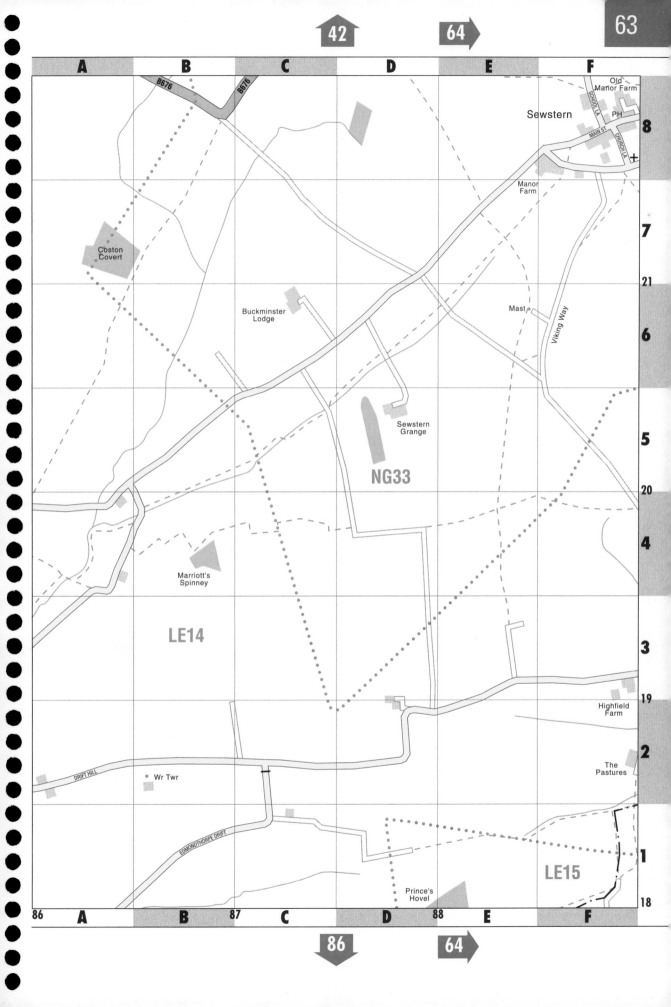

A B C D E F

8

Manor Farm

MAIN ST

TIMBER HILL

PO

STAMFORD RD

Allot Gdns

BACK LA

GUNBY RD

Saw Mill

Mast

Factory

SEWSTERN RD

Brook House

MAIN ST

Gunby

Mill Farm

STAINBY RD

Stainby Warren

Gunby Dale

WITHAM RD

Glebe Farm

7

21

6

THE DRIFT

Gunby Gorse

The Forty Acre

NG33

MOOR LA

5

20

4

Blue Point Farm

LE14

Viking Way

River Witham

3

19

Mill La

Melton Mowbray Quarry

2

Cribb's Lodge

FOSSE LA

Thistleton Gap

LE15

SCHOOL LA

MAIN ST

WITHAM RD

1

LE15

18

89 A B 90 C D 91 E F

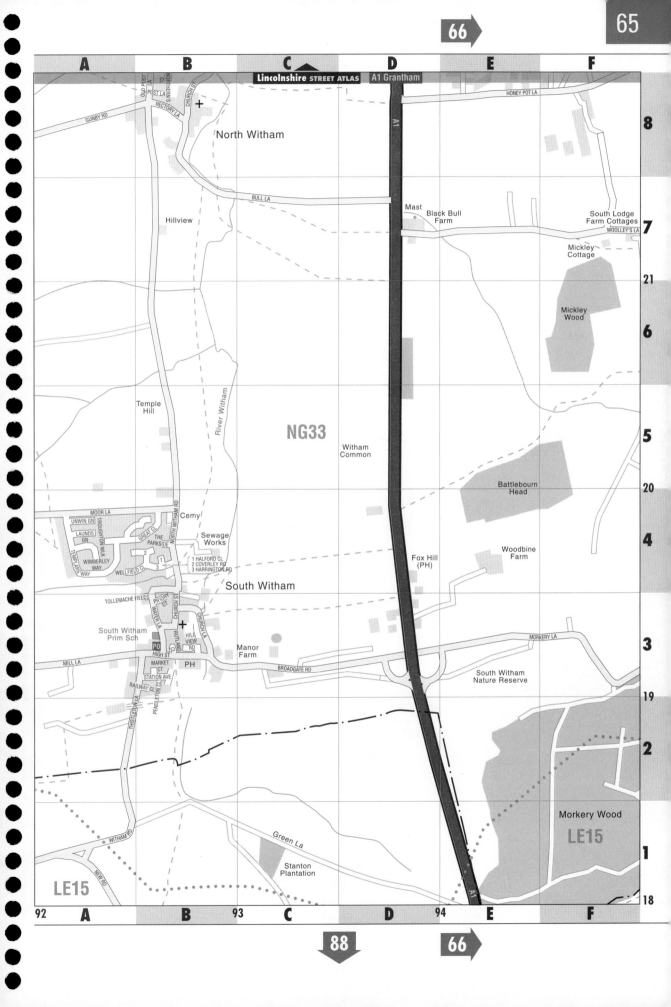

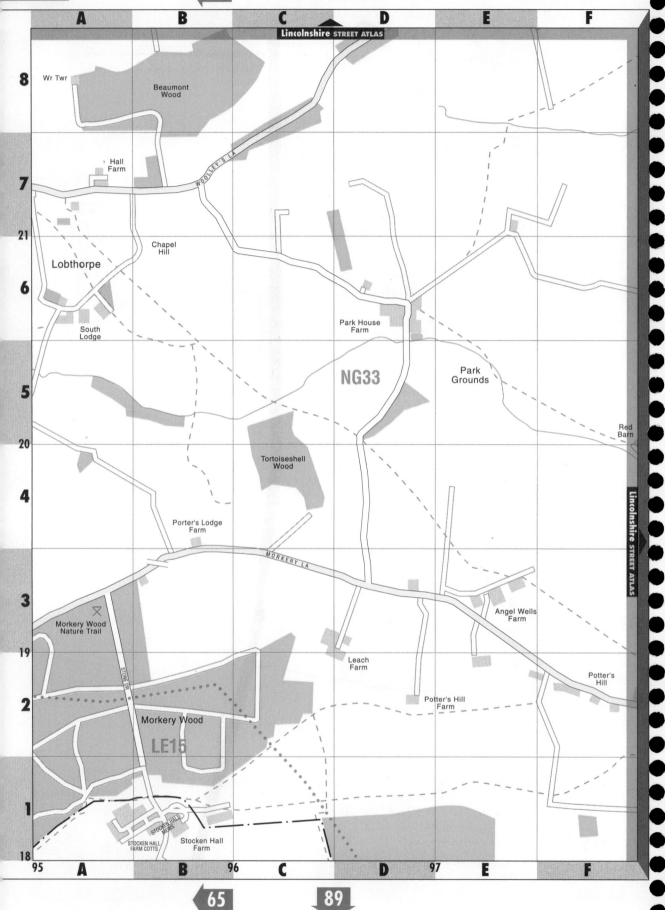

Lincolnshire STREET ATLAS

8

Wr Twr

Beaumont
Wood

7

WOOLLEY'S LA

Hall
Farm

21

Chapel
Hill

Lobthorpe

6

South
Lodge

Park House
Farm

Park
Grounds

NG33

Red
Barn

5

20

Tortoiseshell
Wood

4

Porter's Lodge
Farm

MORKERY LA

3

Morkery Wood
Nature Trail

Angel Wells
Farm

19

Leach
Farm

Potter's
Hill

STONE DR

2

Morkery Wood

Potter's Hill
Farm

LE15

1

STOCKEN HALL MEWS

STOCKEN HALL
FARM COTTS

Stocken Hall
Farm

18

Lincolnshire STREET ATLAS

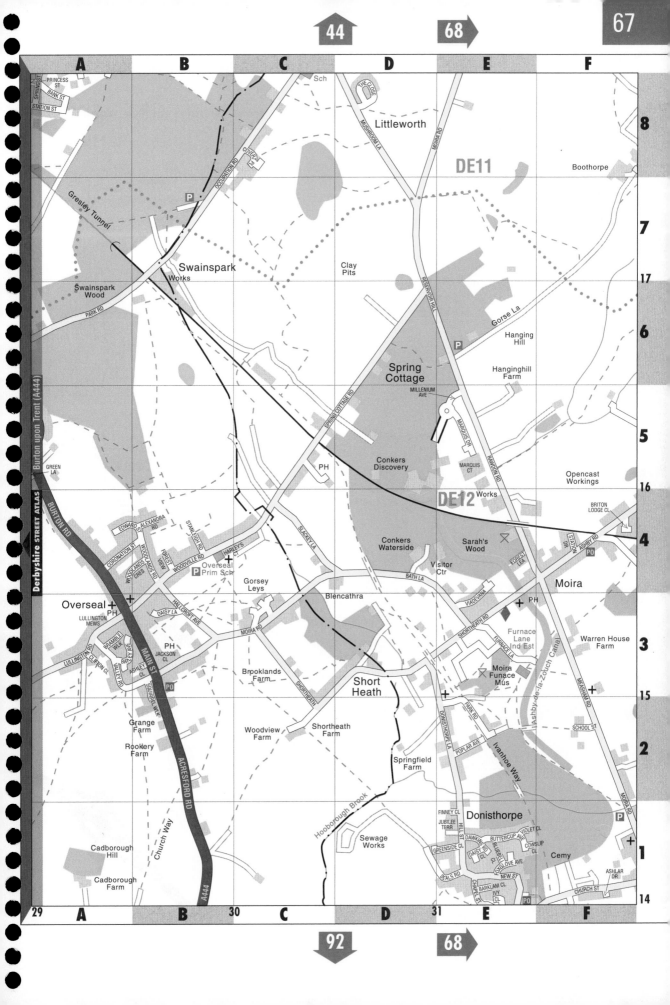

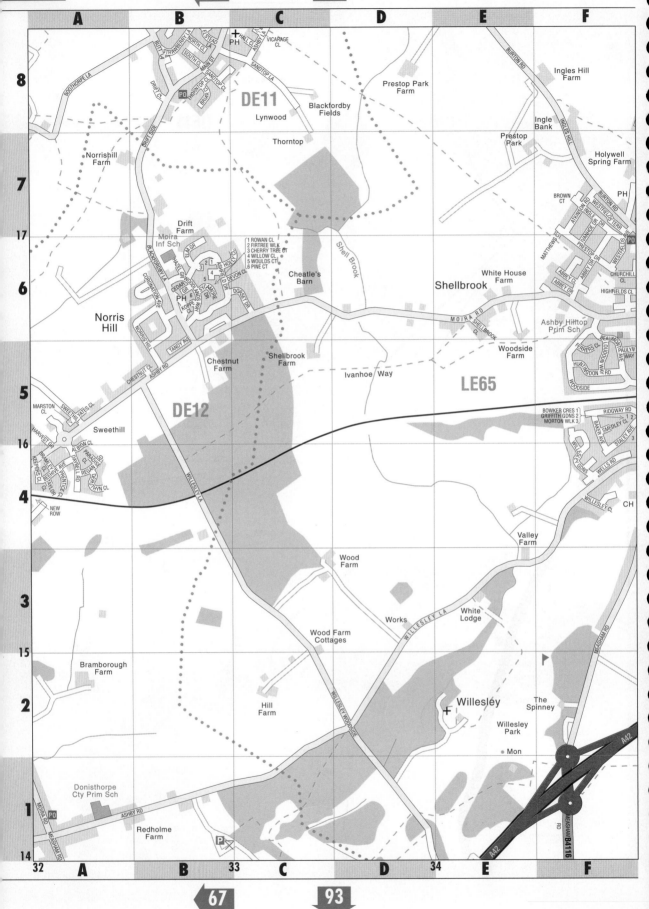

A B C D E F

8

7

17

6

5

16

4

3

15

2

1

14

DE11

Lynwood

Blackfordby Fields

Thorntop

PH
VICARAGE CL
Hall CL
ASH CL
SANDTOP LA

STRAWBERRY LA
ELSTEAD
NORTH CL
SOUTH CL
MAIN ST
BUTT LA
SANDTOP CL
HORNTOP CL
BRIAR CL
PO
DRIFT SIDE

BOOTHORPE LA

Norrishill Farm

Prestop Park Farm

Ingles Hill Farm

BURTON RD

INGLE'S HILL

Ingle Bank

Prestop Park

Holywell Spring Farm

BROWN CT
ATKINSON RD
INGLE CL
WESTFIELDS DR
BURTON RD
PH
IVANHOE DR
PRESTOP DR
ABBEY CL
ABBEY DR
MATTHEWS CL
WESTFIELDS TERR
PO
WESTFIELDS
CHURCHILL CL
HIGHFIELDS CL

Drift Farm

Moira Inf Sch

Cheatle's Barn

Shell Brook

1 ROWAN CL
2 FIRTREE WLK
3 CHERRY TREE CT
4 WILLOW CL
5 WOULDS CT
6 PINE CT

White House Farm

Shellbrook

BLACKFORDBY LA
HAZEL GR
ELM GR
WOODLANDS WAY
CEDAR GR
KOPPE CL
PH
SYCAMORE
HOLLY
ASHFIELD CL
DEVON CL
DORSET DR

MOIRA RD

Norris Hill

CORONATION AVE
NORRIS HILL
TANDY AVE

Chestnut Farm

Shellbrook Farm

Ivanhoe Way

Woodside Farm

SHELLBROOK CL

Ashby Hilltop Prim Sch

FERRERS CL
BEAUMANOR
LOUDON AVE
PAULYN WAY
HUNTINGDON RD
WOODSIDE

LE65

CHESTNUT CL
ASHBY RD

DE12

Sweethill

MARSTON CL
SWEETHILL
YATES CL
ALBION CL
HARVEST GR
BRAMLEY CL
KEEPERS CL
BEECHIVE AVE
PRENTICE CL
DAKYN CL
PARADISE RD
DAKYN CL
REGAN CL
TAYLOR CL

WILLESLEY LA

BOWKER CRES 1
GRIFFITH GDNS 2
MORTON WLK 3
RIDGWAY RD
SMEDLEY CL
BAKER AVE
STALEY AVE
WILSCOT GDNS
WELLS RD
WILLESLEY CL
CH

NEW ROW

Valley Farm

Wood Farm

Bramborough Farm

Hill Farm

Wood Farm Cottages

Works

WILLESLEY LA

White Lodge

WILLESLEY WOODSIDE

Willesley

The Spinney

Willesley Park

Mon

A42

MEASHAM RD

Donisthorpe Cty Prim Sch

PO
MOIRA RD
MEASHAM RD
ASHBY RD

Redholme Farm

P

A42
MEASHAM RD
B4116

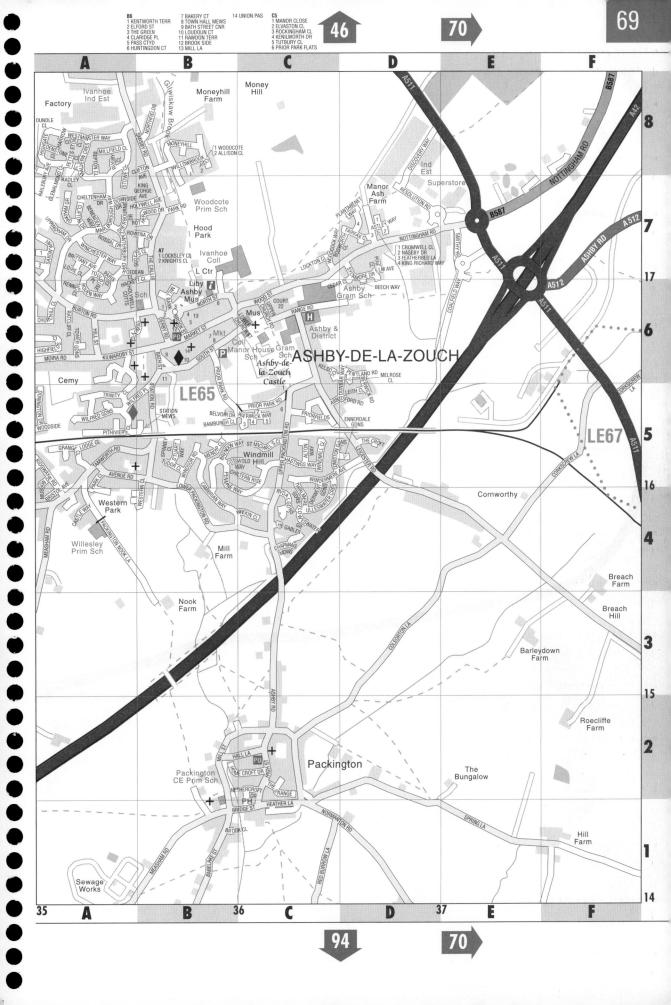

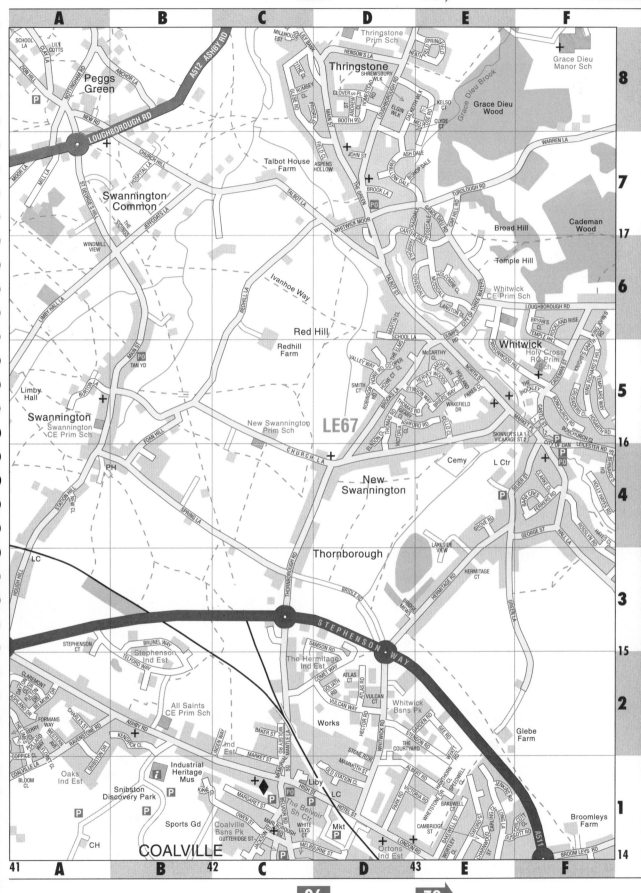

COALVILLE

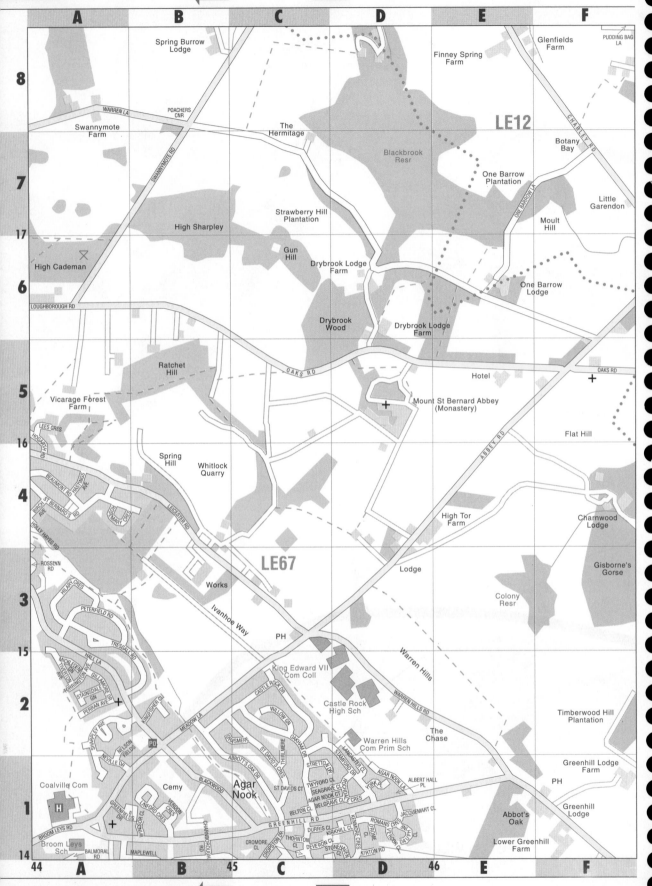

71
49

Spring Burrow Lodge

POACHERS CNR

WARREN LA

Swannymote Farm

The Hermitage

LE12

Finney Spring Farm

Glenfields Farm

PUDDING BAG LA

CHARLEY RD

Botany Bay

Blackbrook Resr

One Barrow Plantation

Little Garendon

High Sharpley

Strawberry Hill Plantation

SWANNYMOTE RD

Moult Hill

17

High Cademan

Gun Hill

Drybrook Lodge Farm

One Barrow Lodge

ONE BARROW LA

6

LOUGHBOROUGH RD

Drybrook Wood

Drybrook Lodge Farm

LEES CRES

Ratchet Hill

OAKS RD

OAKS RD

Hotel

5

Vicarage Forest Farm

Mount St Bernard Abbey (Monastery)

Flat Hill

HOGARTH RD

16

Spring Hill

Whitlock Quarry

ABBEY RD

BEAUMONT RD

HASTINGS AVE

ST BERNARD'S RD

BIRCH AVE

TOR

AVE

ST MARY

CRES

4

LEICESTER RD

High Tor Farm

Charnwood Lodge

HOLLY HAYES RD

ROSSLYN RD

LE67

Lodge

Gisborne's Gorse

Works

HILARY CRES

PETERFIELD RD

Ivanhoe Way

Colony Resr

3

TRESSALL RD

HALL LA

PH

Warren Hills

MICKLEDON DR

HESTON

AVE

GILLAMORE

DR

KINGFISHER CL

15

King Edward VII Com Coll

WARREN HILLS RD

Timberwood Hill Plantation

STAINSDALE

GN

WORRINGTON AVE

PERRAN AVE

MEADOW LA

CASTLE ROCK DR

WILLOW GN

Castle Rock High Sch

The Chase

2

SHARPLEY AVE

NELSON FIELDS

NEVILLE DR

PO

CROSSMERE

ST DAVID'S CRES

THIRLMERE

OAKHAM DR

Warren Hills Com Prim Sch

STRETTON DR

LANCASTER CL

STAMFORD DR

ROCHDAL

AGAR NOOK LA

ALBERT HALL PL

Greenhill Lodge Farm

Cemy

BLACKWOOD

Agar Nook

ST DAVIDS CT

ABBOTT'S OAK DR

AGAR NOOK CT

TWYFORD CL

SEAGRAVE CT

BELGRAVE CL

YORK PL

CRES

PH

Greenhill Lodge

VERNON

DR

LINFORD CRES

GREENFIELDS

DR

BELTON CL

DURRIS CL

Coalville Com

H

Broom Leys Sch

BROOM LEYS RD

BALMORAL RD

MAPLEWELL

CHARNBROUGH

RD

WINDMILL

CROMORE CL

CROPSTON

GREENHILL RD

THORNTON CL

DEVERON CL

KIRKHILL CL

KENMORE CRES

ROMANS CRES

STONEHAVEN CL

JACQUEMART CL

VERNON

DR

DRONE

KIRTON RD

Abbot's Oak

Lower Greenhill Farm

1

14

44

71
97

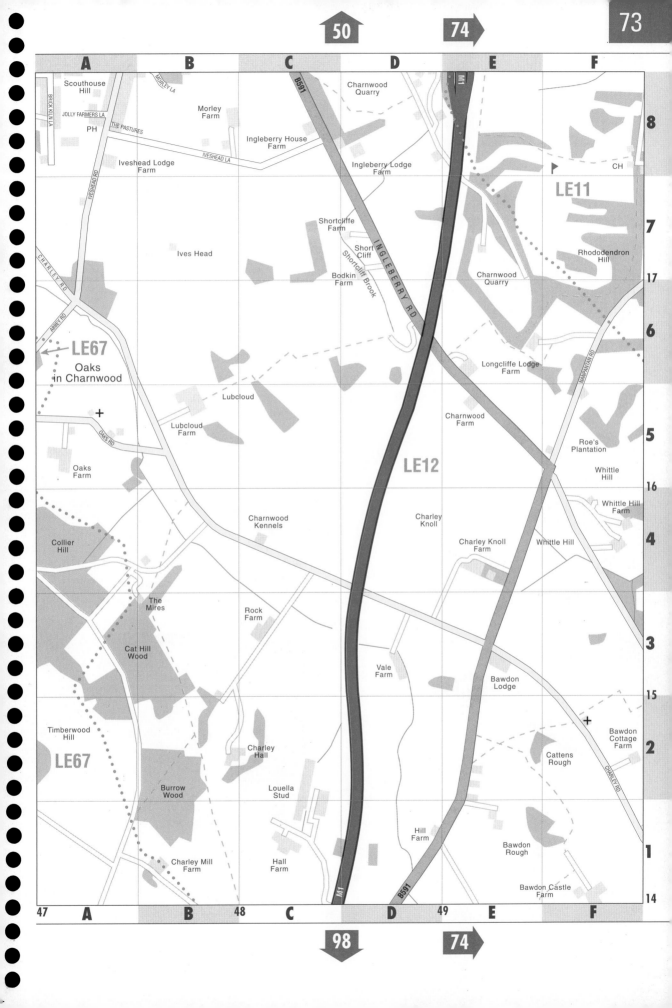

A B C D E F

8

Holywell Hall
Burleigh Wood
AMBLESIDE CL
Holywell Prim Sch
GUILDFORD WAY
EXMOOR CL
MARDALE WAY
THIRLMERE DR
BERKELEY RD
CHICHESTER CL
DULVERTON RD
NICOLSON RD
MONTAGUE DR
LUDLOW CL
TYNEDALE RD
LECONFIELD RD
COMPTON CL
BROOKSIDE
PRIORY RD
THE WIDON
LIVERSCROFT RD
WESTBROOK AVE
PAPTAIN RD
VALLEY RD
SPRINGFIELD
HILL TOP RD
OUTWOODS RD
BEACON RD
PYTCHLEY RD
FARNDALE DR
ULVERTON DR
HAMILEDON CRES
BADGER
POCKET END
CRICKET LA
BROOK LA
BAILEY
LOWER GN
NURSEY CL
WATERRALL PH
BRANGATE RD
MOAT RD
SCOTTESMORE DR
CLEVELAND RD
GRASMERE RD
ATHERSTONE RD
BELVOIR DR
MATO CL
LEDBURY RD
CH
PARK RD
THIRSK CL
CHAVEN
BRAMCOTE RD

7

Nanpantan
NANPANTAN RD
LONGCLIFFE GDNS
PH
SNELL'S NOOK LA
Works
Wood Brooke
Brooke House Farm
Sports Ground
LOUGHBOROUGH
LE11
BRAMCOTE RD

17

Lodge
Nanpantan Hall
Moat House
Woodbrook Vale High Sch
ROSEWOOD WAY

6

The Home Farm
Outwoods Farm
Out Woods
Halfway House

Buck Hill
WOODHOUSE LA
Out Woods Nature Reserve

5

Lodge
Charnwood Hall
Out Woods Nature Trail

16

Outwood Cottage P
Pocket Gate Farm

4

Blackbird's Nest
Hangingstone Hills
BROOK RD

Beacon Cottage
West Beacon Farm
DEAN'S LA
Longhill Farm
Thorntree Farm
Hangingstone Hills
Breakback Plantation
Brook Road Farm
PH

3

LE12
BREAKBACK RD
The Beacon Hill Country Park
CH
P
PERRY CL
HERRICK RD
TUCKETT RD

15

Beacon Hill
Beacon Plantation
WINDMILL RISE

2

P
Leicestershire Round
BIRD HILL RD
Broombriggs Farm Nature Trail
Windmill Hill
PATERSON DR

Broombriggs Cottage Farm
BEACON RD
P
Broombriggs Farm Country Park
HILL RISE 1
THE DRIVE 2
MILL RD
MAPLEWELL RD

1

CHARLEY RD
Broombriggs Hill
Broombriggs House

14

50 A B 51 C D 52 E F

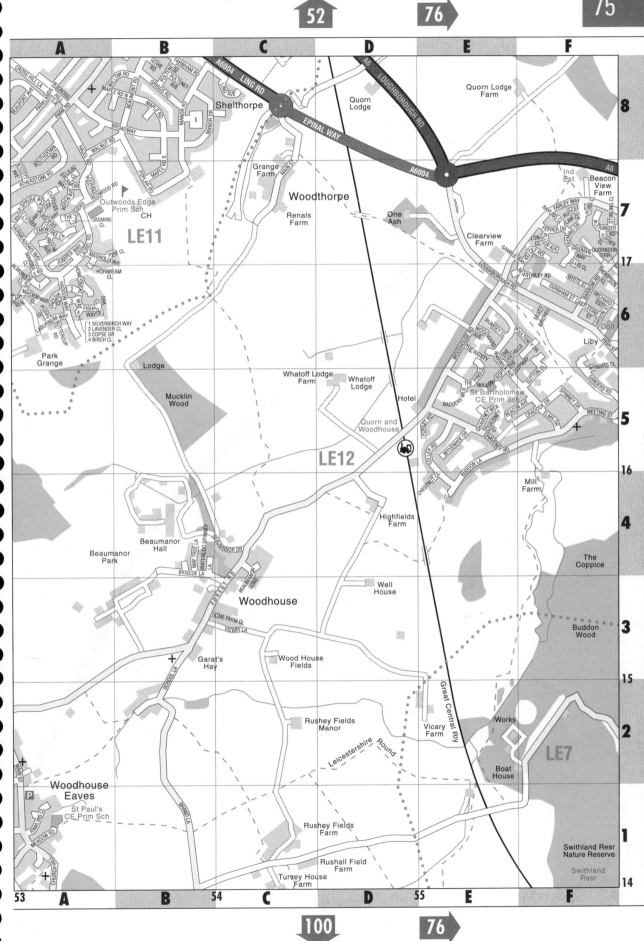

75
53

A B C D E F

8
7
17
6
5
16
4
3
15
2
1
14

Sewage Works
Poole Farm
Humphrey Perkins High Sch
DERWENT RD 1
WINDERMERE RD 2
CONISTON RD
ENNERDALE RD
NOTTINGHAM RD
NURSERY GR
Paudy Rise Farm
Barrow View Farm
THIRLMERE CT
THE RETREAT
BROOK LA
LIME KILNS
ILIFFE'S CL
1 KINGFISHER CL
2 GREBE CL
FLESH HOVEL LA
BARROW RD
BARROW RD
Lodge
CADKINS CT
BARROWCLIFFE CL
WYCLIFFE AVE
BEAUMONT
BRYAN CL
THE BREACHFIELD
NEW CL
NEWTON'S
TOWNSEND CL
SWAN CL
MALLARD RD
BRIGHTON'S
BRINGHSTON AVE
SHIRREFF'S CL
Barrow-upon-Soar
A6
THE ROKERY
WOODS
HIGH ST
CHURCH ST
HIGHFIELDS
THE BANKS
MELTON RD
ILLSTON GDNS
FARLEY WAY
PARKERS FIELDS
Fenny Copse Farm
MEYNELL RD
CROSSLEY CL
BRIDGE ST
PROCTOR'S RD
PARK RD
HOLBORNE CL
CRAMP CL
WARNET RD
CHESTNUT PL
Hall Orchard CE Prim Sch
BREACHFIELD RD
CHERWELL RD
THE MOORINGS
THE PASTURES
SILEBY RD
Works
QUORNDON TERR
Rawlins Com Coll
CASTLEDINE ST
PREVOST GDNS
SWINFORD RD
BROWN AVE
HARRINGTON
VICTORIA ST
CATHERINE'S
HUNTSMAN'S CL
1 WINDSOR CL
2 FREEHOLD ST
SOUTH ST
MARTIN
LODGE
RIBBLE CL
AVON RD
WELLAND RD
PH
Meadow View Farm
Barrow-on-Soar
Grand Union Canal
RIVER VIEW
HISTON ST
MANSFIELD AVE
MANSFIELD ST
DISRAELI ST
NURSERY LA
STATION RD
STOOP
Quorn (Quorndon)
LE12
Marina
CHURCH LA
DOVER HOUSE
SCHOOL LA
WEAVERS CL
QUORN MILL
HALL'ERS
THE MILLS
QUORN CT
MEETING ST
Mills
THE BRINKS
WHALL CL
BARROW RD
MILL LA
MILL LA
River Soar
Works
Quorn House
LEICESTER RD
PADDOCK CL
NORTHAGE CL
SELVESTER DR
UNIT 7 RD
Quorn House Park
THE COPPICE
WOOD LA
Quorn Grange
Cemy
GRANITE WAY
BETTY HENSER'S LA
HAWCLIFFE RD
BROADGATE CL
PEPPER'S CL
LOUGHBOROUGH RD
SLASH LA
MOUNTSORREL LA
Depot
North End
Stonehurst Family Farm & Mus
WHEAT CL
Works
FARNHAM CT
WINDMILL CL
THE HOMESTEAD
BARONS
MARKET PL
PH
Libry
St PETERS
Leicestershire Round
Quarry
Hawcliff Hill
ROAD LA
Quarry (dis)
CROWN LA
WATLING ST
CASTLE HILL
THE NAVINS
LITTLE LA
SOUTH END
ORCHID CL
BUTTERCUP CL
1 SWALLOW CL
2 PARTRIDGE CL
3 CELANDINE CL
4 SKYLARK AVE
1 SORREL CT
2 CHESTNUT CT
LE7
RUSHEY LA
Broad Hill
Mountsorrel
Christ Church & St Peter's CE Prim Sch
GLEBE CL
CHURCH HILL RD
MARTIN AVE
BUDDON CT
LINDEN GR
ROTHLEY RD
ELM GDNS
DANVERS RD
MARSH RD
BERKELEY CL
IRIS CL
MARIGOLD CL
SPEEDWELL CL
MALLARD RD
BULRUSH CL
Swithland Resr Nature Reserve
Leicestershire Round
KINCHLEY LA
SWITHLAND LA
WILLOW CL
THE OSIERS
ROSSLYN AVE
KENILWORTH AVE
EDWIN RICH WAY
WALTON WAY
CONWAY RD
BARNARD WAY
BALMORAL RD
Halstead Rd
HIGHFIELDS
CASTLE RD
KINSTEER RD
BOUNDARY RD
THE ROMANS
ROCKHILL DR
GLENTHORN
LINKFIELD RD
THE PIKE
MERLIN CL
LOUGHBOROUGH RD
A6
LE7
Swithland Resr

56 57 58

75
101

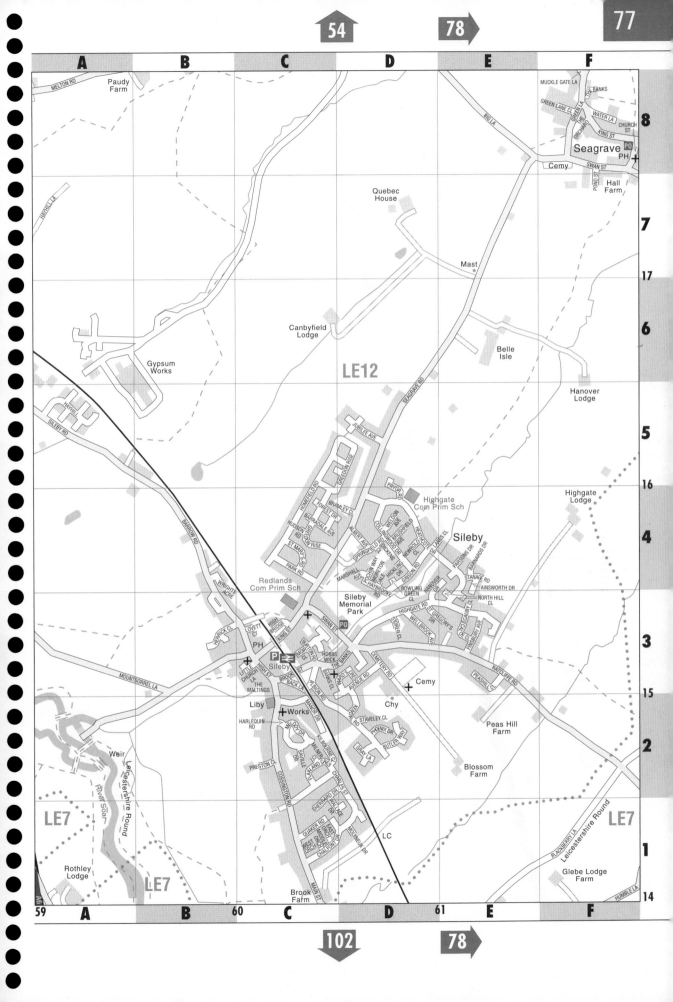

77 55

A B C D E F

8

7

17

6

16

5

4

3

15

2

1

14

62 A B 63 C D 64 E F

77 103

IVY HOUSE CL
BERRYCOTT LA
KING ST
BUTCHERS LA

Park Hill
LE12
Park Hill House
PARK HILL LA
CH

A46
Motel

Jericho Farm
The Lodge Farm

OLD GATE RD
Ox Brook
Hilltop

SEAGRAVE RD

Padge Hall

Ratcliffe Farm
Mast

Longlands
Leicestershire Round

Spinney Farm

Ratcliffe Barn

LE7

Manor Farm

RATCLIFFE RD

River Wreake

Rearsby Mill (disused)

GLEBELAND CL
Thrussington CE Prim. Sch
REGENT ST
HOBY RD
BACK LA
THE GREEN
BLACKSMITHS CL
FERNLEY RISE
PH
CHURCH LA
REARSBY RD
Thrussington

Ratcliffe Coll

The Elms Farm
ROSMINIAN WAY

Ratcliffe on the Wreake

North's Lodge

THRUSSINGTON RD

LC

HEMBLE LA
RATCLIFFE RD

Ratcliffe Hall
CHURCH LA
MAIN ST

Priory Farm

Ratcliffe Mill (disused)
BROOME LA

LC

Rearsby House Farm

MILL RD
ORTON CL
PH
NEW AVE
WESTON CL
MELTON RD

A46

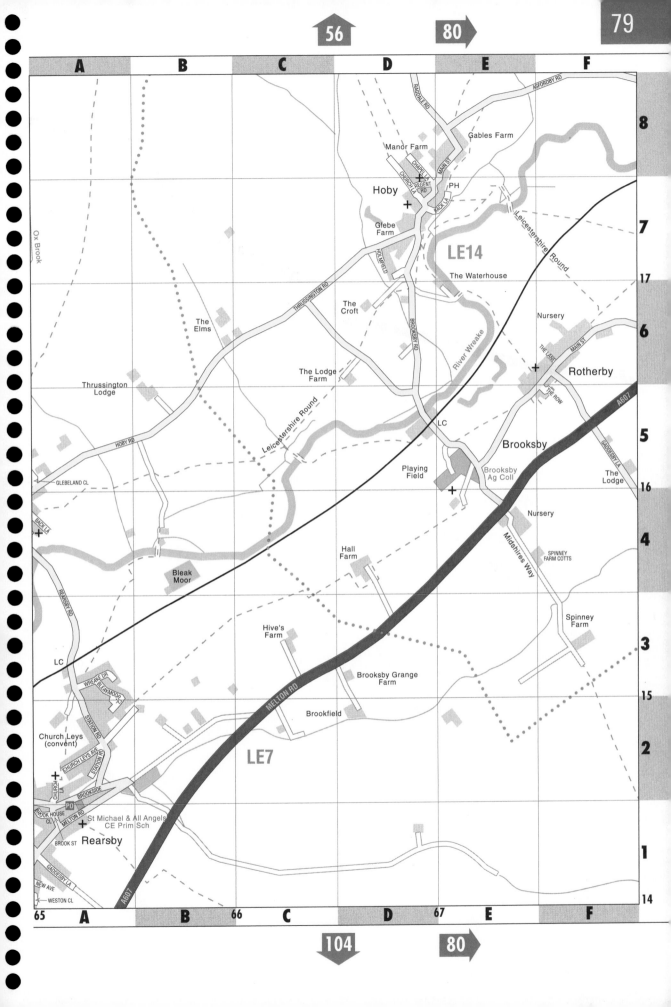

79
57

A B C D E F

8

ASFORDBY RD
HOBY RD
River Wreake
WASHSTONES LA
LC
CARRFIELDS LA
WILL LA
Cemy
Ash Tree
Farm
A607
WELL FIELD LA
CHURCH LA
MAIN ST
GREAT LA
Austen Dyke
Bridge
LC
Washstones
Bridge
Frisby
on the Wreake
HOBY LA
OLD LA
WATER LA
PO
Great Lane
Hill
Chalk Pool
Hill
PH
OAK WAY
YD
ASH WAY
ORCHARD LA
Frisby
CE Prim Sch
Stray Dogs
Home
Pennyhaven

7

ROTHERBY LA
LEICESTER RD

17

6

MAIN ST
A607
Bran Hills

5

The
Barns
LE14
Hickory
Lodge

16

Rotherby
Lodge
Frisby
Grange
GADDESBY LA

4

The
Elms
White
Lodge

3

Brooksby
Spinney
Highfields
Barn
Leicestershire Round
Elm
Cottages

15

GADDESBY LA

2

Messenger's Lodge
Farm
Ash
Close
ROTHERBY RD
LE7
Cream Gorse
(Fox Covert)
Cream Gorse
Farm

Glebe
Farm
Coles
Lodge

The
Grange

1

Midshires Way
Gaddesby
Lodge

14

68 A B 69 C 70 D E F
Carlton Lodge
Farm

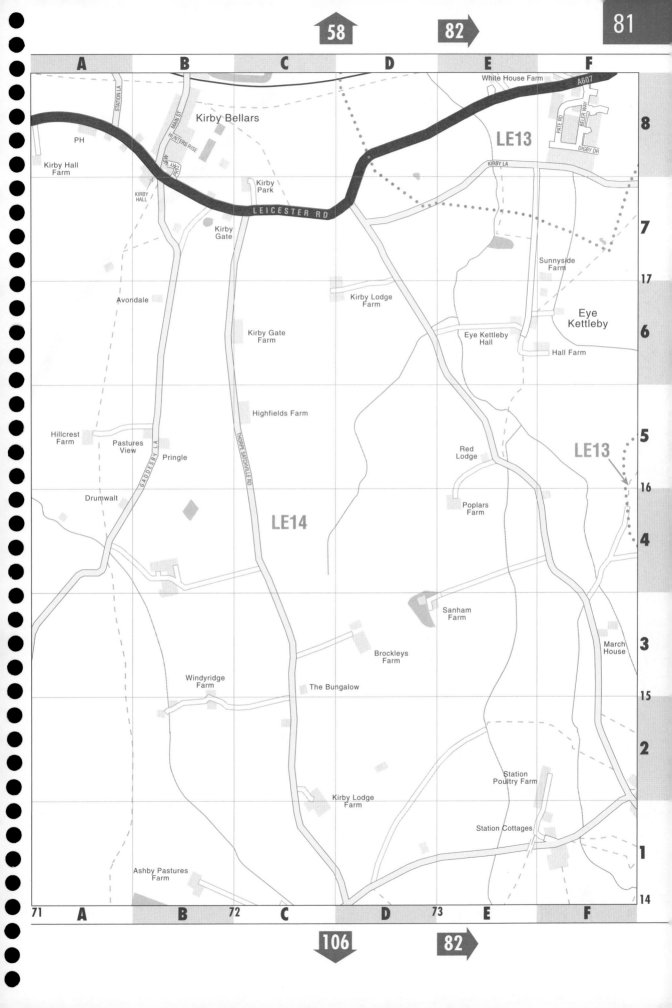

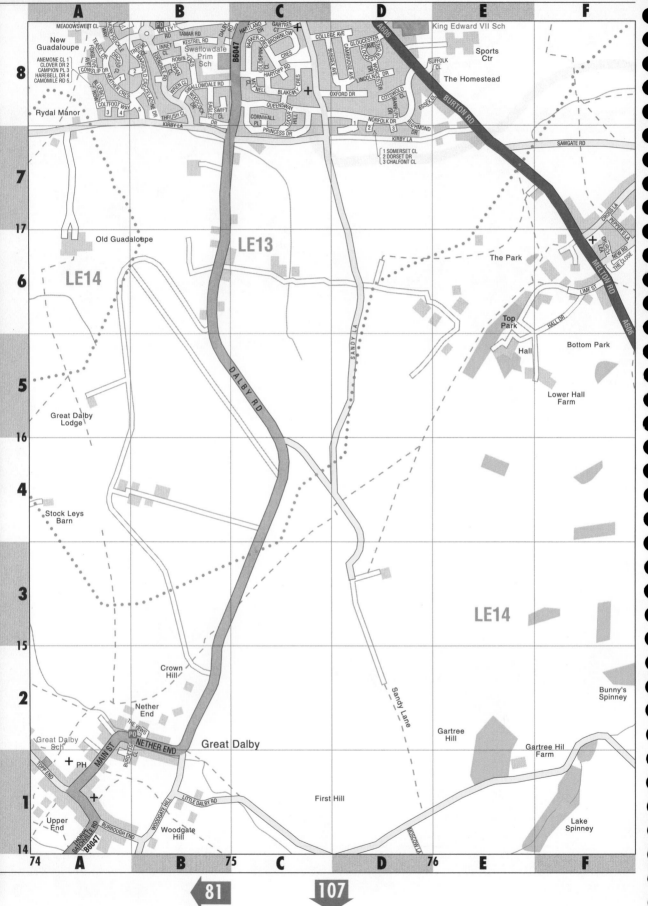

New Guadaloupe

ANEMONE CL 1
CLOVER DR 2
CAMPION PL 3
HAREBELL DR 4
CAMOMILE RD 5

MEADOWSWEET CL

Rydal Manor

Swallowdale Prim Sch

King Edward VII Sch

Sports Ctr

The Homestead

BURTON RD

SAWGATE RD

1 SOMERSET CL
2 DORSET DR
3 CHALFONT CL

KIRBY LA

PRINCESS DR

Old Guadaloupe

LE13

The Park

CHURCH LEA
NEW RD
THE CLOSE
CROSS LA
PEPPER'S LA

MELTON RD

A606

LIME ST

LE14

Top Park

HALL DR

Hall

Bottom Park

Great Dalby Lodge

DALBY RD

SANDY LA

Lower Hall Farm

Stock Leys Barn

Crown Hill

LE14

Nether End

THE JEYS

Bunny's Spinney

Great Dalby Sch

PO

NETHER END

Great Dalby

Sandy Lane

Gartree Hill

Gartree Hil Farm

PH

MAIN ST

BURDETTS CL

LITTLE DALBY RD

First Hill

MOSCOW LA

Upper End

TOPP END

THORPE SATCHVILLE RD

B6047

BURROUGH END

Woodgate Hill

WOODGATE HILL

Lake Spinney

A B C D E F

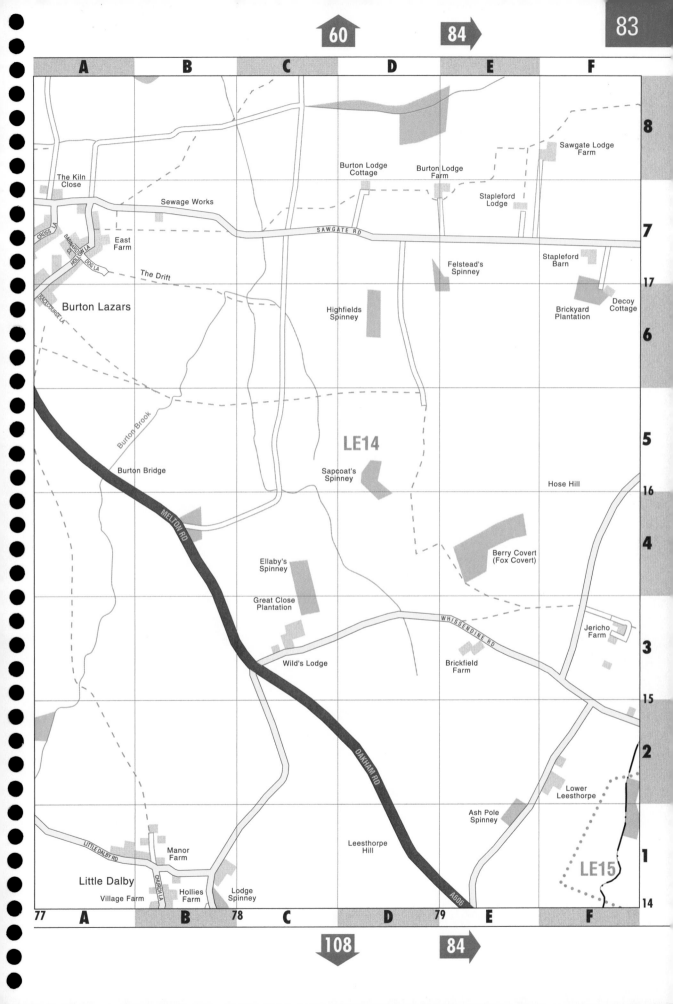

The Kiln Close
Sewage Works
Burton Lodge Cottage
Burton Lodge Farm
Sawgate Lodge Farm
Stapleford Lodge
CROSS LA
BARNABOW CL
HOLLOW LA
DOG LA
East Farm
SAWGATE RD
7
The Drift
Stapleford Barn
Felstead's Spinney
17
RACECOURSE LA
Burton Lazars
Highfields Spinney
Brickyard Plantation
Decoy Cottage
6
Burton Brook
LE14
5
Burton Bridge
Sapcoat's Spinney
Hose Hill
16
MELTON RD
Berry Covert (Fox Covert)
4
Ellaby's Spinney
Great Close Plantation
WHISSENDINE RD
Jericho Farm
3
Wild's Lodge
Brickfield Farm
15
OAKHAM RD
2
Lower Leesthorpe
Ash Pole Spinney
LITTLE DALBY RD
Manor Farm
Leesthorpe Hill
1
CHURCH LA
Little Dalby
Village Farm
Hollies Farm
Lodge Spinney
A606
LE15
14

83
61

A   B   C   D   E   F

8

Cottage Plantation

Stapleford Park

Crossing Covert

LC

7

SAWGATE RD

Bryans Lodge

Laxtons Cottage

17

The Lodge

Paget's Spinney

Holygate Farm

6

Cuckoo Hill

Laxton's Covert

LE14

5

The Grange

16

Waterloo Lodge

4

Whissendine Brook

STAPLEFORD RD

3

15

Browne's Lodge

2

LE15

MELTON RD

WILLOW CL

SHERRARD CL

SHERRARD CL

Whissendine CE Prim Sch

PH

STANILANDS

WALTON CL

ST ANDREWS CL

Whissenthorpe

THORPE GDNS

MAIN ST

BOUVERIE CT

PO

1

Whissendine Windmill

MILL GR

OAKHAM RD

COW LA

THE NOOK

Whissendine Lodge

LAMMAS COTTS

14

Whissendine

83
109

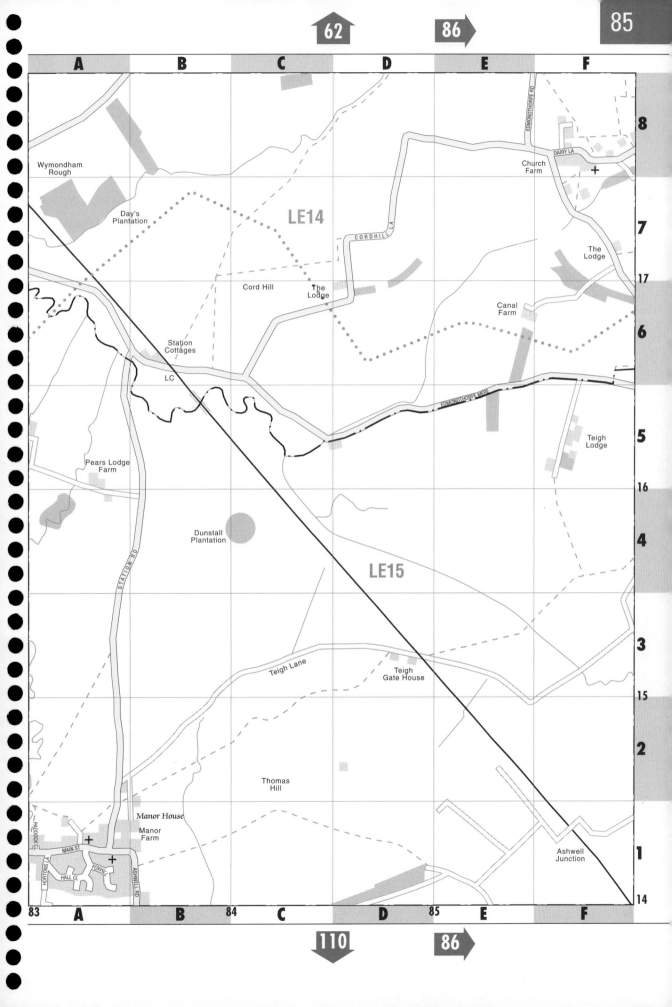

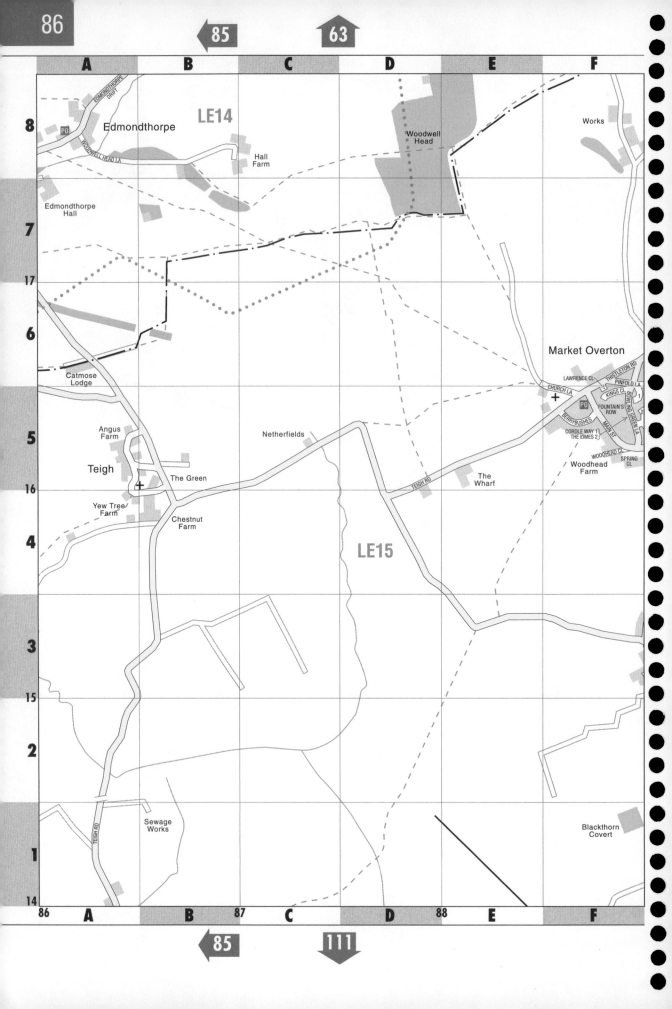

85
63

LE14

Edmondthorpe

PO

WOODWELL HEAD LA

EDMONDTHORPE DRIFT

Hall Farm

Edmondthorpe Hall

Woodwell Head

Works

Catmose Lodge

Market Overton

LAWRENCE CL.
THISTLETON RD
PINFOLD LA
CHURCH LA.
KINGS CL
BOWLING GREEN LA
PO
FOUNTAIN'S ROW
1
BERRYBUSHES
MAIN ST
CORDLE WAY 1
THE LIMES 2
WOODHEAD CL.
SPRING CL

Angus Farm

Netherfields

Woodhead Farm

Teigh

The Green

TEIGH RD

The Wharf

Yew Tree Farm

Chestnut Farm

LE15

TEIGH RD

Sewage Works

Blackthorn Covert

85
111

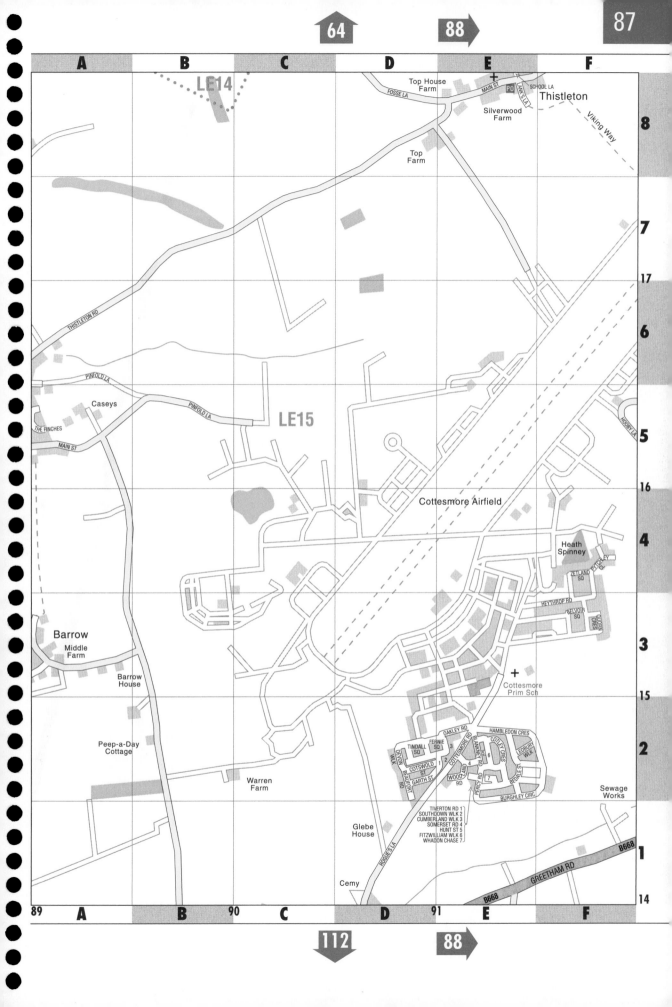

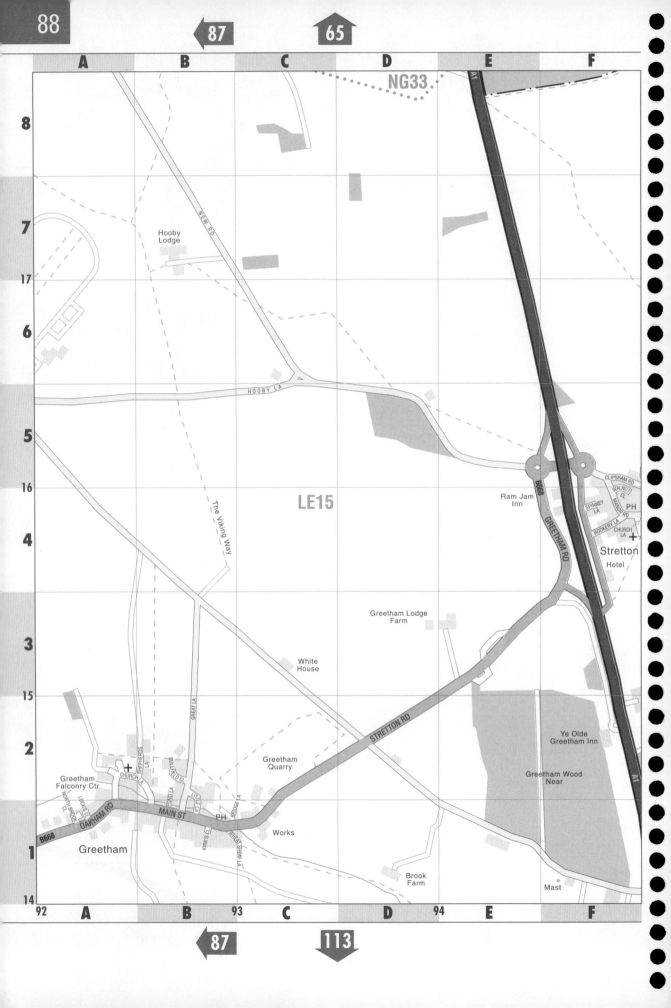

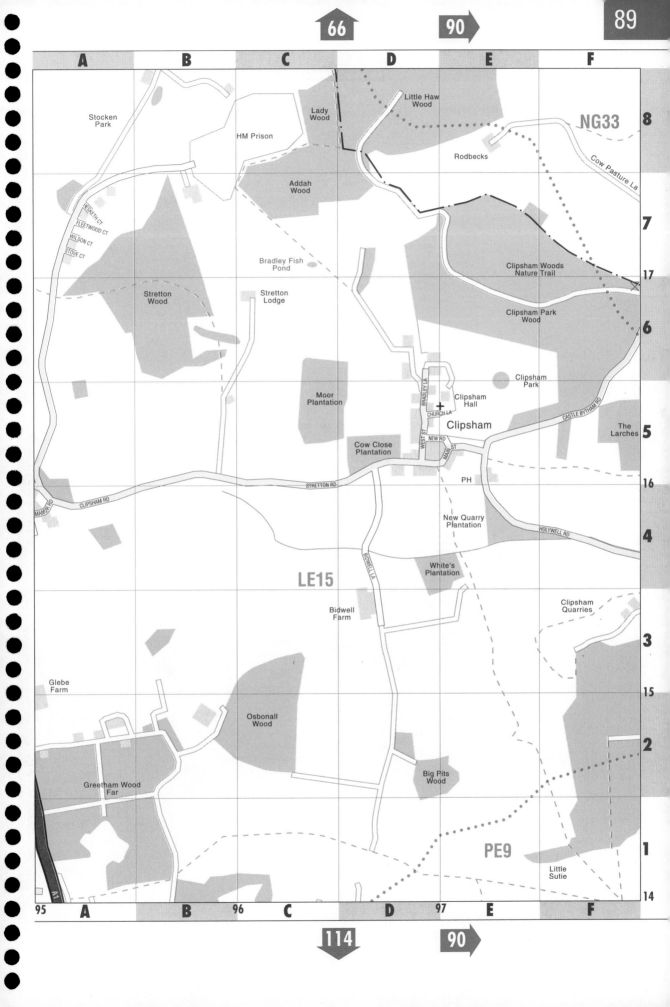

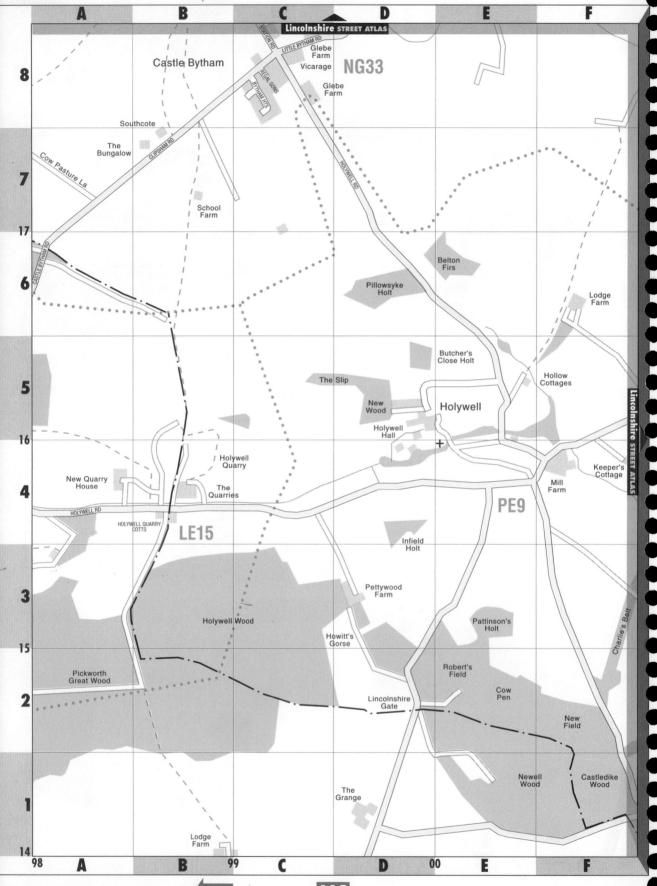

Castle Bytham

NG33

Glebe Farm
Vicarage
Glebe Farm

Southcote

The Bungalow

Cow Pasture La

School Farm

Belton Firs

Pillowsyke Holt

Lodge Farm

Butcher's Close Holt

Hollow Cottages

The Slip

New Wood

Holywell

Holywell Hall

Mill Farm

Keeper's Cottage

New Quarry House

Holywell Quarry

The Quarries

PE9

HOLYWELL RD

HOLYWELL QUARRY COTTS

LE15

Infield Holt

Pettywood Farm

Holywell Wood

Pattinson's Holt

Howitt's Gorse

Robert's Field

Pickworth Great Wood

Cow Pen

Lincolnshire Gate

New Field

Charlie's Belt

The Grange

Newell Wood

Castledike Wood

Lodge Farm

Lincolnshire STREET ATLAS

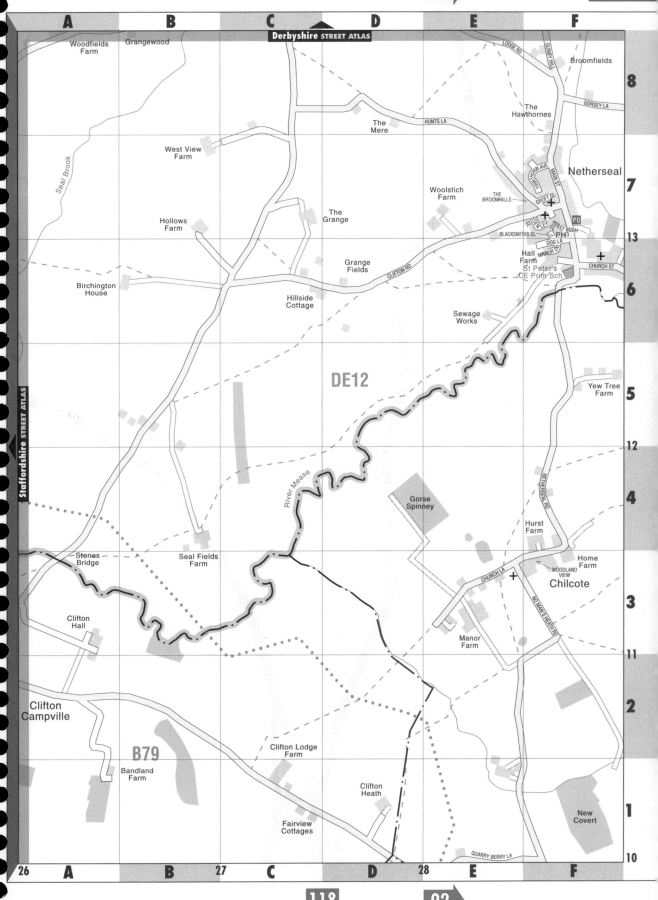

Derbyshire STREET ATLAS

Staffordshire STREET ATLAS

91
67

A B C D E F

8

Mount Pleasant La

Seal Pastures Plantation

Seale Pastures

Gorsey La

Hooborough Brook

Acresford Rd

7

PH

Brookfield Cotts

Coopers Cl

Acresford

Stanleigh Plantation

Stanleigh Gdns

PH

Talbot Pl

Chapel St

Narrow La

Church St

New St

Church Wlk

Hall La

Hall Farm

Rasscliffe Ave

Ivanhoe Way

13

Eastfield

Acresford Rd

Church St

6

Measham Rd

Moneyhill Farm

Saltersford Cottages

Saltersford Bridge

Saltersford Brook

Mine (dis)

Coronation La

Chapel St

Stretton Bridge

Saltersford Farm

River Mease

Oak Villa

5

DE12

Hall Farm

A42

12

Rectory La

4

Stretton en le Field

Repton Rd

3

Park Farm

Manor House Farm

11

2

A42

M42

Tamworth Rd

Heath Lodge

Measham Rd

1

Hill Farm

11

Hotel
The Old Rectory
Appleby Fields

Rectory La

Parkfield Cres

Stoney La

Old End

10

Old House

B5493

M42

A444

29 A 30 B C 30 D 31 E F

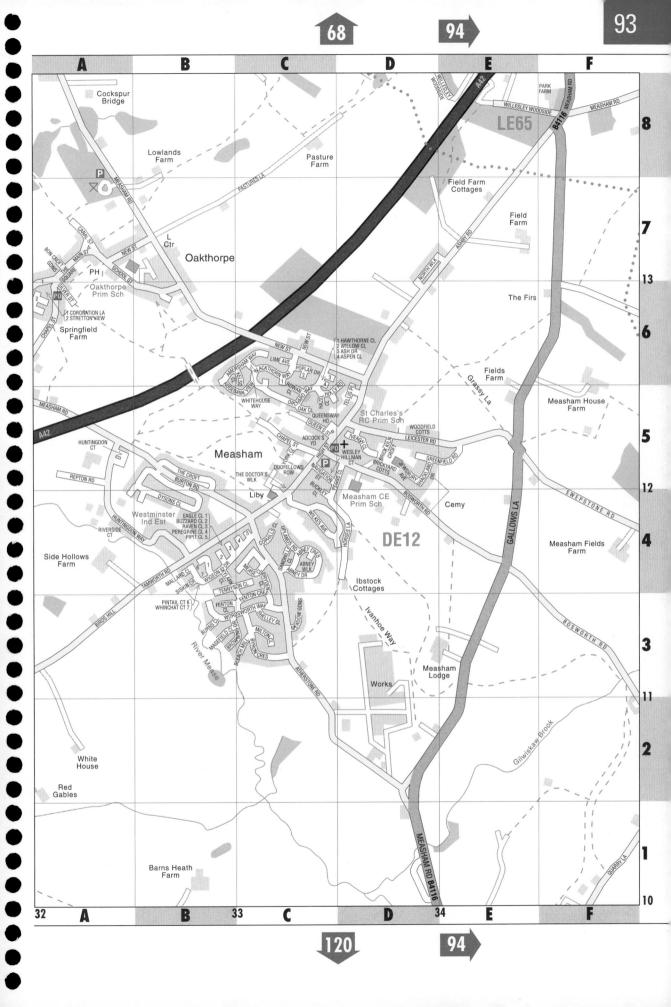

93
69

A **B** **C** **D** **E** **F**

MEASHAM RD

8

LE65

7

BABELAKE ST

Red Burrow Farm

RED BURROW LA

Yew Tree Farm

NORMANTON RD

ASHBY RD

Stonehouse Farm

Home Farm

13

Springs Hydro

BABELAKE ST

Normanton Lodge Farm

Normanton le Heath

SCHOOL LA

HEATHER LA

Highfields Farm

MAIN ST

6

Arlick Farm

The Barn

RED BURROW LA

NORMANTON LA

THE HOLLOW

Hillcrest

Manor Farm

Gilwiskaw Brook

5

12

LE67

Measham Hall

4

SWEPSTONE RD

Mill Top House

Odd Barn

Tempe Farm

DE12

Dishley Farm

ASHBY LA

Upperfields Farm

3

SWEPSTONE RD

11

MAIN ST

2

QUARRY LA

BOSWORTH RD

Swepstone

Manor Farm

CHURCH ST

Valley Farm House

HOME FARM BARNS

Quarry Lane Farm

1

Valley Farm

SWEPSTONE RD

NEWTON RD

10

35 **A** **B** 36 **C** **D** 37 **E** **F**

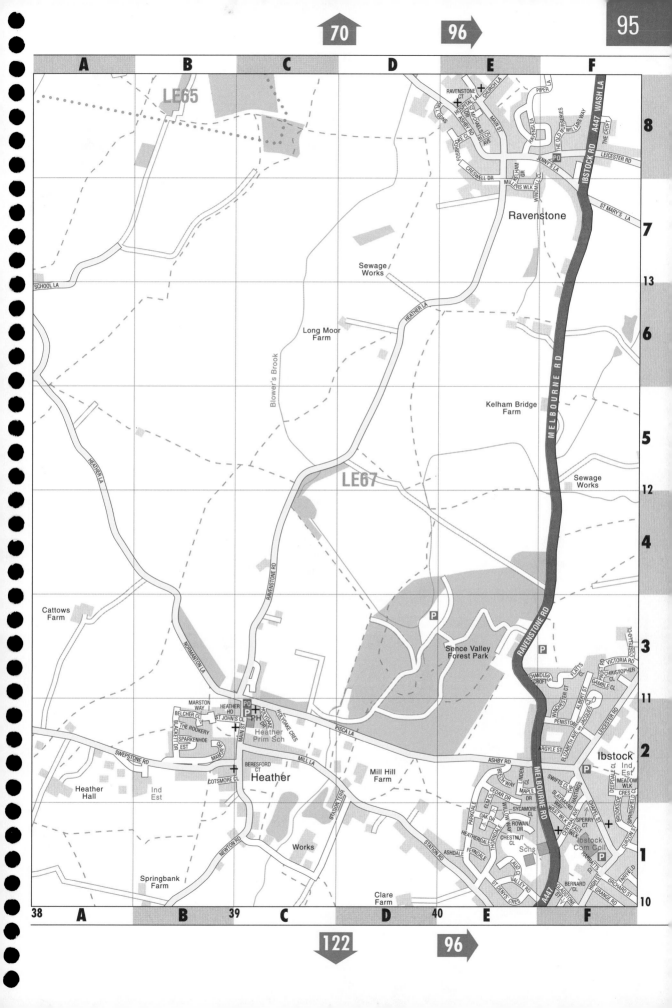

A B C D E F

8

7

13

6

5

12

4

11

2

1

10

41 42 43

St Mary's La

Snibston

Grange Farm

Berryhills Farm

Leicester Rd

Standard Mill

Dksns Way

Snipe

Oak Tree Rd

Ash Tree Rd

Private Rd

Frearson Rd

Jacks Wlk

St Saviours Rd

East St

St Vincents Cl

Highfield

Wentworth Rd

Zetland Cl

Bedale Cl

Vaughan Rd

James St

Ridge La

Belvoir Rd

College Cl

Berrisford Rd

Scotlands Rd

Bridge Rd

Burgess St

Harrison Pl

Stadium Cl

Kemp Rd

Clutsom Rd

Crescent Rd

Cavendish Cres

Heage Rd

Camelford Rd

Croxdale

Totnes

Talkestone Rd

Tavistock

Gray

Woods Rd

Bracken Cl

The Spinney

St Mary's Ave

Manor Rd

Ashburton Rd

Berryhill La

Farm La

Holt's La

Townsend La

Smith's Farm

Donington le Heath

Donington le Heath Manor House

Hugglescote Com Prim Sch

Brambles Cl

Brackenfield

Tweentown

Meadow View

Manor Brook Cl

PH

The Green

Wkspace 17

Workspace 17

Allot Gdns

North Ave

Moreton Ct

Broach Rd

Fairfield Rd

Central Rd

Garfield Rd

Queen St

King St

Prince St

Forest Rd

Convent Dr

St Clares Ct

Avenue Rd

Broad St

Broughton St

Wyggeston St

Stephenson Coll

Belvoirdale Com Prim Sch

St Clares RC Prim Sch

Scotlands Ind Est

Charnwood Ct

London Rd

Charnwood

Scotlands Dr

Amb HQ

Playing Fields

Newbridge High Sch

COALVILLE

Broom Leys Rd

Broom Leys Ave

Bardon Rd

Highgrove Cl

Robin Rd

Heron Cl

Teal Cl

Swan Way

Devana Ave

Clarence Dr

Sunningdale Cl

Hampton Rd

Balmoral Rd

Buckingham Rd

Birmingham Rd

STEPHENSON WAY

BARDON RD A511

PO

Holly Bank

Peggs Grange

Quelch St

Mill Pond

Mill Dam

Links Cl

Highway

River Sence Way

Hawley Rd

Grange Rd

Louella Stud

Grange Farm Bsns Pk

Upper Grange Farm

St John's

Dennis St

Hugglescote

Station Rd

Recn Gd

Cemy

The Elms

River Sence

LE67

River Sence

Richmond Rd

Blackberry La

Blackberry Farm

Byron Cl

Swinfen Cl

Lawrence Cl

Channing Way

Sherwood Cl

Chichester Cl

Pickering

Elinor Cl

Cannock Cl

Kendal Rd

Ibstock Rd

Kendal Rd

South St

Moore Rd

Ind Est

Sports Gd

Ind Est

BEVERIDGE LA

PH

Ellistown

Ellistown Com Prim Sch

Whitehill Rd

Spence View

Derbys

Hallow Cl

Rushby Rd

Colliers Way

David Lees Cl

Francis Way

Battleflat Dr

Sawbridge Cl

East Cres

St Christopher's Rd

PO

Old School Cl

Clay La

LEICESTER RD

REDLANDS EST

Ibstock

Spring Rd

Brooks Side Rd

Cemy

PRETORIA RD

Clay Pit

Pig Farm

MIDLAND RD

Ellistown Farm

Ellistown Terrace Rd

Pickering Grange Farm

Copson St

VICTORIA RD B585

STATION RD

B585

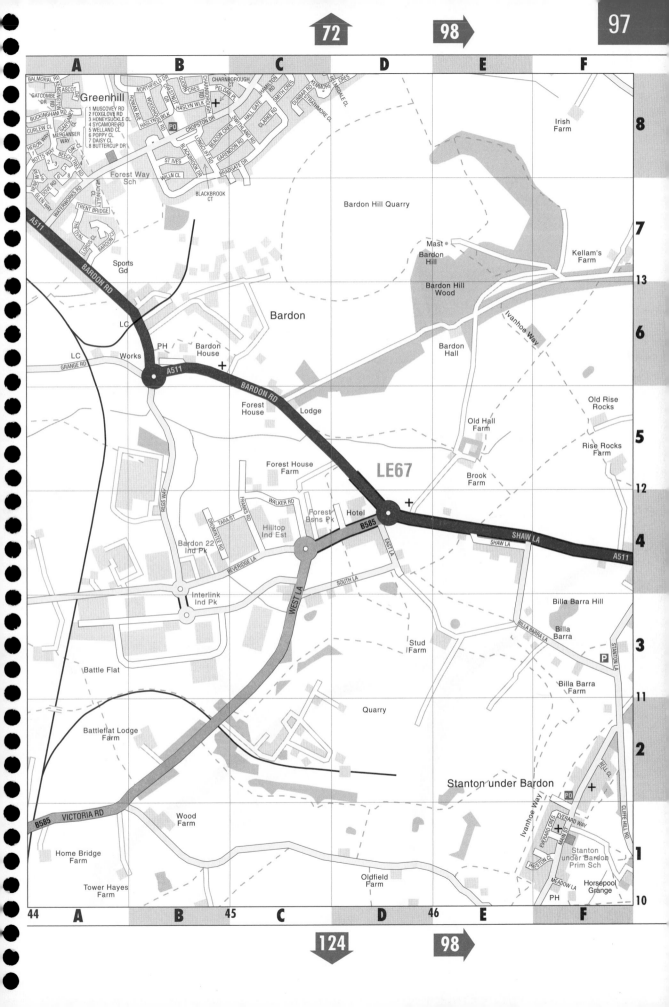

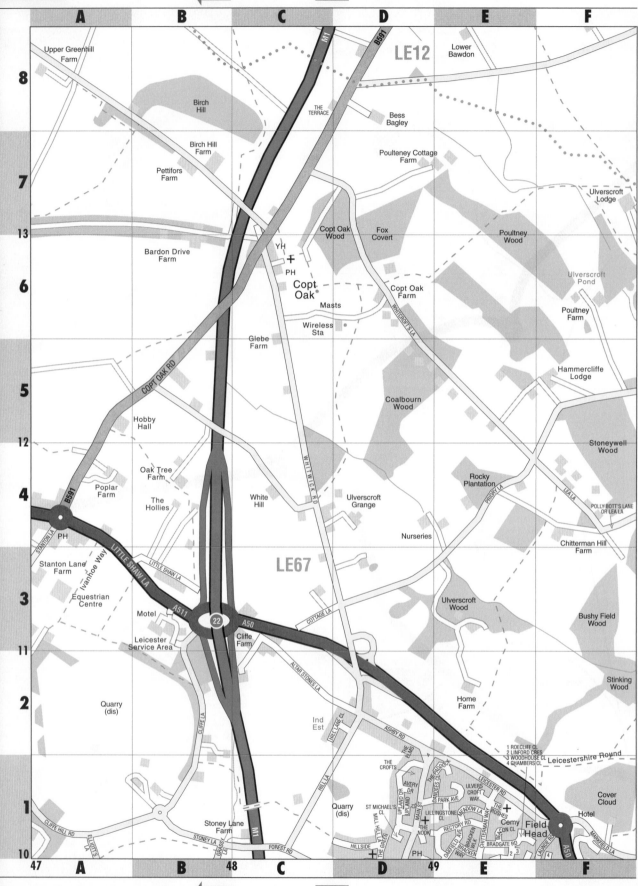

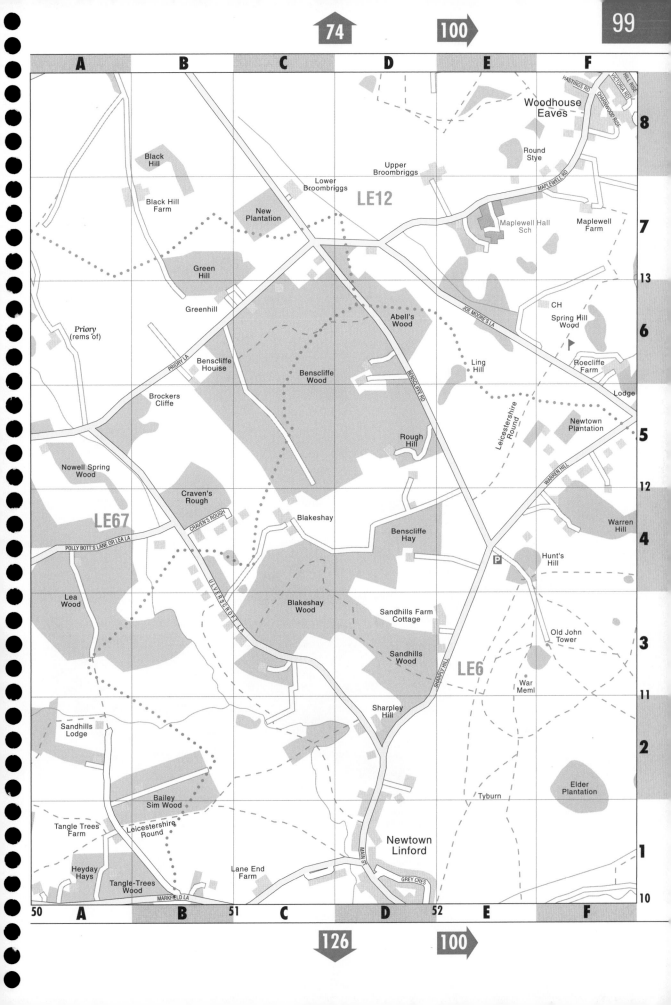

A   B   C   D   E   F

8

THE DRIVE
HILL RISE
NANHILL DR

Hunger
Hill

CHARNWOOD
HO

THE
GRANGE

BRAND HILL

BRAND LA

LE7

Swithland Resr
Nature Reserve

Swithland
Resr

7

Barn
Farm

The
Brand

Brand
Hills

P

Swithland

The
White House

Main St

The Rectory

Swithland St Leonard's
CE Prim Sch

PH

CHARNIA GR

Hall
Farm

13

LE12

Swithland
Hall

6

Roecliffe
Hill

Roecliffe
Manor

Swithland
Camp

Swithland Wood
Farm

Swithland
Wood

Moore
Spinney

Leicester La

The
Rough

5

Swithland Woods
Nature Reserve

Cropston
Leys

Bybrooke Lodge
Farm

12

4

Filter
Sta

P

Roecliffe Rd

Swithland Rd

Bradgate Rd

3

LE6

Sliding Stone
Enclosure

Bradgate
Country Park

Hallgate Hill
Spinney

Hallgates

P

Coppice
Plantation

Reservoir Rd

Lodge La

Water
Works

Cropston Resr
Nature Reserve

Cropston

GUILD CL
STATION RD
SANDHAM
BRIDGE
CAUDLE CL
LATIMER RD
THISTLE CL

11

Dale
Spinney

Cropston Resr

PH

PO

+

FOX HOLLOW
OUTFIELDS DR
STAMFORD DR
PRIORY CL
WAKEFIELD RD

2

Bradgate Park
(Deer Park)

Deer Park
Spinney

Boat
House

LE7

JOSEPH
CL

CAUSEWAY LA

LYCHGATE
CL

Cropston House
Farm

CROPSTON RD

1

Bowling Green
Spinney

Leicestershire Round

Bradgate
(rems of)

Sewage
Works

10

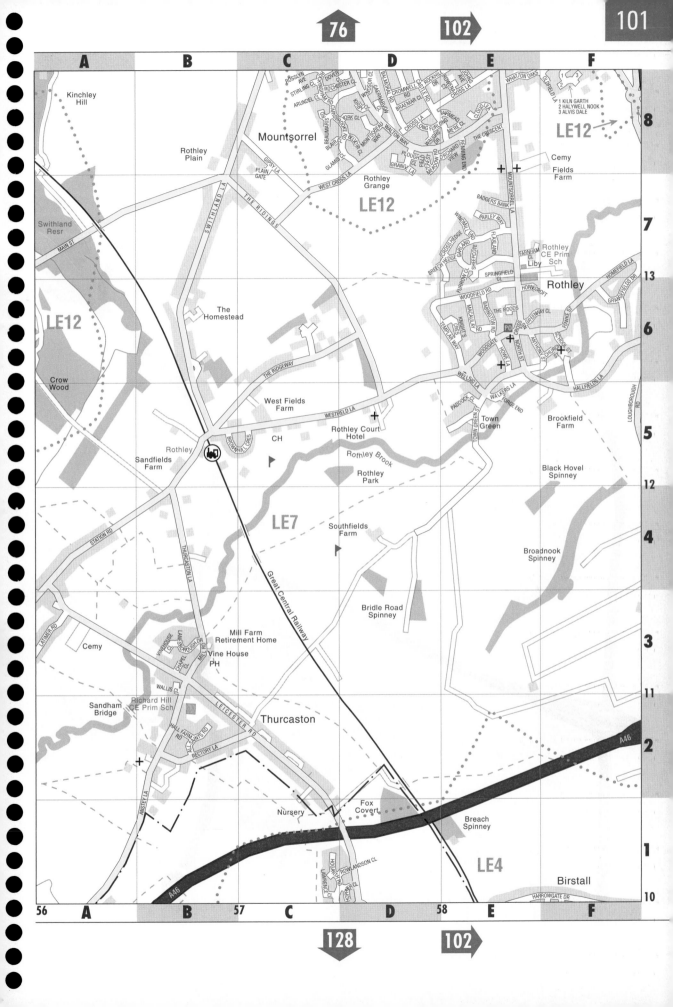

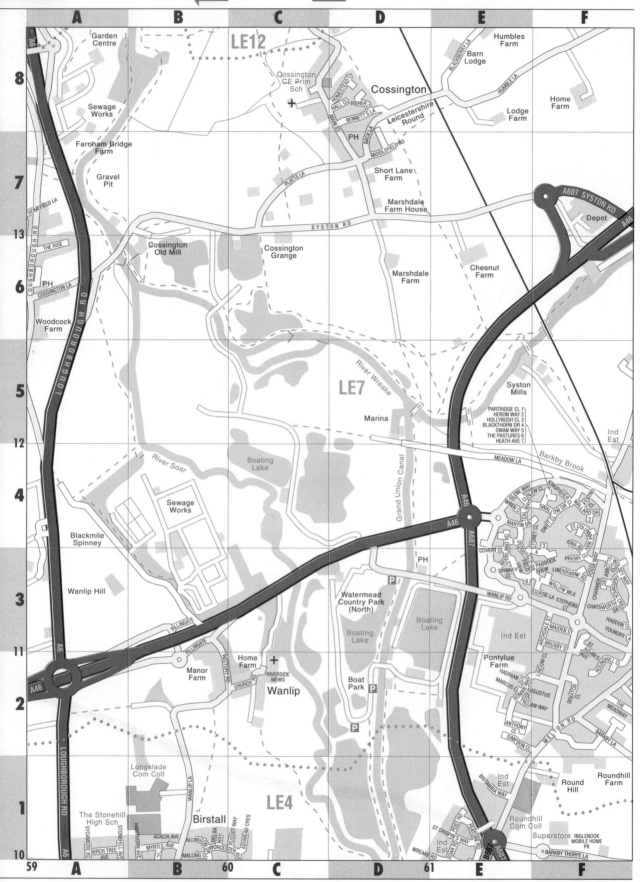

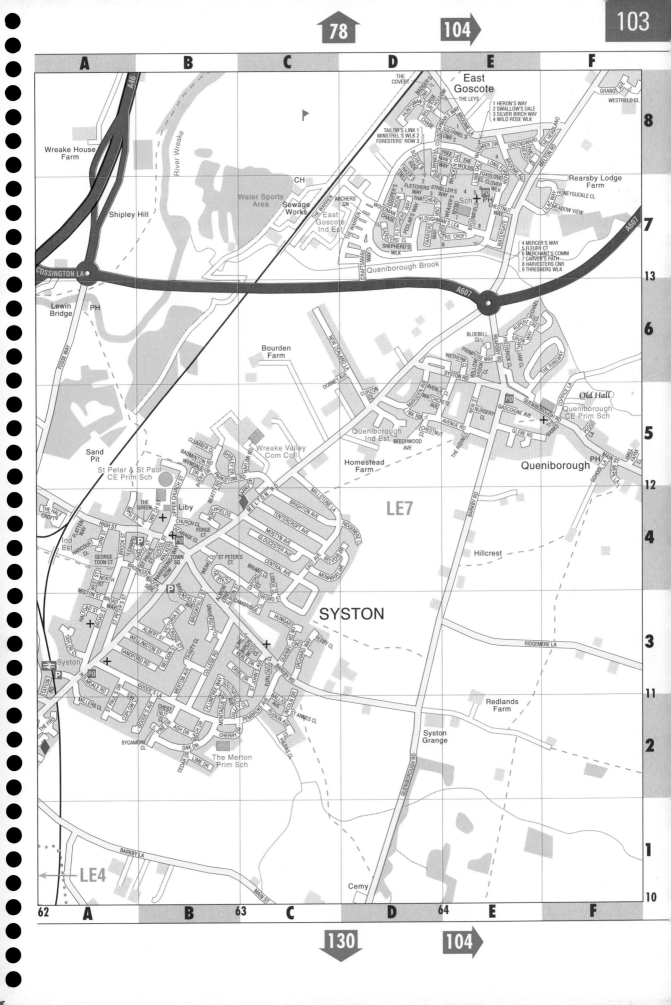

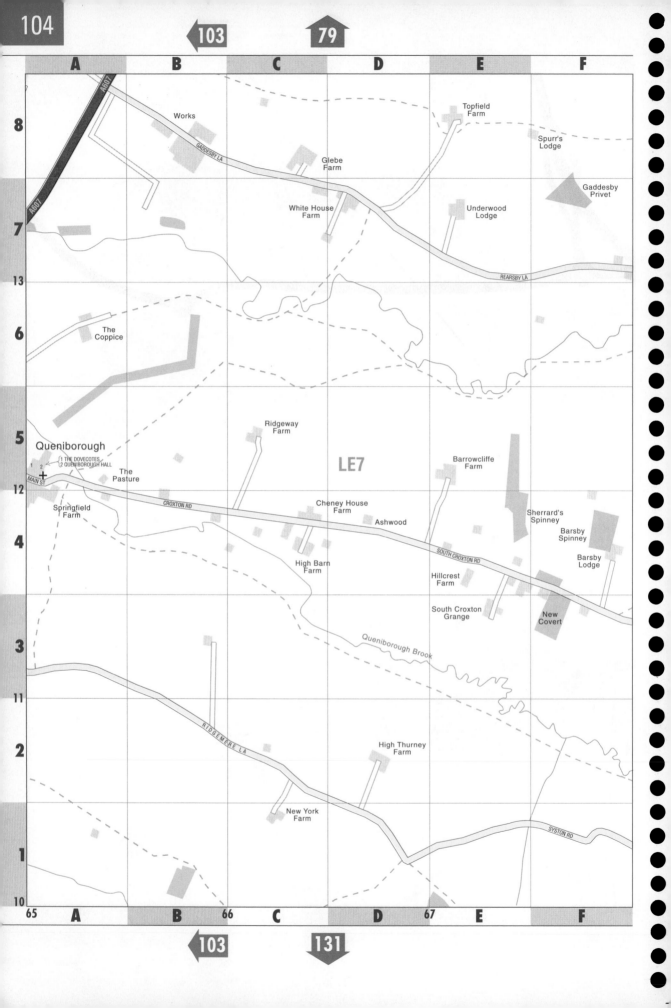

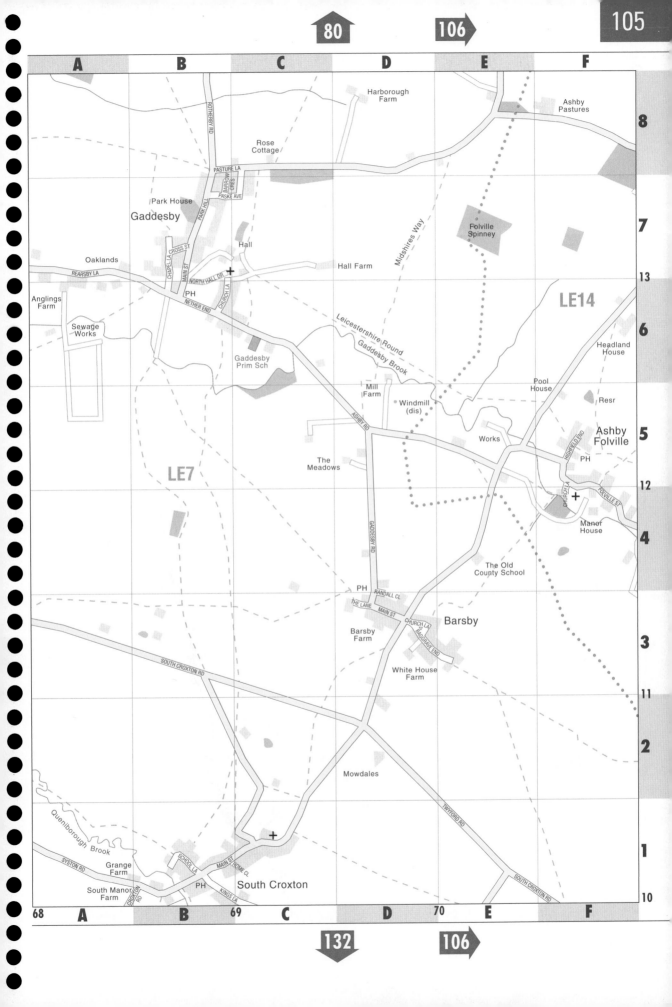

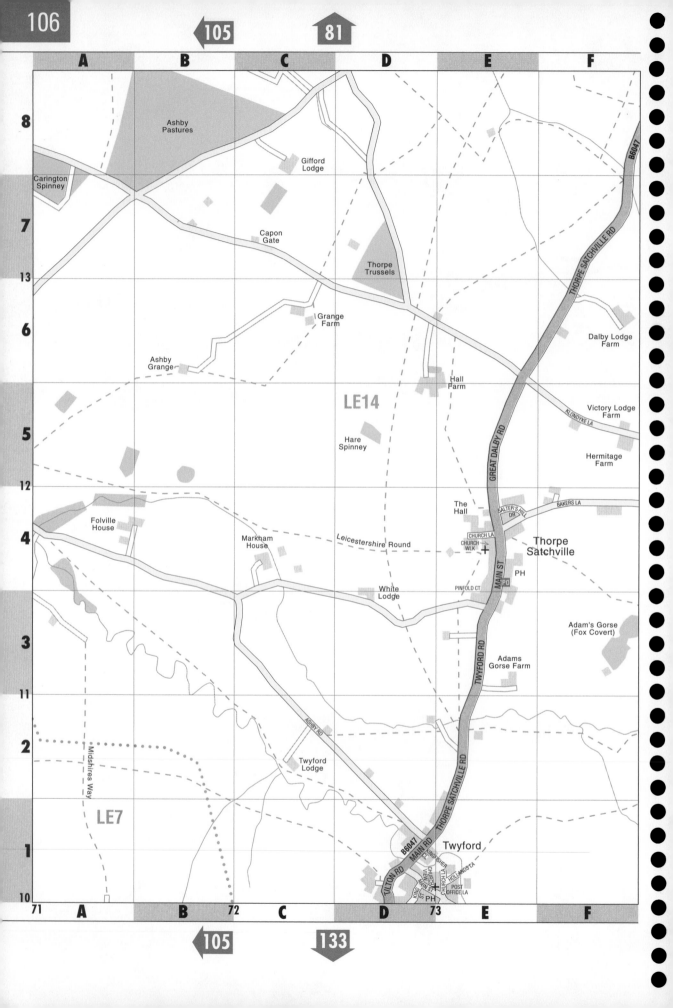

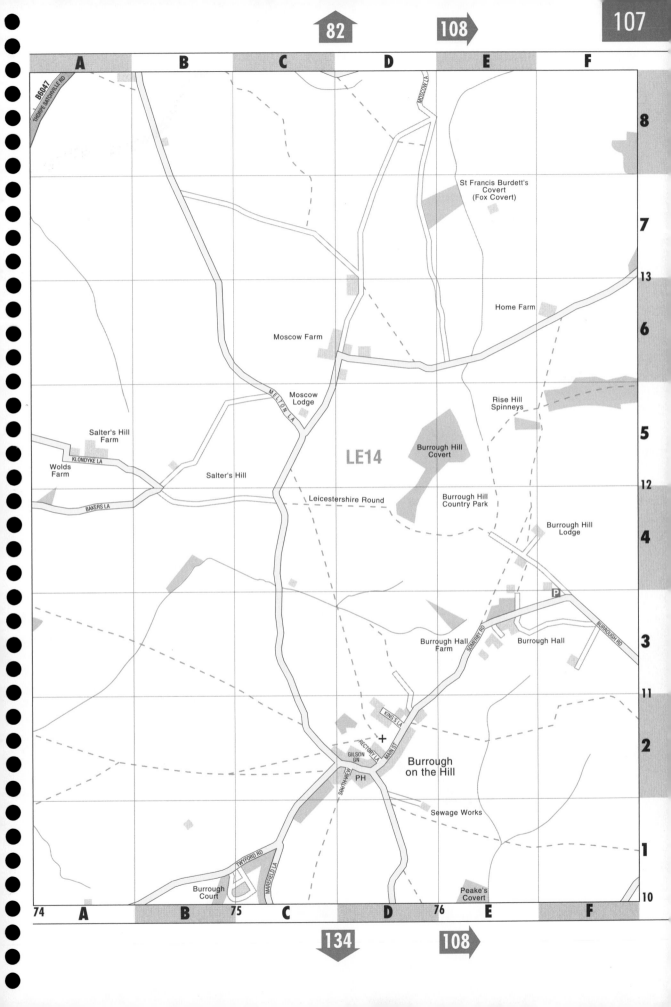

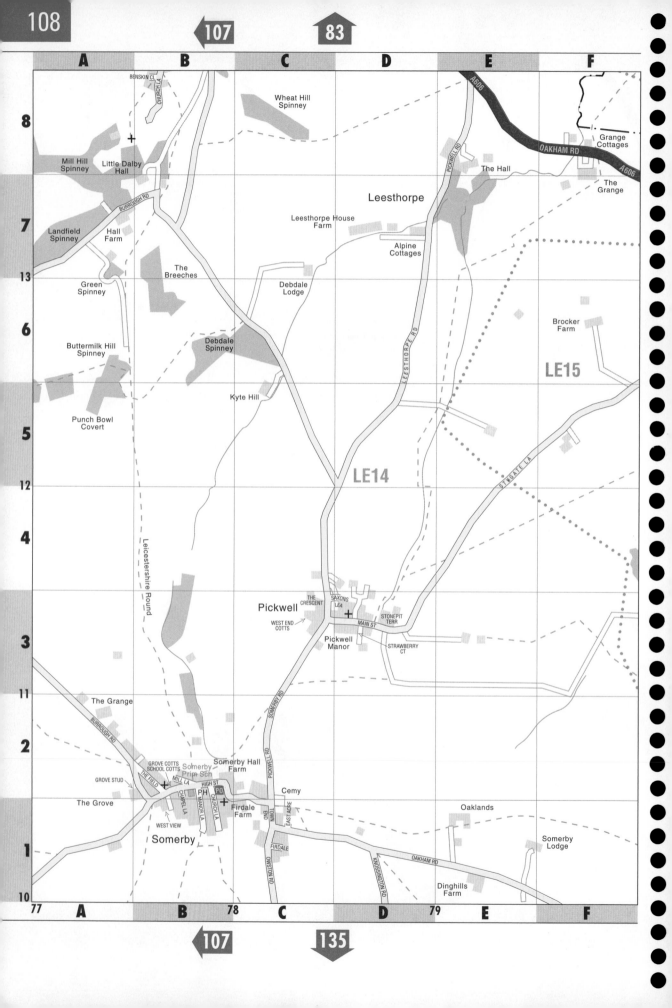

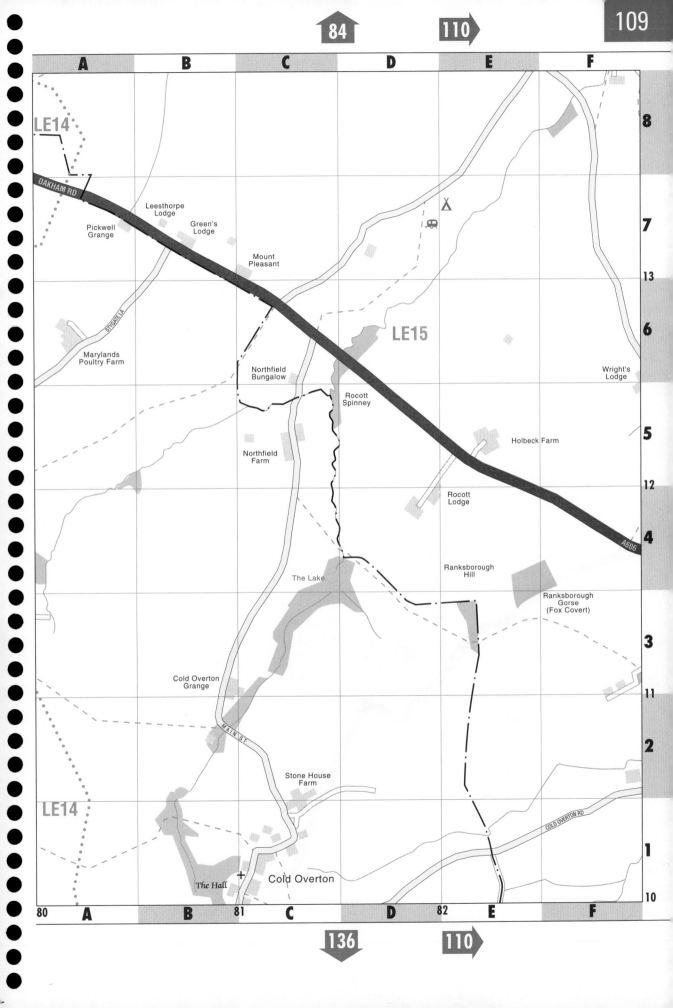

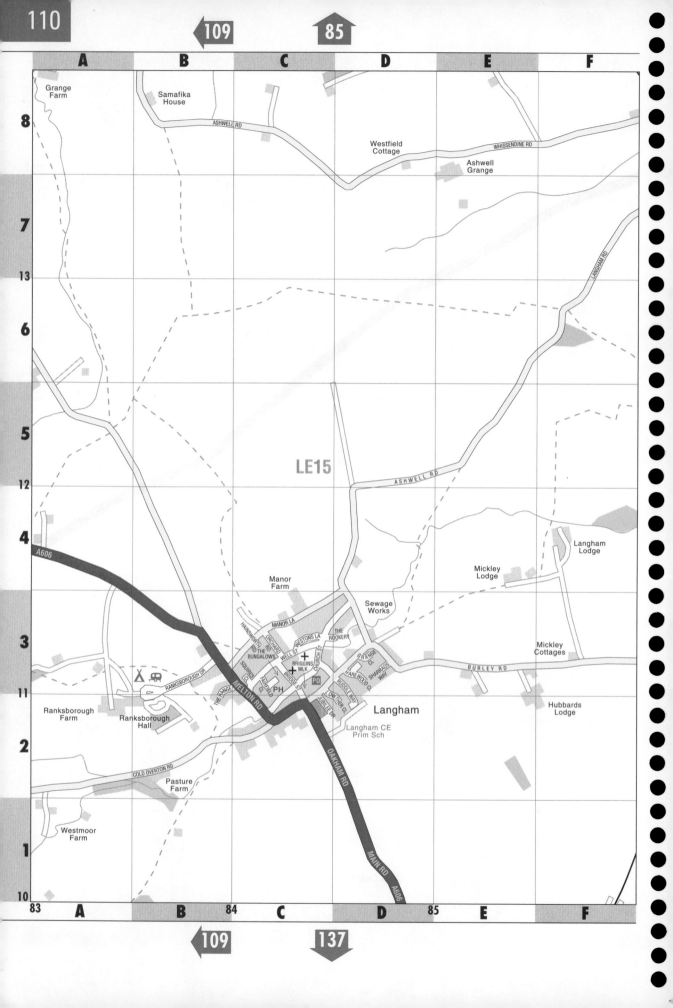

109
85

A B C D E F

8

7

13

6

5

12

4

3

11

2

1

10

109
137

Grange Farm

Samafika House

ASHWELL RD

Westfield Cottage

WHISSENDINE RD

Ashwell Grange

LANGHAM RD

LE15

ASHWELL RD

A606

Langham Lodge

Mickley Lodge

Manor Farm

Sewage Works

Mickley Cottages

MANOR LA

HAINSWORTH RD

ORCHARD RD

THE BUNGALOWS

WELL ST

MELTONS LA

THE ROOKERY

GRANGE CL

SHARBADS WAY

BURLEY RD

SQUIRES CL

FAIRFIELD

BRIGGINS WLK

CHURCH ST

HAREWOOD WAY

RANKSBOROUGH DR

THE RANGE

MELTON RD

BRIDGE ST

PH

PO

RUDDLE WAY

LOW TER CL

JUBILEE DR

Langham

Hubbards Lodge

Ranksborough Farm

Ranksborough Hall

Langham CE Prim Sch

COLD OVERTON RD

Pasture Farm

OAKHAM RD

Westmoor Farm

MAIN RD

A606

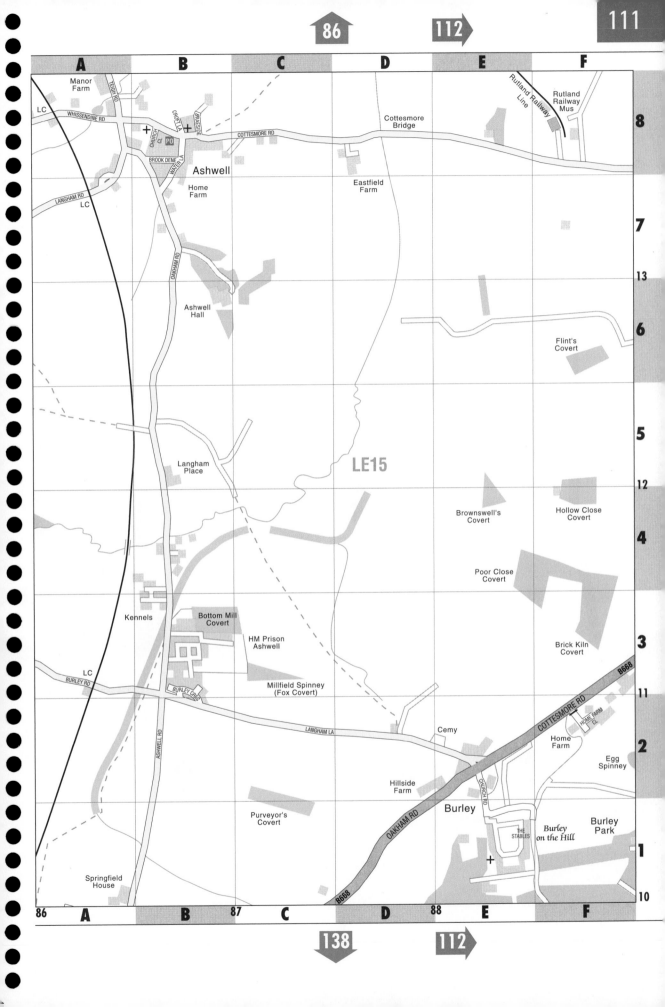

A B C D E F

8
7
13
6
5
12
4
3
11
2
1
10

Manor Farm
TEIGH RD
LC
WHISSENDINE RD
CHURCH CL
CROFT LA
PO
BRAESIDE
COTTESMORE RD
Cottesmore Bridge
Rutland Railway Line
Rutland Railway Mus
BROOK DENE
WATER LA
Ashwell
Home Farm
LANGHAM RD
LC
Eastfield Farm
OAKHAM RD
Ashwell Hall
Flint's Covert
LE15
Langham Place
Brownswell's Covert
Hollow Close Covert
Poor Close Covert
Kennels
Bottom Mill Covert
HM Prison Ashwell
Brick Kiln Covert
B668
LC
BURLEY RD
ASHWELL RD
BURLEY CRES
Millfield Spinney (Fox Covert)
LANGHAM LA
Cemy
COTTESMORE RD
HOME FARM CL
Home Farm
Egg Spinney
Hillside Farm
CHURCH RD
Burley
Purveyor's Covert
OAKHAM RD
THE STABLES
Burley on the Hill
Burley Park
Springfield House
B668

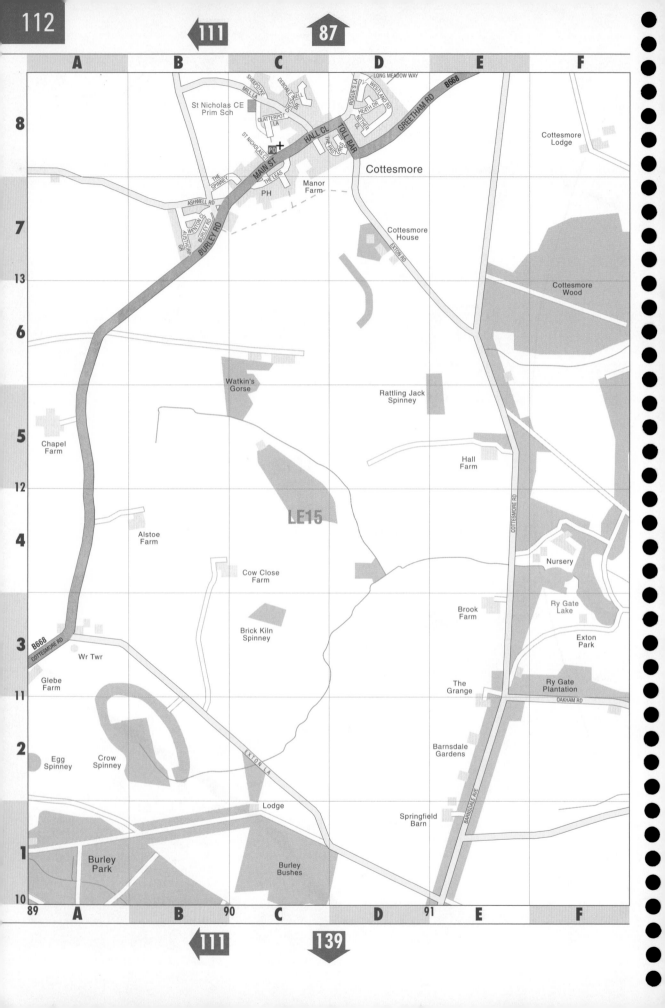

Cottesmore

Cottesmore Lodge

St Nicholas CE Prim Sch

Long Meadow Way

GREETHAM RD   B668

SHEEPDYKE

MILL LA

DERDALE

CRESSWELL DR

CLATTERPOT LA

ROGUE'S LA

WESTLAND RD

HEATH DR

NETHER CL

St NICHOLAS CL

HALL CL

TOLL BAR

THE PADDOCK

PO

MAIN ST

THE SPINNEY

THE LEAS

PH

Manor Farm

ASHWELL RD

WYTON CL

AUSTHORPE DR

BURLEY RD

Cottesmore House

EXTON RD

Cottesmore Wood

Watkin's Gorse

Rattling Jack Spinney

Hall Farm

Chapel Farm

LE15

COTTESMORE RD

Alstoe Farm

Cow Close Farm

Nursery

Brook Farm

Ry Gate Lake

Exton Park

Brick Kiln Spinney

B668

COTTESMORE RD

Wr Twr

Glebe Farm

The Grange

Ry Gate Plantation

OAKHAM RD

Egg Spinney

Crow Spinney

EXTON LA

Barnsdale Gardens

BARNSDALE AVE

Lodge

Springfield Barn

Burley Park

Burley Bushes

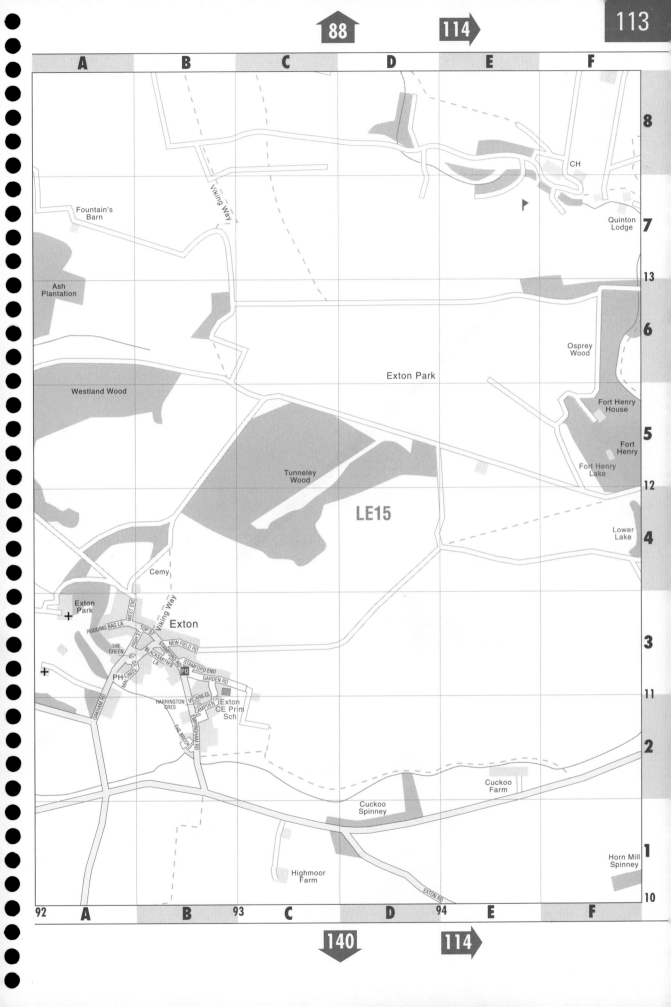

113
89

A B C D E F

8

Woolfox
Wood

Woolfox
Quarry

7

The
Coppice

Airfield
(disused)

13

Toll Bar
Spinney

6

Woolfox
Depot

The
Lodge

Hardwick
Wood

Woolfox
Lodge

Pickworth
Plain

LE15

5

CH

Hardwick
Farm

North Road
Spinney

12

Lower
Lake

Exeter
Gorse

4

Horn
House

GREAT NORTH RD

PE9

Crows
Spinney

Warren
Plantation

Little Oaks

Bloody Oaks

3

North Brook

Pug's Park
Spinney

Tickencote
Warren

11

Middle
Lodge

2

Trout
Hatchery

Old Wood
Lodge

Empingham
Old Wood

Three Corner
Plantation

Wing
Plantations

Horn
Mill

Old Keepers

LOVES LA

1

Horn Mill
Spinney

Tickencote
Laund

10

CROSS ROADS
FARM COTTS

95 A B 96 C D 97 E F

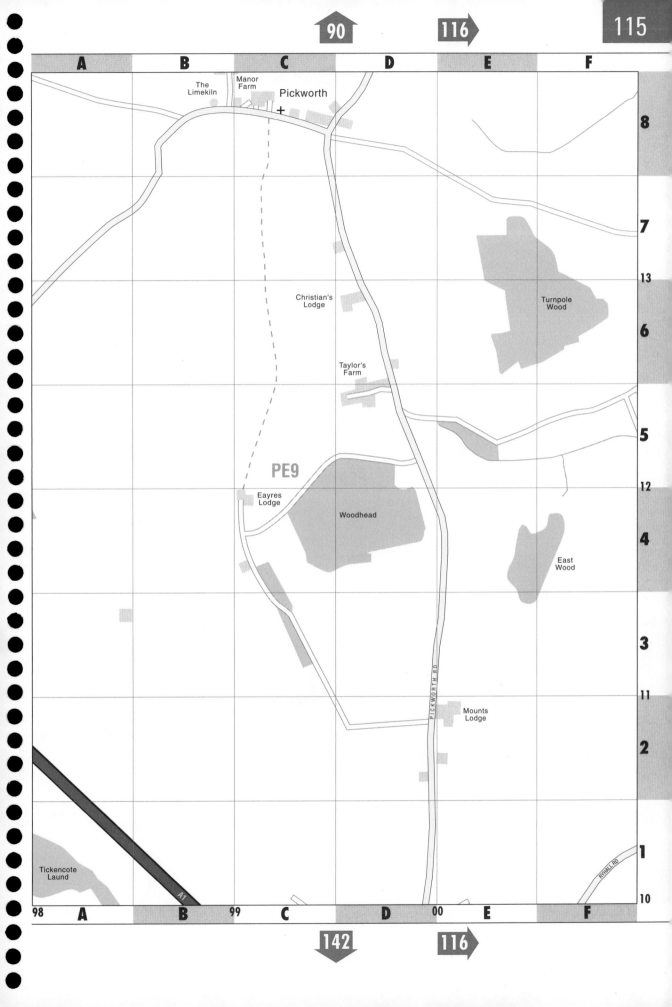

The Limekiln

Manor Farm

Pickworth

8

7

13

Christian's Lodge

Turnpole Wood

6

Taylor's Farm

5

PE9

12

Eayres Lodge

Woodhead

4

East Wood

3

PICKWORTH RD

11

Mounts Lodge

2

A1

1

Tickencote Laund

RYHALL RD

10

98

A

B

99

C

D

00

E

F

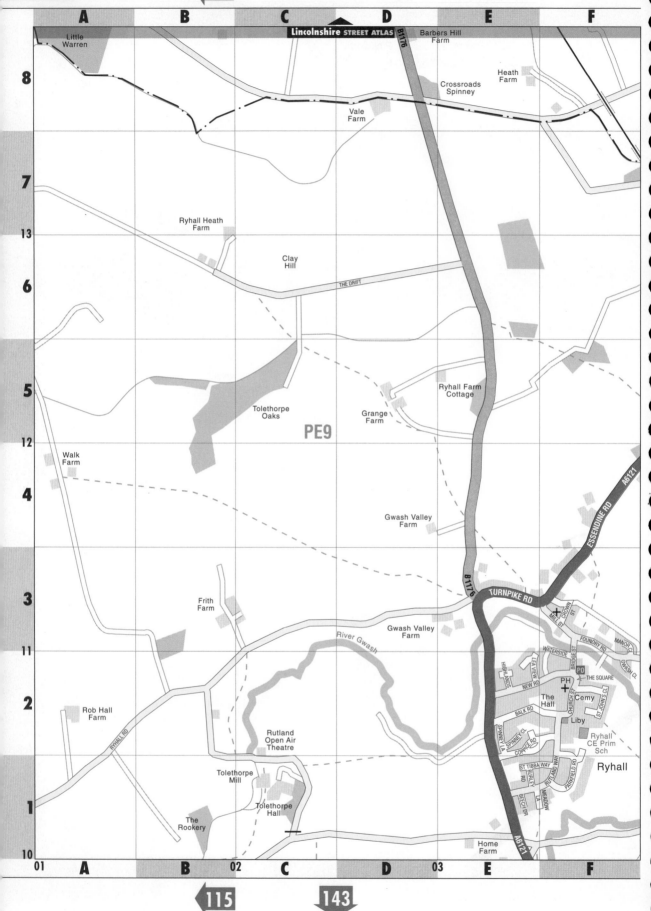

Lincolnshire STREET ATLAS

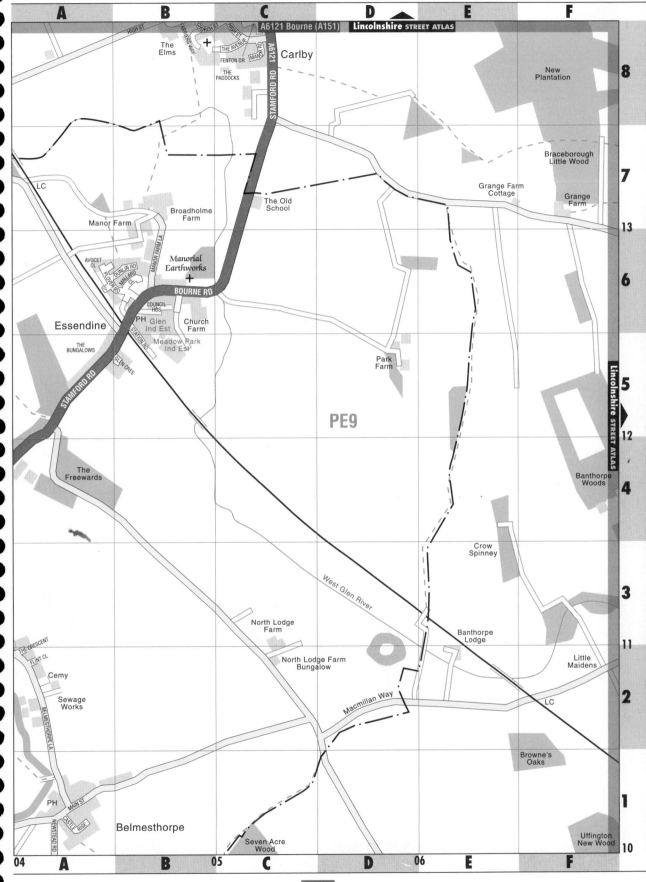

A   B   C   D   E   F

A6121 Bourne (A151)

The Elms

HIGH ST
FARRIERS WAY
CHURCH ST
HIGH ST
THE AVENUE
FENTON DR
THE PADDOCKS
MAIN RD
STAMFORD RD
A6121

Carlby

8

New Plantation

Braceborough Little Wood

7

The Old School

Grange Farm Cottage

Grange Farm

13

LC

Manor Farm

Broadholme Farm

Manorial Earthworks

MANOR FARM LA
AVOCET CL
DUNLIN RD
PLOVER RD
MALLARD CL
BOURNE RD

6

COUNCIL HOS
PH
Glen Ind Est
Church Farm

Essendine

THE BUNGALOWS

Meadow Park Ind Est

Park Farm

STATION RD
GLEN CRES
STAMFORD RD

5

PE9

12

The Freewards

Banthorpe Woods

4

Crow Spinney

West Glen River

3

North Lodge Farm

Banthorpe Lodge

11

North Lodge Farm Bungalow

Little Maidens

THE CRESCENT
FLINT CL

Cemy

Sewage Works

Macmillan Way

LC

2

BELMESTHORPE LA

Browne's Oaks

PH
MAIN ST
CASTLE RISE
NEWSTEAD RD

Belmesthorpe

1

Seven Acre Wood

Uffington New Wood

10

04   A   B   05   C   D   06   E   F

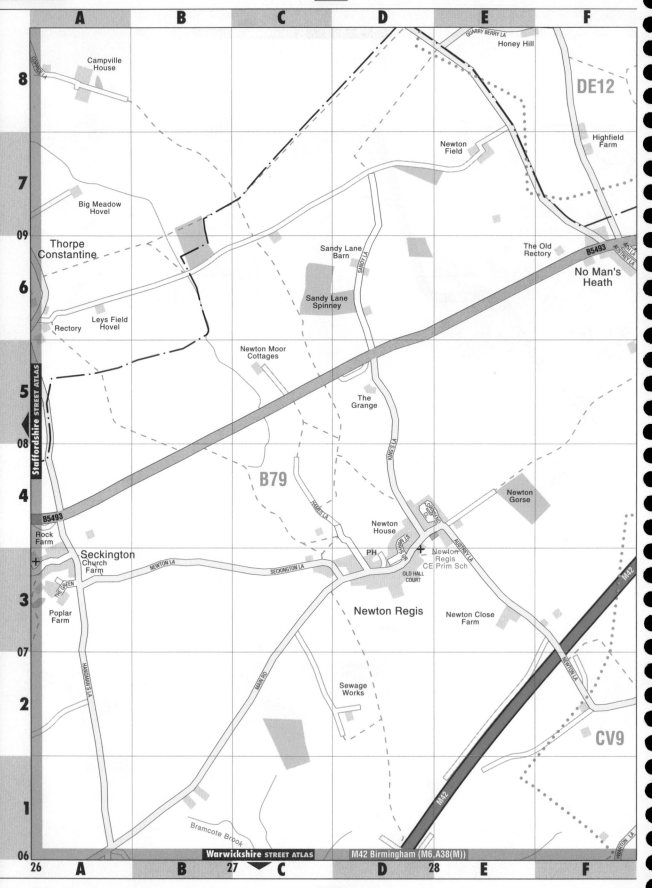

A B C D E F

8

7

09

6

5

08

4

07

2

1

06

Corse La

Campville House

Big Meadow Hovel

Thorpe Constantine

Rectory

Leys Field Hovel

Rock Farm

Seckington

Church Farm

The Green

Poplar Farm

Hangman's La

Newton La

Seckington La

Newton Moor Cottages

Sandy Lane Barn

Sandy La

Sandy Lane Spinney

The Grange

King's La

B79

Hales La

Newton House

PH

Old Hall Court

Main Rd

Newton Regis

Sewage Works

Bramcote Brook

Quarry Berry La

Honey Hill

DE12

Newton Field

Highfield Farm

The Old Rectory

B5493

Asta La

Austrey La

No Man's Heath

Newton Gorse

Knings Rd

St Jams Dr

Newton Regis CE Prim Sch

Newton Close Farm

Austrey La

M42

Newton La

CV9

M42

Newton La

B5493

Staffordshire STREET ATLAS

Warwickshire STREET ATLAS

M42 Birmingham (M6, A38(M))

26 A B 27 C D 28 E F

06

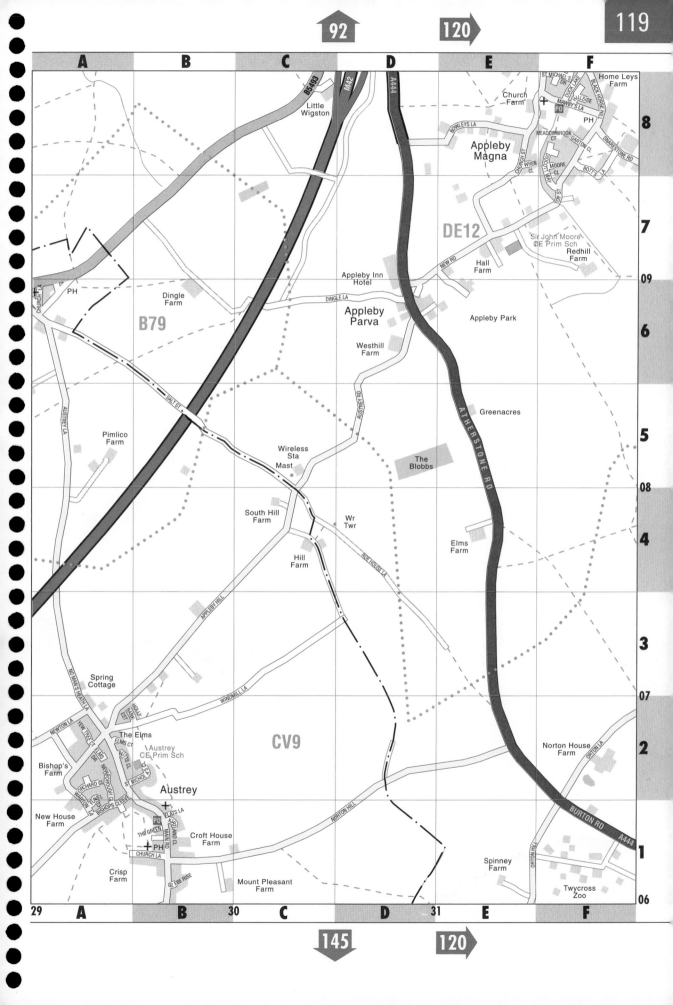

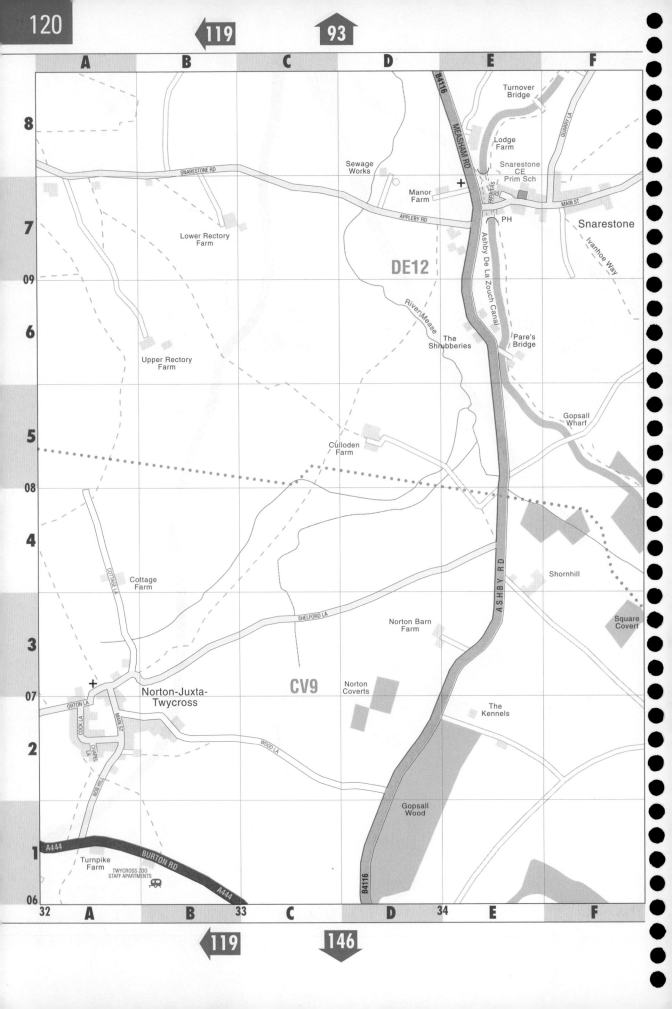

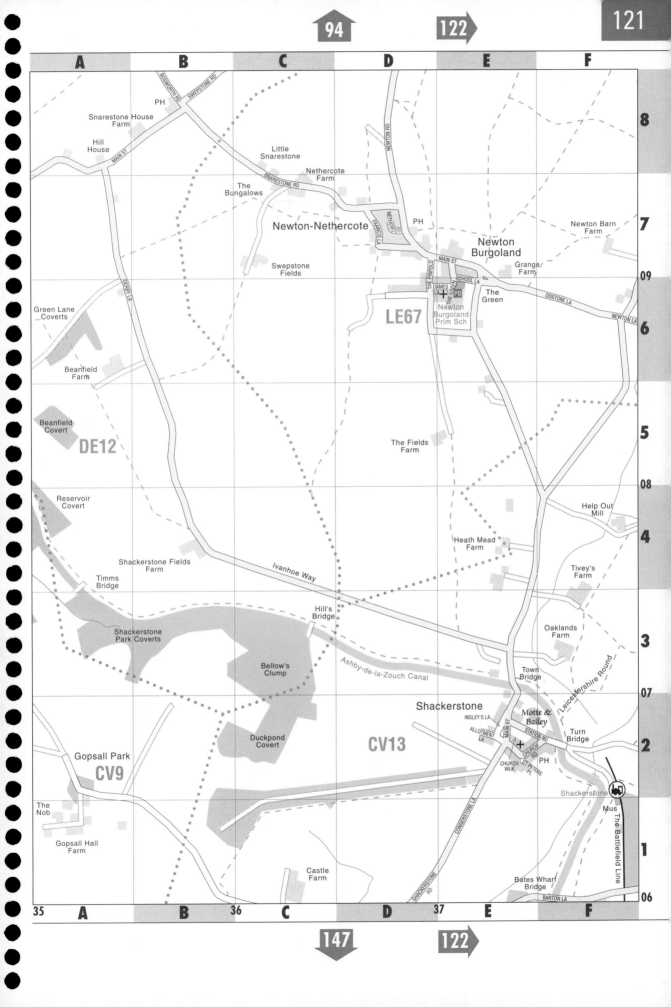

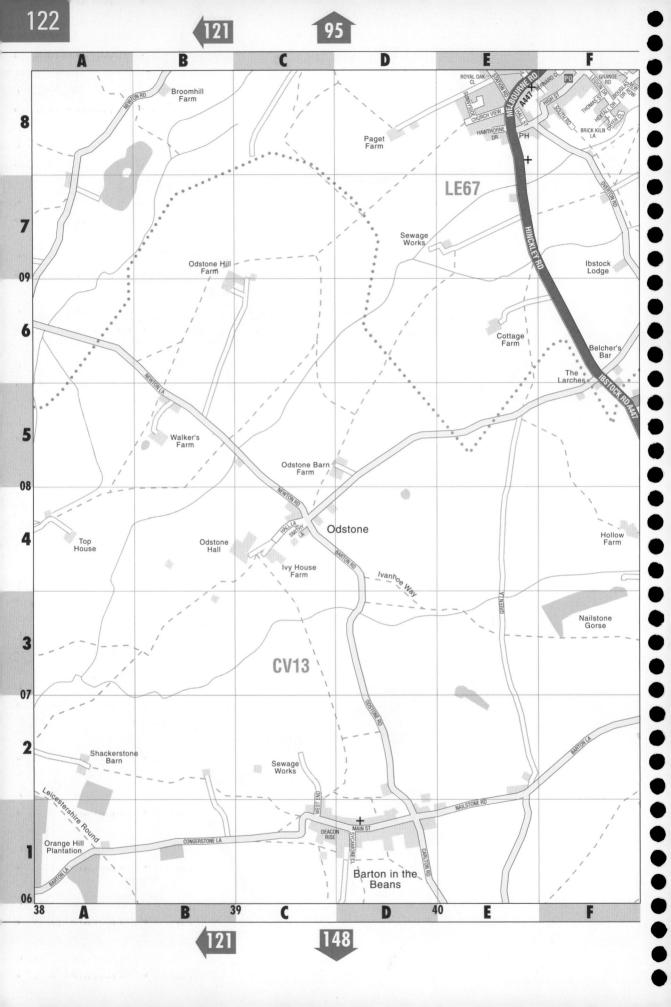

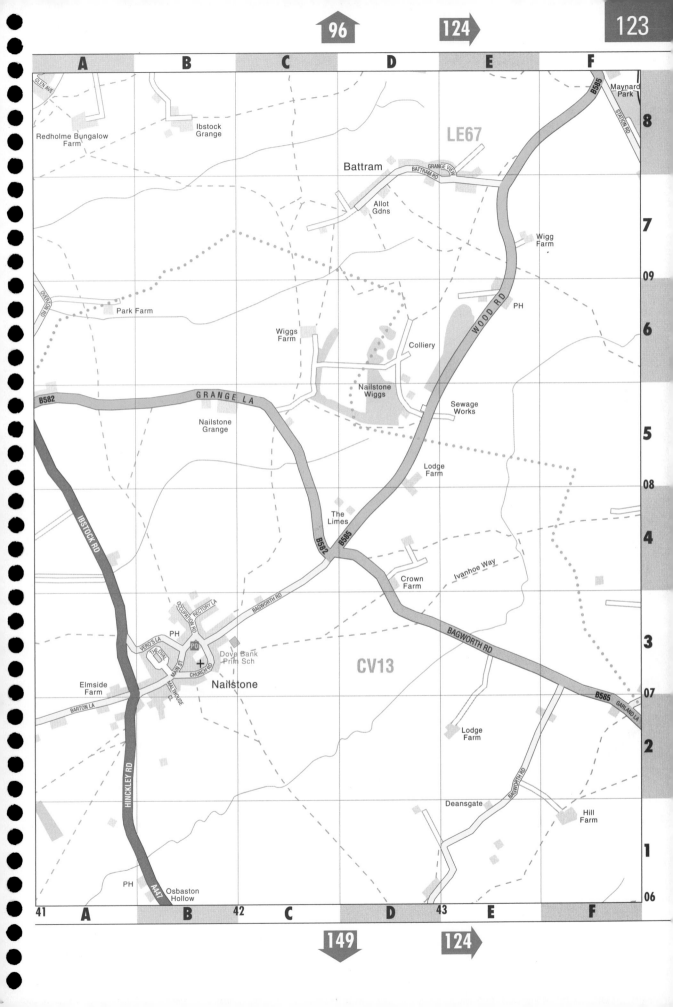

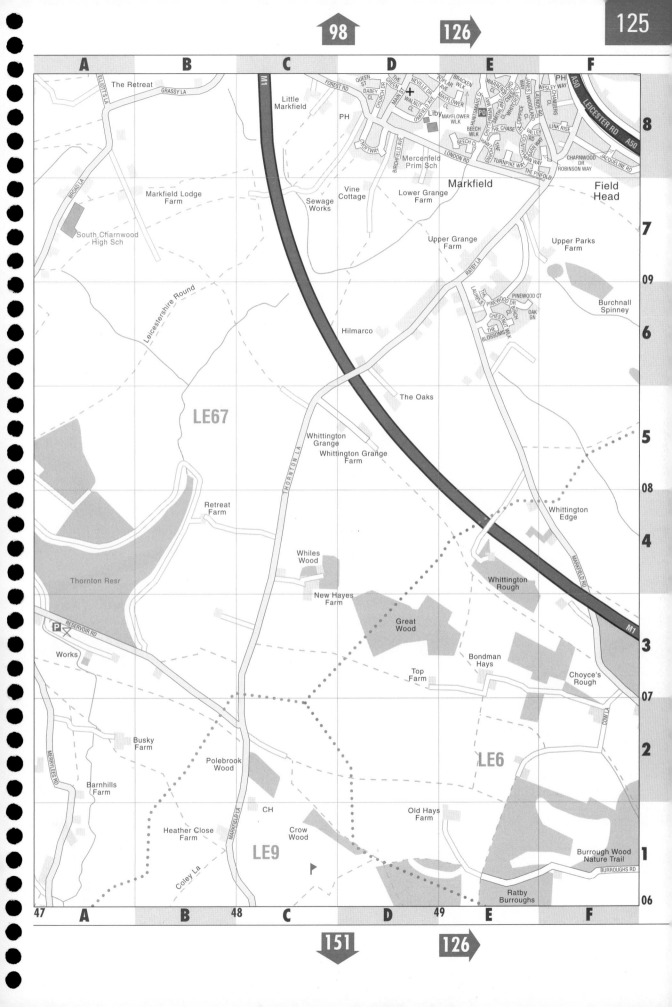

A B C D E F

The Retreat
ELLIOTT'S LA
GRASSY LA
Little Markfield
Forest Rd
Queen St
Dabey Cl
The Green
Main St
Neville Dr
Poplar Ave
Bracken Wlk
Warren Cl
James's Cl
Clifford
Chittenden Cl
Smith Cres
Coppice Cl
Whit Cross
Chambers Cl
Wesley Way
Way
PH
A50
Mayflower Cl
Mayflower Wlk
Link Rise
Laund Rd
LEICESTER RD
PH
Liby
PO
PH
Beech Wlk
Beech Cl
The Chase
Val Ley Rd
Van Way
Jacqueline Rd
Charnwood Dr
Robinson Way
8

Markfield Lodge Farm
South Charnwood High Sch
BROAD LA
Sewage Works
Vine Cottage
Birchfield Ave
London Rd
Mercenfeld Prim Sch
Croft Wa
Huntsmans Cl
Woodland
Main Thorns
Turnpike Wk
The Pinfold
Markfield
Lower Grange Farm
Field Head
7

Leicestershire Round
Upper Grange Farm
Raby La
Upper Parks Farm
09

The Laurels
The Pinewood Dr
Birch
Pinewood Ct
Chestnut Wlk
Oak Gn
Burchnall Spinney
6

LE67
Hilmarco
The Blossoms
The Oaks

Whittington Grange
Whittington Grange Farm
THORNTON LA
5

Retreat Farm
Whittington Edge
08

Whittington Rough
MARKFIELD RD
4

Thornton Resr
Whiles Wood
New Hayes Farm
Great Wood
Bondman Hays
M1
3

P
RESERVOIR RD
Works
Top Farm
Choyce's Rough
07

MERRYLEES RD
Busky Farm
Polebrook Wood
LE6
COW LA
2

Barnhills Farm
MARKFIELD LA
CH
Old Hays Farm
1

Heather Close Farm
LE9
Crow Wood
Burrough Wood Nature Trail
BURROUGHS RD

Coley La
Ratby Burroughs
06

47 A B 48 C D 49 E F

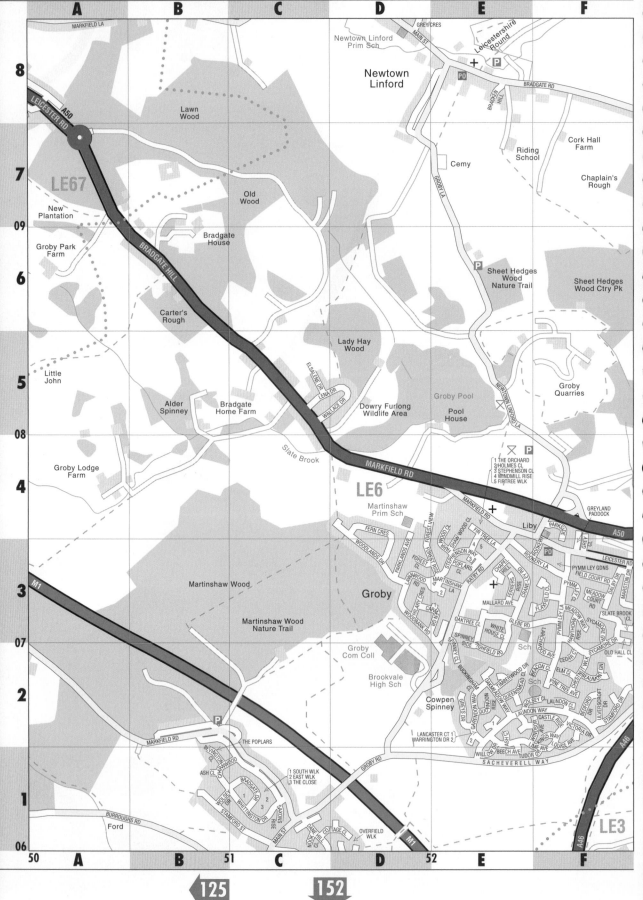

125
99

A   **B**   **C**   **D**   **E**   **F**

MARKFIELD LA

GREY CRES

Newtown Linford Prim Sch

MAIN ST

Leicestershire Round

8

+ P

PO

Newtown Linford

BRADGATE RD

LEICESTER RD A50

BRACKEN HILL

Lawn Wood

Cork Hall Farm

7

LE67

Cemy

Riding School

Chaplain's Rough

GROBY LA

Old Wood

New Plantation

09

Bradgate House

Groby Park Farm

BRADGATE HILL

P Sheet Hedges Wood Nature Trail

Sheet Hedges Wood Ctry Pk

6

Carter's Rough

5

Lady Hay Wood

Groby Quarries

Little John

ELSADENE DR

LENA DR

Alder Spinney

Bradgate Home Farm

WALLACE DR

Dowry Furlong Wildlife Area

Groby Pool

Pool House

NEWTOWN LINFORD LA

08

Slate Brook

MARKFIELD RD

1 THE ORCHARD
2 HOLMES CL
3 STEPHENSON CL
4 WINDMILL RISE
5 FIRTREE WLK

4

Groby Lodge Farm

LE6

Martinshaw Prim Sch

MARKFIELD RD

+

Liby

GREYLAND PADDOCK

PARKSIDE

A50

LEICESTER RD

FERN CRES

WOOD CL

FIR TREE LA

ROONEY

PO

PYMM LEY GDNS

FOREST VIEW

SHAM WOOD CL

FIELD COURT RD

MEADOW COURT RD

WOODLANDS DR

PARKLANDS AVE

FOREST RISE

STEPHENSON WAY

RATBY RD

CHAPEL HILL

FERRERS RISE

CRANE CL

PYMM LEY LA

LARCHWOOD

MARSTON DR

SLATE BROOK CL

SYCAMORE DR

M1

3

Martinshaw Wood

LANWOOD RD

HILARY CRES

WOODBANK DR

MARTINSHAW LA

MALLARD AVE

GLEBE RD

FLATFIELD CL

HAWTHORN CL

CEDAR CL

OLD HALL CL

Martinshaw Wood Nature Trail

Groby

07

Groby Com Coll

Sch

SPINNEY SIDE

HIGHFIELD RD

SPINNEY CL

WHITE HOUSE CL

OAKTREE CL

ELM CL

BEACON CL

PINE TREE AVE

CHESTNUT WLK

SYCAMORE DR

BEAUMONT

2

Brookvale High Sch

Cowpen Spinney

BUCKINGHAM

GREY'S DR

GARENDON WAY

QUEENSWAY

OAKMEADOW RISE

LAUNDE WAY

TIMBERWOOD DR

BEVFORD

WINDSOR CL

LAUNDON WAY

CASTLE RISE

KINGS WAY

VICTORIA DR

ULVERSCROFT DR

STAMFORD DR

A46

P

LANCASTER CT 1
WARRINGTON DR 2

MARKFIELD RD

The Poplars

GROBY RD

WILLOW

BEECH AVE

LIME AVE

LOUISE AVE

TUDOR CL

SACHEVERELL WAY

BEVINGTON CL

FENWOOD

ASH CL

1 SOUTH WLK
2 EAST WLK
3 THE CLOSE

1

WOLSEY DR

WHITTINGTON DR

BRADGATE DR

SAXONS RISE

MAIN ST

LANE

COTTAGE CL

OVERFIELD WLK

M1

LE3

A46

Ford

BURROUGHS RD

STAMFORD ST

06

50   **A**   **B**   **51**   **C**   **D**   **52**   **E**   **F**

125
152

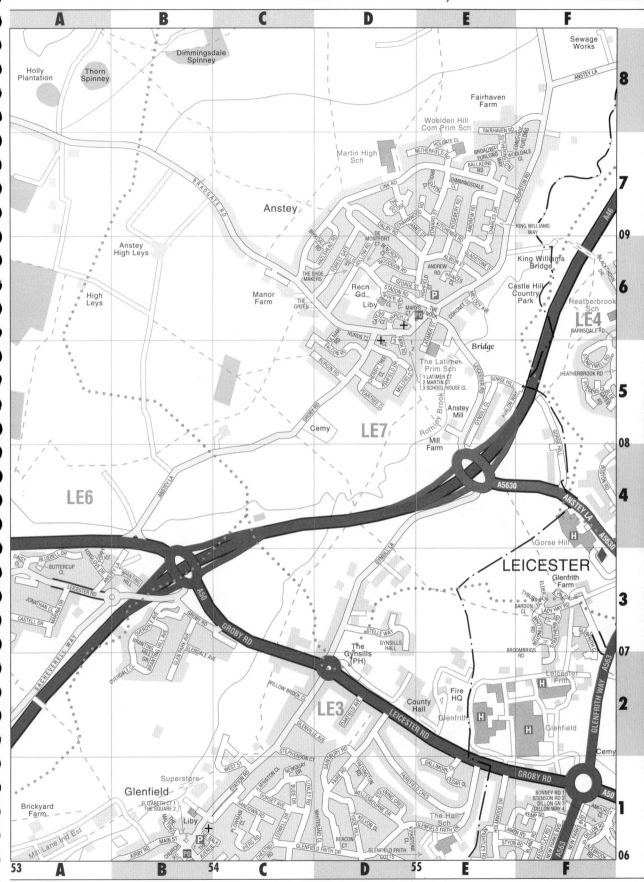

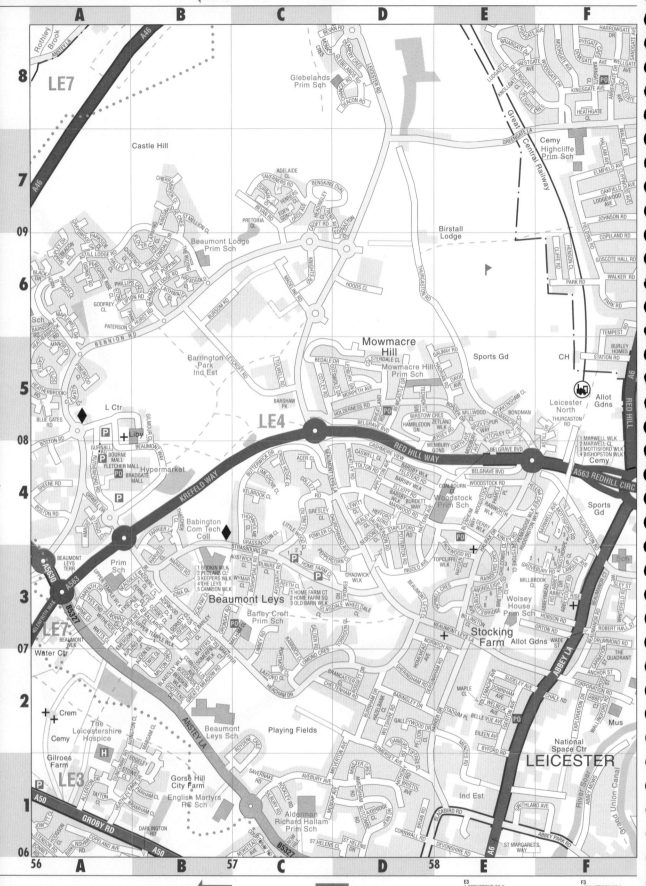

LE7

Castle Hill

Glebelands Prim Sch

Beaumont Lodge Prim Sch

Birstall Lodge

Cemy Highcliffe Prim Sch

Mowmacre Hill

Sports Gd

CH

Leicester North

Allot Gdns

1 MARWELL WLK
2 MARWELL CL
3 MOTTISFORD WLK
4 BISHOPSTON WLK
Cemy

Barrington Park Ind Est

LE4

RED HILL

Mowmacre Hill Prim Sch

L Ctr

Liby

Blue Gates

Hypermarket

Bourne Mall
Fletcher Mall
Bradgate Mall

KREFELD WAY

RED HILL WAY

Woodstock Prim Sch

A563 REDHILL CIRC

Sports Gd

Babington Com Tech Coll

1 BODKIN WLK
2 PEDLARS CL
3 KEEPERS WLK
4 THE LEYS
5 CAMEON WLK

1 HOME FARM CT
2 HOME FARM SQ
3 OLD BARN WLK

Beaumont Leys

Barley Croft Prim Sch

Wolsey House Prim Sch

Prim Sch

Stocking Farm

Allot Gdns

BEAUMONT LEYS TERR

LE7

Water Ctr

Beaumont Leys Sch

THE QUADRANT

Crem

The Leicestershire Hospice

Cemy

Playing Fields

Maple Cl

National Space Ctr

LEICESTER

Mus

Gilroes Farm

LE3

Gorse Hill City Farm

English Martyrs RC Sch

GROBY RD

A50

Alderman Richard Hallam Prim Sch

Ind Est

Grand Union Canal

River Soar

E3
1 GREYSTOKE WLK
2 PIPEWELL WLK
3 KIRKSTEAD WLK
4 CHILCOMBE WLK
5 BRETTON WLK
6 CANONSLEIGH WLK
7 SHELFORD WLK
8 ROBERTSBRIDGE WLK

F3
1 MILLBROOK WLK
2 WAINGROVES WLK
3 LANGLEY WLK
4 GROVEBURY WLK
5 MELCOMBE WLK
6 KIRKSCROFT WLK

A B C D E F

8
7
09
6
5
08
4
3
07
2
1
06

Birstall
Recn Gd

Watermead Country Park

Liby Riverside Com Prim Sch

River Soar

Bridge Bsns Pk

Superstore
Bishop Ellis RC Prim Sch
Eastfield Cty Prim Sch

Thurmaston

Church Hill Inf Sch

Auster Keightley Ind Est

Golf Range

LE4

Works

Sandfield Close Prim Sch

River Soar Grand Union Canal

Sports Gd

Watermead Bridge

WATERMEAD WAY

Ppg Sta

REDHILL CIRC

Outdoor Pursuits Ctr

New Bridge

LOUGHBOROUGH RD

MELTON RD

Herrick Prim Sch

TROON WAY

Sports Gd

Troon Way Bsns Ctr

Rushey Mead Sec Sch

Liby

Rushey Mead

Troon Ind Est

Works

Melton Brook

Rushey Fields Recn Gd

Soar Valley Coll

Old Bridge

Belgrave Hall (Mus)

CHECKETTS RD

MARFITT ST

Allot Gdns

Wyvern Prim Sch

Belgrave

John Ellis Com Coll

Rushey Mead Prim Sch

GIPSY LA

Catherine Street Ind Est

RC Sch

Abbey Prim Com Sch

Works

Belgrave Ind Ctr

Liby Recn Gd

Northfield House Prim Sch

Northfields

LE5

The Towers

59 60 61

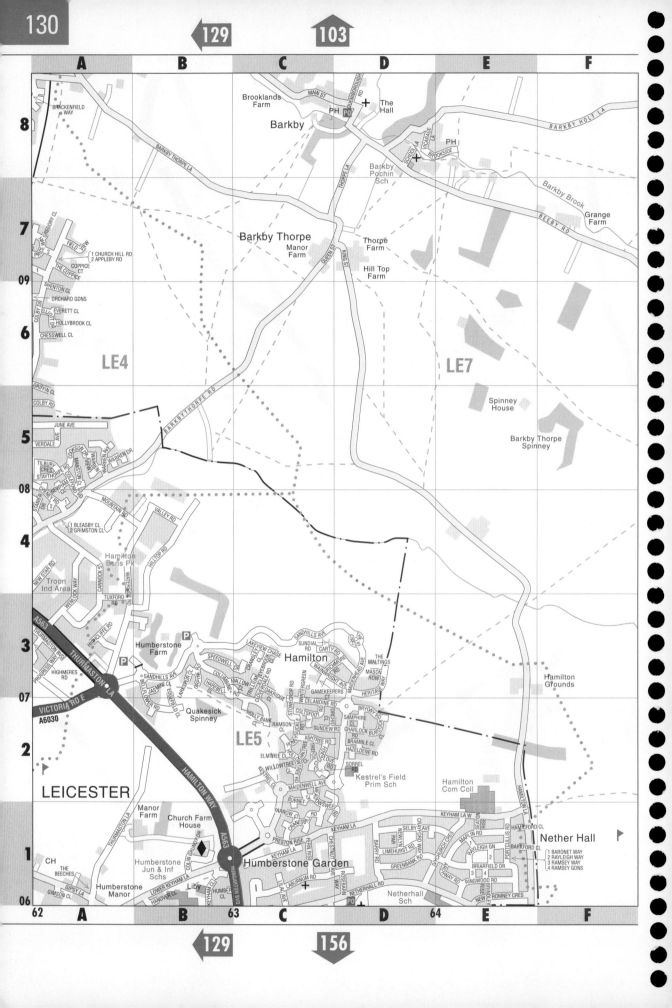

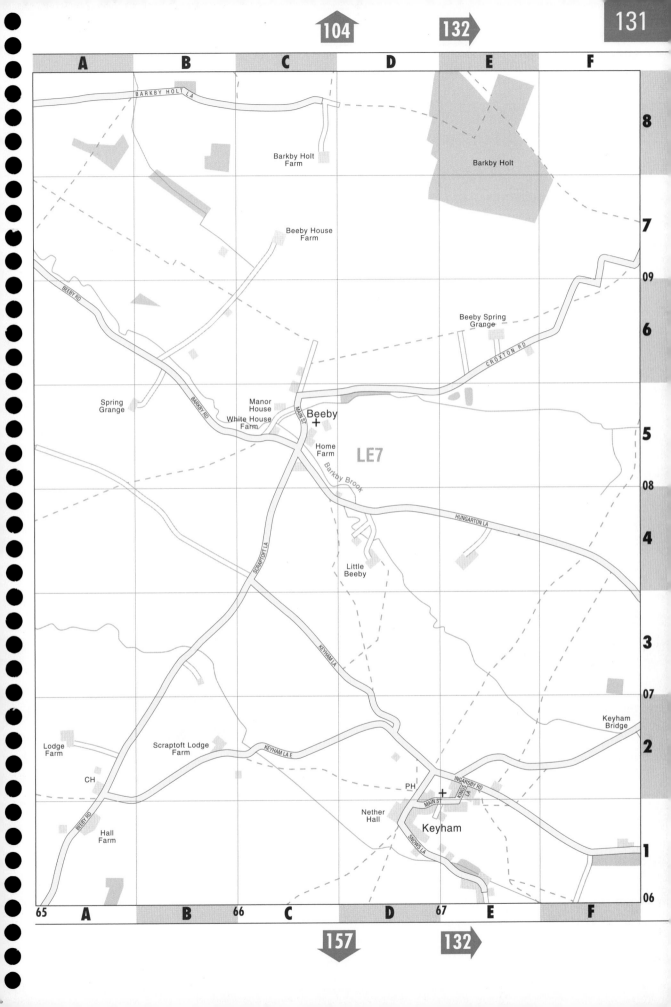

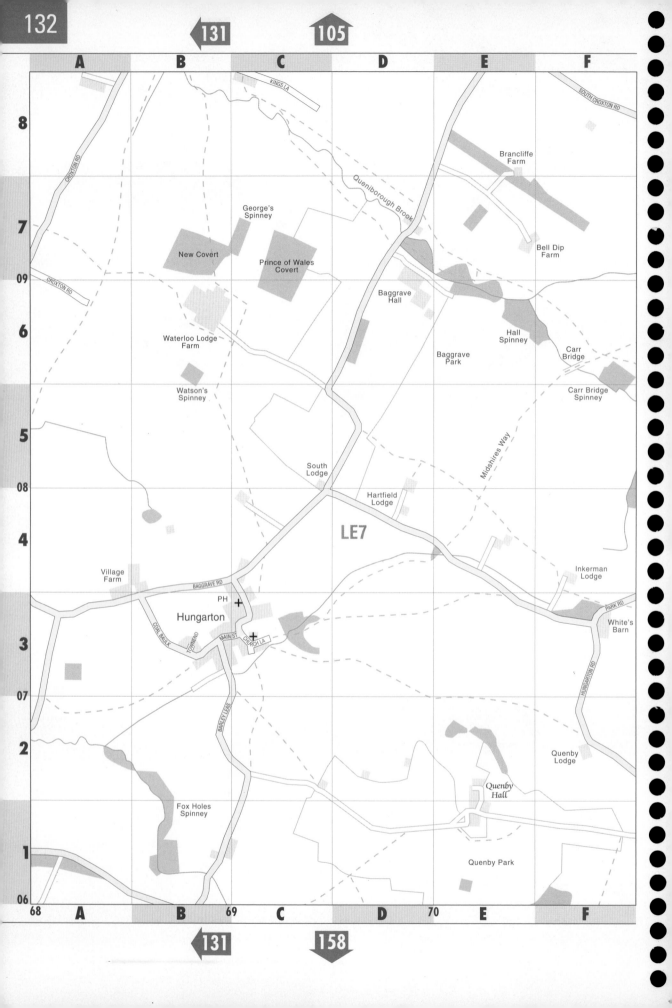

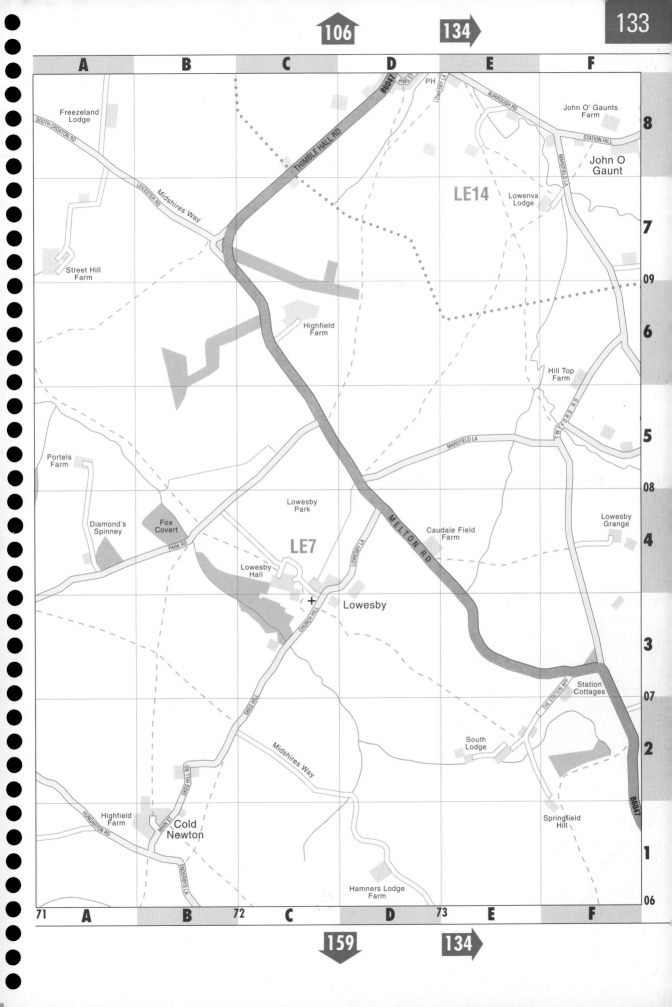

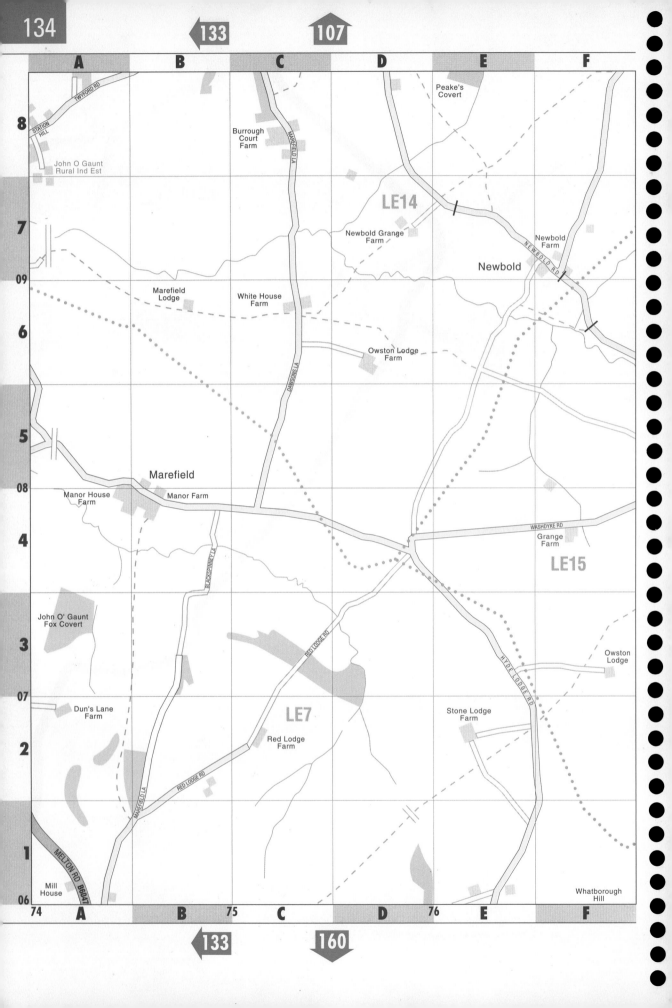

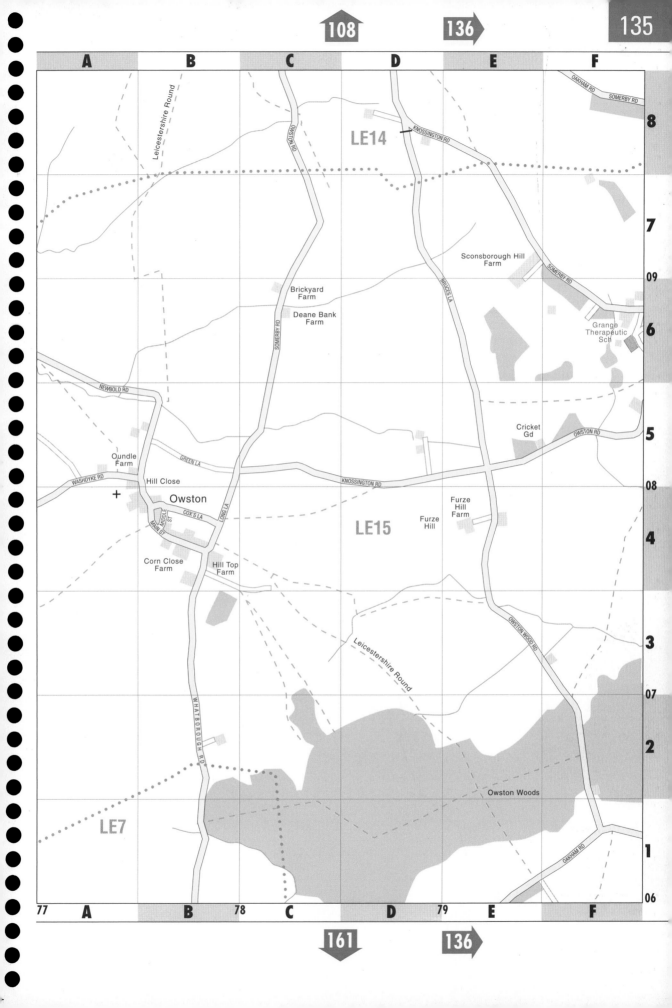

A B C D E F

8

1 RYEFIELD
2 SUMMEFIELD
3 MEADOWFIELD

Superstore

Playing Field

OAKHAM

Our Lady's Well

OAKHAM RD B668

Burley Wood

SCHOFIELD RD
SCHOFIELD CL
WITHERS CL
GRIFFITHS CL
OAKFIELD
LARCHFIELD
SUNNYFIELD
LANE FIELD
MAYFIELD
GREENFIELD
SPRINGFIELD WAY
PLUMER RD
WEN
WHY CL
PARTRIDGE WAY
RIDING CL
KESTREL CL
KINGFISHER
NIGHTINGALE
REDWING

LIVINGSTON CL
TABBERER RD
SUTHERN CL

GILMORE CL

7

Oakham Sch

Oakham CE Prim Sch

BURLEY RD

LADYWELL
LADYWELL
HORN CL
NORMAN CL
BURLEY PARK WAY
HARDWICK

Dog Kennel Spinney

A606

Hereward Way

B668
STATION RD

Oakham Castle

09

Sch Hall (remains of)
Ct P

English Martyr's RC Prim Sch

WOODLAND VIEW
WILLOW CRES
BEECH CL
ELM CL
SMEETON DR
ALSTHORPE RD
PICKWORTH CL
HAMBLETON CL
BROOKE CL
TOLETHORPE CL

Dog Kennel Cottage

Rutland Water (North) Nature Reserve

B668 HIGH ST
A606
Liby
BULL LA
i
Mus P

6

CHURCH ST
CHAPEL
MARKET ST
MARKET PL
THE LODGE
VICARAGE RD
PETERBOROUGH AVE
ST PETER'S
CLARESH
EDMONTON WAY
BANFF CL
CAMBRIDGE
CALGARY CRES
LETHBRIDGE CL
JASPER RD
FAIR VIEW

Sewage Works

CATMOS ST

A6003

Viking Way

STAMFORD RD

BAINES CT
BROOKE RD
BROWN RD
PENN ST
MILL ST
SOUTH ST
ROYCE'S HOMES
THE VALE
THE CL

CATMOSE PARK RD

Mus P

Rutland Farm Park

Swooning Bridge

5

CRICKET LAWNS
BOWLING GREEN CL

Catmose Lodge

LE15

08

Vale of Catmose

UPPINGHAM RD

4

The Grange Farm

Egleton

MEADOW WAY

07

Egleton

RD CL
CHURCH RD
MAIN ST

Barnetts Farm

P ✕

Bird Watching Ctr

Brown's Island

3

HAMBLETON RD

Brook Farm

HAMBLETON RD

Egleton Bay

2

Egleton Nature Reserve

A6003

Lax Hill

Lax Hill Covert

1

Durham Ox Farm

Gorse Close

06

86 A B 87 C 88 D E F

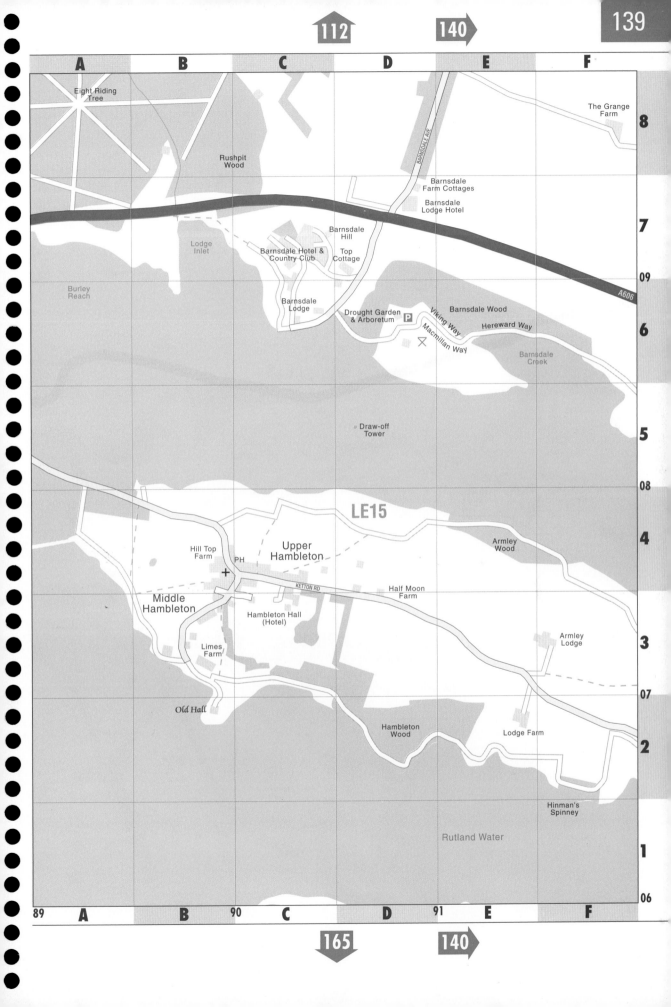

139
113

A   B   C   D   E   F

8

High Moor
Spinney

Hot Hollow
Farm

7

Viking Way

EXTON RD

Warren
Spinney

Lee
Spinney

09

Wind Pump
Farm

Highfields

HIGHFIELD CL

BARN END

A606

PH   Whitwell

High Moor
Farm

Park
House

Cemy

WELL CT HOME
CT
PH   CHURCH
MAIN ST   CT   ST
A606

6

Whitwell
Manor

LE15

NOOK LA

AUDIT HALL RD

Butterfly & Aquatic
Ctr

WHITWELL RD

SYKES LA

Cow Croft
Spinney

Hall Close

Nook
Farm

Nature
Trail

BULL BRIG LA

Water Sports
Area

Whitwell Creek

Hereward Way

Macmillan Way

5

Rescue
Centre

Sykes
Spinney

P

P

Whitwell
Lodge

08

Rutland Belle
Cruise

Bunker's
Hill

4

Limnological
Tower

Normanton
Cottages

3

Rutland Water

Mowmires
Reach

07

Barnhill Creek

Macmillan Way

NORMANTON PARK RD

EMPINGHAM RD

The Belt

Half Moon
Spinney

2

Black
Spinney

Bullock
Spinney

Normanton
Gardens

Normanton
Park

1

Normanton Church
Mus

Hotel

Normanton
Farm

Whare
Koa

Normanton

Howells
Inlet

Normanton Lodge
Farm

06

92   A   B   93   C   D   94   E   F

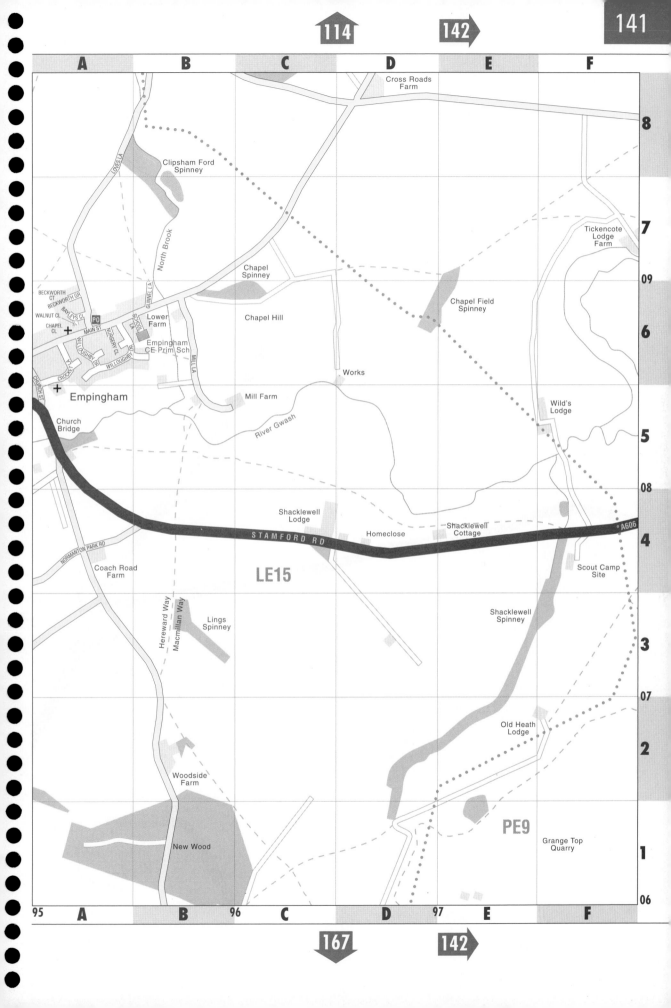

114
142
167
142

Cross Roads Farm

Clipsham Ford Spinney

North Brook

Tickencote Lodge Farm

Chapel Spinney

BECKWORTH CT
BECKWORTH GR
WALNUT CL
CHAPEL CL

Chapel Hill

Chapel Field Spinney

LOVES LA
GUNNEL LA

PO
MAIN ST
BAYLEYS CL
SCHOOL LA
NURSERY CL
WILLOUGHBY DR
CROCKET LA
WILLOUGHBY
A

Lower Farm

Empingham CE Prim Sch

MILL LA

Works

Wild's Lodge

Empingham

Mill Farm

River Gwash

Church Bridge

Shacklewell Lodge

Homeclose

Shacklewell Cottage

A606

Scout Camp Site

NORMANTON PARK RD

STAMFORD RD

LE15

Coach Road Farm

Shacklewell Spinney

HEREWARD WAY
MACMILLAN WAY

Lings Spinney

Old Heath Lodge

Woodside Farm

PE9

New Wood

Grange Top Quarry

95   A   B   96   C   D   97   E   F

141
115

A　B　C　D　E　F

8

Tickencote Park

Tickencote

Mill Pond

Tickencote Hall

A1

B1081

B1081

Glebe Barn

7

WEST VIEW

WINDYRIDGE

ERMINE RISE

PH

HIGH CRES

COLLEGE CL

RYHALL RD

PICKWORTH RD

Casterton Com Coll

Sewage Works

09

Great Casterton CE Prim Sch

Great Casterton

6

Ingthorpe Farm

Ingthorpe

PH

Church Farm

OLD GREAT NORTH RD

Toll Bar

1 LAVENDER WAY
2 BUTTERCUP CL

5

PE9

MEADOWSWEET

SWEETBRIAR

FOXGLOVE RD

HONEYSUCKLE

BLUEBELL RD

PRIMROSE WAY

CAMPION GR

TORAS GR

FOREST GDNS

WILLOW RD

BIRCH RD

B1081

PH Quarry Farm

08

Glebe House

CLOVER GDNS 1
CORNFLOWER CL 2
MARIGOLD CL 3
SORREL CL 4
BRAMBLE GR 5

OAK RD

PINE CL

CEDAR RD

CHARLOCK DR

HAZEL GR

BEECH GR

ASH RD

MORAY CL

ABERDEEN CL

ARRAN RD

FIFE CL

4

A606

STAMFORD RD

EMPINGHAM RD

A606

Sidney House

CHESTNUT GDNS

GARDEN CL

GREAT NORTH RD

3

Mast

Tinwell Lodge Farm Cottages

The Rookery

CASTERTON LA

07

A1

2

Tinwell Lodge Farm

STANFOLD LA

Tinwell House

Tinwell

A6121

TINWELL RD

PH

WELLAND VIEW

MILL LA

Mill Farmhouse

1

Tinwell Grange

The Manor

A6121

River Welland

06

98　A　B　99　C　D　00　E　F

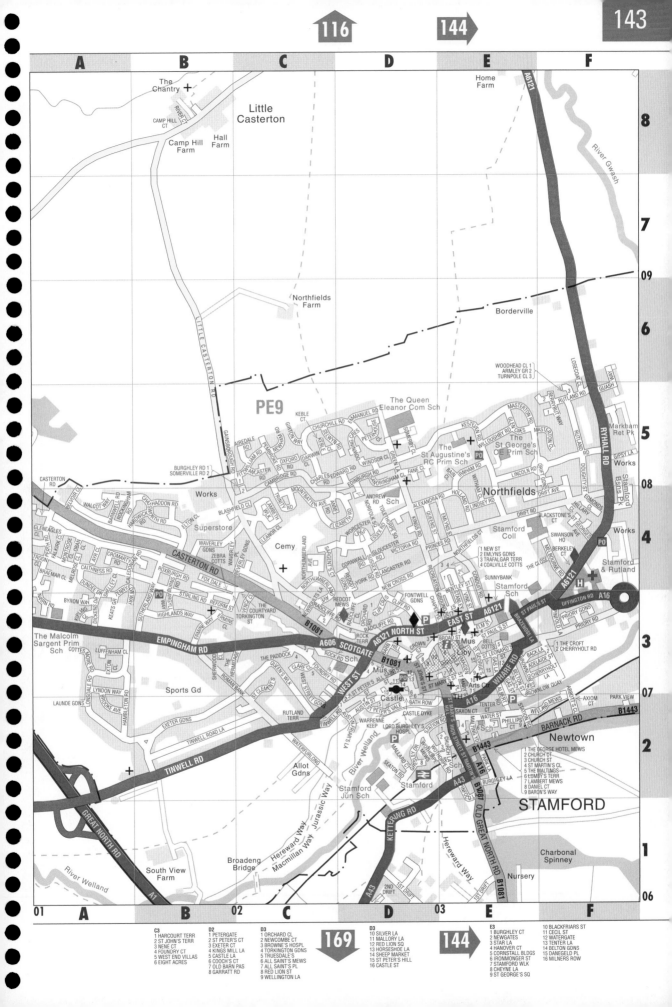

A · B · C · D · E · F

8

Wood Farm
Cottages

Uffington
New Wood

Wood
Farm

Grange
Farm

NEWSTEAD RD

Belmesthorpe
Grange

Macmillan Way

7

Cobbs Nook
Farm

Long
Acres

09

Long Spinney

Morley
Wood

6

Carr's
Lodge

Folly
Farm

The Folly

Grindlepits
Spinney

Lower Home
Farm

5

Works

Mast

08

Newstead
Farm

PE9

Newstead

River Gwash

NEWSTEAD
MILL

Uffington
CE Prim
Sch

SOKES CL

CASEWICK LA

MANNERS CL

4

Works

Allot
Gdns

UFFINGTON RD

West Hall
Farm

Home
Farm

THE CHARTERS

GREATFORD RD

SCHOOL LA

PO

LINDSEY RD

Uffington

A16

MEADOW VIEW

Allot
Gdns

PH

PH

Uffington
House

BERTIE LA

Manor
Farm

Lincolnshire STREET ATLAS

Mill

Uffington
Park

Lodges

MAIN RD

A16
A16 Spalding

3

River Welland

Copthill
Prep Sch

07

B1443

Spring
Wood

2

Pilsgate
Lodges

Sewage
Works

The Dingle
Gardens

Pilgate
Grange

1

Deer Park

Burghley
House

B1443

Jubilee
Plantation

06

04 · A · B · 05 · C · D · 06 · E · F

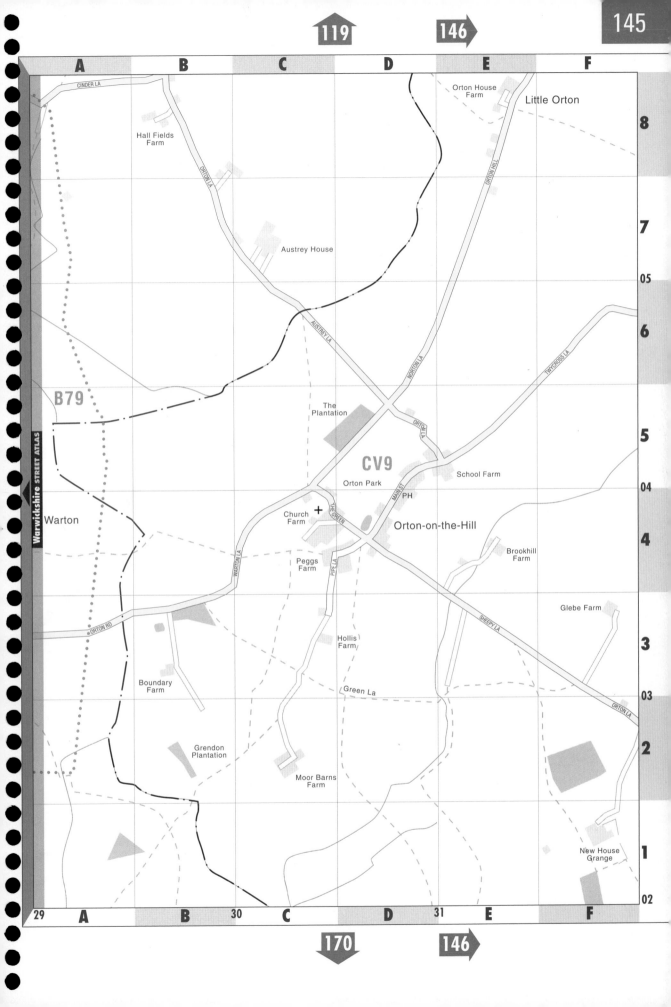

119
146

A B C D E F

8

7

05

6

Orton House Farm

Little Orton

Hall Fields Farm

CINDER LA

ORTON LA

Austrey House

AUSTREY LA

ORTON HILL

TWYCROSS LA

NORTON LA

B79

The Plantation

ORTO LA

CV9

Orton Park

School Farm

5

04

Warton

Church Farm

THE GREEN

MARKT

PH

Orton-on-the-Hill

4

Peggs Farm

WARTON LA

PIPE LA

Brookhill Farm

Glebe Farm

SHEEPY LA

ORTON RD

Hollis Farm

3

03

ORTON LA

Boundary Farm

Green La

2

Grendon Plantation

Moor Barns Farm

New House Grange

1

02

Warwickshire STREET ATLAS

29 A B 30 C D 31 E F

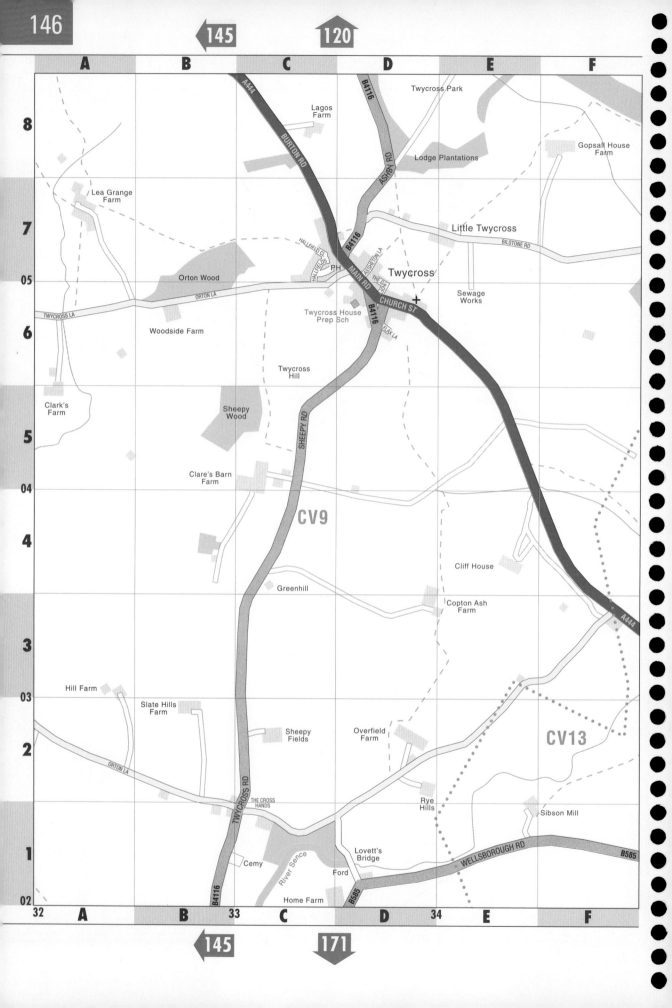

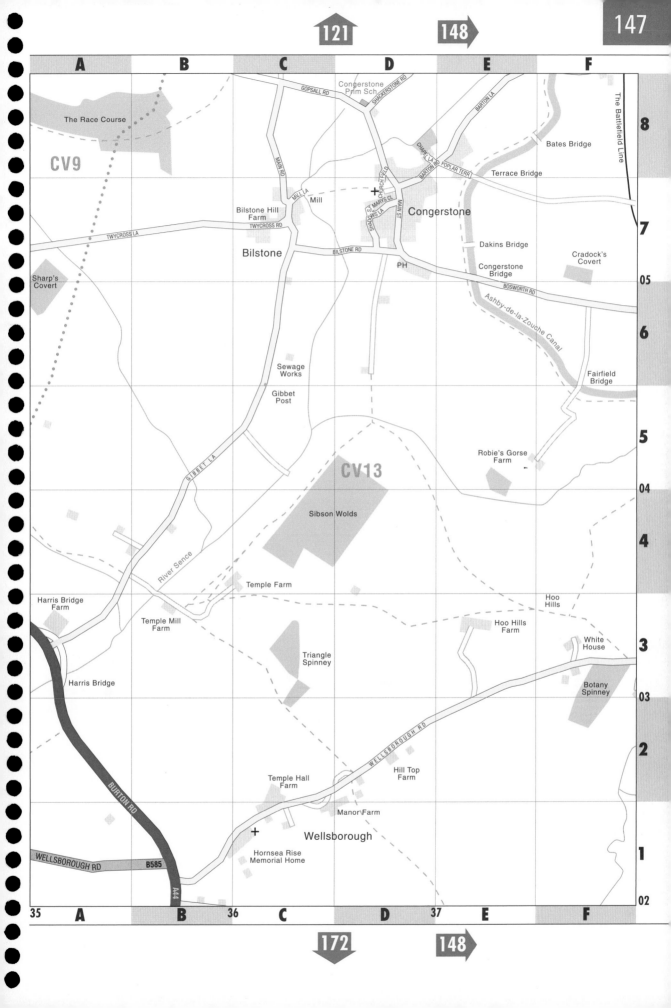

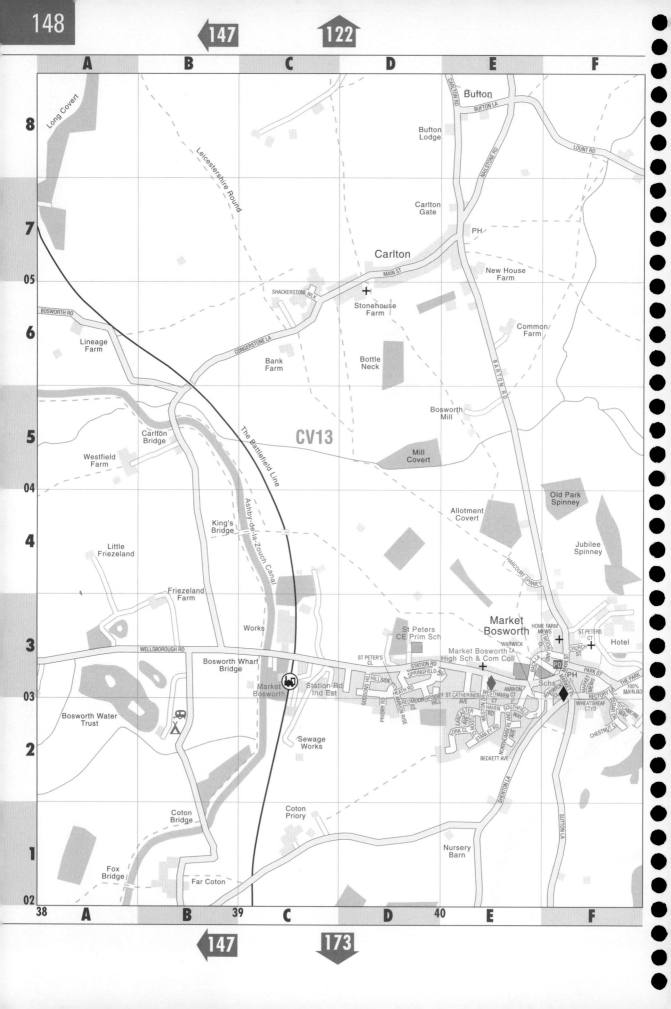

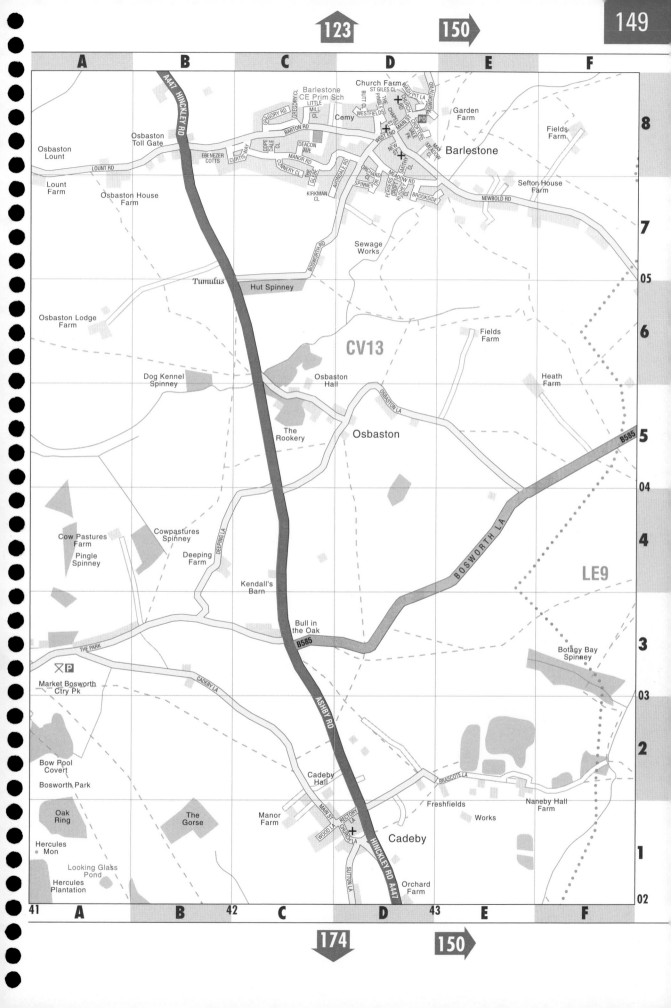

A B C D E F

8

CV13

LE67

Heath Lodge Farm

Merry Lees Ind Est

LE67

Great Fox Covert

HEATH RD

MERRYLEES RD

CV13

7

Newbold Heath

Chater Farm

Halifax Farm

Lindridge Farm

Pool House Farm

05

Spinney Farm

Hook House

Lindridge Hall Farm

Lindridge

6

BARLESTONE RD

BAGWORTH RD

B585

The Fields Farm

Lindridge Wood

B585 BOSWORTH LA

B582

5

St Georges Cl

LE9

Newbold Verdon

MONTAGUE CL

Newbold Verdon Prim Sch

GILLIVER ST

STATHAM ST

DRAGON LA

CADLE ST

HILL ST

PRESTON DR

MILL LA

04

ENSTON ST

HORNBEAM RD

GRANGE CL

SPARKENHOE

Holly Hedges

CHURCH VIEW

BELLS LA

Liby

THE BUNGALOWS

PINE TREE CL

PEDION

Hunt's Lane Farm

4

Main St

PASTURE LA

OAKS DR

PH

THE PADDOCK

SYCAMORE CL

JUBILEE RD

CHADWICK CL

BRAMBLE DR

PETERS AVE

DESFORD RD

HUNTS LA

PO

LORD CREWE

ALANS WAY

Newbold Spinney

LARKFIELD RD

GILBERT'S DR

MALLORY CL

RUSH

WILLOW CL

BARBARA AVE

Tumblin Fields

Allot Gdns

AVE

ARNOLD'S CRES

Cottage Farm

B582

3

Sewage Works

KIRBY LA

BRASCOTE LA

PH

Allot Gdns

Lockey Farm

03

Shericles Farm

2

Manor Farm

Kirby Old Parks

Brascote

Bullacre Spinney

NEWBOLD RD

1

Brascote Covert

Beech Spinney

Stocks House

Brascote House

02

44 A B 45 C D 46 E F

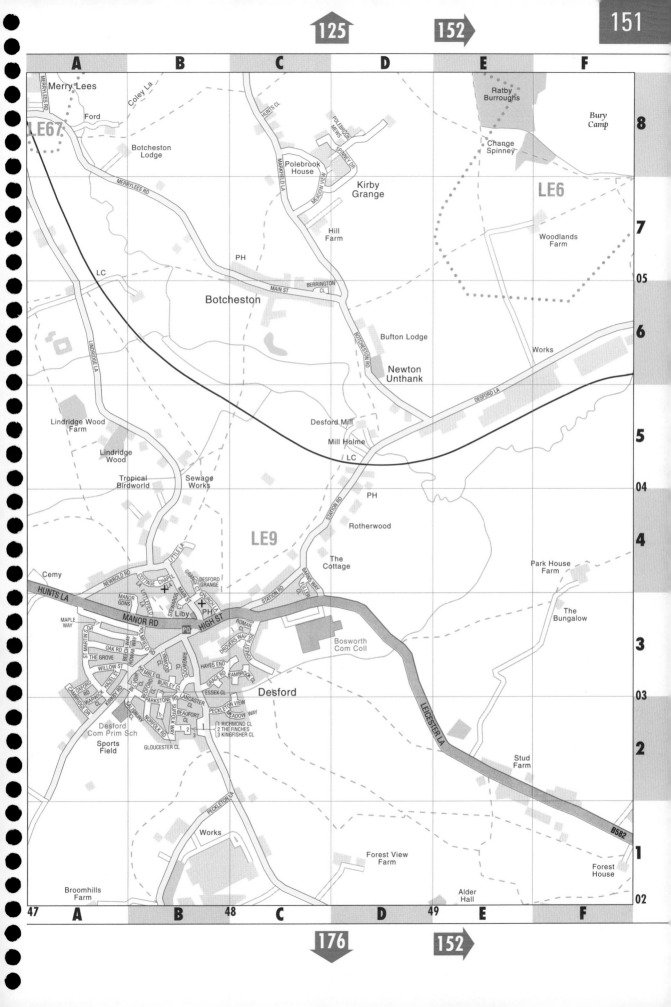

151
126

A B C D E F

8
7
05
6
04
5
4
3
03
2
1
02

50 A B 51 C D 52 E F

BURROUGHS RD
Ratby Prim Sch
Liby
MAIN ST
CHAPEL LA
CHURCH LA
BERRY'S LA
DANE HILL
INGLE DR
WESLEY CL
BANK DR
PO
Ratby
LE6
Hollywell Farm
THE PINFOLD
BROOK DR
DESFORD LA
Works
Works
Poultry Farm
New Bridge
Newbridge Farm
DESFORD LA
Thorneyfields Farm
Rothley Brook
BELL
LEE RISE
GRANGE CL
NICHOLAS DR
HEATHBROOK DR
STATION RD
MILL DR
PARK RD
QUIFLIN LA
BARTON RD
TAVERNER DR
1 JOURNEYMAN'S GN
2 CALVERTON CL
3 CARDINAL CL
FERNDALE DR
COOPER LA
MEADOW CL
ASTILL DR
PRESTON RD
GEARY CL
Kirby Grange
4 SPRING CL
5 PARKFIELD CL
6 WINDMILL CL
7 CENTURION CT
8 FREEMAN'S CT
9 ROBINS FIELD
10 JORDAN CT
11 MARTIN SQ
M1
A46
Mill Lane Ind Est
LE3
B5380
RATBY LA
RATBY LA
RATBY LA
21a
Blood's Hill
VICARAGE CL
GLENFIELD LA
BARLEY WAY
PRIMROSE WAY
BLUEBELL CL
WOODLANDS LA
Cemy
DESFORD RD
MAIN ST
Liby
PO
THE KEEP
THE CROFT
CASTLE RD
CHURCH RD
BARWELL CL
CAREY GDNS
ARNSON AVE
GARFIT RD
OAKCROFT AVE
COURT CL
Kirby Muxloe Castle
Kirby Muxloe
LE3
Kirby Muxloe Prim Sch
Liby
Kirby Fields
LE9
THE HUNTINGS
BARONS LA
BARNS CL
HEDGEROW LA
LADYSMITH RD
PRETORIA RD
FOX LA
Barons Park Farm
The Homestead
GULLET LA
LINKS RD
WILSHERE CL
LIME GR
PRINCESS DR
WENTWORTH GR
STATION RD
STATION DR
STATION CT
TOWERS DR
TOWERS CL
HEWITT DR
LINDEN LA
PORTLAND RD
HASTINGS RD
ROUNDHILL
HOLLYWOOD RD
FOREST DR
THE FAIRWAY
HOLT DR
ROSENDENE CL
STAMFORD RD
WALTON CL
KIRBY LA
SOUTHVIEW CT
FOREST RISE
A47
CH
LC
The Links
Elms Farm
Oaks Farm
Stratho Coppice
The Hollows Farm
Forest Hill Farm
B582
LEICESTER LA
PH
A47
White House
HINCKLEY RD
Forest Farm
SHEPHERD CL
BARRY CT
CHERRY TREE CT
MAYTREE CT
MAYTREE AVE
BARRY DR
CHERRY TREE AVE
BARBARA AVE
MARTIN AVE
ELLIS DR
HAMBLETON CL
HIGHLAND AVE
HARENC CRES
PINE TREE GR
HAWTHORN CL
VALJEAN CRES
STAFFORD RD
ST DAVIDS CT
HENRY CL
SEYMOUR WAY
SCHUNTERS
SOMERVILLE RD
SCH
HEATHLEY
BRACKEN CL
BIRCHWOOD
BRICKMAN CL
BLUE POTS
MAGNA CL
POTTERS
JUNIPER CL
ALDER
OAKWOOD
PLEASANT CL
WARREN CL
RAVEN
KESTREL CL
KINGCUP CL
ROSE CRES
ACACIA CL
TEAL CL
MALLARD WAY
WOODPECKER CL
LARK CL
CARNATION CL
PETUNIA CL
HARVESTER
FOREST HOUSE LA
SWALLOWS CL
CORN CL
BEGGARS LA
YEW CL
PLOUGH CL
HARROW CL
Kingfisher CL
Leicester Forest East
LE3
Kingstand Farm
CH
LE19
LONG LA
FENNY LEYS
BOYERS WLK
BIRCH AVE
FENNY CL

PENNY LEYS

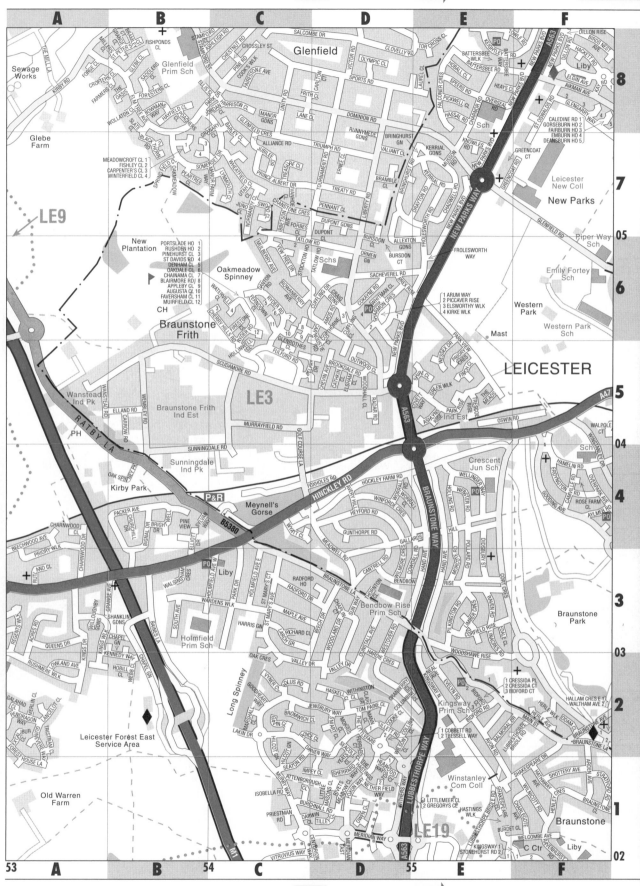

For full street detail of the highlighted area see page 259.

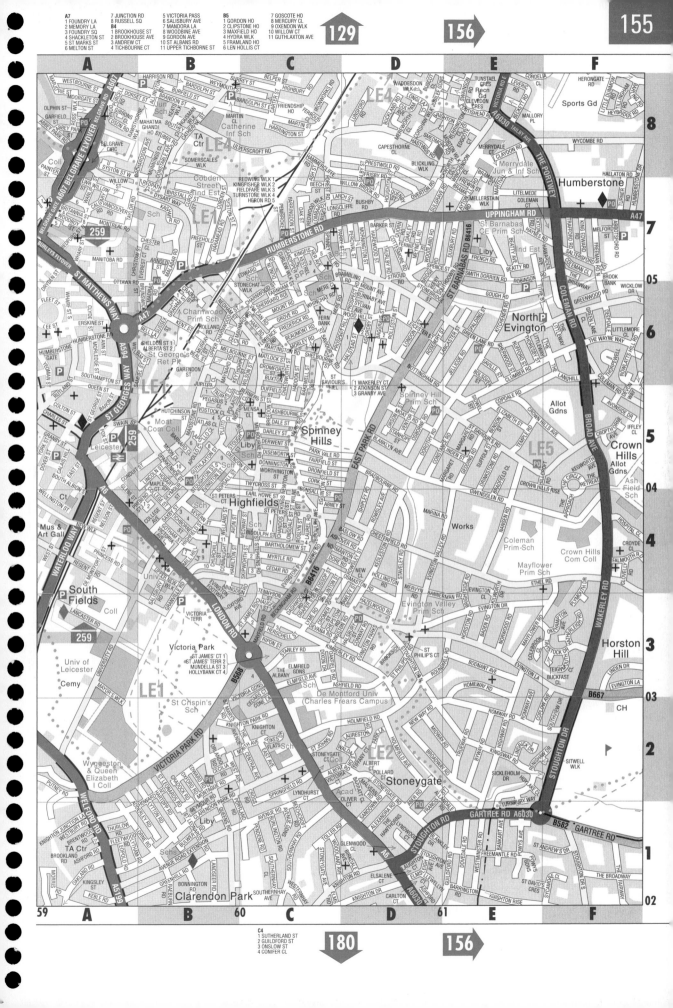

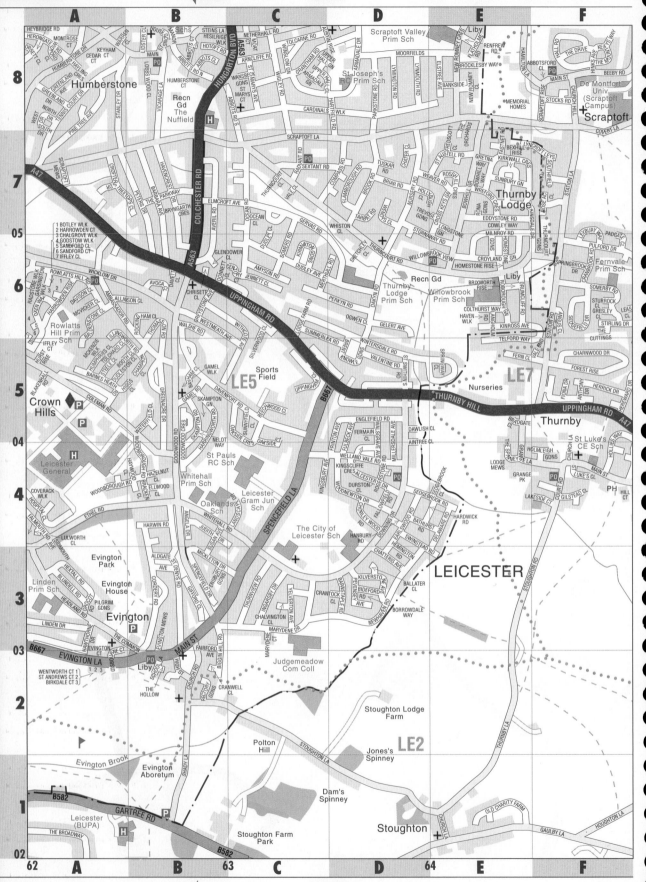

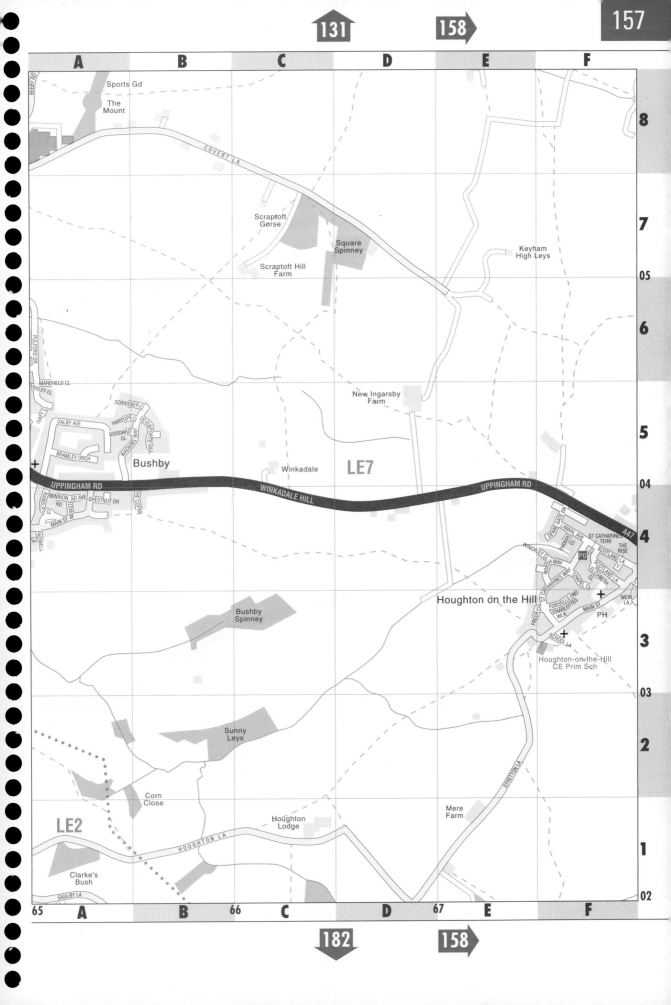

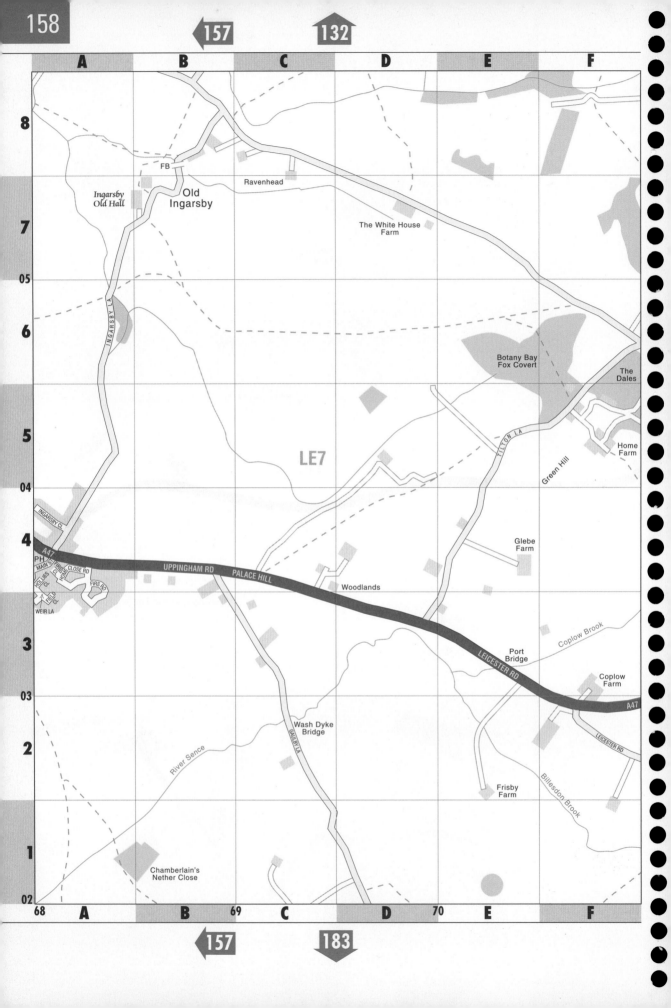

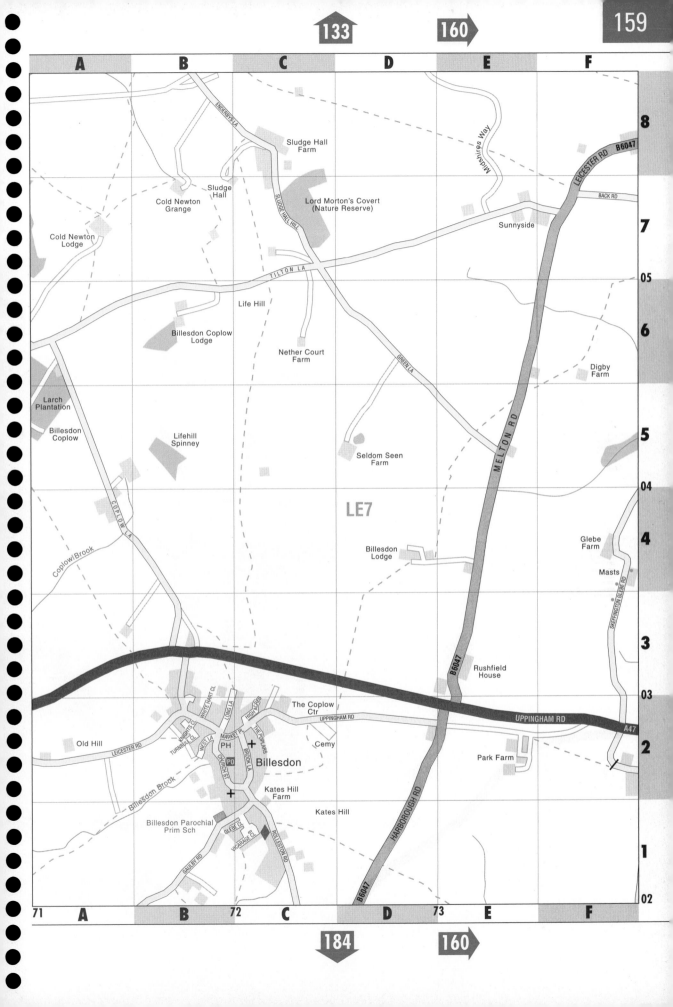

159
134

A   B   C   D   E   F

8

Halstead Ho

Halstead

Stanton Plantation

White Lodge Farm

Mast

British Pony Centre

Halstead Cottages

MELTON RD
B6047
DIGBY CL
MAREFIELD LA
HALSTEAD RISE
ST PETERS TERR
B6047 LEICESTER R
PO
PH
MANOR FARM WLK
MANOR FARM CT
MANOR FARM YD
MAIN ST
Rodhill Farm
THE OLD GRANARY

Tilton on the Hill

OAKHAM RD

PH

HYDE LODGE RD

LAUNDE RD

Tilton Cutting Nature Reserve

7

BACK RD

Sykes Spinney

Tennis Wood

Colborough Hill

05

SKEFFINGTON GLEBE RD

Works

6

LODDINGTON RD

TUGBY RD

Tilton Grange

MIDSHIRES WAY

5

LE7

Tilton Wood

04

Wood Farm

4

Skeffington Wood

3

SKEFFINGTON WOOD RD

Eye Brook

Tryon Spinney

03

New Plantation

Priest Hill

Skeffington

A47

Crow Wood

2

PH
HUNTERS RYE
PO

MAIN ST

UPPINGHAM RD

Welsh Myres Farm

Hoothill Slang

Old Cottage Farm

Skeffington Lodge Farm

Hoothill Wood

Tugby Wood Cottage

1

Brown's Wood

Tugby Wood

02

A47

Skeffington Gap Farm

WOOD LA

74   A   B   75   C   D   76   E   F

159
185

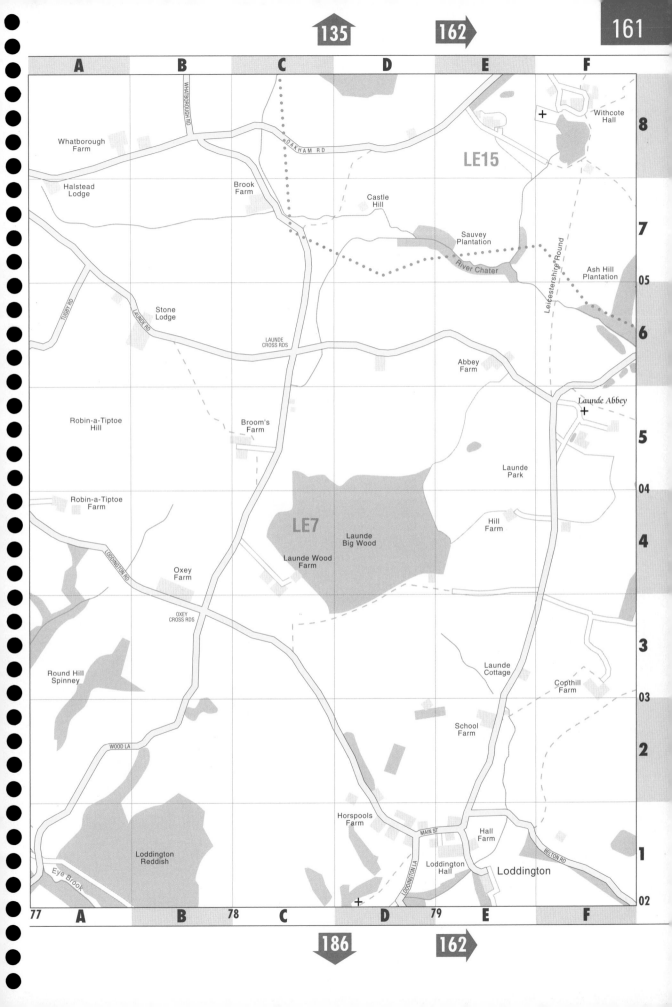

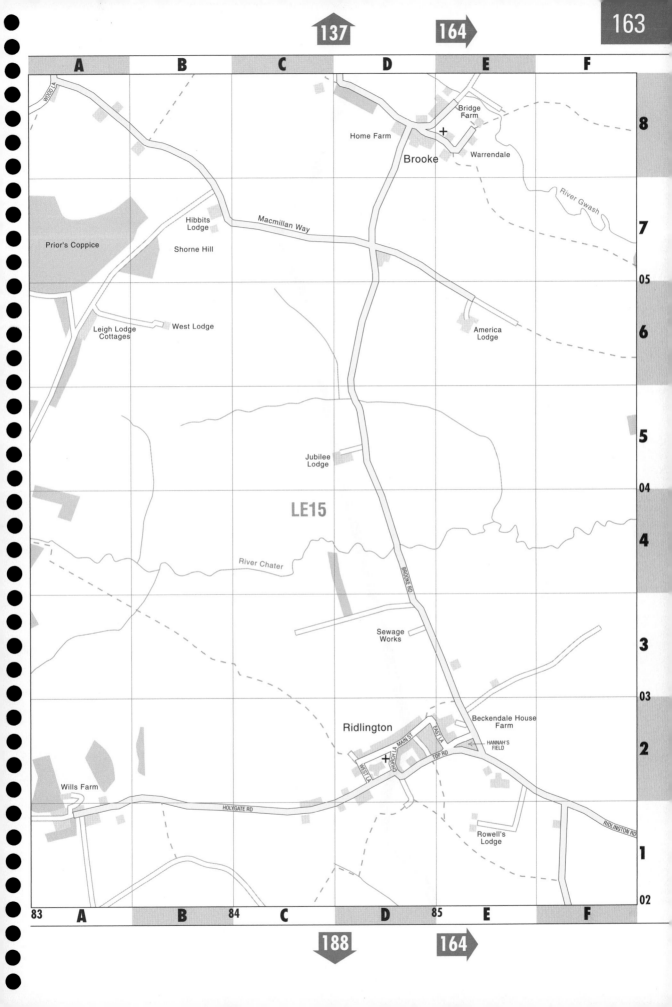

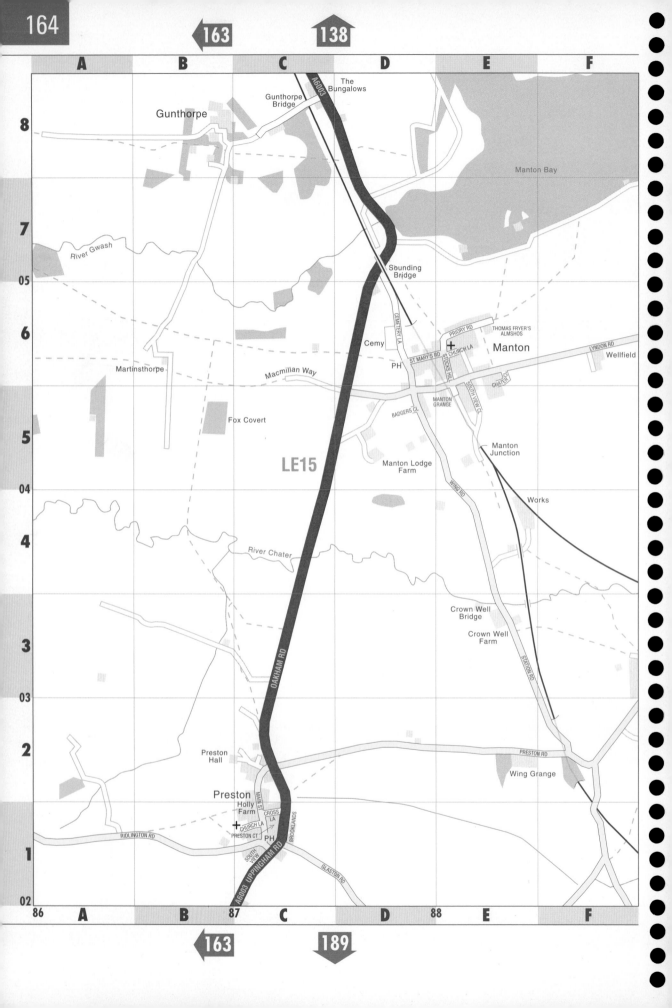

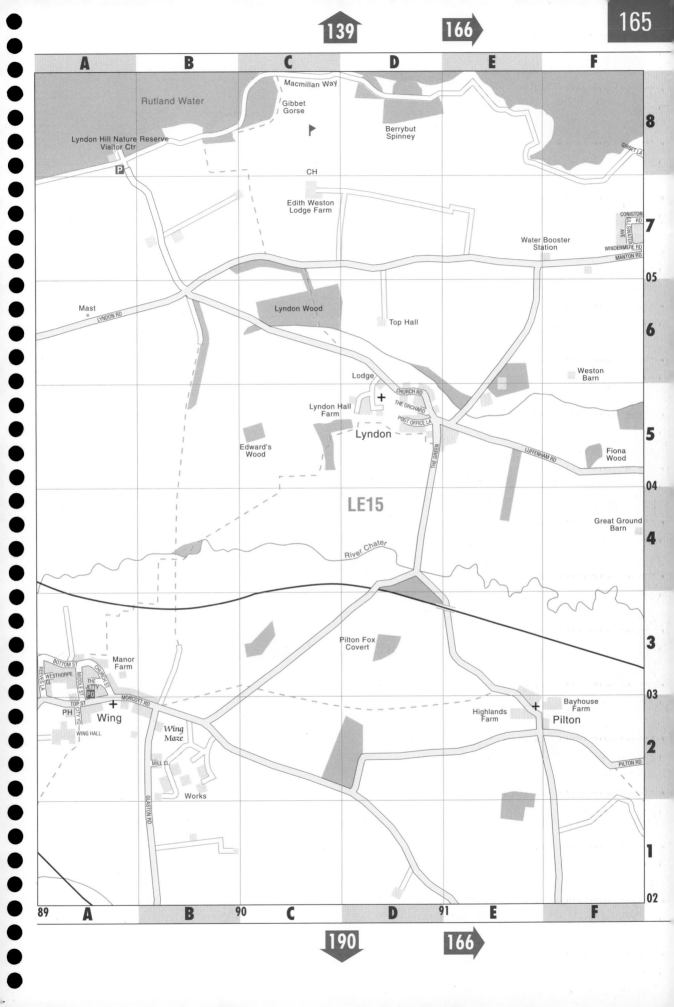

165 140

A B C D E F

8

Rutland Water

Normanton Park Rd

Bracknell House

Top Cottages

Candlesticks Spinney

Sailing Club

Macmillan Way

P

St Mary's Cl

Normanton Rd

Edith Weston

Oak Farm

Gibbet La

Makey's Cl

Weston St

Rectory La

Church La

King Edward Way

Well Cross

Chiltern Dr

Mendip Rd

Severn Cres

Welland Rd

7

Coniston Rd

Derwent Ave

Crummock Ave

Cemy

Edith Weston Prim Sch

PH

Tyler Cl

Pennine Dr

Windermere Rd

Manton Rd

05

Mast

Mast

6

North Luffenham Airfield

PE9

Notwells

5

Sewage Works

LE15

Luffenham Rd

04

Williams Wood

Mast

4

North Luffenham

Butt La

Lyndon Rd

Manor Farm

PH

The Jetties

Pinfold Cl

Pinfold La

Oval Cl

School La

Butt La

Edith Weston Way

Swann Cl

1 Johnson Cl
2 Newmans Cl

Ketton Rd

PO

Church St

Lancaster Ave

Kings Rd

Rose Cl

Sycamore Rd

Glebe Rd

St Mary & St John CE Prim Sch

PH

Chapel La

Dewey's Cl

Digby Rd

3

03

The Briarwood

King's Farm

Station Rd

River Chater

Moor La

Moor Lane Bridge

Works

2

Pilton Rd

North Luffenham Rd

Sewage Works

Mill Farm

Windmill

LC

Settings Farm

A6121

Stamford Rd

1

North Luffenham Rd

Gatehouse La

Cutting La

The Farm

Pinfold La

PO

A6121

02

South Luffenham

West Farm

Angle La

The Street

92 A B 93 C D 94 E F

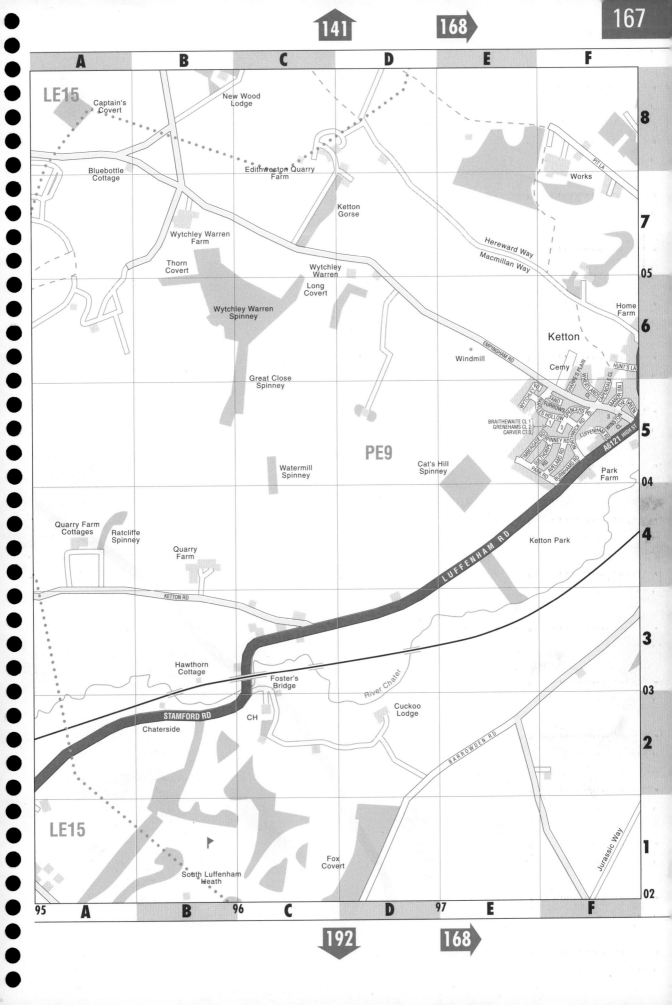

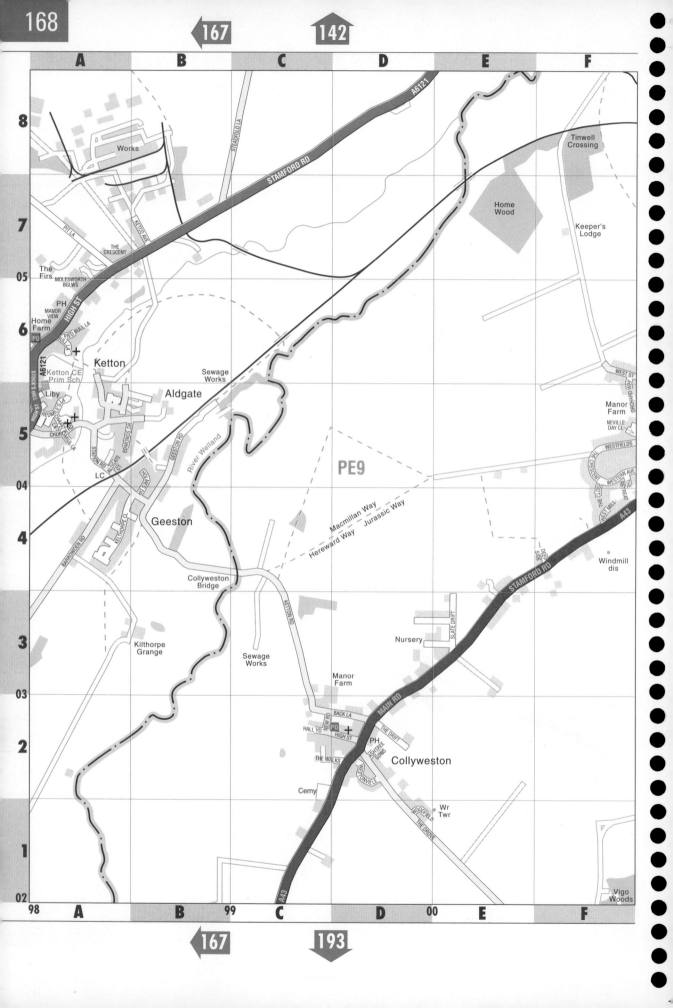

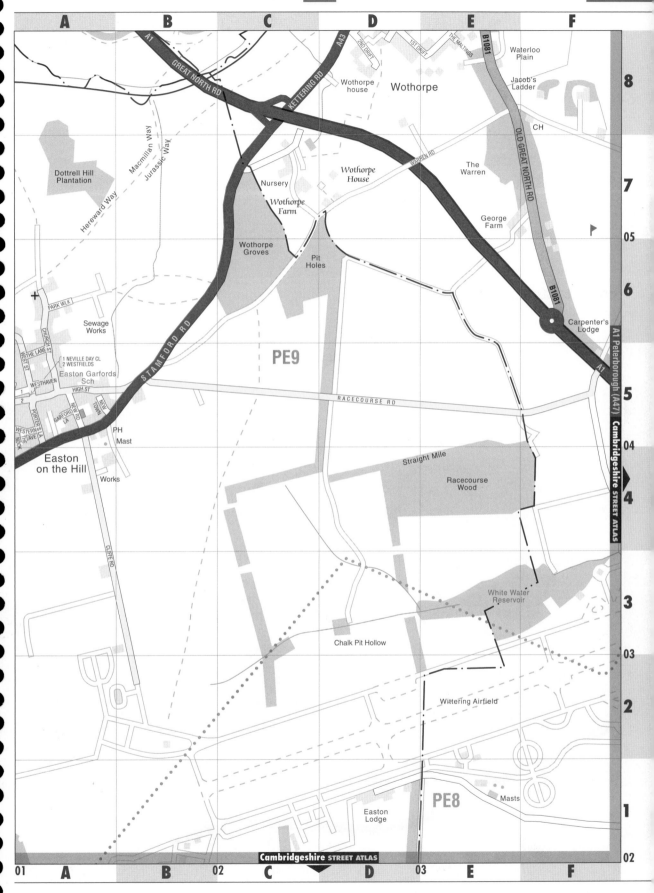

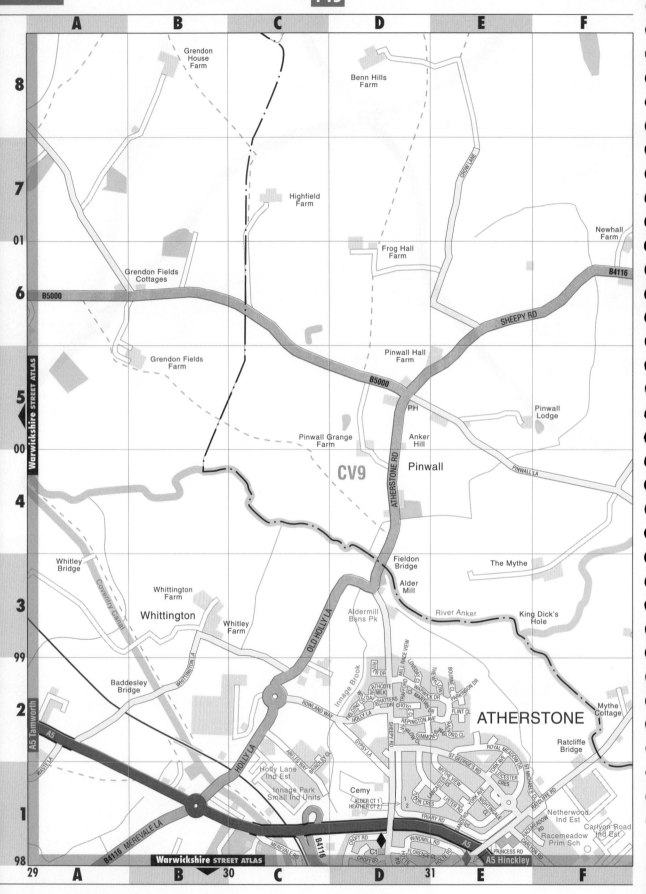

A   B   C   D   E   F

8

7

01

6   B5000

5

00

4

3

99

2

1

98
29   A   B   30   C   D   31   E   F

Grendon
House
Farm

Benn Hills
Farm

Highfield
Farm

Newhall
Farm

Frog Hall
Farm

Grendon Fields
Cottages

B4116

B5000

SHEEPY RD

Grendon Fields
Farm

Pinwall Hall
Farm

Pinwall
Lodge

CROW LANE

PH

Anker
Hill

Pinwall Grange
Farm

CV9   Pinwall

PINWALL LA

ATHERSTONE RD

Whitley
Bridge

Fieldon
Bridge

The Mythe

Whittington
Farm

Alder
Mill

Whittington

Whitley
Farm

Aldermill
Bsns Pk

River Anker

King Dick's
Hole

Coventry Canal

OLD HOLLY LA

Innage Brook

Mythe
Cottage

Baddesley
Bridge

ATHERSTONE

Ratcliffe
Bridge

WHITTINGTON LA

ROWLAND WAY

HOLLY LA

GYPSY LA

SHEEPY RD

Royal Meadow Dr

ST MICHAEL'S CL

A5 Tamworth

WASTE LA

A5

MEREVALE LA

B4116 MEREVALE RD

ABELES WAY

BRINDLEY CL

Holly Lane
Ind Est

Innage Park
Small Ind Units

B4116

MEREVALE RD

Cemy

ALDER CT 1
HEATHER CT 2

TAYLOR CRES

FRIARY RD

CROFT RD

Ct

CROFT RD

WINDMILL RD

FLORENCE CL

HOLTE RD

PRINCESS RD

A5 Hinckley

A5

Netherwood
Ind Est

Racemeadow
Prim Sch

Carlyon Road
Ind Est

RATCLIFFE RD

RACEMEADOW RD

CARLYON RD

Warwickshire STREET ATLAS

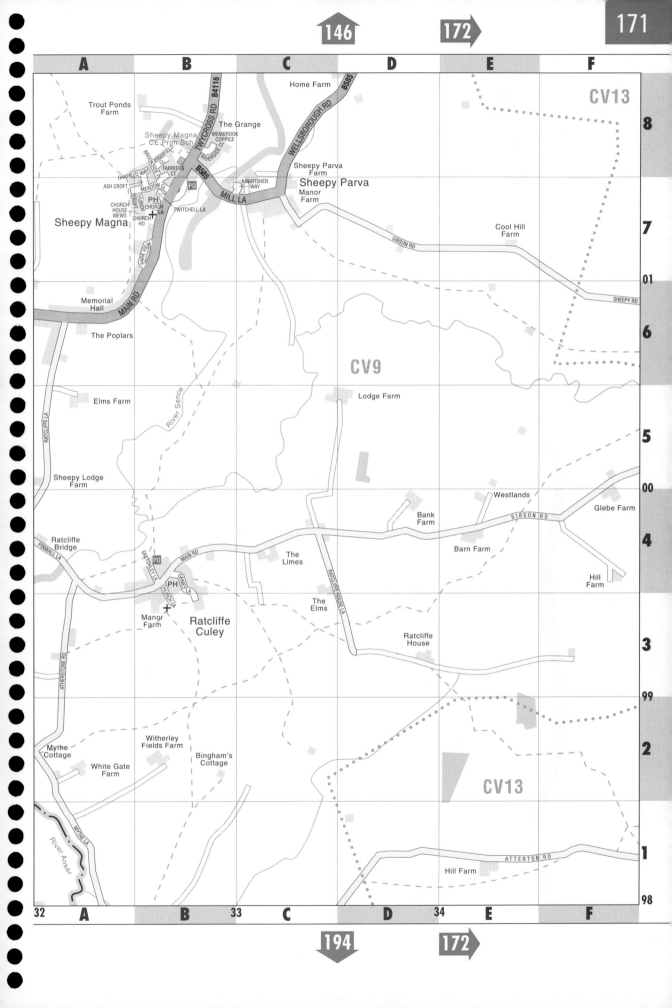

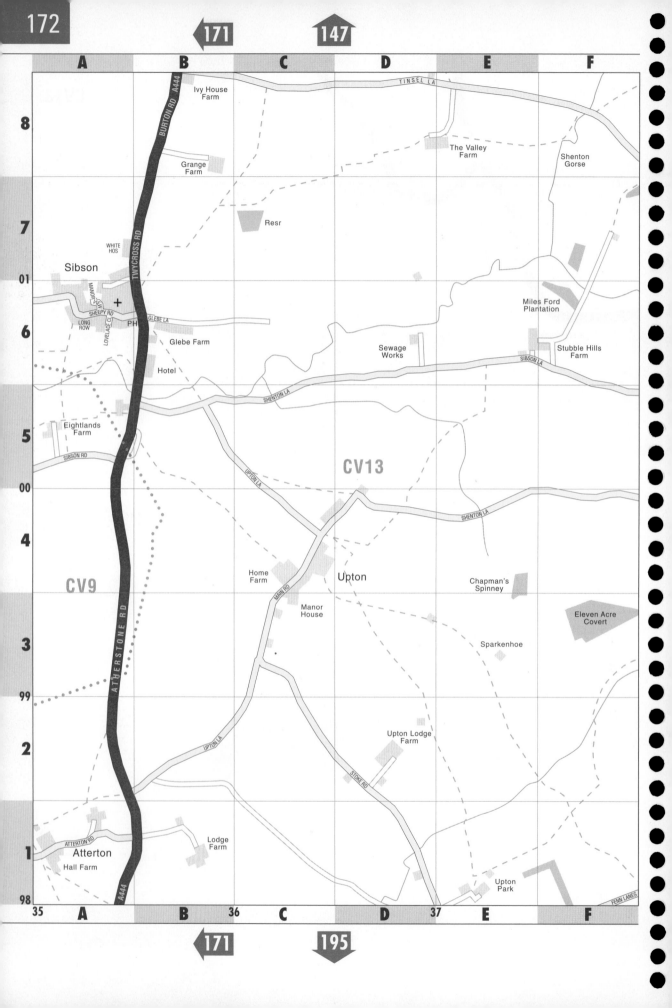

171
147

A B C D E F

8
7
01
6
5
00
4
CV9
CV13
3
99
2
1
98

35 A B 36 C D 37 E F

BURTON RD A444
Ivy House Farm
TINSEL LA
The Valley Farm
Shenton Gorse
Grange Farm
Resr
WHITE HOS
TWYCROSS RD
Sibson
Miles Ford Plantation
MANOR VIEW
SHEEPY RD
+
GLEBE LA
LONG ROW
LOVELACE CL
PH
Glebe Farm
Sewage Works
Stubble Hills Farm
SIBSON LA
Hotel
SHENTON LA
Eightlands Farm
SIBSON RD
UPTON LA
SHENTON LA
ATHERSTONE RD
Home Farm
MAIN RD
Upton
Chapman's Spinney
Manor House
Eleven Acre Covert
Sparkenhoe
UPTON LA
Upton Lodge Farm
STOKE RD
Atterton
ATTERTON RD
Lodge Farm
Hall Farm
A444
Upton Park
Upton Park
FENN LANES

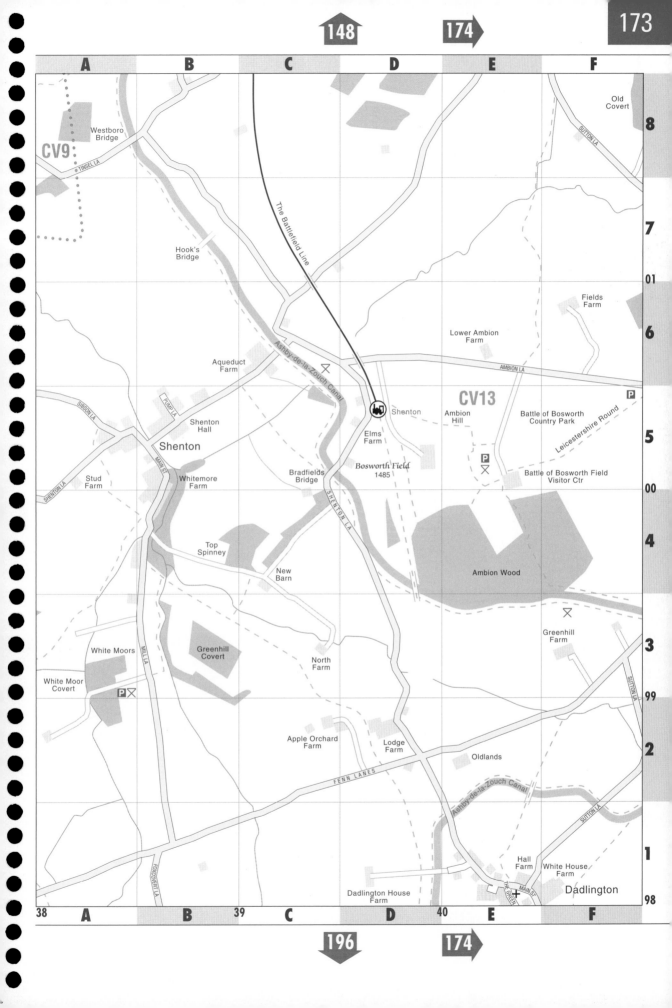

173
149

A B C D E F

8

7

01

6

5

00

4

3

99

2

1

98

Old Covert

Woodhouse Farm

Spring Wood

The Duckery

SUTTON LA

Leicestershire Round

BOSWORTH RD

AMBION LA

Sutton Cheney

Townsend Farm

THE SQUARE

MAIN ST

BLACKSMITHS LA

PH

The Lawn

TWENTY ACRE LA

WHARF LA

CV13

FENN LANES

Sutton Wharf Bridge

Leicestershire Round

Ashby-de-la-Zouch Canal

SUTTON LA

Poplars Farm

St George's Farm

STAPLETON LA

New House Farm

Harper's Hill

Harper's Hill Farm

Bradshaw Farm

Winfrey Farm

Lodge Farm

DADLINGTON LA

The Shade

The Elms

Three Ashes

SUTTON LA

New Farm

Brick Kiln Farm

A447

HINCKLEY RD

Bungalow Farm

Island Lane Farm

Woodside Farm

Woodlands

BOSWORTH RD

Oaks Farm

LE9

STAPLETON LA

Wood View Farm

Manor Lodge Farm

White House Farm

ASHBY RD

Stapleton Brockey

The Farm

Manor Farm

SCHOOL LA

GREEN LA

BEALES CL

MANOR CRES

ST MARTINS

Stapleton

CHAPEL ST

MAIN ST

CHURCH LA

PH

Church Farm

White House Farm

A447

STAPLETON LA

Fox Covert

173
197

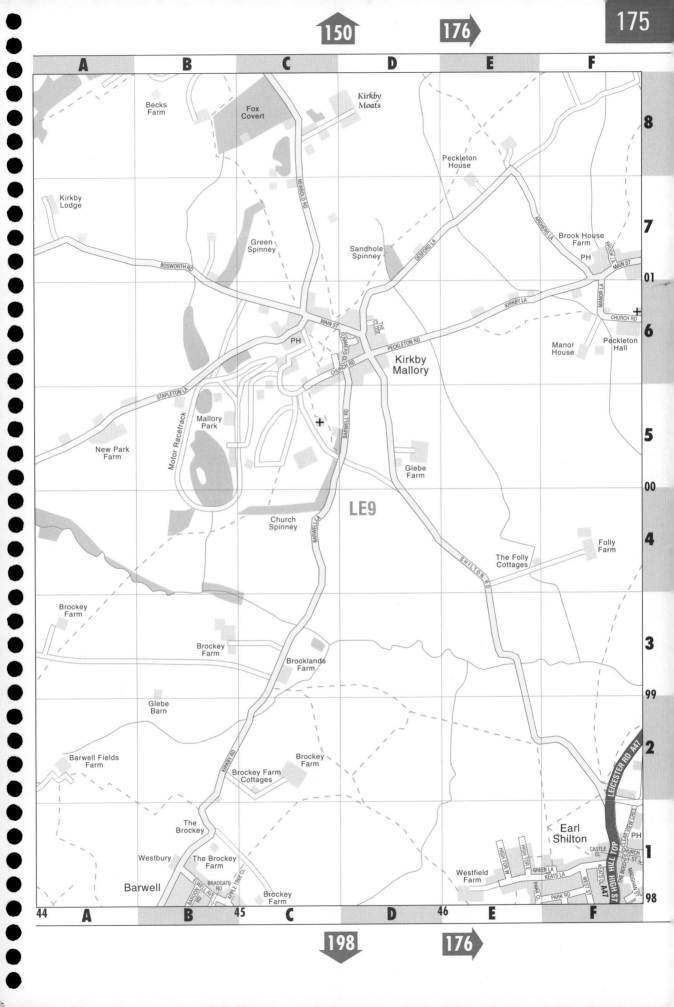

175
151

A B C D E F

8

Mount Pleasant

Works

PECKLETON LA

Oaklands

Peckleton Common

Dan's Barn

Peckleton Rise

A47

7

PECKLETON COMM

Old Brake

Shelbrooke House

Elms Farm House

HILL CL

Tooley Park Farm

DESFORD LA

ELMS DR

01

MAIN ST

Works

Peckleton

New Haven

Stretchnook Farm

CHURCH RD

6

Peckleton Hall

Roundabout Spinney

DAYS LA

The Lodge

HINCKLEY RD

The Knoll

5

Tooley Spinneys

LE9

Knoll Farm

Thurlaston Fields

Tooley Park Cottages

00

North Lodge

Knoll Spinney

DESFORD RD

4

Long Spinneys

Bassett Farm

Clump Farm

Tooley Farm

Bungalow Farm

Hill Farm

The Holt

3

The Spinneys

MOAT CL

The Lodge Farm

99

A47

LEICESTER RD

Riverside Cottages

New Spinney

Bracknell Farm

EARL SHILTON RD

2

North Park

Normanton House Farm

Normanton Thurville

Dairy Farm

Earl Shilton

Church Farm

Normanton

CHURCH ST

KING RICHARD'S

BOSWORTH

THURLASTON LA

Oakfield

1

Sch

THE POPLARS

Marlpit Farm

GEORGE ST

CHAPEL ST

EARL ST

THE FLATS

MILL LA

Normanton Park

98

47 A B 48 C D 49 E F

175
199

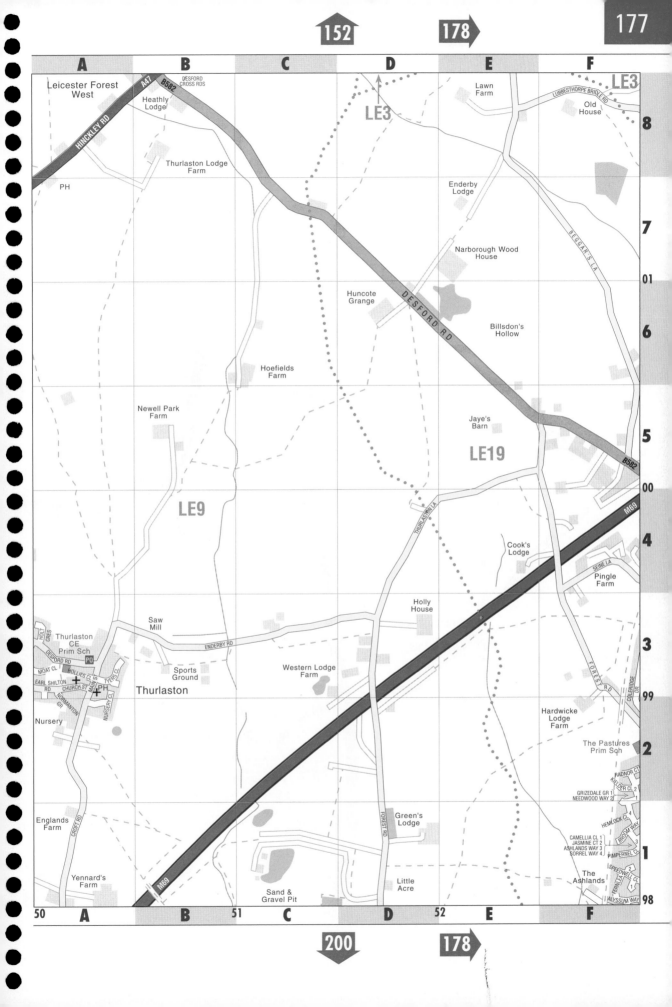

A   B   C   D   E   F

8
7
01
6
5
00
4
3
99
2
1
98

53   A   B   54   C   D   55   E   F

New House Farm
Hopyard Farm
Abbey Farm
Braunstone Town
The Yenwoods
LUBBESTHORPE BRIDLE RD
Fox Covert
Warren Farm
Mast
Fishpool Spinney
Freeboard Spinney
Warren Park Way
Froane's Hill
Mill Hill
Trad Est
The Park
Enderby Hall
Hall Wlk
Leicester La
Enderby
LE19
Liby
Kirk La
Blaby Rd
Brockington Coll
Danemill Prim Sch
L Ctr
Stewart House
Narborough
The Pastures

Centurian Ct Office Pk
Wood Close Plantation
Centurion Way
Legion Way
Dominus Way
Tiber Way
Meridian E
Ind Est
Meridian W
Meridian N
Centre Ct
Meridian S
Ervington Ct
Harcourt Way
M69   21   A563
A5460
Superstore
Grove Farm Triangle
Sh Ctr
Brewery
Fosse Park S
Fosse Park Ave
Soar Valley Way   A563
Penman Way
Thorpe Way
Smith Way
Narborough Rd S
B4114
Mast
Police HQ
St Johns
Ratby Meadow La
St Hill View
Nurseries
Works
River Soar
Gee's Lock
Grand Union Canal
LE2
St Johns
Aldeby Cl
Foxhunter Rdbt
B582
Heron Way
Enderby Bridge
Enderby Rd Ind Est
Merrydale Farm
Sewage Works
Glen Parva Lodge
LE8
Refuse Tip
Grange Bsns Pk
B582
M1
B4114
Leicester Rd
Enderby Rd
Narborough Rd S
LE8
Millfield Com Sch
The Osiers
The Osiers Bsns Pk
Ravenhurst Prim Sch
Lubbesthorpe Way
Works
Narborough Rd S   A5460

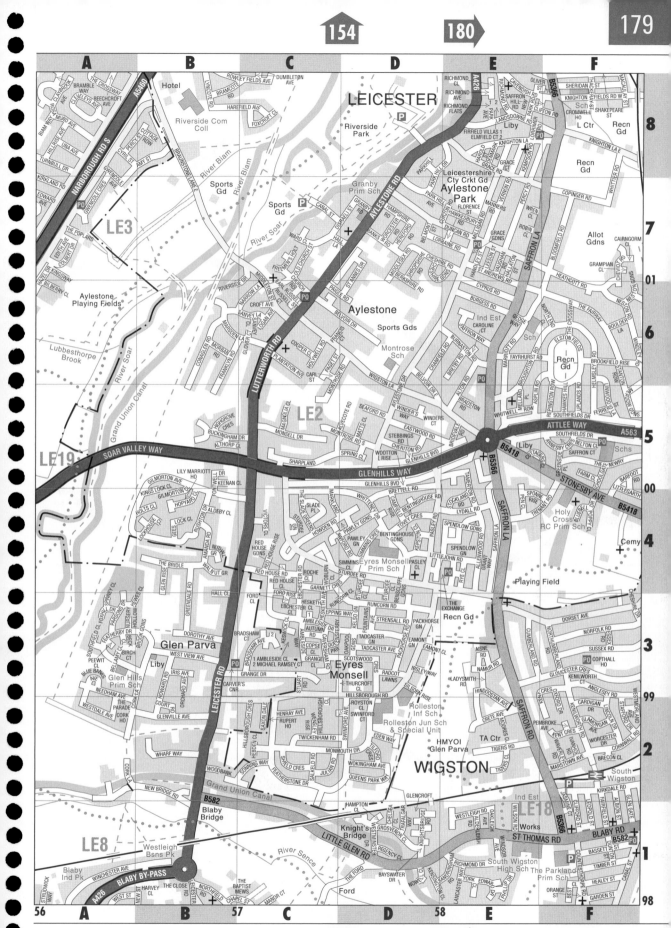

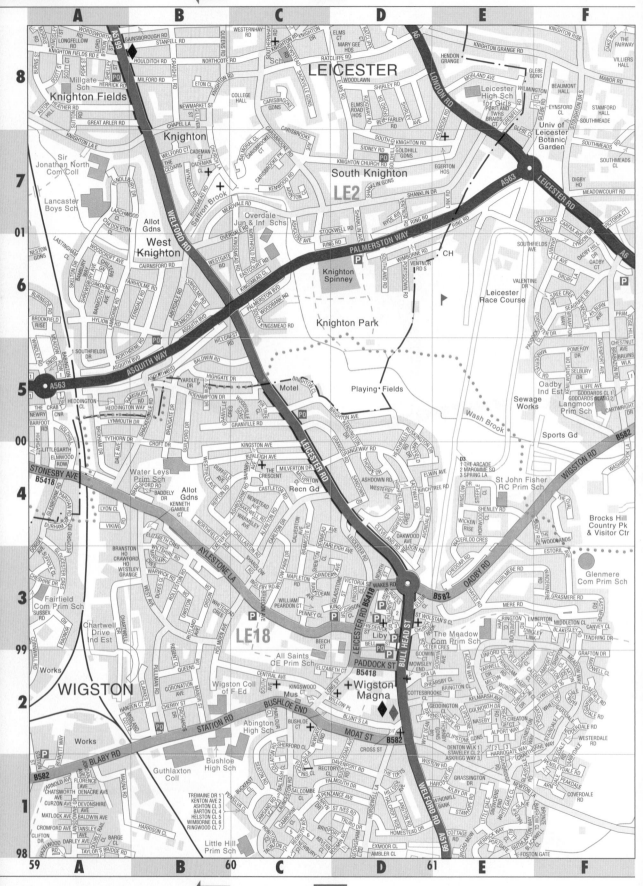

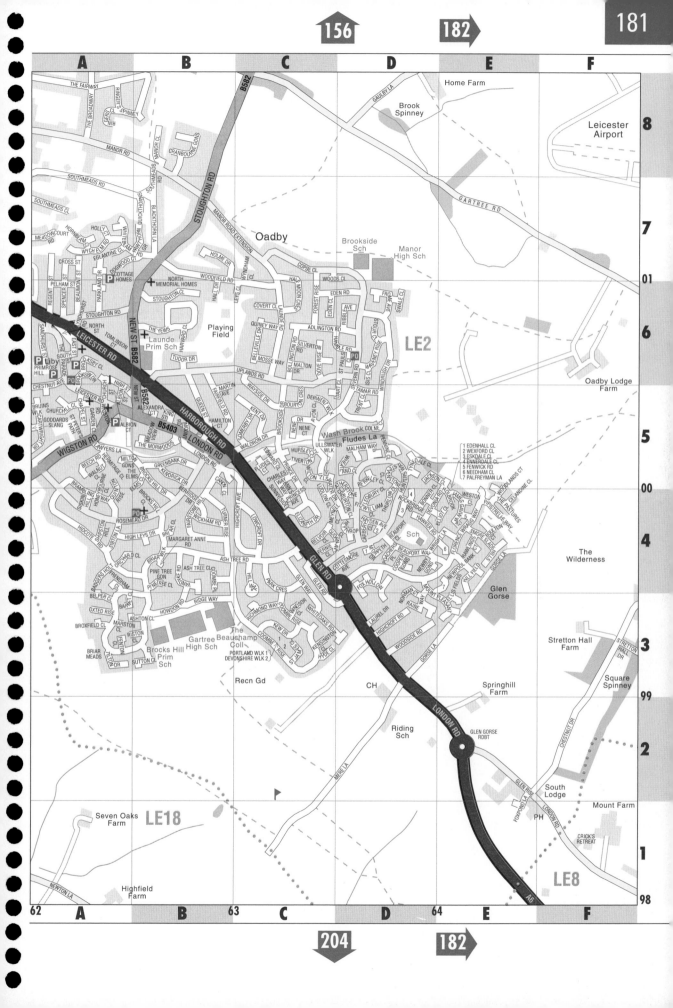

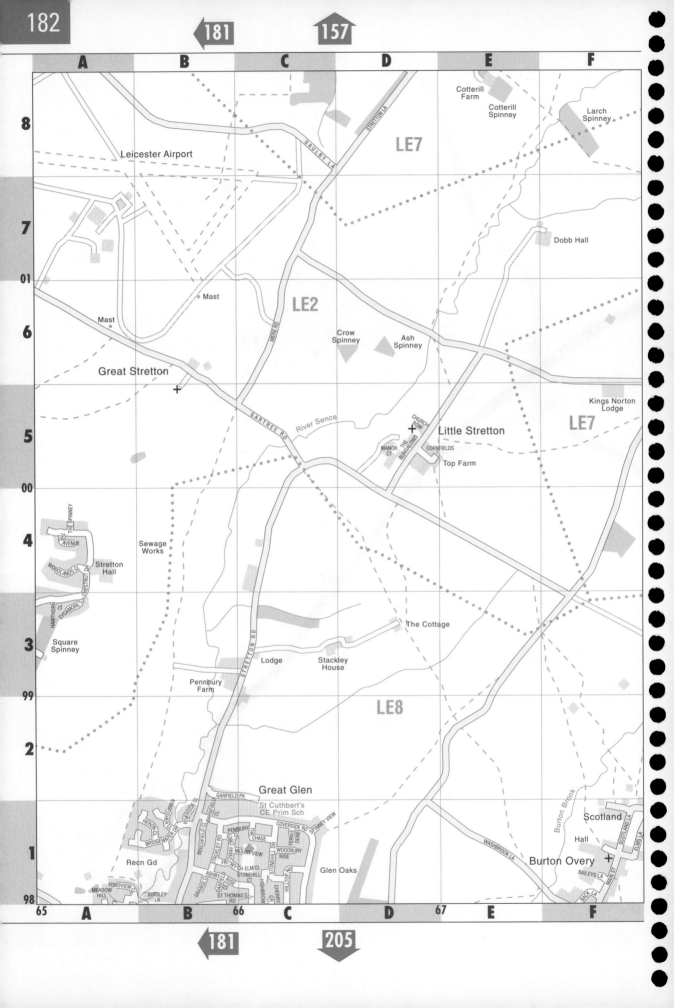

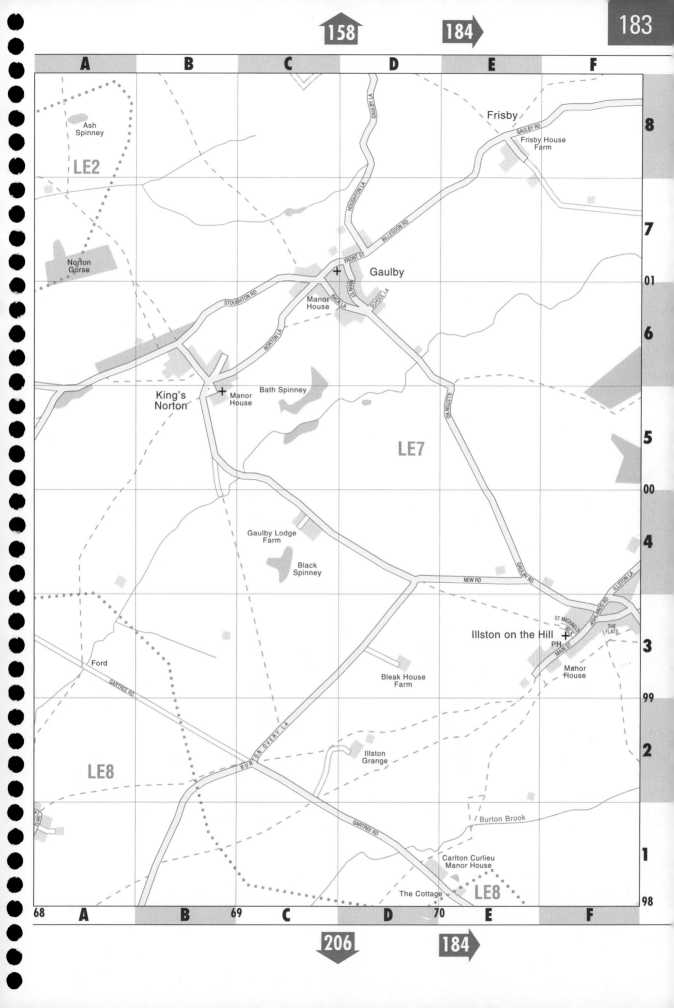

A   B   C   D   E   F

Ash
Spinney

LE2

8

Frisby

Frisby House
Farm

GAULBY RD

GAULBY LA

7

Norton
Gorse

HOUGHTON LA

BILLESDON RD

01

FRONT ST

Gaulby

STOUGHTON RD

Manor
House

BACK LA

MAIN ST

SCHOOL LA

6

NORTON LA

King's
Norton

Manor
House

Bath Spinney

ILLSTON RD

LE7

5

00

4

Gaulby Lodge
Farm

Black
Spinney

NEW RD

GAULBY RD

ILLSTON LA

ASHLANDS RD

ST MICHAEL'S

THE
FLATS

Illston on the Hill

PH

MAIN ST

3

Ford

GARTREE RD

Bleak House
Farm

Manor
House

99

BURTON OVERY LA

2

LE8

Illston
Grange

GARTREE RD

Burton Brook

1

Carlton Curlieu
Manor House

LE8

ELMS

The Cottage

98

183
159

A B C D E F

8

7

01

6

GAULBY RD

Hubbard's
Spinney

Frisby
Lodge
Farm

Frisby
Lodge

ROLLESTON RD

B6047

Rolleston Lodge
Farm

Vale
Cottage

HARBOROUGH RD

BUSBY RD

Blenheim
Plantation

SKEFFINGTON RD

Rolleston

Cranhill
Farm

Ashlands

Long Plantation

ILLSTON LA

LE7

Home Farm

Rolleston
Hall

Pop's Spinney

Crow
Wood

5

00

4

New Inn
The
Lodge

The Farm

Barn
Farm

Barn Close
Spinney

Old Pond
Wood

Whinney Pit
Spinney

Rolleston
Wood

3

99

2

1

98

NOSELEY RD

ILLSTON LA

Burton Brook

CROSS ROADS

Illston Cross
Roads

MERE RD

NEW INN LA

MELTON RD

B6047

Millfield
Clump

ILLSTON RD

Top
Lodge

THE AVENUE

Lodge
Gates

Southfield
Spinney

THREE GATES RD

Home
Plantation

Noseley

BACK DR

Foxhole
Spinney

Turner's Barn
Farm

Three
Gates

KIBWORTH RD

Thistley
Cottages

Long
Acre

Shangton
Holt

Cottons Field
Farm

Coney Hill
Plantation

Round
Spinney

Old Park

Noseley
Wood

Noseley
Hall

New Park

71 A 72 C D 73 E F

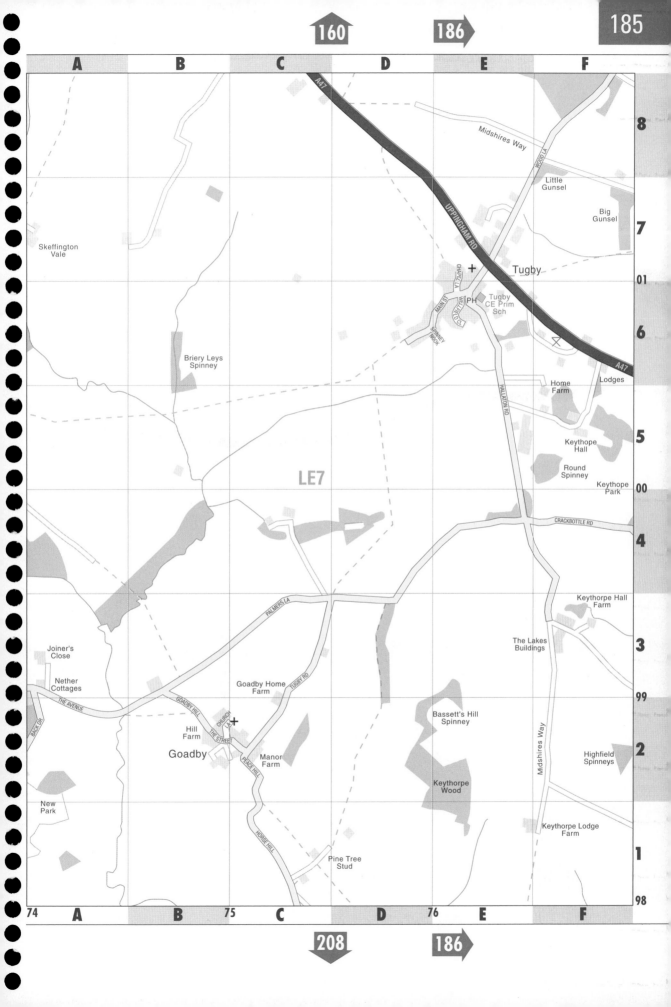

185
161

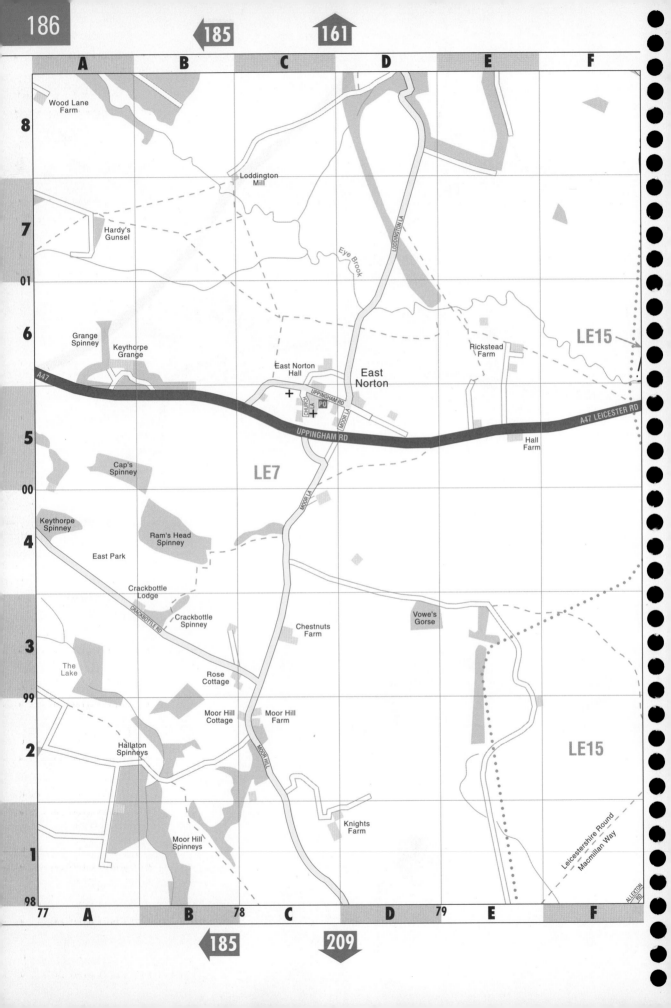

185
209

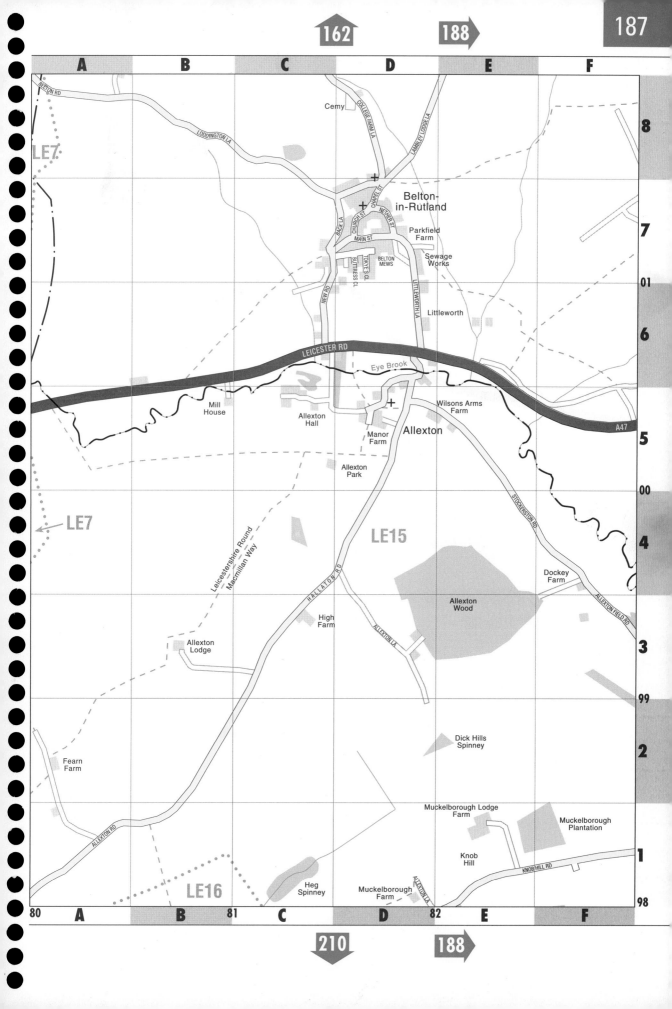

162
188

A B C D E F

Cemy
LE7

8

Belton-
in-Rutland

Parkfield
Farm

7

Sewage
Works

01

BELTON
MEWS

Littleworth

6

LEICESTER RD

Eye Brook

01

Mill
House

Wilsons Arms
Farm

Allexton
Hall

A47

Allexton

5

Manor
Farm

00

Allexton
Park

LE7

LE15

4

Leicestershire Round
Macmillan Way

Allexton
Wood

Dockey
Farm

High
Farm

3

Allexton
Lodge

99

Dick Hills
Spinney

2

Fearn
Farm

Muckelborough Lodge
Farm

Muckelborough
Plantation

Knob
Hill

1

KNOB HILL RD

LE16

Heg
Spinney

Muckelborough
Farm

98

80 A B 81 C D 82 E F

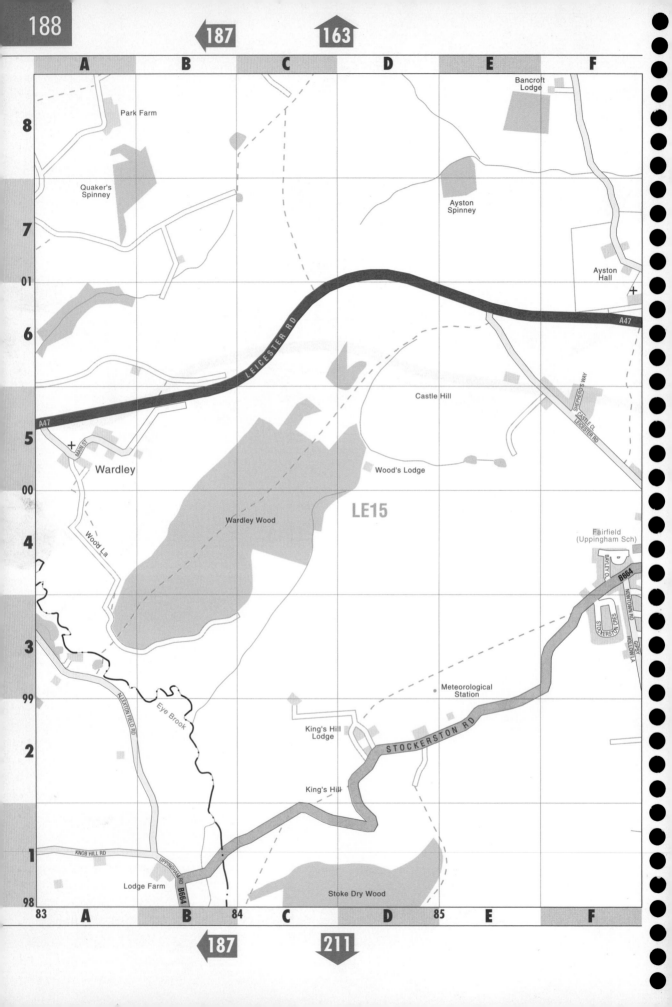

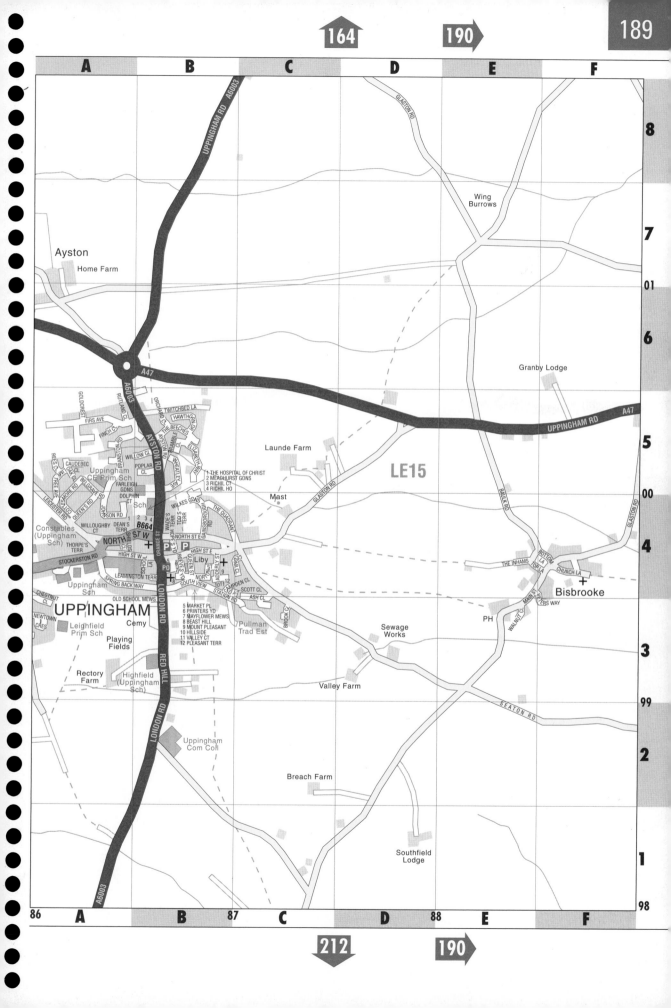

A B C D E F

8

Wing
Burrows

7

Ayston

Home Farm

01

6

Granby Lodge

A47

A6003

UPPINGHAM RD

GLASTON RD

UPPINGHAM RD A47

Lait Farm

LE15

Launde Farm

5

1 THE HOSPITAL OF CHRIST
2 MEADHURST GDNS
3 RICHIL CT
4 RICHIL HO

Mast

00

GOLDCREST

FIRS AVE

RUTLAND CT

ORCHARD CL
TWITCHBED LA
HAWTHORN
THE BEECHES

AYSTON RD

BRAMBLE
ELIZABETH

FINCH C

WILLOW CL

POPLAR CL

Uppingham
CE Prim Sch

WHEATLEY MEW

CAUDEBEC
CL

FARLEIGH
GDNS

DOLPHIN
CT

Sch

WILKES GDNS

THE QUADRANT

GAINSBOROUGH RD

GLASTON RD

REES AVE
THREE AVE

BELGRAVE RD

QUEEN'S RD

WILLOUGHBY
CT

DEAN'S
TERR

1 2 3 4

WADE'S
TERR

OLD SCHOOL
TODD'S
TERR

NORTH ST E

BAULK RD

LECESTER RD

THORPE'S
TERR

NORTH
ST W

B664

ORANGE ST

HIGH ST E

4

00

Constables
(Uppingham
Sch)

STOCKERSTON RD

HIGH ST W

SCHOOL LA

Liby

SOUTH VIEW

AUDLEY ST

NORTH ST

SCOTT CL

THE INHAMS

BOTTOM
LA

TOD LA

Bisbrooke

CHURCH LA

Uppingham
Sch

LEAMINGTON TERR
SPRING BACK WAY

PO

LAMPDEN CL
STATION RD

ASH CL

BROOK CL

MAIN ST

WALNUT CL

FIERS WAY

PH

CHESTNUT
CL

NEWTOWN
CRES

OLD SCHOOL MEWS

5 MARKET PL
6 PRINTERS YD
7 MAYFLOWER MEWS
8 BEAST HILL
9 MOUNT PLEASANT
10 HILLSIDE
11 VALLEY CT
12 PLEASANT TERR

Pullman
Trad Est

Sewage
Works

UPPINGHAM

Leighfield
Prim Sch

Cemy

Playing
Fields

3

Rectory
Farm

Highfield
(Uppingham
Sch)

LONDON RD

RED HILL

Valley Farm

SEATON RD

99

2

Uppingham
Com Coll

Breach Farm

1

Southfield
Lodge

A6003

98

A   B   C   D   E   F

8

7

01

6

Bisbrooke
Hall

Glaston

Glaston Tunnel

WING RD

GLASTON RD

MANOR LA
GLASTON PK
SPRING LA
CHURCH LA
PARK DENFIELD
COTTS CL
PH

A47 UPPINGHAM RD MAIN RD

ORCHARD
CL
Lonsdale
Farm

MORCOTT RD

Glaston Lodge

Motel

GLASTON RD A47

GLASTON RD

5

Wellesley
Spinney

00

LE15

SEATON RD

4

3

99

B672

2

SEATON RD

Seaton

DRURYS LA
THOMPSONS LA
PH
MAIN ST
MOLES LA
BAINES LA
CHURCH LA

NN17

1

Seaton
Grange

GRANGE LA

B672

98

89 A B 90 C D 91 E F

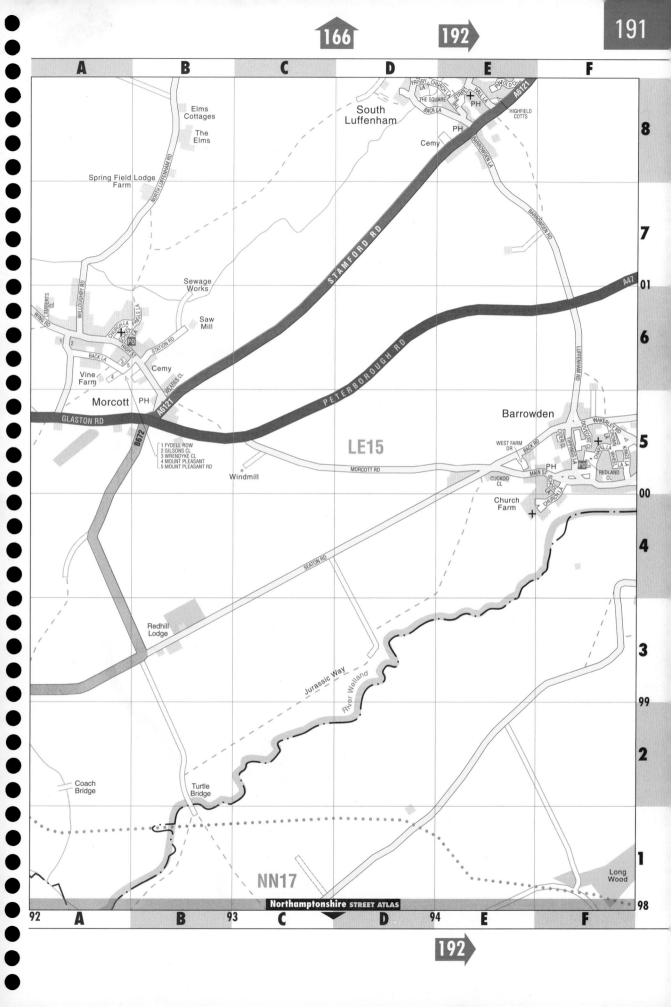

A B C D E F

Elms Cottages

The Elms

South Luffenham

FRISBY LA CHURCH LA THE SQUARE STREET HALL LA PINFOLD CL A6121

PH HIGHFIELD COTTS

BACK LA

PH

Cemy

Spring Field Lodge Farm

NORTH LUFFENHAM RD

STAMFORD RD

BARROWDEN LA

BARROWDEN RD

A47

Sewage Works

WILLOUGHBY RD

WING RD

LAMBERTS CL

CHURCH LA PAGLE LA

PO

STATION RD

HIGH ST

BACK LA

Saw Mill

PETERBOROUGH RD

LUFFENHAM RD

Cemy

1 2

3 5

4

NEARES CL

Vine Farm

Morcott PH

A6121

GLASTON RD

B672

LE15

1 FYDELL ROW
2 GILSONS CL
3 WRENDYKE CL
4 MOUNT PLEASANT
5 MOUNT PLEASANT RD

Windmill

MORCOTT RD

Barrowden

WEST FARM DR

BACK RD

CUCKOO CL

Church Farm

WAKERLEY RD

DOVECOTE CL

CHER CL

TIPPINGS LA

MAIN ST

CHAPEL LA

CROWN LA

KINGS LA

WHEEL LA

PO

PH

SCHOOL LA

CHURCH LA

REDLAND CL

Redhill Lodge

SEATON RD

Jurassic Way

River Welland

Coach Bridge

Turtle Bridge

NN17

Long Wood

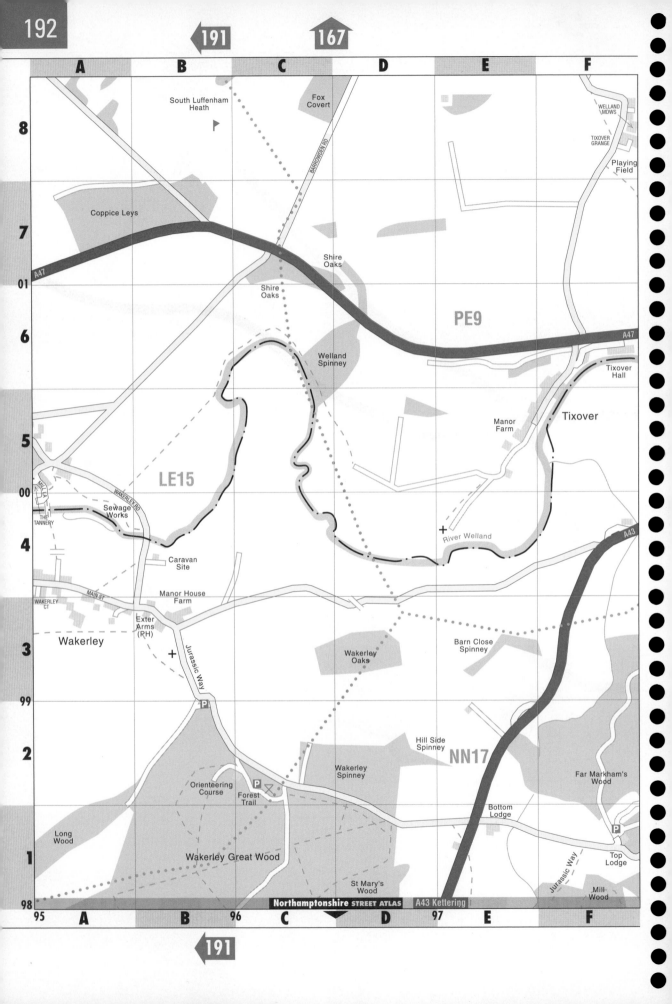

A B C D E F

8

South Luffenham Heath

Fox Covert

WELLAND MDWS

TIXOVER GRANGE

Playing Field

7

Coppice Leys

A47

01

Shire Oaks

PE9

Shire Oaks

A47

6

Welland Spinney

Tixover Hall

Tixover

Manor Farm

5

LE15

00

WAKERLEY RD

Sewage Works

MILL LA

THE TANNERY

River Welland

A43

4

Caravan Site

MAIN ST

Manor House Farm

WAKERLEY CT

Exter Arms (RH)

Wakerley

Jurassic Way

Barn Close Spinney

Wakerley Oaks

3

99

P

Hill Side Spinney

NN17

2

Wakerley Spinney

Far Markham's Wood

Orienteering Course

P

Forest Trail

Bottom Lodge

Long Wood

Jurassic Way

Top Lodge

1

Wakerley Great Wood

St Mary's Wood

Mill Wood

98

95 A B 96 C D 97 E F

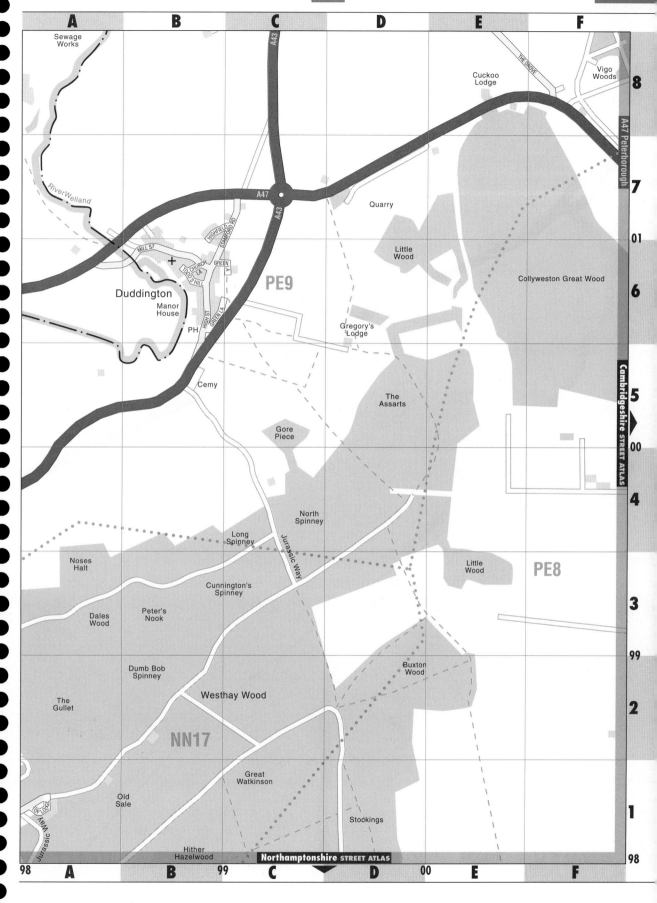

A B C D E F

8

Sewage Works

Cuckoo Lodge

Vigo Woods

THE DROVE

A43

A47 Peterborough

7

River Welland

A47

A43

Quarry

01

Little Wood

PE9

Collyweston Great Wood

6

Duddington

MILL ST
HIGHFIELD
STAMFORD RD
CHURCH LA
GREEN LA
TOUT'S HILL
HIGH ST
GREEN LA

Manor House

PH

Gregory's Lodge

Cambridgeshire STREET ATLAS

Cemy

The Assarts

5

00

Gore Piece

4

North Spinney

Long Spinney

Jurassic Way

Little Wood

PE8

Noses Halt

Cunnington's Spinney

3

Dales Wood

Peter's Nook

99

Dumb Bob Spinney

Buxton Wood

The Gullet

Westhay Wood

2

NN17

Great Watkinson

Old Sale

1

Stockings

Jurassic Way

Hither Hazelwood

98

98 A B 99 C D 00 E F

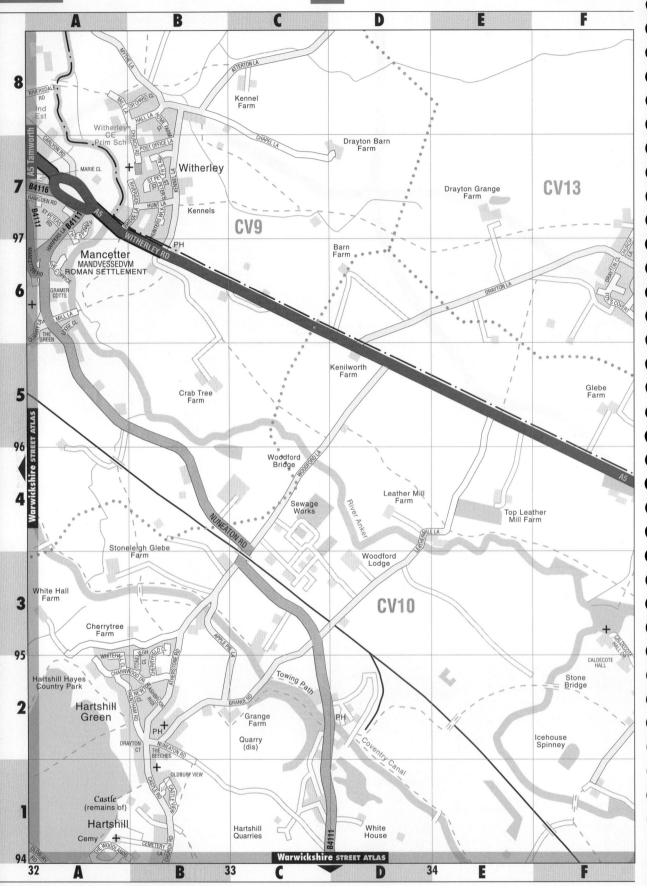

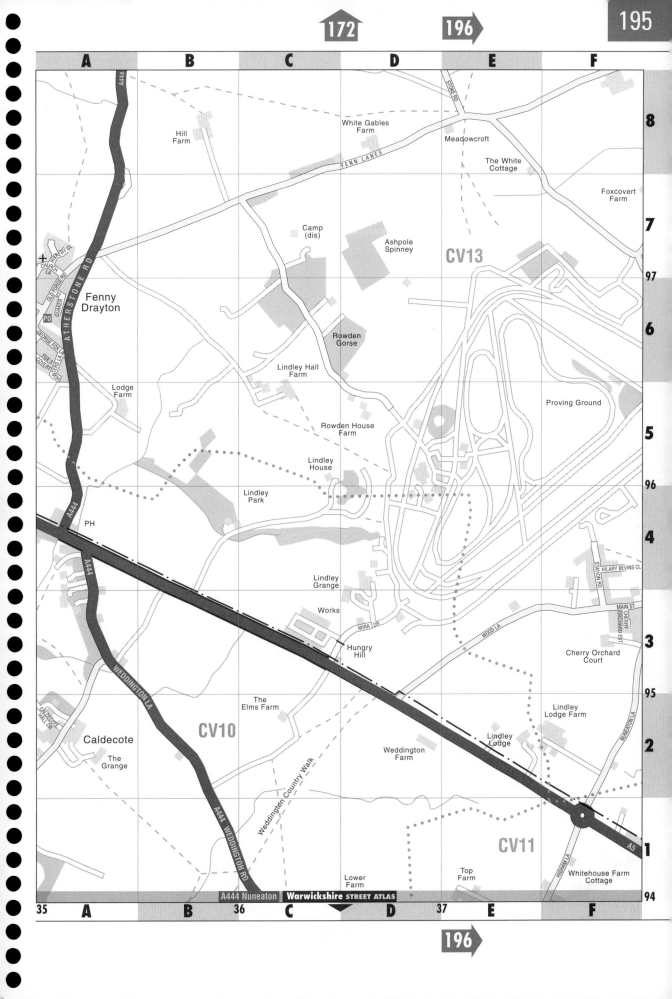

A   B   C   D   E   F

8
7
97
6
5
96
4
95
3
2
1
94

STONE RD

White Gables Farm
Meadowcroft
The White Cottage
Foxcovert Farm

FENN LANES

Hill Farm

Camp (dis)

Ashpole Spinney

CV13

ATHERSTONE RD
A444

+
CHURCH LA
ROKERY CL
OLD FORGE RD
QUAKER LA
GEORGE FOX LA
FOX'S COTERY
HUNTERS LA

PO

Fenny Drayton

Rowden Gorse

Lindley Hall Farm

Proving Ground

Lodge Farm

Rowden House Farm

Lindley House

Lindley Park

A444

PH

A444

A444

Lindley Grange

Works

MIRA DR

Hungry Hill

WOOD LA

STATION RD
Hilary Bevins Cl.
MAIN ST
CHERRY ORCHARD EST

Cherry Orchard Court

WEDDINGTON LA

The Elms Farm

CV10

Weddington Country Walk

Lindley Lodge Farm

Lindley Lodge

CALDECOTE HALL DR

Caldecote

The Grange

Weddington Farm

A444 WEDDINGTON RD

CV11

NUNEATON LA

HIGHAM LA

A5

Lower Farm

Top Farm

Whitehouse Farm Cottage

195
173

A   B   C   D   E   F

8

FOXCOVERT LA

Grange Farm

Marina

Ivy House Farm

STOKE LA

STAPLETON LA

TK GREEN

Fox Covert Farm

Willow Park Ind Est

Stoke Golding
Crown Hill

PH

CHURCH CL
ANDREW CL

HIGH ST
CHURCH ST

ROSEWAY
GREENWAY
TRINITY CL
SHELTON RD
WHITEMOORS RD

WHITEMOORS CL

St Martin's Convent

7

UPTON LA

Brook Farm

STATION RD
THE COURTYARD

CHURCH WLKS
THE STABLE YD

St Margaret's CE Prim Sch

PO

SHERWOOD RD

MARGARET RD
ST
THORNFIELD
HALL DR
PINE CL

GREENWOOD CL

HINCKLEY RD

St Martin's RC Sch

97

MAIN ST

BEVAN CL
Cemy

ARNOLD RD

AVE

Stokefields Farm

STOKE RD

6

Higham Fields Ct

HIGHAM LA

TITHE CL

STONELEY RD

Willow Farm

Brook House

Brook Farm

Millfield Farm

CV13

Highfield Farm

5

Oak Tree Farm

Cuckoo's Nest Farm

Basin Bridge Farm

Compass Fields Farm

WYKIN LA

Oaklands

96

STOKE LA

Vale Farm

Basin Bridge

Higham Fields

Wykin Fields

4

Higham on the Hill CE Prim Sch
PH

Hall Farm

BASIN BRIDGE LA

Ashby de la Zouch Canal

The Hollows

Wykin

PO

MAIN ST

HINCKLEY LA

Spring Hill Farm

WYKIN RD

3

Higham on the Hill

Higham Hall

Wykin House Farm

Wykin Hall

NUNEATON LA

BARR LA

95

A5
WATLING ST

Grange Farm

Hijaz Coll

Higham Thorns

LE10

NORMANDY WAY

A47

2

Harper's Hill

OUTLANDS DR

MADRID CL

STH WAY

1

Hollow Farm

Change Brook

CV11

MARYWELL CL

LEYSMILL CL

FRESWICK CL

CROSSKIRK RD
ST MARTY DR

LOSSIEMOUTH RD

KINROSS WAY
LAXFORD

A47

94

38   A   B   39   C   D   40   E   F

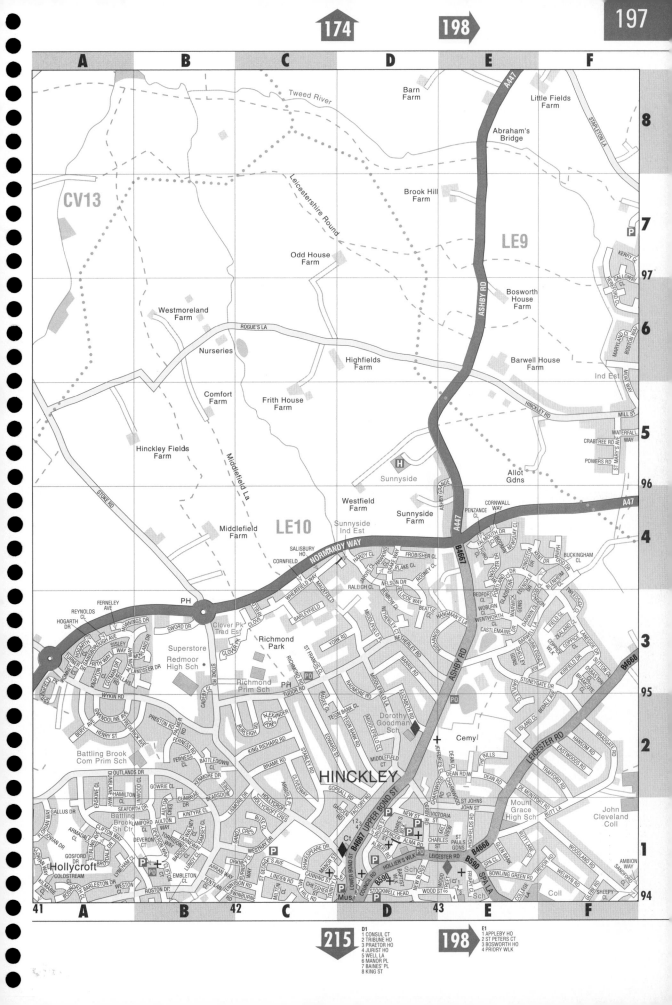

A B C D E F

8 7 97 6 5 96 4 3 95 2 1 94

Glebe Farm

William Bradford Com Coll

Allot Gdns

Recn Gd

WOOD ST · THE HOLLOW

HIGH ST · A47

The Cloisters

Land Society

The Square

OAKS WAY

Liby

B5364 · PO

Townlands CE Prim Sch

Earl Shilton

Heathfield High Sch

HINCKLEY RD

Doctors Fields

Norman Dabley

The Grange

The Breach Farm

STATION RD

Barwell Inf Sch

Liby

CARRS HILL

B581

ELMSTHORPE LA

WILKINSON LA

Church Farm Gram Sch

Breach Lands

B5364

Factory

Inglenook Farm

LE9

Elmsthorpe

STATION RD

The Ivene Farm

Barwell

LEICESTER RD

Nurseries

Elmsthorpe Estate

THE ROUNDHILLS 1
WORTLEY COTTS 2

B581

A47

B4668

Hissar House Farm

BRIDLE PATH RD

Billington Rd W

Billington Rd E

Brick Kiln Hill

Billington Rough

LEICESTER RD

Lynden Lea

FAIRWAYS CT

Burbage Common Visitor Ctr

Bridge Farm

BRIDLE PATH

BURBAGE COMMON RD

B4668

CH

Burbage Common

Leicestershire Round

Woodhouse Farm

M69

Park House

Sheepy Wood

LE10

John Cleveland Coll

Wood House Farm

P

Elmsthorpe Plantation

SMITH LA

Hobbs Hayes

Freeholt Lodge

Burbage Wood

Aston Firs

Freeholt Wood

M69

44 A 45 B C 46 D E F

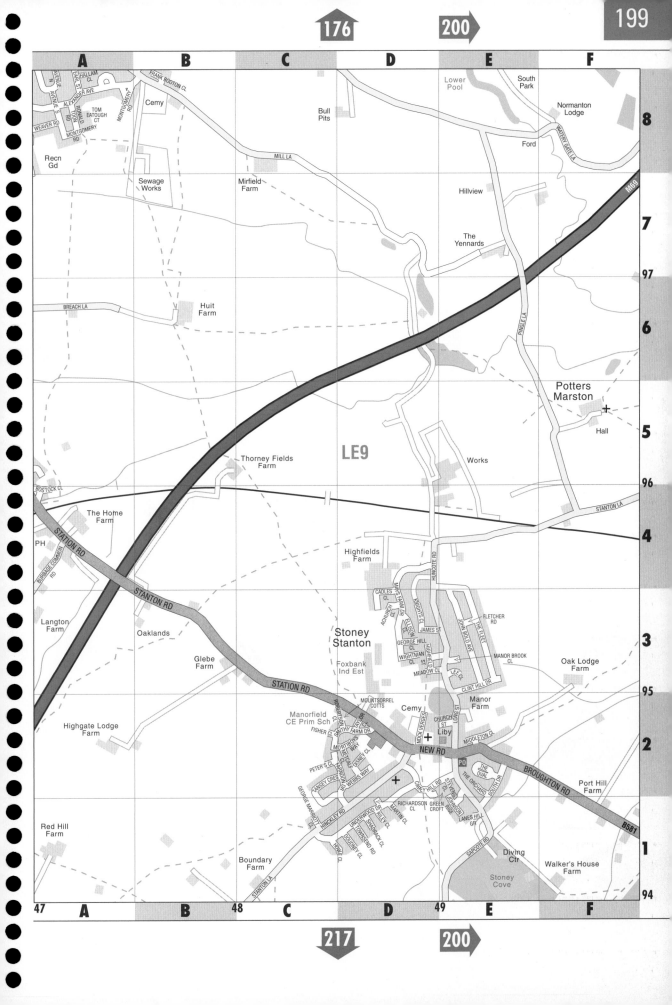

A   B   C   D   E   F

8

M69

Cemy

Forest Road Farm

VETCH CL 1
COWSLIP CL 2
LOBELIA CL 3

COPT OAK RD
PROP CL

L Ctr

SPORTS FIELD LA

LANGLEY CL

Red Hill

Croft Rd

Watery Gate La

Sandpit Cotts

Croft La

Thurlaston Brook

CHENEY CT 1
EUNICE AVE 2

MILL DR
VAN DR
LODGE CL

CREWE END

MAIN ST

Huncote Com Prim Sch

CRITCHLOW

DENHAM LA

HOBILL CL
BENNETT RISE

COOPER CL

Huncote

WOODSIDE CL

BLAKENHALL CL

MARIGOLD WAY
BROOK RD
HARDWICKE RD
TIVERTON

Mill

PH

BROOK ST

ST JAMES CT

DUNCAN LA
SCHOOL LA
PRITCHLEY CL

THE GREEN
MARBOROUGH RD

ROBOTHAM CL

Liby

Stone Quarry

THORNBOROUGH CL

7

97

Thurlaston La

Croft Hill Rd

CAREY RD
RATCLIFFE

Huncote Rd

Elms Farm

LE19

River Soar

6

Hill Foot Farm

Croft Hill

Croft Quarry

Flash Farm

B4114

Stanton La

Huncote Rd

LE9

GUTHLAXTON GAP

5

96

Marston Rd

THE GREEN

HILL ST

DOVECOTE RD

Works

Croft Rd

Cemy

PH

Fosse Farm

Church Farm

Station Rd

TERRACE COTTS

Spinney Ct

SHADS CL

WINSTON AVE

CONISTON WAY
WINDERMERE DR
BALA RD

MARION'S WAY

4

HOLLIERS WAY

KENDALL'S AVE
POCHIN ST
ARBOR RD

Clarke's Spinney

Lowlands Farm

SALISBURY AVE

PETERSFIELD

PO

Fosse House

3

Sewage Works

SPARKENHOE
SOPERS RD
BROUGHTON RD

BRADLEY RD
SCHOOL CL
BROOKS AVE

Croft

Depot

Three Boundary Farm

COVENTRY RD

95

Croft CE Prim Sch

Croft Lodge Farm

Poplars Farm

Ireland House Barn

Paradise Spinney

Sewage Works

Lodge Farm

2

Sopers Bridge

River Soar

Port Hill Farm

Sutton Hill Farm

Highland Farm

1

B581

Sopers Bridge Farm

Fossefield Farm

LEICESTER RD

Messenger's Barn Farm

Sutton Fields Farm

BROUGHTON RD   B581

B4114

Sutton Hill Bridge

Sutton Farm

Walton Lodge Farm

94

50   A   B   51   C   D   52   E   F

A   B   C   D   E   F

LE2

LE18

Blaby

Countesthorpe

LE8

Grand Union Canal

River Sence

Mill Lane Farm

Mill La

Highfields Farm

Blaby Mill

Blaby Hill

Port Hill

Rose Farm

Lodge Farm

Keepers Farm

Crow Mill Bridge

Hospital La

Hall Farm

Cemy

Long Wlk

Thistly Meadow Prim Sch

Stokes CE Prim Sch

Liby

Blaby By-Pass

Lutterworth Rd

A426

B582

Enderby Rd

The Crestway

Willow Farm

Glebe Farm

Beeches Farm

Leysland High Sch

Countesthorpe Com Coll

Hill Farm

Glebe Farm

Stult Bridge

Springwell La

Archway Cottage

Whetstone Brook

Whetstone Gorse

Lilac Cottage

The Bungalow

Bambury La

Willoughby Rd

Westdale Farm

Hill La

Liby

Sch

CH

PH

1 WARNER CL
2 HARRISON CL
3 KINDER CL
4 CHARLES WAY

1 SIMPSON CL
2 KENNY CL

1 CURTIS CL
2 JOHNSON CL
3 HERBERT CL
4 EARLE SMITH CL
5 BUXTON CL

1 CROSSWAYS HO
2 JOHN'S CT
3 PARK HOUSE CT
4 CHURCH WLK

1 NORTHFIELD CL
2 THE GREEN
3 CHAPEL ST
4 MANOR CT

RAILWAY ST 1
COUNTESTHORPE RD 2

BLADEN CL 1
LEOPOLD CL 2

THE SQUARE 1
THE BANK 2

8   7   97   6   5   96   4   3   95   2   1   94

56   57   58

A   B   C   D   E   F

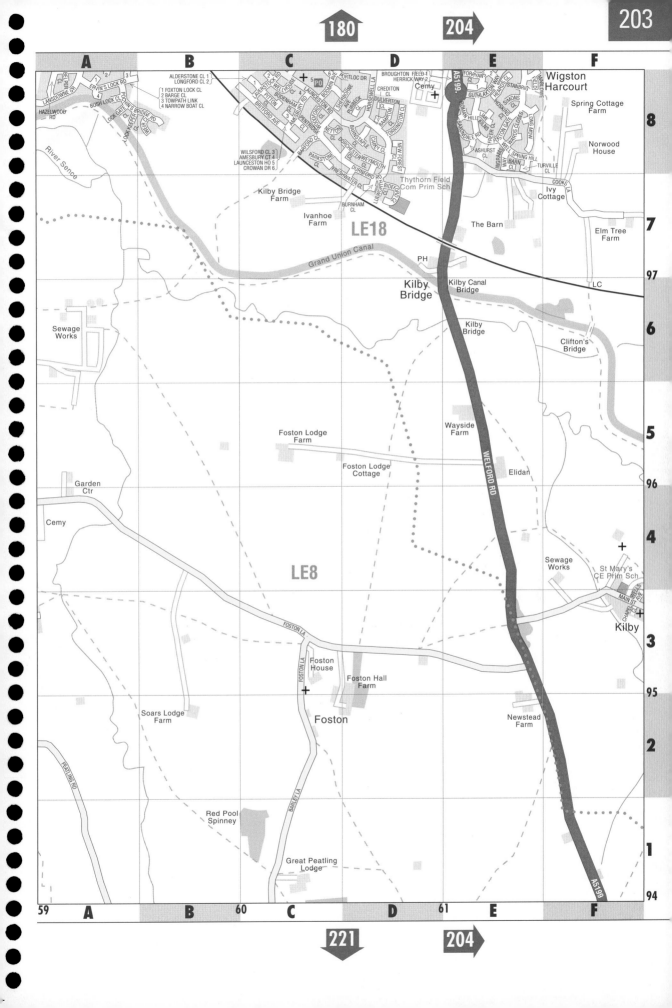

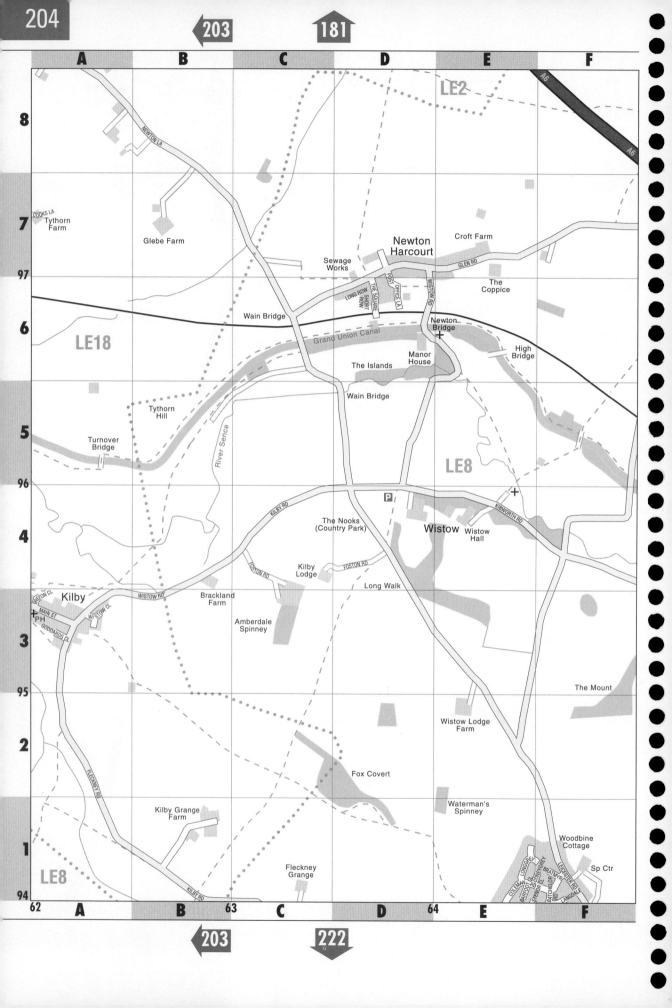

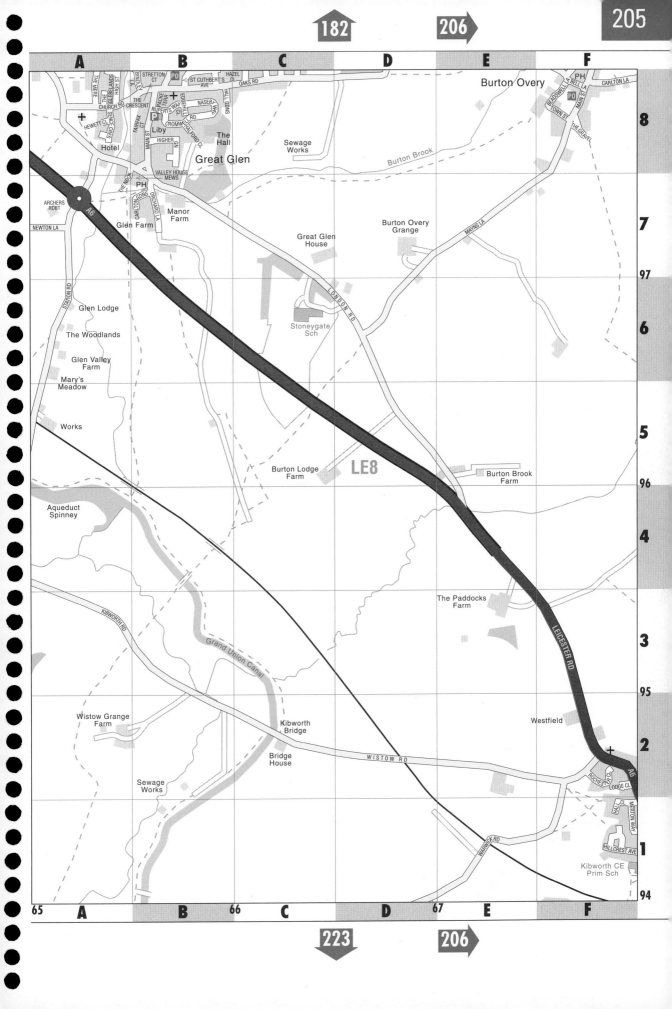

A B C D E F

8

Burton Overy

THE MERE
HIGH ST
GLEBELANDS
CHURCH RD
HEWETT CL
SPENCE CRES
BINDLEY
THE CRESCENT
PACKE TERR
STRETTON CT
ST CUTHBERT'S AVE
HAZEL CL
OAKS RD
HALL GDNS
NASEBY WAY
EDGEHILL RD
RUPERTS WAY
CROMWELL CL
HALFORD CL
BEARSWELL LA
BELL LA
CARLTON LA
TOWN ST
MAIN ST
THE GRAVEL
PH
PO

Hotel
Liby
THE HALL
Great Glen
Sewage Works
Burton Brook
HIGHER
VALLEY HOUSE MEWS

THE NOOK
PH
CARLTON GDNS
ORCHARD LA
Manor Farm
Glen Farm
ARCHERS RDBT
A6

NEWTON LA
STATION RD
Great Glen House
Burton Overy Grange
MAYNS LA

7

97

Glen Lodge
The Woodlands
LONDON RD
Stoneygate Sch

6

Glen Valley Farm
Mary's Meadow

Works

5

Aqueduct Spinney
Burton Lodge Farm
LE8
Burton Brook Farm

96

4

KIBWORTH RD
Grand Union Canal
The Paddocks Farm

3

LEICESTER RD

95

Wistow Grange Farm
Kibworth Bridge
Westfield

Bridge House
WISTOW RD
A6
ROCHESTER CL
LODGE CL
HALL CL
MERTON WAY

2

Sewage Works
WARWICK RD
HILLCREST AVE

1

Kibworth CE Prim Sch

94

65 A B 66 C D 67 E F

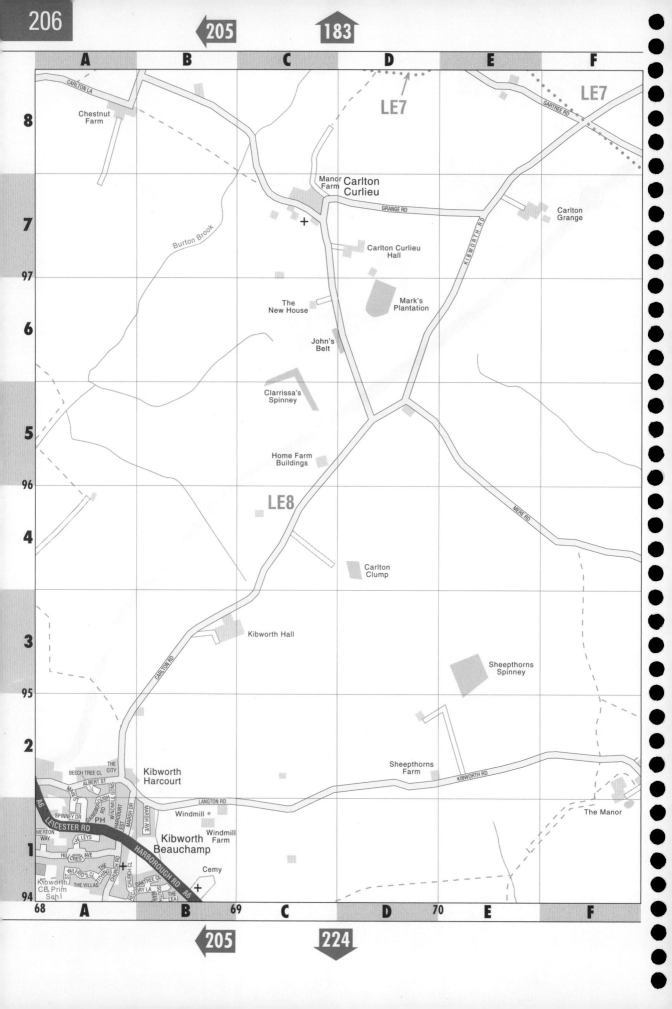

205
183

A B C D E F

8

7

97

6

5

96

4

3

95

2

1

94

CARLTON LA

Chestnut Farm

LE7

GARTREE RD

LE7

Manor Farm

Carlton Curlieu

GRANGE RD

Carlton Grange

Burton Brook

Carlton Curlieu Hall

KIBWORTH RD

The New House

Mark's Plantation

John's Belt

Clarrissa's Spinney

Home Farm Buildings

LE8

MERE RD

Carlton Clump

Kibworth Hall

CARLTON RD

Sheepthorns Spinney

Sheepthorns Farm

KIBWORTH RD

Kibworth Harcourt

THE CITY

BEECH TREE CL

ALBERT ST

MAIN ST

SPINNEY DR

GAINSBOROUGH RD

WINDMILL GDNS

HARBOROUGH RD EST

MARSH DR

MARSH AVE

LANGTON RD

Windmill

Windmill Farm

The Manor

A6

LEICESTER RD

PH

MERTON WAY

THE LEYS

HILL CREST AVE

Kibworth Beauchamp

Cemy

ST WILFRID'S CL

THE TITHINGS

THE CHURCH RD

CHURCH CL

RECTORY LA

OAKTREE CL

SOUTH WAY

THE LEA

HARBOROUGH RD A6

Kibworth CE Prim Schl

THE VILLAS

68 A B 69 C D 70 E F

205
224

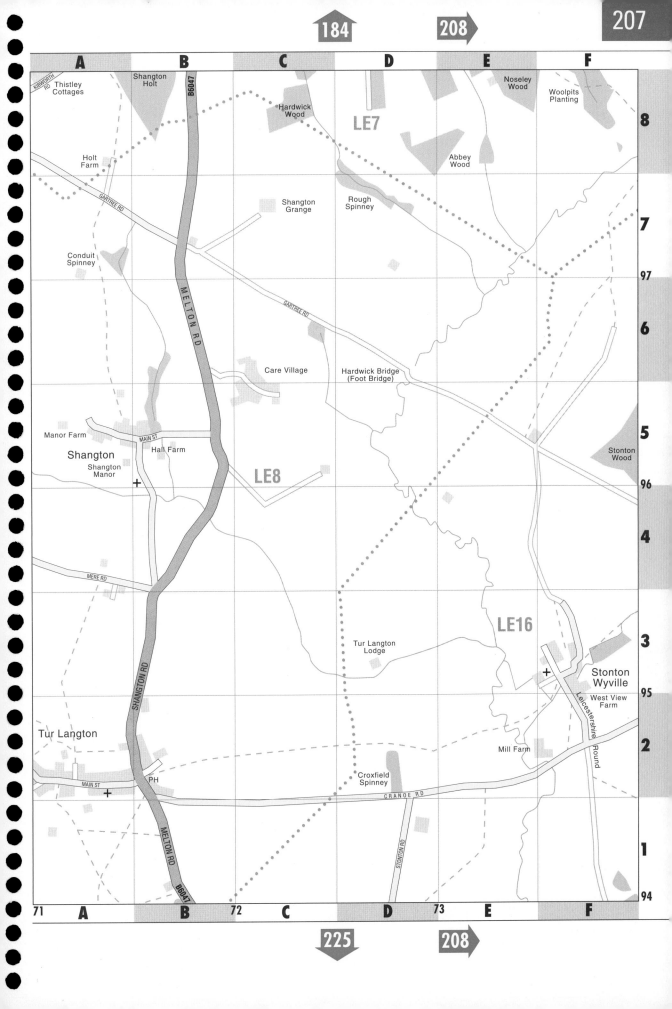

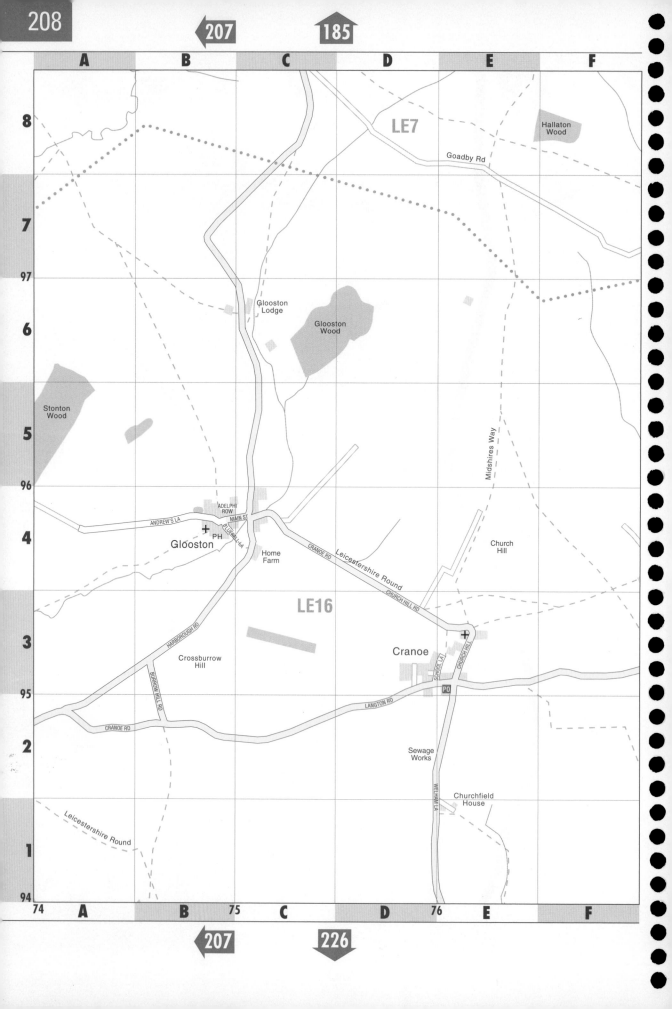

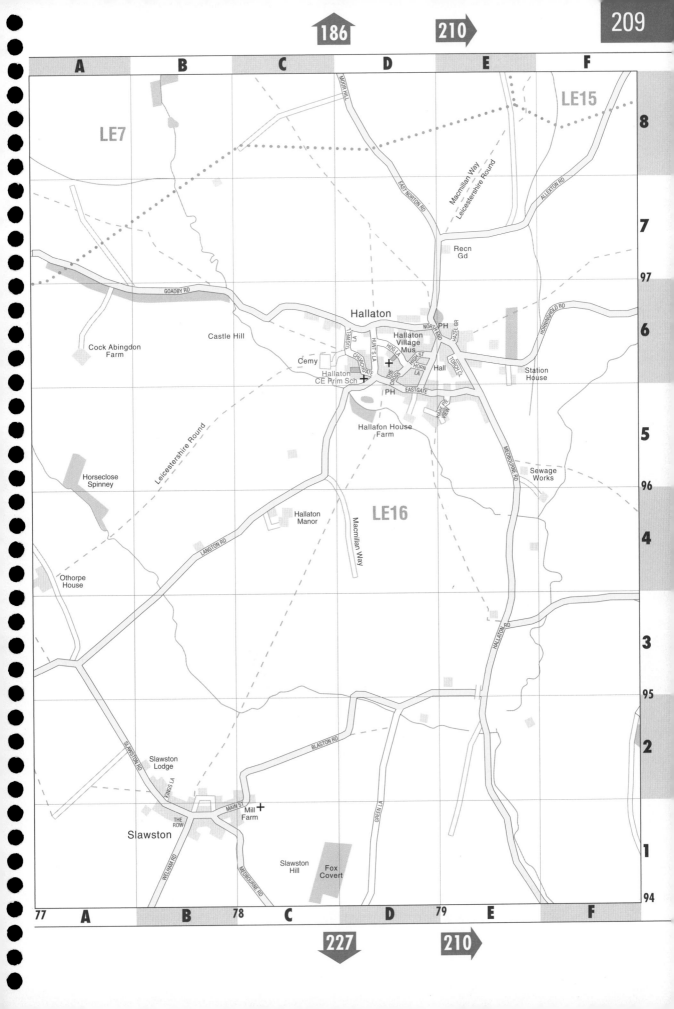

186

210

LE15

LE7

8

7

97

Macmillan Way
Leicestershire Round

EAST NORTON RD

ALLEXTON RD

MOOR HILL

Recn
Gd

6

Hallaton

Castle Hill

HORNINGHOLD RD

Cemy

Hallaton
Village
Mus

Hallaton
CE Prim Sch

NORTH END

PH

HAZEL GR

TUGWELL LA

HUNT'S LA

CHURCHGATE

THE CROSS

HOG LA

HIGH ST

THORN LA

Hall

TORCH CL

Station
House

PH

EASTGATE

Leicestershire Round

Cock Abingdon
Farm

Hallaton House
Farm

HARE PIE VIEW

5

Horseclose
Spinney

MEDBOURNE RD

Sewage
Works

96

Hallaton
Manor

LE16

LANGTON RD

Macmillan Way

4

Othorpe
House

HALLATON RD

3

95

Slawston
Lodge

BLASTON RD

2

SLAWSTON RD

KINGS LA

GREEN LA

THE ROW

Main St
Mill
Farm

Slawston

1

WELHAM RD

MEDBOURNE RD

Slawston
Hill

Fox
Covert

94

77

A

B

78

C

D

79

E

F

227

210

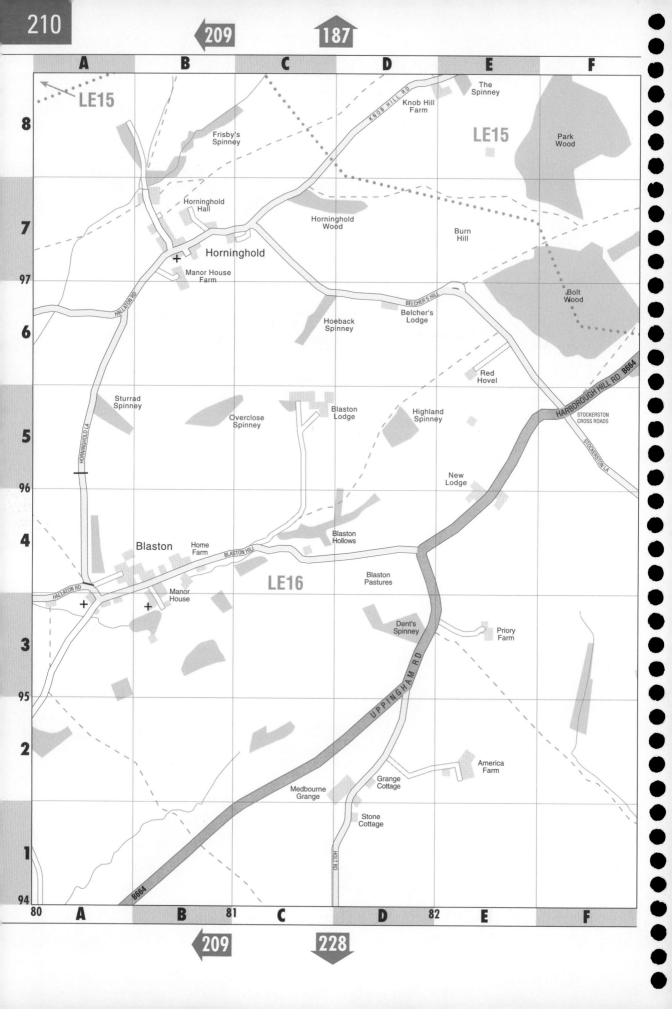

LE15

A B C D E F

8

Frisby's
Spinney

Knob Hill
Farm

The
Spinney

Knob Hill Rd

LE15

Park
Wood

7

Horninghold
Hall

Horninghold
Wood

Burn
Hill

Horninghold

97

Manor House
Farm

Belcher's Hill

Belcher's
Lodge

Bolt
Wood

6

Hallaton Rd

Hoeback
Spinney

Red
Hovel

Harborough Hill Rd   B664

Sturrad
Spinney

Overclose
Spinney

Blaston
Lodge

Highland
Spinney

Stockerston
Cross Roads

5

Horninghold La

New
Lodge

Stockerston La

96

Blaston
Hollows

4

Blaston

Home
Farm

Blaston Hill

LE16

Blaston
Pastures

Hallaton Rd

Manor
House

Dent's
Spinney

Priory
Farm

3

Uppingham Rd

95

America
Farm

2

Grange
Cottage

Medbourne
Grange

Stone
Cottage

Holt Rd

1

94

B664

80   A   B   81   C   D   82   E   F

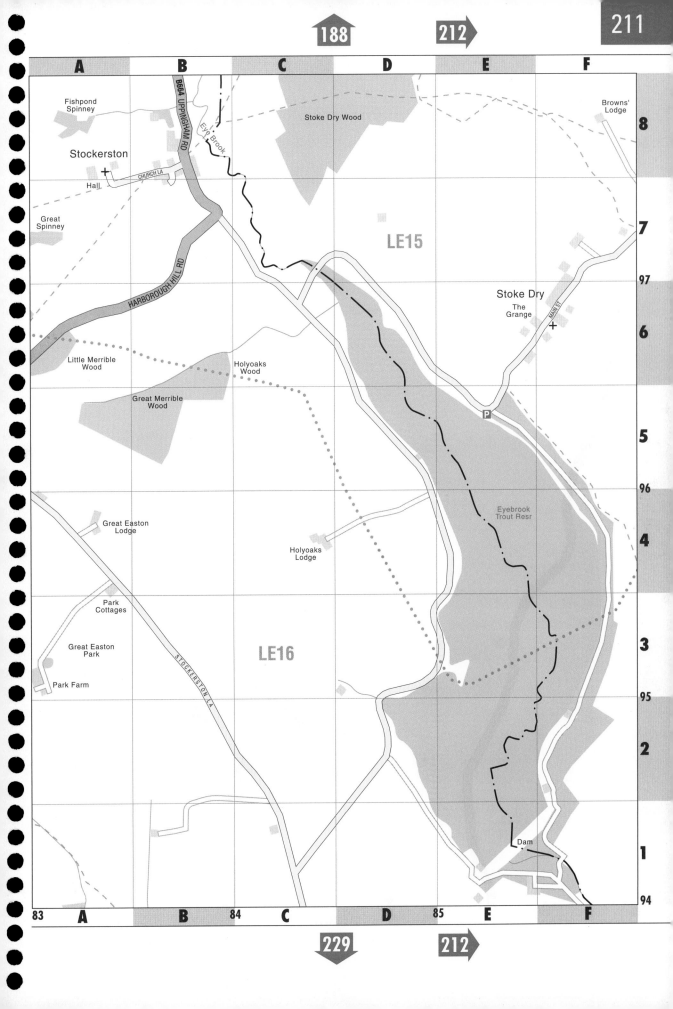

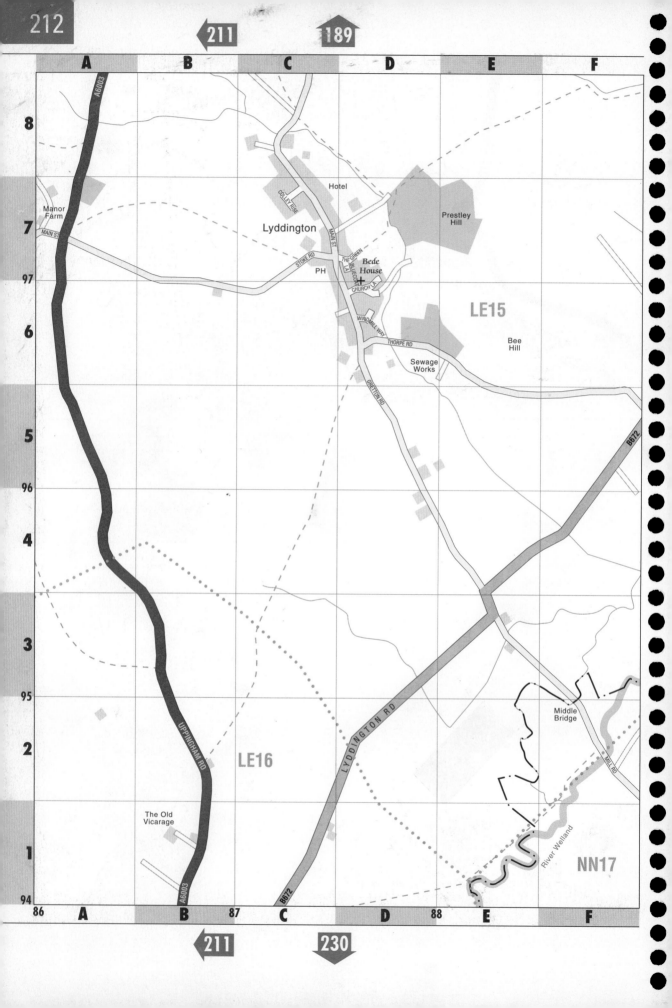

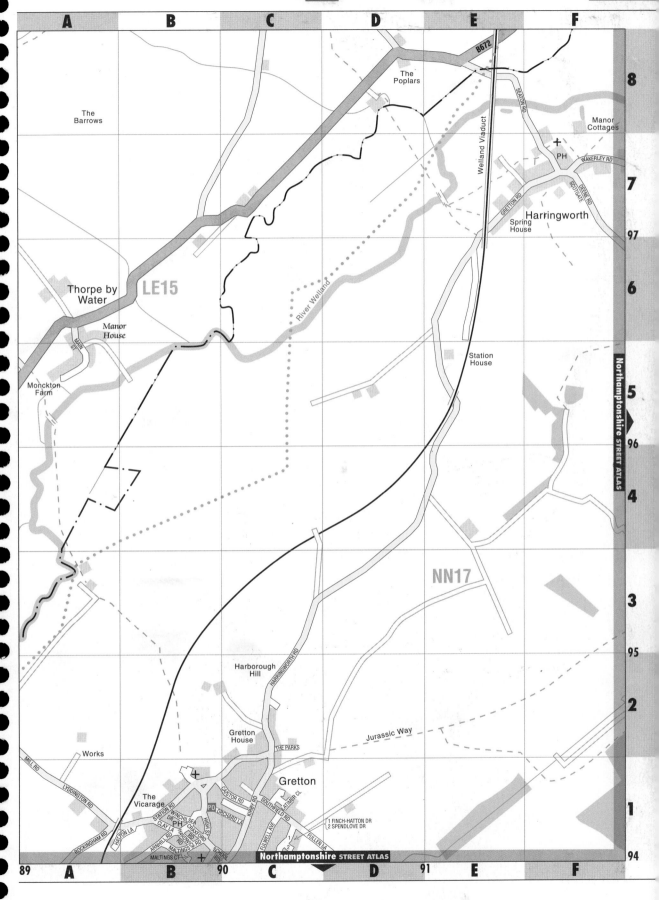

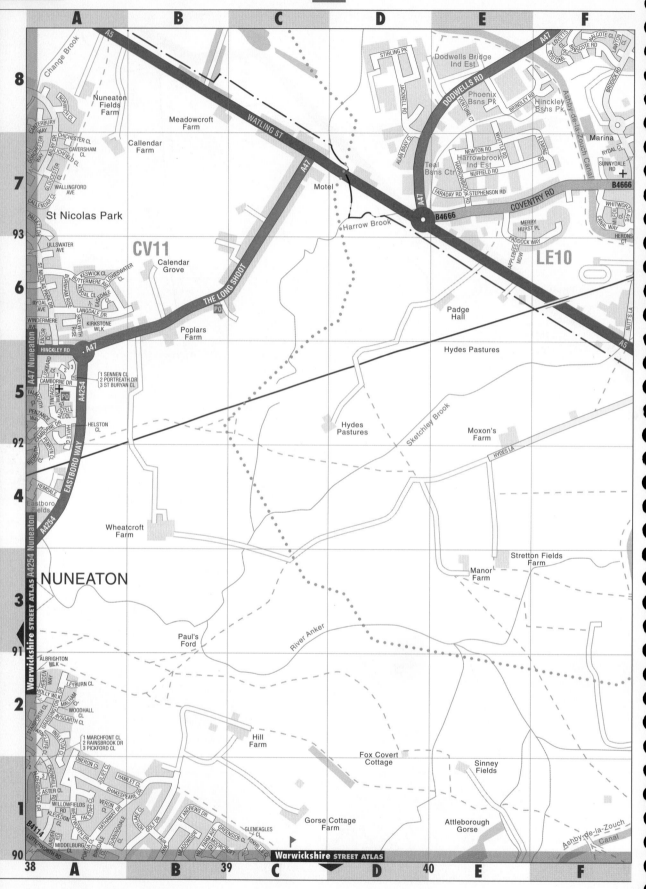

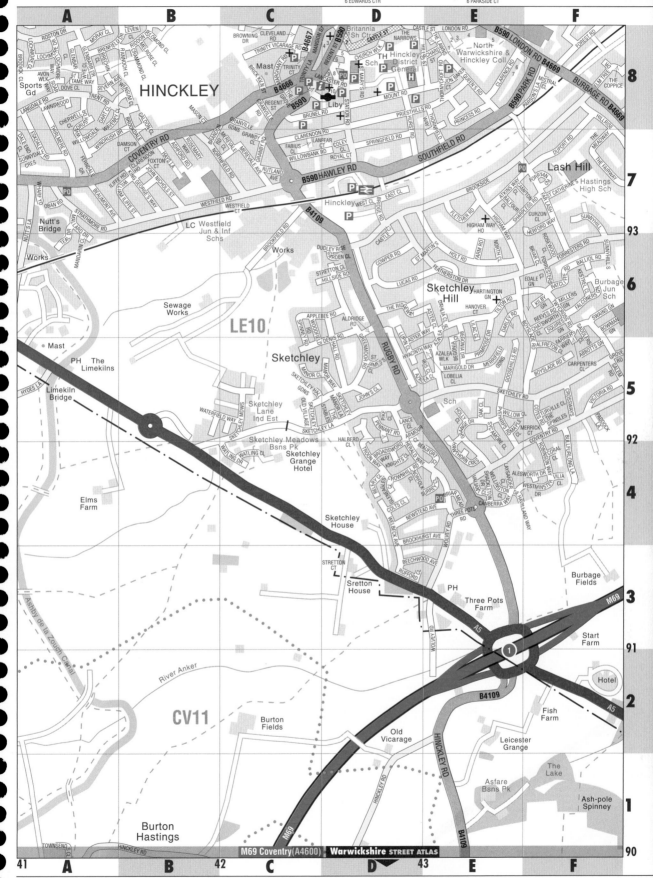

215
198

A   B   C   D   E   F

8

THE COPPICE
Burbage Wood
Aston Firs
Aston Firs
Aston Firs
Freeholt Wood
Brickyard Farm
B4669

WOODGATE RD
HINCKLEY RD
LE9
M69

Threeways Farm
The Homestead

BURBAGE RD
B4669
HILLRISE
SAPCOTE RD
ASTON FLAMVILLE RD

7
MARLBOROUGH CL
THE FAIRWAY
B578
BANK/MDW
WOODBANK
DORCHESTER RD
SHERBORNE RD
MEADOW DR
WINCHESTER DR
WOODLAND AVE
THE MEADOWS
LYNDHURST CL
SEACON CL
CALLSRIUR
ILMINSTER CL
CAMBORNE RD
ASHBURTON CL
Leicestershire Round
HINCKLEY RD

Church Farm

93
FORRESTERS RD
HINCKLEY RD
SCHOOL CL
CROSSLAND ROW
CEDAR CT
ASTON LA

Manor House
MANOR HOUSE CL
Church Farm
Pond Spinney
SHARNFORD RD

6
Sch
GROVE CT
GROVE RD
LOVE LA
NEW RD
Sch
PUGHE'S CL
PILGRIMS GATE
PO
DE LA BERE CRES
WOODS CL
DOCK CL
Burbage
Cottage Farm
Manor House
Aston Flamville

GROSVENOR CRES
WINDSOR CT
WINDSOR ST
STRUTT
FREEMAN'S LA
ORCHARD CL
Liby
CHURCH ST
HORSEPOOL
LIBRARY
LYCHGATE LA
CHURCH CL
FLAMVILLE RD
FOSSE CL
Brickyard Farm
LYCHGATE LA
Oak Farm

5
2 COVENTRY RD
1 SALEM RD
BRITANNIA RD
ORCHARD CL
LODGE CL
Dairy Farm

92
Whitehouse Farm
WORKHOUSE LA
Deepdale Farm

4
Leachmore House
Fields Farm
LE10
Mickle Hill Spinney
Mickle Hill

WORKHOUSE LA
LUTTERWORTH RD

3
M69
Burbage House
Orchard Farm
Mickle Hill Farm

Soar Brook

91
Hogue Hall Spinney

2
A5
Three Corner Spinney
Soar Brook Spinney

Hogue Hall
B4114

1
B578
Lodge Farm
COVENTRY RD
The Shade
Crab-tree Spinney
A5
B4114

90
44   A   B   45   C   D   46   E   F

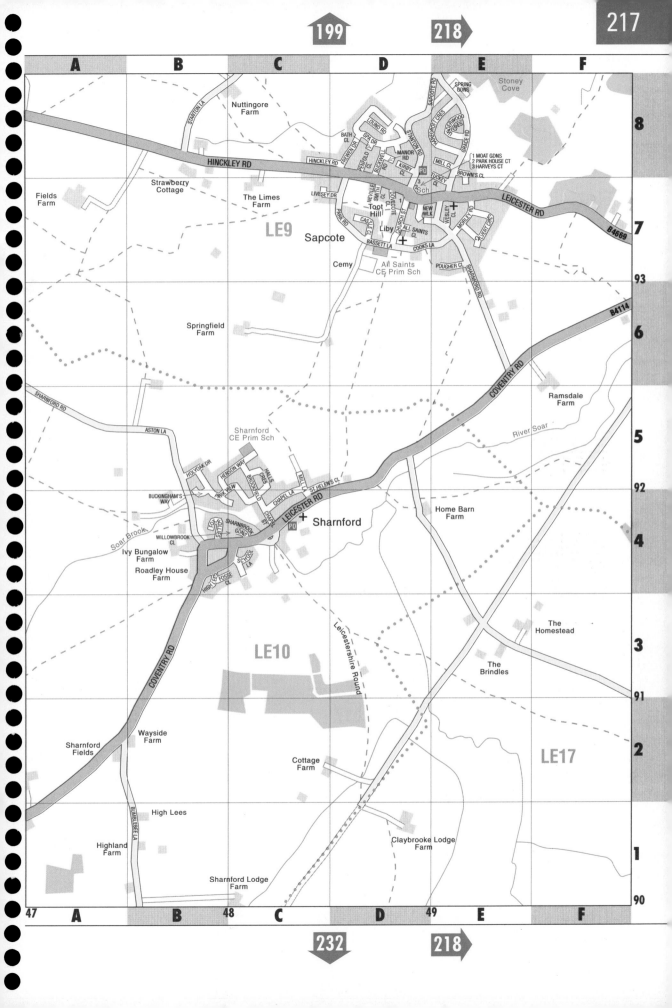

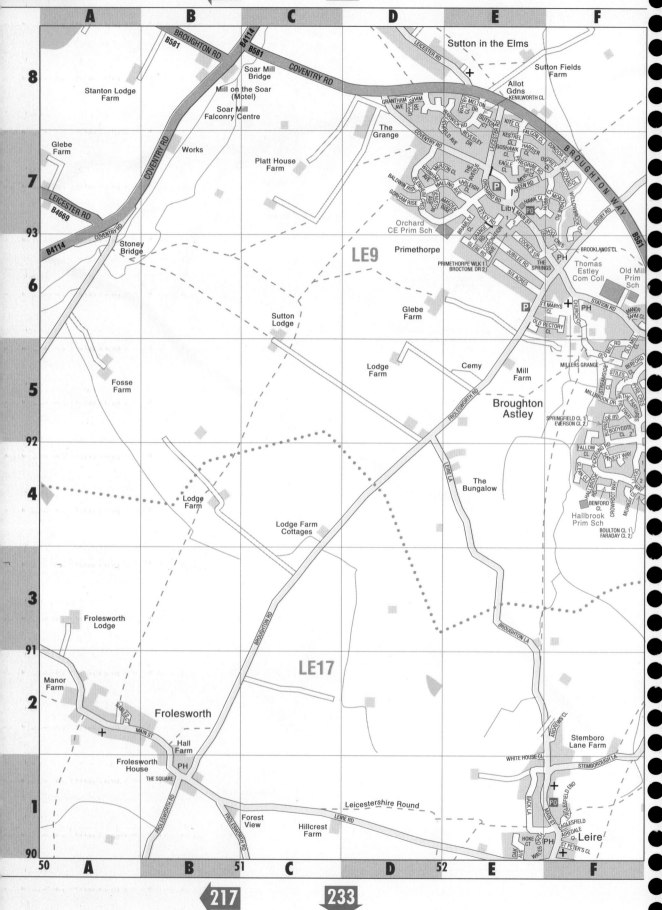

217
200

A B C D E F

8

Stanton Lodge
Farm

Soar Mill
Bridge

Mill on the Soar
(Motel)

Soar Mill
Falconry Centre

Sutton in the Elms

Sutton Fields
Farm

Allot
Gdns

KENILWORTH CL

BROUGHTON RD

B581

B581

COVENTRY RD

B4114

LEICESTER RD

GRANTHAM AVE

UPPINGHAM DR

The
Grange

COVENTRY RD

WHITBY MELTON DR

MELTON
CL

WARWICK RD

SUTTON
CT

BEVERLEY
DR

ENFIELD AVE

LEICESTER RD

KITE CL

FALCON CL

KESTREL
CL

GOSHAWK
CL

HARRIER
CL

OSPREY

PEREGRINE RD

CONDOR CL

BROUGHTON WAY

7

Glebe
Farm

Works

Platt House
Farm

COVENTRY RD

NEWTON CL

WITHINGTON
AVE

MALLING AVE

BALDWIN RISE

BASINGHAM CRES

GORHAM RISE

EARLEIGH
CL

KENISTON
AVE

ORCHARD RD

AMSDEN
RISE

THE
AVENUE

THE
HELIX

EAGLE
CL

MEWS

SEEN RD

BLIZZARD
CL

HAWK
CL

BUZZARD
CL

MONARCH
CL

WILLOWBROOK CL

COSSY RD

93

LEICESTER RD

B4669

B4114

COVENTRY RD

Stoney
Bridge

Orchard
CE Prim Sch

LE9

Primethorpe

BRAMLEY
CL

ESTLEY RD

GRANGE
CL

GLEBE
CL

P

Liby

MAIN ST

PO

SCHOOL
RD

CNES

Primethorpe

PRIMETHORPE WLK 1
BROCTONE DR 2

JUBILEE RD

COOKES
DR

The
Springs

SIX ACRES

BROOKLANDS CL

Thomas
Estley
Com Coll

Old Mill
Prim
Sch

PH

6

Sutton
Lodge

Glebe
Farm

P

ST MARYS
CL

OLD RECTORY
CL

CHURCH CL

OLD RECTORY
CL

PH

STATION RD

MANOR
FARM CL

MILLERS GRANGE

OLD MILL RD

OLD MILL

BERFORD
CL

5

Fosse
Farm

Lodge
Farm

Cemy

Mill
Farm

Broughton
Astley

FROLESWORTH RD

STREAMSIDE

STILES CL

MILLBROOK DR

BYRE CRES

THE PASTURES

THE FIELDS

SPRINGFIELD CL 1
EVERSON CL 2

BODYCOTE
CL 2

92

Lodge
Farm

LEIRE LA

The
Bungalow

FALLOW
CL

PICKERS RD

HARVEST WAY

GLEN LA

MILLBROOK
CL

4

Lodge
Farm

Lodge Farm
Cottages

BROUGHTON RD

HALLBROOK
CL

CROWFOOT WAY

BENFORD
CL

Hallbrook
Prim Sch

MURRAY CL

BOULTON CL 1
FARADAY CL 2

3

Frolesworth
Lodge

BROUGHTON LA

91

Manor
Farm

LE17

2

Frolesworth

GABLES CT

MAIN ST

Hall
Farm

PH

ANDREWS CL

WHITE HOUSE CL

Stemboro
Lane Farm

STEMBOROUGH LA

1

Frolesworth
House

THE SQUARE

FROLESWORTH RD

Forest
View

Hillcrest
Farm

Leicestershire Round

LEIRE RD

BACK LA

MAIN ST

EAGLESFIELD END

EAGLESFIELD

PO

AIREDALE
CL

Leire

WHITE HOUSE CL

HOKE
CT

WYLES CL

PH

ST PETER'S CL

OAK
AVE

90

50 A B 51 C D 52 E F

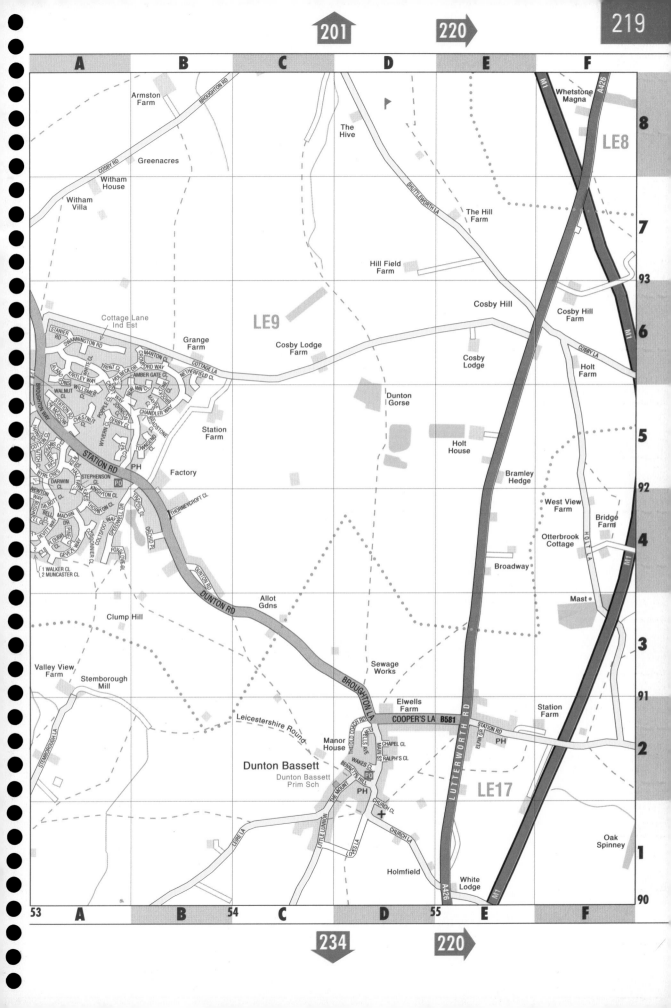

LE8

A B C D E F

8

LE9

7

93

6

Whetstone
Magna

Armston
Farm

BROUGHTON RD

Greenacres

Witham
House

Witham
Villa

COSBY RD

The
Hive

SHUTTLEWORTH LA

The Hill
Farm

Hill Field
Farm

Cosby Hill

Cosby Hill
Farm

Cosby Hill
Farm

COSBY LA

Holt
Farm

Cottage Lane
Ind Est

STANIER RD
SWANNINGTON RD

Grange
Farm

MANTON CL
CROMFORD WAY
COTTAGE LA
NETHERFIELD CL

Cosby Lodge
Farm

Cosby
Lodge

Dunton
Gorse

ALMA CL
CONISTLE
WILLSMER
WALNUT CL
STATION CL

WHITE CL
TRENT CL
MYRTLEY WAY
HOLBECK DR
AMBER GATE CL
NEW INN CL

DERBY CL
JOHNSON WAY
MAYFIELD
CHANDLER WAY
BRADSTONE
TOWNS END CL

Station
Farm

Holt
House

Bramley
Hedge

West View
Farm

Bridge
Farm

5

92

HARRIS CL
THE MEADOW
CHESTNUT CL
WYVERN CL
POPPLE WAY

STATION RD

PH

Factory

THORNEYCROFT CL

Otterbrook
Cottage

HOLT LA

4

NEWTON WAY
BUSHNELL
BELL CL
MACHIN DR
PLOUGH CL
PINE CL
GEVECK WAY

DARWIN CL
STEPHENSON CL
KNIGHTON CL
THORNTON CL
TALBOTT CL
CORDONNIER CL
SPEEDWELL DR
FOXGLOVE CL

TASPOL CL
ORCHID PL

DUNTON RD

Broadway

Mast

1 WALKER CL
2 MUNCASTER CL

Allot
Gdns

Clump Hill

DUNTON RD

3

Valley View
Farm

Stemborough
Mill

Sewage
Works

91

STEMBOROUGH LA

Leicestershire Round

BROUGHTON LA

Elwells
Farm

COOPER'S LA   B581

Station
Farm

Manor
House

THE OLD COACH RD
ELWELLS AVE
WAKES CL
BENNETTS HILL

CHAPEL CL
MAIN ST
ST RALPH'S CL

LUTTERWORTH RD

ELKIN GR
STATION RD
PH

LE17

2

Dunton Bassett

Dunton Bassett
Prim Sch

PO
PH

THE MOUNT
LITTLE LUNNON

LEIRE LA
LOTTS LA
CHURCH CL
CHURCH LA

A426

Oak
Spinney

1

Holmfield

White
Lodge

M1

90

53   A   B   54   C   D   55   E   F

219
202

A   B   C   D   E   F

8

Whetstone
Pastures

Whetstone Gorse
East

Westdale
Farm

Whetstone Gorse
West

Whetstone Brook

WILLOUGHBY RD

BANBURY LA

7

93

LE9

Reatling Lodge
Farm

6

Retreat
Farm

Willoughby
Waterleys

Leicestershire Round

Lodge
Farm

THE
PADDOCKS

MAIN ST

YEW TREE CL.

PH

ORCHARD RD

CHURCH PATH

Cemy

COSBY LA

Manor
Farm

LE8

5

Hill Farm

92

Old Hall

West End
Farm

4

Western
Farm

WILLOUGHBY RD

Leicestershire Round

Nicholls
Farm

3

The Coppice

Willoughby Lodge
Farm

Lodge Farm

GILMORTON LA

91

Gwens
Gorse

2

HUBBARDS
CL

Ashby Magna

OLD FORGE RD

PEVERIL RD

HALL LA

Stresa Glebe
Farm

Manor
Farm

PH

GILMORTON RD

LE17

1

PEATLING RD

Broxtowe
Farm

90

The Retreat

Grange
Farm

Willow
Farm

Orchard
Cottage

56   A   B   57   C   D   58   E   F

219
235

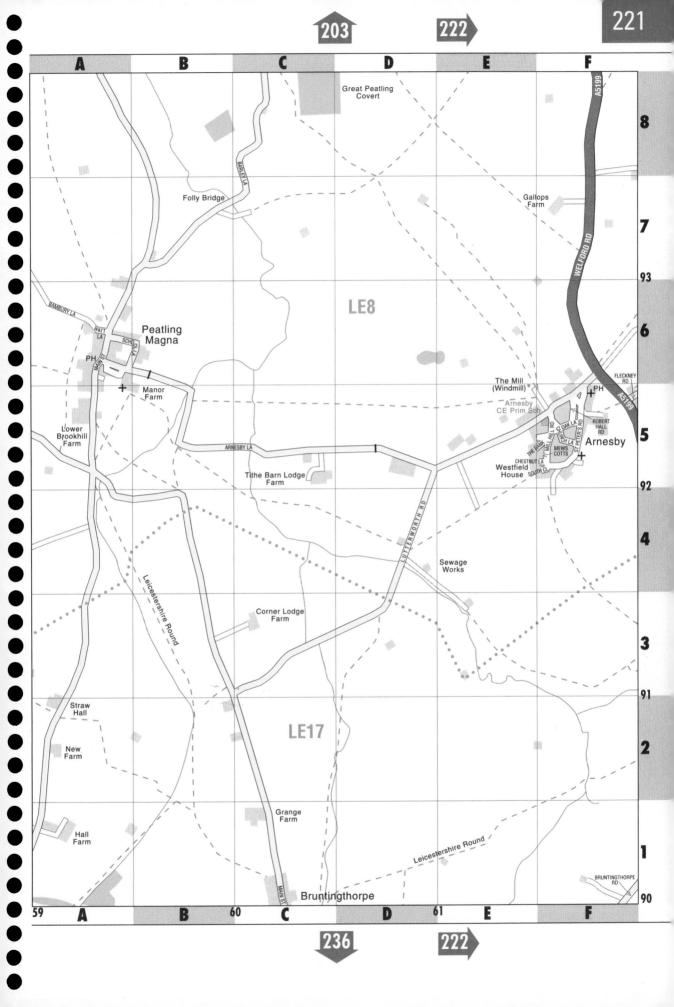

A **B** **C** **D** **E** **F**

LE18

8

Arnesby Lodge Farm

Arnesby Lodge Cottages

KILBY RD

Lyndon Lodge Farm

The Meadows Riding Ctr

PENCLOSE RD
STENOR CL
LANGDALE
Fleckney CE Prim Sch
PARK ST
OLIVE HOS
LEICESTER RD
SHOULBARD
HIGHFIELD ST
MIDDLETONS CL
ALBERT ST
FURNIVAL CL
STORES LA
KIBWORTH RD
PRIEST MDW
CHURCH LA
PO
P
Fleckney
Liby
MAIN ST
LAMPLIGHTERS
BYRON
PH
RICHMOND CL
ORCHARD ST
VICTORIA ST
GLADSTONE ST
SHORT CL
EDNARD RD
ELIZABETH CL
ELIZABETH RD
WESTERN AVE
WITHY
LODGE RD

7

93

6

The Grange

LE8

ARNESBY RD

Fleckney Lodge

5

The White House

Petit-Tor

FLECKNEY RD

Grange Farm

Glebe Farm

Bloxham Farm

92

Brant Hill Farm

The Elms

SHEARSBY RD

4

Leicestershire Round

Rowley Fields Farm

Breach Farm

A5199

3

New Inn Farm

Saddington Lodge Farm

Saddington Brook

91

CHURCH LA
THE SQUARE
BACK LA
WELFORD RD
FENNY LA
PH
WELFORD RD

2

LE17

SADDINGTON RD

MILL LA

Shearsby

BRUNTINGTHORPE RD

1

John Ball Hill

Jane Ball Covert

John Ball Farm

John Ball Covert

Peashill Farm

90

Bath Hotel & Shearsby Spa

A5199

62 **A** 63 **B** **C** 64 **D** **E** **F**

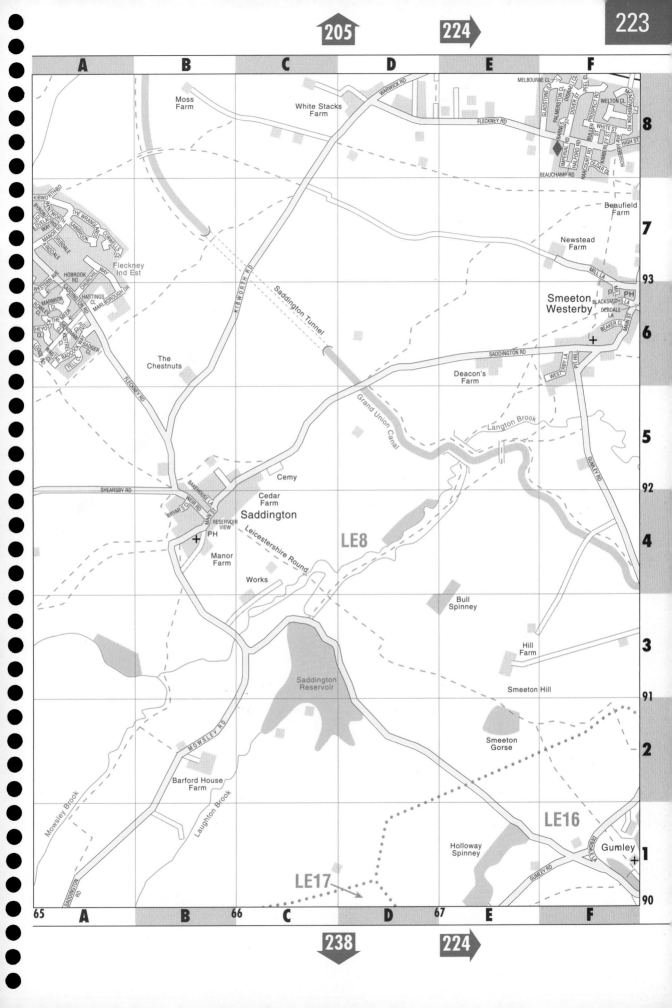

A   B   C   D   E   F

Moss Farm

White Stacks Farm

WARWICK RD

FLECKNEY RD

MELBOURNE CL
GLADSTONE ST
PALMERSTON CL
DISRAELI CL
DOVER ST
PEEL ST
WELTON CL
PROSPECT RD
BULLER RD
WHITE ST
KIMBERLEY ST
McADAMBROOK CL
BARNES
ROSEBERY AVE
HIGH ST
IMPERIAL
HALFORD RD
HARCOURT RD
CEDAR CL
8

Beauchamp Rd

Beaufield Farm

7

Newstead Farm

MILL LA

93

Smeeton Westerby

BLACKSMITHS LA
DEBDALE LA
PH
6

BEAVER LA
MAIN ST
WEST
FERRY LA
PIT HILL

KIBWORTH RD
KENILWORTH
BYRON
LOVELACE RD
MANOR RD
AINSLIE
DREDALE
THE WRANGLANDS
CORWELL'S CL
SAWBROCK
WAY
HOBROOK RD
CHURCHILL
HASTINGS CL
MARLBOROUGH DR
WESTERN AVE
SADDINGTON RD
MARMION
HEYGATE
THE
FOX
KESTREL
BADGER CL
LONGS
THE SADDOCKS
FELL CL

KIBWORTH RD
Fleckney Ind Est

FLECKNEY RD

The Chestnuts

Saddington Tunnel

Deacon's Farm

SADDINGTON RD

Langton Brook

Grand Union Canal

GUMLEY RD

5

SHEARSBY RD

BAKEHOUSE LA

Cemy

WEIR RD
BRYAR'S CL
MAIN ST
RESERVOIR VIEW
PH

Cedar Farm

Saddington

92

LE8

4

Manor Farm

Leicestershire Round

Works

Bull Spinney

Hill Farm

3

Smeeton Hill

91

Saddington Reservoir

MOWSLEY RD

Smeeton Gorse

2

Barford House Farm

Mowsley Brook

Laughton Brook

LE16

Holloway Spinney

GUMLEY RD

Gumley

1

SADDINGTON RD

LE17

90

65   66   67

A   B   C   D   E   F

223
206

A B C D E F

8

LE16

7

Kibworth
Beauchamp

93

LE8

6

Shooting
Gd

92

5

4

3

2

1

90

68 A B 69 C D 70 E F

THE
OLD GRAMMAR
SCHOOL

HOLLOW
STATION

THE LEA

ELLIOT CL

PAGET CT

SCHOOL WLK

CHURCH
RD

RECTORY
LA

RONCHI
CL

LARKSWOOD

BROOKFIELD WAY

A6

MILESTONE
CL

High
Sch

P

PAGET ST

High ST

STATION ST

STUART ST

THE
BANK

MARRIOTT DR

Liby

SMEETON CT

MORRISON
CT

THAME CL

NEW RD

DRIVE

LINKS RD

ASHFIELD
RD

FAIRWAY

FAIRWAY

BIRDIE CL

BRAYMISH CL

WEIR RD

THE PADDOCK

GREENWAY

SPRINGFIELD CL

SMEETON RD

SPRINGFIELD RD

GR MARY CL

WENTWORTH CL

Kibworth
High Sch

CH

Sewage
Works

WEST LANGTON RD

Springfield
Farm

MAIN ST

SPRINGFIELD LA

Masons
Farm

DEBDALE LA

Debdale La

Grange
Farm

HARBOROUGH RD

Beauchamp
Grange

Langton Brook
Plantation

Beauchamp
Farm

A6

Debdale
Wharf

Debdale Wharf
Farm

DEBDALE LA

Grand Union Canal

Towing Path

GUMLEY RD

Debdale
Grange

91

Gumley
Wood

LE16

Fisher's Farm

LANGTON RD

Nursery

NORTH LA

MAIN ST

MIDDLE ST

PARK CL

DALBY'S
LA

GRASE DR

SWINGBRIDGE ST

SWED CRT CL

Schofield
Farm

Foxton

DEBDALE
LA

MAIN ST

Gumley

Sewage
Works

Leicestershire Round

Leicestershire Round

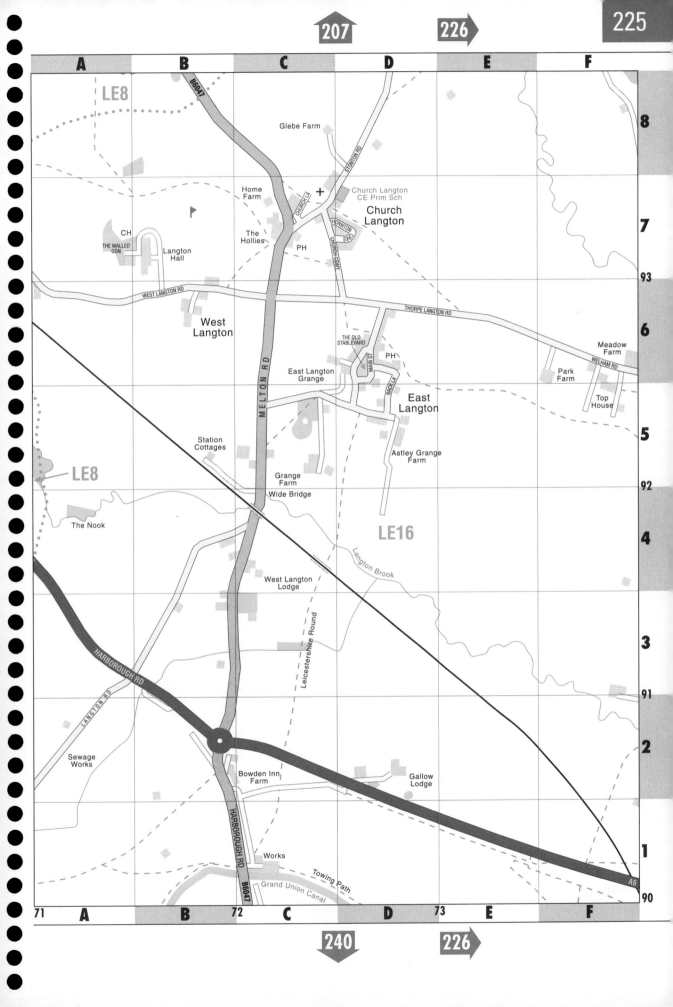

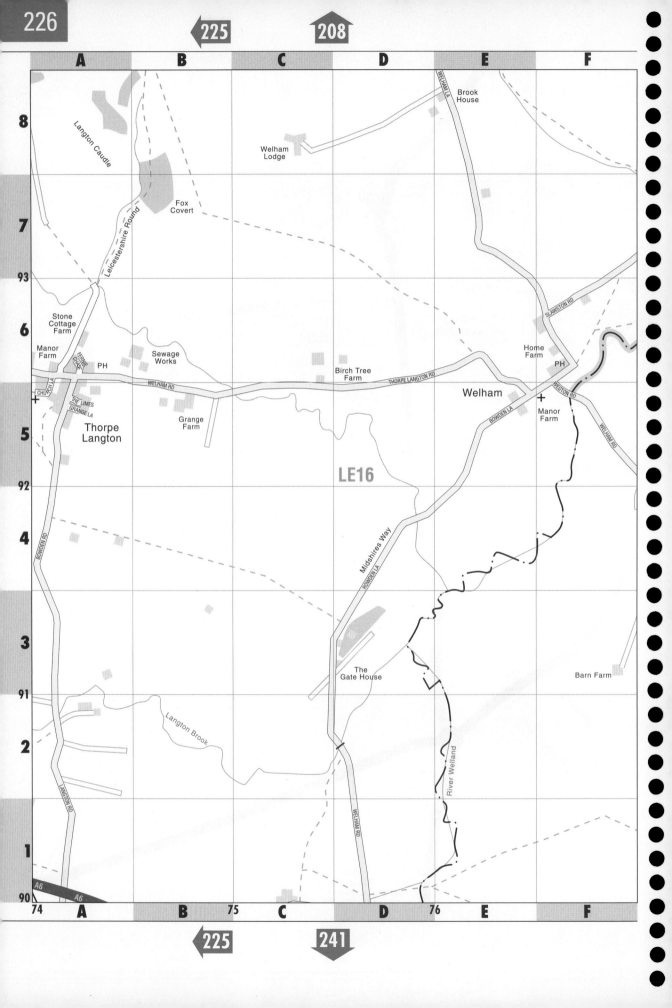

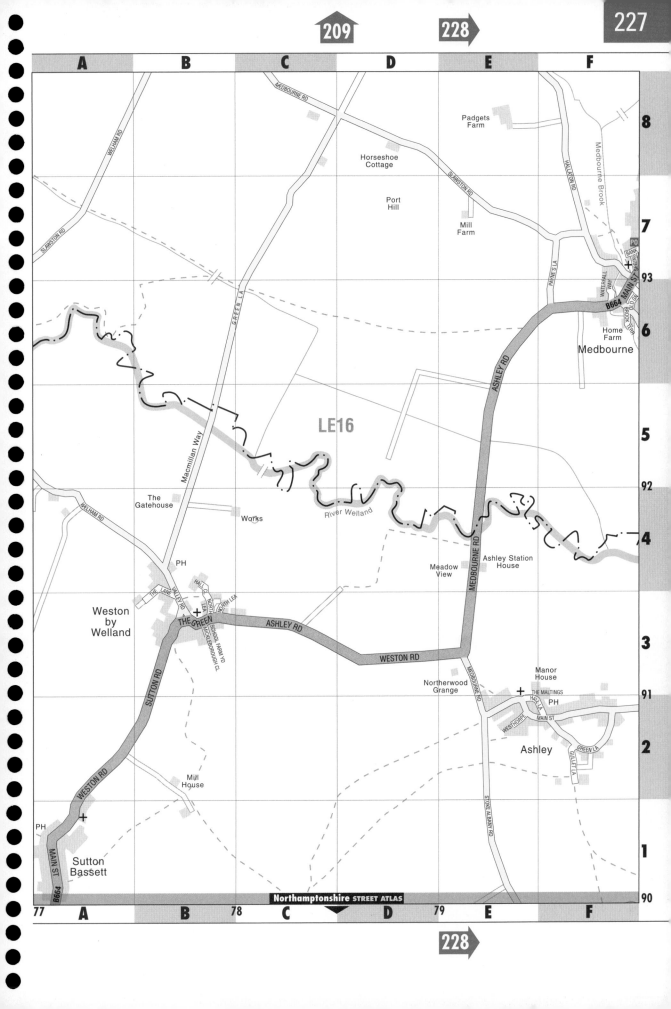

228

A B C D E F

8

UPPINGHAM RD B664

Nevill Holt Farm

Home Farm

Holt Wood

Wignell Hill

Nevill Holt

MARLOW CT

PADDOCK LA

HOLT RD

THE AVENUE

Belvoir Lodge

7

MAIN ST

MANOR RD

Nut Bush

Nevill Holt Quarry (Dis)

DRAYTON RD

Fishpond Spinney

OLD HOLT RD

93

PO

B664

RECTORY LA

P.H.

OLD GN

NEVILL HOLT RD

6

SPRING TERR

5

Works

DRAYTON RD

Upper Leighs

Watson's Gorse

Stoke's Buildings

Medbourne Brook

92

Brookfield House Farm

LE16

MEDBOURNE RD

4

7

River Welland

Holt Crossing

3

MIDDLETON RD

ASHLEY RD

91

WIRE LA

2

1

90

80 A B 81 C D 82 E F

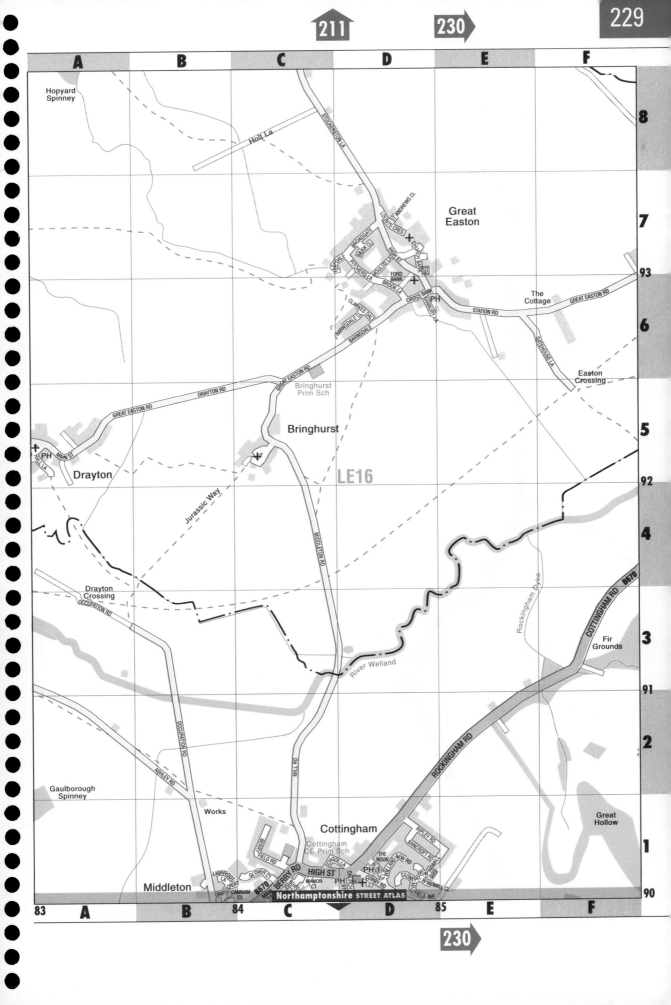

A B C D E F

8

Hopyard
Spinney

Holt La

STOCKERSTON LA

ST ANDREWS CL

Great
Easton

7

BROADGATE

LOUNTS CRES

MASK CT

93

PITCHERS LA

MOULDS LANE

HIGH ST

CHURCH BANK

CHURCH RD

FORD
BANK

BROOK LA

CROSS BANK

BARNSDALE CT

CLARKES DALE

BARNSDALE

BARNSDALE

BANBURY LA

PH

The
Cottage

GREAT EASTON RD

STATION RD

GATEHOUSE LA

6

DRAYTON RD

GREAT EASTON RD

GREAT EASTON RD

Bringhurst
Prim Sch

Easton
Crossing

GREAT EASTON RD

MAIN ST

Bringhurst

5

PH

HALL LA

Drayton

LE16

92

Jurassic Way

MIDDLETON RD

Rockingham Dyke

4

Drayton
Crossing

OCCUPATION RD

COTTINGHAM RD

B670

Fir
Grounds

3

River Welland

91

OCCUPATION RD

ROCKINGHAM RD

2

ASHLEY RD

Gaulborough
Spinney

Works

Great
Hollow

RIPLEY RD

1

Cottingham

BANCROFT RD

BERRY FIELD RD

Cottingham
CE Prim Sch

SCHOOL LA

THE
NOOK

VIEW RD

GLOVER CT

BERRY RD

B670

HIGH ST

MANOR
CT

CORBY RD

PH

WELLAND

STONEY LA

WINDMILL
RISE

WINDMILL
RD

90

LIGHTFOOT
LA

OAK'S SPUR

CANNAM
CL

MAIN ST

CHURCH ST

PH

PO

STONEY LA

FIELD AVE

Middleton

83 A B 84 C D 85 E F

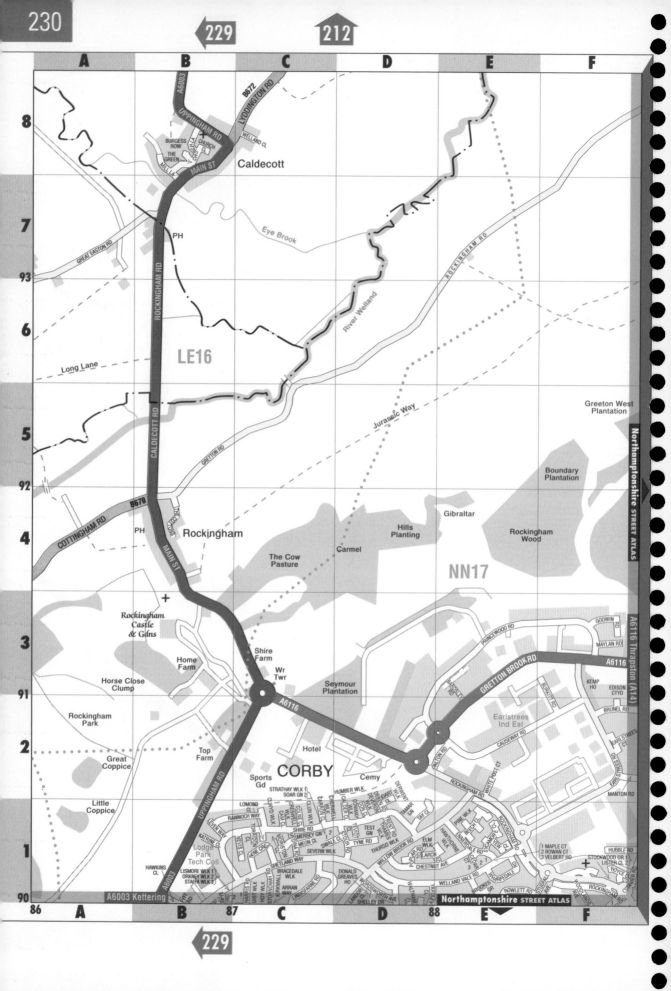

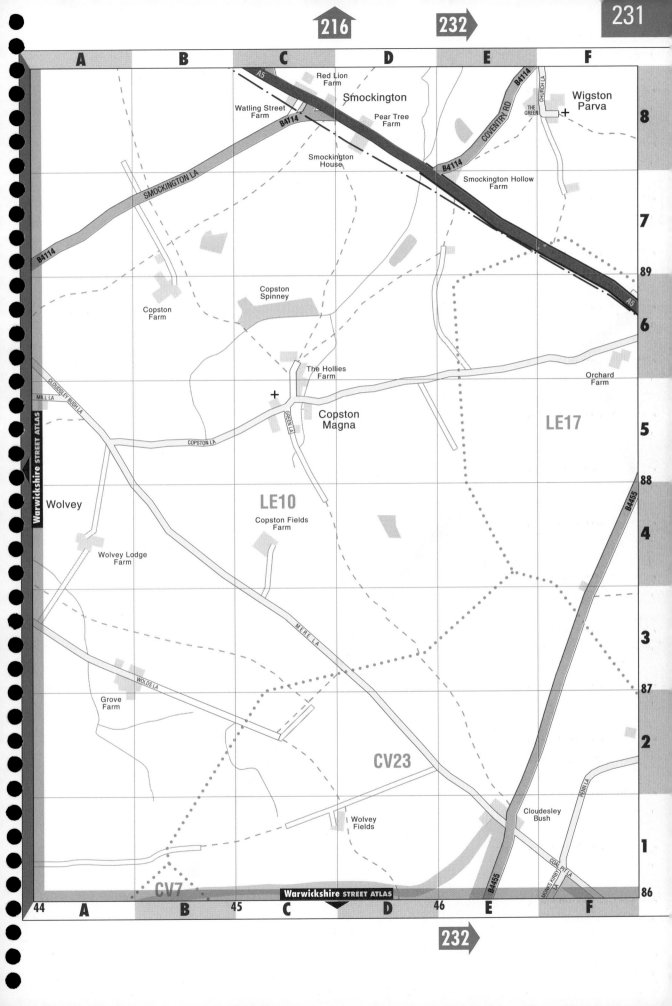

A B C D E F

8

Bumblebee

Sharnford Lodge Farm

Hill Farm

Frolesworth Hill

LE10

Bumble-bee Farm

7

Lodge Farm

89

Manor Farm

MANOR RD

MANOR CL

Gables Farm

FROLESWORTH LA

Mill

High Cross

Victoria Farm

HIGH CROSS RD

Mount Pleasant Cottage

PH

2

COSSEWAY GDNS

WOODLAND AVE

Claybrooke Magna

6

A5

LAUREL FIELDS 1
THE PADDOCK 2

OLD CHAPEL WLK

BACK LA

Sewage Works

B4455

High Cross Grange

Saw Mill

ROMAN CL

BELL ST

HOLLY TREE WLK

Claybrooke Farm

FOSSE WAY

Leicestershire Round

LE17

MAIN RD

GREENDOCK CL

5

B4455

88

WESTERN DR

Claybrooke Hall

CLAYBROOKE CT

Claybrooke Prim Sch

AVENUE VILLAS

Watling House

Claybrooke Parva

+

4

Alma House

Cemy

Wibtoft

Glebe Farm

Manor Farm

WOODWAY LA

Woodway Lodge

Laurel Bank

3

GREEN LA

87

PENN LA

Lodge Farm

2

White House Farm

CV23

A5

1

Tithe Platts Farm

86

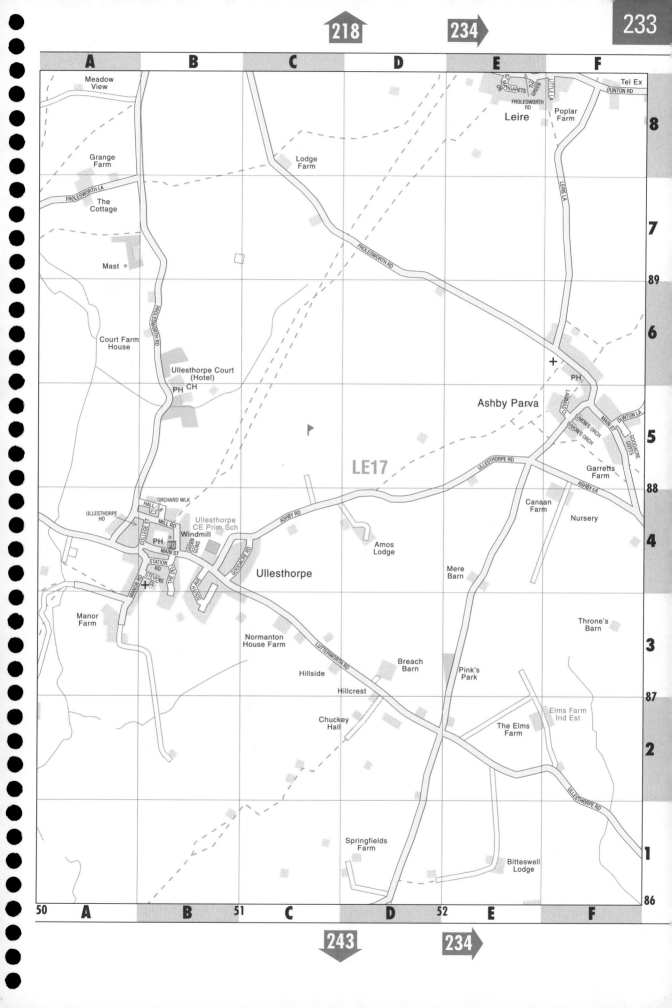

218
234
243
234

A B C D E F

Meadow View

Leire

Tel Ex
DUNTON RD

ST. MARGARETS DR
THE GREEN
LITTLE LA

FROLESWORTH RD

Poplar Farm

8

Grange Farm

Lodge Farm

FROLESWORTH LA

The Cottage

7

Mast

FROLESWORTH RD

89

LEIRE LA

6

Court Farm House

+

PH

Ullesthorpe Court (Hotel)

PH CH

Ashby Parva

LAMMAS CL
SIMON'S ORCH
SIMON'S ORCH

MAIN ST
DUNTON LA

GOODACRE COTTS

5

LE17

ULLESTHORPE RD

Garretts Farm

ASHBY LA

88

HALL
ORCHARD WLK

ULLESTHORPE HO

MILL RD

Ullesthorpe CE Prim. Sch

Windmill

ASHBY RD

Canaan Farm

Nursery

COLLEGE ST

PH PO

MAIN ST

GREEN GDNS

GOODACRE RD

Amos Lodge

4

STATION RD

THE DELL

STEVENS CL

Ullesthorpe

Mere Barn

MANOR RD

+

SOUTH AVE

Throne's Barn

3

Manor Farm

Normanton House Farm

LUTTERWORTH RD

Breach Barn

Pink's Park

87

Hillside

Hillcrest

Elms Farm Ind Est

Chuckey Hall

The Elms Farm

2

Springfields Farm

ULLESTHORPE RD

Bitteswell Lodge

1

86

50 A B 51 C 52 D E F

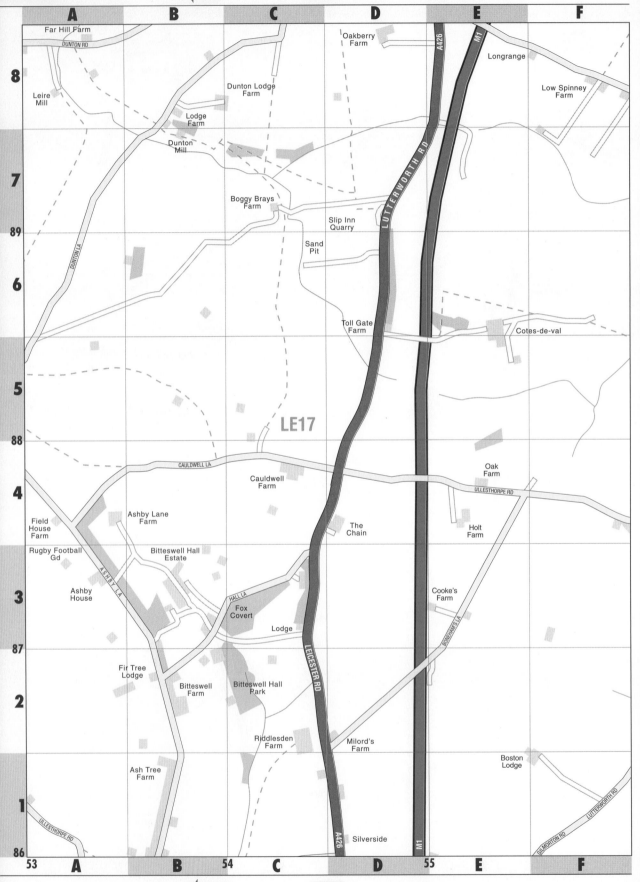

A	B	C	D	E	F

8

Far Hill Farm

Dunton Rd

Oakberry Farm

A426

M1

Longrange

Low Spinney Farm

Leire Mill

Dunton Lodge Farm

Lodge Farm

Dunton Mill

7

LUTTERWORTH RD

89

Boggy Brays Farm

Slip Inn Quarry

Sand Pit

DUNTON LA

6

Toll Gate Farm

Cotes-de-val

5

88

LE17

4

Cauldwell La

Cauldwell Farm

Ullesthorpe Rd

Oak Farm

Field House Farm

Ashby Lane Farm

The Chain

Holt Farm

Rugby Football Gd

Bitteswell Hall Estate

ASHBY LA

Cooke's Farm

3

Ashby House

HALL LA

Fox Covert

Lodge

BONEHAM'S LA

87

Fir Tree Lodge

2

Bitteswell Farm

Bitteswell Hall Park

LEICESTER RD

Boston Lodge

Riddlesden Farm

Milord's Farm

Ash Tree Farm

1

ULLESTHORPE RD

LUTTERWORTH RD

86

A426

Silverside

M1

GILMORTON RD

53	A	B	54	C	D	55	E	F

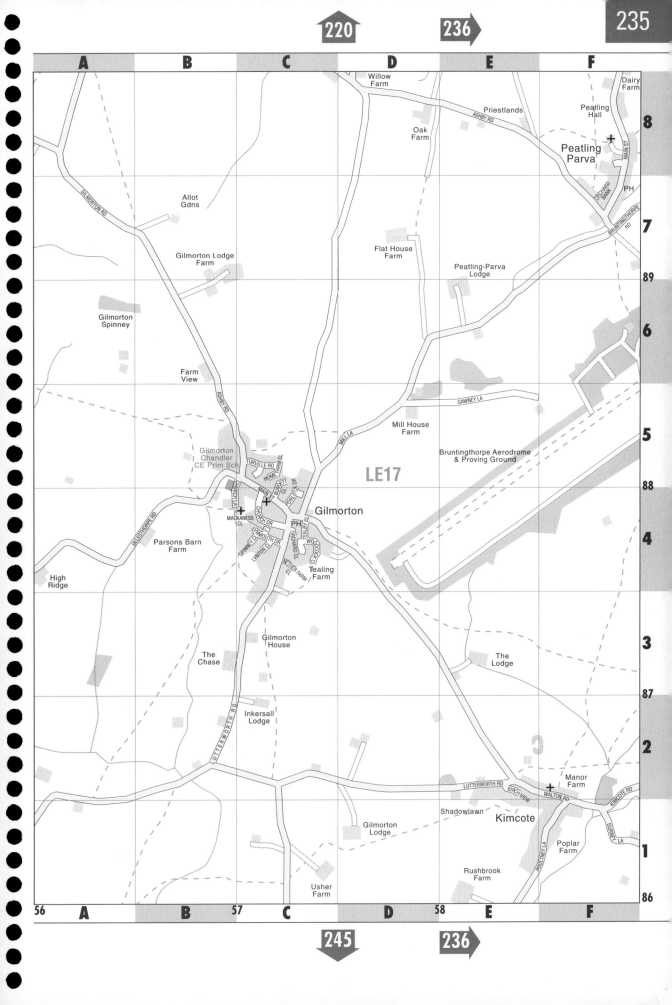

220
236

A B C D E F

8

Willow
Farm

Priestlands

Dairy
Farm

ASHBY RD

Oak
Farm

Peatling
Hall

Peatling
Parva

PH

MAIN ST

GILMORTON RD

Allot
Gdns

ORCHARD BANK

7

Gilmorton Lodge
Farm

Flat House
Farm

Peatling-Parva
Lodge

BRUNTINGTHORPE RD

89

Gilmorton
Spinney

6

Farm
View

GAWNEY LA

Mill House
Farm

5

ASHBY RD

Gilmorton
Chandler
CE Prim Sch

MILL LA

LE17

Bruntingthorpe Aerodrome
& Proving Ground

88

TURVILLE RD

HOME FARM CL

BURDETT CL

PORLOCK DR

Gilmorton

ULLESTHORPE RD

CHURCH LA

MAIN ST

PH

TELBY CL

WOODCOCK CL

4

MACKANESS CL

CHURCH DR

SPINNEY CL

LYMOUTH DR

LYNTON CL

NETHER FARM CL

ORCHARD CL

Parsons Barn
Farm

Tealing
Farm

High
Ridge

Gilmorton
House

The
Chase

The
Lodge

3

87

LUTTERWORTH RD

Inkersall
Lodge

2

LUTTERWORTH RD

BIRCH VIEW

WALTON RD

Manor
Farm

KIMCOTE RD

Shadowlawn

Kimcote

POULTNEY LA

GURNEY LA

Gilmorton
Lodge

Poplar
Farm

1

Rushbrook
Farm

Usher
Farm

86

56 A B 57 C D 58 E F

A B C D E F

8
Manor Ho

CHURCH WK
MAIN ST
LITTLE END
MORRIS CT
PH

Bruntingthorpe

BRUNTINGTHORPE RD

BRUNTINGTHORPE RD

7
Peatling Lodge Farm

BATH LA

Knaptoft House Farm

89

Bruntingthorpe Aerodrome & Proving Ground

Cottage Farm

6
Holt Farm

Holt Farm Cottage

Bruntingthorpe Ind Est

Upper Bruntingthorpe

CHURCHILL DR
PARTRIDGE CL

5
MERE RD

Lockwood Farm

88

LE17

4
Bridgemere Farm

Willowbrook Farm

MOWSLEY LA

Moores Farm

The Lilacs

Holly Tree Farm

3
HIGH ST
AMBION LA
PARK LA

THE CROSS
PO

Walton

87
CHAPEL LA

HALL LA
PO
OLD SCHOOL CL

2
The Bungalow

KIMCOTE RD
Hall

KILWORTH RD

Holt Farm

Grange Farm

BOSWORTH RD

1
Holton Farm

GURNEY LA

Model Farm

Camp Barn Farm

Breach Farm

Walton Holt

86
59 A B 60 C D 61 E F

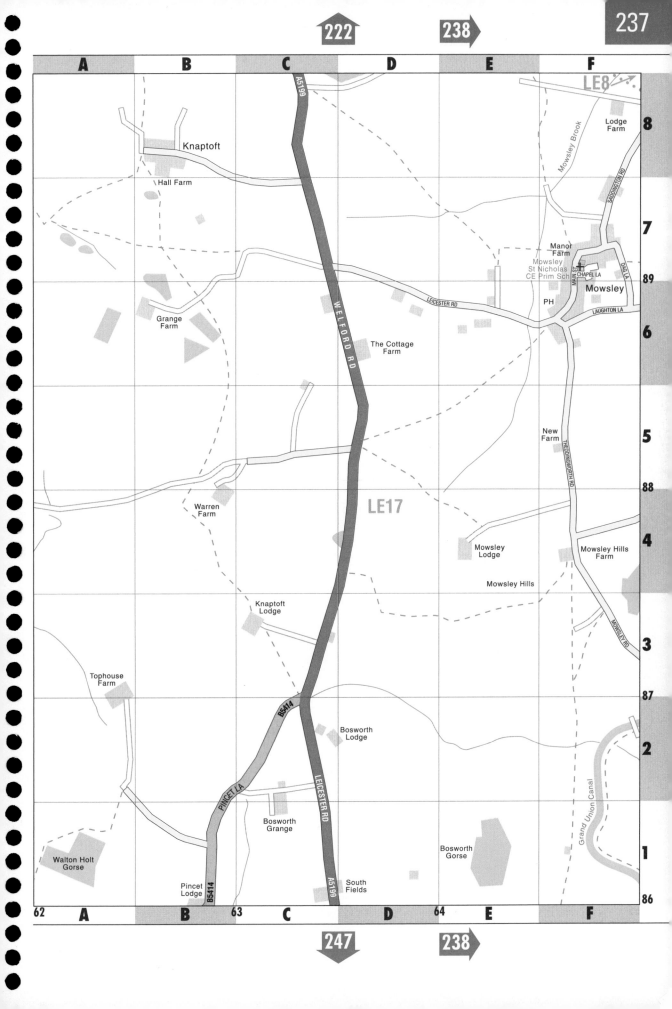

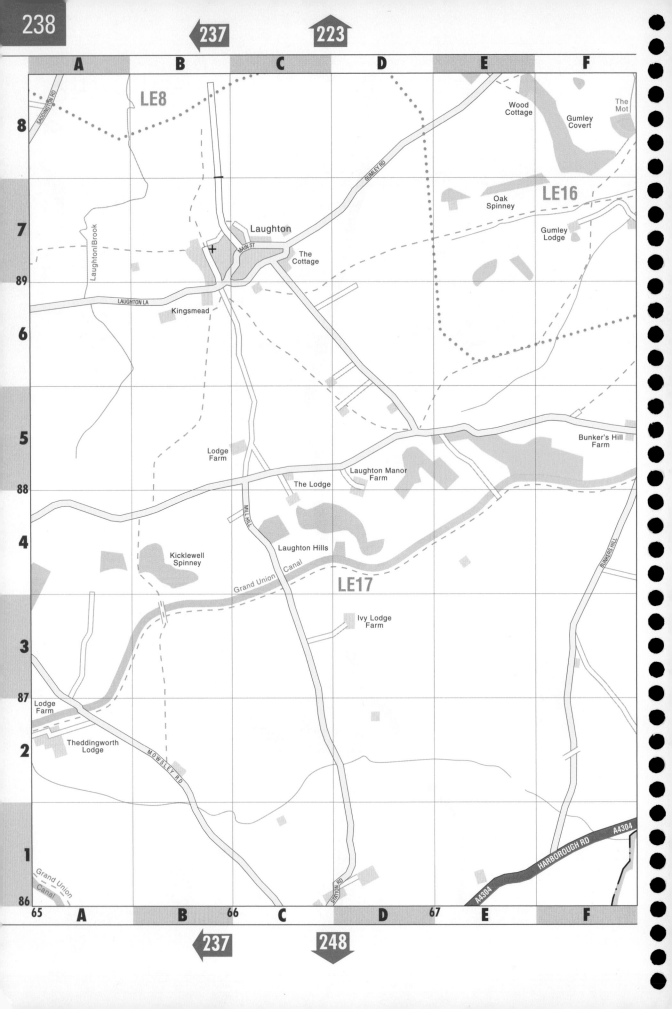

237
223

A B C D E F

LE8

8

Wood
Cottage

Gumley
Covert

The
Mot

SADDINGTON RD

GUMLEY RD

LE16

Oak
Spinney

7

Laughton

Gumley
Lodge

Laughton/Brook

MAIN ST

The
Cottage

89

LAUGHTON LA

Kingsmead

6

5

Bunker's Hill
Farm

Lodge
Farm

88

Laughton Manor
Farm

The Lodge

MILL HILL

4

Kicklewell
Spinney

Laughton Hills

BUNKERS HILL

Grand Union Canal

LE17

Ivy Lodge
Farm

3

87

Lodge
Farm

2

Theddingworth
Lodge

MOWSLEY RD

STATION RD

1

HARBOROUGH RD

A4304

A4304

86

Grand Union
Canal

65 A B 66 C D 67 E F

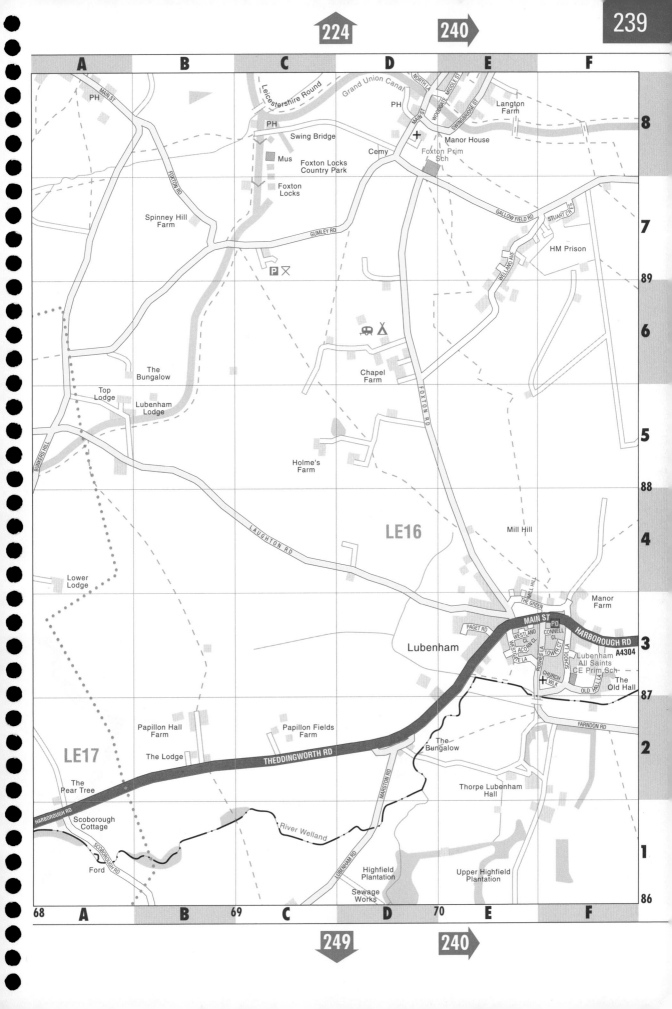

A B C D E F

8
7
89
6
5
88
4
87
2
1
86

MAIN ST
PH

Leicestershire Round
Grand Union Canal
NORTH LA
PH
MAIN ST
WOODGATE
MIDDLE ST
SWINGBRIDGE ST
Langton Farm

Swing Bridge
PH
Mus
Cemy
Foxton Prim Sch
Manor House

FOXTON RD

Foxton Locks Country Park
Foxton Locks

GUMLEY RD

GALLOW FIELD RD
STUART CR

WELLAND AVE
HM Prison

Spinney Hill Farm

P ✗

🚐 ⛺

Chapel Farm

FOXTON RD

The Bungalow
Top Lodge
Lubenham Lodge

BUNKERS HILL

Holme's Farm

LE16

Mill Hill

LAUGHTON RD

Lower Lodge

MILL HILL
THE GREEN
Manor Farm

PAGET RD
MAIN ST
PO
HARBOROUGH RD
A4304

WESTLAND CL
ACORN CL
WEST GATE LA
RUSHES LA
TOWER CL
CONNELL CL
SCHOOL LA
SCHOOL CL

Lubenham
Lubenham All Saints CE Prim Sch

CHURCH WLK
OLD HALL LA
The Old Hall

FARNDON RD

Papillon Hall Farm
The Lodge

Papillon Fields Farm

The Bungalow

LE17

THEDDINGWORTH RD

MARSTON RD

Thorpe Lubenham Hall

The Pear Tree

HARBOROUGH RD
Scoborough Cottage

SCOBOROUGH RD

River Welland

LUBENHAM RD

Upper Highfield Plantation

Ford

Highfield Plantation

Sewage Works

68 A B 69 C D 70 E F

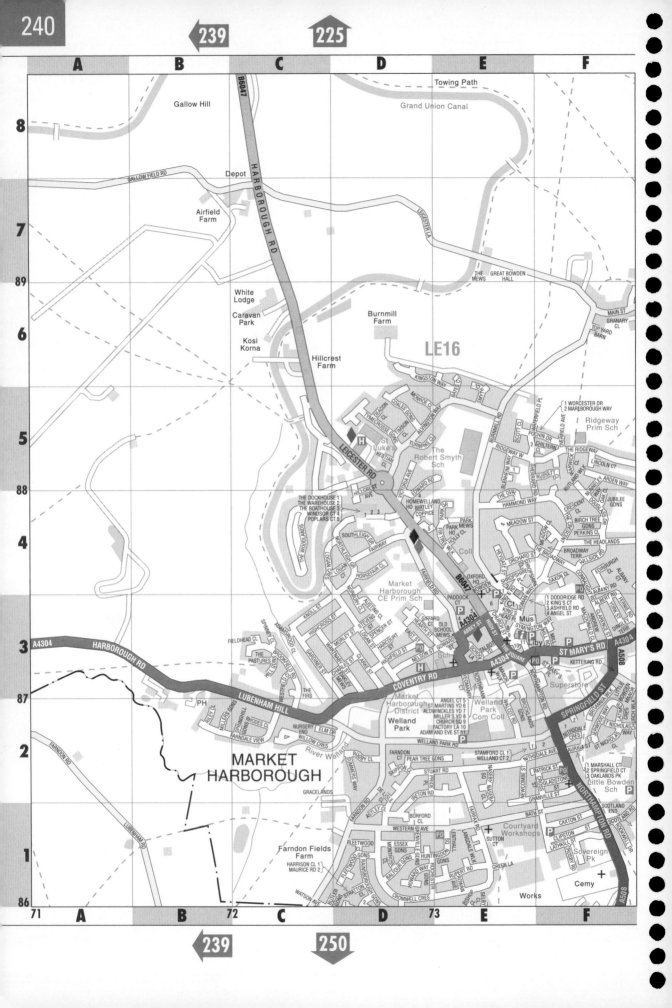

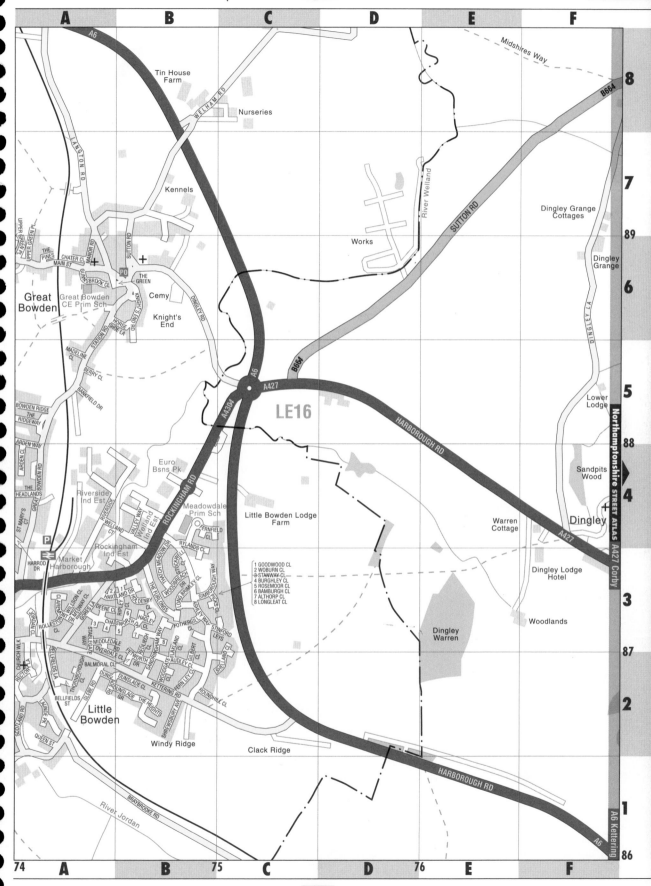

A B C D E F

8

7

89

6

5

88

4

3

87

2

1

86

Midshires Way

Tin House Farm

WELHAM RD

Nurseries

B664

Kennels

LANGTON RD

A6

River Welland

SUTTON RD

Dingley Grange Cottages

Dingley Grange

Works

Dingley Grange

DINGLEY LA

UPPER GREEN PL
THE PINES
CHATER CL
MAIN ST
MANOR RD
SUTTON RD
GUNSBROOK CL
PO
THE GREEN

Great Bowden

Great Bowden CE Prim Sch

KNIGHTS END RD

Cemy

Knight's End

DINGLEY RD

HORSE SHOE LA

Lower Lodge

STATION RD

MADELINE CL

BERRY CL

BANKFIELD DR

A6

A427

B664

A4304

LE16

Sandpits Wood

Northamptonshire STREET ATLAS

A427 Corby

Warren Cottage

Dingley

A427

BOWDEN RIDGE
THE RIDGEWAY
ARDEN WAY
ARDEN CL
GREAT BOWDEN RD
THE HEADLANDS
ST MARYS CT

Euro Bsns Pk

ROCKINGHAM RD

Riverside Ind Est

RIVERSIDE
WELLAND CT
VALLEY WAY
WELLAND IND EST

Meadowdale Prim Sch

FERNFIELD CL

Little Bowden Lodge Farm

RYLANDS CL

Dingley Lodge Hotel

Woodlands

P

HARROD DR

Market Harborough

Rockingham Ind Est

CHURCH WLK
CLARENDON DR
ROLLESTON CL
TO WOBURN
WILSON CL
MEDWAY CL
GORSE LA
DEENE CL
CHATSWORTH DR
HARTLAND DR
STRAELEGATE WAY
MIDDLEDALE
OVERDALE CL
PEWORTH DR
REDLEIGH
SANDRINGHAM WAY
WOODGATE
FLAXLAND
AUDLEY CL
GILBERT

HANTHORN MEADOW DR
WOODBREACH DR
STOCKWELL DR
LONG BRIMLEY CL
SIMBOROUGH WAY
ASHLEY WAY
STINFORD LEYS
FOTHERGILL WAY
RILEY CL

1 GOODWOOD CL
2 WOBURN CL
3 STANWAY CL
4 BURGHLEY CL
5 ROSEMOOR CL
6 BAMBURGH CL
7 ALTHORP CL
8 LONGLEAT CL

Dingley Warren

THE FURLONGS
HAGLEY
DENBY
BALMORAL CL
THORNBOROUGH RD
GLEBE RD
DUNSLADE CL
DUNSLADE RD
THE HEIGHTS
BELLFIELDS LA
BELLFIELDS ST
KETTERING RD
ROUNDHILL CL
SHRELLAND CL

SCOTLAND RD
LAUNDE PK
QUEEN ST

Little Bowden

Windy Ridge

Clack Ridge

BRAYBROOKE RD

River Jordan

HARBOROUGH RD

HARBOROUGH RD

A6 Kettering

A6

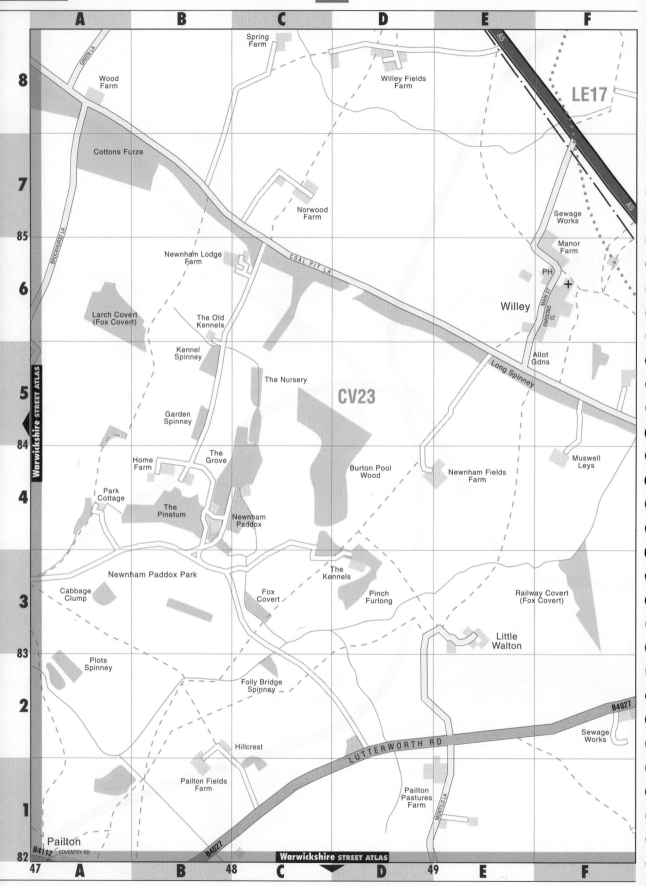

Spring Farm

Wood Farm

Willey Fields Farm

LE17

Cottons Furze

Norwood Farm

Sewage Works

Newnham Lodge Farm

COAL PIT LA

Manor Farm

PH

Larch Covert (Fox Covert)

The Old Kennels

Willey

Kennel Spinney

Allot Gdns

Long Spinney

The Nursery

CV23

Garden Spinney

Home Farm

The Grove

Burton Pool Wood

Newnham Fields Farm

Muswell Leys

Park Cottage

The Pinetum

Newnham Paddox

Newnham Paddox Park

The Kennels

Cabbage Clump

Fox Covert

Pinch Furlong

Railway Covert (Fox Covert)

Little Walton

Plots Spinney

Folly Bridge Spinney

B4027

Hillcrest

Sewage Works

LUTTERWORTH RD

Pailton Fields Farm

Pailton Pastures Farm

Pailton

COVENTRY RD

B4112

Warwickshire STREET ATLAS

BROCKHURST LA

GREEN LA

MAIN ST

PARSONS CL

MONTILO LA

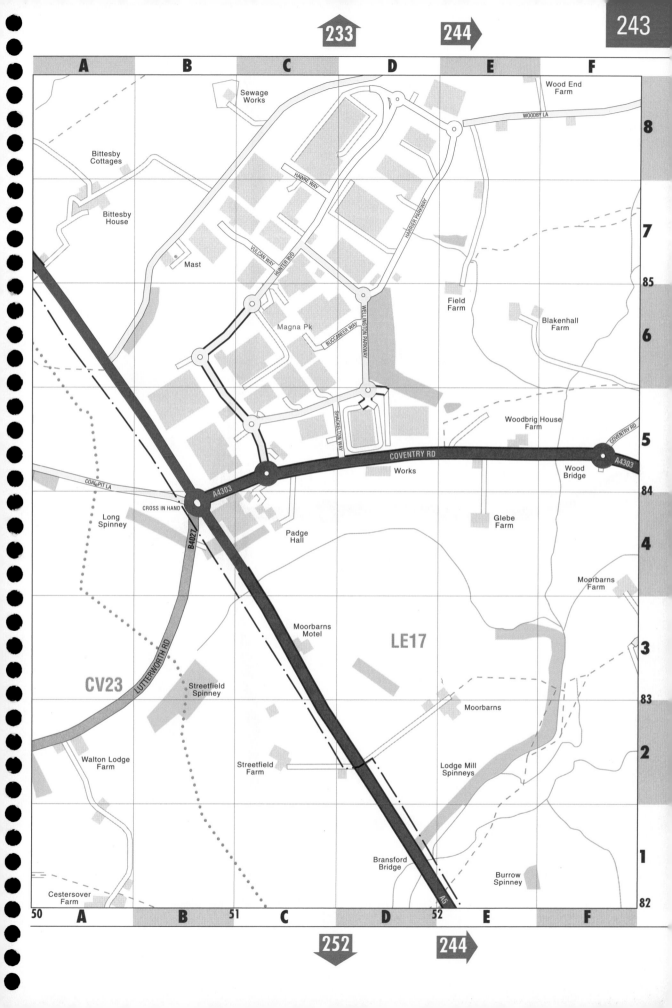

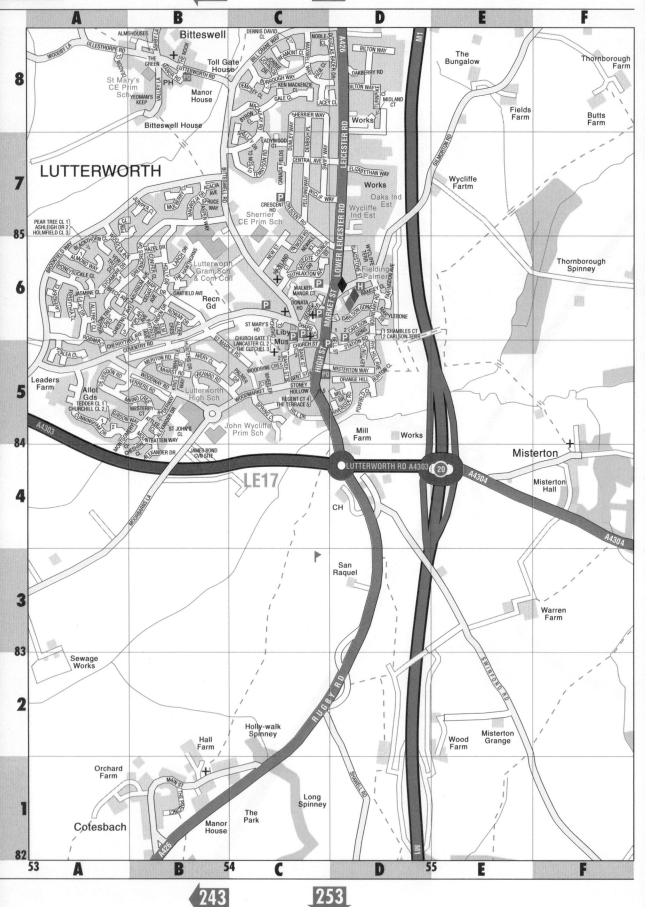

243
234

LUTTERWORTH

Bitteswell

8

7

85

6

84

LE17

5

4

3

83

2

1

82

53   A   B   54   C   D   55   E   F

A   B   C   D   E   F

Cotesbach
Misterton

243
253

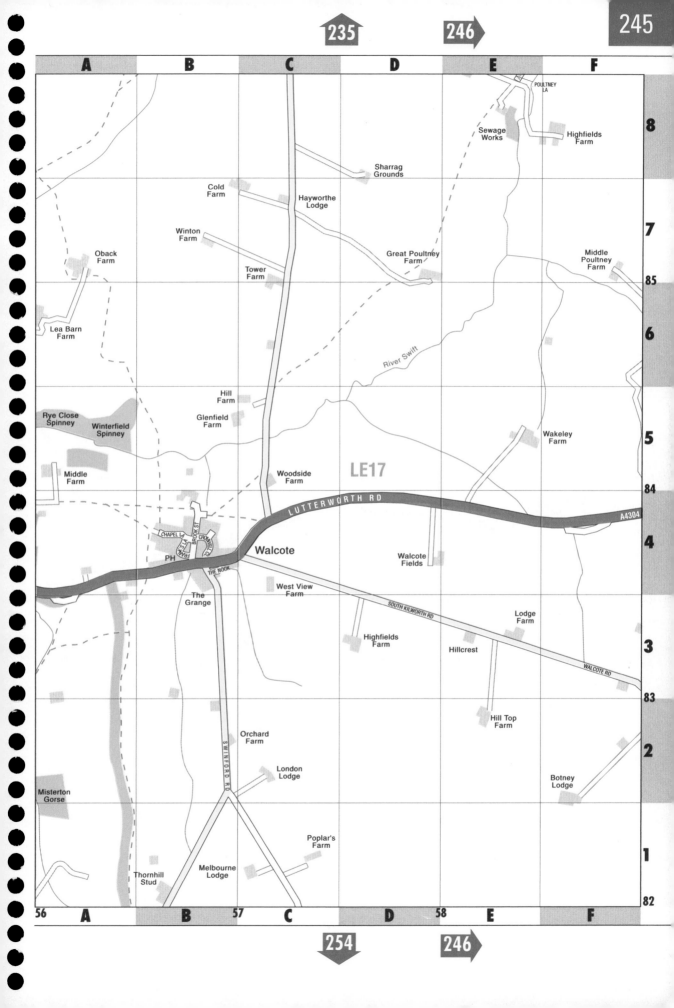

A B C D E F

8

POULTNEY LA

Sewage Works

Highfields Farm

Sharrag Grounds

Cold Farm

Hayworthe Lodge

7

Winton Farm

Great Poultney Farm

Oback Farm

Middle Poultney Farm

Tower Farm

85

Lea Barn Farm

6

River Swift

Hill Farm

Glenfield Farm

Rye Close Spinney

Winterfield Spinney

Wakeley Farm

5

Middle Farm

Woodside Farm

LE17

84

LUTTERWORTH RD

A4304

4

CHAPEL LA
BROOK ST
FRANK LA
CROMWELL CT

Walcote Fields

PH

Walcote

THE NOOK

West View Farm

The Grange

SOUTH KILWORTH RD

Lodge Farm

Highfields Farm

Hillcrest

WALCOTE RD

3

83

Hill Top Farm

Orchard Farm

SWINFORD RD

2

London Lodge

Botney Lodge

Misterton Gorse

Poplar's Farm

1

Thornhill Stud

Melbourne Lodge

82

56 A B 57 C D 58 E F

245
236

	A	B	C	D	E	F

8

Camp Barn

Windmill Farm

BOSWORTH RD

Hill Top Farm

Walton Holt

7

Walton Lodge

Tabbermear's Farm

Hill Top Lodge

85

KILWORTH RD

6

Snowdon Lodge

North Kilworth Sticks

The Grange

5

Poultney Grange

Kilworth Sticks Farm

B5414

Greenacre Cottage

PINCET LA

84

The Belt

LE17

A4304

LUTTERWORTH RD

WHEELWRIGHT CL

WESTERN COTTS

KNIGHTON YD

MILLENNIUM CL

B5414

A4304

STATION RD

4

Buckwell Lodge

Ainsloe Spinney

WASH PIT LA

PH

PO

HOLLOW RD

HAWTHORNE RD

THE ELMS GREEN

MARKET ST

THORNE ST

SCOFF RD

3

Caldicote Spinney

North Kilworth House

Playing Field

St Andrew's CE Prim Sch

BACK ST

ARNSBY LA

CHURCH ST

DAG LA

CRANMER LA

Nether Hall

North Kilworth

83

South Kilworth Lodge

Church Spinney

SOUTH KILWORTH RD

2

Roseneath

The Elms

WALCOTE RD

CH

Nurseries

1

Malt Shovel

Tollgate Farm

NORTH RD

LEYS PBS

THE BELT

North Kilworth Mill Farm

82

South Kilworth CE Prim Sch

	A		B		C		D		E		F
59				60				61			

245
255

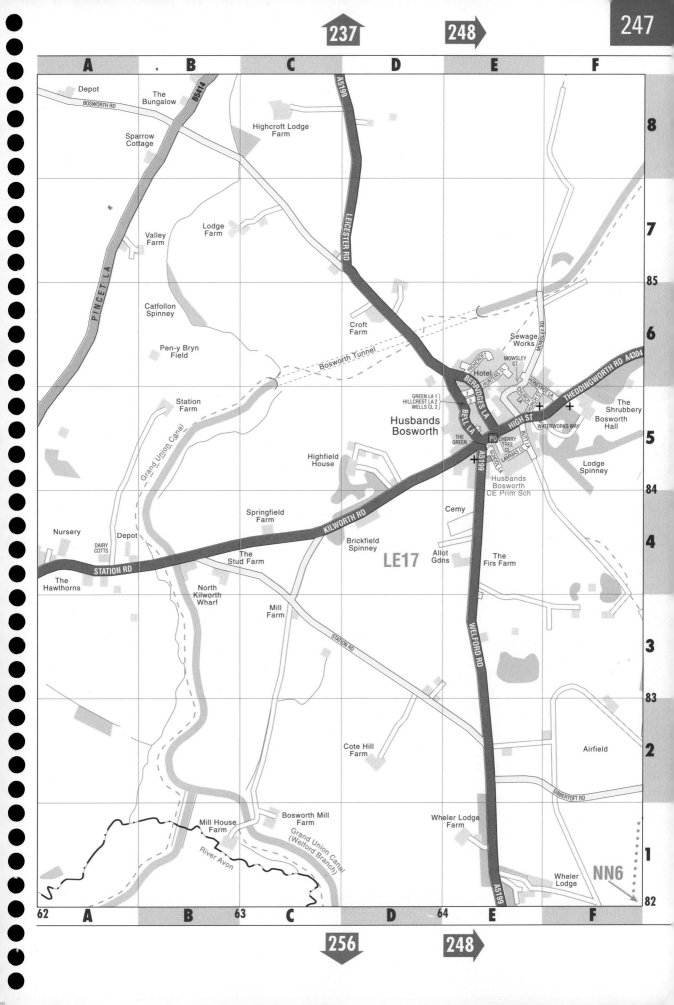

247
238

A   B   C   D   E   F

Grand Union Canal

8

The Crown
(PH)

HARBOROUGH RD
A4304

Cemy

MONSLEY RD

STATION RD

MAIN ST

THE
BUNGALOWS

Works

TOMS CL

Theddingworth

BANK
COTTS

PEBBLE
COTT

HOTHORPE RD

BOSWORTH RD

THEDDINGWORTH RD

7

Dene
Lodge

Damside
Spinney

Old
Folly

Quiet
Fields

Home
Farm

Pebble
Hall

85

Woodside
Farm

Hothorpe
Hall

THEDDINGWORTH RD

A4304

6

LE17

Broxhill
Buildings

River Welland

5

Spring
Hollow

Nichol's Hill
Spinney

Gravel Pit
Spinney

84

Long
Spinney

Hothorpe
Hills

Barn-hill
Spinney

Coombe-hill
Spinney

4

LE16

3

Carland
Spinney

The
Roserie

83

The
Wrongs

Coombes
Farm

2

WELFORD RD

WESTHORPE

BEECHES CL

WELLAND RISE
PH

Airfield

SIBBERTOFT RD

BERKELEY ST

NASEBY RD

Sibbertoft

NN6

CHURCH
ST

1

Depot

SULBY RD

SULBY HALL OLD DR

Sulby
Lodge

Jurassic Way

The
Kennels

82

65   A   B   66   C   D   67   E   F

247

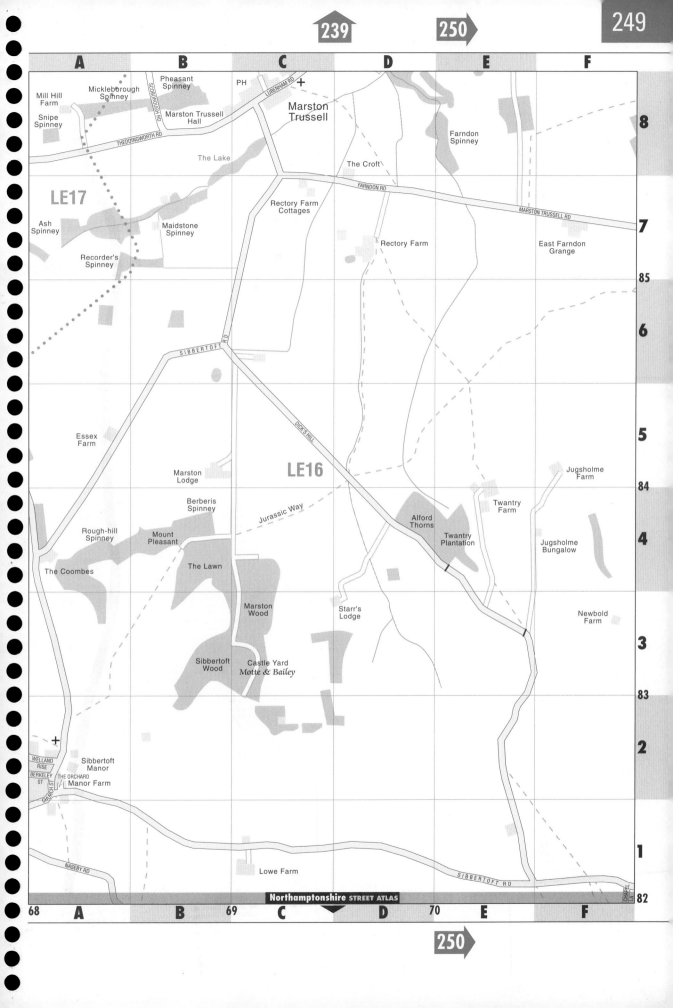

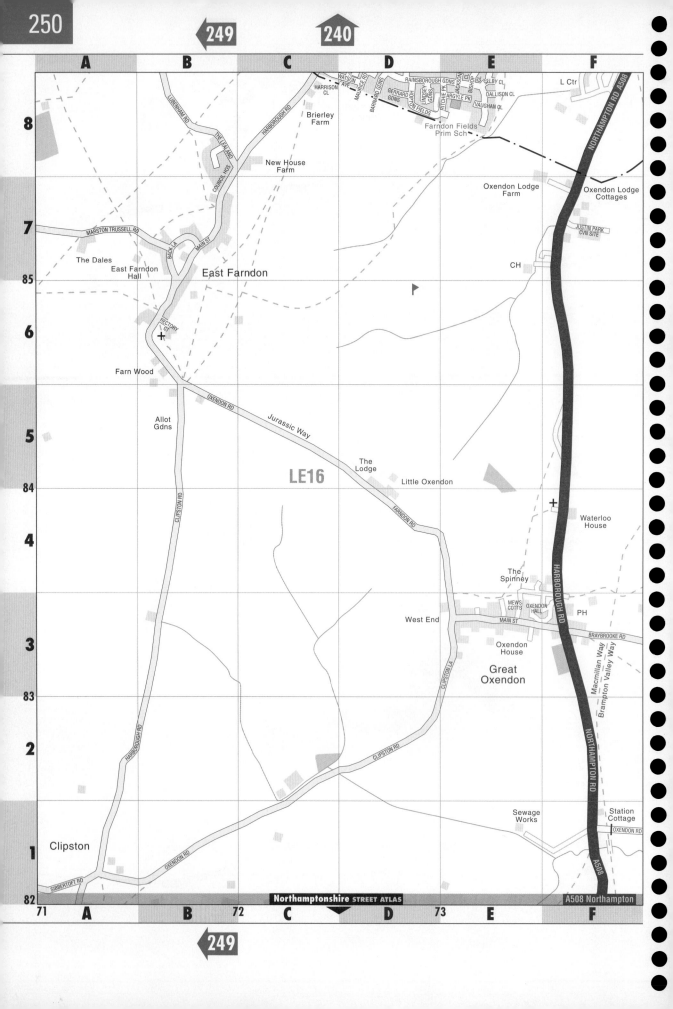

249
240

A   B   C   D   E   F

8

7

85

6

5

84

4

3

83

2

1

82

L Ctr

NORTHAMPTON RD A508

Brierley Farm

Harrison CL

WATSON RD

MAURICE AVE

BARNARD GDNS

GERRARD GDNS

HOPTON FIELDS

LINDSEY GDNS

RAINSBOROUGH GDNS

RITCHIE PK

ARGYLE PK

JACKSON

BISHOP

CL

SELBY CL

DALLISON CL

VAUGHAN QL

Farndon Fields Prim Sch

New House Farm

Oxendon Lodge Farm

Oxendon Lodge Cottages

JUSTIN PARK CVN SITE

LUBENHAM RD

THE EALAND

HARBOROUGH RD

COUNCIL HOS

MARSTON TRUSSELL RD

BACK LA

MAIN ST

The Dales

East Farndon Hall

East Farndon

CH

RECTORY CL

+

Farn Wood

OXENDON RD

Allot Gdns

Jurassic Way

CLIPSTON RD

LE16

The Lodge

Little Oxendon

FARNDON RD

+

Waterloo House

HARBOROUGH RD

The Spinney

MEWS COTTS

OXENDON HALL

PH

West End

MAIN ST

BRAYBROOKE RD

Oxendon House

Great Oxendon

CLIPSTON LA

Macmillan Way

Brampton Valley Way

NORTHAMPTON RD

HARBOROUGH RD

CLIPSTON RD

Clipston

Sewage Works

Station Cottage

OXENDON RD

OXENDON RD

SIBBERTOFT RD

A508

A508 Northampton

249

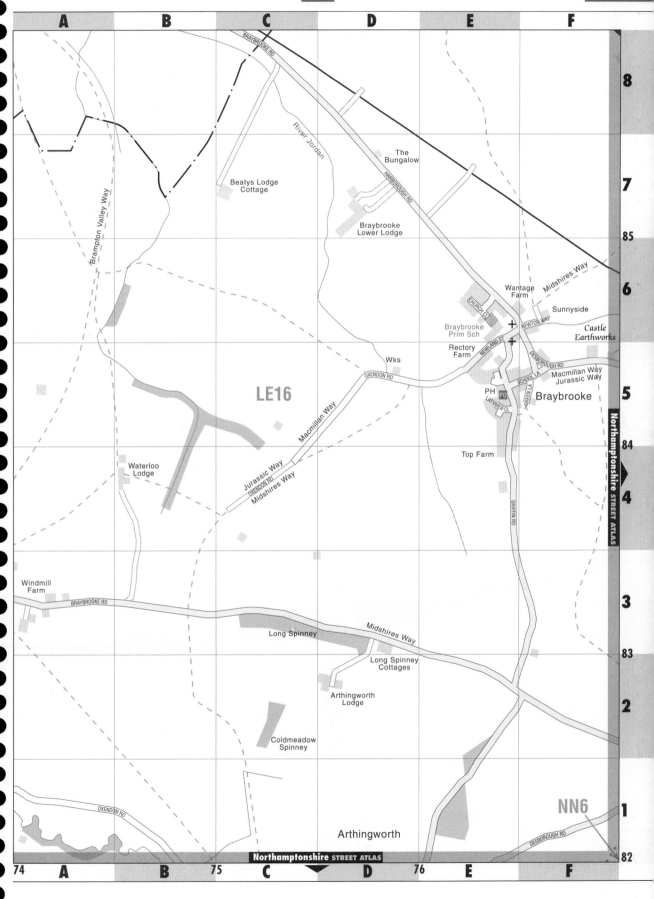

| | A | B | C | D | E | F |

BRAYBROOKE RD

River Jordan

Brampton Valley Way

Beatys Lodge Cottage

The Bungalow

HARBOROUGH RD

Braybrooke Lower Lodge

Midshires Way

Wantage Farm

Sunnyside

CHURCH CL

NEWTON WAY

Castle Earthworks

Braybrooke Prim Sch

NEWLAND ST

Rectory Farm

Macmillan Way
Jurassic Way

Wks

OXENDON RD

DESBOROUGH RD

SCHOOL LA

GREEN LA

PH

PO

Braybrooke

LATYMER CL

LE16

Macmillan Way

Top Farm

Waterloo Lodge

Jurassic Way

OXENDON RD

Midshires Way

GRIFFIN RD

Windmill Farm

BRAYBROOKE RD

Long Spinney

Midshires Way

Long Spinney Cottages

Arthingworth Lodge

Coldmeadow Spinney

NN6

OXENDON RD

Arthingworth

DESBOROUGH RD

| 74 | A | B | 75 | C | D | 76 | E | F | 82 |

8 7 85 6 5 84 4 3 83 2 1

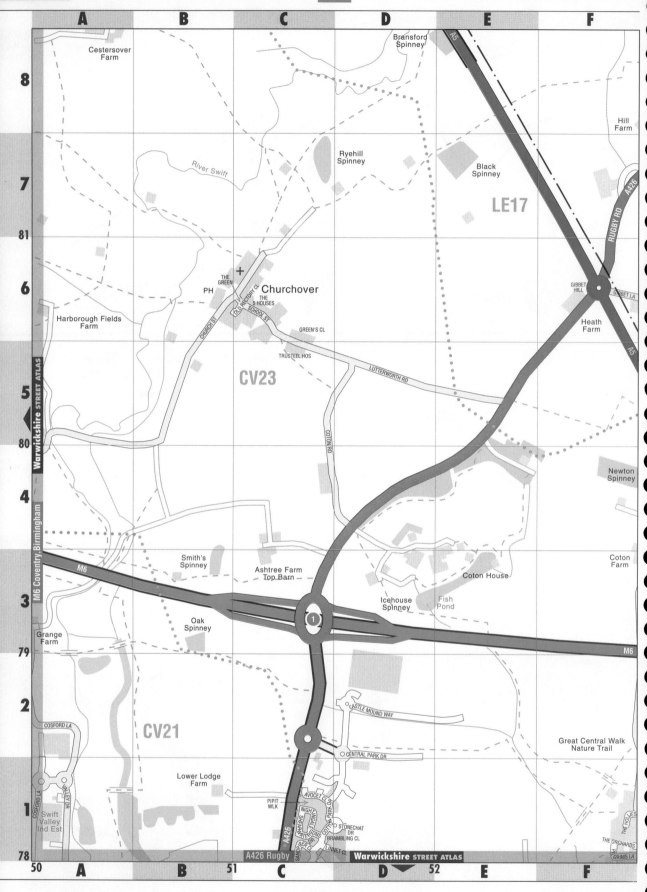

Cestersover
Farm

Bransford
Spinney

Hill
Farm

8

Ryehill
Spinney

River Swift

Black
Spinney

LE17

7

81

THE
GREEN

Churchover

PH

THE
5 HOUSES

GIBBET
HILL

GIBBET LA

6

Harborough Fields
Farm

CHURCH ST

OLD RECTORY CL

SCHOOL ST

GREEN'S CL

TRUSTEEL HOS

LUTTERWORTH RD

Heath
Farm

A5

CV23

5

80

Newton
Spinney

COTON RD

Coton
Farm

4

Smith's
Spinney

Ashtree Farm
Top Barn

Coton House

Icehouse
Spinney

Fish
Pond

M6

M6

3

Oak
Spinney

1

Grange
Farm

79

COSFORD LA

CV21

2

Great Central Walk
Nature Trail

Lower Lodge
Farm

PIPIT
WLK

AVOCET CL

CASTLE MOUND WAY

CENTRAL PARK DR

1

Swift
Valley
Ind Est

NIGHTINGALE GDNS

SHEARWATER DR

COTTON PARK DR

STONECHAT
DR

BRAMBLING CL

LINNET CL

THE HOLLIES

THE ORCHARDS

GRIMS LA

78

50

A

B

51

C

D

52

E

F

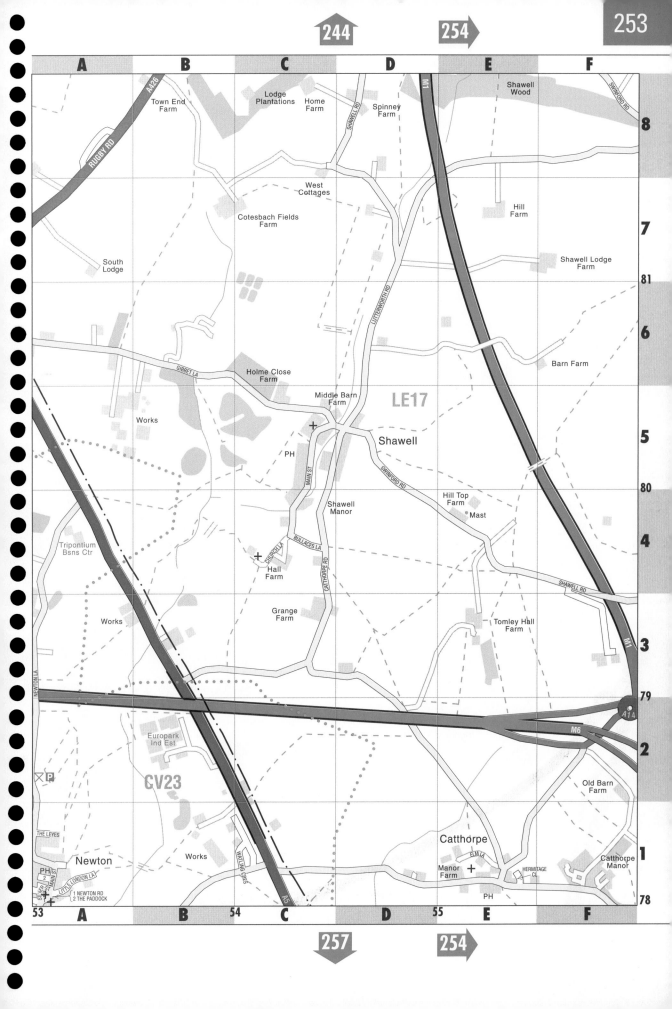

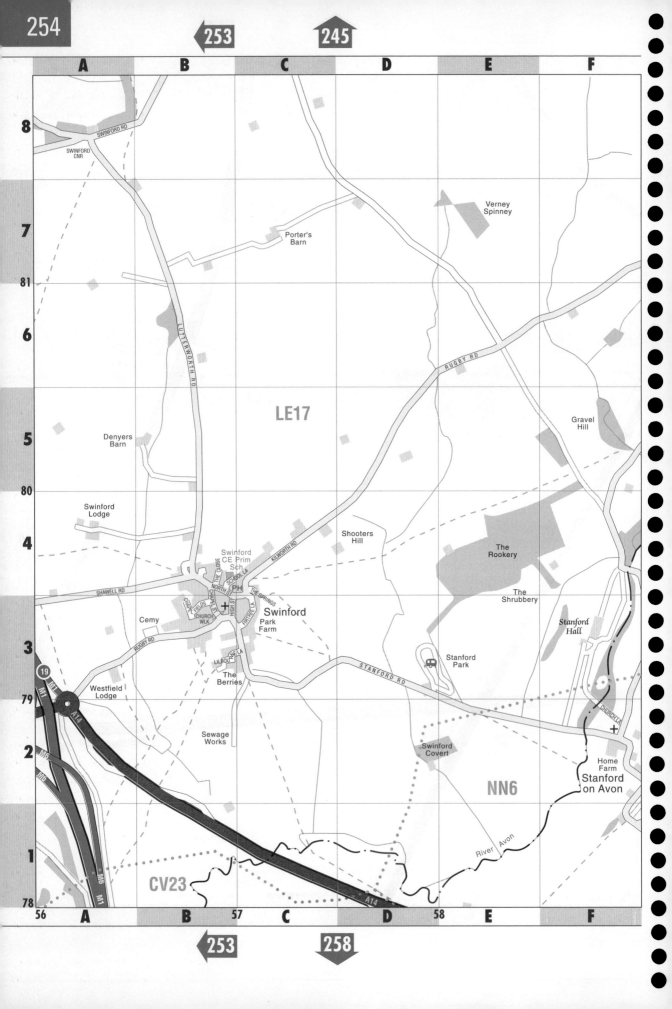

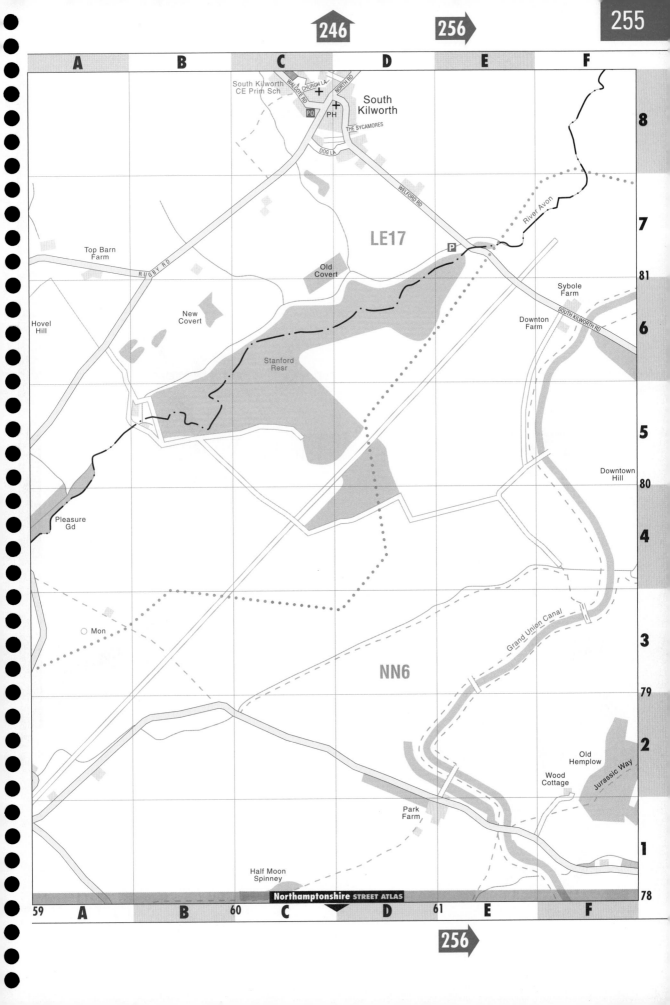

A B C D E F

South Kilworth
CE Prim Sch
CHURCH LA
WALCOTE RD
NORTH RD
PO
PH
South
Kilworth
THE SYCAMORES
DOG LA
WELFORD RD

LE17

8

River Avon

7

Top Barn
Farm
RUGBY RD
Old
Covert
P
81
Sybole
Farm
Downton
Farm
SOUTH KILWORTH RD

New
Covert

Hovel
Hill
6

Stanford
Resr
Downtown
Hill
80

5

Pleasure
Gd
4

Grand Union Canal

Mon
3

NN6
79

Old
Hemplow
2
Wood
Cottage
Jurassic Way

Park
Farm

Half Moon
Spinney
1

78

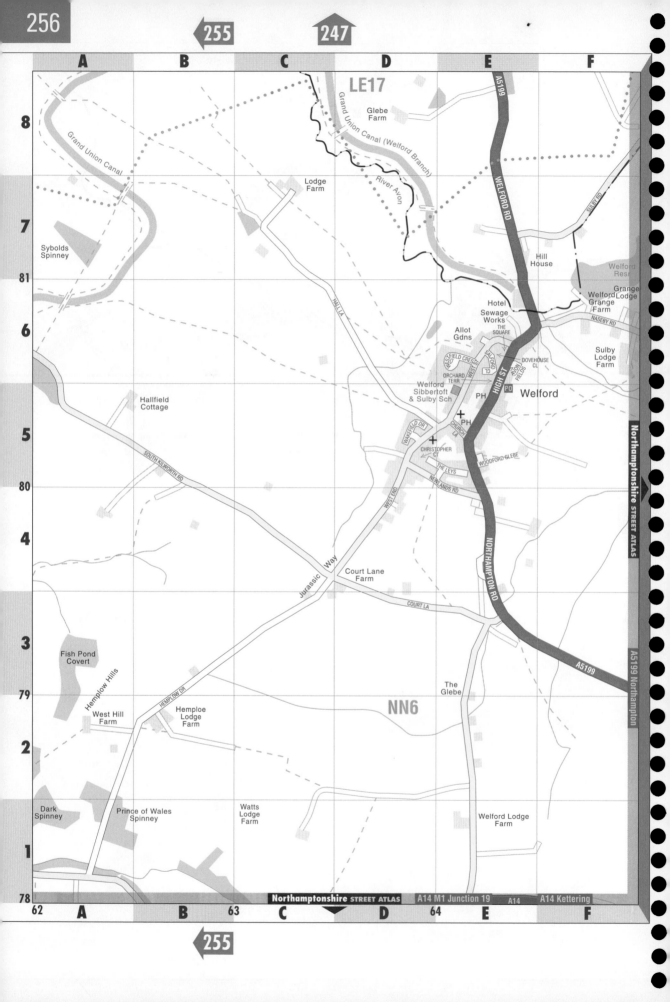

LE17

Glebe
Farm

Grand Union Canal

Grand Union Canal (Welford Branch)

River Avon

A5199

Lodge
Farm

Sybolds
Spinney

Hill
House

SULBY RD

Welford Resr

WELFORD RD

Grange
Welford Lodge
Grange
Farm

Hotel
Sewage
Works

HALL LA

Allot
Gdns

THE
SQUARE

NASEBY RD

Sulby
Lodge
Farm

FIELD CRESC
WEST
ORCHARD
TERR

SEAFORD
RD

DOVEHOUSE
CL

AVON
FIELDS

Hallfield
Cottage

Welford
Sibbertoft
& Sulby Sch

WEST
END

HIGH ST

PH

PO

Welford

SOUTH KILWORTH RD

WANSFORD DR

CHURCH
LA

PH

CHRISTOPHER
CT

THE LEYS

WOODFORD GLEBE

Jurassic Way

WEST END

NEWLANDS RD

Court Lane
Farm

NORTHAMPTON RD

COURT LA

Fish Pond
Covert

Hemplow Hills

HEMPLOW DR

NN6

The
Glebe

A5199

West Hill
Farm

Hemploe
Lodge
Farm

Dark
Spinney

Prince of Wales
Spinney

Watts
Lodge
Farm

Welford Lodge
Farm

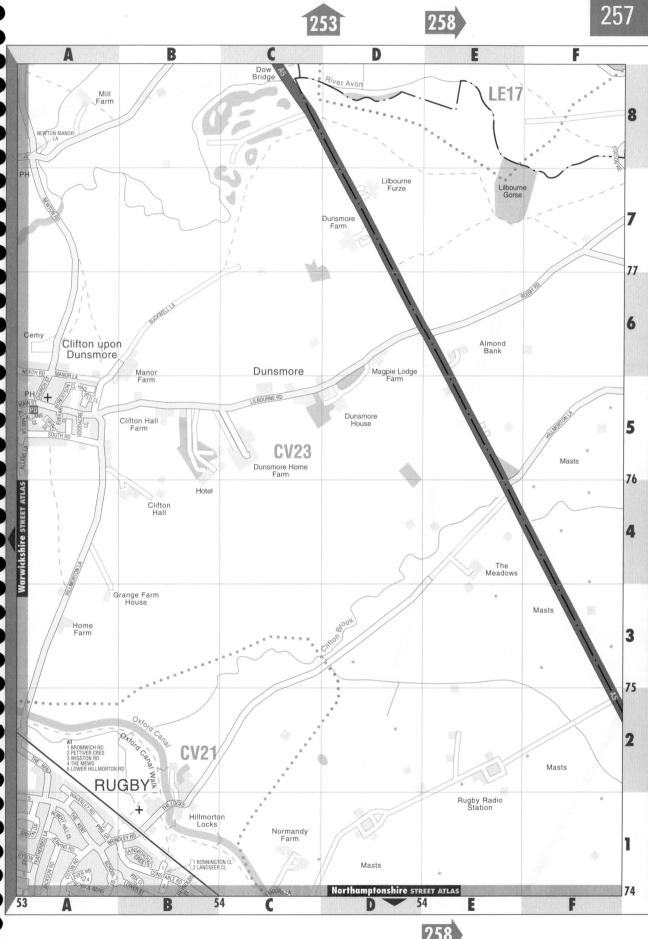

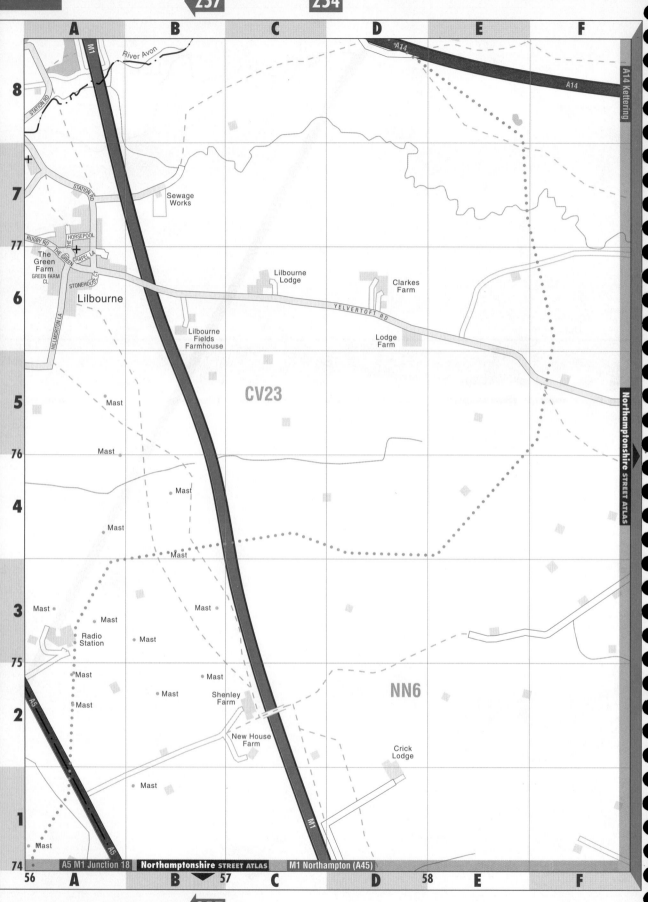

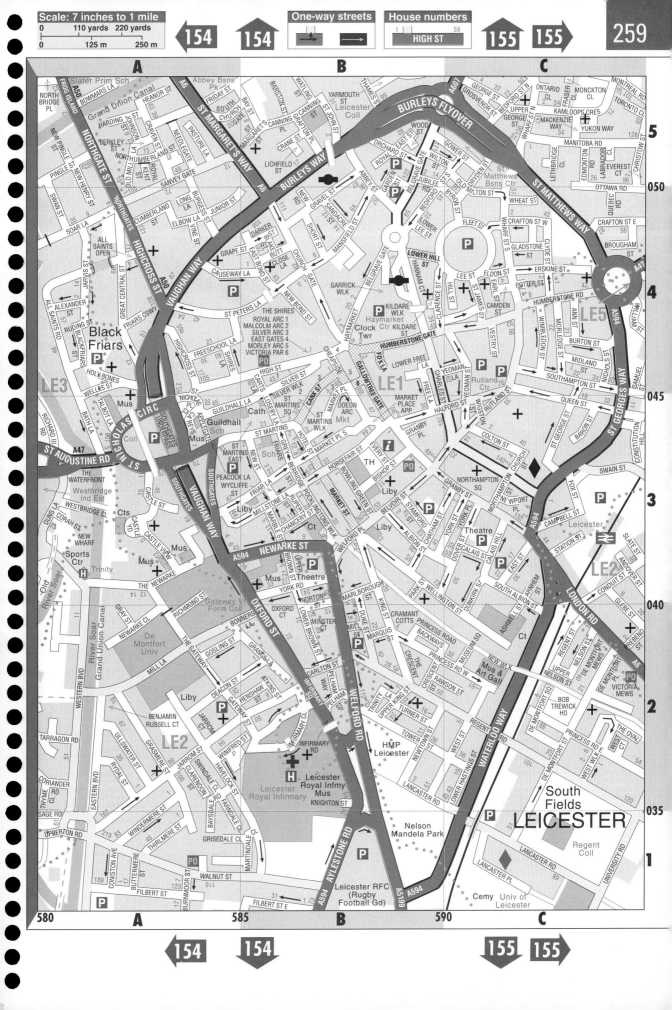

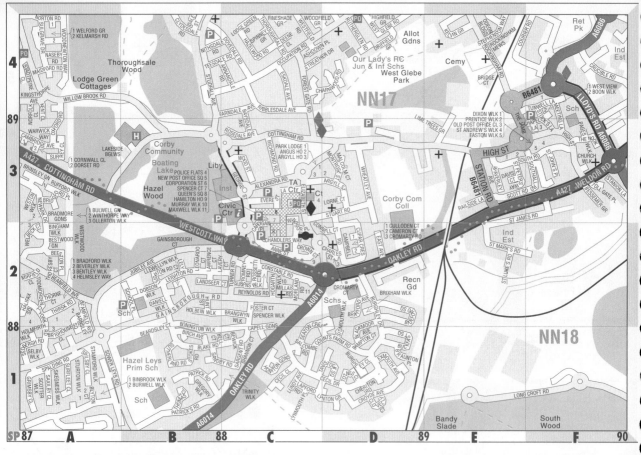

Corby

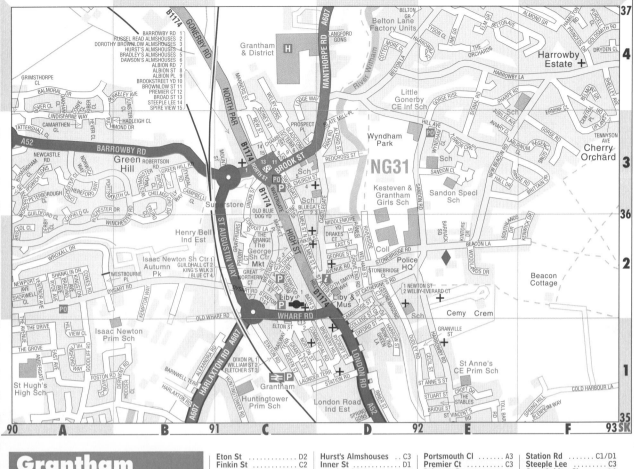

Grantham

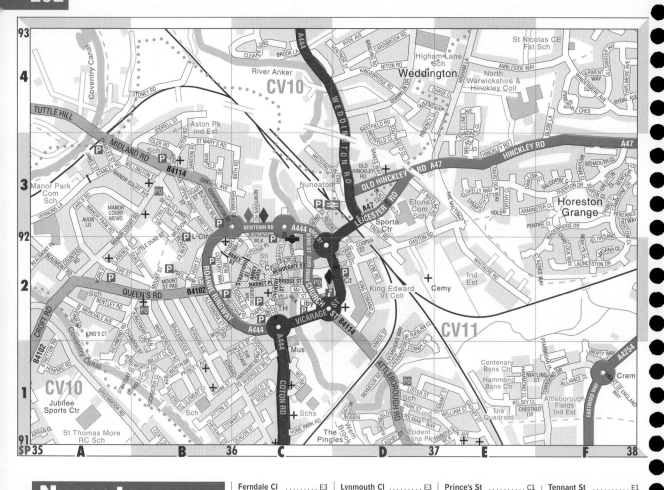

Nuneaton

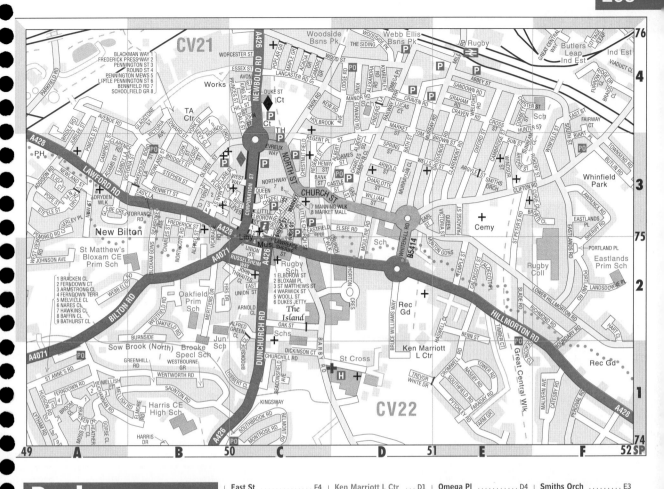

Rugby

Index

Church Rd **6** **Beckenham BR2.......53** **C6**

Place name	Location number	Locality, town or village	Postcode district	Page and grid square
May be abbreviated on the map	Indicates the place's position in a crowded area of mapping	Shown when more than one place has the same name	District for the indexed place	

Public and commercial buildings are highlighted in magenta
Places of interest are highlighted in blue with a star★

Index of localities, towns and villages

Braybrooke Rd
Great Oxendon LE16 ... 251 A3
Leicester LE4 ... 129 E1
Market Harborough LE16 ... 241 B1
Braymish Cl LE8 ... 224 B8
Brazenose La PE9 ... 143 E3
Brazil St LE2 ... 154 E3
Breachfield Rd LE12 ... 76 E7
Breach La LE9 ... 198 F6
Breach Rd LE67 ... 96 D7
Breadcroft La LE12 ... 76 D8
Breadsall Cl DE11 ... 44 A7
Breakback Rd LE12 ... 74 E3
Breaston Ind Est DE72 ... 9 C7
Brechin Cl LE10 ... 215 A8
Brecknock Dr NG10 ... 10 A7
Brecon Cl
Long Eaton NG10 ... 10 A8
Wigston LE18 ... 179 F2
Bredon Cl NG10 ... 10 A8
Breech Hedge LE7 ... 101 E7
Breedon Ave LE18 ... 180 C3
Breedon La
Osgathorpe LE12 ... 48 C5
Worthington LE65 ... 47 F6
Breedon St LE2 ... 155 C5
Brendon Cl LE12 ... 50 C1
Brendon Way LE65 ... 69 B5
Brenfield Dr LE10 ... 215 B8
Brent Ct LE3 ... 178 F7
Brentingby Cl LE13 ... 59 E1
Brent Knowle Gdns LE5 ... 156 D5
Brentnall Cl NG10 ... 10 B7
Brentwood Rd LE2 ... 155 A1
Bretby Bsns Pk DE15 ... 44 A8
Bretby Rd LE2 ... 179 E6
Bretby View DE11 ... 45 A4
Breton Cl LE18 ... 204 A3
Brettell Rd LE2 ... 179 D4
Bretton Cl LE4 ... 128 E3
Bretton Wlk 5 LE4 ... 128 E3
Breward Way LE13 ... 59 D6
Brewer Cl LE4 ... 129 E5
Brex Rise LE3 ... 153 D6
Breydon Ind Ctr NG10 ... 10 F7
Brian Rd LE4 ... 128 D1
Brians Cl LE7 ... 103 C4
Brianway The LE5 ... 155 F7
Briar Cl
Blackfordby DE11 ... 68 B8
Coalville LE67 ... 96 C7
Hinckley LE10 ... 215 F6
Leicester, Oadby LE2 ... 181 B4
Briarfield Dr LE5 ... 130 E1
Briargate Dr LE4 ... 128 E8
Briarmead LE10 ... 215 E4
Briar Meads LE2 ... 181 B3
Briar Rd LE5 ... 156 D7
Briar Wlk LE2 ... 181 B4
Brick Kiln Croft DE12 ... 93 D5
Brick Kiln La
Ibstock LE67 ... 122 F8
Shepshed LE12 ... 50 A1
Brick Kiln St LE10 ... 215 C8
Brickman Cl LE3 ... 152 F2
Brickwood Pl LE12 ... 53 F1
Brickyard Cotts DE12 ... 93 D5
Brickyard La
East Leake LE12 ... 31 A8
Wymondham LE14 ... 62 D3
Bridegate La LE14 ... 19 B6
Bridevale Rd LE2 ... 179 E5
Bridge Bsns Pk LE4 ... 129 D7
Bridge Cl
Swadlincote DE11 ... 44 C2
Thurmaston LE4 ... 129 F8
Bridge Field DE72 ... 9 C7
Bridge Fields DE74 ... 18 D3
Bridge Ho LE11 ... 52 B4
Bridge Jun Sch LE5 ... 155 C7
Bridge La
Greetham LE15 ... 88 B1
Witherley CV9 ... 194 B7
Bridgeland Rd LE11 ... 52 C5
Bridge Mews LE67 ... 71 D3
Bridge Park Rd LE4 ... 129 D7
Bridge Rd Coalville LE67 ... 96 D8
Hinckley LE10 ... 215 D7
Leicester LE5 ... 155 D7
Bridgeside Cotts LE11 ... 52 A5
Bridge St
Barrow-u-S LE12 ... 76 C7
Langham LE15 ... 110 C3
Long Eaton NG10 ... 10 D8
Loughborough LE11 ... 52 A4
Packington LE65 ... 69 C1
Ryhall PE9 ... 116 F2
Shepshed LE12 ... 50 B4
Swadlincote DE11 ... 44 C2
Bridgewater Dr LE8 ... 182 B1
Bridge Way LE8 ... 201 F7
Bridle Cl Croft LE9 ... 200 C3
Melton Mowbray LE13 ... 59 A5
Bridle Path Rd LE9 ... 198 D5
Bridle Rd LE67 ... 111 B8
Bridlespur Way LE4 ... 128 E5
Bridle The LE2 ... 179 B4
Bridport Cl LE18 ... 180 D1
Brierfield Rd LE9 ... 201 D2
Briers Cl LE19 ... 201 B7
Briers Way LE67 ... 71 E5
Briggins Wlk LE15 ... 110 C3
Brightman Ho DE11 ... 44 B5
Brighton Ave
Syston LE7 ... 103 C4
Wigston LE18 ... 180 D5
Brighton Cl LE18 ... 180 C5
Brighton Rd LE5 ... 155 E8
Brightside Ave LE13 ... 59 A4
Brightside Rd LE5 ... 155 E4
Brightwell Dr LE3 ... 153 B4
Brindle Path LE9 ... 198 D4
Brindley Cl CV9 ... 170 C1
Brindley Rd
Hinckley LE10 ... 214 E8
Rugby CV21 ... 257 B1
Brindley Rise LE5 ... 130 E1
Bringhurst Gn LE3 ... 153 E7
Bringhurst Prim Sch LE16 ... 229 C6
Bringhurst Rd LE3 ... 153 E7
Brington Cl LE18 ... 180 E2
Brinks The LE12 ... 76 B5
Brinsmead Rd LE2 ... 180 B7
Brisco Ave LE11 ... 51 F6
Briscoe La LE12 ... 75 B4
Bristol Ave
Ashby-De-La-Z LE65 ... 69 A4
Leicester LE4 ... 128 D1
Britannia Rd LE10 ... 216 A5
Britannia Sh Ctr LE10 ... 215 D8
Britannia St
Leicester LE1 ... 155 A7
Shepshed LE12 ... 50 B4
Britannia Way LE4 ... 102 E1
Britannia Wlk LE16 ... 240 F2
Britford Ave LE18 ... 203 C8
British School Gdns LE13 ... 59 C3
Briton Lodge Cl DE12 ... 67 F4
Briton St LE3 ... 154 D4
Brittany Ave LE65 ... 69 A7
Brixham Dr LE2,LE18 ... 180 A5
Brixworth Rise LE5 ... 156 E6
Broad Ave LE5 ... 155 F5
Broadbent Cl LE8 ... 201 F7
Broadfield Way LE8 ... 202 D4
Broadford Cl LE4 ... 129 D4
Broadgate LE16 ... 229 D7
Broadgate Cl LE4 ... 129 A8
Broadgate Rd NG33 ... 65 C3
Broadhill Rd DE74 ... 18 C2
Broadhurst St LE4 ... 129 B2
Broad La LE67 ... 125 A7
Broad Mdw LE18 ... 180 E1
Broadmead Rd LE8 ... 202 A6
Broad St Coalville LE67 ... 96 D8
Enderby LE19 ... 178 B3
Long Eaton NG10 ... 10 D7
Loughborough LE11 ... 52 A4
Stamford PE9 ... 143 E3
Syston LE7 ... 103 A3
Broadsword Way LE10 ... 215 D4
Broadway
Loughborough LE11 ... 75 B8
Syston LE7 ... 103 A3
Broadway Furlong LE7 ... 127 E7
Broadway Rd LE5 ... 155 D2
Broadway Terr LE16 ... 240 F4
Broadway The
Leicester LE2 ... 156 A1
Market Harborough LE16 ... 240 F4
Brockenhurst Dr LE3 ... 178 E8
Brockey Cl LE9 ... 198 B7
Brockhurst Ave LE10 ... 215 D4
Brockhurst La CV23 ... 242 A6
Brockington Coll LE19 ... 178 C2
Brocklehurst Rd LE13 ... 59 E5
Brocklesby Way LE5 ... 156 E8
Brocks Hill Cl LE2 ... 181 B4
Brocks Hill Country Pk & Visitor Ctr★ LE2 ... 180 F4
Brocks Hill Dr LE2 ... 181 B5
Brocks Hill Prim Sch LE2 ... 181 B3
Brocktone Cl LE9 ... 219 B5
Broctone Dr LE9 ... 218 E7
Brodick Cl LE10 ... 215 A8
Brodick Rd LE10 ... 214 F8
Bromhead St LE11 ... 52 C5
Bromley La LE12 ... 49 B7
Bromwich Cl LE3 ... 153 C2
Bromwich Rd 1 CV21 ... 257 A1
Bronte Cl Leicester LE3 ... 154 A4
Long Eaton NG10 ... 10 A7
Bronze Barrow Cl LE18 ... 180 F1
Brook Bank LE5 ... 155 F7
Brook Cl
Long Eaton NG10 ... 10 E5
Packington LE65 ... 69 B1
Uppingham LE15 ... 189 C3
Brook Cres LE14 ... 58 B3
Brook Ct LE8 ... 202 F4
Brookdale LE10 ... 215 B7
Brookdale Rd
Hartshorne DE11 ... 44 F4
Leicester LE3 ... 153 D5
Brook Dene LE15 ... 111 B8
Brook Dr LE6 ... 152 C8
Brooke Ave PE9 ... 143 A2
Brooke Cl LE15 ... 138 B7
Brooke Hill Prim Sch LE15 ... 137 E4
Brooke House Coll LE16 ... 240 E4
Brooke Priory Sch LE15 ... 137 F7
Brooke Rd
Braunston-in-R LE15 ... 137 B2
Oakham LE15 ... 137 F4
Ridlington LE15 ... 163 D4
Brookes Ave LE9 ... 200 C3
Brookes Gr NN17 ... 230 E1
Brook Farm Ct
Hoton LE12 ... 32 D2
Willoughby-on-t-W LE12 ... 34 C7
Brookfield LE10 ... 217 C5
Brookfield Ave
Loughborough LE11 ... 51 E1
Syston LE7 ... 103 B3
Brookfield Cotts DE12 ... 92 C7
Brookfield Ct LE13 ... 59 B5
Brookfield Rd
Hinckley LE10 ... 215 C6
Market Harborough LE16 ... 240 C3
Brookfield Rise LE2 ... 179 F6
Brookfield St
Melton Mowbray LE13 ... 59 B5
Syston LE7 ... 103 B3
Brookfield Way
Kibworth Beauchamp LE8 ... 224 B8
Lutterworth LE17 ... 244 A6
Brook Gdns LE2 ... 179 B3
Brookhouse Ave 2 LE2 ... 155 B4
Brook House Cl LE7 ... 79 A1
Brook House Mews DE11 ... 44 A7
Brookhouse St 1 LE2 ... 155 B4
Brook La Asfordby LE14 ... 57 F2
Barrow-u-S LE12 ... 76 E8
Billesdon LE7 ... 159 C2
Great Easton LE16 ... 229 D6
Loughborough LE11 ... 74 D8
Melton Mowbray LE13 ... 59 D2
Peckleton LE9 ... 175 F7
Thringstone LE67 ... 71 D7
Brookland Rd LE2 ... 155 A1
Brooklands LE15 ... 164 C1
Brooklands Cl
Broughton Astley LE9 ... 218 F6
Whetstone LE8 ... 201 F7
Brooklands Gdns LE16 ... 240 E2
Brooklands Prim Sch NG10 ... 10 D6
Brooklands Rd LE9 ... 201 D4
Brook Rd Leicester LE5 ... 156 D7
Woodhouse Eaves LE12 ... 74 E4
Brooksby Ag Coll LE14 ... 79 E5
Brooksby Cl LE2 ... 181 A6
Brooksby Dr LE2 ... 181 A6
Brooksby Rd LE14 ... 79 D6
Brooksby St LE2 ... 154 E1
Brookside Barkby LE7 ... 130 E8
Barlestone CV13 ... 149 D7
Diseworth DE74 ... 28 C5
East Leake LE12 ... 31 E8
Hinckley LE10 ... 215 E7
Leicester LE5 ... 155 D3
Rearsby LE7 ... 79 A2
Syston LE7 ... 103 B4
Whetstone LE8 ... 201 F6
Brook Side
12 Ashby-De-La-Z LE65 ... 69 B6
3 Loughborough LE11 ... 52 A4
Brookside Ave LE12 ... 31 E8
Brookside Cl
Barrow-u-S LE12 ... 53 D1
Long Eaton NG10 ... 10 B8
Shepshed LE12 ... 50 C2
Brookside Cres LE67 ... 95 F1
Brookside Dr LE2 ... 181 C5
Brookside Ho LE67 ... 96 A2
Brookside Pl CV9 ... 171 B8
Brookside Rd LE11 ... 74 D8
Brookside Sch LE2 ... 181 D7
Brooks La LE67 ... 71 D5
Brook St
Ashby-De-La-Z LE65 ... 69 B6
Burton o t W LE12 ... 53 F7
Enderby LE19 ... 178 B3
Hartshorne DE11 ... 45 A7
Huncote LE9 ... 200 D7
Melton Mowbray LE13 ... 59 D3
Rearsby LE7 ... 79 A1
Shepshed LE12 ... 50 C5
Sileby LE12 ... 77 C3
Swadlincote DE11 ... 44 A3
Syston LE7 ... 103 A4
Thurmaston LE4 ... 129 D7
Walcote LE17 ... 245 B4
Whetstone LE8 ... 201 F7
Wymeswold LE12 ... 33 D3
Brooks The LE15 ... 113 B2
Brook Terr LE16 ... 227 F6
Brookvale High Sch LE6 ... 126 D2
Broom Ave LE11 ... 75 A7
Broombriggs Farm Ctry Pk★ LE12 ... 74 E1
Broombriggs Farm Nature Trail★ LE12 ... 74 F1
Broombrigs Rd LE3 ... 127 F3
Broome Ave LE7 ... 103 E8
Broome La LE7 ... 78 C1
Broomfield LE7 ... 103 E7
Broomfield Com Prim Sch LE7 ... 103 E7
Broomhills Rd LE19 ... 200 F8
Broomhills The DE12 ... 91 F7
Broomleys LE8 ... 202 D4
Broom Leys Ave LE67 ... 96 F8
Broom Leys Rd LE67 ... 72 A1
Broom Leys Sch LE67 ... 72 A1
Broom Way LE19 ... 177 F1
Brosdale Dr LE10 ... 197 A1
Brougham St LE1 ... 259 C4
Broughton Cl
Anstey LE7 ... 127 E7
Loughborough LE11 ... 51 C4
Broughton Field LE18 ... 203 E8
Broughton La
Dunton Bassett LE17 ... 219 D2
Leire LE17 ... 218 E3
Long Clawson LE14 ... 20 A2
Broughton Rd
Cosby LE9 ... 201 C1
Croft LE9 ... 200 C3
Frolesworth LE17 ... 218 C3
Leicester LE2 ... 179 E6
Stoney Stanton LE9 ... 199 F2
Broughton St LE67 ... 96 D8
Broughton Way LE9 ... 218 F7
Brown Ave LE12 ... 76 A6
Brown Ct LE65 ... 68 F7
Browne's Hospl 3 PE9 ... 143 D3
Brownhill Cres LE7 ... 101 C5
Browning Cl LE13 ... 59 C6
Browning Dr
Hinckley LE10 ... 215 C8
Measham DE12 ... 93 C3
Browning Rd
Loughborough LE11 ... 51 D4
Oakham LE15 ... 137 E6
Swadlincote DE11 ... 44 C5
Browning St
Leicester LE3 ... 154 C4
Narborough LE19 ... 178 A1
Brownlow Cres LE13 ... 82 C8
Brownlow Prim Sch LE13 ... 59 D4
Brownlow Quay PE9 ... 143 E3
Brownlow St PE9 ... 143 E3
Brown's Cl LE9 ... 217 E8
Browns La LE11 ... 52 A3
Browns Rd NG10 ... 10 E8
Brown's Way LE8 ... 201 F5
Broxburn Cl LE4 ... 129 D4
Broxfield Cl LE2 ... 181 A3
Bruces La LE14,LE15 ... 135 E6
Bruce St LE3 ... 154 D3
Bruce Way LE8 ... 201 E5
Bruin St LE4 ... 129 A1
Bruins Wlk LE2 ... 180 F5
Brunel Ave LE3 ... 154 A8
Brunel Rd LE10 ... 215 C8
Brunel Way LE67 ... 71 B3
Brunswick St LE1 ... 155 B6
Bruntingthorpe Aerodrome & Proving Ground LE17 ... 236 B6
Bruntingthorpe Ind Est LE17 ... 236 C6
Bruntingthorpe Rd
Peatling Parva LE17 ... 236 B8
Shearsby LE17 ... 222 A1
Brushfield Ave LE12 ... 77 D4
Bruxby St LE7 ... 102 F3
Bryan Cl LE12 ... 76 D8
Bryan's Cl LE67 ... 71 F6
Bryar's Cl LE8 ... 223 B4
Bryngarth Cres LE5 ... 156 B7
Bryony Rd LE5 ... 130 D2
Buccaneer Way LE17 ... 243 D6
Buchan Wlk LE3 ... 154 A5
Buckfast Cl
Leicester LE5 ... 155 F3
Wigston LE18 ... 180 C1
Buckhaven Cl LE4 ... 129 D4
Buckingham Cl
Groby LE6 ... 126 E2
Hinckley LE10 ... 197 F4
Buckingham Dr
Leicester LE2 ... 179 B5
Loughborough LE11 ... 51 C5
Buckingham Rd
Coalville LE67 ... 96 F8
Countesthorpe LE8 ... 202 F4
Oakham LE15 ... 137 F5
Buckingham's Way LE9 ... 217 B4
Buckland Rd LE5 ... 155 D8
Buckley Cl
Measham DE12 ... 93 C4
Woodville DE11 ... 45 A2
Buckminster Cl LE13 ... 59 E2
Buckminster La NG33 ... 43 A6
Buckminster Prim Sch NG33 ... 42 E1
Buckminster Rd
Leicester LE3 ... 154 D8
Sproxton LE14 ... 41 F5
Stainby NG33 ... 43 C2
Bucksburn Wlk LE4 ... 129 D4
Buck's La LE12 ... 30 A7
Buckwell La CV23 ... 257 B6
Buckwell Rd LE9 ... 217 D8
Buddon Ct LE12 ... 76 E1
Buddon La LE12 ... 75 E5
Bude Dr LE3 ... 127 C1
Bude Rd LE18 ... 180 D1
Bufton La CV13 ... 148 E8
Bullaces La LE17 ... 253 C4
Bull Brig La LE15 ... 140 A5
Buller Rd LE4 ... 129 A1
Buller St LE8 ... 223 F8
Bullfield Cl LE15 ... 88 B2
Bullfinch Cl LE15 ... 138 A8
Bullfurlong La LE10 ... 215 F4
Bull Head St LE18 ... 180 D3
Bull Hill LE12,LE65 ... 48 A5
Bull La Ketton PE9 ... 168 A6
North Witham NG33 ... 65 C7
Oakham LE15 ... 138 A6
Bull Ring LE12 ... 50 B4
Bull's Head Row DE73 ... 26 E6
Bulrush Cl LE12 ... 76 F1
Bulstode Pl DE74 ... 18 C2
Bulwer Rd LE2 ... 155 B1
Bumblebee La LE9 ... 217 B1
Bungalows The
Essendine PE9 ... 117 A5
Langham LE15 ... 110 C3
Little Stretton LE2 ... 182 D5
Newbold Verdon LE9 ... 150 B4
Theddingworth LE17 ... 248 D8
Bunkers Hill LE17 ... 238 F4
Burbage CE Inf Sch LE10 ... 216 A5
Burbage Cl LE11 ... 51 E6
Burbage Common★ LE10 ... 198 A3
Burbage Common Rd LE9 ... 198 D3
Burbage Common & Woods Visitor Centre★ LE10 ... 198 B3
Burbage Jnr Sch LE10 ... 216 A6
Burbage Jun Sch LE10 ... 215 F6
Burbage Rd LE10 ... 215 F8
Burchnall Rd LE3 ... 153 D1
Burden La LE14 ... 12 B3
Burder St LE11 ... 52 C5
Burdet Cl LE3 ... 153 E1
Burdett Cl LE17 ... 235 C4
Burdetts Cl LE14 ... 82 A1
Burdett Way LE4 ... 128 D4
Burdock Cl LE5 ... 130 D2
Burfield Ave LE11 ... 52 A3
Burfield St LE4 ... 155 B8
Burford Cl LE16 ... 240 D1
Burgess Rd
Coalville LE67 ... 96 C8
Leicester LE2 ... 179 E6
Burgess Row LE16 ... 230 B8
Burgess St
Leicester LE1 ... 259 A4
Wigston LE18 ... 180 D3
Burghley Circ LE15 ... 87 E2
Burghley Cl LE16 ... 241 A3
Burghley Ct 1 PE9 ... 143 E3
Burghley Ho★ PE9 ... 144 B1
Burghley La PE9 ... 143 E2
Burghley Rd PE9 ... 143 C5
Burgin Rd LE7 ... 127 D5
Burgins La LE14 ... 40 A7
Burkitt Rd NN17 ... 230 F3
Burleigh Ave LE18 ... 180 C4
Burleigh Com Coll LE11 ... 51 C3
Burleigh Rd
Hinckley LE10 ... 197 C2
Loughborough LE11 ... 52 A4
Burley Cl Cosby LE9 ... 201 D3
Desford LE9 ... 151 B3
Burley Cres LE15 ... 111 B3
Burley Homes LE4 ... 128 F5
Burley Park Way LE15 ... 138 C7
Burley Rd
Cottesmore LE15 ... 112 B7
Langham LE15 ... 110 E3
Oakham LE15 ... 138 B7
Ryhall PE9 ... 116 E1
Burley Rise DE74 ... 18 D1
Burleys Flyover LE1 ... 259 B5
Burleys Way LE1 ... 259 B5
Burlington Cl DE72 ... 9 D8
Burlington Rd LE2 ... 155 C1
Burnaby Ave LE5 ... 155 D6
Burnaby Pl LE14 ... 57 F3
Burnaston Rd LE2 ... 179 E6
Burnell Rd LE3 ... 154 B2
Burneston Way LE18 ... 180 E2
Burnet Cl LE5 ... 130 C2
Burney La DE73 ... 26 C2
Burnham Cl LE18 ... 203 D7
Burnham Dr
Leicester LE4 ... 128 D2
Whetstone LE8 ... 201 F6
Burnham Rise CV11 ... 214 A6
Burnhams Rd PE9 ... 167 F5
Burnmill Rd LE16 ... 240 E5
Burnmoor St LE2 ... 154 E3
Burns Cl Measham DE12 ... 93 B3
Melton Mowbray LE13 ... 59 B6
Burnside Rd
Broughton Astley LE9 ... 218 F5
Leicester LE2 ... 180 A6
Burns Rd
Loughborough LE11 ... 51 D4
Stamford PE9 ... 143 B4
Burns St Leicester LE2 ... 180 A8
Narborough LE19 ... 178 B1
Burnsway LE10 ... 197 C1
Burrough End LE14 ... 82 A1
Burrough Hill Ctry Pk★ LE14 ... 107 E4
Burrough Rd
Little Dalby LE14 ... 108 A7
Somerby LE14 ... 108 A2
Twyford LE14 ... 133 E8
Burroughs Rd LE6 ... 126 A1
Burrough Way LE17 ... 244 C8
Burrough Wood Nature Trail★ LE6 ... 125 F1
Burrow Hill Rd LE16 ... 208 B3
Burrows Cl LE19 ... 201 B7
Burrows The LE19 ... 201 A8
Bursdon Cl LE3 ... 153 D6
Bursdon Ct LE3 ... 153 D6
Bursnells La LE14 ... 62 D2
Bursom Rd LE4 ... 128 B6
Burton Cl Harby LE14 ... 12 A3
Leicester, Oadby LE2 ... 181 D4
Lutterworth LE17 ... 244 D5
Burton La LE67 ... 71 A5
Burton on the Wolds Prim Sch LE12 ... 53 F6
Burton Overy La LE7, LE8 ... 183 C2
Burton Rd
Ashby-De-La-Z LE65 ... 69 A6
Boundary LE65 ... 45 E1
Measham DE12 ... 93 B5
Melton Mowbray LE13 ... 59 D1
Overseal DE12 ... 67 A4
Sileby LE12 ... 77 C3
Twycross CV9 ... 146 C8
Wellsborough CV13 ... 147 A2
Woodville DE11 ... 44 D6
Burton's La NG32 ... 4 F5
Burton St Leicester LE1 ... 259 C4
Loughborough LE11 ... 52 B2
Melton Mowbray LE13 ... 59 C2
Burton Wlk LE12 ... 31 E8
Burton Wlks LE11 ... 52 B2
Bury Cl LE16 ... 229 C1
Buscot Cl LE4 ... 155 D8
Bushby Rd LE5 ... 155 D7
Bushey Cl LE19 ... 201 B8
Bush Lock Cl LE18 ... 203 A8
Bushloe Ct LE18 ... 180 C2
Bushloe End LE18 ... 180 C2
Bushnell Cl LE9 ... 219 A4
Bushy Cl NG10 ... 10 B6
Bushy Rd LE7 ... 184 D7
Buswells Lodge Prim Sch LE4 ... 128 A3
Butchers La LE12 ... 78 A7
Butcombe Rd LE4 ... 128 D1
Bute Cl LE10 ... 197 C1
Bute Way LE8 ... 202 F3
Butler Cl LE4 ... 129 E4
Butler Ct LE11 ... 51 F3
Butler Gdns LE16 ... 240 C1
Butler Way LE12 ... 77 D2
Butt Cl
Barlestone CV13 ... 149 D8
Wigston LE18 ... 180 E1
Butt Close La LE1 ... 259 B4
Buttercup Ave DE12 ... 67 E1
Buttercup Cl
Groby LE6 ... 127 A3
Mountsorrel LE12 ... 76 F2
Narborough LE19 ... 178 A1
Stamford PE9 ... 142 F5
Buttercup Dr LE67 ... 97 A8
Buttercup Rd LE11 ... 75 A6
Butterley Dr LE11 ... 51 B2
Buttermere Ave CV11 ... 214 A6
Buttermere St LE2 ... 259 A1
Buttermere Way LE12 ... 53 C1
Butterwick Dr LE4 ... 128 C4
Butthole La DE74 ... 50 D5
Butt La Blackfordby DE11 ... 45 A1
Hinckley LE10 ... 197 F1
Husbands Bosworth LE17 ... 247 E5
Normanton on S LE12 ... 30 F4
North Luffenham LE15 ... 166 D3
Wymondham LE14 ... 62 E3
Butt Lane Cl LE10 ... 197 E1
Buttress Cl LE15 ... 187 D7
Butts Cl CV9 ... 119 A2
Butts The LE14 ... 24 E1
Buxton Cl
Swadlincote DE11 ... 44 A7
Whetstone LE8 ... 201 F7
Buxton St LE2 ... 155 C6
Buzzard Cl
Broughton Astley LE9 ... 218 F7
Measham DE12 ... 93 B4
Byfield Dr LE18 ... 180 E2
Byford Rd LE4 ... 128 E2
Byland Way LE11 ... 51 B5
Byre Cres LE9 ... 218 F5
Byron Cl Fleckney LE8 ... 223 A7
Lutterworth LE17 ... 244 C8
Narborough LE19 ... 178 A2
Byron Cres DE12 ... 93 C3
Byron Ct LE8 ... 222 F7
Byron Rd DE11 ... 44 C6
Byron St Barwell LE9 ... 198 B8
Earl Shilton LE9 ... 198 E7
Leicester LE1 ... 259 C4
Loughborough LE11 ... 51 E5
Byron St Extension LE11 ... 51 F5
Byron Way
Melton Mowbray LE13 ... 59 B5
Stamford PE9 ... 143 A3
Byrton Dr LE67 ... 96 C4
Bytham Hts NG33 ... 90 C8
Byway Rd LE5 ... 155 E2

C

Cabin Leas LE11 ... 52 B5
Cadeby Cl LE10 ... 197 B3
Cadeby La CV13 ... 149 B3

Cad – Che 269

Cademan Cl LE2 ... **180** B7
Cademan Ct LE2 ... **180** B7
Cademan St LE67 ... **71** F5
Cadles Cl LE9 ... **199** D3
Cadle St LE9 ... **150** B5
Caernarvon Cl
Mountsorrel LE12 ... **101** D8
Shepshed LE12 ... **50** A4
Cairngorm Cl LE2 ... **179** F7
Cairnsford Rd LE2 ... **180** B6
Caistor Rd NN17 ... **213** C1
Caithness Rd PE9 ... **143** A4
Calais Hill LE1 ... **259** C3
Calais St LE1 ... **259** C3
Caldecote Hall CV10 ... **194** F2
Caldecote Hall Dr
CV10 ... **194** F3
Caldecote Prim Sch
LE3 ... **154** A1
Caldecote Rd LE3 ... **154** A1
Caldecott Cl LE18 ... **180** F2
Caldecott Rd LE16 ... **230** B5
Calder Cl Corby NN17 ... **230** D1
Oakham LE15 ... **137** E5
Calderdale Dr NG10 ... **10** A6
Calder Rd LE4 ... **128** C3
Caldon Cl LE10 ... **215** B8
Caldwell St LE11 ... **52** A4
Caledine Rd LE3 ... **155** A8
Caledonian Rd PE9 ... **143** B4
Calgary Cres LE15 ... **138** B6
Calgary Rd LE1 ... **155** A7
Callan Cl LE19 ... **201** A8
Callan's La LE65 ... **46** D7
Callendar Cl CV11 ... **214** A7
Callis The LE65 ... **69** B7
Caloe Cl LE12 ... **77** E3
Calver Hey Rd LE4 ... **128** B3
Calvert Cres LE9 ... **217** E7
Calverton Ave LE18 ... **180** C4
Calverton Cl LE6 ... **152** D8
Camborne Cl LE18 ... **180** C1
Camborne Dr CV11 ... **214** A5
Cambourne Rd LE10 ... **216** A6
Cambrian Cl LE9 ... **201** D2
Cambrian Way
Ashby-De-La-Z LE65 ... **69** B4
Swadlincote DE11 ... **44** A3
Cambridge Ave LE13 ... **82** D8
Cambridge Cl LE7 ... **103** C3
Cambridge Dr LE9 ... **151** A2
Cambridge Rd
Cosby LE8,LE9 ... **201** E5
Stamford PE9 ... **143** C5
Cambridge St
Coalville LE67 ... **71** E1
Leicester LE3 ... **154** C4
Loughborough LE11 ... **52** B5
Shepshed LE12 ... **50** B2
Cam Cl NN17 ... **230** C1
Camden Rd LE3 ... **154** A1
Camden St LE1 ... **259** C4
Camelford Rd LE67 ... **96** C7
Camellia Cl LE19 ... **177** F1
Camelot Way LE19 ... **178** A1
Cameron Ave LE4 ... **129** B3
Camfield Rise LE2 ... **179** D4
Camomile Rd LE13 ... **82** B8
Campbell Ave LE4 ... **129** E5
Campbell St LE1 ... **259** C3
Campden Cl
Exton LE15 ... **113** B2
Uppingham LE15 ... **189** B4
Camp Hill Ct PE9 ... **143** B8
Campion Cl LE19 ... **201** A8
Campion Gr PE9 ... **142** F5
Campion Hill DE74 ... **17** A4
Campion Pl LE13 ... **82** A8
Campion Rd DE11 ... **44** E4
Campion Wlk LE4 ... **128** B3
Campton Cl LE10 ... **215** E7
Camrose Cl LE15 ... **138** B6
Camville Rd LE3 ... **153** F4
Canada Fields LE17 ... **244** C7
Canal Bank
Loughborough LE11 ... **52** A5
Shardlow DE72 ... **9** A1
Canal La Harby LE14 ... **12** D5
Hose LE14 ... **20** E8
Long Clawson LE14 ... **20** C6
Canal St Leicester LE2 ... **179** C7
Oakthorpe DE12 ... **93** A7
Thurmaston LE4 ... **129** E8
Wigston LE18 ... **179** F1
Canal Way LE10 ... **214** F7
Canberra Way LE10 ... **215** E4
Candle La LE9 ... **198** F8
Cank St LE1 ... **259** B4
Cannam Cl
Middleton LE16 ... **229** B1
Whetstone LE8 ... **202** A5
Canner Cl DE11 ... **45** A2
Canning Pl LE1 ... **259** B5
Canning St
Hinckley LE10 ... **197** C1
Leicester LE1 ... **259** B5
Canning Way LE11 ... **51** C6
Cannock Cl LE67 ... **96** D4
Cannock St LE4 ... **130** A4
Cannock Way NG10 ... **10** F7
Canon Cl LE2 ... **181** B5
Canons Cl LE19 ... **201** B8
Canonsleigh Rd LE4 ... **128** E3
Canonsleigh Wlk 6
LE4 ... **128** E3
Canon St LE4 ... **129** C1
Canterbury Dr
Ashby-De-La-Z LE65 ... **69** A7
Canterbury Dr *continued*
Melton Mowbray LE13 ... **59** A6
Canterbury Terr LE3 ... **154** B3
Canterbury Way CV11 **214** A8
Cantrell Rd LE3 ... **153** D3
Canvey Cl LE18 ... **180** F3
Capendale Cl PE9 ... **167** F5
Capers Cl LE19 ... **178** A3
Capesthorne Cl LE5 ... **155** D8
Captains Close Prim Sch
LE14 ... **57** E3
Carbery Cl LE2 ... **181** D4
Cardigan Dr LE18 ... **179** F2
Cardinal Cl LE6 ... **152** D8
Cardinals Wlk LE5 ... **156** C8
Carey Cl LE18 ... **203** D8
Carey Gdns LE9 ... **152** D5
Carey Hill Rd LE9 ... **199** D2
Carey Rd LE9 ... **200** D7
Careys Cl LE1 ... **259** A3
Carfax Ave LE2 ... **180** F7
Car Hill Rd LE67 ... **71** E7
Carillon Ct LE11 ... **52** B4
Carillon Tower & War
Meml★ LE11 ... **52** A3
Carington St LE11 ... **51** F5
Carisbrooke Ave LE2 ... **180** C7
Carisbrooke Ct LE2 ... **180** C7
Carisbrooke Gdns
LE2 ... **180** C8
Carisbrooke Pk LE2 ... **180** C7
Carisbrooke Rd
Leicester LE2 ... **180** C7
Mountsorrel LE12 ... **101** D8
Carlin Cl DE72 ... **9** E8
Carling Cl LE67 ... **71** E1
Carlisle St LE3 ... **154** C5
Carl Moult Ho DE11 ... **44** A2
Carlson Gdns LE17 ... **244** D6
Carlson Terr LE17 ... **244** D6
Carl St LE2 ... **179** C6
Carlton Ave LE19 ... **201** C8
Carlton Ct
Glenfield LE3 ... **153** D8
Leicester LE2 ... **155** D1
Carlton Dr LE18 ... **180** C4
Carlton Gdns LE8 ... **205** B7
Carlton La LE8 ... **205** F8
Carlton Rd
Barton in t B CV13 ... **122** D1
Kibworth Beauchamp
LE8 ... **206** B3
Long Eaton NG10 ... **10** B5
Carlton St LE1 ... **259** B2
Carlyon Rd
Atherstone CV9 ... **170** F1
Atherstone CV9 ... **194** A7
Carlyon Rd Ind Est
CV9 ... **194** A8
Carlyon Road Ind Est
CV9 ... **170** F1
Carmen Gr LE6 ... **126** E3
Carnation Cl LE3 ... **152** F2
Carnation St LE4 ... **128** F2
Carnegie Cres LE13 ... **59** E6
Carnegie Mus★ LE13 ... **59** D3
Carnival Way DE74 ... **17** B4
Carnoustie Rd LE3 ... **153** D6
Caroline Ct LE2 ... **179** E6
Carpenters Cl LE10 ... **215** F5
Carpenter's Cl LE3 ... **153** B7
Carpe Rd LE4 ... **129** D1
Carrfield Ave 5 NG10 ... **10** F8
Carrfields La LE14 ... **80** D8
Carriageway The
LE15 ... **136** A6
Carron Cl NN17 ... **230** C1
Carrow Rd LE3 ... **153** B5
Carrs Cl DE74 ... **17** A3
Carr's Dr LE9 ... **198** F8
Carrs Hill LE9 ... **198** C6
Carr's Rd LE9 ... **198** F8
Carter Cl Enderby LE19 **178** A3
Long Eaton NG10 ... **10** B6
Carter Dale LE67 ... **71** D7
Carter St LE4 ... **155** C8
Cartland Dr LE11 ... **51** C6
Carts La LE1 ... **259** B4
Cartwright Dr LE2 ... **181** A5
Cartwright St LE11 ... **52** C5
Carty Rd LE5 ... **130** C3
Carver Ct PE9 ... **167** F5
Carver's Cnr LE2 ... **179** B3
Carver's Path LE7 ... **103** E7
Casewick La PE9 ... **144** F4
Cashmore View LE4 ... **128** D4
Castell Dr LE6 ... **127** A3
Casterton Com Coll
PE9 ... **142** E7
Casterton La PE9 ... **142** E2
Casterton Rd PE9 ... **143** B4
Castle Bytham Rd LE15 **89** F5
Castle Cl Bottesford NG13 **3** D2
Earl Shilton LE9 ... **175** F1
Sapcote LE9 ... **217** D7
Uppingham LE15 ... **188** F5
Castle Ct LE10 ... **215** D7
Castledine Ave LE12 ... **76** A6
Castledine St
Loughborough LE11 ... **52** B2
Quorn LE12 ... **75** F6
Castledine St Extension
LE11 ... **52** B2
Castle Donington Com Coll
DE74 ... **17** B3
Castle Dyke PE9 ... **143** D3
Castle Fields LE4 ... **128** A5
Castleford Rd LE3 ... **178** E8
Castlegate Ave LE4 ... **128** F8
Castle Hill
Castle Donington DE74 ... **17** B4
East Leake LE12 ... **31** F8
Mountsorrel LE12 ... **76** E2
Castle La
Melbourne DE73 ... **26** B7
5 Stamford PE9 ... **143** D2
Castlemaine Dr LE10 ... **197** E3
Castle Mews DE73 ... **26** B7
Castle Mews The DE11 ... **44** A7
Castle Mills DE73 ... **26** B7
Castle Mound Way
CV23 ... **252** D2
Castle Rd
Castle Gresley DE11 ... **44** A1
Hartshill CV10 ... **194** B1
Kirby Muxloe LE9 ... **152** D5
Mountsorrel LE12 ... **101** D8
Castle Rise
Belmesthorpe PE9 ... **117** A1
Groby LE6 ... **126** F2
Castle Rock Dr LE67 ... **72** C2
Castle Rock High Sch
LE67 ... **72** D2
Castle St Hinckley LE10 **215** D8
Leicester LE1 ... **259** A3
Melbourne DE73 ... **26** B7
16 Stamford PE9 ... **143** D3
Whitwick LE67 ... **71** F5
Castleton Rd LE18 ... **180** C4
Castle View
Hartshill CV10 ... **194** B1
Leicester LE1 ... **259** A3
Castle View Rd NG13 ... **7** C8
Castle Way LE65 ... **69** A4
Castle Yd LE1 ... **259** A3
Caswell Cl LE4 ... **128** D4
Caters Cl LE7 ... **127** D6
Catesby St LE3 ... **154** D5
Catherine Inf Sch LE4 **155** B8
Catherine Jun Sch
LE4 ... **155** B8
Catherine Rise DE11 ... **44** A6
Catherines Cl LE12 ... **76** B6
Catherine St LE4 ... **129** C1
Catherine Street Ind Est
LE4 ... **129** D2
Cathkin Cl LE3 ... **153** D5
Catmose Park Rd
LE15 ... **138** B5
Catmos St LE15 ... **138** A6
Catthorpe Rd LE17 ... **253** C4
Cattle Market LE11 ... **52** B3
Cauby Cl LE12 ... **77** E3
Caudebec Cl LE15 ... **189** A5
Caudle Cl LE7 ... **100** F3
Cauldwell La LE17 ... **234** B4
Causeway La
Cropston LE7 ... **100** E2
Leicester LE1 ... **259** A4
Causeway Rd NN17 ... **230** E2
Cavalry Cl LE13 ... **59** A6
Cavendish Bridge DE72 **17** B8
Cavendish Cl
Castle Donington DE74 ... **17** A2
Shardlow DE72 ... **9** B2
Swadlincote DE11 ... **44** A7
Cavendish Cres LE67 ... **96** C7
Cavendish Ct DE72 ... **9** A1
Cavendish Rd LE2 ... **179** E8
Cave Rd LE12 ... **76** E8
Caversham Cl CV11 ... **214** A7
Caversham Rd LE2 ... **179** C3
Cawdell Dr LE12 ... **29** D2
Cawsand Rd LE18 ... **180** C1
Caxton St LE16 ... **240** F1
Cecil Ct 11 PE9 ... **143** E3
Cecilia Rd LE2 ... **155** B2
Cecil Rd LE2 ... **155** B6
Cedar Ave Birstall LE4 ... **129** A7
East Leake LE12 ... **31** D8
Long Eaton NG10 ... **10** C5
Lutterworth LE17 ... **244** B6
Wigston LE18 ... **180** D2
Cedar Cl
Ashby-De-La-Z LE65 ... **69** C6
Glenfield LE3 ... **127** E1
Kibworth Beauchamp
LE8 ... **223** F8
Uppingham LE15 ... **189** C4
Cedar Cres LE19 ... **201** B7
Cedar Croft DE72 ... **16** A7
Cedar Ct Burbage LE10 **216** A6
Corby NN17 ... **230** E1
Groby LE6 ... **126** F2
Leicester LE5 ... **156** A8
Cedar Dr Ibstock LE67 ... **95** E2
Market Bosworth CV13 ... **148** F2
Melton Mowbray LE13 ... **59** B5
Syston LE7 ... **103** B2
Cedar Gr Moira DE12 ... **68** B6
Mountsorrel LE12 ... **76** E1
Swadlincote DE11 ... **44** A7
Cedar Rd Blaby LE8 ... **202** B6
Castle Donington DE74 ... **17** B2
Earl Shilton LE9 ... **198** D7
Leicester LE2 ... **155** C4
Loughborough LE11 ... **52** C1
Stamford PE9 ... **142** F4
Cedars Ct LE2 ... **155** C3
Cedar St LE15 ... **137** A2
Cedars The LE2 ... **180** B7
Cedarwood Cl LE4 ... **129** D1
Celandine Cl
Leicester, Oadby LE2 ... **181** E4
Mountsorrel LE12 ... **76** F2
Celandine Dr LE13 ... **82** B8
Celandine Pl DE11 ... **44** E4
Celandine Rd LE5 ... **130** C2
Cello Cl LE67 ... **71** E5
Celt St LE3 ... **154** D4
Cemetery La
Hartshill CV10 ... **194** B1
Manton LE15 ... **164** D6
Cemetery Rd
Sileby LE12 ... **77** D3
Whetstone LE8 ... **201** F7
Central Ave
Ibstock LE67 ... **95** F1
Leicester LE2 ... **155** C2
Lutterworth LE17 ... **244** C7
Shepshed LE12 ... **50** B3
Syston LE7 ... **103** C4
Wigston LE18 ... **180** C2
Central Cl LE8 ... **201** F8
Central Park Dr CV23 ... **252** D2
Central Rd
Coalville LE67 ... **96** D7
Leicester LE3 ... **154** D7
Central St LE8 ... **202** F4
Centre Ct LE19 ... **178** D7
Centurian Ct Office Pk
LE19 ... **178** D8
Centurion Ct LE6 ... **152** D8
Centurion Way LE19 ... **178** D7
Century Ct LE5 ... **156** C6
Chadderton Cl LE2 ... **180** A7
Chadwell Cl
Asfordby LE14 ... **57** E2
Melton Mowbray LE13 ... **59** E2
Chadwell Rd LE3 ... **153** E7
Chadwick Cl LE9 ... **150** B4
Chadwick Wlk LE4 ... **128** D3
Chaffinch Cl
Leicester LE4 ... **128** B6
Oakham LE15 ... **138** B8
Chainama Cl LE3 ... **153** C6
Chainbridge Cl LE11 ... **52** A5
Chale Rd LE4 ... **128** F2
Chalfont Cl LE13 ... **82** D7
Chalfont Dr LE12 ... **77** C1
Chalgrove Wlk LE5 ... **156** A6
Challottee LE12 ... **50** C3
Chalmondley Dr LE13 ... **59** D6
Chalvington Cl LE5 ... **156** C3
Chambers Cl LE67 ... **125** F8
Champion Cl LE5 ... **156** B5
Chancel Rd LE4 ... **128** D8
Chancery St LE1 ... **259** B3
Chandlers Croft LE67 ... **95** F3
Chandler Way LE9 ... **219** B5
Chandos St LE2 ... **155** C4
Channing Way LE67 ... **96** C4
Chantrell Cl LE67 ... **124** B5
Chantry Cl
Huncote LE9 ... **200** D7
Long Eaton NG10 ... **10** A4
Melbourne DE73 ... **26** B7
Chapel Bar LE12 ... **33** C3
Chapel Cl
Ab Kettleby LE14 ... **37** C2
Albert Village DE11 ... **44** C1
Dunton Bassett LE17 ... **219** D2
Empingham LE15 ... **141** A6
Houghton on t H LE7 ... **157** F4
Kilby LE18 ... **203** F3
Oakham LE15 ... **138** A6
Ravenstone LE67 ... **70** F1
Syston LE7 ... **103** A4
Thurcaston LE7 ... **101** B3
Chapel Fields LE17 ... **254** B3
Chapel Flats LE9 ... **198** B6
Chapel Gn LE3 ... **153** B3
Chapel Hill Groby LE6 ... **126** E3
Woolsthorpe by B NG32 ... **15** B8
Chapel La
Ab Kettleby LE14 ... **37** C2
Barrowden LE15 ... **191** F5
Clipston LE16 ... **249** F1
Coleorton LE67 ... **70** E8
Congerstone CV13 ... **147** D8
Cosby LE9 ... **201** D2
Croxton Kerrial NG32 ... **24** A7
Desford LE9 ... **151** B4
Gaddesby LE7 ... **105** B7
Granby NG13 ... **5** B5
Hoby LE14 ... **79** D8
Hose LE14 ... **20** F8
Ketton PE9 ... **168** A5
Leicester LE2 ... **180** B8
Lilbourne CV23 ... **258** A6
Mowsley LE17 ... **237** F7
Nether Broughton LE14 ... **36** C8
North Luffenham LE15 ... **166** D3
Norton-J-T CV9 ... **120** A2
Old Dalby LE14 ... **35** E4
Osgathorpe LE12 ... **48** E3
Ratby LE6 ... **152** C8
Sharnford LE10 ... **217** C4
Somerby LE14 ... **108** B2
Tugby LE7 ... **185** E6
Upper Broughton LE14 ... **19** A1
Walcote LE17 ... **245** B4
Walton LE17 ... **236** B2
Willoughby-on-t-W LE12 ... **34** D7
Witherley CV9 ... **194** C7
Wymondham LE14 ... **62** E2
Chapel Rise LE65 ... **47** F5
Chapel Row NG33 ... **43** B8
Chapel St
Barkestone-le-V NG13 ... **6** B2
Barlestone CV13 ... **149** D8
Barwell LE9 ... **198** B6
Belton-in-R LE15 ... **187** D7
Blaby LE8 ... **179** C1
Chapel St *continued*
Bottesford NG13 ... **3** B3
Donisthorpe DE12 ... **67** E1
Earl Shilton LE9 ... **176** A1
Eaton NG32 ... **22** F6
Enderby LE19 ... **178** A3
Ibstock LE67 ... **95** F1
Leicester, Oadby LE2 ... **181** A5
Long Eaton NG10 ... **10** E7
Lutterworth LE17 ... **244** C6
Measham DE12 ... **93** C5
Melbourne DE73 ... **26** B7
Melton Mowbray LE13 ... **59** C3
Oakthorpe DE12 ... **93** A6
Sharnford LE10 ... **217** C4
Shepshed LE12 ... **50** B5
Smisby LE65 ... **45** F3
Stapleton LE9 ... **174** F1
Swadlincote DE11 ... **44** A1
Swinford LE17 ... **254** B3
Syston LE7 ... **103** B4
Woodville DE11 ... **44** E2
Chapel Yd PE9 ... **143** E3
Chaplin Ct LE3 ... **153** D3
Chapmans Mdws LE65 ... **69** C4
Chapman St LE11 ... **52** C4
Chappell Cl LE4 ... **129** E7
Charlecote Ave LE3 ... **153** F1
Charles Dr LE7 ... **127** E7
Charles Rd PE9 ... **143** C5
Charles St
Hinckley LE10 ... **197** E1
Leicester LE1 ... **259** B4
Long Eaton NG10 ... **10** D6
Loughborough LE11 ... **52** B5
Market Harborough
LE16 ... **240** D3
Ravenstone LE67 ... **71** A2
Sileby LE12 ... **77** C2
Swadlincote DE11 ... **44** B2
Charleston Cl DE11 ... **44** A7
Charleston Cres LE9 ... **198** A6
Charles Way
Leicester, Oadby LE2 ... **181** C5
Whetstone LE8 ... **202** A5
Charley Dr LE11 ... **51** E2
Charley Rd
Shepshed LE12 ... **72** F7
Woodhouse Eaves LE12 ... **73** F2
Charlock Dr PE9 ... **142** F4
Charlock Rd LE5 ... **130** D2
Charlotte Ct LE8 ... **202** A8
Charlotte St LE13 ... **59** C3
Charlottes Wlk LE7 ... **157** F3
Charlton Ave 6 NG10 ... **10** F8
Charlton Cl LE8 ... **202** A6
Charnborough Ct LE67 ... **97** B8
Charnborough Rd LE67 **97** B8
Charnia Gr LE12 ... **100** F6
Charnor Rd LE3 ... **153** E8
Charnwood LE6 ... **126** B1
Charnwood Ave
Asfordby LE14 ... **57** F3
Castle Donington DE74 ... **17** C3
Long Eaton NG10 ... **10** B4
Sutton Bonington LE12 ... **30** C5
Thurmaston LE4 ... **129** F8
Whetstone LE8 ... **201** F8
Charnwood Cl
Hinckley LE10 ... **197** E2
Leicester Forest East
LE3 ... **153** A4
Thurmaston LE4 ... **129** F8
Charnwood Ct LE67 ... **96** E8
Charnwood Dr
Hartshill Green CV10 ... **194** B2
Leicester Forest East
LE3 ... **153** A3
Markfield LE67 ... **125** F8
Melton Mowbray LE13 ... **59** A4
Thurnby LE7 ... **156** F5
Charnwood Fields
LE12 ... **30** C5
Charnwood Ho LE12 ... **100** A8
Charnwood Mus★
LE11 ... **52** A4
Charnwood Prim Sch
LE2 ... **155** B6
Charnwood Rd
Anstey LE7 ... **127** D7
Barwell LE9 ... **198** B8
Hinckley LE10 ... **197** D2
Loughborough LE11 ... **52** B2
Shepshed LE12 ... **50** B2
Charnwood Rise LE12 ... **99** F8
Charnwood St
Coalville LE67 ... **71** E1
Leicester LE5 ... **155** C6
Charteris Cl LE11 ... **51** D6
Charter St LE1 ... **154** F7
Charters The PE9 ... **144** E4
Chartley Rd LE3 ... **154** C3
Chartwell Dr LE18 ... **180** A3
Chartwell Drive Ind Est
LE18 ... **180** A3
Chase The
Braunstone LE3 ... **178** F7
East Goscote LE7 ... **103** D8
Great Glen LE8 ... **182** C1
Markfield LE67 ... **125** E8
Chater Cl
Great Bowden LE16 ... **241** A6
Leicester LE5 ... **156** D7
Manton LE15 ... **164** E6
Chater Rd LE15 ... **137** F5
Chatham St LE1 ... **259** B3
Chatsworth Ave LE18 ... **180** A1
Chatsworth Cl
Hinckley LE10 ... **215** F6
Shepshed LE12 ... **50** A3
Chatsworth Dr
Market Harborough
LE16 ... **241** B3
Syston LE7 ... **102** F3
Chatsworth Rd
Loughborough LE11 ... **51** D5
Stamford PE9 ... **143** B4
Swadlincote DE11 ... **44** A6
Chatsworth St LE2 ... **155** C6
Chatteris Ave LE5 ... **156** D3
Chaucer St
Leicester LE2 ... **155** C3
Narborough LE19 ... **178** A1
Chaveney Ct LE12 ... **75** E5
Chaveney Rd LE12 ... **75** E5
Chaveney Wlk LE12 ... **75** E5
Cheapside
Leicester LE1 ... **259** B4
Melton Mowbray LE13 ... **59** C3
Shepshed LE12 ... **50** C4
Checketts Cl LE4 ... **129** B2
Checketts Rd LE4 ... **129** B3
Checkland Rd LE4 ... **129** E8
Cheddar Rd LE18 ... **180** E3
Cheer Cl LE8 ... **201** F4
Chelker Way LE11 ... **51** C3
Chellaston La DE72 ... **16** A8
Chellaston Rd LE18 ... **180** C4
Chelsea Cl LE2 ... **179** D1
Cheltenham Dr LE65 ... **69** A7
Cheltenham Rd LE4 ... **128** D2
Cheney Ct LE9 ... **200** D8
Cheney End LE9 ... **200** D7
Cheney Rd LE4 ... **130** A4
Chepstow Rd LE2 ... **155** C3
Cheribough Rd DE74 ... **17** A3
Cheriton Rd LE2 ... **179** D5
Cherrybrook Cl LE4 ... **128** B7
Cherry Cl Breaston DE72 ... **9** E8
Loughborough LE11 ... **75** A7
Cherry Dr LE7 ... **103** B2
Cherryfield Cl CV10 ... **194** B2
Cherry Gr LE8 ... **182** C1
Cherry Hills Rd LE3 ... **153** C6
Cherryholt La PE9 ... **143** F3
Cherryholt Rd PE9 ... **143** F3
Cherryleas Dr LE3 ... **154** C4
Cherry Orchard Est
CV13 ... **195** F3
Cherry Rd LE8 ... **202** B7
Cherry St LE18 ... **180** B2
Cherrytree Ave LE17 ... **244** A5
Cherry Tree Ave LE3 ... **152** E3
Cherrytree Cl LE8 ... **202** E4
Cherry Tree Cl
Anstey LE7 ... **127** D5
Husbands Bosworth
LE17 ... **247** E5
Cherry Tree Ct
Leicester Forest East
LE3 ... **152** E3
Moira DE12 ... **68** B6
Cherry Tree Dr
Barwell LE9 ... **198** B8
Plungar NG13 ... **6** A1
Cherry Tree Gr LE19 ... **178** A3
Cherry Tree Mews
DE11 ... **44** F2
Cherwell Cl LE10 ... **215** A8
Cherwell Rd LE12 ... **76** D7
Cherwell Wlk NN17 ... **230** C1
Cheshire Cl LE17 ... **244** B4
Cheshire Dr LE18 ... **180** A3
Cheshire Gdns LE2 ... **179** D7
Cheshire Rd LE2 ... **179** D7
Chessher St LE10 ... **197** C1
Chester Cl Blaby LE8 ... **202** C7
Leicester LE1 ... **155** B7
Loughborough LE11 ... **51** F3
Chesterfield Ave NG10 ... **10** F7
Chesterfield Rd LE5 ... **155** D4
Chesterfield Way LE9 ... **198** C7
Chester Gdns DE11 ... **44** B2
Chester Rd LE8 ... **202** C7
Chesterton Ct LE19 ... **178** A2
Chesterton Wlk LE3 ... **154** A5
Chestnut Ave
Corby NN17 ... **230** D1
Leicester LE5 ... **130** D1
Leicester, Oadby LE2 ... **181** A5
Lutterworth LE17 ... **244** A6
Swadlincote DE11 ... **44** B7
Chestnut Cl
Bottesford NG13 ... **3** C3
Broughton Astley LE9 ... **219** A5
Ibstock LE67 ... **95** E1
Littlethorpe LE19 ... **201** B6
Market Bosworth CV13 ... **148** F2
Moira DE12 ... **68** B5
Queniborough LE7 ... **103** D5
Quorn LE12 ... **75** E4
Shepshed LE12 ... **50** C3
Syston LE7 ... **103** B2
Uppingham LE15 ... **189** A3
Chestnut Ct LE12 ... **76** E2
Chestnut Dr LE7 ... **157** A4
Chestnut Gdns PE9 ... **142** F3
Chestnut Gn DE11 ... **44** B2
Chestnut Gr LE67 ... **97** B8
Chestnut La LE8 ... **221** F5
Chestnut Pl LE12 ... **76** D7

Chestnut Rd
Glenfield LE3 ... 153 C8
Oakham LE15 ... 138 A7
Chestnut St LE11 ... 52 A4
Chestnuts The
Countesthorpe LE8 ... 202 E4
Long Eaton NG10 ... 10 A8
Chestnut Way
East Goscote LE7 ... 103 E7
Melton Mowbray LE13 ... 59 C1
Chestnut Wlk
Groby LE6 ... 126 F2
Markfield LE67 ... 125 E6
Chettle Rd LE3 ... 154 A7
Chetwynd Dr LE13 ... 58 F3
Chevin Ave LE3 ... 153 D5
Cheviot Cl
Oakham LE15 ... 137 E6
Swadlincote DE11 ... 44 A3
Cheviot Dr LE12 ... 50 C3
Cheviot Rd
Leicester LE2 ... 179 F7
Long Eaton NG10 ... 10 A8
Cheyne La 8 PE9 ... 143 E3
Chichester Cl
Ellistown LE67 ... 96 C4
Loughborough LE11 ... 74 C8
Nuneaton CV11 ... 214 A7
Chilcombe Cl LE4 ... 128 E3
Chilcombe Wlk 4
LE4 ... 128 E3
Chilcott Cl LE67 ... 71 F1
Chiltern Ave
Cosby LE9 ... 201 D2
Shepshed LE12 ... 50 D3
Chiltern Cl
Market Harborough
LE16 ... 240 F5
Oakham LE15 ... 137 D6
Chiltern Dr LE15 ... 166 C7
Chiltern Gn LE2 ... 180 A6
Chiltern Rd DE11 ... 44 A3
Chiltern Rise LE65 ... 69 C5
Chislehurst Ave LE3 ... 178 F8
Chiswick Dr LE11 ... 51 C4
Chiswick Rd LE2 ... 154 F1
Chitterman Way LE67 ... 125 E8
Chorley Wood Rd LE5 ... 156 D4
Choyce Cl CV9 ... 170 D2
Chrisett Cl LE5 ... 156 B6
Christ Church & St Peter's CE Prim Sch LE12 ... 76 E2
Christie Dr LE11 ... 51 D6
Christopher Cl
Countesthorpe LE8 ... 202 E3
Heather LE67 ... 95 F3
Christopher Ct NN6 ... 256 D5
Christopher Dr LE4 ... 129 F4
Christow St LE1 ... 155 B7
Christ the King RC Prim Sch LE3 ... 154 B6
Chrysanthemum Ct
DE11 ... 44 A5
Church Ave
Leicester LE3 ... 154 C5
Swadlincote DE11 ... 44 B3
Church Bank LE16 ... 229 D7
Church Cl
Ashwell LE15 ... 111 B8
Barwell LE9 ... 198 A6
Blackfordby DE11 ... 45 B1
Braybrooke LE16 ... 251 E6
Broughton Astley LE9 ... 218 F6
Burbage LE10 ... 216 A5
Caldecott LE16 ... 230 B8
Dunton Bassett LE17 ... 219 D1
Hose LE14 ... 20 F7
Kibworth Beauchamp
LE8 ... 206 A1
Lutterworth LE17 ... 244 C6
Stoke Golding CV13 ... 196 D7
Syston LE7 ... 103 B4
Church Cnr NG13 ... 6 F4
Church Croft CV9 ... 171 B7
Church Cswy LE16 ... 225 C7
Church Ct PE9 ... 143 E2
Church Dr
Gilmorton LE17 ... 235 C4
Markfield LE67 ... 125 D8
Church End LE14 ... 19 D1
Church Farm Gram Sch
LE9 ... 198 D6
Church Farm La LE8 ... 220 D5
Church Field CV13 ... 147 D8
Churchgate LE16 ... 209 D6
Church Gate
Kegworth DE74 ... 18 D2
Leicester LE1 ... 259 B4
Loughborough LE11 ... 52 B4
Lutterworth LE17 ... 244 C5
Shepshed LE12 ... 50 C4
Churchgate Mews LE11 ... 52 B4
Church Gresley Inf Sch
DE11 ... 44 B2
Church Hill
Bagworth LE67 ... 124 B4
Birstall LE4 ... 129 B6
Cranoe LE16 ... 208 E3
Knipton NG32 ... 14 E3
Scraptoft LE7 ... 156 F8
Swannington LE67 ... 71 B7
Tilton on t H LE7 ... 133 C3
Woodhouse Eaves LE12 ... 75 A1
Church Hill CE Jun & Inf Schs LE4 ... 129 F7
Church Hill Rd
Cranoe LE16 ... 208 D3
Mountsorrel LE12 ... 76 D1
Thurmaston LE4 ... 129 F7
Church Ho CV9 ... 171 B7
Church House Mews
CV9 ... 171 B7
Churchill Cl
Ashby-De-La-Z LE65 ... 69 A6
Breaston DE72 ... 9 D8
Leicester, Oadby LE2 ... 181 A5
Lutterworth LE17 ... 244 A5
Melton Mowbray LE13 ... 59 C5
Churchill Dr
Leicester Forest East
LE3 ... 153 B4
Upper Bruntingthorpe
LE17 ... 236 D5
Churchill Rd
Oakham LE15 ... 137 E6
Stamford PE9 ... 143 C5
Churchill St LE2 ... 155 B4
Churchill Way LE8 ... 223 A7
Church La
Ab Kettleby LE14 ... 37 C3
Anstey LE7 ... 127 D6
Arnesby LE8 ... 221 F5
Asfordby LE14 ... 57 F2
Ashby Folville LE14 ... 105 F4
Austrey CV9 ... 119 B1
Barrowden LE15 ... 191 F4
Barrow-u-S LE12 ... 76 D8
Barsby LE7 ... 105 D3
Barwell LE9 ... 198 A6
Bisbrooke LE15 ... 189 F4
Bottesford NG13 ... 3 B3
Cadeby CV13 ... 149 D1
Caldecott LE16 ... 230 B8
Castle Donington DE74 ... 17 B3
Chilcote DE12 ... 91 E3
Church Langton LE16 ... 225 C7
Clipsham LE15 ... 89 D5
Croxton Kerrial NG32 ... 24 B7
Desford LE9 ... 151 B3
Duddington PE9 ... 193 B6
Dunton Bassett LE17 ... 219 D1
East Norton LE7 ... 186 C5
Eaton NG32 ... 22 F7
Edith Weston LE15 ... 166 B7
Fenny Drayton CV13 ... 194 F6
Fleckney LE8 ... 222 F7
Frisby on t W LE14 ... 80 D8
Gaddesby LE7 ... 105 B6
Gilmorton LE17 ... 235 B4
Glaston LE15 ... 190 B6
Goadby LE7 ... 185 B2
Greetham LE15 ... 88 A2
Grimston LE14 ... 57 B8
Hemington DE74 ... 17 E4
Hoby LE14 ... 79 D7
Hungarton LE7 ... 132 C3
Husbands Bosworth
LE17 ... 247 E5
Leicester LE2 ... 180 B7
Leicester,Stoughton LE2 ... 156 E1
Little Dalby LE14 ... 108 B8
Long Clawson LE14 ... 20 C3
Lyddington LE15 ... 212 D6
Manton LE15 ... 164 E6
Market Overton LE15 ... 86 F5
Morcott LE15 ... 191 A6
Muston NG13 ... 7 F8
Narborough LE19 ... 201 C8
No Mans Heath B79 ... 119 A6
Old Dalby LE14 ... 35 E4
Osgathorpe LE12 ... 48 E4
Plungar NG13 ... 5 F1
Preston LE15 ... 164 C1
Quorn LE12 ... 76 A6
Ratby LE6 ... 152 C8
Ratcliffe Culey CV9 ... 171 B3
Ratcliffe on t W LE7 ... 78 C2
Ravenstone LE67 ... 70 E1
Rearsby LE7 ... 79 A2
Redmile NG13 ... 6 F3
Ridlington LE15 ... 163 D2
Saxelbye LE14 ... 57 E6
Seaton LE15 ... 190 C1
Sedgebrook NG32 ... 4 F1
Sewstern NG33 ... 63 F8
Shawell LE17 ... 253 C4
Shearsby LE17 ... 222 A3
Sheepy Magna CV9 ... 171 B7
Somerby LE14 ... 108 B1
South Kilworth LE17 ... 255 C8
South Luffenham LE15 ... 191 E8
South Witham NG33 ... 65 B3
Sproxton LE14 ... 41 F6
Stamford PE9 ... 143 E2
Stapleton LE9 ... 174 E1
Stathern LE14 ... 13 A2
Stockerston LE15 ... 211 B8
Stretton LE15 ... 88 F4
Swannington LE67 ... 71 C4
Swinford NN6 ... 254 F2
Thorpe Langton LE16 ... 226 A5
Thorpe Satchville LE14 ... 106 E4
Thrussington LE7 ... 78 F4
Thurmaston LE4 ... 129 E7
Thurnby LE7 ... 156 F4
Twyford LE14 ... 106 E1
Upper Broughton LE14 ... 19 A1
Waltham on t W LE14 ... 40 A7
Welford NN6 ... 256 E5
Whetstone LE8 ... 201 F8
Wigston Parva LE10 ... 231 F8
Willoughby-on-t-W LE12 ... 34 C7
Wymondham LE14 ... 62 E2
Church Lands LE11 ... 52 B6
Church Langton CE Prim Sch LE16 ... 225 D7
Church Lea LE14 ... 82 F6
Church Leys Ave LE7 ... 79 A2
Church Nook LE18 ... 180 D3
Church Rd
Barlestone CV13 ... 149 D8
Burley LE15 ... 111 E2
Egleton LE15 ... 138 D3
Glenfield LE3 ... 127 B1
Great Glen LE8 ... 205 A8
Hartshill CV10 ... 194 B1
Ketton PE9 ... 168 A5
Kibworth Beauchamp
LE8 ... 206 A1
Kirby Muxloe LE9 ... 152 D5
Kirkby Mallory LE9 ... 175 C6
Leicester, Aylestone
LE2 ... 179 C6
Leicester,Evington LE5 ... 156 B2
Leicester LE4 ... 129 A3
Lyndon LE15 ... 165 D5
Nailstone CV13 ... 123 B3
Peckleton LE9 ... 176 A6
Shackerstone CV13 ... 121 E2
Swadlincote DE11 ... 44 A6
Wanlip LE7 ... 102 C2
Witherley CV9 ... 194 B7
Church Row LE2 ... 182 D5
Church Side LE12 ... 50 C4
Church Sq
Market Harborough
LE16 ... 240 E3
Melbourne DE73 ... 26 B6
Church St
Appleby Magna DE12 ... 119 E8
Barrow-u-S LE12 ... 76 D8
Belton-in-R LE15 ... 187 D7
Belton LE12 ... 49 B6
Billesdon LE7 ... 159 B2
Blaby LE8 ... 202 C8
Bottesford NG13 ... 3 B3
Braunston-in-R LE15 ... 137 A2
Burbage LE10 ... 216 A5
Carlby PE9 ... 117 B8
Churchover CV23 ... 252 B6
Clifton u D CV23 ... 257 A5
Cottingham LE16 ... 229 D1
Countesthorpe LE8 ... 202 F3
Donisthorpe DE12 ... 67 F1
Earl Shilton LE9 ... 176 A1
Easton on t H PE9 ... 169 A6
Empingham LE15 ... 141 A6
Granby NG13 ... 5 B5
Hartshorne DE11 ... 45 B6
Hathern LE12 ... 30 A1
Husbands Bosworth
LE17 ... 247 E5
Langham LE15 ... 110 C3
Leicester LE1 ... 259 C3
Leicester, Oadby LE2 ... 181 A5
Lockington DE74 ... 17 F4
Lutterworth LE17 ... 244 C5
Market Bosworth CV13 ... 148 F3
Market Harborough
LE16 ... 240 E3
Melbourne DE73 ... 26 B7
Melton Mowbray LE13 ... 59 C3
Netherseal DE12 ... 91 F6
North Kilworth LE17 ... 246 F3
North Luffenham LE15 ... 166 D3
North Witham NG33 ... 65 B8
Oakham LE15 ... 138 A6
Orston NG13 ... 2 A7
Rothley LE7 ... 101 F6
Ryhall PE9 ... 116 F2
Sapcote LE9 ... 217 D7
Scalford LE14 ... 38 E5
Seagrave LE12 ... 77 F8
Shepshed LE12 ... 50 C4
Sibbertoft LE16 ... 249 A2
Skillington NG33 ... 43 B8
South Witham NG33 ... 65 B3
Stamford PE9 ... 143 E2
Stoney Stanton LE9 ... 199 E2
Swadlincote DE11 ... 44 A6
Swadlincote DE11 ... 44 B1
Swadlincote DE11 ... 44 C4
Swepstone LE67 ... 94 D2
Thurlaston LE9 ... 177 A3
Thurmaston LE4 ... 129 D7
Twycross CV9 ... 146 D6
Wing LE15 ... 165 A3
Worthington LE65 ... 47 F6
Wymeswold LE12 ... 33 C3
Church Terr LE13 ... 59 C3
Church View
Bottesford NG13 ... 3 A3
Breaston DE72 ... 9 D7
Ibstock LE67 ... 122 E8
Narborough LE19 ... 201 C8
Newbold Verdon LE9 ... 150 A4
Osgathorpe LE12 ... 48 E4
Twyford LE14 ... 106 D1
Churchward Ave LE4 ... 128 D4
Church Wlk Blaby LE8 ... 202 B8
Bruntingthorpe LE17 ... 236 C8
Donisthorpe DE12 ... 92 E8
Hinckley LE10 ... 215 D8
Hose LE14 ... 20 F7
Lubenham LE16 ... 239 F3
Market Harborough
LE16 ... 241 A2
Shackerstone CV13 ... 121 E2
Swinford LE17 ... 254 B3
Thorpe Satchville LE14 ... 106 E4
Church Wlks CV13 ... 196 D7
Cider Cl LE15 ... 191 F5
Cinder La CV9 ... 145 A8
Circle The LE5 ... 155 F5
Circus The LE5 ... 130 D3
City Of Dan LE67 ... 71 F4
City of Leicester Sch The
LE5 ... 156 C3
City Of Three Waters
LE67 ... 71 E6
City Rd LE14 ... 12 F3
City The
Kibworth Beauchamp
LE8 ... 206 A2
Woodville DE11 ... 45 A2
City Yd LE15 ... 165 A2
Civic Way DE11 ... 44 B4
Clamp Dr DE11 ... 44 B3
Clapgun St DE74 ... 17 B3
Clare Cl PE9 ... 143 C3
Clarefield Rd LE3 ... 154 B5
Clare Gr LE3 ... 153 D2
Claremont Dr
Market Harborough
LE16 ... 241 A3
Ravenstone LE67 ... 70 F2
Claremont St LE4 ... 129 A3
Clarence Ct 7 LE10 ... 215 E8
Clarence Dr LE67 ... 96 F8
Clarence Rd
Hinckley LE10 ... 215 E8
Long Eaton NG10 ... 10 C6
Narborough LE19 ... 178 D2
Clarence St
Leicester LE1 ... 259 B4
Loughborough LE11 ... 52 C5
Market Harborough
LE16 ... 240 F3
Clarendon Ho LE10 ... 215 B7
Clarendon Park Rd
LE2 ... 155 B1
Clarendon Rd LE10 ... 215 C7
Clarendon St LE2 ... 259 A2
Claresholm Cres LE15 ... 138 B6
Claridge Pl 4 LE65 ... 69 B6
Clark Cardens LE8 ... 202 A8
Clark Dr LE13 ... 59 C6
Clarke Cl LE67 ... 71 F4
Clarke Dr NG10 ... 10 A4
Clarke Gr LE4 ... 129 A6
Clarke Rd LE67 ... 97 C8
Clarkes Dale LE16 ... 229 D6
Clarkes La DE72 ... 16 B8
Clarkes Rd LE18 ... 180 B2
Clarke St Leicester LE4 ... 129 B3
Market Harborough
LE16 ... 240 D3
Clatterpot La LE15 ... 112 C8
Clawson Cl LE11 ... 51 D6
Clawson La
Ab Kettleby LE14 ... 37 D4
Hickling LE14 ... 19 D7
Long Clawson LE14 ... 21 C1
Upper Broughton LE14 ... 19 E1
Claxton Rise LE14 ... 20 C2
Claybrook Ave LE3 ... 179 A8
Claybrooke Ct LE17 ... 232 F5
Claybrooke Prim Sch
LE17 ... 232 E4
Clay Cl DE11 ... 44 D5
Claydon Rd LE5 ... 155 E8
Claye St NG10 ... 10 E7
Clay La Ellistown LE67 ... 96 E2
Gretton NN17 ... 213 B1
Peggs Green LE67 ... 71 A8
Claymar Dr DE11 ... 44 A7
Claymill Rd LE4 ... 129 F4
Clay St Draycott DE72 ... 9 A7
Wymeswold LE12 ... 33 C3
Clayton Dr LE4 ... 129 F6
Clear View Cres LE9 ... 175 F1
Cleeve Mount LE11 ... 51 C4
Clematis Cl LE4 ... 128 A5
Clement Ave LE4 ... 129 A3
Clements Gate DE74 ... 28 D6
Clevedon Cres LE4 ... 155 E8
Cleveland Ave 4 NG10 ... 10 F8
Cleveland Cl DE11 ... 44 B3
Cleveland Rd
Hinckley LE10 ... 215 C8
Loughborough LE11 ... 74 F7
Wigston LE18 ... 180 D3
Cleveleys Ave LE3 ... 179 A8
Cliff Ave LE11 ... 51 F5
Cliff Cres PE9 ... 143 D3
Cliffe Hill Rd LE67 ... 98 A1
Cliffe House Mews
LE8 ... 201 F8
Cliffe La LE67 ... 98 B2
Cliffe Rd Birstall LE4 ... 128 F6
Easton on t H PE9 ... 169 A3
Clifford Cl NG10 ... 10 A4
Clifford Rd LE11 ... 51 F5
Clifford St
Leicester LE3 ... 154 D6
Long Eaton NG10 ... 10 E7
Wigston LE18 ... 179 F1
Cliff Rd Stamford PE9 ... 143 D3
Woolsthorpe by B NG32 ... 8 C1
Cliffwood Ave LE4 ... 128 F7
Clifton Ave
Ashby-De-La-Z LE65 ... 69 B8
Long Eaton NG10 ... 10 F7
Clifton Cl Overseal DE12 ... 67 A3
Swadlincote DE11 ... 44 A2
Clifton Ct
Hinckley LE10 ... 197 B1
Oakham LE15 ... 137 F6
Clifton Dr
Ashby-De-La-Z LE65 ... 69 A7
Wigston LE18 ... 180 A1
Clifton Rd
Leicester LE2 ... 179 F8
Netherseal DE12 ... 91 D6
Clifton Thorpe Mdws
DE11 ... 46 B1
Clifton Way LE10 ... 197 A1
Clint Hill Dr LE9 ... 199 E3
Clipper Rd LE4 ... 129 F3
Clipsham Rd
Castle Bytham NG33 ... 90 B7
Stretton LE15 ... 89 A4
Clipsham Woods Nature Trail★ LE15 ... 89 E7
Clipstone Cl LE18 ... 180 E2
Clipstone Gdns LE18 ... 180 E2
Clipstone Ho 2 LE2 ... 155 B5
Clipston La LE16 ... 250 E3
Clipston Rd
East Farndon LE16 ... 250 B4
Great Oxendon LE16 ... 250 D2
Clipston St LE16 ... 240 F1
Clivesway LE10 ... 197 C2
Clock House Ct LE15 ... 137 D8
Cloisters The LE9 ... 198 E8
Close The
Albert Village DE11 ... 67 D8
Anstey LE7 ... 127 D7
Barwell LE9 ... 198 B7
Blaby LE8 ... 179 B1
Burton Lazars LE14 ... 82 F6
Easton on t H PE9 ... 168 F4
Kirkby Mallory LE9 ... 175 D6
Narborough LE19 ... 178 A2
Ratby LE6 ... 126 C1
Stamford PE9 ... 143 F4
Swinford LE17 ... 254 B4
Cloud Hill View LE67 ... 47 E3
Cloud Lea LE12 ... 101 E8
Cloudsley Bush La
LE10 ... 231 A5
Cloud Way Ct LE11 ... 52 A6
Clovelly Rd
Glenfield LE3 ... 153 D8
Leicester LE5 ... 155 F4
Clover Cl LE19 ... 201 A8
Cloverdale DE11 ... 44 B7
Cloverdale Rd LE5 ... 130 C3
Clover Dr LE13 ... 82 B8
Cloverfield LE10 ... 197 C3
Clover Gdns PE9 ... 142 E4
Clover La LE12 ... 76 F1
Clover Pk LE10 ... 197 B3
Clover Pk Trad Est
LE10 ... 197 B3
Clover Pl LE67 ... 71 D8
Clover Wlk LE7 ... 103 E7
Clowbridge Dr LE11 ... 51 C3
Clumber Cl LE7 ... 103 B5
Clumber Rd LE5 ... 155 E6
Clumber St
Long Eaton NG10 ... 10 D7
Melton Mowbray LE13 ... 59 B4
Clun Wlk NN17 ... 230 C1
Clutsom Rd LE67 ... 96 C7
Clwyd Wlk NN17 ... 230 C1
Clyde Ct LE67 ... 71 E8
Clydesdale Cl LE13 ... 59 A6
Clyde St LE1 ... 259 C4
Coachhouse Mews
DE11 ... 44 A7
Coachmans Ct LE12 ... 50 C5
Coachouse Ct LE11 ... 52 B3
Coach Rd LE12 ... 50 D3
Coal Baulk LE7 ... 132 B3
Coalbourn Cl LE4 ... 128 E4
Coales Ave LE8 ... 202 A5
Coales Gdns LE16 ... 240 D5
Coalfield Way LE65 ... 69 E6
Coal La
Hartshorne DE11,DE73 ... 45 D8
Hose LE14 ... 20 F8
Coal Pit La
Lutterworth CV23,LE17 ... 243 A5
Willey CV23 ... 242 C6
Wolvey CV23 ... 231 F1
Coalville Bsns Pk LE67 ... 71 C1
Coalville Com Hospl
LE67 ... 72 A1
Coalville Cotts PE9 ... 143 E4
Coalville La LE67 ... 71 A1
Coatbridge Ave LE4 ... 129 D4
Coates Ave LE3 ... 154 A7
Cobbett Rd LE3 ... 153 D2
Cobden Prim Sch LE11 ... 52 C4
Cobden St
Leicester LE1 ... 155 B7
Long Eaton NG10 ... 10 E7
Loughborough LE11 ... 52 C4
Cobden Street Ind Est
LE1 ... 155 B7
Cobleas NG32 ... 15 B7
Cobwells Cl LE8 ... 223 A7
Cock La CV9 ... 120 A2
Cockleys NG10 ... 10 C6
Cockshut La DE73 ... 26 A8
Coe Ave LE11 ... 51 B5
Cokayne Rd LE3 ... 153 D6
Colbert Dr LE3 ... 179 A7
Colby Dr LE4 ... 130 A6
Colby Rd LE4 ... 129 F5
Colchester Rd LE5 ... 156 B7
Cold Overton Rd
Knossington LE15 ... 136 B7
Langham LE15 ... 110 B2
Oakham LE15 ... 137 D6
Coldstream Cl LE10 ... 197 A1
Colebrook Cl LE5 ... 155 E3
Coleford Rd LE4 ... 130 A5
Coleman Cl LE5 ... 155 F7
Coleman Ct LE5 ... 155 F7
Coleman Prim Sch
LE5 ... 155 E4
Coleman Rd
Fleckney LE8 ... 204 E1
Leicester LE5 ... 156 A5
Coleorton La LE65 ... 69 D3
Coleridge Dr LE19 ... 178 A2
Coles Cl LE4 ... 129 D5
Coley Cl LE10 ... 215 D7
Colgrove Rd LE11 ... 52 A2
Colindale Ave LE4 ... 129 A8
Colin Grundy Dr LE5 ... 130 B1
Collaton Rd LE18 ... 180 C1
College Ave
Leicester LE2 ... 155 B4
Melton Mowbray LE13 ... 82 C8
College Cl Coalville LE67 ... 96 C8
Great Casterton PE9 ... 142 E7
College Farm La LE15 ... 187 D8
College Hall LE2 ... 180 C8
College La LE10 ... 197 E1
College Rd
Sutton Bonington LE12 ... 30 A8
Syston LE7 ... 103 B3
Whetstone LE8 ... 202 A8
College St
Leicester LE2 ... 155 B4
Ullesthorpe LE17 ... 233 B4
Collett Rd LE4 ... 128 C4
Colley Rise LE15 ... 212 C7
Colliers Way LE67 ... 96 E3
Colliery Rd DE11 ... 44 A1
Colliery Row DE11 ... 44 A1
Collingham Rd LE3 ... 154 C1
Collingwood Cl LE13 ... 58 F3
Collingwood Cres LE13 ... 58 F3
Collingwood Dr LE12 ... 77 D4
Collingwood Rd NG10 ... 10 E6
Collin Pl LE4 ... 129 C2
Collins Cl LE3 ... 153 D2
Colne Cl Corby NN17 ... 230 C1
Leicester, Oadby LE2 ... 181 D5
Colonel's La LE14 ... 19 A1
Colsterdale Cl LE4 ... 128 D5
Colsterworth Rd
Skillington NG33 ... 43 C7
Stainby NG33 ... 43 F3
Colston La LE14 ... 11 E4
Coltbeck Ave LE19 ... 201 A7
Coltfoot Way LE13 ... 82 A8
Colthurst Way LE5 ... 156 E6
Colton St LE1 ... 259 C3
Colts Cl LE10 ... 215 D4
Coltsfoot Cl DE11 ... 44 F4
Coltsfoot Rd LE5 ... 130 C2
Coltsfoot Way LE9 ... 219 A4
Columbia Cl LE19 ... 178 A3
Columbine Cl LE3 ... 153 E2
Columbine Rd LE5 ... 130 B3
Colwell Rd LE3 ... 154 D8
Combe Cl LE3 ... 154 C8
Comet Cl LE3 ... 154 B7
Comet Way LE67 ... 71 D2
Commerce St DE73 ... 26 A7
Commercial Sq LE2 ... 154 F1
Common Rd DE11 ... 44 B2
Common Side DE11 ... 44 B2
Common The
Barwell LE9 ... 198 B5
Leicester LE5 ... 156 A3
Compass Rd LE5 ... 156 D7
Compton Ave DE72 ... 16 A8
Compton Cl LE11 ... 74 C8
Compton Dr LE9 ... 200 D8
Compton Rd LE3 ... 154 C2
Conaglen Rd LE2 ... 179 B6
Condon Rd LE12 ... 76 E7
Condor Cl LE9 ... 218 F7
Conduit Rd PE9 ... 143 E4
Conduit St LE2 ... 259 C3
Cone La LE2 ... 155 C3
Coneries The LE11 ... 52 B4
Coneygrey LE8 ... 204 F1
Congerstone La
Barton in t B CV13 ... 122 B1
Carlton CV13 ... 148 C6
Shackerstone CV13 ... 121 E1
Congerstone Prim Sch
CV13 ... 147 D8
Conifer Cl
4 Leicester LE2 ... 155 C4
Lutterworth LE17 ... 244 B6
Coninsby Cl LE3 ... 154 B1
Coniston Ave LE2 ... 259 A1
Coniston Cl LE9 ... 198 F8
Coniston Cres LE11 ... 51 D1
Coniston Ct LE9 ... 198 F8
Coniston Gdns LE65 ... 69 C5
Coniston Rd
Barrow-u-S LE12 ... 76 D8
Edith Weston LE15 ... 166 A7
Melton Mowbray LE13 ... 59 A6
Coniston Way LE9 ... 200 D4
Conkers Discovery Ctr★
DE12 ... 67 D5
Conkers Waterside Ctr★
DE12 ... 67 D4
Connaught Ho LE11 ... 52 B3
Connaught Rd LE16 ... 240 F4
Connaught St LE2 ... 155 B4
Connell Cl LE16 ... 239 F3
Constable Ave LE4 ... 155 B8

272 Dav – Eld

Davett Cl LE5 156 B6
David Ave LE4 128 E5
David Lees Cl LE67 96 E3
Davison Cl LE5 156 A6
Davis Rd DE11 44 B4
Dawkins Rd DE12 67 E1
Dawlish Cl LE5 156 D5
Dawsons La LE7,LE14 134 C6
Dawson's La LE9 198 B6
Dawson's Rd LE12 48 D4
Daybell Cl
Bottesford NG13 3 B3
Whetstone LE8 178 F1
Daybell Rd DE12 68 A4
Day St LE4 129 A3
Dayton Cl LE67 71 A2
Deacon Ave CV13 149 C8
Deacon Cl
Bitteswell LE17 244 A8
Market Harborough
LE16 240 D5
Shepshed LE12 50 C3
Deacon Rd LE4 128 D8
Deacon Rise CV13 122 C1
Deacon St LE2 259 A2
Dean Cl LE10 197 E2
Deancourt Rd LE2 180 B6
Deane Gate Dr LE7 157 F4
Deanery Cres LE4 128 D8
Deane St LE11 51 E5
Dean Rd Hinckley LE10 197 E2
Leicester LE4 129 C1
Dean Rd W LE10 197 E2
Deansburn Ho LE3 153 F8
Deanside Dr LE11 51 E6
Dean's La LE12 74 B3
Dean's St LE15 137 F6
Dean's Terr LE15 189 A4
Debdale LE15 112 C8
Debdale Hill LE14 35 E4
Debdale La
Gumley LE16 224 C3
Smeeton Westerby LE8 224 A6
Debdale Pl LE14 57 E2
Deben Rd NN17 230 D1
Dee Cl LE15 137 E4
Deeming Dr LE12 75 F7
Deene Cl LE16 241 A3
Deene Rd NN17 213 F7
Deepdale
Great Easton LE16 229 D7
Leicester LE5 155 F6
Deepdale Cl LE67 95 F2
Deepdale Rd NG10 10 A5
Deepdene Cl DE11 44 C1
Deeping La CV13 149 B4
Deep Side PE9 168 F4
Deepway The LE12 75 E5
Deers Acre LE11 52 B6
Degens Way LE67 96 B7
De Havilland Way
LE10 215 E4
Deighton Way LE11 51 C6
De La Bere Cres LE10 216 A6
Delamare Rd LE13 59 D6
Delamere Cl DE72 9 D8
Delaware Rd LE5 156 E4
De Lisle Cl LE16 240 D2
De Lisle Ct LE11 51 B2
De Lisle RC Sch LE11 51 D3
Dell The Oakham LE15 138 A5
Ullesthorpe LE17 233 B4
Delph The DE73 26 F2
Delven La DE74 17 B3
De Montford University
(Charles Frears Campus)
LE2 155 C2
De Montfort LE13 59 C5
De Montfort Cl LE11 51 C5
De Montfort Ct LE7 127 D6
De Montfort Mews
LE1 259 C2
De Montfort Pl LE1 259 C2
De Montfort Rd LE10 197 E1
De Montfort Sq LE1 259 C2
De Montfort St LE1 259 C2
De Montfort University
LE2 259 A2
De Montfort Univ
(Scraptoft Campus)
LE7 156 F8
Dempsey Cl LE17 244 C8
Denacre Ave LE18 180 A1
Denbigh Pl LE17 244 C7
Denbydale LE18 180 F1
Denegate Ave LE4 128 F8
Denfield Cl LE15 190 B5
Denham Cl LE3 153 C6
Denis Cl LE3 154 B5
Denis Rd LE10 215 D5
Deniston Ave LE9 218 D7
Denman La LE9 200 D8
Denmark Rd LE2 179 E8
Denmead Ave LE18 180 C4
Dennis David Cl LE17 244 C8
Dennis St LE67 96 D6
Denstone Cl LE65 69 A8
Denton La Harston NG32 15 C4
Sedgebrook NG32 8 F6
Denton Rise LE13 59 E4
Denton St LE3 154 B5
Denton Wlk LE18 180 E2
Derby Cl LE9 219 A5
Derby La DE12 121 A6
Derby Rd
Ashby-De-La-Z LE65 69 B6
Aston-on-T DE72 16 A8
Draycott DE72 9 A7
Hathern LE12 29 F2
Hinckley LE10 197 D1
Kegworth DE74 18 C2
Long Eaton NG10 10 A8
Long Eaton NG10 10 D8
Loughborough LE11 51 E6
Melbourne DE73 26 A8
Smisby LE65,DE11,DE73 45 F6
Swadlincote DE11 44 C3
Derby Sq 5 LE11 52 A4
Derrys Hollow LE67 96 E3
Derry Wlk LE4 128 E4
Dersingham Rd LE4 128 E2
De Ruthyn Cl DE12 68 A4
Derwent Ave LE15 166 A7
Derwent Cl
Castle Gresley DE11 44 A1
Earl Shilton LE9 198 F8
Derwent Dr
Loughborough LE11 51 D1
Melton Mowbray LE13 59 B1
Oakham LE15 137 F5
Derwent Gdns LE65 69 C5
Derwent Rd LE12 76 D8
Derwent St Draycott DE72 9 A7
Leicester LE2 155 C5
Long Eaton NG10 10 C6
Derwent Street Ind Est
NG10 10 C6
Derwent Wlk
Corby NN17 230 D2
Leicester, Oadby LE2 181 C5
Desborough Rd
Arthingworth LE16 251 F1
Braybrooke LE16 251 F5
Desford Com Prim Sch
LE9 151 A2
Desford Cross Roads
LE9 177 B8
Desford Grange LE9 151 B4
Desford La
Kirkby Mallory LE9 175 D7
Peckleton LE9 176 B8
Ratby LE6,LE9 152 B7
Desford Rd
Enderby LE9,LE19 177 D6
Kirby Muxloe LE9 152 D6
Narborough LE19 201 B8
Newbold Verdon LE9 150 D4
Thurlaston LE9 176 F4
Desford Tropical Bird
Gdns★ LE9 151 B5
Devana Ave LE67 96 F8
Devana Rd LE2 155 C3
Devenports Hill LE7 157 B5
De Verdon Rd LE17 244 A5
De Verdun Ave LE12 49 B6
Deveron Cl LE67 72 C1
Deveron Ct LE10 197 B1
Deveron Way LE10 197 B1
Deveron Wlk NN17 230 D1
Devitt Way LE9 218 F4
Devon Cl DE12 68 C6
Devonia Rd LE2 181 D4
Devon La NG13 3 B3
Devonshire Ave LE18 180 A1
Devonshire La LE11 52 B3
Devonshire Rd LE4 128 E1
Devonshire Sq LE11 52 B3
Devonshire Wlk LE2 181 C3
Devon Way LE5 155 F5
Devon Wlk LE15 87 D2
Deweys Cl LE15 166 D3
Dexters Cl LE12 76 A7
Dickens Cl LE12 77 D4
Dickens Ct LE3 154 A5
Dickens Dr
Melton Mowbray LE13 59 B6
Stamford PE9 143 A3
Swadlincote DE11 44 C5
Dicken The LE8 201 F7
Dickinson Way LE4 129 F7
Dickman's La LE14 12 B3
Dick's Hill LE16 249 C5
Didcott Way DE12 119 F8
Didsbury St LE3 153 E3
Dieppe Way LE13 59 B5
Digby Cl Leicester LE3 154 B3
Tilton on t H LE7 160 A8
Digby Dr
Melton Mowbray LE13 81 F8
Oakham LE15 137 E6
Digby Ho LE2 180 F7
Digby Rd LE15 166 D3
Dillon Gn LE3 153 F8
Dillon Rd LE3 153 F8
Dillon Rise LE3 153 F8
Dillon Way LE3 127 F1
Dimmingsdale Cl LE7 127 E7
Dingle La B79,DE12 119 C6
Dingley Ave LE4 129 C1
Dingley La LE16 241 F6
Dingley Link LE18 180 E3
Dingley Rd LE16 241 B6
Dingley Terr LE16 240 F3
Dinmore Grange DE11 45 B6
Discovery Way LE65 69 D7
Diseworth CE Prim Sch
DE74 28 C6
Diseworth Rd DE74 17 A1
Diseworth St LE2 155 C5
Disney Cl LE9 199 D2
Disraeli Cl LE8 223 F8
Disraeli St
Leicester LE2 179 D7
Quorn LE12 76 A6
Ditchling Ave LE3 154 A6
Dixie Gram Sch The
CV13 148 F3
Dixon Dr LE2 155 C3
Dobney Ave LE7 103 C6
Dockhouse The LE16 240 D4
Doctor Cookes Cl LE9 198 A6
Doctors Fields LE9 198 D7
Doctor's La
Breedon on the Hill DE73 26 F2
Melton Mowbray LE13 59 E4
Doctor's Wlk The DE12 93 C5
Doddridge Rd LE16 240 E4
Dodgeford La LE12 48 F6
Dodwells Bridge Ind Est
LE10 214 E8
Dodwells Rd LE10 214 E8
Dog And Gun La LE8 201 F5
Dog La
Burton Lazars LE14 83 A7
Netherseal DE12 91 F6
South Kilworth LE17 255 C8
Wilson DE73 26 E6
Dogwood Ct LE2 181 A7
Dolphin Ct LE15 189 A4
Dominion Rd
Glenfield LE3 153 D8
Swadlincote DE11 44 B5
Dominus Way LE19 178 D8
Domont Cl LE12 50 B3
Donald Cl LE4 129 F4
Donald Greaves Ho
NN17 230 D1
Donaldson Rd LE4 155 A8
Donata Ho LE17 244 C6
Doncaster Rd LE4 129 B1
Don Cl Corby NN17 230 D1
Oakham LE15 137 E4
Donington Dr LE65 68 F5
Donington Grand Prix
Collection Museum★
DE74 27 D8
Donington La
Shardlow DE72 17 C8
Shardlow DE72,DE74 17 C7
Donington le Heath Manor
House★ LE67 96 C6
Donisthorpe La DE12 67 E2
Donisthorpe Prim Sch
DE12 68 A1
Donnett Cl LE5 156 B6
Donnington Park Motor
Racing Circuit DE74 27 C8
Donnington St LE2 155 C5
Dorchester Cl
Blaby LE8 202 B6
Wigston LE18 203 D8
Dorchester Rd
Burbage LE10 216 B7
Leicester LE3 154 B4
Dorchester Way CV11 214 A7
Dore Rd LE5 155 C4
Dorfold Wlk LE4 129 D1
Dorian Rise LE13 59 B2
Dorothy Ave
Glen Parva LE2 179 B3
Melton Mowbray LE13 59 A4
Thurmaston LE4 129 D6
Dorothy Goodman Sch
LE10 197 D2
Dorothy Rd LE5 155 D5
Dorset Ave
Glenfield LE3 127 C1
Wigston LE18 179 F3
Dorset Dr
Melton Mowbray LE13 82 D7
Moira DE12 68 C6
Dorset St LE4 155 A8
Double Rail Cl LE18 180 A1
Doudney Cl LE9 199 D1
Doughty St PE9 143 F5
Douglas Bader Dr
LE17 244 D8
Douglas Dr LE67 122 F8
Douglas Jane Cl LE13 59 A4
Douglas Rd NG10 10 C8
Douglass Dr LE16 240 F4
Dove Bank Prim Sch
CV13 123 B3
Dove Cl Hinckley LE10 215 A8
Oakham LE15 137 E5
Woodville DE11 44 F3
Dovecote
Breedon on the Hill DE73 27 B3
Castle Donington DE74 17 B3
Shepshed LE12 50 C4
Dovecote Cl
Barrowden LE15 191 F5
Sapcote LE9 217 D7
Dovecote Rd LE9 200 C5
Dovecote St LE12 30 A1
Dovecotes The LE7 104 A5
Dovecote The DE73 26 F2
Dovecote Way LE9 198 B6
Dovedale Ave
Blaby LE8 202 B7
Long Eaton NG10 10 B6
Dovedale Cl LE13 59 B1
Dovedale Ct NG10 10 B6
Dovedale Prim Sch
NG10 10 B6
Dovedale Rd
Leicester LE2 155 E1
Thurmaston LE4 129 E7
Dovehouse Cl NN6 256 E6
Dove La NG10 10 C8
Dovelands Prim Sch
LE3 154 B5
Dover Cl LE12 101 D8
Dove Rd Coalville LE67 97 A7
Diseworth DE74 28 C8
Dove Rise LE2 181 C6
Dover St
Kibworth Beauchamp
LE8 223 F8
Leicester LE1 259 C3
Dower House Gdns
LE12 76 A6
Downham Ave LE4 128 E2
Downing Cres PE9 143 D5
Downing Dr LE5 156 D4
Downside Dr LE65 69 A7
Down St LE4 129 B1
Dowry Furlong Wildlife
Area★ LE6 126 D5
Doyle Cl LE11 51 D6
Dragon La LE9 150 A5
Dragon St NG13 5 B5
Dragwell DE74 18 D2
Drake Way LE10 197 D4
Draper St LE2 155 C3
Draycott Com Prim Sch
DE72 9 A7
Draycott Rd
Breaston DE72 9 C7
Long Eaton NG10 10 A4
Drayton Cl CV13 194 F6
Drayton Ct CV10 194 B2
Drayton La CV13 194 E6
Drayton Rd
Bringhurst LE16 229 B5
Drayton LE16 228 D7
Leicester LE3 153 E7
Medbourne LE16 228 A5
Drayton St DE11 44 C4
Dribdale LE8 223 A7
Drift Ave PE9 143 F4
Drift Cl DE11 68 B8
Drift Gdns PE9 143 F5
Drift Hill Redmile NG13 6 F4
Wymondham LE14 63 A2
Drift Rd PE9 143 E4
Drift Side DE11 68 B7
Drift The
Collyweston PE9 168 D2
Denton NG32 15 E3
Essendine PE9 116 D6
Sewstern NG33 42 F2
Thistleton NG33 64 B5
Drinkstone Rd LE5 155 E5
Drive, Dalby Rd LE13 59 C1
Drive The Barwell LE9 198 C8
Birstall LE4 129 A6
Countesthorpe LE8 202 C4
Kibworth Beauchamp
LE8 224 B8
Scraptoft LE7 156 F8
Woodhouse Eaves LE12 100 A8
Drome Cl LE67 72 D1
Dromintee Rd LE67 97 B4
Dronfield St LE5 155 C5
Drought Gdn &
Arboretum★ LE15 139 D6
Drovers Way
Desford LE9 151 C3
Narborough LE19 201 B7
Drove The PE9 168 D1
Druid St LE10 197 D1
Drumcliff Rd LE5 156 E6
Drummond Rd
Enderby LE19 178 A3
Leicester LE4 128 F3
Drummond Wlk LE13 59 B5
Drury La LE2 180 F6
Drurys La LE15 190 C1
Dryden Cl DE12 93 C4
Dryden St LE1 259 C5
Dryer Cl LE67 122 F8
Dry Pot La LE12 28 F2
Duck Lake DE12 119 F8
Dudleston Cl LE5 156 A5
Dudley Ave LE5 156 C6
Dudley Cl LE5 156 C6
Dudley Rise LE10 215 D6
Duffield Ave LE18 180 B4
Duffield Cl NG10 10 A5
Duffield St LE2 155 C5
Dukes Cl
Thurmaston LE4 129 F7
Wigston LE18 180 B3
Dukes Dr Flats LE2 155 C2
Dukes Rd LE14 36 B6
Duke St Leicester LE1 259 B2
Loughborough LE11 52 B5
Melton Mowbray LE13 59 E4
Dulverton Cl
Loughborough LE11 74 D8
Wigston LE18 203 D8
Dulverton Rd
Leicester LE3 154 C5
Melton Mowbray LE13 59 A5
Dumbleton Ave LE3 154 C1
Dumps Rd LE67 71 E6
Dunbar Rd
Coalville LE67 97 C8
Leicester LE4 129 E2
Dunbar Way LE65 69 D6
Dunblane Ave LE4 129 D4
Dunblane Way LE10 197 A2
Duncan Ave LE9 200 D7
Duncan Rd LE2 179 E7
Duncan Way LE11 51 C6
Duncombe Rd LE3 128 A1
Dundee Dr PE9 143 A4
Dundee Rd Blaby LE8 202 B6
Swadlincote DE11 44 D5
Dundonald Rd LE4 129 A1
Dunholme Ave LE11 51 B4
Dunholme Rd LE4 129 E1
Dunire Cl LE4 128 C3
Dunkirk St LE1 259 C3
Dunley Way LE17 244 C7
Dunlin Rd
Essendine PE9 117 B6
Leicester LE5 155 C7
Dunnicliffe La DE73 26 A7
Dunnsmoor La DE11 44 E7
Duns La LE3 259 A3
Dunslade Cl LE16 241 B2
Dunslade Gr LE16 241 B2
Dunslade Rd LE16 241 A2
Dunsmore Cl LE11 74 D8
Dunsmore Way DE11 44 E5
Dunstall Ave LE3 153 D3
Dunster Rd LE12 76 D1
Dunster St LE3 154 B5
Dunston Cl 4 NG10 10 F7
Dunsville Wlk LE4 129 D3
Dunton Bassett Prim Sch
LE17 219 D2
Dunton La LE17 234 A6
Dunton Rd
Broughton Astley LE17,
LE9 219 B3
Leire LE17 234 A8
Dunton St
Leicester LE3 154 D7
Wigston LE18 179 F1
Dupont Cl LE3 153 D7
Dupont Gdns LE3 153 D7
Duport Rd LE10 215 F7
Durban Rd LE4 128 C7
Durham Cl
Bagworth LE67 124 A6
Swadlincote DE11 44 E5
Durham Dr LE18 180 A4
Durham Rd LE11 51 E6
Durham Wlk LE67 124 A6
Durnford Rd LE18 203 D7
Durrell Cl LE11 51 C6
Durris Cl LE67 72 C1
Durston Cl LE5 156 D4
Duxbury Rd LE5 155 E7
Dyers Ct LE11 52 C5
Dysart Way LE1 155 B7
Dyson Cl
Lutterworth LE17 244 C7
Rugby CV21 257 A1
Dysons Cl DE12 93 B4

E

Eagle Cl
Broughton Astley LE9 218 E7
Measham DE12 93 B4
Eagles Dr LE13 82 B8
Eaglesfield LE17 218 F1
Eaglesfield End LE17 218 E1
Ealing Rd LE2 154 F1
Eamont Cl LE2 179 D3
Eamont Gn LE2 179 D3
Earle Smith Cl LE8 202 A7
Earl Howe St LE2 155 C4
Earl Howe Terr 5
LE3 154 D5
Earl Russell St LE2 179 C6
Earls Cl LE4 129 F7
Earl Shilton Rd LE9 176 D2
Earls Rd LE14 36 B6
Earl St Earl Shilton LE9 176 A1
Leicester LE1 259 C4
Earlstrees Ct NN17 230 F2
Earlstrees Ind Est
NN17 230 E2
Earlstrees Rd NN17 230 F2
Earls Way LE4 129 F7
Earlswood Cl DE72 9 D8
Earlswood Rd LE5 156 D4
Easby Cl LE11 51 B5
Easedale Cl CV11 214 A6
East Acre LE14 108 C1
East Ave Leicester LE2 155 C2
Melton Mowbray LE13 59 A4
Syston LE7 103 C4
Whetstone LE8 201 F8
East Bond St LE1 259 B4
Eastboro Fields CV11 214 A4
Eastboro Way CV11 214 A4
East Cl LE10 215 D7
Eastcourt Rd LE2 180 C6
East Cres LE67 96 E2
East End LE14 20 D4
East End Dr DE11 44 C4
Eastern Bvd LE2 259 A2
Eastfield Ave LE13 59 C4
Eastfield Ct LE3 154 B5
Eastfield Cty Prim Sch
LE4 129 F8
Eastfield Rd
Leicester LE3 154 B5
Swadlincote DE11 44 C6
Thurmaston LE4 129 F8
Eastgate LE16 209 D5
East Gates LE1 259 B4
East Gn LE9 198 A6
East Goscote Ind Est
LE7 103 C7
Easthorpe La
Muston NG13 3 E1
Redmile NG13 6 F4
Easthorpe Rd NG13 3 C2
Easthorpe View NG13 3 C2
East La Bardon LE67 97 D4
Ridlington LE15 163 E2
Eastleigh Rd LE3 154 D3
East Link LE19 178 E7
Eastmere Rd LE18 180 F3
East Midlands Airport
DE74 28 C8
East Midlands Airport
Aeropark★ DE74 17 A1
East Norton Rd LE16 209 D7
Easton Garfords Sch
PE9 169 A5
East Orch LE12 77 C1
East Park Rd LE5 155 D5
East Rd Birstall LE4 129 A5
Wymeswold LE12 33 E4
East Side Croft LE13 59 D6
East St Leicester LE1 259 C3
Leicester, Oadby LE2 181 A6
Long Eaton NG10 10 F8
Market Harborough
LE16 240 D3
Stamford PE9 143 E3
Eastway DE74 17 B3
Eastway Rd LE18 180 D4
East Wlk Ibstock LE67 95 F1
Ratby LE6 126 C1
Eastwood Rd LE2 179 D5
Eastwoods Rd LE10 197 F2
Eaton Ct NG32 22 F7
Eaton Grange Dr NG10 10 A8
Eaton Rd DE74 17 B3
Ebchester Cl LE2 179 C3
Ebchester Rd LE2 179 C4
Ebenezer Cotts CV13 149 B8
Edale Cl Leicester LE3 153 E3
Long Eaton NG10 10 B6
Edale Gn LE10 215 F6
Eddystone Rd LE5 156 E7
Edelin Rd LE11 52 B1
Eden Cl
Leicester, Oadby LE2 181 C6
Loughborough LE11 51 C5
Edendale Dr LE10 197 E4
Edendale Rd LE13 82 B8
Eden Gdns LE4 128 C7
Edenhall Cl
Leicester LE4 129 D3
Leicester, Oadby LE2 181 D4
Edenhurst Ave LE3 178 F7
Eden Rd LE2 181 D6
Edensor St LE4 129 C3
Eden Way LE2 179 D2
Edgbaston Cl LE4 128 D7
Edgcote Ct LE5 155 E8
Edgecote Dr DE11 44 A7
Edgefield Cl LE5 130 B2
Edgehill Cl LE8 205 B8
Edge Hill Ct NG10 10 D4
Edgehill Rd LE4 129 E2
Edgeley Cl LE3 128 B1
Edgeley Rd LE8 202 F4
Edinburgh Cl LE16 240 F4
Edinburgh Rd
Earl Shilton LE9 198 D7
Stamford PE9 143 D5
Edinburgh Way LE12 76 C1
Edison Ctyd NN17 230 F3
Edith Ave LE3 179 A7
Edith Weston Prim Sch
LE15 166 A7
Edith Weston Rd
LE15 166 D4
Edmonds Cl PE9 143 F4
Edmonds Dr PE9 168 A5
Edmondthorpe Drift
LE14 63 B1
Edmondthorpe Mere
LE15 85 E5
Edmondthorpe Rd
LE14 62 E1
Edmonton Rd LE1 259 C5
Edmonton Way LE15 138 B6
Edward Ave LE3 178 F8
Edward Cl LE2 181 C5
Edward Dr LE2 179 E1
Edward Rd
Fleckney LE8 222 F7
Leicester LE2 155 B2
Long Eaton NG10 10 D8
Market Harborough
LE16 240 D5
Stamford PE9 143 D5
Edwards Ctr 6 LE10 215 D8
Edward St
Albert Village DE11 44 C1
Anstey LE7 127 E7
Hartshorne DE11 45 A3
Hinckley LE10 197 C2
Leicester LE5 155 C7
Loughborough LE11 52 A5
Overseal DE12 67 B4
Egerton Ave LE4 128 E2
Egerton Hos LE2 180 E7
Egerton View LE13 59 B3
Eggington Ct LE11 51 E2
Eggington St LE5 155 C5
Eglantine Cl LE2 181 A7
Egleton Nature Reserve★
LE15 138 F2
Eider Cl LE8 201 F4
Eight Acres 6 PE9 143 C3
Eileen Ave LE4 128 E2
Elbow La LE1 259 A4
Elder Cl LE3,LE7 127 F3
Elder La LE67 48 A2

Goldcrest LE15 .... 189 A5
Golden Sq LE12 .... 51 A8
Goldfinch Cl LE11 .... 51 F3
Goldhill LE18 .... 180 D4
Goldhill Gdns LE2 .... 180 D7
Goldhill Rd LE2 .... 180 D7
Golding Cl LE11 .... 51 B6
Goldsmith Rd LE3 .... 154 A4
Goldspink Cl LE13 .... 82 C8
Golf Course La LE3 .... 153 C5
Golf Dr CV11 .... 214 B1
Goliath Rd LE67 .... 71 D2
Gonerby La NG32 .... 4 F5
Goodacre Cl CV23 .... 257 A5
Goodacre Cotts LE17 .... 233 F5
Goodacre Rd LE17 .... 233 C4
Goode's Ave LE7 .... 103 B2
Goode's La LE7 .... 103 B3
Goodheart Way LE3 .... 153 C2
Gooding Ave LE3 .... 154 A3
Gooding Cl LE3 .... 154 B3
Goodriche Ho LE13 .... 59 D3
Goodriche St LE13 .... 59 D3
Goodwood Cl LE16 .... 241 B3
Goodwood Cres LE5 .... 156 B4
Goodwood Rd LE5 .... 156 B4
Goosehills Rd LE10 .... 215 E5
Goose La LE9 .... 198 A5
Gopsall Rd
Congerstone CV13 .... 147 C8
Hinckley LE10 .... 197 D2
Gopsall St LE2 .... 155 B5
Gordon Ave 9 LE2 .... 155 B4
Gordon Ho 1 LE2 .... 155 B5
Gordon Rd LE11 .... 52 B6
Gores La LE16 .... 241 A3
Gorham Rise LE9 .... 218 D7
Gorseburn Ho LE3 .... 153 F8
Gorse Hill Anstey LE7 .... 127 E5
Anstey LE7 .... 127 F5
Gorse Hill City Farm*
LE4 .... 128 B1
Gorse Hill Hospl LE7 .... 127 F4
Gorse La
Leicester, Oadby LE2 .... 181 D3
Moira DE12 .... 67 E6
Syston LE7 .... 102 F3
Gorse Rd LE67 .... 96 C6
Gorsey La DE12 .... 92 A7
Gorsty Cl LE4 .... 128 B3
Goscote Dr LE17 .... 244 C6
Goscote Hall Rd LE4 .... 128 F6
Goscote Ho 7 LE2 .... 155 B5
Goseley Ave DE11 .... 45 A4
Goseley Cres DE11 .... 45 A4
Gosford Dr LE10 .... 197 A1
Goshawk Cl LE9 .... 218 E7
Gosling St LE2 .... 259 A2
Gotham St LE2 .... 155 B4
Gough Rd LE5 .... 155 E6
Goward St LE16 .... 240 E3
Gower St LE1 .... 259 C5
Gowrie Cl LE10 .... 197 B2
Grace Ct LE2 .... 179 E8
Gracedieu La LE67,LE12 .... 48 F2
Grace Dieu Manor Sch
LE67 .... 71 F8
Gracedieu Rd LE11 .... 51 D3
Grace Dieu Rd LE67 .... 71 E7
Grace Gdns LE2 .... 179 E7
Gracelands LE16 .... 240 C2
Grace Rd Desford LE9 .... 151 B3
Leicester LE2 .... 179 E8
Sapcote LE9 .... 217 E8
Grafton Dr LE18 .... 180 F2
Grafton Pl LE1 .... 259 B5
Grafton Rd LE11 .... 51 E6
Graham Rise LE11 .... 51 D6
Graham St LE1 .... 155 B6
Gramer Cotts CV9 .... 194 A6
Grampian Cl LE2 .... 179 F7
Grampian Way
Long Eaton NG10 .... 10 A8
Oakham LE15 .... 137 D6
Granary Cl
Glenfield LE3 .... 153 C8
Kibworth Beauchamp
LE8 .... 224 B7
Market Harborough
LE16 .... 240 F6
Granby Ave LE5 .... 155 D6
Granby Cl LE10 .... 215 C7
Granby Dr NG13 .... 3 A2
Granby Hill NG13 .... 5 B6
Granby Ho LE13 .... 59 C3
Granby La Granby NG13 .... 5 A7
Plungar NG13 .... 5 E2
Granby Pl LE1 .... 259 B3
Granby Prim Sch LE2 .... 179 D7
Granby Rd
Hinckley LE10 .... 215 C7
Leicester LE2 .... 179 D7
Melton Mowbray LE13 .... 59 D6
Granby St
Leicester LE1 .... 259 C3
Loughborough LE11 .... 52 A4
Grange Ave
Breaston DE72 .... 9 D8
Leicester Forest East
LE3 .... 153 B3
Rearsby LE7 .... 103 F8
Grange Bsns Pk LE8 .... 178 F1
Grange Cl
Ashby-De-La-Z LE65 .... 69 A5
Glenfield LE3 .... 153 B8
Great Glen LE8 .... 182 B1
Langham LE15 .... 110 D3
Leicester LE2 .... 179 C3
Grange Cl *continued*
Melbourne DE73 .... 26 B8
Newbold Verdon LE9 .... 150 B4
Ratby LE6 .... 152 D8
Grange Dr
Castle Donington DE74 .... 17 A3
Glen Parva LE2 .... 179 C3
Hinckley LE10 .... 215 E5
Long Eaton NG10 .... 10 F8
Melton Mowbray LE13 .... 59 E1
Whetstone LE8 .... 201 F8
Grange Farm Bsns Pk
LE67 .... 96 E5
Grange Farm Cl DE74 .... 17 D5
Grangefields Dr LE7 .... 101 F6
Grange La Coston LE14 .... 62 E8
Leicester LE2 .... 259 B2
Mountsorrel LE12 .... 101 D8
Nailstone CV13 .... 123 B5
Seaton LE15 .... 190 B1
Thorpe Langton LE16 .... 226 A5
Thurnby LE7 .... 156 E4
Grange Pk
Leicester LE7 .... 156 E4
Long Eaton NG10 .... 10 F8
Grange Prim Sch NG10 .... 10 F8
Granger Ct LE11 .... 52 A4
Grange Rd
Broughton Astley LE9 .... 218 E7
Carlton Curlieu LE8 .... 206 D7
Coalville LE67 .... 96 E6
Hartshill Green CV10 .... 194 C2
Ibstock LE67 .... 95 F1
Long Eaton NG10 .... 10 F8
Shepshed LE12 .... 50 A3
Wigston LE18 .... 180 D4
Grange St LE11 .... 52 A5
Grange The
Earl Shilton LE9 .... 198 E7
Packington LE65 .... 69 C2
Woodhouse Eaves LE12 .... 100 B8
Grange Therapeutic Sch
LE15 .... 135 F6
Grange View LE67 .... 123 E8
Grangeway Rd LE18 .... 180 D4
Granite Cl LE19 .... 178 A4
Granite Way LE12 .... 76 C4
Grantham Ave LE9 .... 218 D8
Grantham Rd
Bottesford NG13 .... 3 D2
Leicester LE5 .... 156 C8
Skillington NG33 .... 43 B8
Grant Way LE2 .... 179 E4
Grantwood Rd LE13 .... 59 E5
Granville Ave LE2 .... 180 F6
Granville Com Sch
DE11 .... 44 E4
Granville Cres LE18 .... 180 B5
Granville Gdns LE10 .... 215 C8
Granville Rd
Hinckley LE10 .... 215 C8
Leicester LE1 .... 155 B4
Melton Mowbray LE13 .... 59 A5
Wigston LE18 .... 180 C5
Granville St
Loughborough LE11 .... 52 A4
Market Harborough
LE16 .... 240 F2
Woodville DE11 .... 44 E3
Grape St LE1 .... 259 B4
Grasmere LE67 .... 72 C2
Grasmere Cl LE12 .... 76 D8
Grasmere Rd
Loughborough LE11 .... 74 F7
Wigston LE18 .... 180 F3
Grasmere St LE2 .... 259 A2
Grass Acres LE3 .... 178 E7
Grassholme Dr LE11 .... 51 A3
Grassington Cl LE4 .... 128 C4
Grassington Dr
Nuneaton CV11 .... 214 A2
Wigston LE18 .... 180 E1
Grassy La LE67 .... 125 B8
Gravel St LE1 .... 259 B4
Gravel The LE8 .... 205 F8
Gray La LE12 .... 77 D2
Grays Cl DE74 .... 17 B3
Grays Ct LE19 .... 178 A3
Gray St Leicester LE2 .... 259 A2
Loughborough LE11 .... 52 B2
Grayswood Dr LE4 .... 128 A6
Great Arler Rd LE2 .... 180 A8
Great Bowden CE Prim Sch
LE16 .... 241 A6
Great Bowden Hall
LE16 .... 240 E7
Great Bowden Rd
LE16 .... 241 A4
Great Casterton CE Prim
Sch PE9 .... 142 E7
Great Central Railway
LE4 .... 128 E7
Great Central Railway
Mus* LE11 .... 52 C3
Great Central Rd LE11 .... 52 C3
Great Central Rly*
LE4 .... 128 E7
Great Central Rly*
LE7 .... 75 E2
Great Central St LE1 .... 259 A4
Great Central Walk Nature
Trail* CV23 .... 252 F2
Great Central Way
LE3 .... 154 D2
Great Cl NG33 .... 65 B4
Great Dalby Rd LE14 .... 106 E5
Great Dalby Sch LE14 .... 82 A1
Great Easton Rd
Bringhurst LE16 .... 229 C6
Drayton LE16 .... 229 A5
Great Easton LE16 .... 229 F6
Greatford Rd PE9 .... 144 E4
Great La
Frisby on t W LE14 .... 80 D8
Greetham LE15 .... 88 B2
Great Meadow Rd
LE4 .... 128 B2
Great North Rd
Great Casterton PE9 .... 114 D4
Stamford PE9 .... 142 F3
Wothorpe PE9 .... 169 B8
Greaves Ave
Melton Mowbray LE13 .... 59 B4
Old Dalby LE14 .... 36 C6
Grebe Cl LE12 .... 76 E8
Grebe Way LE8 .... 201 F5
Greedon Rise LE12 .... 77 C4
Greenacre Dr LE5 .... 156 B5
Greenacres Dr LE17 .... 244 B6
Green Bank LE13 .... 59 E3
Greenbank Dr LE2 .... 181 B5
Greenbank Rd LE5 .... 130 D1
Greenclose La 1 LE11 .... 52 A4
Greencoat Ct LE3 .... 153 E7
Greencoat Rd LE3 .... 153 E7
Green Croft LE9 .... 199 E1
Greendale Rd LE2 .... 179 B3
Green Farm Cl CV23 .... 258 A6
Greenfield Prim Sch
LE8 .... 202 E4
Greenfield Rd
Measham DE12 .... 93 E5
Oakham LE15 .... 138 A8
Greenfields LE8 .... 201 F7
Greenfields Dr LE67 .... 72 A1
Greengate La LE4 .... 128 E7
Green Gdns LE17 .... 233 B4
Green Hill LE12 .... 30 A1
Greenhill Cl
Melton Mowbray LE13 .... 59 D5
Narborough LE19 .... 201 A7
Greenhill Dr LE9 .... 198 B7
Greenhill Rd
Coalville LE67 .... 72 C1
Leicester LE2 .... 155 B1
Stoke Golding CV13 .... 196 D7
Green Hill Rise LE12 .... 30 A2
Greenhithe Rd LE2 .... 154 D1
Green La Ashley LE16 .... 227 F2
Barton in t B CV13 .... 122 E3
Braybrooke LE16 .... 251 F5
Breedon on the Hill DE73 .... 26 C2
Countesthorpe LE8 .... 202 F4
Diseworth DE74 .... 28 B6
Duddington PE9 .... 193 B6
Earl Shilton LE9 .... 175 F1
Easthorpe NG13 .... 3 C1
Goadby Marwood LE14 .... 22 E3
Granby NG13 .... 5 C5
Harby LE14 .... 12 C2
Husbands Bosworth
LE17 .... 247 E5
Market Harborough
LE16 .... 240 E1
North Kilworth LE17 .... 246 F3
Owston LE15 .... 135 B5
Seagrave LE12 .... 77 F8
Stamford PE9 .... 143 D5
Stapleton LE9 .... 174 E2
Tilton on t H LE7 .... 159 D6
Upper Broughton LE14 .... 19 B4
Weston by W LE16 .... 227 C6
Whitwick LE67 .... 71 E3
Wibtoft LE17 .... 232 B2
Wilson DE73 .... 26 E5
Wolvey LE10 .... 231 C5
Greenland Ave LE5 .... 156 A8
Greenland Dr LE5 .... 156 A8
Green Lands DE11 .... 44 B7
Green Lane Cl
Leicester LE5 .... 155 F6
Seagrave LE12 .... 77 F8
Green Lane Inf Sch
LE5 .... 155 C7
Green Lane Rd LE5 .... 155 E6
Greenlawn Wlk LE3 .... 154 D8
Green Leas DE72 .... 16 A8
Greenmoor Rd LE10 .... 215 D5
Green Rd LE9 .... 218 E7
Green's Cl CV23 .... 252 C6
Greenside Cl
Donisthorpe DE12 .... 67 E1
Long Eaton NG10 .... 10 E7
Nuneaton CV11 .... 214 C1
Greenside Pl LE2 .... 179 F5
Greenslade LE13 .... 59 D3
Greensward LE7 .... 103 E8
Green The Allington NG32 .... 4 F5
Anstey LE7 .... 127 C6
3 Ashby-De-La-Z LE65 .... 69 B6
Aston-on-T DE72 .... 16 B8
Atherstone CV9 .... 194 A6
Austrey CV9 .... 119 B1
Barkestone-le-V NG13 .... 6 B3
Bitteswell LE17 .... 244 B8
Blaby LE8 .... 202 C8
Breaston DE72 .... 9 D8
Breedon on the Hill DE73 .... 26 E2
Caldecott LE16 .... 230 B8
Castle Donington DE74 .... 17 A3
Churchover CV23 .... 252 C6
Coalville LE67 .... 96 C5
Croft LE9 .... 200 C5
Dadlington CV13 .... 196 E8
Diseworth DE74 .... 28 B5
Green The *continued*
Draycott DE72 .... 9 A7
Exton LE15 .... 113 A3
Great Bowden LE16 .... 241 B6
Hathern LE12 .... 30 A1
Hickling LE14 .... 19 C6
Hose LE14 .... 20 F7
Huncote LE9 .... 200 D7
Husbands Bosworth
LE17 .... 247 E5
Ketton PE9 .... 167 F5
Leire LE17 .... 233 E8
Lilbourne CV23 .... 258 A6
Long Whatton LE12 .... 29 C3
Lubenham LE16 .... 239 E3
Lyddington LE15 .... 212 D7
Lyndon LE15 .... 165 D5
Markfield LE67 .... 98 D1
Mountsorrel LE12 .... 76 E2
Muston NG13 .... 7 F8
Newton Burgoland LE67 .... 121 E6
North Kilworth LE17 .... 246 F3
Old Dalby LE14 .... 35 E4
Orton-on-t-H CV9 .... 145 C4
Seckington B79 .... 118 A3
Stathern LE14 .... 13 A3
Stonesby LE14 .... 40 E6
Syston LE7 .... 103 B4
Thringstone LE67 .... 71 D7
Thrussington LE7 .... 78 F4
Walton o t W LE12 .... 54 A4
Weston by W LE16 .... 227 B3
Wigston Parva LE10 .... 231 E8
Greenway LE8 .... 224 B8
Greenway Cl LE7 .... 101 E6
Greenway The LE4 .... 129 A2
Greenwich Cl LE19 .... 201 B8
Green Wlk LE3 .... 153 E5
Greenwood Rd
Leicester LE5 .... 155 F6
Stoke Golding CV13 .... 196 E7
Greetham Falconry Ctr*
LE15 .... 88 A2
Greetham Rd
Cottesmore LE15 .... 87 F1
Stretton LE15 .... 88 F4
Gregory Ave DE72 .... 9 C8
Gregory Cl
Barlestone CV13 .... 149 C8
Thurmaston LE4 .... 130 A7
Gregory Rd CV13 .... 149 C8
Gregorys Cl LE3 .... 153 D1
Gregory St LE11 .... 52 B3
Gregson Cl
Leicester LE4 .... 129 D5
Swadlincote DE11 .... 44 B5
Grendon Cl LE18 .... 180 E3
Grenehams Cl PE9 .... 167 F5
Grenfell Rd LE2 .... 180 E8
Grenville Gdns LE16 .... 240 D1
Gresley Cl
Leicester, Beaumont Leys
LE4 .... 128 C4
Leicester,Thurnby LE7 .... 156 F6
Gresley Dr PE9 .... 143 D2
Gresley Woodlands
DE11 .... 44 A2
Gresley Wood Rd DE11 .... 44 A2
Gretna Way LE5 .... 156 E7
Gretton Brook Rd
NN17 .... 230 E3
Gretton Ct LE13 .... 59 B3
Gretton Gdns LE14 .... 62 C2
Gretton Rd
Harringworth NN17 .... 213 E7
Lyddington LE15 .... 212 D5
Rockingham LE16 .... 230 B5
Grewcock Cl LE17 .... 232 E6
Grey Cl LE6 .... 126 F3
Grey Cres LE6 .... 99 D1
Grey Friars LE1 .... 259 B3
Greylag Way LE8 .... 201 F4
Greyland Paddock
LE6 .... 126 F3
Greys Dr LE6 .... 126 E2
Greystoke Cl LE4 .... 128 E3
Greystoke Prim Sch
LE19 .... 201 C8
Greystoke Wlk 1 LE4 .... 128 E3
Greystone Ave LE5 .... 156 B6
Griffin Cl Shepshed LE12 .... 50 A3
Thurmaston LE4 .... 130 A5
Griffin Rd LE16 .... 251 E4
Griffith Gdns LE65 .... 68 F5
Griffiths Cl LE15 .... 138 A8
Griffydam Prim Sch
LE67 .... 48 A2
Griggs Rd LE11 .... 75 B8
Grimes Gate DE74 .... 28 C6
Grimston Cl LE4 .... 130 A4
Grisedale Cl LE2 .... 259 A1
Grizedale Gr LE19 .... 177 F2
Groby Com Coll LE6 .... 126 D2
Groby La LE6 .... 126 E7
Groby Rd Anstey LE7 .... 127 C5
Glenfield LE3 .... 127 C3
Leicester LE3 .... 128 A1
Ratby LE6 .... 126 D1
Grocot Rd LE5 .... 156 A3
Grosvenor Ave
Breaston DE72 .... 9 F8
Long Eaton NG10 .... 10 A4
Grosvenor Cl LE2 .... 179 D1
Grosvenor Cres
Burbage LE10 .... 216 A6
Leicester, Oadby LE2 .... 180 F7
Grosvenor St LE1 .... 259 C5
Grovebury Rd LE4 .... 128 F3
Grovebury Wlk 4 LE4 .... 128 F3
Grove Cotts LE14 .... 108 B2
Grove Farm Triangle
LE19 .... 178 E5
Grove La LE12 .... 76 D7
Grove Pk LE10 .... 216 A6
Grove Prim Sch The
LE13 .... 59 B3
Grove Rd Burbage LE10 .... 216 A6
Leicester LE5 .... 155 C6
Loughborough LE11 .... 51 E3
Whetstone LE8 .... 202 A7
Whitwick LE67 .... 71 E4
Grove St DE11 .... 44 B4
Grove Stud LE14 .... 108 A2
Grove The
Asfordby LE14 .... 57 E3
Breaston DE72 .... 9 F8
Desford LE9 .... 151 A3
Hinckley LE10 .... 215 C8
Grove Way LE19 .... 178 F5
Guadaloupe Ave LE13 .... 59 E1
Guash Way PE9 .... 143 F5
Guild Cl LE7 .... 100 F3
Guildford Ave DE11 .... 44 E6
Guildford Way LE11 .... 74 C8
Guildhall La LE1 .... 259 A3
Guilford Dr LE18 .... 180 B5
Guilford Rd LE2 .... 155 E1
Guilford St 2 LE2 .... 155 C4
Guinea Cl NG10 .... 10 A7
Guinevere Way LE3 .... 153 A2
Gullet La Ashley LE16 .... 227 F2
Kirby Muxloe LE9 .... 152 C5
Gumley Rd
Foxton LE16 .... 239 C7
Laughton LE16,LE17 .... 238 D8
Smeeton Westerby LE8 .... 223 F5
Gumley Sq LE19 .... 178 B3
Gunby Hill DE12 .... 91 F8
Gunby Rd
North Witham NG33 .... 65 A8
Sewstern NG33 .... 64 B8
Stainby NG33 .... 43 E1
Gunnel La LE15 .... 141 B6
Gunnsbrook Cl LE16 .... 241 A6
Gunthorpe Cl LE15 .... 138 B7
Gunthorpe Rd LE3 .... 153 D4
Gurnall Rd LE4 .... 128 A4
Gurney Cres LE19 .... 201 C6
Gurney La LE17 .... 236 A1
Guscott Rd LE67 .... 71 E1
Guthlaxton Ave
11 Leicester LE2 .... 155 B5
Lutterworth LE17 .... 244 C6
Guthlaxton Coll LE18 .... 180 B2
Guthlaxton Gap LE19,
LE19 .... 200 F5
Guthlaxton St LE2 .... 155 B5
Guthlaxton Way LE18 .... 180 E1
Guthridge Cres LE3 .... 154 B3
Gutteridge St LE67 .... 96 C8
Gwash Cl PE9 .... 116 F2
Gwencole Ave LE3 .... 179 A8
Gwencole Cres LE3 .... 179 A7
Gwendolen Rd LE5 .... 155 E4
Gwendolin Ave LE4 .... 129 B8
Gwendoline Ave LE10 .... 197 A2
Gwendoline Dr LE8 .... 202 E4
Gynsill Cl LE7 .... 127 E5
Gynsill La LE7 .... 127 D3
Gynsills Hall LE7 .... 127 D3
Gypsy La CV9 .... 170 D2

H

Hackett Cl LE65 .... 69 B7
Hackett Rd LE3 .... 153 F8
Haddenham Rd LE3 .... 154 C2
Haddon Cl LE7 .... 102 F3
Haddon Rd PE9 .... 143 B4
Haddon St LE2 .... 155 C6
Haddon Way
Long Eaton NG10 .... 9 F4
Loughborough LE11 .... 75 A6
Hades La LE12 .... 34 D4
Hadfield Cl CV23 .... 257 A5
Hadfield Dr LE13 .... 59 C4
Hadrian Cl
Hinckley LE10 .... 196 F1
Syston LE7 .... 102 E2
Hadrian Rd
Leicester LE4 .... 128 E5
Thurmaston LE4 .... 129 E7
Hagley Cl LE16 .... 241 B3
Haig Pl LE3 .... 154 A2
Hailebury Ave LE65 .... 69 A8
Hailey Ave LE11 .... 51 C5
Hainsworth Rd LE15 .... 110 C3
Halberd Cl LE10 .... 215 D5
Halcroft Rise LE18 .... 180 D1
Half Croft The LE7 .... 103 A4
Half Moon Cres LE2 .... 181 C6
Halford Cl
Great Glen LE8 .... 205 B8
South Witham NG33 .... 65 B4
Whetstone LE8 .... 201 F6
Halford Rd LE8 .... 223 F8
Halford St
Leicester LE1 .... 259 C3
Syston LE7 .... 103 A3
Halifax Dr LE4 .... 128 E4
Halkin St LE4 .... 129 B1
Hallam Ave LE4 .... 128 F7
Hallam Cl LE9 .... 199 A8
Hallam Cres E LE3 .... 154 A2
Hallam Fields DE74 .... 17 B2
Hallamford Rd LE12 .... 50 A6
Hallaton CE Prim Sch
LE16 .... 209 D6
Hallaton Rd
Allexton LE15 .... 187 C4
Horninghold LE16 .... 210 A6
Leicester LE5 .... 155 F8
Medbourne LE16 .... 227 F7
Slawston LE16 .... 209 E3
Tugby LE7 .... 185 E5
Hallaton St LE2 .... 179 E7
Hallaton Village Mus*
LE16 .... 209 D6
Hallbrook Prim Sch
LE9 .... 218 F4
Hallbrook Rd LE9 .... 218 F4
Hall Cl Blackfordby DE11 .... 68 C8
Cossington LE7 .... 102 D8
Cottesmore LE15 .... 112 C8
Glen Parva LE2 .... 179 B3
Kibworth Beauchamp
LE8 .... 205 F1
Weston by W LE16 .... 227 B4
Whissendine LE15 .... 85 A1
Hall Croft LE12 .... 50 B4
Hallcroft Ave
Countesthorpe LE8 .... 202 E3
Overseal DE12 .... 67 B3
Hallcroft Gdns LE8 .... 202 E3
Hall Dr Asfordby LE14 .... 57 E2
Burton Lazars LE14 .... 82 F6
Burton o t W LE12 .... 54 A7
Leicester, Oadby LE2 .... 181 B6
Stoke Golding CV13 .... 196 E7
Halley Cl LE4 .... 128 A6
Hall Farm Cl
Castle Donington DE74 .... 17 B3
Queniborough LE7 .... 103 F5
Swadlincote DE11 .... 44 C4
Hall Farm Cres LE9 .... 219 A5
Hall Farm Rd
Swadlincote DE11 .... 44 C4
Thurcaston LE7 .... 101 B2
Hallfield Cl CV9 .... 146 C7
Hallfields CV9 .... 146 C7
Hallfields La LE7 .... 101 F5
Hall Gate Coalville LE67 .... 97 C8
Diseworth DE74 .... 28 C6
Hall Gdns
East Leake LE12 .... 31 F8
Great Glen LE8 .... 205 B8
Hemington DE74 .... 17 D4
Ravenstone LE67 .... 95 D8
Hall La
Ashby Magna LE17 .... 220 A2
Ashley LE16 .... 227 E2
Bitteswell LE17 .... 234 C3
Coalville LE67 .... 72 A2
Donisthorpe DE12 .... 92 E8
Drayton LE16 .... 229 A5
Eastwell LE14 .... 22 B5
Leicester LE2 .... 179 C7
Odstone CV13 .... 122 C4
Packington LE65 .... 69 C2
South Luffenham LE15 .... 191 E8
Stainby NG33 .... 43 D2
Ullesthorpe LE17 .... 233 B4
Walton LE17 .... 236 A2
Welford NN6 .... 256 D6
Witherley CV9 .... 194 B8
Hall Leys LE12 .... 76 A5
Hall Orchard CE Prim Sch
LE12 .... 76 D7
Hall Orchard La LE14 .... 80 D8
Hall Rd Hinckley LE10 .... 215 D5
Scraptoft LE7 .... 156 F8
Hall Sch The LE3 .... 127 E1
Halls Cres LE10 .... 217 C5
Hall St Ibstock LE67 .... 122 E8
Swadlincote DE11 .... 44 A2
Hall Wlk LE19 .... 178 B4
Hall Yd PE9 .... 168 C2
Halsbury St LE2 .... 155 D3
Halstead Rd LE12 .... 76 D1
Halstead Rise LE7 .... 160 A8
Halstead St LE5 .... 155 D6
Halter Slade LE18 .... 180 E1
Halywell Nook LE7 .... 101 F8
Hamble Cl LE9 .... 151 B3
Hambledon Cres
Cottesmore LE15 .... 87 E2
Loughborough LE11 .... 74 F8
Hambledon Gn LE4 .... 128 D5
Hamble Rd LE2 .... 181 D6
Hambleton Cl
Leicester Forest East
LE3 .... 152 F2
Oakham LE15 .... 138 B6
Hambleton Rd
Egleton LE15 .... 138 C3
Stamford PE9 .... 143 A2
Hamelin Rd LE3 .... 153 F4
Hames La B79 .... 118 C4
Hamilford Cl LE7 .... 130 E1
Hamilton Bsns Pk LE4 .... 130 A4
Hamilton Cl LE10 .... 197 A2
Hamilton Com Coll
LE5 .... 130 E2
Hamilton Ct LE2 .... 181 B5
Hamilton Dr
Melton Mowbray LE13 .... 59 C1
Swadlincote DE11 .... 44 C5
Hamilton La LE7 .... 130 E2
Hamilton Rd
Coalville LE67 .... 97 C8

Hamilton Rd *continued*
Long Eaton NG10 ... 10 D8
Hamilton St LE2 ... 155 B4
Hamilton Way LE5 ... 130 B2
Hamlet Cl CV11 ... 214 B1
Hammercliffe Rd LE5 ... 155 C8
Hammond Way LE16 ... 240 E4
Hampden Rd LE4 ... 129 E2
Hampshire Rd LE2 ... 179 D7
Hampstead Cl LE19 ... 201 B8
Hampton Cl
Glen Parva LE2 ... 179 D1
Wigston LE18 ... 180 E2
Hanbury Cl LE15 ... 137 D5
Hanbury Gdns LE15 ... 137 A2
Hanbury Rd LE5 ... 156 D4
Hand Ave LE3 ... 153 E3
Handley St LE2 ... 179 E7
Hand's Wlk NG13 ... 3 A2
Hanford Way LE11 ... 52 B5
Hanger Bank DE72 ... 16 B8
Hangman's La
Hinckley LE10 ... 197 E3
Newton Regis B79 ... 118 A2
Hannah Par LE4 ... 129 A7
Hannah's Field LE15 ... 163 E2
Hannam Ct LE1 ... 259 B4
Hanover Cl LE5 ... 130 B1
Hanover Ct
Hinckley LE10 ... 215 E6
Loughborough LE11 ... 51 D5
4 Stamford PE9 ... 143 E3
Hanover Dr LE12 ... 77 D4
Hansen Ct LE18 ... 180 B2
Hansom Ct 1 LE10 ... 215 D8
Hansom Rd LE10 ... 197 F2
Haramead Rd LE1 ... 155 B7
Harborough Hill Rd
LE15 ... 211 B6
Harborough Rd
Billesdon LE7 ... 184 C6
Braybrooke LE16 ... 251 D7
Clipston LE16 ... 250 A2
Dingley LE16 ... 241 D5
East Farndon LE16 ... 250 C8
Glooston LE16 ... 208 B3
Great Oxendon LE16 ... 250 F4
Kibworth Beauchamp
LE8, LE16 ... 224 E5
Leicester, Oadby LE2 ... 181 B5
Lubenham LE16 ... 240 A3
Market Harborough
LE16 ... 240 C7
Theddingworth LE17 ... 238 F1
Harby CE Prim Sch
LE14 ... 12 B3
Harby La Harby NG13 ... 11 B5
Hose LE14 ... 20 F7
Plungar NG13 ... 12 E6
Stathern LE14 ... 12 F3
Harcourt Cl LE7 ... 103 A4
Harcourt Est LE8 ... 206 A1
Harcourt Pl DE74 ... 17 B4
Harcourt Rd
Kibworth Beauchamp
LE8 ... 223 F8
Wigston LE18 ... 180 E1
Harcourt Spinney
CV13 ... 148 E4
Harcourt St LE16 ... 240 D3
Harcourt Terr 1 PE9 ... 143 C3
Harcourt Way LE19 ... 178 D6
Hardacre Cl DE73 ... 26 A8
Hardie Cres LE3 ... 153 D2
Harding St LE1 ... 259 A5
Hardwick Cl LE15 ... 138 B7
Hardwick Cres LE7 ... 102 F3
Hardwick Ct LE3 ... 154 C3
Hardwick Dr LE11 ... 51 C4
Hardwicke Rd LE19 ... 200 F8
Hardwick Rd
Gretton NN17 ... 213 B1
Leicester LE5 ... 156 E4
Stamford PE9 ... 143 B4
Hardy Cl Hinckley LE10 ... 197 D4
Long Eaton NG10 ... 10 D6
Hardy's Ave LE4 ... 129 C4
Harebell Cl
Hamilton LE5 ... 130 B3
Woodville DE11 ... 44 E4
Harebell Dr LE13 ... 82 A8
Harecroft Cres LE9 ... 217 D8
Harefield Ave LE3 ... 179 C8
Harene Cres LE3 ... 152 E3
Hare Pie View LE16 ... 209 E5
Harewood Cl LE15 ... 110 D3
Harewood St LE5 ... 155 D7
Harland Cl
Asfordby LE14 ... 57 F2
Cosby LE9 ... 201 D3
Harlaxton St LE3 ... 154 C2
Harlech Cl LE11 ... 51 E5
Harlech Wlk LE13 ... 59 C5
Harlequin Rd LE12 ... 77 C2
Harlequin Way LE8 ... 201 F4
Harles Acres LE14 ... 19 C6
Harley Cl LE12 ... 50 B2
Harley's Ct DE12 ... 67 B4
Harolds La LE19 ... 178 B5
Harold St LE2 ... 179 E8
Harpers La CV9 ... 194 A7
Harratts Cl LE67 ... 95 F1
Harrier Cl LE9 ... 218 E7
Harrier Parkway LE17 243 D7
Harriman Cl LE12 ... 50 B4
Harrimans Dr DE72 ... 9 F8
Harrington Cl LE12 ... 76 A6
Harrington Cres LE15 ... 113 B2
Harrington Rd
Shepshed LE12 ... 50 C3
South Witham LE15 ... 65 B4
Wigston LE18 ... 180 E3
Harrington St
Draycott DE72 ... 9 B7
Leicester LE4 ... 155 C8
Long Eaton NG10 ... 10 B5
Harrington Way LE15 ... 137 E5
Harringworth Rd
Gretton NN17 ... 213 C2
Leicester LE5 ... 156 B5
Harris Cl LE9 ... 219 A5
Harris Gn LE3 ... 153 C3
Harrison Cl
Earl Shilton LE9 ... 198 F8
Glenfield LE3 ... 153 C8
Market Harborough
LE16 ... 250 D8
Whetstone LE8 ... 202 A5
Wigston LE18 ... 180 B1
Harrison Pl LE67 ... 96 C8
Harrison Rd LE4 ... 129 B2
Harrisons Row LE7 ... 103 B4
Harrison St LE4 ... 129 E8
Harris Rd Corby NN17 ... 230 C1
Leicester LE4 ... 128 B3
Harrod Dr LE16 ... 241 A4
Harrogate Rd LE4 ... 129 C1
Harrogate Way LE18 ... 180 E2
Harrowbrook Ind Est
LE10 ... 214 E7
Harrowbrook Rd LE10 214 E7
Harrow Cl
Ashby-De-La-Z LE65 ... 69 A8
Leicester Forest East
LE3 ... 152 F1
Harrowden Ct LE5 ... 156 A6
Harrowden Rise LE5 ... 156 A6
Harrowgate Dr LE4 ... 101 F1
Harrow Rd
Leicester LE3 ... 154 C4
Swadlincote DE11 ... 44 B7
Harry French Ct LE11 ... 51 E4
Harston Rd NG32 ... 15 F5
Hart Cl LE8 ... 201 F5
Hartfield Rd LE5 ... 156 D8
Hartington Gn LE10 ... 215 E6
Hartington Rd LE2 ... 155 C6
Hartland Dr
Market Harborough
LE16 ... 241 B3
Melton Mowbray LE13 ... 82 C8
Hartopp Cl LE7 ... 157 A5
Hartopp Rd
Leicester LE2 ... 155 B1
Melton Mowbray LE13 ... 82 C8
Hart Rd LE5 ... 155 C6
Hartshill Hayes Ctry Pk★
CV10 ... 194 A2
Hartshill Rd DE11 ... 45 A4
Hartshorn Cl LE4 ... 129 F6
Hartshorne CE Prim Sch
DE11 ... 45 B6
Hartshorne Rd DE11 ... 44 F3
Hartside Gdns NG10 ... 10 A8
Harvard Cl LE2 ... 181 B6
Harvest Cl
Leicester LE4 ... 128 B3
Littlethorpe LE19 ... 201 D6
Harvester Cl LE3 ... 152 F1
Harvesters Cnr LE7 ... 103 E7
Harvest Gr DE12 ... 68 A5
Harvest Hill DE11 ... 44 B7
Harvest Way LE9 ... 218 F4
Harvey Cl LE8 ... 179 B1
Harvey Ct DE74 ... 17 B3
Harvey Rd DE74 ... 17 B2
Harveys Ct LE9 ... 217 D7
Harwin Rd LE5 ... 156 B4
Harwood Dr LE10 ... 197 F4
Haskell Cl LE3 ... 153 D2
Haslemere Rd NG10 ... 10 B8
Haslyn Wlk LE67 ... 97 B8
Hassal Rd LE3 ... 153 E8
Hastings Ave LE67 ... 72 A4
Hastings Cl
Breedon on the Hill DE73 ... 26 E2
Fleckney LE8 ... 223 A6
Hastings Dr LE9 ... 198 C7
Hastings High Sch
LE10 ... 215 F7
Hastings Rd
Kirby Fields LE9 ... 152 E4
Leicester LE5 ... 155 D8
Swadlincote DE11 ... 44 B3
Woodhouse Eaves LE12 ... 99 F8
Hastings St
Castle Donington DE74 ... 17 B2
Loughborough LE11 ... 52 A4
Hastings The
Braunstone LE3 ... 153 D1
Ibstock LE67 ... 95 F2
Hastings Way LE65 ... 69 C5
Hastings Wlk LE3 ... 153 E1
Hathaway Ave LE3 ... 153 F1
Hathaway Dr CV11 ... 214 A1
Hatherleigh Rd LE5 ... 155 F3
Hathern CE Prim Sch
LE12 ... 30 A1
Hathern Cl NG10 ... 10 D5
Hathern Dr LE11,LE12 ... 50 F6
Hathern Rd
Long Whatton LE12 ... 29 D3
Shepshed LE12 ... 50 D6
Hathern Turn LE12 ... 29 F2
Hathernware Ind Est
LE12 ... 30 C5
Hathersage Ave NG10 ... 9 F5
Hat Rd LE3 ... 178 E7
Hattern Ave LE4 ... 128 D4
Hatters Dr CV9 ... 170 D2
Hatton Crofts NG10 ... 10 C6
Hatton Ct DE73 ... 26 A7
Hatton La NN17 ... 213 B1
Haulton Dr DE74 ... 17 A4
Havelock St
Leicester LE2 ... 259 A2
Loughborough LE11 ... 51 F4
Haven Cl Belton LE12 ... 49 B6
Leicester Forest East
LE3 ... 152 F2
Havencrest Dr LE5 ... 156 B7
Haven Pk LE11 ... 51 E5
Haven Rd CV13 ... 148 E2
Haven Wlk LE5 ... 156 E6
Hawarden Ave LE5 ... 155 F7
Hawcliffe Rd LE12 ... 76 C4
Hawk Cl LE9 ... 218 E7
Hawker Rd LE2 ... 181 D4
Hawkesbury Rd LE2 ... 179 E7
Hawkes Hill LE2 ... 179 F5
Hawke Way LE17 ... 243 C7
Hawkins Cl
Corby NN17 ... 230 B1
Hinckley LE10 ... 197 D4
Hawley Cl LE67 ... 96 E6
Hawley Rd LE10 ... 215 D7
Hawthorn Ave
Birstall LE4 ... 129 B8
Breaston DE72 ... 9 F8
Netherseal DE12 ... 91 F7
Hawthorn Cl
Coalville LE67 ... 71 E1
Leicester Forest East
LE3 ... 152 E2
Leicester, Oadby LE2 ... 182 A3
Old Dalby LE14 ... 35 E4
Hawthorn Cres LE10 ... 215 E4
Hawthorn Dr
Blaby LE8 ... 202 B6
Uppingham LE15 ... 189 B5
Hawthorne Ave
Hathern LE12 ... 30 A2
Long Eaton NG10 ... 10 C6
Hawthorne Cl DE12 ... 93 C6
Hawthorne Dr
Ibstock LE67 ... 122 E8
Leicester LE5 ... 156 A3
Thornton LE67 ... 124 E4
Hawthorne Rd LE17 ... 246 F3
Hawthorne St LE3 ... 154 C7
Hawthorne Way LE9 ... 198 B6
Hawthorne Wlk NN17 ... 230 E1
Hawthorn Gr LE2 ... 181 B7
Hawthorn Rd
Castle Donington DE74 ... 17 B5
Mountsorrel LE12 ... 76 E2
Hawthorn Rise LE6 ... 126 F3
Hawthorns The
Countesthorpe LE8 ... 202 E4
Leicester LE2 ... 155 D1
Lutterworth LE17 ... 244 B6
Markfield LE67 ... 125 E8
Haybarn Cl LE19 ... 201 D6
Haybrooke Rd LE12 ... 77 D4
Hayden Ave LE2 ... 181 D4
Hayden Cl LE4 ... 128 E3
Haydon Rd LE11 ... 51 E4
Hayes Ave DE72 ... 9 B7
Hayes Cl LE67 ... 71 F4
Hayes End LE9 ... 151 B3
Hayes Rd LE18 ... 180 E3
Hayfield Cl LE3 ... 153 B8
Hayhill LE12 ... 77 A5
Hayhill La LE12 ... 76 F6
Hayle Cl CV11 ... 214 A5
Hayling Cres LE5 ... 156 A8
Haymarket LE1 ... 259 B4
Haymarket Ctr LE1 ... 259 B4
Haynes Rd LE5 ... 155 F7
Hays La LE10 ... 215 B7
Hay Wain La DE11 ... 44 B7
Hayward Ave LE11 ... 52 C2
Haywood Cl LE5 ... 156 B4
Hazeland Ct LE17 ... 244 C6
Hazelbank Cl LE4 ... 128 D2
Hazelbank Rd LE8 ... 202 F4
Hazel Cl Birstall LE4 ... 129 B8
Great Glen LE8 ... 205 B8
Littlethorpe LE19 ... 201 C6
Measham DE12 ... 93 C5
Swadlincote DE11 ... 44 A5
Hazeldene Rd LE5 ... 130 D2
Hazel Dr
Braunstone LE3 ... 178 F6
Lutterworth LE17 ... 244 B6
Hazel Gr Hallaton LE16 ... 209 E6
Moira DE12 ... 68 B6
Stamford PE9 ... 142 F4
Hazelnut Cl LE5 ... 156 B4
Hazel Prim Sch LE2 ... 154 F3
Hazel Rd LE11 ... 75 A8
Hazelrigg Cl DE74 ... 16 F4
Hazel St Desford LE9 ... 151 A3
Leicester LE2 ... 154 F3
Hazel Way LE9 ... 198 A7
Hazelwood Rd
Leicester LE5 ... 155 D3
Wigston LE18 ... 180 A1
Hazlehead Rd LE7 ... 127 D6
Hazlemere Cl LE8 ... 202 B7
Hazlewood Cres LE14 ... 57 E3
Heacham Dr LE4 ... 128 C2
Headingley Cl
Coalville LE67 ... 97 A7
Leicester LE4 ... 128 C7
Headland Rd LE5 ... 156 A3
Headlands The LE16 ... 240 F4
Headland The LE7 ... 103 F8
Headley Rd LE3 ... 178 F7
Heafield Dr DE74 ... 18 D2
Healey Cl LE4 ... 128 D4
Healey St LE18 ... 179 F1
Heanor St LE1 ... 259 A5
Heards Cl LE18 ... 203 E8
Hearthcote Rd DE11 ... 44 A3
Hearth St LE16 ... 240 D3
Heath Ave
Narborough LE19 ... 178 E2
Syston LE7 ... 102 F3
Heathbrook Dr LE6 ... 152 D8
Heathcoat St LE11 ... 52 A4
Heathcote Dr LE12 ... 77 D4
Heathcott Rd LE2 ... 179 F7
Heath Ct LE9 ... 198 D7
Heath Dr LE15 ... 112 D8
Heatherbrook Rd LE4 128 A5
Heatherbrook Sch
LE4 ... 127 F6
Heather Cres
Breaston DE72 ... 9 F7
Melton Mowbray LE13 ... 82 A8
Heather Ct CV9 ... 170 D1
Heatherdale LE67 ... 95 E1
Heather Ho LE67 ... 95 C2
Heather La
Normanton Le H LE67 ... 95 A5
Packington LE65 ... 69 C1
Ravenstone LE67 ... 95 D6
Heather Prim Sch LE67 95 C2
Heather Rd LE2 ... 180 A8
Heather Way LE8 ... 202 F3
Heathfield LE67 ... 71 E8
Heathfield High Sch
LE9 ... 198 C7
Heathfield Rd LE18 ... 180 D5
Heathgate Cl LE4 ... 128 F8
Heath Gdns DE72 ... 10 A8
Heath La Boundary DE11 45 C2
Earl Shilton LE9 ... 198 D8
Southwood DE11 ... 46 B6
Wyville NG32 ... 25 F8
Heath La S LE9 ... 198 D8
Heathley Cl LE3 ... 152 F2
Heathley Park Dr LE3 128 A1
Heath Rd
Bagworth LE67 ... 124 C3
Market Bosworth CV13 ... 148 D3
Heawood Way LE3 ... 153 D1
Heays Cl LE3 ... 153 F8
Hebden Cl LE2 ... 179 C2
Hebden Way CV11 ... 214 A2
Hecadeck La LE14 ... 36 C8
Hector Rd LE67 ... 71 D2
Heddington Cl LE2 ... 180 A5
Heddington Way LE2 ... 180 A5
Hedge Gr DE11 ... 44 B7
Hedge Rd LE67 ... 96 C7
Hedgerow La LE9 ... 152 D5
Hedgerow Rd LE3 ... 154 A4
Hefford Gdns LE4 ... 128 D4
Heighton Cres LE19 ... 201 C6
Heights The LE16 ... 241 B2
Helena Cres LE4 ... 128 F4
Helmsdale Cl LE67 ... 97 C8
Helmsley Rd LE2 ... 179 F6
Helston Cl
Nuneaton CV11 ... 214 A5
Wigston LE18 ... 180 C1
Hemdale CV11 ... 214 A4
Hemington Ct DE74 ... 17 C5
Hemington Hill DE74 ... 17 C4
Hemington La DE74 ... 17 E5
Hemington Prim Sch
DE74 ... 17 D5
Hemington Rd LE5 ... 156 D3
Hemlock Cl LE19 ... 177 F1
Hemplow Dr NN6 ... 256 B2
Hendon Grange LE2 ... 180 E8
Henley Cres LE3 ... 153 F1
Henley Rd LE3 ... 154 C6
Henray Ave LE2 ... 179 C2
Henry Cl LE3 ... 152 F2
Henry Dane Way LE67 ... 47 E3
Henry St LE10 ... 197 A2
Henshaw St LE2 ... 259 B2
Hensman Cl LE8 ... 223 A6
Henson Cl LE4 ... 128 F6
Henson's La LE67 ... 71 D8
Henson Way LE10 ... 217 C5
Henton Rd LE3 ... 154 C5
Herald Way LE10 ... 215 D4
Herbert Ave LE4 ... 129 B2
Herbert Cl LE8 ... 202 A7
Herbert St LE11 ... 52 B5
Herdsmans Cl LE19 ... 201 C7
Hereford Cl LE9 ... 197 F6
Hereford Cres DE11 ... 44 D6
Hereford Rd LE2 ... 179 D7
Hereward Dr LE7 ... 156 F5
Herford Way LE10 ... 215 E6
Heritage Way LE5 ... 130 D3
Herle Ave LE3 ... 153 F2
Herle Wlk LE3 ... 153 F2
Hermitage Cl
Leicester, Oadby LE2 ... 181 A5
Newton CV23 ... 253 E1
Hermitage Ct LE67 ... 71 E3
Hermitage Ind Est The
LE67 ... 71 C2
Hermitage Park Way
DE11 ... 44 A7
Hermitage Rd
Birstall LE4 ... 129 A5
Loughborough LE11 ... 51 C2
Whitwick LE67 ... 71 E3
Hermitage The PE9 ... 143 C3
Heron Cl
Great Glen LE8 ... 182 B1
Mountsorrel LE12 ... 76 F2
Heron Dr DE11 ... 44 F3
Herongate Rd LE5 ... 156 A8
Heron Rd
Barrow-u-S LE12 ... 76 E8
Leicester LE5 ... 155 C7
Oakham LE15 ... 138 B8
Herons Ct LE10 ... 214 F7
Heron's Way LE7 ... 103 E8
Heron Way
Coalville LE67 ... 97 A8
Narborough LE19 ... 178 D2
Syston LE7 ... 102 F4
Herrick Cl
Enderby LE19 ... 178 A3
Sileby LE12 ... 77 B3
Herrick Dr LE7 ... 156 F5
Herrick Prim Sch LE4 129 D4
Herrick Rd
Leicester LE2 ... 180 A8
Loughborough LE11 ... 52 B2
Woodhouse Eaves LE12 ... 74 F2
Herricks Ave LE4 ... 129 F5
Herrick Way LE18 ... 180 E1
Herriot Way LE11 ... 51 D5
Herschell St LE2 ... 155 C3
Hervey Woods LE67 ... 71 E5
Hesilrige Wlk LE5 ... 156 B8
Hesketh Ave LE2 ... 179 C3
Hesketh Cl LE2 ... 179 C3
Hesketh Ct LE15 ... 89 A7
Hewes Cl LE2 ... 179 B3
Hewett Cl LE8 ... 205 A8
Hewitt Dr LE9 ... 152 F4
Hextall Dr LE67 ... 122 F8
Hextall Rd LE5 ... 156 A3
Hexter Cl LE8 ... 201 F4
Heybridge Rd LE5 ... 155 F8
Heybrook Ave LE8 ... 202 A7
Heycock Cl LE8 ... 223 A6
Heyford Rd LE3 ... 153 D4
Heygate St LE16 ... 240 E4
Hey St NG10 ... 10 C4
Heythrop Cl LE2 ... 181 D4
Heythrop Rd LE15 ... 87 F3
Heyworth Rd LE3 ... 154 C1
Hickling Ct LE11 ... 51 F4
Hickling Dr LE12 ... 77 D4
Hickling La
Long Clawson LE14 ... 20 A4
Upper Broughton LE14 ... 19 A2
Hickling Rd LE14 ... 19 B8
Hidcote Rd LE2 ... 181 A4
Higgs Cl LE5 ... 156 A5
High Acres LE7 ... 159 C2
Higham La
Higham on t H CV11 ... 195 F1
Stoke Golding CV13 ... 196 C6
Higham on the Hill CE Prim
Sch CV13 ... 196 A4
Higham Way LE10 ... 215 E7
Higham Way Ho LE10 ... 215 E7
Highbridge LE12 ... 77 C3
Highbrow LE8 ... 182 C1
Highbury Rd LE4 ... 155 C8
Highcliffe Prim Sch
LE4 ... 128 F7
Highcliffe Rd LE5 ... 130 A3
High Cres PE9 ... 142 D7
Highcroft LE17 ... 247 E6
Highcroft Ave LE2 ... 181 C4
Highcroft Cl NG10 ... 10 E5
Highcroft Rd LE2 ... 181 D3
High Cross Rd LE17 ... 232 C6
Highcross St
Leicester LE1 ... 259 A4
Market Harborough
LE16 ... 240 C3
Higher Gn LE8 ... 205 B8
Highfield PE9 ... 193 B7
Highfield Ave LE13 ... 59 A5
Highfield Cl
Empingham LE15 ... 140 F6
Sheepy Magna CV9 ... 171 B8
Shepshed LE12 ... 50 C5
Highfield Cotts LE15 ... 191 E8
Highfield Cres
Croxton Kerrial NG32 ... 24 B7
Wigston LE18 ... 180 D4
Highfield Ct LE9 ... 198 E7
Highfield Dr LE18 ... 180 D4
Highfield End LE14 ... 105 F5
Highfield Rd
Groby LE6 ... 126 E2
Swadlincote DE11 ... 44 B3
Highfields
Barrow-u-S LE12 ... 76 D8
Thornton LE67 ... 124 F3
Highfields Cl LE65 ... 68 F6
Highfields Dr LE11 ... 51 E1
Highfields Rd
Hinckley LE10 ... 197 E1
Mountsorrel LE12 ... 76 D1
Highfield St
Anstey LE7 ... 127 E6
Coalville LE67 ... 96 C7
Earl Shilton LE9 ... 198 E7
Fleckney LE8 ... 222 E8
Leicester LE2 ... 155 B4
Highfield St *continued*
Market Harborough
LE16 ... 240 D3
Stoney Stanton LE9 ... 199 D3
Swadlincote DE11 ... 44 B3
Highfield (Uppingham Sch)
LE15 ... 189 B3
Highgate
Ashby-De-La-Z LE65 ... 69 A8
Leicester LE2 ... 180 A4
Highgate Ave LE4 ... 128 E8
Highgate Com Prim Sch
LE12 ... 77 D4
Highgate Dr LE2 ... 180 B5
Highgate La NG13 ... 13 A7
Highgate Rd LE12 ... 77 D3
Highgrove Cres LE2 ... 179 B5
Highland Ave LE3 ... 152 E2
Highlands PE9 ... 116 E2
Highlands Way PE9 ... 143 B3
High Lees LE10 ... 217 B4
High Mdw LE12 ... 30 A1
Highmeres Rd LE4 ... 129 F3
High St Barrow-u-S LE12 76 D7
Barwell LE9 ... 198 A6
Bottesford NG32 ... 3 A2
Braunston-in-R LE15 ... 137 A2
Carlby PE9 ... 117 B8
Carlby PE9 ... 117 C8
Castle Donington DE74 ... 17 A2
Coalville LE67 ... 71 C1
Collyweston PE9 ... 168 D2
Cottingham LE16 ... 229 C1
Desford LE9 ... 151 B3
Duddington PE9 ... 193 B6
Earl Shilton LE9 ... 198 F8
Easton on t H PE9 ... 169 A5
Enderby LE19 ... 178 B3
Exton LE15 ... 113 A3
Fleckney LE8 ... 222 F8
Great Easton LE16 ... 229 D7
Great Glen LE8 ... 205 A8
Gretton NN17 ... 213 B1
Hallaton LE16 ... 209 D6
Husbands Bosworth
LE17 ... 247 E5
Ibstock LE67 ... 122 F8
Kegworth DE74 ... 18 C2
Ketton PE9 ... 168 A5
Kibworth Beauchamp
LE8 ... 224 A8
Leicester LE1 ... 259 B4
Leicester LE5 ... 156 B2
Leicester, Oadby LE2 ... 181 A5
Long Eaton NG10 ... 10 E8
Loughborough LE11 ... 52 B4
Lutterworth LE17 ... 244 C5
Market Harborough
LE16 ... 240 E3
Measham DE12 ... 93 C5
Melbourne DE73 ... 26 A7
Melton Mowbray LE13 ... 59 C3
Morcott LE15 ... 191 A6
North Kilworth LE17 ... 246 F4
Oakham LE15 ... 137 F6
Packington LE65 ... 69 C2
Quorn LE12 ... 75 F6
Sileby LE12 ... 77 C3
Somerby LE14 ... 108 B2
South Witham NG33 ... 65 B3
Stamford PE9 ... 143 E3
Staunton in t V NG13 ... 1 B4
Stoke Golding CV13 ... 196 D7
Swadlincote DE11 ... 44 C4
Swinford LE17 ... 254 B3
Syston LE7 ... 103 A4
Waltham on t W LE14 ... 40 A6
Walton LE17 ... 236 B3
Welford NN6 ... 256 E6
Whetstone LE8 ... 201 F7
Woodville DE11 ... 44 F2
High St E LE15 ... 189 B4
High Street St Martin's
PE9 ... 143 E2
High St W LE15 ... 189 A4
High Tor E LE9 ... 175 E1
High Tor W LE9 ... 175 E1
Highway Rd
Leicester LE5 ... 155 E2
Thurmaston LE4 ... 129 F8
Hijaz Coll CV11 ... 196 C2
Hilary Bevins Cl CV13 ... 195 F4
Hilary Cl LE13 ... 59 E6
Hilary Cres
Coalville LE67 ... 72 A3
Groby LE6 ... 126 D3
Hilcot Gn LE3 ... 153 C2
Hilders Rd LE3 ... 154 A6
Hildyard Rd LE4 ... 129 A1
Hillary Cl PE9 ... 143 F4
Hillary Pl LE3 ... 154 A2
Hillberry Cl LE19 ... 201 A8
Hill Cl LE9 ... 176 A7
Hillcrest Ave
Kibworth Beauchamp
LE8 ... 206 A1
Market Harborough
LE16 ... 240 D4
Hillcrest La LE17 ... 247 E5
Hillcrest Rd LE2 ... 180 C6
Hillcroft Cl LE4 ... 129 F8
Hillcroft Rd LE5 ... 155 E5
Hill Ct LE7 ... 156 F4
Hill Dr LE17 ... 244 C5
Hill Farm Ave CV11 ... 214 B1
Hill Field LE2 ... 181 E4
Hill Gdns LE16 ... 240 C3

Lords Cl LE67 97 A7
Lordship La NG13 2 A6
Lord's La NG33 43 B8
Lorne Rd LE2 155 B1
Lorraine Rd LE2 179 E7
Lorrimer Rd LE2 179 E8
Lorrimer Way LE11 51 C5
Loseby La LE1 259 B3
Losecoat Cl PE9 143 F5
Lossiemouth Rd LE10 196 F1
Lothair Rd LE2 154 E1
Lothian Pl DE74 17 A3
Loudoun Ct 10 LE65 69 B6
Loudoun Pl DE74 17 A4
Loudoun Way LE65 68 F5
Loughbon NG13 2 A7
Loughborough CE Prim Sch
LE11 51 F3
Loughborough Coll
LE11 51 F3
Loughborough General
Hospl LE11 52 B4
Loughborough Gram Sch
LE11 52 B2
Loughborough High Sch
LE11 52 B3
Loughborough Hospl
LE11 51 E4
Loughborough Rd
Asfordby LE14 57 D3
Birstall LE4 129 A7
Burton o t W LE12 53 E7
Burton o t W LE12 53 F4
Cotes LE12 53 B6
East Leake LE12 31 F7
Hathern LE12 51 A8
Hoton LE12 53 B8
Loughborough LE12 75 D8
North End LE12 76 D3
Peggs Green LE67 71 A7
Quorn LE12 75 E6
Rothley LE7 102 A5
Shepshed LE12 50 C4
Thringstone LE67 71 D8
Whitwick LE67 71 F6
Loughborough Sta
LE11 52 C5
Loughborough Tech Ctr
LE11 51 F3
Loughborough Univ
LE11 51 E3
Loughborough Univ of Tech
LE11 51 C1
Loughborough Univ Sch of
Art & Design
Loughborough LE11 51 F3
Loughborough LE11 52 A4
Louise Ave LE6 126 F2
Lound Rd LE9 217 D8
Lount Rd CV13 148 F8
Lounts Cres LE16 229 D7
Loveday Cl CV9 170 D2
Love La LE10 216 A6
Lovelace Cl CV13 172 A6
Lovelace Cres LE9 198 F5
Lovelace Way LE8 223 A7
Loves La
Dunton Bassett LE17 219 D1
Empingham LE15 141 A8
Lovett Cl LE12 77 C3
Lovetts Cl LE10 214 F8
Loveys Croft DE73 26 E2
Lowcroft Dr LE2 181 C4
Lower Bond St LE10 197 D1
Lower Brand LE67 48 A4
Lower Brook St NG10 10 E7
Lower Brown St LE1 259 B2
Lower Cambridge St
LE11 52 B5
Lower Church St
Ashby-De-La-Z LE65 69 B6
Syston LE7 103 B4
Lower Free La LE1 259 B4
Lower Gladstone St
LE11 52 B5
Lower Gn LE11 74 D8
Lower Hastings St
LE1 259 C2
Lower Hillmorton Rd 5
CV21 257 A1
Lower Hill St LE1 259 B4
Lower Holme LE12 30 B3
Lower Keyham La LE5 130 B1
Lower Lee St LE1 259 B4
Lower Leicester Rd
LE17 244 D6
Lower Moor Rd LE67 70 E8
Lower Packington Rd
LE65 69 B4
Lower St CV21 257 B1
Lower Willow St LE1 155 A7
Lowesby Cl LE13 59 E2
Lowesby La
Tilton on t H LE7 133 D4
Twyford LE14 133 E8
Loweswater Cl
Barrow-u-S LE12 53 D1
Nuneaton CV11 214 A6
Loweswater Dr LE11 51 D1
Loweswater Gr LE65 69 C4
Lowfields La NG32 4 E6
Lowick Dr LE18 180 E2
Lowland Ave LE3 153 A2
Lowther Cl LE15 110 C2
Lowther Way LE11 52 B1
Low Woods La LE12 49 B3
Loxley Dr LE13 59 B1
Loxley Rd LE3 127 C1
Lubbesthorpe Bridle Rd
Braunstone LE3 153 E1
Enderby LE19,LE3 177 F8
Lubbesthorpe Rd LE3 178 E6
Lubbesthorpe Way
LE19 178 E7
Lubenham All Saints CE
Prim Sch LE16 239 F3
Lubenham Hill LE16 240 C2
Lubenham Rd
East Farndon LE16 240 B1
Marston Trussell LE16 239 D1
Lucas Rd LE10 215 D6
Lucas Way LE9 198 E7
Ludgate Cl LE4 128 E8
Ludlam Cl LE8 202 C4
Ludlow Cl
Leicester, Oadby LE2 181 C4
Loughborough LE11 74 C8
Ludlow Dr LE13 59 C5
Ludlow Pl LE12 50 A2
Luffenham Cl PE9 143 A3
Luffenham Rd
Barrowden LE15 191 F6
Ketton PE9 167 E4
Lyndon LE15 165 E5
Lullington Mews DE12 67 A3
Lullington Rd DE12 67 A3
Lulworth Cl
Leicester LE5 156 A4
Wigston LE18 203 D7
Lumby's Terr PE9 143 E2
Lundy Cl LE10 197 B1
Lunsford Rd LE5 155 D8
Lupin Cl LE10 215 D5
Luther St LE3 154 C4
Lutterworth Gram Sch &
Com Coll LE17 244 B6
Lutterworth High Sch
LE17 244 B5
Lutterworth Mus*
LE17 244 C5
Lutterworth Rd
Arnesby LE8, LE17 221 D4
Bitteswell LE17 244 B8
Blaby LE8 202 B7
Burbage LE10 216 C3
Churchover CV23,LE17 252 D5
Dunton Bassett LE17 219 E2
Gilmorton LE17 235 B2
Kimcote LE17 235 E2
Leicester LE2 179 C6
Lutterworth LE17 244 D4
Nuneaton CV11 214 A1
Pailton CV23,LE17 243 B3
Shawell LE17 253 D6
Swinford LE17 254 B6
Ullesthorpe LE17 233 C3
Walcote LE17 245 C4
Whetstone LE8 202 A3
Lyall Cl LE11 51 D6
Lychgate Cl
Burbage LE10 216 A5
Cropston LE7 100 E2
Lychgate La LE10 216 C5
Lydall Rd LE2 179 E4
Lyddington Bede Ho*
LE15 212 D7
Lyddington Rd
Caldecott LE15, L16 212 D2
Gretton NN17 213 A1
Lydford Rd LE4 129 E2
Lyle Cl Leicester LE4 129 E5
Melton Mowbray LE13 59 C6
Lyme Rd LE2 155 C3
Lymington Rd LE5 156 D8
Lyn Cl LE3,LE7 127 F3
Lyncote Rd LE3 179 B8
Lyncroft Leys LE7 156 F7
Lyndale Cl LE4 129 E6
Lyndale Rd LE3 178 F8
Lynden Ave NG10 10 D5
Lyndene Cl LE9 198 F7
Lyndhurst Cl LE10 216 A7
Lyndhurst Ct LE2 155 C2
Lyndhurst Rd LE2 181 A6
Lyndon Dr LE2 180 F6
Lyndon Hill Nature Reserve
Visitor Ctr* LE15 165 A8
Lyndon Rd
Manton LE15 164 F6
North Luffenham LE15 166 B4
Lyndon Way PE9 143 A3
Lyndwood Ct LE2 155 D1
Lyneham Cl LE10 197 A1
Lyngate Ave LE4 129 A8
Lynholme Rd LE2 180 B6
Lynmouth Cl LE3 153 C7
Lynmouth Dr
Gilmorton LE17 235 C4
Wigston LE18 180 A5
Lynmouth Rd LE5 156 D8
Lynton Cl LE17 235 C4
Lynton Rd LE13 59 A6
Lynwood Cl LE9 151 B3
Lyon Cl LE18 180 A4
Lysander Cl LE10 215 E4
Lytham Rd LE2 155 A1
Lytton Rd LE2 155 B1

M

Mablowe Field LE18 203 E8
Macaulay Rd
Lutterworth LE17 244 C8
Rothley LE7 101 E6
Macaulay St LE2 179 F8
MC Carthy Rd LE12 50 A3
Macdonald Rd LE4 129 A1
McDowell Way LE19 201 B7
Machin Dr LE9 219 A4
Mackaness Cl LE17 235 C4
Mackenzie Way LE1 259 C5
McKenzie Wlk LE5 156 A5
Mackworth Cl DE11 44 B7
Maclean Ave LE11 51 C6
McNeil Gr DE72 9 A7
McVicker Cl LE5 156 A6
Madeline Cl LE16 241 A5
Madeline Rd LE4 128 C6
Madras Rd LE1 155 B6
Magee Cl LE10 197 C2
Magna Pk LE17 243 C6
Magna Rd LE18 180 A1
Magnolia Ave LE11 75 A7
Magnolia Cl
Leicester Forest East
LE3 152 E2
Leicester LE2 179 C5
Magnolia Dr LE17 244 B7
Magnus Rd LE4 129 C2
Mahatma Ghandi Ho
LE4 155 B8
Maidenhair Cl LE11 75 A6
Maidenhead Ave LE5 130 D3
Maiden La PE9 143 E3
Maiden St LE7 102 F3
Maidenwell Ave LE5 130 C2
Maidstone Rd LE2 155 B5
Maidwell Cl LE18 180 F2
Maino Cres LE17 244 B5
Main Rd
Asfordby Valley LE14 58 B3
Austrey CV9 119 B1
Barleythorpe LE15 137 E8
Bilstone CV13 147 C8
Brentingby LE14 60 D2
Claybrooke Parva LE17 232 E5
Collyweston PE9 168 D2
Glaston LE15 190 B5
Granby NG13 5 A4
Nether Broughton LE14 36 C7
Newton Regis B79 118 C2
Old Dalby LE14 35 E4
Ratcliffe Culey CV9 171 B4
Redmile NG13 6 E4
Sheepy Magna CV9 171 A6
Stainby NG33 43 D2
Twycross CV9 146 D7
Twyford LE14 106 D1
Uffington PE9 144 E3
Upton CV13 172 C4
Wycomb LE14 39 A6
Main St
Albert Village DE11 44 C1
Allington NG32 4 F5
Asfordby LE14 57 F3
Ashby Parva LE17 233 F5
Ashley LE16 227 F2
Bagworth LE67 124 B5
Barkby LE7 130 C8
Barlestone CV13 149 D8
Barrowden LE15 191 F5
Barsby LE7 105 D4
Barton in t B CV13 122 D1
Beeby LE7 131 C5
Belmesthorpe PE9 117 A1
Belton-in-R LE15 187 D7
Bisbrooke LE15 189 E4
Blackfordby DE11 68 B8
Botcheston LE9 151 C6
Branston NG32 23 C8
Breaston DE72 9 D8
Breedon on the Hill DE73 26 F2
Broughton Astley LE9 218 E7
Bruntingthorpe LE17 221 C1
Buckminster NG33 42 D2
Burrough on t H LE14 107 D2
Burton Overy LE8 182 F1
Cadeby CV13 149 C1
Caldecott LE16 230 B8
Carlton CV13 148 D7
Clifton u D CV23 257 A5
Clipsham LE15 89 E5
Cold Overton LE15 109 B2
Congerstone CV13 147 D7
Cosby LE9 201 D2
Cossington LE7 102 D8
Cotesbach LE17 244 B1
Cottesmore LE15 112 C8
Countesthorpe LE8 202 F3
Croxton Kerrial LE14 24 B7
Dadlington CV13 173 E1
Drayton LE16 229 A5
Dunton Bassett LE17 219 D2
East Farndon LE16 250 B7
East Langton LE16 225 D6
Eastwell LE14 22 B6
Eaton NG32 22 F7
Egleton LE15 138 D3
Empingham LE15 141 A6
Fleckney LE8 222 F7
Foxton LE16 224 E1
Frisby on t W LE14 80 D8
Frolesworth LE17 218 B2
Gaddesby LE7 105 B7
Gaulby LE7 183 D6
Gilmorton LE17 235 C4
Glenfield LE3 127 B1
Glooston LE16 208 C4
Main St continued
Goadby Marwood LE14 22 C1
Granby NG13 5 C5
Great Dalby LE14 82 A1
Great Glen LE8 205 B8
Great Oxendon LE16 250 E3
Greetham LE15 88 B1
Grimston LE14 57 B8
Gumley LE16 239 A8
Gunby NG33 64 E8
Harby LE14 12 A2
Hartshorne DE11 45 B6
Heather LE67 95 C2
Hemington DE74 17 D4
Hickling LE14 19 C6
Higham on t H CV13 196 A3
Hoby LE7 37 E8
Holwell LE14 37 F4
Houghton on t H LE7 157 F3
Huncote LE9 200 D7
Hungarton LE7 132 C3
Illston on t H LE7 183 F3
Keyham LE7 131 D1
Kibworth Beauchamp
LE8 206 A2
Kilby LE18 204 A3
Kirby Bellars LE14 81 B8
Kirby Muxloe LE9 152 E6
Kirkby Mallory LE9 175 C6
Knossington LE15 136 A6
Laughton LE17 238 C7
Leicester,Evington LE5 156 B3
Leicester,Humberstone
LE5 156 B8
Leicester LE3 153 F2
Leire LE17 218 F1
Lockington DE74 17 F5
Loddington LE7 161 D1
Long Eaton NG10 10 D7
Long Whatton LE12 29 B4
Lubenham LE16 239 F3
Lyddington LE15 213 A6
Market Bosworth CV13 148 F3
Market Overton LE15 86 F5
Markfield LE67 98 D1
Medbourne LE16 228 A7
Mowsley LE17 237 F7
Muston NG13 7 F8
Nailstone CV13 123 B3
Netherseal DE12 91 F7
Newbold Verdon LE9 150 B4
Newton Burgoland LE67 121 E7
Newton CV23 253 A1
Newtown Linford LE6 126 D8
Normanton Le H LE67 94 F6
Normanton on S LE12 30 D3
Norton-J-T CV9 120 A2
Oakthorpe DE12 93 A7
Old Dalby LE14 36 A5
Orton-on-t-H CV9 145 D4
Osgathorpe LE12 48 D3
Overseal DE12 67 B3
Owston LE15 135 B4
Peatling Magna LE8 221 A6
Peatling Parva LE17 235 F8
Peckleton LE9 175 F7
Pickwell LE14 108 D3
Preston LE15 164 C2
Queniborough LE7 103 F5
Ragdale LE14 56 C4
Ratby LE6 152 C8
Ratcliffe on t W LE7 78 C2
Ravenstone LE67 95 E8
Redmile NG13 6 F3
Rempstone LE12 32 D5
Ridlington LE15 163 D2
Rockingham LE16 230 B4
Rotherby LE14 79 F6
Saddington LE8 223 B4
Saltby LE14 24 E1
Saxelbye LE14 57 E7
Scraptoft LE7 156 F8
Seaton LE15 190 C1
Sewstern NG33 63 F8
Shackerstone CV13 121 E2
Shangton LE8 207 B5
Shawell LE17 253 C5
Shearsby LE17 222 A2
Shenton CV13 173 B5
Skeffington LE7 160 A2
Slawston LE16 209 B1
Smeeton Westerby LE8 223 F6
Smisby LE65 45 F3
Snarestone DE12 121 A8
South Croxton LE7 105 B1
Sproxton LE14 41 F5
Stanford on S LE12 31 C1
Stanton u B LE67 97 F1
Stapleton LE9 174 F1
Stathern LE14 13 A3
Stoke Dry LE15 211 F6
Stoke Golding CV13 196 D7
Stonesby LE14 40 E6
Sutton Bassett LE16 227 A1
Sutton Bonington LE12 30 B7
Sutton Cheney CV13 174 B6
Swannington LE67 71 B5
Swepstone LE67 94 D2
Swithland LE12 100 E7
Theddingworth LE17 248 D8
Thistleton LE15 87 E8
Thornton LE67 124 E4
Thorpe Satchville LE14 106 E4
Thringstone LE67 71 D8
Thurlaston LE9 177 A3
Thurmaston LE7 103 C1
Thurnby LE7 157 A4
Tilton on t H LE7 133 B1
Main St continued
Tilton on t H LE7 160 A8
Tugby LE7 185 E6
Tur Langton LE16 207 A2
Twyford LE14 106 D1
Ullesthorpe LE17 233 B4
Wakerley LE15 192 A4
Wardley LE15 188 A5
Whissendine LE15 84 F1
Willey CV23 242 F6
Willoughby-on-t-W LE12 34 D7
Willoughby Waterleys
LE8 220 C5
Wilson DE73 26 E5
Woodhouse Eaves LE12 75 A2
Woodthorpe LE12 75 C7
Worthington LE65 47 F5
Wymondham LE14 62 E2
Zouch LE12 30 B3
Maitland Ave LE12 76 E1
Maizefield LE10 197 C4
Makey's Cl LE15 166 A7
Malabar Rd LE1 155 B7
Malcolm Arc LE1 259 B4
Malcolm Sargent Prim Sch
The PE9 143 A3
Malham Cl
Leicester LE4 128 C3
Nuneaton CV11 214 A2
Malham Way LE2 181 D5
Mallard Ave LE6 126 E3
Mallard Cl
Essendine PE9 117 B6
Measham DE12 93 B4
Mallard Ct PE9 143 D2
Mallard Dr
Hinckley LE10 215 A7
Syston LE7 102 F4
Mallard Rd
Barrow-u-S LE12 76 E8
Mountsorrel LE12 76 F2
Mallard Way LE3 152 E2
Malling Ave LE9 218 E7
Malling Cl LE4 102 B1
Mallory Cl LE9 150 B3
Mallory La 11 PE9 143 D3
Mallory Pl LE5 155 E8
Mallory St LE9 198 C8
Mallow Cl LE5 130 C3
Malmesbury Ave DE11 44 D6
Malthouse Cl CV13 123 B3
Maltings Ct NN17 213 B1
Maltings Rd NN17 213 B1
Maltings The
Ashley LE16 227 F3
Glenfield LE3 127 B1
Hamilton LE5 130 D3
Shardlow DE72 9 B1
Sileby LE12 77 C3
Stamford PE9 143 E2
Wothorpe PE9 169 E8
Maltings Yd LE15 113 A3
Malting Yd PE9 143 E2
Malt Mill Bank LE9 198 A6
Malton Dr LE2 181 C6
Malvern Ave LE12 50 C2
Malvern Cres
Ashby-De-La-Z LE65 69 A8
Cosby LE9 201 D3
Malvern Gdns NG10 10 A8
Malvern Rd LE2 155 D2
Malvern Wlk LE15 137 D6
Mammoth St LE67 71 D1
Mancetter Rd CV9 194 A6
Manchester La DE11 45 C5
Manchester St NG10 10 D6
Mandarin Cl LE10 215 A6
Mandarin Way LE8 201 F4
Mandervell Rd LE2 180 F5
Mandora La 7 LE2 155 B4
Manitoba Rd LE1 259 C5
Mann Cl LE3 153 D2
Manners Cl PE9 144 F4
Manners Dr LE13 59 D6
Manners Rd LE2 179 E7
Mannion Cres NG10 10 B5
Manor Brook Cl
Coalville LE67 96 C5
Stoney Stanton LE9 199 E3
Manor Cl
Claybrooke Magna LE17 232 D6
Hinckley LE10 215 C5
Leicester, Oadby LE2 181 B8
Long Whatton LE12 29 B4
Melton Mowbray LE13 59 E5
Ryhall PE9 116 F3
Manor Close 1 LE65 69 C5
Manor Cres LE9 174 E2
Manor Ct Blaby LE8 179 C1
Breaston DE72 9 E8
Cottingham LE16 229 C1
Little Stretton LE2 182 D5
Waltham on t W LE14 40 A6
Willoughby-on-t-W LE12 34 C7
Manor Dr Leicester LE4 128 A5
Loughborough LE11 75 B8
Netherseal DE12 91 F6
Sileby LE12 77 C2
Worthington LE65 47 F6
Manor Farm Cl LE9 218 F6
Manor Farm Ct LE7 160 A8
Manor Farm La PE9 117 B6
Manor Farm Mews
DE72 16 B8
Manor Farm Rd DE72 16 B8
Manor Farm Way LE3 153 C7
Manor Farm Wlk LE7 160 A8
Manor Farm Yd LE7 160 A8
Manorfield CE Prim Sch
LE9 199 D2
Manor Gdns
Desford LE9 151 B3
Glenfield LE3 153 C8
Shepshed LE12 50 B4
Manor Gn PE9 167 F5
Manor High Sch LE2 181 D7
Manor House Cl LE10 216 E6
Manor House Gdns
LE5 156 B8
Manor House Prep Sch
LE65 69 C6
Manor House Rd NG10 10 F6
Manor La
Barleythorpe LE15 137 D8
Clifton u D CV23 257 A6
Glaston LE15 190 B6
Granby NG13 5 A8
Langham LE15 110 C3
Peckleton LE9 175 F6
Somerby LE14 108 B1
Manorleigh DE72 9 E8
Manor Paddock NG32 4 F5
Manor Pl 6 LE10 197 D1
Manor Rd
Barlestone CV13 149 C8
Bitteswell LE17 244 B8
Carlby PE9 117 C8
Claybrooke Magna LE17 232 D6
Coalville LE67 96 C6
Cosby LE9 201 D4
Desford LE9 151 B3
Easthorpe NG13 3 C2
Fleckney LE8 223 A7
Great Bowden LE16 241 A6
Heather LE67 95 B2
Leicester, Oadby LE2 181 A8
Loughborough LE11 75 B8
Medbourne LE16 228 A7
Sapcote LE9 217 D8
Stretton LE15 88 F4
Thurmaston LE4 129 D6
Ullesthorpe LE17 233 A4
Manor Road Extension
LE2 181 B7
Manor St Hinckley LE10 197 C1
Wigston LE18 180 B2
Manor View
Ketton PE9 168 A6
Sibson CV13 172 A6
Manor Way LE10 215 D5
Manor Wlk LE16 240 E3
Mansfield Ave LE12 76 A6
Mansfield Cl DE11 44 D4
Mansfield St
Leicester LE1 259 B4
Quorn LE12 76 A6
Mansion House Gdns
LE13 59 C6
Mansion St LE10 215 D8
Manston Cl LE4 130 A5
Mantle La LE67 71 C2
Mantle Rd LE3 154 D6
Manton Cl LE9 219 B6
Manton Grange LE15 164 E5
Manton Rd LE15 166 A7
Maple Ave Blaby LE8 202 B7
Braunstone LE3 153 C3
Countesthorpe LE8 202 F4
Maple Cl
East Leake LE12 31 D8
Hinckley LE10 215 E5
Leicester LE4 128 E2
Melton Mowbray LE13 59 B5
Maple Ct NN17 230 E1
Maple Dr
Aston-on-T DE72 16 A7
Ibstock LE67 95 E2
Lutterworth LE17 244 B6
Maple Gr DE72 9 F8
Maple Rd
Loughborough LE11 75 B8
Swadlincote DE11 44 B6
Thurmaston LE4 129 D6
Maple Rd N LE11 75 B8
Maple Rd S LE11 75 B7
Maple St LE2 155 B5
Mapleton Rd
Draycott DE72 9 A8
Wigston LE18 180 C3
Maple Tree Wlk LE19 201 C7
Maple Way
Desford LE9 151 A3
Earl Shilton LE9 198 E6
Maplewell LE67 72 B1
Maplewell Dr LE4 128 A6
Maplewell Hall Sch
LE12 99 E7
Maplewell Rd LE12 99 F7
Maplin Rd LE5 130 E1
Mapperley Ho LE13 59 D3
Marble St LE1 259 B3
Marchant Rd LE10 215 C8
Marchfont Cl CV11 214 A1
Marcus Cl LE7 102 E2
Mardale Way LE11 74 D8
Marefield Cl LE7 157 A5
Marefield La
Burrough on t H LE14 134 C8
Lowesby LE7 133 E5
Tilton on t H LE7 134 B1
Twyford LE14 133 F8
Marfitt St LE4 129 B2
Margam Cl LE3 128 B2
Margaret Anne Rd
LE2 181 B4
Margaret Cl LE4 129 E8

Mar – Mil 281

Margaret Cres LE18 180 B3
Margaret Rd LE5 155 E5
Margaret St LE67 71 C1
Marie Cl CV9 194 A7
Marigold Cl PE9 142 E4
Marigold Cres LE13 82 B8
Marigold Dr LE10 215 E5
Marigold La LE12 76 F2
Marigold Pl DE11 44 F4
Marigold Way LE19 200 F8
Marina Dr LE6 127 A3
Marina Rd LE5 155 D4
Marion's Way LE9 200 D4
Marjorie St LE4 155 A8
Market Bosworth Ctry Pk★ CV13 149 A3
Market Bosworth High Sch & Com Coll CV13 148 E3
Market Bosworth Sta★ CV13 148 C3
Market Ct NG33 65 B3
Market Harborough CE Prim Sch LE16 240 D3
Market Harborough District Hospl LE16 240 D2
Market Harborough Mus★ LE16 240 E3
Market Harborough Sta LE16 241 A3
Market Mews CV13 148 F3
Market Pl Belton LE12 49 B6
Billesdon LE7 159 B2
5 Hinckley LE10 215 D8
Kegworth DE74 18 D2
Leicester LE1 259 B3
Long Eaton NG10 10 E8
Loughborough LE11 52 B4
Market Bosworth CV13 148 F3
Melbourne DE73 26 B7
Melton Mowbray LE13 59 C3
Mountsorrel LE12 76 E3
Oakham LE15 138 A6
Shepshed LE12 50 B4
Uppingham LE15 189 B4
Whitwick LE67 71 F5
Market Place App LE1 259 B3
Market Pl S LE1 259 B3
Market St
Ashby-De-La-Z LE65 69 B6
Bottesford NG13 3 B2
Castle Donington DE74 17 B3
Coalville LE67 71 C1
Draycott DE72 9 A7
Leicester LE1 259 B3
Loughborough LE11 52 A4
Lutterworth LE17 244 C6
Oakham LE15 138 A6
Swadlincote, Church Gresley DE11 44 B1
Swadlincote DE11 44 B4
Markfield La
Botcheston LE9 151 C8
Markfield LE67 98 F1
Thornton LE67 124 F6
Markfield Rd
Groby LE6 126 D4
Ratby LE6 126 B2
Markham Ret Pk PE9 143 F5
Markland LE2 179 C4
Marlborough Cl LE10 216 B7
Marlborough Dr LE8 223 A6
Marlborough Rd
Breaston DE72 9 D7
3 Long Eaton NG10 10 F8
Marlborough Sq LE67 71 C1
Marlborough St LE1 259 B3
Marlborough Way
Ashby-De-La-Z LE65 69 A7
Market Harborough LE16 240 E5
Marle Pit Hill LE12 30 A8
Marl Fields LE7 76 F1
Marlow Ct LE16 228 A8
Marlow Rd LE3 154 D2
Marmion Cl LE8 223 A6
Maromme Sq 2 LE18 180 D3
Marquis Ct DE12 67 E5
Marquis Dr DE12 67 E5
Marquis Rd LE14 36 B6
Marquis St LE1 259 B2
Marriott Dr LE8 224 B8
Marriott Prim Sch LE2 179 E6
Marriott Rd LE2 179 E6
Marsden Ave LE7 103 D5
Marsden Cl LE67 70 F2
Marsden La LE2 179 B6
Marshall Ave LE12 77 D4
Marshall Cl LE3 153 C2
Marshall Ct LE16 240 F2
Marshall Farm Cl NG13 6 B2
Marshall St LE3 154 D7
Marsh Ave LE8 206 B1
Marsh Cl LE4 129 E5
Marsh Ct NG13 3 B3
Marsh Dr LE8 206 A1
Marsh Rd LE12 76 F1
Marsh's Paddock LE14 19 C6
Marston Cl
Leicester, Oadby LE2 181 A3
Moira DE12 68 A5
Marston Cres LE8 202 E3
Marston Dr LE6 126 F3
Marston La NG32 4 F5
Marston Rd Croft LE9 200 B5
Leicester LE4 129 E2
Lubenham LE16 239 D2
Marston Trussell Rd LE16 249 F7
Marston Way LE67 95 B2
Marstown Ave LE18 179 F2
Marteg Cl LE13 59 B1
Martin Ave
Barrow-u-S LE12 76 D7
Leicester Forest East LE3 152 F3
Leicester, Oadby LE2 181 B5
Mountsorrel LE12 76 D1
Martin Cl Leicester LE4 155 B8
Oakham LE15 138 B8
Stoney Stanton LE9 199 D1
Whitwick LE67 71 D6
Martin Ct LE7 127 D5
Martindale Cl
Leicester LE2 259 B1
Loughborough LE11 51 D1
Martin Dr LE7 102 E4
Martin High Sch LE7 127 D7
Martins Dr CV9 170 E2
Martinshaw La LE6 126 E3
Martinshaw Prim Sch LE6 126 D4
Martinshaw Wood Nature Trail★ LE6 126 C3
Martin Square LE6 152 D8
Martin St LE4 155 C8
Martival LE5 155 E7
Marvin Cl LE3 154 B7
Marwell Cl LE4 128 F4
Marwell Wlk LE4 128 F4
Marwood Rd LE4 128 D4
Marydene Ct LE5 156 C3
Marydene Dr LE5 156 C3
Mary Gee Hos LE2 180 D8
Mary La LE14,NG32 40 C8
Maryland Cl LE9 197 F6
Maryland Ct DE11 44 A7
Marylebone Dr LE17 244 D6
Mary Rd LE3 154 B8
Mary's Cl LE12 33 C3
Marys Ct LE7 127 D6
Mary St LE9 198 F8
Marywell Cl LE10 196 F1
Masefield Ave
Narborough LE19 178 A2
Swadlincote DE11 44 C6
Masefield Cl
Barwell LE9 198 C8
Measham DE12 93 B3
Mason Cres DE11 44 E4
Mason Ct LE10 215 B8
Mason Row LE5 130 D3
Masons Cl LE19 201 B7
Masterton Cl PE9 143 F5
Masterton Rd PE9 143 E5
Matlock Ave LE18 180 A1
Matlock Ct NG10 9 F5
Matlock St LE2 155 C6
Matthew Arnold Ct LE11 51 D5
Matthew Ct LE11 52 D4
Matthews Ct LE65 68 F7
Matts Cl LE2 179 D5
Maughan St LE9 175 F1
Maura Cl LE8 201 F5
Maurice Dr LE8 202 D3
Maurice Rd LE16 250 D8
Mavis Ave LE3 154 C2
Mawby Cl LE8 202 A5
Mawby's La DE12 119 F8
Maxfield Ho 8 LE2 155 B5
Maxwell Dr LE11 51 C5
Maxwell St Breaston DE72 9 F8
Long Eaton NG10 10 E7
Maxwell Way LE17 244 C8
May Cl LE3 154 A4
Mayfield LE15 138 A8
Mayfield Dr
Loughborough LE11 52 B2
Wigston LE18 180 D4
Mayfield Rd LE2 155 C3
Mayfield St LE13 59 B5
Mayfield Way LE9 198 C7
Mayflower Cl LE67 125 E8
Mayflower Jun Sch LE5 155 F4
Mayflower Mews LE15 189 B4
Mayflower Rd LE5 155 E3
Mayflower Wlk LE67 125 E8
Maylands Ave DE72 9 E8
Maylan Rd NN17 230 F3
May Meadow Cl CV13 149 D8
Maynard Cl LE67 124 A6
Maynard Pk★ LE67 123 F8
Maynard Rd LE2 155 B6
Maynard Wlk LE67 124 A6
Mayns La LE8 205 E7
Mayo Cl LE11 74 F7
Mayor's Wlk LE1 155 A3
Maypole Hill DE11 44 A6
Mayre Cl LE9 219 B5
Mays Farm Dr LE9 199 D3
Maytree Cl LE3 152 E3
Maytree Ct LE3 152 E3
Maytree Dr LE3 152 E2
May Tree La LE12 75 B4
Meadhurst Gdns LE15 189 B4
Meadhurst Rd LE3 154 A5
Meadow Ave LE11 52 B6
Meadowbrook Ct DE12 119 F8
Meadowbrook Rd LE8 223 F8
Meadow Cl
Bagworth LE67 124 B5
Meadow Cl *continued*
Barrow-u-S LE12 76 E8
Breaston DE72 9 E7
Draycott DE72 9 A7
Market Harborough LE16 240 F4
Ratby LE6 152 D8
Sheepy Magna CV9 171 B7
Stoney Stanton LE9 199 D3
Meadow Com Prim Sch The LE18 180 E3
Meadowcourt Rd LE2 180 F7
Meadow Court Rd
Earl Shilton LE9 198 F7
Groby LE6 126 F3
Meadow Cres DE74 17 B2
Meadowcroft Cl LE3 153 B7
Meadow Ct LE19 178 A1
Meadowdale Prim Sch LE16 241 B4
Meadow Dr LE10 216 A7
Meadow Edge LE19 178 A2
Meadowfield LE15 138 A8
Meadow Gdns
Leicester LE2 180 A5
Measham DE12 93 C3
Meadow Hill LE8 182 A1
Meadow La
Birstall LE4 129 C8
Coalville LE67 72 B2
Long Eaton NG10 10 F7
Loughborough LE11,LE12 52 B7
Markfield LE67 98 E1
Ryhall PE9 116 E1
Stanton u B LE67 97 F1
Swadlincote DE11 44 A6
Syston LE7 102 E4
Meadow Lane Ind Est LE11 52 B6
Meadow Park Ind Est PE9 117 B5
Meadow Rd
Barlestone CV13 149 D7
Barwell LE9 198 C7
Mountsorrel LE12 101 D8
Woodhouse Eaves LE12 75 A1
Meadowside CV11 214 B1
Meadows La LE14 11 D1
Meadows Rise LE14 62 D2
Meadow St LE16 240 E4
Meadows The
Burbage LE10 216 A7
East Goscote LE7 103 E8
Littlethorpe LE19 201 D7
Shepshed LE12 50 A3
Meadowsweet PE9 142 E5
Meadowsweet Cl LE13 82 A8
Meadow The LE9 219 A5
Meadow View
Botcheston LE9 151 C8
Coalville LE67 96 C5
East Goscote LE7 103 F7
Leicester, Oadby LE2 181 B5
Stamford PE9 144 A4
Meadow Way
Desford LE9 151 C2
Egleton LE15 138 D3
Groby LE6 126 F3
Melton Mowbray LE13 59 D1
Swadlincote DE11 44 A6
Wigston LE18 180 F2
Meadow Wlk LE67 95 F2
Meads The LE3 153 E5
Meadvale Rd LE2 180 C7
Meadway LE3 154 A6
Meadway The
Birstall LE4 129 A8
Hinckley LE10 215 F7
Syston LE7 102 F2
Meadwell Rd LE3 153 D3
Mease Cl DE12 93 C4
Measham CE Prim Sch DE12 93 D5
Measham Rd
Acresford DE12 92 D6
Ashby-De-La-Z LE65 68 F3
Measham DE12 92 F1
Moira DE12 67 F3
Oakthorpe DE12 93 A7
Packington LE65 69 B1
Packington LE65 93 F8
Snarestone DE12 120 E8
Medbourne Rd
Ashley LE16 227 E4
Drayton LE16 228 E4
Hallaton LE16 209 E5
Slawston LE16 209 C1
Medhurst Cl LE8 202 A5
Medina Rd Corby NN17 230 C1
Leicester LE3 154 D8
Medway Cl LE16 241 A3
Medway Com Prim Sch LE2 155 C4
Medway Dr LE13 59 B6
Medway St LE2 155 C4
Meer The LE8 223 A6
Meeting House Cl LE12 31 F8
Meeting St LE12 75 F5
Melba Way LE4 102 B1
Melbourn Brothers Brewery Mus★ PE9 143 D3
Melbourne Cl LE8 223 F8
Melbourne Ct NG10 9 F4
Melbourne Dr LE13 59 A3
Melbourne Hall & Gdns★ DE73 26 C7
Melbourne Ho LE13 59 D3
Melbourne Inf & Jun Sch DE73 26 B8
Melbourne La DE73 26 E3
Melbourne Rd
Ibstock LE67 122 E8
Leicester LE2 155 C5
Newbold LE67 47 D2
Ravenstone LE67 95 F5
Stamford PE9 143 F4
Melbourne St
Coalville LE67 71 D1
Leicester LE2 155 B6
Melbray Dr LE13 59 C6
Melbreak Ave LE11 74 E8
Melcombe Wlk 5 LE4 128 F3
Melcroft Ave LE3 154 B5
Melford St LE5 155 F7
Melland Pl LE2 179 E5
Mellerstain Wlk LE5 155 E7
Mellier Cl LE19 178 A2
Mellor Com Prim Sch LE4 129 B3
Mellor Rd LE3 154 A5
Melody Ave LE7 127 E6
Melody Dr LE12 77 C2
Melrose Cl
Ashby-De-La-Z LE65 69 D6
Hinckley LE10 215 B8
Stamford PE9 143 A4
Melrose Rd LE67 71 E8
Melrose St LE4 129 B1
Melton Ave
Leicester LE4 129 C5
Melbourne DE73 26 A8
Melton & District War Meml Hospl LE13 59 C2
Melton Dr LE9 218 E8
Melton La LE14 107 C5
Melton Mowbray Coll of F Ed LE13 59 B3
Melton Mowbray Coll of F Ed (Annexe) LE13 59 C3
Melton Mowbray Ctry Pk★ LE13 59 D6
Melton Mowbray Sta LE13 59 C2
Melton Mowbray Visitor Ctr★ LE13 59 D6
Melton Rd
Asfordby Hill LE14 58 C3
Barrow-u-S LE12 76 E8
Burton Lazars LE14 83 B4
Burton o t W LE12 54 C7
East Goscote LE7 103 F8
East Langton LE16 225 C5
East Leake LE12 31 E5
Langham LE15 110 C2
Leicester LE4 129 C3
Long Clawson LE14 20 B1
Oakham LE15 137 F6
Rearsby LE7 79 C2
Scalford LE14 38 C3
Shangton LE8 207 B6
Syston LE7 103 C4
Thurmaston LE4 129 D7
Tilton on t H LE7 159 E5
Twyford LE7 133 D4
Upper Broughton LE14 19 A1
Waltham on t W LE14 40 A6
Whissendine LE15 84 C2
Wymondham LE14 62 C2
Melton Spinney Rd LE14,LE13 59 F7
Melton St
Earl Shilton LE9 198 E8
6 Leicester LE1 155 A7
Melville Cl LE11 51 B6
Memorial Homes LE7 156 E8
Memorial Sq LE67 71 C1
Memory La 2 LE1 155 A7
Mendip Ave LE4 128 D1
Mendip Cl
Ashby-De-La-Z LE65 69 B5
Shepshed LE12 50 C3
Mendip Rd
Edith Weston LE15 166 C7
Oakham LE15 137 D6
Mennecy Cl LE8 202 D3
Mensa Cl LE2 155 C5
Menzies Rd LE4 128 E2
Meon Cl NN17 230 C1
Mercenfeld Prim Sch LE67 125 D8
Mercer's Way LE7 103 E7
Merchant's Comm LE7 103 E7
Mercia Dr LE2 180 F6
Mercury Cl 8 LE2 155 B5
Mere Cl Leicester LE5 155 C6
Mountsorrel LE12 101 E8
Meredith Rd LE3 154 B1
Mere La
Leicester, Oadby LE2 181 D2
Queniborough LE7 103 F5
Wolvey LE10 231 C3
Mereoak La DE11,DE73 45 E7
Mere Rd
Great Stretton LE2 182 C6
Illston on t H LE7 184 C3
Leicester LE5 155 C5
Shangton LE8 206 F4
Upper Bruntingthorpe LE17 236 C5
Waltham on t W LE14 40 A7
Wigston LE18 180 E3
Mere The LE8 205 A8
Merevale Ave LE10 215 C7
Merevale Cl LE10 215 C7
Merevale La CV9 170 B1
Merevale Rd CV9 170 C1
Mereworth Cl LE5 155 D8
Merganser Way LE67 97 A8
Meridian E LE19 178 D7
Meridian N LE19 178 D7
Meridian S LE19 178 D6
Meridian W LE19 178 D7
Meridian Way LE3 153 D1
Meriton Rd LE17 244 B5
Merlin Cl
Broughton Astley LE9 218 E7
Leicester Forest East LE3 153 A2
Mountsorrel LE7 76 F1
Merlin Way DE11 44 F3
Merrick Ct LE10 215 F5
Merrifield Gdns LE10 215 E5
Merrin Ct LE11 52 B4
Merrydale Inf Sch LE5 155 E8
Merrydale Jun Sch LE5 155 E8
Merry Hurst Pl LE10 214 E7
Merry Lees Ind Est LE9 150 F8
Merrylees Rd
Desford LE9 125 A2
Newbold Verdon LE9 150 D8
Mersey Gn NN17 230 C1
Merthull Rd LE5 156 C6
Merton Ave
Leicester LE3 154 C5
Syston LE7 103 B3
Merton Cl LE9 218 D7
Merton Prim Sch The LE7 103 B2
Merton Way LE8 205 F1
Mervyn Rd LE5 155 D4
Messenger Cl LE11 51 E7
Metcalf Cl LE9 199 D2
Metcalfe St LE9 198 E7
Methuen Ave LE4 129 E8
Mews Cotts
Arnesby LE8 221 F5
Great Oxendon LE16 250 E3
Mews The
Great Bowden LE16 240 E7
Melbourne DE73 26 B7
4 Rugby CV21 257 A1
Meynell Cl
Leicester, Oadby LE2 181 C4
Melton Mowbray LE13 82 C8
Meynell Rd
Leicester LE5 155 D7
Long Eaton NG10 10 D5
Quorn LE12 76 A7
Meynell St DE11 44 A1
Michael Cl LE7 103 E6
Michael Lewis Ho LE3 154 B6
Michael Ramsey Ct LE2 179 C3
Mickleborough Cl LE16 227 B3
Mickleden Gn LE67 72 A2
Mickledon Cl NG10 10 B8
Mickleton Cl DE11 44 B1
Mickleton Dr LE5 156 B3
Middelburg Cl CV11 214 A1
Middle Ave LE11 51 F6
Middle Cl DE11 44 B4
Middledale Rd LE16 241 A3
Middlefield Cl LE10 197 D2
Middlefield Ct LE10 197 D2
Middlefield La LE10 197 D3
Middlefield Pl LE10 197 D3
Middlefield Rd LE7 102 D7
Middle La LE14 36 D8
Middle Orch LE12 77 C1
Middle Rd LE67 48 A1
Middlesex Rd LE2 179 D7
Middle St
Barkestone-le-V NG13 6 C2
Croxton Kerrial NG32 24 B7
Foxton LE16 224 E1
Hose LE14 20 F7
Owston LE15 135 B4
Skillington NG33 43 B8
Stainby NG33 43 D2
Wing LE15 165 A3
Middleton Cl
Stoney Stanton LE9 199 E2
Wigston LE18 180 F3
Middleton Pl LE11 52 B2
Middleton Rd
Ashley LE16 228 B3
Bringhurst LE16 229 C4
Middletons Cl LE8 222 F8
Middleton St LE2 179 C6
Midhurst Ave LE3 178 F8
Midland Cotts LE18 180 B2
Midland Ct LE17 244 D8
Midland Rd
Ellistown LE67 96 D4
Swadlincote DE11 44 B5
Midland Rd Ind Est DE11 44 B5
Midland St
Leicester LE1 259 C4
Long Eaton NG10 10 E8
Midway La LE17 236 B3
Midway Rd
Leicester LE5 155 D2
Swadlincote DE11 44 C5
Mikado Rd NG10 10 C5
Milby Dr CV11 214 A7
Mildenhall Rd LE11 51 C4
Mildmay Cl LE13 59 C6
Milestone Cl LE8 224 C8
Milfoil Cl LE10 214 F7
Milford Cl LE19 201 A8
Milford Rd LE2 180 B8
Millais Rd LE10 197 A3
Mill Bank LE65 69 B6
Millbrook Cl LE4 128 F3
Millbrook Dr LE9 218 F5
Millbrook Wlk 1 LE4 128 F3
Mill Cl Birstall LE4 129 B6
Sapcote LE9 217 E8
Shepshed LE12 50 C5
Smeeton Westerby LE8 223 F6
Swadlincote DE11 44 C5
Wigston LE18 202 F8
Wing LE15 165 B2
Milldale Rd NG10 10 B6
Mill Dam LE67 96 D6
Mill Dr LE6 152 D7
Millenium Ave DE12 67 E5
Millennium Cl LE17 246 F4
Miller Cl LE4 129 E5
Millers Cl Glenfield LE3 153 B8
Syston LE7 103 A2
Millersdale Ave LE5 156 D5
Millers Gdns LE16 240 B2
Millers Gn LE10 215 F6
Millers Grange LE9 218 F5
Millers Wlk LE67 95 E7
Miller's Yd LE16 240 E3
Millfield DE72 9 B2
Millfield Ave LE16 229 D1
Millfield Cl Anstey LE7 127 D5
Ashby-De-La-Z LE65 69 A8
Millfield Com Sch LE3 178 E7
Millfield Cres LE3 178 F6
Millfield Croft DE11 44 B7
Millfield St DE11 45 A2
Millgate Sch LE2 180 A8
Mill Gn DE72 9 A1
Mill Gr
Lutterworth LE17 244 D5
Whissendine LE15 84 E1
Mill Hill Enderby LE19 178 A4
Laughton LE17 238 C4
Leicester LE4 129 A2
Lubenham LE16 239 E3
Stathern LE14 13 B2
Mill Hill Cl LE8 202 A7
Mill Hill La
Leicester LE2 155 B4
Markfield LE67 98 D1
Mill Hill Rd
Arnesby LE8 221 F5
Hinckley LE10 197 C1
Market Harborough LE16 240 F3
Millhouse Ct DE72 9 B7
Millhouse Est LE67 71 C8
Milligan Rd LE2 179 E7
Mill La Asfordby LE14 57 F2
13 Ashby-De-La-Z LE65 69 B6
Atherstone CV9 194 A6
Barrowden LE15 192 A5
Barrow-u-S LE12 76 D6
Belton LE12 49 B7
Bilstone CV13 147 C7
Blaby LE8 202 E8
Caldecott LE16 230 B8
Cottesmore LE15 112 C8
Croxton Kerrial NG32 24 B7
Earl Shilton LE9 199 C8
East Leake LE12 31 F8
Empingham LE15 141 B6
Enderby LE19 178 B2
Frisby on t W LE14 80 D8
Gilmorton LE17 235 D5
Heather LE67 95 C2
Hickling LE14 19 B7
Kegworth DE74 18 D2
Ketton PE9 168 A5
Leicester LE2 259 A2
Long Clawson LE14 20 D3
Long Whatton LE12 29 D4
Loughborough LE11 52 C5
Melton Mowbray LE13 59 D2
Newbold Verdon LE9 150 B4
Orston NG13 2 A8
Peggs Green LE67 71 A7
Sharnford LE10 217 C5
Shearsby LE17 222 A2
Sheepy Magna CV9 171 B7
Shenton CV13 173 B3
Smeeton Westerby LE8 223 F7
Somerby LE14 108 B2
South Witham NG33 64 E2
Thornton LE67 124 E4
Thurmaston LE4 129 D8
Tinwell PE9 142 F1
Waltham on t W LE14 40 A6
Willoughby-on-t-W LE12 34 D8
Witherley CV9 194 A8
Wolvey LE10 231 A5
Mill Lane Ind Est LE3 127 A1
Mill La The LE3 153 A8
Mill Pond LE67 96 D6
Millpool Cl DE11 45 A7
Mill Race View CV9 170 D2
Mill Rd
Cottingham LE16 229 C2
Gretton LE15, NN17 212 F2
Rearsby LE7 78 F1
Thurcaston LE7 101 B3
Ullesthorpe LE17 233 B4

282 Mil – Nor

Mill Rd continued
Woodhouse Eaves LE12 74 F1
Mills Cl DE72 9 A7
Mill St Barwell LE9 198 A5
Duddington PE9 193 B6
Leicester LE2 259 B2
Melton Mowbray LE13 59 C2
Oakham LE15 138 A6
Packington LE65 69 B2
Ryhall PE9 116 F3
Mills The LE12 76 A5
Millstone La
Leicester LE1 259 B3
Syston LE7 103 C4
Mills Yd LE11 52 B3
Mill View Hinckley LE10 197 E1
Huncote LE9 200 D7
Millwood Cl LE4 128 E5
Milner Ave DE72 9 A7
Milner Cl LE12 77 C2
Milner Rd NG10 10 D8
Milners Row 16 PE9 143 E3
Milnroy Rd LE5 156 E7
Milton Ave DE11 44 C6
Milton Cl Hinckley LE10 197 C1
Measham DE12 93 C3
Melton Mowbray LE13 59 B5
Wigston LE18 180 E2
Milton Cres LE4 128 A2
Milton Ct LE11 51 D5
Milton Gdns LE2 181 A5
Milton St
Long Eaton NG10 10 D7
Loughborough LE11 51 E5
Narborough LE19 178 A1
Milton Terr NG10 10 D7
Milverton Ave LE4 128 D1
Milverton Cl LE18 180 C4
Milverton Dr LE18 180 C4
Mimosa Cl LE11 75 A6
Minehead St LE3 154 B5
Minster Cres LE4 128 D1
Minster Ct LE2 259 B2
Minstrel's Wlk LE7 103 D7
Mint Gr NG10 10 A7
Minton Rd DE74 16 F4
Mint Rd LE2 154 D4
Mira Dr CV10 195 D3
Misterton Way LE17 244 D5
Mistral Cl LE10 215 F8
Mitchell Dr LE11 51 B6
Mitchell Rd LE19 178 A3
Mitchell St NG10 10 E7
Moat Cl LE9 176 F3
Moat Com Coll LE2 155 B5
Moat Ct LE5 156 C8
Moat Gdns LE9 217 D7
Moat Rd Leicester LE5 155 D5
Loughborough LE11 74 E8
Moat St
Swadlincote DE11 44 B1
Wigston LE18 180 D2
Moat The DE74 17 B4
Moat Way LE9 197 F6
Modbury Ave LE4 128 E4
Model Farm Cl LE11 51 E1
Moira Dale DE74 17 C3
Moira Funace Mus★
DE12 67 E3
Moira Inf Sch DE12 68 B6
Moira Rd
Donisthorpe DE12 68 A1
Overseal DE12 67 C3
Shellbrook LE65 68 E6
Woodville DE11 44 E2
Moira St Leicester LE4 129 B1
Loughborough LE11 52 B3
Melbourne DE73 26 A7
Moir Cl LE12 77 C3
Moles La LE15 190 C1
Molesworth Bglws
PE9 168 A6
Molyneux Dr LE12 77 D1
Monal Cl LE8 201 F4
Monarch Cl LE4 129 C8
Monarch Way LE11 52 A6
Monar Cl LE4 129 D4
Mona St LE9 198 E7
Monckton Cl LE1 259 C5
Moneyhill LE65 69 B8
Monica Rd LE3 178 F7
Monks Cres LE4 128 C8
Monks Kirby La CV23 231 F1
Monmouth Dr LE2 179 D2
Monroe Cl LE16 240 D5
Monsaldale Cl NG10 10 B6
Monsarrat Way LE11 51 D6
Monsell Dr LE2 179 C5
Montague Ave LE7 103 B2
Montague Cl LE9 150 B5
Montague Dr LE11 74 C8
Montague Rd
Broughton Astley LE9 218 F7
Leicester LE2 155 B2
Monteith Pl DE74 17 B4
Montford Mews DE74 17 B4
Montgomery Cl LE17 244 A5
Montgomery Rd LE9 199 A8
Montilo La CV23 242 E1
Montreal Rd LE1 155 A7
Montrose Cl
Market Harborough
LE16 240 D1
Stamford PE9 143 A4
Montrose Ct LE5 156 A8
Montrose Rd LE2 179 C6
Montrose Rd S LE2 179 D5
Montrose Sch LE2 179 D6
Montsoreau Way
LE12 101 D8
Montvale Gdns LE3 154 D8
Moon Cl LE2 155 B5
Moorbarns La LE17 244 B4
Moorcroft Cl CV11 214 B1
Moore Ave DE74 18 D3
Moore Cl DE12 119 F8
Moore Rd Barwell LE9 198 C7
Ellistown LE67 96 E4
Moores Cl LE18 179 E2
Moores La LE19 178 B4
Moores Rd LE4 129 B2
Moorfield Pl LE12 50 B4
Moorfields LE5 156 D8
Moorgate Ave LE4 128 F8
Moorgate St LE4 155 A8
Moorhen Way LE11 51 F3
Moor Hill LE7 186 C2
Moorings The LE12 76 E6
Moor La
Aston-on-T DE72 16 B8
Breedon on the Hill DE73,
DE74 27 B4
Coleorton LE67 70 F6
East Norton LE7 186 C4
East Norton LE7 186 D5
Long Bennington NG23 1 E6
Loughborough LE11 52 E3
Normanton on S LE12 30 C4
North Luffenham LE15 166 D2
South Witham NG33 64 D4
Stathern LE14 13 A4
Moorland Cl CV13 148 F3
Moorland Rd LE7 102 E3
Moorlands The LE67 70 E4
Moors La CV23 257 C1
Moor The LE67 70 E6
Moray Cl Hinckley LE10 215 A8
Stamford PE9 142 F4
Morban Rd LE2 179 B6
Morcote Rd LE3 153 E3
Morcott Rd
Barrowden LE15 191 D5
Glaston LE15 190 D5
Wing LE15 165 A2
Moreton Ct LE67 96 D7
Moreton Dale LE12 77 D4
Morgans Orch LE12 76 D8
Moriston Cl NN17 230 C1
Morkery La NG33 66 C3
Morkery Wood Nature
Trail★ LE15 66 A3
Morland Ave LE2 180 E8
Morland Dr LE10 197 B3
Morledge St LE1 259 C4
Morley Arc LE1 259 B4
Morley Cl LE13 59 A4
Morley La LE12 50 B1
Morley Rd
Leicester LE5 155 C6
Sapcote LE9 217 E7
Morley St
Loughborough LE11 52 C5
Market Harborough
LE16 240 D3
Mornington St LE5 155 D7
Morpeth Ave LE4 128 D5
Morpeth Dr LE2 181 D4
Morris Cam Wlk LE14 57 E3
Morris Cl
Braunstone LE3 153 D2
Loughborough LE11 52 C4
Morris Ct LE17 236 C8
Morrison Ct LE8 224 A8
Morris Rd LE2 155 A1
Mortiboys Way LE9 199 D2
Mortimer Pl LE3 154 B1
Mortimer Rd
Melton Mowbray LE13 59 C4
Narborough LE19 201 A7
Mortimer Way
Leicester LE3 154 B1
Loughborough LE11 51 B6
Mortoft Rd LE4 129 B3
Morton Wlk
Ashby-De-La-Z LE65 68 F5
Leicester LE5 155 E8
Morwoods The LE2 181 B5
Moscow La
Great Dalby LE14 107 D8
Shepshed LE12 50 A1
Mossdale LE67 71 E6
Mossdale Rd LE3 178 E8
Mosse Way LE2 181 C6
Mossgate LE3 154 A7
Mosswithy LE8 222 F6
Mostyn Ave LE7 103 C4
Mostyn St LE3 154 B5
Mottisford Rd LE4 128 F4
Mottisford Wlk LE4 128 F4
Moulds La LE16 229 D7
Mountain Rd LE4 130 A4
Mount Ave Barwell LE9 198 C7
Leicester LE5 155 D6
Mountbatten Ave PE9 143 C4
Mountbatten Rd LE15 137 E6
Mountbatten Way
LE17 244 B5
Mountcastle Rd LE3 154 C2
Mountfield Rd LE9 198 E8
Mountfields Dr LE11 51 E2
Mountfields Lodge Sch
LE11 51 F2
Mount Grace High Sch
LE10 197 E1
Mount Grace Rd LE11 51 B5
Mount Pleasant
Castle Donington DE74 17 B3
Kegworth DE74 18 C2
Leicester, Oadby LE2 181 E3
Morcott LE15 191 A6
Uppingham LE15 189 B4
Mount Pleasant La
DE12 92 A8
Mount Pleasant Rd
Morcott LE15 191 A6
Swadlincote DE11 44 A1
Mount Rd Cosby LE9 201 D3
Hartshorne DE11 45 A4
Hinckley LE10 215 D8
Leicester LE5 155 C6
Leicester, Oadby LE2 181 B5
Mount Sch The LE13 59 B2
Mountsorrel Cotts
LE9 199 D2
Mountsorrel La
Rothley LE7 101 E7
Sileby LE12 77 A3
Mount St DE72 9 F7
Mount St Bernard Abbey
(Monastery)★ LE67 72 D5
Mount The
Dunton Bassett LE17 219 D2
Scraptoft LE7 156 F8
Mount View LE8 182 B1
Mowbray Ct LE13 59 B3
Mowbray Dr LE7 103 C4
Mowmacre Hill LE4 128 E5
Mowmacre Hill Prim Sch
LE4 128 D5
Mowsley Ct LE17 247 E6
Mowsley End LE18 180 D2
Mowsley La LE17 236 D4
Mowsley Rd
Husbands Bosworth
LE17 247 E6
Saddington LE8 223 B2
Theddingworth LE17 238 B2
Mowsley St Nicholas CE
Prim Sch LE17 237 F7
Muckle Gate La LE12 54 F1
Muirfield Cl LE3 153 C6
Mulberry Ave LE3 153 C6
Mulberry Cl LE17 244 B7
Mulberry Way DE72 16 A6
Mull Way LE8 202 F3
Muncaster Cl LE9 219 A4
Mundella St LE2 155 C3
Mundy Cl LE12 53 F7
Munnings Cl LE4 155 B8
Munnings Dr LE10 197 A3
Muntjack Rd LE8 201 F5
Murby Way LE3 153 C1
Murdoch Rise LE11 51 D6
Muriel Rd LE3 154 C5
Murray Cl LE9 218 F4
Murrayfield Rd LE3 153 C5
Murray St LE2 155 B6
Muscovey Rd LE67 97 A8
Museum Sq LE1 259 C2
Musgrove Cl 3 LE3 154 D5
Mushill La LE12 33 D5
Mushroom La DE11 67 D8
Musk Cl LE16 229 D7
Musson Dr LE65 69 A5
Musson Rd LE3 153 E7
Muston La NG13 3 D1
Myrtle Ave Birstall LE4 102 B1
Long Eaton NG10 10 C6
Myrtle Cl LE9 198 A7
Myrtle Rd LE2 155 C4
Mythe La CV9 194 A8
Mythe View CV9 170 E1

N

Nagle Gr LE4 129 D5
Nailstone Rd
Barton in t B CV13 122 E1
Carlton CV13 148 E8
Nairn Rd PE9 143 A3
Namur Rd LE18 179 E3
Nanhill Dr LE12 100 A8
Nanpantan Rd LE11 74 B7
Nansen Rd LE5 155 E4
Narborough Rd
Cosby LE9,LE19 201 D4
Huncote LE9 200 D7
Leicester LE3 154 C3
Narborough Rd N LE3 154 D5
Narborough Rd S
LE19 178 E4
Narborough Sta LE19 201 C7
Narrow Boat Cl LE18 203 A8
Narrow La
Donisthorpe DE12 92 E8
Hathern LE12 30 A1
Leicester LE2 179 C6
Stathern LE14 13 A3
Wymeswold LE12 34 B2
Narrows The LE10 215 E8
Naseby Cl
Market Harborough
LE16 240 E2
Wigston LE18 180 E2
Naseby Dr
Ashby-De-La-Z LE65 69 D7
Long Eaton NG10 10 E4
Loughborough LE11 51 A2
Naseby Rd
Leicester LE4 129 E2
Sibbertoft LE16 248 F6
Welford NN6 256 F6
Naseby Sq LE16 240 E2
Naseby Way LE8 205 B8
Nathaniel Rd NG10 10 F7
National Forest Visitors
Ctr★ DE12 67 E4
National Space Ctr★
LE4 128 F2
Navigation St
Leicester LE1 154 F7
Measham DE12 93 C5
Navigation Way LE11 52 A5
Navins The LE12 76 E2
Naylor Ave LE11 52 D2
Naylor Rd LE7 103 C5
Neal Ave LE3 153 E2
Neale St NG10 10 E7
Near Mdw NG10 10 E5
Necton St LE7 103 A3
Nedham St LE2 155 B6
Needham Ave LE2 179 A3
Needham Cl
Leicester, Oadby LE2 181 E4
Melton Mowbray LE13 59 C4
Needlegate LE1 259 A5
Needwood Way LE19 177 F2
Nelot Way LE5 156 B5
Nelson Cl LE12 50 D4
Nelson Dr LE10 197 D4
Nelson Fields LE67 72 A2
Nelson Pl LE65 45 F3
Nelson St
Leicester LE1 259 C2
Long Eaton NG10 10 D6
Market Harborough
LE16 240 D3
Swadlincote DE11 44 B5
Syston LE7 103 B3
Nene Cl LE13 59 B1
Nene Cres Corby NN17 230 C1
Oakham LE15 137 F5
Nene Ct
Leicester, Oadby LE2 181 C5
3 Stamford PE9 143 C3
Nene Dr LE2 181 C5
Nene Way LE67 97 A7
Neptune Cl LE2 155 C5
Neston Gdns LE2 179 F6
Neston Rd LE2 179 F6
Nether Cl LE15 112 D8
Nethercote LE67 121 D7
Nethercroft Dr LE65 69 C2
Nether End
Gaddesby LE7 105 B6
Great Dalby LE14 82 B2
Nether Farm Cl LE17 235 C4
Netherfield Cl LE9 219 B6
Netherfield La DE72,
DE74 17 F8
Netherfield Rd
Anstey LE7 127 E7
Long Eaton NG10 10 C4
Nether Field Way LE3 153 D1
Netherhall La LE4 129 B6
Netherhall Rd LE5 130 D1
Netherhall Sch LE5 130 D1
Netherley Ct LE10 197 D3
Netherley Rd LE10 197 D3
Netherseal Rd DE12 91 F4
Nether St
Belton-in-R LE15 187 D7
Harby LE14 12 A3
Netherwood Ind Est
CV9 170 F1
Netton Cl LE18 203 C8
Nevanthon Rd LE3 154 B5
Neville Cl LE12 50 B4
Neville Day Cl PE9 168 F5
Neville Dr Coalville LE67 72 A1
Markfield LE67 125 D8
Neville Rd LE3 154 B5
Neville Smith Cl LE9 217 D7
Nevill Holt Rd LE16 228 F6
Nevis Cl NN17 230 C1
Newall Cl LE17 244 C7
Newark Cl LE12 49 F3
Newarke Cl LE2 259 A2
Newarke Houses Mus★
LE1 259 A3
Newarke St LE1 259 B3
Newarke The LE2 259 A3
Newark Rd LE4 129 E7
New Ashby Ct LE11 51 B2
New Ashby Rd LE11 51 B2
New Ave LE7 79 A1
Newbery Ave NG10 10 F6
New Bldgs LE10 197 D1
Newbold CE Prim Sch
LE67 47 E2
Newbold Cl LE12 77 D4
Newbold Dr DE74 17 B5
Newbold La LE65 47 E5
Newbold Rd
Barlestone CV13 149 E7
Desford LE9 151 A4
Kirkby Mallory LE9 175 C7
Owston LE14,LE15 134 F7
Newbold Verdon Prim Sch
LE9 150 A4
Newbon Cl LE11 51 E4
New Bond St LE1 259 B4
Newborough Cl CV9 119 A2
Newboults La PE9 143 C3
New Brickyard La
DE74 18 D1
Newbridge High Sch
LE67 96 D7
New Bridge Rd LE2 179 B2
New Bridge St LE2 154 E3
Newbury Ave LE13 59 A5
Newbury Cl LE18 180 C1
Newby Cl LE8 178 F1
Newby Gdns LE2 181 D4
New Causeway NG13 6 C2
New Cl Leicester LE5 155 D4
Swannington LE67 71 A4
Newcomb Ct 2 PE9 143 D3
Newcombe Rd LE3 154 B2
Newcombe St LE16 240 E2
New Cotts NG32 15 D5
Newcroft Prim Sch
LE12 50 C2
New Cross Rd PE9 143 D4
New Field Rd LE15 113 B3
New Fields Ave LE3 154 A2
New Fields Sq LE3 154 B1
New Forest Cl LE18 203 D8
Newgate End LE18 180 C2
Newgates 2 PE9 143 E3
Newhall Rd DE11 44 B5
Newham Cl LE4 130 A5
Newham Rd PE9 143 C5
Newhaven Rd LE5 156 D3
New Henry St LE3 259 A5
Newington St LE4 129 B2
Newington Wlk LE4 129 B2
New Inn Cl LE9 219 B5
New Inn La LE7 184 B2
New King St LE11 52 C3
New La LE12 54 A4
Newlands Ave LE12 50 C2
Newlands Cl DE11 44 A2
Newlands Rd
Barwell LE9 198 B7
Welford NN6 256 E5
Newland St LE16 251 E5
New Lount (Nature Trail)★
LE67 47 D2
Newlyn Par LE5 130 D1
Newmans Cl LE15 166 D3
Newmarket St LE2 180 B8
New Park Rd LE2 179 E8
New Parks Bvd LE3 153 E7
New Parks Cres LE3 154 A8
New Park St LE3 154 D5
New Parks Way LE3 153 E7
New Pingle St LE3 259 A5
Newpool Bank LE2 181 E4
Newport Ave LE13 59 C4
Newport Lo LE13 59 C4
Newport Pl LE1 259 C3
Newport St LE3 154 C7
Newquay Cl LE10 197 E4
Newquay Dr LE3 127 C1
New Rd
Appleby Magna DE12 119 E7
Belton-in-R LE15 187 C6
Burbage LE10 216 A6
Burton Lazars LE14 82 F6
Clipsham LE15 89 D5
Collyweston PE9 168 C2
Easton on t H PE9 169 A5
Illston on t H LE7 183 E4
Kibworth Beauchamp
LE8 224 B8
Leicester LE1 259 B4
Peggs Green LE67 71 A8
Ryhall PE9 116 E2
Staunton in t V NG13 1 D3
Stoney Stanton LE9 199 D2
Stretton LE15 88 B7
Woodville DE11 44 E2
New Romney Cl LE5 156 E8
New Romney Cres
LE5 156 E8
New Row Ibstock LE67 122 F8
Moira DE12 68 A4
Willoughby-on-t-W LE12 34 E7
Woolsthorpe by B NG32 8 B1
Newry Jun Sch LE2 179 F5
Newry The LE2 179 F5
New St Asfordby LE14 57 F3
Barlestone CV13 149 D8
Barrow-u-S LE12 76 D7
Blaby LE8 202 B8
Countesthorpe LE8 202 F4
Donisthorpe DE12 67 E1
Draycott DE72 9 A7
Earl Shilton LE9 198 E7
Hinckley LE10 197 D1
Kegworth DE74 18 E3
Leicester LE1 259 B3
Leicester, Oadby LE2 181 B6
Long Eaton NG10 10 E8
Loughborough LE11 52 B3
Lutterworth LE17 244 C6
Measham DE12 93 C6
Melton Mowbray LE13 59 C3
Oakham LE15 137 F6
Oakthorpe DE12 93 A7
Queniborough LE7 103 E5
Scalford LE14 38 E5
Stamford PE9 143 E4
Swadlincote DE11 44 B2
New Star Rd LE4 130 A4
Newstead Ave
Bushby LE7 157 A4
Hinckley LE10 215 D4
Leicester LE3 128 C1
Wigston LE18 180 C4
Newstead Mill PE9 144 B4
Newstead Rd
Belmesthorpe PE9 144 A8
Newstead Rd continued
Leicester LE2 180 C8
New Swannington Prim Sch
LE67 71 C5
Newton Burgoland Prim
Sch LE67 121 E6
Newton Cl
Barrow-u-S LE12 76 E8
Hartshill Green CV10 194 B2
Loughborough LE11 51 D6
Newton Dr LE4 129 B8
Newton La
Austrey B79, CV9 118 F2
Great Glen LE8 205 A7
Newton CV23 253 A3
Newton Regis B79 118 B3
Odstone CV13 122 B5
Wigston LE18 180 E1
Newton Manor La
CV23 257 A8
Newton Park Cl DE11 44 A7
Newton Rd
Clifton u D CV23 257 A7
Heather LE67 95 B1
Hinckley LE10 214 E7
Odstone CV13 122 C4
Swepstone LE67 121 D8
Newton Regis CE Prim Sch
B79 118 D3
Newton Way
Braybrooke LE16 251 F6
Broughton Astley LE9 219 A4
New Town PE9 169 A5
Newtown Cres LE15 189 A3
Newtown Linford La
LE6 126 E5
Newtown Linford Prim Sch
LE6 126 D8
Newtown Rd LE15 188 F3
Newtown St LE1 259 B2
New Tythe St NG10 10 F7
New Walk Mus & Art Gall★
LE1 259 C2
New Way Rd LE5 155 D2
New Wharf LE2 259 A3
New Wlk Leicester LE1 259 C2
Sapcote LE9 217 D7
Shepshed LE12 50 B4
New Zealand La LE7 103 C6
Nicholas Dr LE6 152 D8
Nichols St LE1 259 C4
Nicklaus Rd LE4 129 E5
Nicolson Rd LE11 74 C8
Nidderdale Rd LE18 180 F2
Nightingale Ave LE12 30 B1
Nightingale Cl CV9 170 E1
Nightingale Dr DE11 44 F3
Nightingale Gdns
CV23 252 C1
Nightingale Way LE15 138 B7
Nine Acres DE74 18 C2
Nithsdale Ave LE16 240 F2
Nithsdale Cres LE16 240 F2
Nob Hill CV9 120 A2
Noble Cl LE17 244 C8
Noble St LE3 154 D6
Nock Verges
Earl Shilton LE9 176 A1
Stoney Stanton LE9 199 D2
Noel Ave LE15 137 E5
Noel St LE3 154 D3
No Man's Heath La
CV9 119 A3
No Man's Heath Rd
DE12 91 F3
Nook Cl Ratby LE6 126 C1
Shepshed LE12 50 C2
Nook La LE15 140 F5
Nooks Country Park The★
LE8 204 D6
Nook St LE3 154 B7
Nook The Anstey LE7 127 E6
Bitteswell LE17 244 B8
Cosby LE9 201 D2
Cottingham LE16 229 D1
Croxton Kerrial NG32 24 A7
Easton on t H PE9 169 A5
Enderby LE19 178 A3
Great Glen LE8 205 A8
Markfield LE67 98 D1
Sproxton LE14 41 F5
Walcote LE17 245 B4
Whetstone LE8 201 F7
Whissendine LE15 84 F1
Wymeswold LE12 33 C3
Norbury Ave LE4 129 C1
Norbury Cl LE16 240 D3
Norfolk Cl LE10 215 D4
Norfolk Dr LE13 82 D8
Norfolk Rd
Desford LE9 151 B2
1 Long Eaton NG10 10 F8
Wigston LE18 179 F3
Norfolk Sq PE9 143 D4
Norfolk St LE3 154 D5
Norfolk Wlk LE3 154 D5
Norman Ct
Kegworth DE74 18 D1
Leicester, Oadby LE2 181 D4
Norman Dagley Cl
LE9 198 E7
Normandy Cl LE3 153 C7
Normandy Way LE10 197 A3
Norman Rd LE4 129 E8
Norman St LE3 154 D4
Normanton Church Mus★
LE15 140 C1

Normanton Dr
Loughborough LE11 52 B6
Oakham LE15 138 B7
Normanton Gdns★
LE15 140 D2
Normanton Gr LE9 177 A3
Normanton La
Bottesford NG13 3 B4
Heather LE67 95 B3
Normanton Le H LE67 94 E6
Stanford on S LE12 31 B1
Normanton on Soar Prim
Sch LE12 30 D3
Normanton Park Rd
Empingham LE15 141 A4
Normanton LE15 140 E2
Normanton Rd
Edith Weston LE15 166 B8
Leicester LE5 155 D4
Packington LE65 69 C1
Norman Way LE13 59 C3
Norris Cl LE4 128 A3
Norris Hill DE12 68 B6
Northage Cl LE12 76 B4
Northampton Rd
Market Harborough
LE16 240 F3
Welford NN6 256 E4
Northampton Sq LE1 259 C3
Northampton St LE1 259 C3
North Ave Coalville LE67 96 D7
Leicester LE2 155 C2
Northbank LE16 240 E3
North Bridge Pl LE3 154 E7
North Brook Cl LE15 88 A1
North Cl
Blackfordby DE11 68 B8
Hinckley LE10 215 E6
Northcote Rd LE2 180 B8
Northcote St NG10 10 E7
Northcote Wlk CV9 170 D2
North Cres NG13 3 A2
Northdene Rd LE2 180 B5
Northdown Dr LE4 129 E6
North Dr LE5 156 A8
North End LE16 209 D6
North End Cl LE2 179 F6
Northern's Cl NG33 65 B8
Northfield LE67 124 A7
Northfield Ave
Birstall LE4 129 B8
Long Eaton NG10 10 B4
Wigston LE18 180 B4
Northfield Cl LE13 59 C4
Northfield Dr LE67 97 B8
Northfield House Prim Sch
LE4 129 E1
Northfield Rd
Blaby LE8 179 B1
Hinckley LE10 215 C7
Leicester LE4 129 E1
Northfields
Ashby-De-La-Z LE65 69 B8
Long Eaton NG10 10 B4
Syston LE7 103 B4
Northfields Ct PE9 143 E4
Northfold Rd LE2 180 C6
Northgate LE15 137 F6
Northgates LE1 259 A4
Northgate St LE3 259 A5
North Hall Dr LE7 105 B7
North Hill Cl LE12 77 E3
North La LE16 224 D1
North Lea LE16 227 B3
Northleigh Gr LE16 240 D4
Northleigh Way LE9 198 F7
North Luffenham Rd
Morcott LE15 191 B8
North Luffenham LE15 166 B2
South Luffenham LE15 166 D1
North Memorial Homes
LE2 181 B6
North Rd
Clifton u D CV23 257 A6
Long Eaton NG10 10 C6
Loughborough LE11 52 B6
South Kilworth LE17 246 D1
North St
Asfordby Valley LE14 58 B3
Ashby-De-La-Z LE65 69 B6
Barrow-u-S LE12 76 D8
Leicester, Oadby LE2 181 A6
Melbourne DE73 26 A7
Melton Mowbray LE13 59 C4
Rothley LE7 101 E6
Stamford PE9 143 D3
Swadlincote DE11 44 B5
Swinford LE17 254 B4
Syston LE7 103 A4
Whitwick LE67 71 E5
Wigston LE18 180 D3
North St E LE15 189 A4
North St W LE15 189 A4
Northumberland Ave
Leicester LE4 129 C2
Market Bosworth CV13 148 E2
Stamford PE9 143 C4
Northumberland Rd
LE18 179 F3
Northumberland St
LE1 259 A5
North View Cl LE14 58 B3
North Warwickshire &
Hinckley Coll LE10 215 F8
North Way LE7 157 F4
Northwick Rd PE9 167 F5
North Witham Rd NG33 65 B4
North Wlk DE12 93 D7
Northwood Dr LE12 50 C6
Norton Hill CV9 119 D1
Norton La Gaulby LE7 183 C6
Orton-on-t-H CV9 145 D6
Norton Rd LE9 198 C8
Norton St Leicester LE1 259 B2
Uppingham LE15 189 B4
Norwich Cl
Nuneaton CV11 214 A8
Shepshed LE12 50 A2
Norwich Rd LE4 128 E3
Norwood Cl LE10 197 E3
Norwood Rd LE5 155 E3
Noseley Rd LE7 184 A3
Notley Ct LE9 198 C8
Notley Manor Dr LE9 198 C8
Nottingham La LE14 35 C5
Nottingham Rd
Ab Kettleby LE14 37 C4
Ashby-De-La-Z LE65 69 D7
Barrow-u-S LE12 53 E3
Bottesford NG13 2 F2
Kegworth DE74 18 D2
Leicester LE5 155 D6
Long Eaton NG10 10 F8
Loughborough LE11,LE12 52 D6
Melton Mowbray LE13 59 B5
Peggs Green LE67 71 A8
Worthington LE65 47 C5
Nottingham St LE13 59 C3
Nowell Cl LE2 179 D1
Nuffield Hospl The
LE5 156 B8
Nuffield Rd LE10 214 E7
Nugent St LE3 154 D6
Nuneaton La CV13 195 F2
Nuneaton Rd
Atherstone CV9, CV10 194 B4
Hartshill Green CV10 194 B2
Nunneley Way LE16 240 F5
Nursery Cl
Empingham LE15 141 A6
Queniborough LE7 103 E5
Shepshed LE12 50 C6
Swadlincote DE11 44 B6
Thurlaston LE9 177 A2
Thurmaston LE4 129 D6
Nursery End
Loughborough LE11 74 D8
Market Harborough
LE16 240 C2
Nursery Gdns LE9 198 D7
Nursery Gr LE12 76 E8
Nursery Hollow LE2 179 A3
Nursery La Holwell LE14 37 D4
Knipton NG32 14 E3
Quorn LE12 76 A6
Nursery Rd LE5 156 D7
Nurses La LE14 62 E2
Nutfield Rd LE3 154 C3
Nuthall Gr LE2 179 B4
Nutkin Cl LE11 51 F2
Nutt's La LE10 215 A7

O

Oadby Ct LE2 180 F6
Oadby Hill Dr LE2 180 F6
Oadby Ind Est LE2 180 F5
Oadby Rd LE18 180 E3
Oak Ave LE17 218 E1
Oakberry Rd LE17 244 D8
Oak Cl Coalville LE67 97 A8
Hinckley LE10 215 E5
Loughborough LE11 75 A6
Market Harborough
LE16 240 F4
Measham DE12 93 C5
Uppingham LE15 189 A5
Oak Cres
Braunstone LE3 153 C2
East Leake LE12 31 D8
Oakcroft Ave LE9 152 E5
Oakdale Cl LE3 153 C6
Oakdale Rd LE9 198 D7
Oakdene Rd LE2 180 A6
Oak Dr Ibstock LE67 95 E1
Syston LE7 103 B2
Oakenshaw Cl LE4 128 E5
Oakfield LE15 138 A8
Oakfield Ave
Birstall LE4 128 F7
Glenfield LE3 127 D2
Lutterworth LE17 244 B6
Markfield LE67 125 D8
Oakfield Cl LE8 182 B1
Oakfield Cres LE8 202 C6
Oakfield Rd LE2 155 C3
Oakfield Way CV9 171 B8
Oak Gn LE67 125 E6
Oakham Castle Hall★
LE15 138 A6
Oakham CE Prim Sch
LE15 138 A7
Oakham Cl LE11 51 E6
Oakham Dr LE67 72 C2
Oakham Gr LE65 69 A7
Oakham Rd
Ashwell LE15 111 B7
Braunston-in-R LE15 137 B3
Exton LE15 113 A2
Greetham LE15 88 A1
Halstead LE7,LE15 161 C8
Knossington LE15 136 A6
Langham LE15 110 D2
Leesthorpe LE14 83 D2
Oakham LE15 138 C8
Oakham Rd *continued*
Preston LE15 164 C3
Somerby LE14 108 D1
Whissendine LE15 84 F1
Oakham Sch (Old Sch)
LE15 138 A6
Oakham Sta LE15 137 F7
Oakhurst Ct LE11 51 C4
Oak La LE8 221 F5
Oakland Ave
Leicester LE4 129 C4
Long Eaton NG10 10 C5
Oakland Rd LE2 155 A1
Oaklands Ave LE11 51 F2
Oaklands Pk LE16 240 F2
Oaklands Sch LE5 156 B4
Oaklands Way DE73 26 B8
Oakland Terr NG10 10 C5
Oakleigh Ave LE2 179 E1
Oakley Ave LE12 50 B5
Oakley Cl LE12 50 B5
Oakley Dr
Long Whatton LE12 29 D2
Loughborough LE11 51 F1
Oakley Mews LE16 240 D3
Oakley Rd
Cottesmore LE15 87 E2
Leicester LE5 155 D7
Shepshed LE12 50 B5
Oakley's Rd NG10 10 E7
Oakley's Rd W NG10 10 D6
Oakmeadow LE3 153 B7
Oakmeadow Way LE6 126 E2
Oakpool Gdns LE2 179 D3
Oak Rd Desford LE9 151 A3
Littlethorpe LE19 201 C6
Melton Mowbray LE13 59 C3
Stamford PE9 142 F4
Oakridge Cl LE5 130 C3
Oaks Ct LE19 201 A8
Oaks Dr Blaby LE8 202 C7
Newbold Verdon LE9 150 C4
Oakside Cl LE5 156 C4
Oakside Cres LE5 156 C5
Oaks Ind Est
Loughborough LE11 52 A6
Lutterworth LE17 244 D7
Ravenstone LE67 71 A1
Oaks Ind Est The
LE19 201 A7
Oak Spinney Pk LE3 153 B4
Oaks Rd Great Glen LE8 205 C8
Whitwick LE67 72 C5
Oak St Leicester LE5 155 C7
Swadlincote DE11 44 A2
Oaks Way
Earl Shilton LE9 198 E8
Leicester, Oadby LE2 180 F8
Oakthorpe Ave LE3 154 B4
Oakthorpe Prim Sch
DE12 93 A7
Oaktree Cl Groby LE6 126 E3
Hamilton LE5 130 C2
Kibworth Beauchamp
LE8 206 B1
Oaktree Rd LE67 96 B7
Oak Way LE14 80 D8
Oakwood Ave LE18 180 D4
Oakwood Cl
Leicester Forest East
LE3 152 F2
Thornton LE67 124 F3
Oakwood Dr LE11 51 B1
Oasis The LE3 153 B8
Oban Cl PE9 143 A4
Oban Rd LE10 215 A7
Oban St LE3 154 C7
Oberon Cl CV11 214 A1
Occupation La
Willoughby-on-t-W LE12 34 E5
Woodville DE11 44 D1
Occupation Rd
Albert Village DE11 44 C1
Middleton LE16 229 B2
Nailstone CV13 123 B3
Ocean Cl LE5 156 C7
Ocean Rd LE5 156 C7
Odam Cl LE3 153 F2
Oddfellows Row DE12 93 C5
Odeon Arc LE1 259 B4
Odstone Dr LE10 214 F8
Odstone La LE67 121 F6
Odstone Rd CV13 122 D2
Offranville Cl LE4 129 F6
Ogwen Cl LE5 156 D6
Okehampton Ave LE5 155 F3
Old Ashby Rd LE11 51 B2
Old Barn Pas 7 PE9 143 D3
Old Barn Wlk LE4 128 C3
Old Bridewell LE13 59 D6
Oldbury Rd CV10 194 A1
Oldbury View CV10 194 B1
Old Chapel Wlk LE17 232 E6
Old Charity Farm LE2 156 E1
Old Church St LE2 179 C7
Old Coach Rd The
LE17 219 D2
Old Dalby CE Prim Sch
LE14 35 E4
Old Dalby La LE14 36 C6
Old Dalby Trad Est
LE14 36 A5
Old End DE12 92 F1
Old Engine Yd The
LE12 32 E5
Oldershaw Ave DE74 18 E2
Oldershaw Rd LE12 31 F8
Old Field Cl LE8 202 C4
Oldfield Dr DE11 44 C5
Oldfield La LE7 101 F8
Old Forge Cl LE12 30 A1
Old Forge La NG13 5 C5
Old Forge Rd
Ashby Magna LE17 220 A2
Fenny Drayton CV13 195 A6
Old Garden Cl LE8 202 A7
Old Gate Rd LE7 78 E7
Old Gn LE16 227 F6
Old Grammar Sch The
LE8 224 A8
Old Granary The LE7 160 A7
Old Great North Rd
Great Casterton PE9 142 E6
Wothorpe PE9 169 F7
Old Hall Cl Groby LE6 126 F3
Thurmaston LE4 129 E8
Old Hall Court B79 118 D3
Old Hall Gdns DE11 44 A2
Old Hall La LE16 239 F3
Old Hill The NG32 14 F3
Old Holly La CV9 170 C3
Old Holt Rd LE16 228 A7
Old La The NG13 6 C2
Old Mill Cl LE9 218 F5
Old Mill La LE1 259 A5
Old Mill Prim Sch LE9 218 F6
Old Mill Rd LE9 218 F5
Old Milton St LE1 259 C4
Old Nurseries The LE67 95 F8
Old Park Cl NG11 18 F6
Old Parsonage La LE12 32 C1
Old Post La NG33 65 B8
Old Rectory Cl
Broughton Astley LE9 218 F6
Churchover CV23 252 C6
Old Rectory Mus★
LE11 52 B4
Old School Cl
Ellistown LE67 96 E2
North Luffenham LE15 166 D3
Walton LE17 236 A2
Old School La LE67 124 B4
Old School Mews
Aston-on-T DE72 16 B8
Market Harborough
LE16 240 E3
Uppingham LE15 189 B3
Old Stableyard The
LE16 225 D6
Old Station Cl
Coalville LE67 71 D1
Shepshed LE12 50 B2
Old Station Dr LE14 61 C3
Old Station Yd NG13 3 C3
Old Vicarage Gdns
LE14 37 D3
Old Water Mill The
LE12 30 B3
Old Way LE12 30 A1
Old Woodyard The
LE12 30 A1
Olive Hos LE8 222 F8
Oliver Ct LE2 155 D2
Oliver Rd Leicester LE4 129 D2
Loughborough LE11 52 B2
Oliver St LE2 179 E8
Olphin St LE4 155 A8
Olympic Cl LE3 153 D8
One Barrow La LE12 72 E7
Onslow St 3 LE2 155 C4
Ontario Cl LE1 259 C5
Orange Hill LE17 244 D5
Orange St
Uppingham LE15 189 B4
Wigston LE18 202 F8
Orchard Ave
Castle Donington DE74 17 A3
Glen Parva LE2 179 B3
Orchard Bank LE17 235 F8
Orchard CE Prim Sch
LE9 218 D7
Orchard Cl
Austrey CV9 119 A2
Barkestone-le-V NG13 6 B2
Barlestone CV13 149 D8
Breaston DE72 9 F8
Burbage LE10 216 A5
Diseworth DE74 28 C5
East Leake LE12 31 D8
Egleton LE15 138 C3
Gilmorton LE17 235 C4
Glaston LE15 190 B5
Leicester, Oadby LE2 181 A4
Melbourne DE73 26 A7
Osgathorpe LE12 48 C4
Ravenstone LE67 70 F2
Shepshed LE12 50 B3
1 Stamford PE9 143 D3
Sutton Bonington LE12 30 C5
Uppingham LE15 189 B5
Witherley CV9 194 B8
Orchard Com Prim Sch
DE74 17 A4
Orchard Est LE12 75 F6
Orchard Gdns LE4 129 F6
Orchard La
Countesthorpe LE8 202 F3
Great Glen LE8 205 B7
Gretton NN17 213 C1
Orchard Rd
Birstall LE4 129 B7
Broughton Astley LE9 218 E7
Langham LE15 110 C3
Lutterworth LE17 244 B5
Stamford PE9 143 D3
Orchard Rd *continued*
Willoughby Waterleys
LE8 220 C5
Orchards Dr LE18 180 B2
Orchardson Ave LE4 155 B8
Orchard St
Fleckney LE8 222 F7
Hinckley LE10 215 E8
Ibstock LE67 95 F1
Leicester LE1 259 B5
Long Eaton NG10 10 E7
2 Loughborough LE11 52 A4
Market Harborough
LE16 240 E4
Orchards The
Leicester LE5 156 E8
Newton CV23 252 F1
Thornton LE67 124 F4
Orchard Terr NN6 256 E6
Orchard The
Groby LE6 126 E3
Lyndon LE15 165 D5
Seagrave LE12 77 F8
Sibbertoft LE16 249 A2
Stoney Stanton LE9 199 E2
Orchard View LE12 101 E8
Orchard Way
Easton on t H PE9 168 F6
Measham DE12 93 C5
Syston LE7 103 C3
Wymeswold LE12 33 D4
Orchard Wlk LE17 233 B4
Orchid Cl Hamilton LE5 130 C2
Melton Mowbray LE13 82 A8
Mountsorrel LE12 76 F2
Narborough LE19 178 A1
Orchid Pl LE9 219 B4
Oriel Dr LE7 103 C3
Orkney Cl LE10 197 C1
Orkney Way LE8 202 F3
Orkney Wlk NN17 230 C1
Orlando Rd LE2 155 B2
Orly Ave DE74 17 A2
Orme Cl LE4 128 A3
Ormen Gn LE3 153 D6
Ormes La CV9 171 B4
Ormond Cl LE9 198 A7
Oronsay Rd LE4 128 B3
Orpine Rd LE5 130 B3
Orsett Cl LE5 156 A8
Orson Dr LE18 180 B3
Orson St LE5 155 D5
Orston La NG13 2 E4
Orston Prim Sch NG13 2 A7
Orton Cl LE7 78 F1
Orton Hill CV9 145 E8
Orton La Austrey CV9 145 B8
Norton-J-T CV9 120 A2
Orton-on-t-H CV9 145 D5
Sheepy Magna CV9 146 A2
Twycross CV9 146 B6
Orton Rd Leicester LE4 128 F3
Warton B79 145 A3
Ortons Ind Est LE67 71 D1
Orwell Cl
Clifton u D CV23 257 A5
Loughborough LE11 51 D6
Orwell Dr LE4 128 A4
Osbaston Cl LE10 197 F3
Osbaston La CV13 149 D5
Osborne Rd
Leicester LE5 155 D5
Loughborough LE11 51 C6
Osbourne Ct LE8 201 F8
Osiers Business Pk The
LE19 178 E6
Osiers The
Braunstone LE3 178 F7
Kegworth DE74 18 E2
Loughborough LE11 75 A7
Mountsorrel LE12 76 C1
Osmaston Cl NG10 9 F5
Osmaston Rd LE5 155 D4
Osprey Cl LE9 218 F7
Osprey Rd LE4 128 A6
Osterley Cl LE11 51 C4
Ostler La LE14 57 D7
Oswin Rd LE3 153 E5
Ottawa Rd LE1 259 C4
Otter La LE12 76 F2
Otter Way LE8 201 F5
Oundle Cl LE65 69 A8
Our Lady's Convent Sch
LE11 52 B2
Outfields Dr LE7 100 F2
Outlands Dr LE10 197 A2
Outram Dr DE11 44 D4
Outwood Cl LE3 153 D5
Outwoods Ave LE11 51 F1
Outwoods Dr LE11 51 F1
Outwoods Edge Prim Sch
LE11 75 A7
Outwoods La LE67 70 E8
Out Woods Nature
Reserve★ LE11 74 C5
Out Woods Nature Trail★
LE11 74 C5
Outwoods Rd LE11 74 F8
Oval Cl LE15 166 D4
Oval The Coalville LE67 97 A7
Leicester LE1 259 C2
Leicester, Oadby LE2 180 F4
Market Harborough
LE16 240 E4
Nailstone CV13 123 B3
Stoney Stanton LE9 199 E2
Overdale Ave LE3 127 B3
Overdale Cl Anstey LE7 127 B2
Overdale Cl *continued*
Long Eaton NG10 10 A6
Market Harborough
LE16 241 A3
Overdale Inf Sch LE2 180 C6
Overdale Jun Sch LE2 180 C7
Overdale Rd
Leicester LE2 180 C7
Thurmaston LE4 129 F6
Overfield Ave LE16 240 F5
Overfield Cl
Narborough LE19 201 A7
Ratby LE6 152 D8
Overfield Wlk LE6 126 D1
Overing Cl LE4 129 A3
Overpark Ave LE3 154 A3
Overseal Prim Sch
DE12 67 B4
Overseal Rd LE3 153 E8
Overton Cl LE67 70 E7
Overton Rd
Ibstock LE67 122 F7
Leicester LE5 155 D7
Owen Ave NG10 10 F5
Owen Cl
Braunstone LE3 153 D1
Leicester LE4 129 E5
Owen Cres LE13 59 D4
Owen Dr LE13 59 D4
Owen St LE67 71 C1
Owston Dr LE18 180 B3
Owston Rd
Knossington LE15 135 F5
Somerby LE14 108 C1
Owston Wood Rd
LE15 135 E3
Oxbow Cl LE13 59 A2
Oxburgh Cl LE11 51 C5
Oxendon Hall LE16 250 E3
Oxendon Rd
Arthingworth LE16 251 A1
Braybrooke LE16 251 D5
Clipston LE16 250 B1
East Farndon LE16 250 B5
Oxendon St LE2 155 B5
Oxendon Wlk 9 LE2 155 B5
Oxen Way LE5 156 A6
Oxey Cross Rds LE7 161 B3
Oxford Ave LE2 155 B3
Oxford Ct Leicester LE1 259 B2
Syston LE7 103 C4
Oxford Dr
Melton Mowbray LE13 82 D8
Wigston LE18 179 F2
Oxford Ho LE16 240 E4
Oxford Rd Desford LE9 151 A3
Leicester LE2 155 B2
Stamford PE9 143 C5
Oxford St Barwell LE9 198 B7
Coalville LE67 71 E1
Earl Shilton LE9 198 F8
Leicester LE1 259 B2
Long Eaton NG10 10 E8
Loughborough LE11 51 F4
Shepshed LE12 50 B2
Swadlincote DE11 44 A1
Syston LE7 103 C3
Oxley Cl LE12 50 A3
Oxley Prim Sch LE12 50 A3
Oxted Rise LE2 181 A3
Ozier Holt NG10 10 C6

P

Packer Ave LE3 153 B4
Packe St LE11 52 A4
Packe Horse LE8 205 B8
Packhorse Dr LE19 178 D2
Packhorse Gn LE2 179 D3
Pack Horse La LE11 52 B3
Packhorse Rd LE2 179 D3
Pack Horse Rd DE73 26 B8
Packington CE Prim Sch
LE65 69 B2
Packington Hill DE74 18 C2
Packington Nook La
LE65 69 A4
Packman Gn LE8 202 F3
Packwood Rd LE4 128 E3
Paddock Cl
Castle Donington DE74 16 F3
Countesthorpe LE8 202 E4
Leicester, Oadby LE2 180 F6
Melton Mowbray LE13 59 D1
Quorn LE12 76 B5
Rothley LE7 101 E5
Whissendine LE15 85 A1
Paddock Ct LE16 240 E3
Paddock La
Hinckley LE10 215 F5
Medbourne LE16 228 D8
Paddock St LE18 180 D2
Paddocks The
Bottesford NG13 3 A2
Carlby PE9 117 C8
Littlethorpe LE19 201 D7
Sedgebrook NG32 8 F8
Sutton Bonington LE12 30 B6
Waltham on t W LE14 40 A7
Willoughby Waterleys
LE8 220 C5
Paddocks View NG10 10 B8
Paddock The
Allington NG32 4 F5

St Peter's Ct
2 Stamford PE9 143 D2
Syston LE7 103 B4
St Peters Dr LE8 201 F8
St Peter's Dr LE67 124 F3
St Peter's Hill 15 PE9 143 D3
St Peters La LE1 259 B4
St Peter's Path LE2 181 A5
St Peters Pl CV13 121 E2
St Peter's RC Prim Sch
Earl Shilton LE9 176 A1
Hinckley LE10 197 E1
St Peters Rd
Atherstone CV9 194 A7
Leicester LE2 155 C4
St Peter's Rd LE8 221 F5
St Peter's St
Stamford PE9 143 D3
Syston LE7 103 A3
St Peters Terr LE7 160 A8
St Peter & St Paul CE Prim Sch LE7 103 B5
St Peter's Vale PE9 143 D2
St Philip's Ct LE5 155 D3
St Philips Rd
Burton o t W LE12 54 A7
Leicester LE5 155 D3
St Saviour's Hill LE5 155 C6
St Saviours Rd
Coalville LE67 96 C8
Leicester LE5 155 C6
St Saviour's Rd LE5 155 E5
St Stephens Ct DE11 44 E3
St Stephens Rd LE2 155 C4
St Swithin's Rd LE5 156 D5
St Thomas More RC Prim Sch LE2 180 C8
St Thomas Rd LE2, LE18 179 E1
St Thomas's Rd LE8 182 C1
St Tibba Way PE9 116 E1
St Vincent Cl NG10 10 E6
St Vincents Cl LE67 96 C7
St Wilfrid's Cl LE8 206 A1
St Winefride Rd LE12 50 B3
St Winefride's RC Prim Sch LE12 50 B4
St Wolstan's Cl LE18 180 E3
Salcombe Cl LE18 180 C1
Salcombe Dr LE3 153 C8
Salem Rd LE10 215 F5
Salford Cl NN6 256 E6
Salisbury Ave
Croft LE9 200 C4
6 Leicester LE2 155 B4
Melton Mowbray LE13 59 D4
Salisbury Cl Blaby LE8 202 B6
Desford LE9 151 A2
Salisbury Dr DE11 44 E5
Salisbury Ho LE10 197 C4
Salisbury La DE73 26 B7
Salisbury Rd
Burbage LE10 216 B7
Leicester LE1 155 B4
Salisbury St
Long Eaton NG10 10 E7
Loughborough LE11 52 C4
Salkeld Rd LE2 179 C2
Salmon Mews LE12 50 B4
Saltash Cl LE18 180 C1
Saltby Rd
Croxton Kerrial NG32 24 B7
Sproxton LE14 41 F6
Saltcoates Ave LE4 129 C4
Salter Cl DE74 16 F4
Saltersford Rd LE5 155 F7
Saltersgate Dr LE4 129 A8
Salter's Hill Dr LE14 106 E4
Salt's Cl LE19 178 B2
Salt St B79,CV9 119 B5
Samphire Cl LE5 130 D2
Samson Rd
Coalville LE67 71 D3
Leicester LE3 154 B7
Samuel St LE1 155 B6
Sanara Cl LE4 129 B3
Sandacre St LE1 259 B4
Sandalwood Rd LE11 51 E1
Sandcliffe Pk DE11 44 D7
Sandcliffe Rd DE11 44 D6
Sandcroft Cl DE11 44 D5
Sanders Cl CV9 170 E1
Sanderson Cl LE8 202 A6
Sanders Rd LE12 75 F5
Sandfield Cl LE4 129 E5
Sandfield Close Prim Sch LE4 129 E5
Sandford Ave NG10 10 E7
Sandford Cl
Hinckley LE10 197 F1
Leicester LE5 156 A6
Sandford Ct LE5 156 A6
Sandford Rd LE7 103 A3
Sand Furrows PE9 167 F5
Sandgate Ave LE4 128 F8
Sandham Bridge Rd LE7 100 F3
Sandhill Dr LE19 178 D1
Sandhills Ave LE5 130 C3
Sandhills Cl Belton LE12 49 B6
Measham DE12 93 C4
Sandhills The LE12 75 E6
Sandhole La LE12 49 D1
Sandhurst Cl LE3 154 B6
Sandhurst Gdns LE3 154 B6
Sandhurst Rd LE3 154 B6
Sandhurst St LE2 181 A6
Sandiacre Dr LE4 129 F8
Sandlands The DE11 44 D6
Sandown Rd
Glenfield LE3 127 C1
Leicester LE5 155 D1
Wigston LE18 180 D4
Sandpiper Cl
Leicester LE5 155 C7
Rugby CV23 252 C1
Sand Pit La LE14 20 C2
Sandringham Ave
Earl Shilton LE9 198 D7
Leicester LE4 129 B3
Sandringham Cl
Oakham LE15 137 E5
Stamford PE9 143 D5
Sandringham Dr LE11 51 D5
Sandringham Rd
Coalville LE67 96 F8
Glen Parva LE2 179 E1
Sandringham Rise LE12 49 F2
Sandringham Way LE16 241 B3
Sands The LE14 20 D3
Sandtop Cl DE11 68 B8
Sandtop La DE11 68 C8
Sandwell Cl NG10 10 A6
Sandy Cres LE10 197 C1
Sandy La
Melton Mowbray LE13, LE14 82 D5
Newton Regis B79 118 D6
Scalford LE14 38 E5
Sandy Rise LE18 180 F4
Sankey Dr DE11 44 C1
Sanvey Cl LE2 179 C6
Sanvey Gate LE1 259 A5
Sanvey La LE2 179 C6
Sapcote Dr LE13 59 E1
Sapcote Rd
Burbage LE10 216 B7
Stoney Stanton LE9 199 E1
Sargent's Ct PE9 143 C4
Sarson Cl LE14 58 A2
Sarson St LE12 75 F6
Saunderson Rd LE4 128 D4
Savernake Rd LE4 128 C1
Saville Cl LE10 197 E2
Saville Dr LE12 77 C2
Saville Rd LE8 202 C6
Saville St LE5 155 E6
Sawbridge Cl LE67 96 E3
Sawbrook LE8 223 A7
Sawday St LE2 154 E3
Sawgate Rd LE14 83 D7
Sawley Jun & Inf Sch NG10 10 A5
Sawley Rd Breaston DE72 9 E6
Draycott DE72 9 B6
Sawley St LE5 155 D3
Sawmand Cl NG10 10 C6
Saxby Rd LE13 59 E3
Saxby St LE2 155 B4
Saxelbye La LE14 57 B8
Saxelby Rd LE14 57 E4
Saxon Cl
Breedon on the Hill DE73 26 F2
Market Harborough LE16 240 F4
Saxon Ct PE9 143 E2
Saxon Dale LE2 179 C2
Saxondale Rd LE18 203 E8
Saxons Lea LE14 108 D3
Saxons Rise LE6 126 C1
Saxon St LE3 154 D4
Saxon Way LE65 69 A7
Scalborough Cl LE8 202 C4
Scalford CE Prim Sch LE14 38 E5
Scalford Rd
Eastwell LE14 22 A5
Melton Mowbray LE13 59 C6
Scalpay Cl LE4 128 B3
Scarborough Rd LE4 129 C2
Schofield Rd
Loughborough LE11 51 C3
Oakham LE15 138 A8
School Cl
Albert Village DE11 44 C1
Burbage LE10 216 A6
Croft LE9 200 C3
School Cotts LE14 108 B2
School Cres LE9 218 F7
School Farm Yd LE16 227 B3
Schoolgate LE2 179 F5
School Gdns CV21 257 A1
School Hill
Sproxton LE14 41 F5
Walton o t W LE12 54 A4
School House Cl LE7 127 D5
School La Barkby LE7 130 D8
Barrowden LE15 191 F5
Belton LE12 49 B6
Birstall LE4 129 A6
Braybrooke LE16 251 F5
Castle Donington DE74 17 A4
Cottingham LE16 229 C1
Cranoe LE16 208 E3
Croxton Kerrial NG32 24 A7
Empingham LE15 141 B6
Gaulby LE7 183 D6
Harby LE14 12 B3
Houghton on t H LE7 157 F3
Huncote LE9 200 D7
Husbands Bosworth LE17 247 E5
Leicester LE5 156 B2
Long Clawson LE14 20 C3
School La *continued*
Lubenham LE16 239 F3
Market Harborough LE16 240 E3
Morcott LE15 191 A6
Narborough LE19 201 B7
Newbold LE67 47 E2
Newton Burgoland LE67 121 E6
Normanton Le H LE67 94 F6
Peatling Magna LE8 221 B6
Peggs Green LE67 48 A1
Queniborough LE7 103 F5
Quorn LE12 76 A6
Rempstone LE12 32 D5
Scalford LE14 38 E5
Sedgebrook NG32 8 F8
Sewstern NG33 42 E1
Sharnford LE10 217 C4
South Croxton LE7 105 B1
Stapleton LE9 174 E2
Stathern LE14 13 A2
Swinford LE17 254 B4
Thistleton LE15 64 E1
Uffington PE9 144 E4
Uppingham LE15 189 B4
Whitwick LE67 71 D6
Woodhouse LE12 75 B3
School Rd
Gretton NN17 213 B1
Kibworth Beauchamp LE8 224 A8
Oakham LE15 138 A7
School St
Churchover CV23 252 C6
Donisthorpe DE12 67 F2
Fleckney LE8 222 F7
Loughborough LE11 52 B4
Oakthorpe DE12 93 A7
Rothley LE7 101 F6
Rugby CV21 257 A1
Swadlincote DE11 44 B2
Syston LE7 103 B4
School View NG13 3 A2
School Wlk LE8 224 A8
Scoborough Rd LE16, LE17 239 A1
Scotgate
Harringworth NN17 213 F7
Stamford PE9 143 D3
Scotland End LE16 240 F1
Scotland La
Burton Overy LE8 182 F1
Houghton on t H LE7 157 F4
Scotland Rd LE16 241 A2
Scotlands Dr LE67 96 D8
Scotlands Ind Est LE67 96 E8
Scotlands Rd LE67 96 D8
Scotland Way LE8 202 F3
Scotswood Cres LE2 179 D3
Scott Cl
Market Harborough LE16 240 E5
Uppingham LE15 189 B4
Scott Ct LE2 180 A8
Scotts Cl LE65 69 B7
Scott St LE2 180 A8
Scraptoft La
Beeby LE7 131 C4
Leicester LE7 156 C7
Scraptoft Mews LE5 156 A7
Scraptoft Rise LE7 156 F8
Scraptoft Valley Prim Sch LE5 156 E8
Scrivener Cl LE7 157 B5
Scudamore Rd LE3 153 C5
Seacole Cl LE3 153 D2
Seaford Rd LE2 179 D5
Seaforth Dr LE10 197 A1
Seagrave Cl LE67 72 D1
Seagrave Dr LE2 180 F6
Seagrave Rd
Sileby LE12 77 D5
Thrussington LE7 78 E5
Seals Cl LE12 54 A7
Seals Rd DE12 67 E1
Seaton Cl LE10 216 B7
Seaton Rd
Barrowden LE15 191 C4
Braunstone LE3 153 C1
Glaston LE15 190 B4
Harringworth NN17 213 E8
Stamford PE9 143 D2
Uppingham LE15 189 E2
Wigston LE18 180 C1
Seaton Rise LE5 130 E1
Seckington La B79 118 C3
Seddons Cl LE4 128 D4
Sedgebrook Cl LE5 156 E4
Sedgebrook Rd
Allington NG32 4 F4
Leicester LE5 156 E4
Woolsthorpe by B NG32 B3
Sedgefield Dr
Leicester LE7 156 F6
Syston LE7 102 E3
Sedgemoor Rd NG10 10 E5
Segrave Rd LE3 154 B2
Seine La LE19 177 F4
Selbourne Ct LE11 52 C4
Selbourne St LE11 52 C4
Selbury Dr LE2 180 F5
Selby Ave LE5 130 D1
Selby Cl LE16 250 E8
Selina Cl DE74 17 A4
Selina St DE73 26 A7
Selkirk Rd LE4 129 D4
Selvester Dr LE12 76 B5
Selwyn Rd PE9 143 C5
Senator Cl LE7 102 F2
Sence Cres LE8 205 A8
Sence Valley Forest Pk* LE67 95 E3
Sennen Cl CV11 214 A5
Seton Cl LE11 51 C7
Severn Ave LE10 215 A8
Severn Cl Cosby LE9 201 D3
Oakham LE15 137 E5
Severn Cres LE15 166 D7
Severn Hill LE13 59 B1
Severn Rd LE2 181 D6
Severn St LE2 155 B4
Severn Wlk NN17 230 C1
Seward St LE11 52 A3
Sewstern La
Allington NG23 4 B8
Muston NG32 8 B8
Sewstern Rd NG33 64 D8
Sextant Rd LE5 156 C7
Seymour Cl LE11 51 B5
Seymour Rd
Burton o t W LE12 53 F7
Leicester LE2 155 B1
Seymour St LE2 155 B4
Seymour Way LE3 152 F3
Shackelton Way LE17 243 D5
Shackerdale Rd LE2, LE18 180 B5
Shackerstone Rd CV13 147 D8
Shackerstone Sta* CV13 121 F2
Shackerstone Wlk CV13 148 C6
Shackland Dr DE12 93 D5
Shackleton Dr LE10 215 E4
Shackleton St 4 LE1 155 A7
Shades Cl LE9 200 C4
Shadows La CV13 147 D7
Shadrack Cl LE9 199 D1
Shady La LE2 156 B1
Shaeffer Ct LE4 128 B2
Shaftesbury Ave
Leicester LE4 129 B2
Long Eaton NG10 10 B4
Shaftesbury Jun Sch LE3 154 D4
Shaftesbury Rd LE3 154 D4
Shakespear Cl DE74 28 C5
Shakespeare Cl
Braunstone LE3 153 E1
Swadlincote DE11 44 C6
Shakespeare Dr
Diseworth DE74 28 C5
Hinckley LE10 197 C1
Leicester LE3 153 F1
Nuneaton CV11 214 A1
Shakespeare St
Leicester LE2 179 F8
Loughborough LE11 52 B4
Shambles Ct LE17 244 D6
Shangton Rd LE8 207 B3
Shanklin Ave LE2 180 D7
Shanklin Dr LE2 180 D7
Shanklin Gdns
Leicester Forest East LE3 153 B3
Leicester LE2 180 D7
Shannon Way LE15 137 E5
Shanti Margh LE4 129 C2
Shardlow Rd
Aston-on-T DE72 16 C7
Wigston LE18 180 C3
Sharmon Cres LE3 153 D6
Sharnbrook Gdns LE10 217 C4
Sharnford Rd
Aston Flamville LE10 216 F6
Sapcote LE9 217 E6
Sharp Cl NG10 10 C6
Sharpe's Plain PE9 167 F5
Sharpe Way LE19 201 B7
Sharpland LE2 179 C5
Sharpless Rd LE10 215 F7
Sharpley Ave LE67 72 A2
Sharpley Dr LE4 128 A6
Sharpley Rd LE11 51 C2
Sharply Hill LE6 99 E3
Sharp's Cl LE67 124 F4
Sharpswood Manor DE11 44 E4
Sharrads Way LE15 110 D3
Shaw Cl LE8 201 F6
Shawell Rd
Cotesbach LE17 244 D1
Swinford LE17 254 A4
Shaw La LE67 97 E4
Shaw Wood Cl LE6 126 E3
Shearer Cl LE4 129 E4
Shearers Ct LE11 52 C5
Shearsby Cl LE18 180 D2
Shearsby Rd LE8 222 E4
Shearwater Dr CV23 252 C1
Sheene Rd LE4 128 A4
Sheepcote LE7 101 E7
Sheepdyke LE15 112 C8
Sheep Market 14 PE9 143 D3
Sheepy Cl LE10 197 F1
Sheepy La CV9 145 E3
Sheepy Magna CE Prim Sch CV9 171 B8
Sheepy Rd
Atherstone CV9 170 D2
Sheepy Magna CV9 170 E6
Sibson CV13 172 A6
Twycross CV9 146 C5
Sheet Hedges Wood Ctry Pk* LE6 126 F6
Sheet Hedges Wood Nature Trail* LE6 126 E6
Sheet Stores Ind Est NG10 10 D5
Sheffield St LE3 154 D3
Shelbourne St LE5 155 C6
Sheldon Cl LE11 51 B6
Sheldon St LE1 155 B6
Shelford La CV9 120 C3
Shelford Wlk 7 LE4 128 E3
Shelland Cl LE16 241 C2
Shellbrook Cl LE65 68 E6
Shellduck Cl LE8 201 F4
Shelley Ave LE13 59 B5
Shelley Cl
Measham DE12 93 C3
Stamford PE9 143 A4
Shelley Dr Corby NN17 230 D1
Lutterworth LE17 244 C7
Shelley Gdns LE10 197 E3
Shelley Rd
Narborough LE19 178 A2
Swadlincote DE11 44 C5
Shelley St
Leicester LE2 180 A8
Loughborough LE11 51 D5
Shelthorpe Ave LE11 52 B1
Shelthorpe Prim Sch Special Unit LE11 52 C1
Shelthorpe Rd LE11 52 B2
Shenley Rd LE18 180 E4
Shenton Cl
Stoke Golding CV13 196 E7
Thurmaston LE4 130 A6
Whetstone LE8 201 F7
Wigston LE18 180 C3
Shenton La
Market Bosworth CV13 148 E2
Shenton CV13 173 C4
Sibson CV13 172 C5
Upton CV13 172 E4
Shenton Prim Sch LE5 155 C7
Shenton Rd LE9 198 B7
Shenton Sta* CV13 173 D5
Shepherd Cl LE3 152 E3
Shepherds Cl
Loughborough LE11 51 D1
Shepshed LE12 50 C5
Shepherd's Cl LE12 30 C5
Shepherds Croft LE13 59 B5
Shepherds La LE15 88 B2
Shepherd's Way LE15 188 F5
Shepherd's Wlk LE7 103 D7
Shepherd Wlk DE74 18 C1
Sheppards Orch LE12 33 C4
Shepshed High Sch LE12 50 C4
Shepshed Rd LE12 50 E8
Sherard Prim Sch LE13 59 E1
Sherborne Ave LE18 203 D8
Sherborne Rd LE10 216 B7
Sherbourne Dr LE65 69 A7
Sherford Cl LE18 180 C2
Sheridan Cl LE19 178 A2
Sheridan St LE2 179 F8
Sheringham Rd LE4 128 D2
Sherloyd Cl LE4 129 F4
Sherrard Cl LE15 84 F2
Sherrard Dr LE12 77 C1
Sherrard Rd
Leicester LE5 155 C6
Market Harborough LE16 240 E5
Sherrard St LE13 59 C3
Sherrard Way LE3 153 D1
Sherrier CE Prim Sch LE17 244 C7
Sherrier Way LE17 244 C8
Sherwood Cl
Ellistown LE67 96 D4
Stamford PE9 143 B3
Sherwood Dr LE13 59 A4
Sherwood Rd CV13 196 E7
Sherwood St LE5 155 E6
Shetland Rd LE4 129 C1
Shetland Way
Corby NN17 230 C1
Countesthorpe LE8 202 F4
Shield Cres LE2 179 C2
Shields Cl LE15 189 A4
Shields Cres DE74 17 A3
Shilling Way NG10 10 A7
Shilton Rd Barwell LE9 198 B6
Kirkby Mallory LE9 175 E4
Shipley Rd LE5 155 D4
Shipston Hill LE2 181 A4
Shipton Cl LE18 180 F2
Shire Cl LE3 153 E5
Shire Rd NN17 230 C1
Shires La LE1 259 A4
Shires Orch NG32 24 B7
Shires The LE1 259 B4
Shirley Ave LE2 180 D8
Shirley Cl DE74 17 A4
Shirley Cres DE72 9 D8
Shirley Dr LE7 103 B5
Shirley Pk DE72 16 B7
Shirley Rd LE2 180 D8
Shirley St
Leicester LE4 129 A2
Long Eaton NG10 10 A4
Shirreffs Cl LE12 76 E8
Shoby La LE14 57 A8
Shoe Makers The LE7 127 D6
Shoesmith Cl LE9 198 A6
Shooting Close La LE12 76 D7
Short Cl LE8 222 F7
Shortheath DE12 67 C2
Shortheath Rd DE12 67 E3
Short Hill DE73 26 F6
Short La DE74 16 F4
Shortridge La LE19 178 B2
Short Row LE8 204 D6
Short St LE1 259 B4
Shottens Cl LE4 128 B2
Shottery Ave LE3 153 F1
Shoulbard LE8 222 E8
Shrewsbury Ave
Leicester LE2 180 A6
Market Harborough LE16 241 B2
Shrewsbury Cl LE9 198 A7
Shrewsbury Wlk LE67 71 D8
Shropshire Cl LE16 240 E4
Shropshire Pl LE16 240 E4
Shropshire Rd LE2 179 D7
Shrubbery The DE11 45 A2
Shuttleworth La LE9 219 D7
Sibbertoft Rd
Clipston LE16 249 E1
Husbands Bosworth LE17 247 F2
Marston Trussell LE16 249 B6
Sibson Dr DE74 18 B2
Sibson La CV13 172 E6
Sibson Rd Birstall LE4 129 A7
Ratcliffe Culey CV9 171 E4
Sheepy Magna CV9 171 D7
Sibton La LE2 181 A4
Sickleholm Dr LE5 155 E2
Side Ley DE74 18 C3
Side St NG32 4 F5
Sidings The
Bottesford NG13 2 F3
Swannington LE67 71 B7
Sidmouth Ave LE5 156 A4
Sidney Ho LE13 59 D3
Sidney Rd LE2 180 D7
Sidney St NG10 10 D6
Sidwell St LE5 155 E5
Signal Rd LE14 36 A5
Silbury Rd LE4 128 C1
Sileby Rd
Barrow-u-S LE12 76 E6
Mountsorrel LE12 76 E3
Sileby Sta LE12 77 C3
Silkstone Cl DE11 44 B1
Silsden Rise LE2 179 D3
Silver Arc LE1 259 B4
Silver Birches LE12 75 F6
Silverbirch Way LE11 75 A6
Silver Birch Way LE7 103 E8
Silverdale Dr LE4 129 F6
Silver La 10 PE9 143 D3
Silver St Leicester LE1 259 B4
Newton CV23 253 A1
Oakthorpe DE12 93 A6
Whitwick LE67 71 F4
Silverstone Dr LE4 129 D5
Silverton Rd
Leicester, Oadby LE2 181 C6
Loughborough LE11 74 F8
Silver Wlk LE1 259 B4
Silverwood Cl LE5 156 C6
Silverwood Rd NG13 3 A2
Simborough Way LE16 241 B3
Simmins Cl LE2 179 D4
Simmins Cres LE2 179 D4
Simmonds Way CV9 170 D2
Simons Cl LE18 203 E8
Simon's Orch LE17 233 F5
Simpson Cl Blaby LE8 202 A6
Syston LE7 102 E2
Sir Henry's La DE73 26 A4
Sir John Moore CE Prim Sch DE12 119 E7
Sir Jonathan North Com Coll LE2 180 A7
Sir Robert Martin Ct LE11 51 D5
Siskin Dr DE12 93 B4
Siskin Hill LE2 181 A4
Sisley Way LE10 197 A3
Sitch Cl LE9 219 A5
Sitwell Wlk LE5 155 F2
Six Acres LE9 218 E6
Six Hills La LE14 56 C8
Six Hills Rd
Ragdale LE14 56 C4
Walton o t W LE12 54 D4
Skampton Gn LE5 156 B5
Skampton Rd LE5 156 B5
Skeffington Glebe Rd LE7 160 A6
Skeffington Rd LE7 184 E6
Skeffington Wood Rd LE7 160 C3
Skeg Hill LE7 133 C2
Skeg Hill Rd LE7 133 B2
Skelton Dr LE2 180 A6
Skelwith Rise CV11 214 A6
Skerry La NG13 4 A2
Sketchley Cl LE5 156 D6
Sketchley Hall Gdns LE10 215 C5
Sketchley Hill Prim Sch LE10 215 E5

Sketchley La
Hinckley LE10 .... 215 C5
Ratcliffe Culey CV9 .... 171 B4
Sketchley Lane Ind Est LE10 .... 215 C5
Sketchley Manor La LE10 .... 215 D5
Sketchley Mdws LE10 215 C5
Sketchley Meadows Bsns Pk LE10 .... 215 C5
Sketchley Old Village LE10 .... 215 C5
Sketchley Rd LE10 .... 215 E5
Skevington Ave LE11 .... 51 E4
Skillington Rd NG33 .... 43 D3
Skinner's La LE67 .... 71 F5
Skinners Way DE11 .... 44 D5
Skippon Cl LE16 .... 240 D2
Skipworth St LE2 .... 155 C4
Skye Rd NN17 .... 230 B1
Skye Way LE8 .... 202 F3
Skylark Ave LE12 .... 76 F1
Skylark Cl DE12 .... 93 B4
Slackey La DE12 .... 67 C4
Slack La DE11 .... 45 B6
Slade Gns The LE2 .... 179 C4
Slade La DE73,DE74 .... 27 A7
Slade Pl LE2 .... 179 C4
Slash La LE12 .... 76 F4
Slate Brook Cl LE6 .... 126 F3
Slate Cl LE3 .... 153 B8
Slate Drift PE9 .... 168 E3
Slater Prim Sch LE3 .... 259 A5
Slater St LE3 .... 154 E7
Slate St LE2 .... 259 C3
Slawston Rd
Medbourne LE16 .... 227 E7
Slawston LE16 .... 209 A2
Welham LE16 .... 226 F6
Slaybarns Way LE67 .... 95 F2
Sloane Cl LE19 .... 178 A3
Sludge Hall Hill LE7 .... 159 C7
Small Thorn Pl DE11 .... 44 F2
Smart Cl LE3 .... 153 D2
Smedley Cl LE65 .... 68 F5
Smedmore Rd LE5 .... 155 D8
Smeeton Rd LE8 .... 224 A7
Smisby Rd LE65 .... 69 B8
Smith Ave LE4 .... 129 F6
Smith Cres LE67 .... 97 C8
Smith Ct LE67 .... 71 D5
Smith Dorrien Rd LE5 155 E7
Smith Way LE19 .... 178 E4
Smithy Cl CV13 .... 149 D8
Smithy Farm Dr LE9 .... 199 D2
Smithy La
Burbage LE9, LE10 .... 198 C1
Long Whatton LE12 .... 29 A2
Odstone CV13 .... 122 C4
Smithy Rd LE65 .... 69 E7
Smithy Way LE12 .... 50 C4
Smockington La LE10 231 B7
Smore Slade Hills LE2 .... 181 E4
Smyth Cl LE16 .... 240 E5
Snarestone CE Prim Sch DE12 .... 120 E7
Snarestone Rd
Appleby Magna DE12 .... 120 B8
Newton Burgoland LE67 121 C7
Snarrow's Rd LE67 .... 48 E2
Snell's Nook La LE11 .... 74 A8
Snelston Cl LE15 .... 138 B7
Snibston Discovery Pk★ LE67 .... 71 B1
Snibston Dr LE67 .... 71 A1
Snipe Cl LE67 .... 96 B7
Snowdens End LE18 .... 180 E1
Snowdon Ave LE15 .... 137 E6
Snowdon Cl LE12 .... 50 C2
Snowdrop Cl LE19 .... 200 F8
Snow Hill Leicester LE4 128 C1
Melton Mowbray LE13 .... 59 D4
Snows La LE7 .... 131 D1
Soarbank Way LE11 .... 51 E7
Soar Cl LE13 .... 59 B1
Soar Gn NN17 .... 230 C1
Soar La Leicester LE3 .... 259 A4
Normanton on S LE12 .... 30 D3
Sutton Bonington LE12, DE74 .... 30 A8
Soar Mill Falconry Ctr★ LE9 .... 218 B8
Soar Rd Quorn LE12 .... 76 B6
Thurmaston LE4 .... 102 E1
Soar Valley Coll LE4 .... 129 D3
Soar Valley Way LE2, LE19 .... 179 A5
Soar Way LE10 .... 215 A8
Soho St LE13 .... 59 C3
Solway Cl LE13 .... 59 B1
Somerby Cl PE9 .... 143 D5
Somerby Dr LE2 .... 181 C5
Somerby Prim Sch LE14 .... 108 B2
Somerby Rd
Burrough on t H LE14 .... 107 E3
Cold Overton LE14,LE16 136 A8
Knossington LE15 .... 135 C6
Leicester LE7 .... 156 F6
Owston LE15 .... 135 F7
Pickwell LE14 .... 108 C2
Somerfield Way LE3 .... 152 F2
Somerfield Wlk LE4 .... 128 B2
Somerscales Wlk LE4 155 B7
Somerset Ave LE4 .... 128 D2
Somerset Cl
Burton o t W LE12 .... 53 F7
Melton Mowbray LE13 .... 82 D8
Somerset Dr LE3 .... 153 C7
Somerset Rd LE15 .... 87 E2
Somers Rd LE5 .... 156 C6
Somerville Rd
Leicester LE3 .... 154 C1
Stamford PE9 .... 143 C4
Somes Cl PE9 .... 144 E4
Sonning Way LE2 .... 179 C2
Sopers Rd LE9 .... 200 C3
Sorrel Cl PE9 .... 142 F4
Sorrel Ct LE12 .... 76 E2
Sorrel Dr DE11 .... 44 E4
Sorrel Rd LE5 .... 130 C2
Sorrel Way LE19 .... 177 F1
South Albion St LE1 .... 259 C3
Southampton St LE1 .... 259 C4
South Ave
Leicester Forest East LE3 .... 153 B3
Ullesthorpe LE17 .... 233 B4
Wigston LE18 .... 180 C2
South Charnwood High Sch LE67 .... 125 A7
South Church Gate LE1 .... 259 A5
South Cl Arnesby LE8 .... 221 F5
Blackfordby DE11 .... 68 B8
Scalford LE13 .... 38 E5
South Cres NG13 .... 3 A2
South Croxton Rd
Queniborough LE7 .... 104 E4
South Croxton LE7 .... 132 F8
Southdown Dr LE4 .... 129 E5
Southdown Rd
Leicester LE5 .... 155 D6
Loughborough LE11 .... 75 A8
Southdown Wlk LE15 .... 87 E2
South Dr Leicester LE5 .... 156 A8
Stoney Stanton LE9 .... 199 E2
Southernhay Ave LE2 .... 155 C1
Southernhay Cl LE2 .... 155 C1
Southernhay Rd LE2 .... 155 C1
Southey Cl
Enderby LE19 .... 178 A2
Leicester LE4 .... 155 B8
Southfield Ave LE7 .... 103 B3
Southfield Cl
Glen Parva LE2 .... 179 A3
Scraptoft LE7 .... 156 F7
Southfield Prim Sch LE15 .... 137 E5
Southfield Rd
Gretton NN17 .... 213 C1
Hinckley LE10 .... 215 E7
Loughborough LE11 .... 52 B3
Southfields 3 NG10 .... 10 E7
Southfields Ave LE2 .... 180 F6
Southfields Dr LE2 .... 179 F5
Southfields Inf Sch LE2 .... 179 F5
Southfield Way CV13 .... 148 E2
Southgates LE1 .... 259 A3
Southgates Underpass LE1 .... 259 A3
South Kilworth CE Prim Sch LE17 .... 255 C8
South Kilworth Rd
North Kilworth LE17 .... 246 E2
Walcote LE17 .... 245 D3
Welford NN6 .... 256 B5
South Kingsmead Rd LE2 .... 180 C6
South Knighton Rd LE2 .... 180 D7
South La LE67 .... 97 D4
Southland Rd LE2 .... 180 D6
Southleigh Gr LE16 .... 240 D4
Southmeade LE2 .... 180 F8
Southmeads Cl LE2 .... 181 A7
Southmeads Rd LE2 .... 181 A7
South Par LE13 .... 59 C3
South Rd
Clifton u D CV23 .... 257 A5
Ibstock LE67 .... 122 F8
South St
Asfordby Hill LE14 .... 58 D3
Ashby-De-La-Z LE65 .... 69 B6
Barrow-u-S LE12 .... 76 D7
Draycott DE72 .... 9 A7
Ellistown LE67 .... 96 D4
Leicester, Oadby LE2 .... 181 A6
Long Eaton NG10 .... 10 E7
Loughborough LE11 .... 52 B3
Melbourne DE73 .... 26 A7
Oakham LE15 .... 137 F6
Oakham LE15 .... 138 A6
Scalford LE14 .... 38 E4
Woodville DE11 .... 44 F1
South View
Asfordby LE14 .... 57 E2
Burrough on t H LE14 .... 107 D2
Preston LE15 .... 164 C1
Uppingham LE15 .... 189 B4
South View Cl LE15 .... 164 E5
Southview Ct LE3 .... 152 F3
Southview Dr LE5 .... 155 F6
Southway LE8 .... 202 B6
South Way LE8 .... 206 B1
South Wigston High Sch LE2,LE18 .... 179 E1
South Wigston Sta LE18 .... 179 F2
South Witham Nature Res★ NG33 .... 65 E3
South Witham Prim Sch NG33 .... 65 A4
South Wlk LE6 .... 126 C1
Southworth Rd DE73 .... 26 E2
Sovereign Ct LE11 .... 52 B3
Sovereign Gr NG10 .... 10 B7
Sovereign Pk LE16 .... 240 F1
Sowters La LE12 .... 54 B6
Spa Cl LE10 .... 197 E1
Spa Dr LE9 .... 217 D8
Spa La Hinckley LE10 .... 197 E1
Orston NG13 .... 2 B7
Wigston LE18 .... 180 D2
Spalding St LE5 .... 155 E6
Sparkenhoe Croft LE9 .... 200 C3
Newbold Verdon LE9 .... 150 C4
Sparkenhoe Com Prim Sch LE2 .... 155 B4
Sparkenhoe Com Prim Sch (Gopsall Annexe) LE2 .... 155 B5
Sparkenhoe Est LE67 .... 95 B2
Sparkenhoe St LE2 .... 155 B5
Sparrow Hill LE11 .... 52 B4
Sparsis Gdns LE19 .... 178 D1
Spear Gate NG10 .... 10 C8
Speeds Pingle LE11 .... 52 A4
Speedwell Cl
Coalville LE67 .... 71 E1
Narborough LE19 .... 177 F1
Woodville DE11 .... 44 F4
Speedwell Dr
Broughton Astley LE9 .... 219 A4
Hamilton LE5 .... 130 B3
Speedwell Rd LE12 .... 76 F2
Speers Rd LE3 .... 153 E8
Spencefield Dr LE5 .... 156 B3
Spencefield La LE5 .... 156 C4
Spencer Ave LE4 .... 129 E7
Spencer Rd LE17 .... 244 C6
Spencers Rd PE9 .... 167 F5
Spencer St
Hinckley LE10 .... 197 D1
Leicester, Oadby LE2 .... 181 A6
Market Harborough LE16 .... 240 D3
Spencer View LE67 .... 96 E3
Spence St LE5 .... 155 D7
Spendlove Dr NN17 .... 213 C1
Spendlow Gdns LE2 .... 179 E4
Spendlow Gn LE2 .... 179 E4
Sperry Ct LE67 .... 95 F1
Spey Dr LE15 .... 137 E4
Spiers Cl LE19 .... 201 B7
Spindle Rd LE11 .... 75 A6
Spindles The LE10 .... 215 F5
Spinney Ave LE8 .... 202 F4
Spinney Cl
Ashby-De-La-Z LE65 .... 69 B5
Gilmorton LE17 .... 235 C4
Glen Parva LE2 .... 179 A3
Groby LE6 .... 126 E2
Market Harborough LE16 .... 240 C3
Melton Mowbray LE13 .... 59 E5
Ryhall PE9 .... 116 E2
Syston LE7 .... 102 E3
Spinney Ct LE9 .... 200 C4
Spinney Dr
Barlestone CV13 .... 149 D7
Botcheston LE9 .... 151 C8
Kibworth Beauchamp LE8 .... 206 A1
Quorn LE12 .... 75 F5
Spinney Farm Cotts LE14 .... 79 F4
Spinney Halt LE8 .... 201 F7
Spinney Hill
Market Bosworth CV13 .... 148 D3
Melbourne DE73 .... 26 A7
Spinney Hill Dr LE11 .... 51 D2
Spinney Hill Prim Sch LE5 .... 155 D5
Spinney Hill Rd LE5 .... 155 C7
Spinney La Ryhall PE9 .... 116 E2
Stretton LE15 .... 88 F4
Spinney Nook LE7 .... 185 E6
Spinney Rd
Hinckley LE10 .... 215 C6
Ketton PE9 .... 167 F5
Spinney Rise LE4 .... 129 A7
Spinneyside LE6 .... 126 E2
Spinney The
Atherstone CV9 .... 194 A7
Castle Donington DE74 .... 17 A4
Coalville LE67 .... 96 C6
Cottesmore LE15 .... 112 B7
Leicester, Oadby LE2 .... 182 A4
Thurnby LE7 .... 156 E4
Spinney View LE8 .... 182 C1
Spire View NG13 .... 3 B3
Spittal DE74 .... 17 A4
Spittal Hill DE74 .... 17 A4
Sponne Rise LE2 .... 179 E4
Sports Field La LE9 .... 200 D8
Sports Rd LE3 .... 153 D8
Spring Back Way LE15 .... 189 A4
Spring Bank LE16 .... 227 F7
Springbrook Dr LE7 .... 156 F6
Spring Cl Breaston DE72 .... 9 C8
Castle Gresley DE11 .... 44 A1
Lutterworth LE17 .... 244 C5
Market Overton LE15 .... 86 F5
Ratby LE6 .... 152 D8
Shepshed LE12 .... 50 C2
Spring Close LE2 .... 179 D5
Spring Cottage Rd DE12 .... 67 D5
Springdale Rd LE4 .... 129 E6
Springfield
Kegworth DE74 .... 18 B2
Thringstone LE67 .... 71 E8
Springfield Ave
Long Eaton NG10 .... 10 F8
Market Bosworth CV13 .... 148 D3
Springfield Cl
Broughton Astley LE9 .... 218 F5
Burton o t W LE12 .... 53 F7
Ibstock LE67 .... 95 F1
Kibworth Beauchamp LE8 .... 224 B7
Loughborough LE11 .... 74 E8
Rothley LE7 .... 101 E7
Swadlincote DE11 .... 44 B6
Spring Field Cl LE3 .... 153 B7
Springfield Cres LE8 .... 224 B8
Springfield Ct LE16 .... 240 F2
Springfield Jun Sch DE11 .... 44 C5
Springfield La LE8 .... 224 A6
Springfield Pk LE10 .... 197 A3
Springfield Rd
Hinckley LE10 .... 215 D7
Leicester LE2 .... 155 C2
Shepshed LE12 .... 50 B3
Sileby LE12 .... 77 D4
Swadlincote DE11 .... 44 B6
Springfield St
Market Harborough LE16 .... 240 F2
Melton Mowbray LE13 .... 59 B5
Springfield Way LE15 .... 138 A8
Spring Gdns
Littlethorpe LE19 .... 201 C6
Sapcote LE9 .... 217 E8
Springhill DE11 .... 45 A8
Springhill Gdns LE16 .... 240 C2
Spring La
Ab Kettleby LE14 .... 37 A3
Glaston LE15 .... 190 B5
Long Whatton LE12 .... 29 D2
Packington LE65 .... 69 E1
Shepshed LE12 .... 50 B2
Swannington LE67 .... 71 B4
3 Wigston LE18 .... 180 D3
Wymondham LE14 .... 62 D2
Spring Rd LE67 .... 96 A2
Spring St DE11 .... 44 A1
Springs The
Broughton Astley LE9 .... 218 E6
Swinford LE17 .... 254 C4
Spring Terr LE16 .... 228 A6
Spring The NG10 .... 10 D5
Springway Cl LE5 .... 156 E5
Springwell Cl LE8 .... 202 E4
Springwell Dr LE8 .... 202 D4
Springwell La LE8 .... 201 F4
Springwood Farm Rd DE11 .... 44 B7
Sproxton Rd
Buckminster NG33 .... 42 D2
Skillington NG33 .... 43 A3
Spruce Ave LE11 .... 75 A7
Spruce Way LE17 .... 244 B7
Square Ct LE4 .... 129 B7
Square The
Bagworth LE67 .... 124 B5
Bottesford NG13 .... 3 A3
Countesthorpe LE8 .... 202 F3
Earl Shilton LE9 .... 198 E8
Frolesworth LE17 .... 218 B1
Glenfield LE3 .... 127 B1
Littlethorpe LE19 .... 201 C6
Long Whatton LE12 .... 29 B4
Market Harborough LE16 .... 240 E3
Newton Harcourt LE8 .... 204 D6
Oakthorpe DE12 .... 93 A7
Ryhall PE9 .... 116 F2
Shearsby LE17 .... 222 A2
Skillington NG33 .... 43 B8
South Luffenham LE15 .... 191 D8
Sutton Cheney CV13 .... 174 B6
Welford NN6 .... 256 E6
Squires Cl LE15 .... 110 C3
Squires Gn LE10 .... 215 F6
Squire's Ride LE7 .... 103 D8
Squirrel Cl LE19 .... 201 A7
Squirrel La DE73 .... 26 E4
Squirrel's Cnr LE7 .... 103 E8
Squirrel Wlk LE11 .... 51 F2
Squirrel Wlk DE12 .... 67 B3
Stable Cl LE19 .... 201 C7
Stable Ct DE73 .... 26 B7
Stablegate Way LE16 .... 241 A3
Stable Mews DE11 .... 44 F2
Stables Ct LE15 .... 137 F6
Stables The
Burley LE15 .... 111 E1
Hinckley LE10 .... 215 D5
Stable Yd The CV13 .... 196 D7
Stackley Rd LE8 .... 182 B1
Stadium Cl LE67 .... 96 C8
Stadium Ind Pk NG10 .... 10 F8
Stadium Pl LE4 .... 128 E2
Stadon Rd LE7 .... 127 D6
Staffa Wlk NN17 .... 230 B1
Stafford Ave LE13 .... 59 D4
Stafford Dr LE18 .... 179 F2
Stafford Leys LE3 .... 152 F3
Stafford Leys Com Prim Sch LE3 .... 152 F2
Staffords Acre DE74 .... 18 C2
Stafford St Barwell LE9 198 A6
Stafford St *continued*
Leicester LE4 .... 129 C3
Long Eaton NG10 .... 10 F8
Stainby Rd
Buckminster NG33 .... 42 E2
Gunby NG33 .... 64 E8
Staindale LE18 .... 180 F2
Stainforth Cl CV11 .... 214 A2
Stainmore Ave LE19 .... 178 A2
Stainsdale Gn LE67 .... 72 A2
Staley Ave LE65 .... 68 F5
Stamford Bsns Pk PE9 .... 143 F4
Stamford Cl
Glenfield LE3 .... 153 C8
Long Eaton NG10 .... 10 E4
Market Harborough LE16 .... 240 E2
Stamford Coll PE9 .... 143 E4
Stamford Dr
Coalville LE67 .... 72 D1
Cropston LE7 .... 100 F2
Groby LE6 .... 126 F2
Stamford End LE15 .... 113 B3
Stamford Hall LE2 .... 180 F8
Stamford High Sch PE9 .... 143 E2
Stamford Jun Sch PE9 .... 143 D2
Stamford Mus★ PE9 .... 143 D2
Stamford Rd
Carlby PE9 .... 117 C8
Duddington PE9 .... 193 C7
Easton on t H PE9 .... 169 B5
Empingham LE15, PE9 .... 141 C4
Essendine PE9 .... 117 A5
Exton LE15 .... 113 B3
Ketton PE9 .... 168 C8
Kirby Fields LE9 .... 152 E4
Oakham LE15 .... 138 B5
Sewstern NG33 .... 64 A8
South Luffenham LE15, PE9 .... 191 D7
Stamford & Rutland Hospl PE9 .... 143 F4
Stamford Sch PE9 .... 143 E3
Stamford Sch (Welland Ho) PE9 .... 143 E2
Stamford St
Glenfield LE3 .... 153 B8
Leicester LE1 .... 259 B3
Ratby LE6 .... 126 C1
Stamford Sta PE9 .... 143 D2
Stamford St Gilbert CE Prim Sch The PE9 .... 143 D3
Stamford Wlk 7 PE9 .... 143 E3
Stanage Rd LE12 .... 77 E4
Stanbrig LE18 .... 203 E8
Stancliff Rd LE4 .... 129 F5
Standard Hill LE67 .... 96 B7
Stanfell Rd LE2 .... 180 B8
Stanford Hall★ LE17 .... 254 F3
Stanford Hill LE11 .... 52 B6
Stanford La LE12 .... 52 D7
Stanford Rd
Normanton on S LE12 .... 30 F2
Swinford LE17 .... 254 D3
Stanhope Glade DE15 .... 44 A8
Stanhope Rd
Swadlincote DE11 .... 44 B3
Wigston LE18 .... 180 E1
Stanhope St
Leicester LE5 .... 155 D5
Long Eaton NG10 .... 10 D8
Stanier Dr LE4 .... 130 A4
Stanier Rd
Broughton Astley LE9 .... 219 A6
Corby NN17 .... 230 F1
Stanilands LE15 .... 84 E1
Stanleigh Gdns DE12 .... 92 E8
Stanleigh Rd DE12 .... 67 B4
Stanley Cl
Netherseal DE12 .... 91 F7
Woodville DE11 .... 44 F3
Stanley Dr LE5 .... 156 A8
Stanley Rd
Hinckley LE10 .... 197 C2
Leicester LE2 .... 155 C3
Market Bosworth CV13 .... 148 E2
Stanleys La LE14 .... 22 A6
Stanley St Barwell LE9 .... 198 A6
Long Eaton NG10 .... 10 E7
Loughborough LE11 .... 52 B2
Stamford PE9 .... 143 E3
Swadlincote DE11 .... 44 C4
Stanton La Croft LE9 .... 200 A5
Sapcote LE9 .... 217 B8
Stanton u B LE67 .... 97 F3
Thornton LE67 .... 124 E6
Stanton Rd
Asfordby Hill LE14 .... 58 D3
Elmesthorpe LE9 .... 199 B3
Sapcote LE9 .... 217 D8
Stanton Row LE2 .... 179 F6
Stanton under Bardon Prim Sch LE67 .... 97 F1
Stanton Vale Sch NG10 10 C7
Stanway Cl LE16 .... 241 A3
Stanyon Cl LE8 .... 202 F4
Stapleford Rd
Leicester LE4 .... 128 D4
Whissendine LE15 .... 84 E3
Staplehurst Ave LE3 .... 178 E8
Stapleton La
Barwell LE9 .... 197 F8
Dadlington CV13 .... 174 A1
Kirkby Mallory LE9 .... 175 B5
Starkie Ave DE74 .... 16 F3
Star La 3 PE9 .... 143 E3
Starmer Cl LE9 .... 201 E3
Statham St LE9 .... 150 B5
Stathern Prim Sch LE14 .... 13 A2
Stathern Rd
Eastwell LE14 .... 22 B6
Harby LE14 .... 12 C3
Station App LE15 .... 137 F7
Station App The LE7 .... 133 F3
Station Ave
Loughborough LE11 .... 51 F5
South Witham NG33 .... 65 B3
Station Cl LE9 .... 152 E4
Station Cotts LE14 .... 21 B2
Station Dr
Kirby Fields LE9 .... 152 E4
Moira DE12 .... 67 F4
Station Hill
Swannington LE67 .... 71 A4
Twyford LE14 .... 133 F8
Station Hollow LE8 .... 224 A8
Station La Asfordby LE14 57 F2
Old Dalby LE14 .... 35 F5
Scraptoft LE7 .... 156 F7
Station Mews LE65 .... 69 B5
Station Rd
Ashby-De-La-Z LE65 .... 69 B5
Bagworth LE67 .... 124 A6
Birstall LE4 .... 128 F5
Bottesford NG13 .... 3 B3
Broughton Astley LE9 .... 219 A5
Castle Bytham NG33 .... 90 C8
Castle Donington DE74 .... 17 B6
Coalville LE67 .... 96 D6
Countesthorpe LE8 .... 202 E3
Croft LE9 .... 200 C4
Cropston LE7 .... 101 A4
Desford LE9 .... 151 C3
Draycott DE72 .... 9 B7
Dunton Bassett LE17 .... 219 E2
Earl Shilton LE9 .... 198 E7
Ellistown LE67 .... 96 F1
Elmesthorpe LE9 .... 198 F5
Essendine PE9 .... 117 B6
Glenfield LE3 .... 127 C1
Great Bowden LE16 .... 241 A6
Great Easton LE16 .... 229 E6
Great Glen LE8 .... 205 A6
Gretton NN17 .... 213 B1
Hemington DE74 .... 17 C5
Higham on t H CV13 .... 195 F4
Hinckley LE10 .... 215 D8
Husbands Bosworth LE17 .... 247 D3
Ibstock LE67 .... 95 D1
Kegworth DE74,LE12 .... 18 E3
Ketton PE9 .... 168 A5
Kirby Fields LE9 .... 152 E4
Leicester LE5, LE7 .... 156 F6
Lilbourne CV23 .... 258 A7
Littlethorpe LE19 .... 201 C7
Long Eaton NG10 .... 10 F8
Lutterworth LE17 .... 244 D5
Market Bosworth CV13 .... 148 D3
Melbourne DE73 .... 26 C8
Morcott LE15 .... 191 B6
North Kilworth LE17 .... 247 A4
Oakham LE15 .... 137 F7
Quorn LE12 .... 76 A6
Ratby LE6 .... 152 D7
Rearsby LE7 .... 79 A2
Shackerstone CV13 .... 121 E2
South Luffenham LE15 .... 166 E2
Stamford PE9 .... 143 D2
Stoke Golding CV13 .... 196 C7
Stoney Stanton LE9 .... 199 C3
Syston LE7 .... 103 A3
Theddingworth LE17 .... 248 C8
Ullesthorpe LE17 .... 233 B4
Upper Broughton LE14 .... 35 C8
Uppingham LE15 .... 189 B4
Waltham on t W LE14 .... 22 F3
Whissendine LE15 .... 85 A4
Wigston LE18 .... 180 B2
Wing LE15 .... 164 E3
Woodville DE11 .... 44 F2
Station Rd Ind Est CV13 .... 148 C3
Station St
Castle Gresley DE11 .... 67 A8
Kibworth Beauchamp LE8 .... 224 A8
Leicester LE1 .... 259 C3
Long Eaton NG10 .... 10 E7
Loughborough LE11 .... 51 F5
Whetstone LE8 .... 201 F8
Wigston LE18 .... 180 A1
Station Terr
Bagworth LE67 .... 124 A7
Heather LE67 .... 95 D2
Staunton Cl DE74 .... 17 A4
Staveley Cl Sileby LE12 .... 77 D2
Wigston LE18 .... 180 E2
Staveley Ct LE11 .... 52 B5
Staveley Rd
Leicester LE5 .... 155 D4
Melton Mowbray LE13 .... 59 A4
Staythorpe Rd LE4 .... 130 A5
Steadfold La PE9 .... 168 C8
Steadman Ave LE9 .... 201 E3
Stebbings Rd LE2 .... 179 D5
Steele Cl LE5 .... 156 A5
Steeple Cl LE18 .... 180 E4
Steeple Ct LE11 .... 52 B4
Steeple Row LE11 .... 52 B4
Steins La LE5 .... 156 B8
Stelle Way LE7 .... 127 D3

Stemborough La LE17 219 A2
Stenor Cl LE8 222 E8
Stenson Rd
Coalville LE67 71 E2
Leicester LE3 128 A1
Stephens Ct LE7 102 F3
Stephenson Cl
Broughton Astley LE9 219 A5
Groby LE6 126 E3
Stephenson Coll
Ashby-De-La-Z LE65 69 C6
Coalville LE67 96 D8
Stephenson Ct
Glenfield LE3 127 C2
Ravenstone LE67 71 A3
Stephenson Dr LE3 154 C7
Stephenson Ind Est
LE67 71 B2
Stephenson Rd LE10 214 E7
Stephenson Way
Coalville LE67 71 D3
Groby LE6 126 E3
Sterndale Rd NG10 10 B6
Stevens Cl
Stoney Stanton LE9 199 E2
Ullesthorpe LE17 233 B4
Stevens La DE72 9 D8
Stevenson Ave DE72 9 B8
Stevenson Gdns LE9 201 D4
Stevens St LE16 240 D3
Stevenstone Cl LE2 181 D5
Stewards Ct LE9 151 B3
Stewart Ave LE19 178 A2
Stewart Dr LE11 51 C6
Steyning Cres LE3 127 D1
Stiles Cl LE9 218 F5
Stiles The LE7 103 B4
Stinford Leys LE16 241 C3
Stinson Way LE67 71 E5
Stirling Ave
Hinckley LE10 197 A1
Loughborough LE11 51 D5
Stirling Cl
Mountsorrel LE12 101 C8
Quorn LE12 75 F7
Stirling Dr LE7 156 F6
Stirling Pk LE10 214 D8
Stirling Rd
Melton Mowbray LE13 59 B4
Stamford PE9 143 B3
Stocken Hall Farm Cott
LE15 66 B1
Stocken Hall Mews
LE15 66 B1
Stockerston Cres
LE15 188 F3
Stockerston Cross Rds
LE16 210 F5
Stockerston La LE16 211 B3
Stockerston Rd
Allexton LE15 187 E4
Uppingham LE15 188 D2
Stockingers Ct LE11 52 C5
Stocking La DE73 48 B8
Stockland Rd LE2 179 E4
Stocks Hill LE15 164 E6
Stock's Hill PE9 168 A5
Stocks Rd LE7 156 F8
Stockton Ho LE3 153 C6
Stockton Rd LE4 129 E1
Stockwell Cl LE16 241 B3
Stockwell Head LE10 197 D1
Stockwell Rd LE2 180 D7
Stockwell The LE12 33 C3
Stockwood Dr NN17 230 E1
Stoke Albany Rd LE16 227 E1
Stoke La
Higham on t H CV13 196 A4
Stoke Golding CV13 196 E8
Stoke Rd
Hinckley LE10,CV13 197 A4
Lyddington LE15 212 C7
Upton CV13 172 D2
Stokes CE Prim Sch
LE8 202 A7
Stokes Dr LE3 154 B8
Stokes Paddock LE14 20 B3
Stokes Wood Prim Sch
LE3 154 B8
Stonebow Cl LE11 51 B6
Stonebow Prim Sch
LE11 51 B6
Stonebridge St LE5 155 D6
Stonechat Dr CV23 252 C1
Stonechat Wlk LE5 155 C6
Stone Cl LE4 128 A6
Stonecroft LE8 202 C3
Stonecrop Rd LE5 130 C2
Stone Dr NG33,LE15 66 A2
Stonehaven Cl LE67 72 D1
Stonehaven Rd LE4 129 D4
Stonehill DE74 17 B2
Stonehill Ave LE4 129 A8
Stonehill Ct LE8 182 C1
Stonehill Dr LE8 182 C1
Stonehill High Sch The
LE4 102 B1
Stonehills DE74 18 C2
Stonehouse Ct CV23 258 A6
Stonehurst Family Farm &
Mus★ LE12 76 D3
Stonehurst La LE12 30 D3
Stonehurst Rd LE3 178 F8
Stoneleigh Cl CV10 194 B2
Stoneleigh Way LE3 154 C8
Stoneley Rd CV13 196 D6
Stone Mdws NG10 10 E5
Stonepit Dr LE16 229 D1
Stonepit La NG33 43 B8
Stonepit Terr LE14 108 D3
Stone Row LE67 71 D1
Stonesby Ave LE2 179 F4
Stonesby Rd
Saltby LE14 24 D1
Sproxton LE14 41 E5
Waltham on t W LE14 40 B6
Stoneycroft Rd LE9 198 E7
Stoneygate Ave LE2 155 C1
Stoneygate Coll LE2 155 C2
Stoneygate Ct LE2 155 C2
Stoneygate Dr LE10 197 F3
Stoneygate Rd LE2 155 D2
Stoneygate Sch
Great Glen LE8 205 C6
Leicester LE2 155 C3
Stoney Hollow LE17 244 C5
Stoney La
Appleby Magna DE12 92 F1
Coleorton LE67 70 F8
Stanton u B LE67 98 B1
Stoneywell Rd LE4 127 F5
Stonton Rd LE16 225 D8
Stoop La LE12 76 A6
Stordon La LE67 48 B2
Storer Cl LE12 77 D3
Storer Rd LE11 51 F4
Stores La LE8 222 F7
Storey St LE3 154 D7
Stornaway Rd LE5 156 D6
Stornoway Rd NN17 230 C1
Stoughton Ave LE2 155 D1
Stoughton Cl LE2 181 B6
Stoughton Dr LE5 155 F2
Stoughton Dr N LE5 155 D3
Stoughton Dr S LE2 180 F8
Stoughton Farm Pk★
LE2 156 C1
Stoughton La LE2 156 C2
Stoughton Rd
Gaulby LE7 183 C6
Leicester LE2 155 D1
Leicester, Oadby LE2 181 B7
Thurnby LE5,LE7 156 F3
Stoughton St LE2 155 B5
Stoughton St S LE2 155 B5
Stour Cl LE2 181 D6
Stourdale Cl NG10 10 A6
Stour Rd NN17 230 D1
Stove Ct LE15 89 A7
Stowe Cl
Ashby-De-La-Z LE65 69 A7
Leicester LE3 128 A1
Stow Hill LE14 41 F5
Strachan Cl LE12 76 F1
Strancliffe La LE12 53 C1
Strasbourg Dr LE4 128 C3
Stratford Rd LE3 153 F1
Strathaven Rd LE4 129 D4
Strathay Wlk NN17 230 C1
Strathern Rd LE3,LE7 127 F3
Strathmore Ave LE4 129 D3
Strathmore Cl LE67 97 C8
Strathmore Rd LE10 215 A7
Stratton Cl LE16 240 D1
Strawberry Ct LE14 108 D3
Strawberry La DE11 68 B8
Streamside Cl LE9 218 F5
Street The Goadby LE7 185 B2
South Luffenham LE15 191 E8
Strensall Rd LE2 179 D3
Stretton Cl LE10 215 D6
Stretton Ct
Great Glen LE8 205 B8
Hinckley LE10 215 D3
Stretton Dr LE67 72 C1
Stretton Hall Dr LE2 181 F3
Stretton La LE7 157 E2
Stretton Raod LE15 88 D2
Stretton Rd
Clipsham LE15 89 C4
Great Glen LE8 182 C3
Leicester LE3 154 C5
Stretton View DE12 93 A6
Stroller's Way LE7 103 E7
Stroma Way LE8 202 F3
Stroud Ct NG13 3 B3
Stroud Rd LE5 155 D7
Stroud's Cl LE14 20 F8
Strudwick Way LE8 179 A1
Strutt Rd LE10 216 A5
Stuart Cres LE16 239 F7
Stuart Rd
Glen Parva LE2 179 C3
Market Harborough
LE16 240 E2
Stuart St
Kibworth Beauchamp
LE8 224 A8
Leicester LE3 154 D3
Stuart Way LE65 69 B5
Stubbs Rd LE4 155 B8
Studbrook Cl DE74 16 F3
Studfall Ave NN17 230 F1
Studfarm Cl DE73 26 E2
Sturdee Cl LE2 179 D4
Sturdee Gn LE2 179 C4
Sturdee Rd LE2 179 D4
Sturrock Cl LE7 156 F6
Stygate La LE14 108 E5
Styon Rd LE3 127 E1
Sudeley Ave LE4 128 E2
Suffolk Cl
Melton Mowbray LE13 82 D8
Wigston LE18 180 A3
Suffolk St LE5 155 E5
Suffolk Way LE9 151 B2
Sulby Hall Old Dr
NN6 248 B1
Sulby Rd NN6 248 B1
Sulgrave Rd LE5 155 D7
Sullington Rd LE12 50 C3
Sullivan Way LE11 51 F6
Sulthorpe Rd PE9 167 F5
Summerfield LE15 138 A8
Summerlea Rd LE5 156 D6
Summerpool Rd LE11 51 F7
Summers Cl LE9 175 D6
Summers Way LE16 240 D2
Sunbury Gn LE5 156 E7
Sunbury Rise LE8 202 C4
Sundew Rd LE5 130 C2
Sunningdale Cl CV11 214 A1
Sunningdale Ind Pk
LE3 153 B4
Sunningdale Rd LE3 153 B4
Sunnybank PE9 143 E3
Sunnycroft Rd LE3 154 A5
Sunnydale Cres LE10 215 A7
Sunnydale Rd LE10 214 F7
Sunnyfield LE15 138 A8
Sunnyfield Cl LE5 156 C5
Sunnyhill LE10 215 F7
Sunnyhill Rd LE11 51 F1
Sunnyhill S LE10 215 F6
Sunnyside
Hinckley LE10 197 D3
Ibstock LE67 122 E8
Sunny Side LE2 181 C4
Sunnyside Cl LE8 178 F1
Sunnyside Hospl LE10 197 D5
Sunnyside Ind Est
LE10 197 D4
Sun St DE11 44 F2
Sun Way LE3 153 D3
Surrey Cl LE10 215 E4
Surrey St LE4 155 B8
Susan Ave LE5 156 B4
Sussex Ave LE13 82 D8
Sussex Rd
Stamford PE9 143 D4
Wigston LE18 179 F3
Sussex St LE1 155 B6
Sutherington Way
LE7 127 E7
Sutherland St 1 LE2 155 C4
Sutherland Way PE9 143 B3
Suthern Cl LE15 138 A8
Suthers Rd DE74 18 C2
Sutton Ave LE4 129 C2
Sutton Bonington Prim Sch
LE12 30 B6
Sutton Cl Hinckley LE10 197 F3
Leicester, Oadby LE2 181 B3
Quorn LE12 75 F5
Sutton Bonington LE12 30 C5
Sutton Ct
Broughton Astley LE9 218 E8
Market Harborough
LE16 240 E1
Sutton La
Dadlington CV13 173 F1
Granby NG13 5 D6
Market Bosworth CV13 148 F1
Sutton Cheney CV13 174 D8
Sutton Pl LE4 129 C2
Sutton Rd
Great Bowden LE16 241 B6
Kegworth DE74 18 C1
Leicester LE2 180 A8
Little Bowden LE16 241 E7
Weston by W LE16 227 B3
Suttons Bsns Pk DE11 44 E3
Swadlincote Rd DE11 44 E3
Swains Gn LE10 215 F6
Swainson Rd LE4 155 E8
Swain St LE1 259 C3
Swale Cl Corby NN17 230 D1
Leicester, Oadby LE2 181 D6
Melton Mowbray LE13 59 B1
Swallow Cl LE12 76 F2
Swallow Dale LE67 71 D7
Swallowdale Dr LE4 128 B6
Swallowdale Prim Sch
LE13 82 B8
Swallowdale Rd LE13 82 B8
Swallow Dr LE7 102 F4
Swallow Rd DE11 44 F3
Swallows Cl LE3 152 E1
Swallow's Dale LE67 103 E8
Swallows Dr LE14 12 F3
Swallow Wlk LE12 30 A1
Swan Cl Barrow-u-S LE12 76 E8
Melton Mowbray LE13 82 B8
Mountsorrel LE12 76 F2
Swan Ct LE12 30 B6
Swann Cl LE15 166 D3
Swannington CE Prim Sch
LE67 71 A5
Swannington Rd
Broughton Astley LE9 219 A6
Leicester LE3 154 C7
Ravenstone LE67 70 F2
Swannymote Rd LE67,
LE12 72 B7
Swanscombe Rd LE2 154 D1
Swanson Ho PE9 143 F4
Swan St Leicester LE3 259 A4
Loughborough LE11 52 B4
Seagrave LE12 77 F8
Sileby LE12 77 C3
Swan Way Coalville LE67 96 F8
Syston LE7 102 E4
Swedish Cl LE16 224 E1
Sweetbriar PE9 142 E5
Sweetbriar Rd LE3 154 C3
Sweethill DE12 68 A5
Swepstone Rd
Heather LE67 95 A2
Measham DE12 94 B4
Snarestone DE12,LE67 94 C1
Swift Cl
Melton Mowbray LE13 82 B8
Syston LE7 102 F4
Woodville DE11 44 F3
Swifts Cl LE67 95 F2
Swift's Cl LE12 33 C3
Swift Valley Ind Est
CV21 252 A1
Swift Way LE17 244 C7
Swinburne Rd LE10 197 C1
Swindale Cl LE2 259 A2
Swinfen Cl LE67 96 C3
Swinfield Rd LE12 76 A6
Swinford Ave LE2 179 D2
Swinford CE Prim Sch
LE17 254 B4
Swinford Cnr LE17 254 A8
Swinford Ct LE2 179 D2
Swinford Rd
Cotesbach LE17 244 E2
Walcote LE17 245 B2
Swingbridge Rd LE11 51 F7
Swingbridge St LE16 239 E8
Swinstead Rd LE5 156 D4
Swithland Ave LE4 128 F1
Swithland Cl
Loughborough LE11 51 C5
Markfield LE67 125 E8
Swithland Ct LE3 178 F7
Swithland La LE7 101 B7
Swithland Rd
Coalville LE67 97 C8
Swithland LE12 100 E4
Swithland Resr Nature
Reserve★ LE7 75 F1
Swithland St Leonard's CE
Prim Sch LE12 100 E7
Swithland Woods Nature
Reserve★ LE12 100 B5
Sword Cl LE3 153 C7
Sword Dr LE10 197 B3
Sybil Rd LE3 154 B1
Sycamore Ave DE11 44 A7
Sycamore Cl
Barton in t B CV13 122 D1
Corby NN17 230 E1
Hinckley LE10 215 E5
Ibstock LE67 95 E1
Leicester LE2 155 F1
Leicester, Oadby LE2 182 A3
Melton Mowbray LE13 59 B5
Newbold Verdon LE9 150 A4
Syston LE7 103 B2
Sycamore Dr
Ashby-De-La-Z LE65 69 D7
Groby LE6 126 F2
Lutterworth LE17 244 A6
Moira DE12 68 B6
Sycamore Gr LE6 126 F3
Sycamore La LE14 62 D2
Sycamore Rd
Birstall LE4 129 A8
Castle Donington DE74 17 B5
Coalville LE67 97 A8
East Leake LE12 31 D8
Long Eaton NG10 10 C5
North Luffenham LE15 166 D3
Sycamore St LE8 202 B8
Sycamores The LE17 255 D8
Sycamore Way
Littlethorpe LE19 201 B6
Loughborough LE11 75 A7
Market Bosworth CV13 148 F2
Sydney Rd DE72 9 B7
Sykefield Ave LE3 154 C4
Sykes La LE15 140 E5
Sylvan Ave LE5 155 D6
Sylvan St LE3 154 C7
Sylvan Way LE3 153 B4
Symington Way LE16 240 E3
Sysonby Grange La
LE13 58 F2
Sysonby St LE13 59 A4
Syston Rd
Cossington LE7 102 C7
Queniborough LE7 103 E6
South Croxton LE7 104 F1
Syston Sta LE7 103 A3
Syston St E LE1 155 B7
Syston St W LE1 155 A8
Sywell Ave LE11 51 C3
Sywell Dr LE18 180 F2

T

Tabberer Cl LE15 138 A8
Tadcaster Ave LE2 179 D3
Tadcaster Gn LE2 179 D3
Tailby Ave LE5 155 E8
Tailor's Link LE7 103 D7
Talbot La Leicester LE1 259 A3
Whitwick LE67 71 C7
Talbot Pl DE12 92 E8
Talbot St Leicester LE4 129 A3
Swadlincote DE11 44 A1
Whitwick LE67 71 D6
Talbott Cl LE9 219 A4
Talbot Yd LE16 240 E3
Tamar Gn NN17 230 D1
Tamar Rd Leicester LE4 129 E2
Leicester, Oadby LE2 181 D5
Tamar Rd *continued*
Melton Mowbray LE13 59 B1
Tamerton Rd LE2 179 E5
Tame Way LE10 215 A8
Tamworth Cl LE12 49 F2
Tamworth Rd
Appleby Magna DE12 92 E2
Ashby-De-La-Z LE65 69 A5
Long Eaton NG10 10 C5
Measham DE12 93 B4
Tandy Ave DE12 68 B5
Tanner's La LE12 30 A1
Tannery The LE15 192 A5
Tanni Gray Ho 6 LE11 52 A4
Tansey Cres LE9 199 C2
Tansley Ave LE18 180 A1
Tanyard Cl DE74 17 B4
Tan Yd LE67 71 B5
Tara St LE67 97 B4
Tarbat Rd LE5 156 D7
Tarragon Rd LE2 154 D4
Tatlow Ho LE3 153 D6
Tatlow Rd LE3 153 C6
Tatmarsh LE11 52 B5
Tatton Cl LE3 128 A1
Tatwin Ct DE73 26 F2
Taunton Cl LE18 180 C1
Taunton Rd LE3 154 B5
Taurus Cl LE2 155 B5
Taverner Dr LE6 152 D7
Taverners Rd LE4 128 C7
Tavistock Cl LE67 96 C6
Tavistock Dr LE5 155 F3
Tay Cl Corby NN17 230 D1
Oakham LE15 137 E4
Taylor Cl Moira DE12 68 A4
Syston LE7 103 A3
Taylor Ho LE11 52 C4
Taylor Rd LE1 155 A7
Taylor Road Prim Sch
LE1 155 B7
Taylor's Bridge Rd
LE18 180 A1
Taylors Cl LE9 199 D2
Teal Bsns Ctr LE10 214 E7
Tealby Cl LE17 235 C4
Teal Cl Coalville LE67 96 F8
Leicester Forest East
LE3 152 F2
Teal Dr LE10 215 A6
Teal Way LE7 102 E4
Teasel Cl LE19 201 A8
Teasel Dr
Melton Mowbray LE13 82 A8
Woodville DE11 44 F4
Tebbs Cl LE8 202 C4
Tedder Cl LE17 244 A5
Tedworth Gn LE4 128 D5
Tees Cl LE15 137 F5
Teesdale Rd NG10 10 A6
Teigh Rd Ashwell LE15 86 A1
Market Overton LE15 86 D5
Teign Bank Cl LE10 197 D2
Teign Bank Rd LE10 197 D2
Teignmouth Cl LE5 155 F3
Telford Way
Coalville LE67 71 B2
Leicester LE5 156 E5
Tellis Pl DE12 93 D5
Tempest Rd LE4 128 F6
Templars Way
South Witham NG33 65 A4
Whitwick LE67 71 F5
Templar Way LE7 101 E6
Temple Cl LE12 50 C1
Temple Hill LE67 71 F6
Temple Rd LE5 155 E5
Tendring Dr LE18 180 F3
Tennis Ave LE13 59 C1
Tennis Court Dr LE5 156 A8
Tennyson Ave DE11 44 C6
Tennyson Cl DE12 93 B4
Tennyson Rd
Hinckley LE10 197 C1
Loughborough LE11 51 D4
Lutterworth LE17 244 C7
Tennyson St
Leicester LE2 155 C3
Narborough LE19 178 A1
Tennyson Way
Melton Mowbray LE13 59 B6
Stamford PE9 143 A4
Tentas The LE67 48 A2
Tenter Cl NG10 10 D5
Tentercroft Ave LE7 103 C4
Tenter Ct PE9 143 E2
Tenter La 13 PE9 143 E3
Tern Ave DE11 44 F3
Terrace Cotts LE9 200 C4
Terrace The
Copt Oak LE67 98 C8
Lutterworth LE17 244 C5
Test Gn NN17 230 D1
Tetbury Dr LE12 49 F2
Tetuan Rd LE3 154 C6
Teviot Cl NN17 230 D1
Tewkesbury Rd NG10 10 E5
Tewkesbury St LE3 154 D6
Thackeray St LE2 179 F8
Thames Dr LE13 59 B1
Thames St LE1 259 B5
Thames Wlk NN17 230 D1
Thatcher Cl LE4 128 B4
Thatchers' Cnr LE7 103 D7
Thatch Meadow Dr
LE16 241 B3
Theddingworth Rd
Husbands Bosworth
LE17 248 A6
Lubenham LE16 239 C2
Marston Trussell LE16 249 B8
Mowsley LE17 237 F5
Thimble Hall Rd LE7,
LE14 133 C8
Thirlmere LE67 72 C1
Thirlmere Ct LE12 76 D8
Thirlmere Dr LE11 74 D8
Thirlmere Gdns LE65 69 C4
Thirlmere Rd
Barrow-u-S LE12 76 D8
Hinckley LE10 215 A7
Wigston LE18 180 E3
Thirlmere St LE2 259 A1
Thistle Cl Cropston LE7 100 F2
Narborough LE19 201 A8
Thistleton La NG33 65 A2
Thistleton Rd LE15 87 A6
Thistly Meadow Prim Sch
LE8 202 C7
Thomas Cl LE7 157 F4
Thomas Cook Cl DE73 26 A7
Thomas Dalby Wlk
LE15 137 F6
Thomas Estley Com Coll
LE9 218 F6
Thomas Fryer's Almshouses
LE15 164 E6
Thomas Rd
Kegworth DE74 18 C1
Whitwick LE67 71 D5
Thomasson Rd LE5 156 B6
Thomas St
Ibstock LE67 122 F8
Loughborough LE11 52 D3
Thompson Ave LE12 49 B6
Thompson Cl
Quorn LE12 75 F6
Woodville DE11 44 E4
Thompsons La LE15 190 C1
Thomson Cl LE4 129 D6
Thoresby Rd NG10 10 C7
Thoresby St LE5 155 E6
Thornborough Cl
Market Harborough
LE16 241 A2
Narborough LE19 200 F7
Thornborough Rd LE67 71 C3
Thornby Gdns LE18 180 E2
Thorndale LE67 95 E1
Thorndale Rd LE4 129 F7
Thorneycroft Cl LE9 219 B4
Thorneywood Rd NG10 10 F8
Thornfield Ave CV13 196 E7
Thornfield Way LE10 215 E8
Thornhills LE19 178 A2
Thornhills Gr LE19 178 A2
Thornholme Cl LE4 128 C4
Thorn St DE11 44 F2
Thorn Street Mews
DE11 44 F2
Thornton Cl
Braunstone LE3 153 D3
Broughton Astley LE9 219 A4
Coalville LE67 72 C1
Thornton Com Prim Sch
LE67 124 E4
Thornton Cres LE16 225 D7
Thornton Dr LE19 201 C8
Thornton La
Bagworth LE67 124 C4
Markfield LE67 125 C5
Stanton u B LE67 124 E7
Thorntop Cl DE11 68 B8
Thorntree Cl
Breaston DE72 9 E8
Ravenstone LE67 70 F2
Thornville Cl LE4 129 E1
Thorny Cl LE11 51 D6
Thornycroft Rd LE10 215 E8
Thorpe Acre Inf Sch
LE11 51 D4
Thorpe Acre Jun Sch
LE11 51 D4
Thorpe Acre Rd LE11 51 D5
Thorpe Downs Rd
DE11 44 B1
Thorpe Dr LE18 180 D4
Thorpe End LE13 59 D3
Thorpe Field Dr LE4 129 F8
Thorpe Gdns LE15 84 E1
Thorpe Hill LE11 51 C4
Thorpe La LE7 130 D8
Thorpe Langton Rd
East Langton LE16 225 D6
Welham LE16 226 D6
Thorpe Leys NG10 10 D5
Thorpe Rd
Lyddington LE15 212 D6
Melton Mowbray LE13 59 E4
Shepshed LE12 50 A3
Thorpe Satchville Rd
Great Dalby LE14 82 A1
Kirby Bellars LE14 81 C5
Thorpe Satchville LE14 106 F7
Twyford LE14 106 E2
Thorpe Side LE14 38 F4
Thorpes La NG32 24 B7
Thorpe St LE3 154 D5
Thorpe's Terr LE15 189 A4
Thorpe Way LE19 178 D4
Thorpewell LE5 155 F6

Name and Address	Telephone	Page	Grid reference